History and Images

MEDIEVAL TEXTS AND CULTURES OF NORTHERN EUROPE

5

History and Images

Towards a New Iconology

edited by

Axel Bolvig and Phillip Lindley

BREPOLS

British Library Cataloguing in Publication Data.
A catalogue record for this book is available from the British Library.

D/2003/0095/29
ISBN 2-503-51155-4

Printed in the EU on acid-free paper.

Contents

List of Illustrations

2. Haus Altenkamp, räumliche Darstellung des Entrées überlagert mit Schadenskartierung, Ansicht von Nordwesten. © Landesamt für Denkmalpflege, Hannover *(Plate 20)*
3. Haus Altenkamp, Entrée, Wandmalerei-Ausschnitt der Südwand, Überlagerung der Farbauszüge. Das Farbbild wurde aus den schwarz/weißen Spektralbildern berechnet. Durch Kalibrierung des fotografischen Prozesses läßt sich so eine langzeitstabile, rekonstruierbare colormetrische Abbildung realisieren. © Landesamt für Denkmalpflege, Hannover *(Plate 21)*
4. Haus Altenkamp, Entrée, Wandmalerei-Ausschnitt der Südwand, UV-Fluoreszenz-Aufnahme. © Landesamt für Denkmalpflege, Hannover
5. Das Bild entsteht durch Beleuchtung mit 320-380 nm und durch Filterung mit 440-660 nm. Die Verwendung unterschiedlicher Farben bei früheren Restaurierungen der linken Figur wird deutlich sichtbar. © Landesamt für Denkmalpflege, Hannover
6. Haus Altenkamp, Entrée, Bildplan der Südwand, überlagert mit Thermobild. © Landesamt für Denkmalpflege, Hannover
7. Das Thermobild setzt sich aus 4 Einzelbildern zusammen. Vom Objekt reflektierte Strahlungen im Bereich zwischen 8 und 14 μm wurden registriert. Die Abbildung zeigt Kältebrücken an den Seiten der Wände (Anschluß zur Außenwand bzw. zu unbeheizten Nachbarräumen). Der wärmere (grüne) Bereich in Bildmitte weist darauf hin, daß durch einen offenen Kamin im Nachbarraum Wärme abgesogen wird. © Landesamt für Denkmalpflege, Hannover *(Plate 22)*
8. Haus Altenkamp, Entrée, Thermobild der Südwand, überlagert mit Schadenskartierung. © Landesamt für Denkmalpflege, Hannover *(Plate 23)*
9. Die Überlagerung korreliert die Schadenskartierung mit bauphysikalischen Aussagen. © Landesamt für Denkmalpflege, Hannover *(Plate 24)*
10. Haus Altenkamp, Entrée, nach der Restaurierung. © Landesamt für Denkmalpflege, Hannover *(Plate 25)*

Frank Colson, Jean Colson, Ross Parry, Andrew Sawyer
Cutting off the king's head: images and the (dis)location of power.

1. 'Penning' dated 1588: from H. E. Greve, *De Tijd van den Tachtigjarigen Oorlog in Beeld* (Amsterdam: Elsevier, 1908), p. 67
2. C. J. Visscher, 'Afbeelding van 't Nederlandts Bestandt' [Image of the Netherlands Truce], *c.* 1609. FM1267. Reproduced by permission of the Rijksprentenkabinet, Rijksmuseum, Amsterdam
3. Detail, 'Afbeelding van 't Nederlandts Bestandt' [Image of the Netherlands Truce], *c.* 1609. FM1267. Reproduced by permission of the Rijksprentenkabinet, Rijksmuseum, Amsterdam

4. 'Livre', *Revista Illustrada*, Rio de Janeiro, 14 October 1884
5. 'Não vos aproximeis de mim! Vossas mãos ainda tintas de sangue dos escravos manchariam as minhas vistas! Retirae-vos, tu não vos quero.' *Revista Illustrada* 15 June 1888 [original orthography]
6. Inigo Jones, 'Pallas of Perfection', Devonshire Collection, Chatsworth. Reproduced by permission of the Duke of Devonshire and the Chatsworth Settlement Trustees. © Photographic Survey, Courtauld Institute of Art, London
7. Representation of a view from the west balcony of the first Jacobean Banqueting House (*c.* 1607–1619) looking towards Inigo Jones' scenery for *The Vision of Delight* (1617). Computer-generated model, Ross Parry, 1999. Details from Inigo Jones, 'A Street in Perspective' and 'Proscenium and Hunt Scene', Devonshire Collection, Chatsworth. Reproduced by permission of the Duke of Devonshire and the Chatsworth Settlement Trustees. © Photographic Survey, Courtauld Institute of Art, London *(Plate 26)*

Gerhard Jaritz
'Serra ex ferro'—'Serra ex vitro': Medieval history—computers—image messages reconsidered

1. 'Visitation of the Virgin', Master of the Schottenaltar, panel painting, Austrian, 1469/1480. Vienna, Schottenstift. © Institut für Realienkunde des Mittelalters und der frühen Neuzeit, Krems
2. 'Christ Visiting St George in Prison', panel painting, 1516. Spišská Sobota (Slovakia), parish church. © Institut für Realienkunde des Mittelalters und der frühen Neuzeit, Krems
3. 'The Dream of St Joseph', Friedrich Pacher, (detail: the hard road to Egypt), panel painting, Tirol, before 1500. Innsbruck, Landesmuseum Ferdinandeum. © Institut für Realienkunde des Mittelalters und der frühen Neuzeit, Krems
4. 'The Temptation of St Martin by the Disguised Devil', panel painting, before 1500. Göflan (Südtirol), parish church. © Institut für Realienkunde des Mittelalters und der frühen Neuzeit, Krems
5. 'St Florian and St Sebastian' (detail: Emperor Frederick III as St Sebastian), panel painting, Styrian, *c.* 1480. Obdach (Steiermark), church of the hospital. © Institut für Realienkunde des Mittelalters und der frühen Neuzeit, Krems
6. 'Parable of Dives and Lazarus' (detail: the servant of Dives), panel painting, Upper Rhine, end of the fifteenth century. St Paul im Lavanttal (Kärnten), collections of the Benedictine monastery. © Institut für Realienkunde des Mittelalters und der frühen Neuzeit, Krems
7. 'Labours of the Months', month of August (detail: hairstyle of an 'im-

5. Chartres Cathedral, north transept, right porch, right outer archivolts, 'December pig killing'. © James Austin
6. Chartres Cathedral, north transept, left porch, left outer archivolts, 'Women carding and spinning'. © James Austin
7. 'Woman with distaff defecating'. Wooden 'aisselier' from an apothecary's shop, late fifteenth century, Nantes, Musée Dobrée. © Author
8. 'Spinning sow'. Wood. Malestroit, Brittany, fifteenth century. © Author
9. 'Spinning sow and monkeys', *Livre des simples médecines*, Paris Bibliothèque nationale de France, ms. fr. 9136 fol. 1, late fifteenth century. © Bibliothèque nationale de France, Paris
10. Chartres, 'Salmon' from the 'Maison du Saumon'. © Author
11. Chartres Cathedral, north transept, right porch, left outer archivolts, Pisces. © James Austin
12. 'À la Truie qui file' sign of a charcutier, early seventeenth century, Paris, Musée Carnavalet. © Musée Carnavalet, Paris

Jean Wirth
Les marges à drôleries des manuscrits gothiques: problèmes de méthode

1. Heures de Jeanne d'Evreux, New York, Cloisters, MS. 54.1.2, fols 15ᵛ–16, 'Arrestation du Christ et Annonciation'. © The Cloisters, New York
2. Bréviaire de Renaud de Bar, Verdun, Bibliothèque municipale, ms. 107, fol. 138ʳ, 'Siège d'un château'. © Bibliothèque municipale, Verdun
3. Psautier de Gorleston, Londres, British Library, MS. Add. 49622, fol. 162ᵛ, 'Chevalier effrayé par un escargot'. © British Library, London
4. Psautier gantois, Oxford, Bodleian Library, MS. Douce 6, fol. 92ᵛ, 'Couvade'. © Bodleian Library, Oxford
5. Psautier, Oxford, Bodleian Library, MS. Laud. lat. 84, fol. 19, 'Initiale *Beatus*'. © Bodleian Library, Oxford
6. Livre d'heures, New York, Pierpont Morgan Library, MS. M. 754, fol. 48ᵛ, 'Singes boulangers'. © Pierpont Morgan Library, New York
7. Psautier gantois, Oxford, Bodleian Library, MS. Douce 5, fol. 146, 'Ecole des singes'. © Bodleian Library, Oxford
8. Psautier-Heures de Geoffroy d'Aspremont et d'Isabelle de Kievraing, Oxford, Bodleian Library, MS. Douce 118, fol. 101ᵛ, 'David en singe couronné'. © Bodleian Library, Oxford

Helena Edgren
'Primitive' paintings: the visual world of populus rusticus

1. Church of St Mary (Maaria), Southern Finland, 'Primitive paintings'. © Author
2. Church of Borgund, Norway, 'Graffiti', from Martin Blindheim, *Grafitti in Norwegian Stave churches c. 1150–c. 1350* (Oslo: Universitetsforlaget, 1985)

12. Tensta church. 'Revelations of St Birgitta'. © Author

Ulla Haastrup
Representations of Jews in Danish medieval art—can images be used as source material on their own?

1. Jelling church, fresco, 1080–1100, 'St John the Baptist preaching to a gathering of Jews', Watercolour by the restorer J. Magnus-Petersen 1874. © Nationalmuseet, Copenhagen
2. Raasted church, fresco, about 1125, 'judex barbatus', in the scene of the Magi at the court of King Herod. © Author
3. Altarpiece from Boeslunde church, now at the National Museum in Copenhagen, about 1425–35, Lübeck. 'The Virgin Mary's Training in Reading'. © Nationalmuseet, Copenhagen
4. Altarpiece in St Mary in Helsingborg, 1449–52. 'The Circumcision'. © Author
5. Tuse church, wall painting, 1460–80. 'The Circumcision'. © www.kalkmalerier.dk
6. Fanefjord church, wallpainting, about 1500. 'Jesus among the Doctors'. © Author
7. Haggadah. German, *c.* 1460, London, British Library, MS. Add. 14762, fol. 7^{v}. 'German Jews' (from Metzger: *Jewish Life*, fig. 175)
8. Fanefjord church, wall painting, *c.* 1500. 'The Circumcision'. © Author
9. Hebrew manuscript, Naples, Third quarter of the fifteenth century. Nîmes, Bibliothèque municipale, ms. 13, fol. 181^{v}. 'The Circumcision' (from Metzger: *Jewish Life*, fig. 333)
10. Master of The Tuscher-altar, Nürnberg, *c.* 1450, 'The Circumcision'. Aachen, Suermondt-Museum, from Mellinkoff, *Outcasts*, vol. II, fig. II.23
11. Stege church, wall painting 1494. '*Kristen iude* and figures with Jewish hats'. © Author

Norbert Schnitzler
Anti-semitism, image desecration, and the problem of 'Jewish Execution'

1. Engraving representing the panel-painting with the Miracle of Notre-Dame de Cambron, *c.* 1890, J. van Péteghem, Brussels
2. First field of the panel-painting: The image desecration, detail, *c.* 1890, J. van Péteghem, Brussels
3. Fifth field of the panel-painting: Mary appears in a vision to the blacksmith, detail, *c.* 1890, J. van Péteghem, Brussels
4. Tenth field of the panel painting: Execution of the baptized Jew *capite traverso*, detail, *c.* 1890, J. van Péteghem, Brussels
5. Oath-Taking, from *Enderung vnd Schmach der Bildung Mariae von den Juden bewiesen*, Strasbourg *c.* 1515

and ‘The Fall’, last ‘The Annunciation’, ‘The Nativity’, and ‘The Adoration of the Three Kings’. *c.* 1379–83. © Elke Walford, Kunsthalle, Hamburg

Lena Liepe
On the epistemology of images

1. Unknown artist: frontispiece, Giles of Rome, *De regimine principum*, translation to French by Jean Wauquelin, copy from 1452 by Jacques Pilavaine. Brussels, Bibliothèque Royale Albert Ier, ms. 9043, fol. 2r. © Bibliothèque Royale Albert Ier, Brussels
2. Unknown artist: frontispiece, Jacques de Guise, *Annales Hannoniae*, translation into French by Jean Wauquelin, copy from 1448 by Wauquelin and Jacotin du Bois. Brussels, Bibliothèque Royale Albert Ier, ms. 9242, fol. 1r. © Bibliothèque Royale Albert Ier, Brussels

Acknowledgements

Both editors would like to record their great debt of gratitude to Dr Brian Levy, Reader in French at the University of Hull, for his exemplary translation of Jean-Claude Schmitt's article, his checking of the French throughout the book, his assistance with many of the other translations and for his general care and attention throughout the book's progress to the printers. No general editor could have done more. We also would like to thank Dr Simon Forde of Brepols Publishers for his great interest in the present volume.

Axel Bolvig would also like to record his thanks to Annedorte Vad for all her practical work.

The Editors, and the Editorial Board of Medieval Texts and Cultures of Northern Europe, deeply regret that the essays of Michael Camille and Francis Haskell are here published as posthumous testimony to the scholarship of two eminent and sadly missed colleagues. This volume is dedicated to their memory.

Photographic Acknowledgements

Austin, James

Bayerische Staatsbibliothek, Munich
Biblioteca apostolica vaticana
Bibliothèque municipale, Amiens
Bibliothèque municipale, Verdun
Bibliothèque nationale de France, Paris
Bibliothèque Royale Albert Ier, Brussels
Bodleian Library, Oxford
British Library, London

Church of St Gumbert, Ansbach
Cloisters, New York
Courtauld Institute of Art, London

Dean & Chapter, Lincoln
Duke of Devonshire and the Chatsworth Settlement Trustees

Gabinetto di disegni Uffizii, Florence
Groeninge Museum, Bruges

Herzog August Bibliothek, Wolfenbüttel

Institut für Realienkunde des Mittelalters und der frühen Neuzeit, Krems
Institute of Information and Computing Sciences, Utrecht University

Keble College Library, Oxford
Kongelige Bibliotek, Copenhagen
Kunsthalle, Hamburg

Landesamt für Denkmalpflege, Hannover
Larsen, Lennart, Nationalmuseet, Copenhagen

Musée Carnavalet, Paris
Musée des Beaux-Arts, Dijon

National Board of Antiquities, Finland
National Buildings Board
National Gallery, London
Nationalmuseet, Copenhagen

Rijksprentenkabinet, Rijksmuseum, Amsterdam

Trinity College, Cambridge

University of Leicester

Walford, Elke, Kunsthalle, Hamburg
Walters Art Gallery, Baltimore

Introduction

AXEL BOLVIG

In 1999, the History and Images Congress was held at the University of Copenhagen. It was arranged as part of a research project initiated by the Faculty of Humanities under the heading *The Visual Construction of Realities*. Historians and art historians presented a variety of new approaches to research on visual material. The papers of the congress form the basis of this volume. The main object was, and remains, not only to show how the images may be understood as an equal partner to the text in historical research but also to demonstrate that imagery constitutes a separate category of source material with its own category of meaning and information and requiring its own interpretative methodologies. The subtitle 'Towards a New Iconology' indicates that traditional approaches to images are becoming inadequate. Historians who have expected art to reveal directly aspects of the historical society under investigation as a mimetic reproduction of the past, art historians who have looked solely at the aesthetic qualities of images, those who have investigated in iconography or iconology, all those who from Gregory the Great to the present day have linked image to text, all now seem insufficient.[1] The contributions to the present volume demonstrate that the visual construction of realities represents a unique temporally located world of our own times as well as the 'reality' of an historical past. And they demonstrate that this world of the eye is as complex and ubiquitous as the world of the word.

[1] Concerning an evaluation of the famous statement of Gregory the Great, see Jérôme Baschet, 'Introduction: l'image-objet', in *L'image. Fonctions et usages des images dans l'occident médiéval,* ed. by J. Baschet and J.-C. Schmitt (Paris: Le Léopard d'Or, 1996), pp. 7–26; Mary Carruthers, *The Book of Memory. A Study of Memory in Medieval Culture* (Cambridge: Cambridge University Press, 1990; repr. 1999), pp. 221–29.

It was *written* that in the beginning was the Word, but God soon felt obliged to place the prohibition of the making of images in the Ten Commandments on equal terms with the prohibition of killing. Modern research has discovered that among our five senses the eye is the most active. The eye sends ten million bits a second to the brain, the skin sends one million, the ear 100,000, the sense of smell 100,000, and the sense of taste only 1000 bits a second.[2] The sense of sight is then by far the strongest of our senses, sending enormous amounts of information to the brain. This in itself is a weighty argument for dealing with images. The text is also apprehended as an image by the eye, but being a visual representation of the linear system of the spoken words, the contents of a text is only understood in the course of time. A picture, in contrast, represents all its information within the same syntax.[3]

In the present volume, Keith Moxey argues for the establishment of Visual Studies: 'Rather than seek consensus, it benefits from the radical disagreement between different styles of interpretation'. The contributions to this volume present many different approaches to research in pictures as images and art and as visual communication and should, therefore, accord with his definition of visual studies. The film director Michelangelo Antonioni's credo reads:

> But we know that behind every image revealed there is another image more fateful to reality and in back of that image there is another and yet another behind the last one and so on up the true image of that absolute mysterious reality that no one will ever see.[4]

This is what modern researchers on the visual world of the historic past have also realized: every picture has many layers and contains many scientific 'truths'. The end of the last millennium was accompanied by the pluralism of deconstruction, which initiated the 'meltdown' of historical and art historical methods, described by Jean-Claude Schmitt in 'Images and the historian'. Are we facing a new constructive era based on a deconstructivist fragmentary inheritance?

In 1928, René Magritte painted a picture with visual configurations which resembled a pipe. Over this simple and rather un-aesthetic depiction he wrote: 'Ceci n'est pas une pipe'. The title of the picture reads: 'La trahison des images'. It took decades for researchers in history and art history to realize that their work with images was embedded in 'treachery'. In my opinion Magritte's simple and 'un-

---

[2] Bent Fausing, *Synet som sans* (Copenhagen: Samlerens Bogklub, 1995), pp. 17, 54.

[3] Michael Baxandall argues that analysing an image is equal to scanning a text (M. Baxandall, *Patterns of Intention. On the Historical Explanation of Pictures* (New Haven: Yale University Press, 1985; repr. 1992), p. 3). In my view this has nothing to do with the non-linearity of an image. The textualizing of an image is caused by the fact that when analysing we 'translate' the visual contents to a linear linguistic system.

[4] Michelangelo Antonioni (dir.), *Al di là delle nuvole* (*Beyond the clouds*), 1995; lines spoken by John Malkovich (The Director).

artistic' combination of a mimetic configuration and a linguistic statement is one of the many examples showing that artistic creativity most often forms the avant-garde in raising questions. In my view, the contributions to this volume demonstrate an inspiring willingness during the last couple of decades to deal with the 'treachery' of images by accepting the uniqueness of visual information. The 'treachery' we find is within the words, which are connected to an image as a title or as a description, not within the image itself. And why not think that medieval artists, too, often formed an avant-garde?

One could argue that iconographic studies for centuries have realized the 'treachery' of images if we define iconography as a conventional codified distance between expression and content. From the ancient hieroglyphs and culminating in medieval Christian imagery, such conventions have dominated image making. The more or less arbitrary linkage between content and expression is a 'treachery' towards the apparent analogue visual presentation. This is not the intriguing point in Magritte's canvas. He is, so I think, alluding to our belief in the analogue aspect in visual representation. With the rise of portrait and especially landscape painting, iconography lost influence in the visual arts. At least its role is no longer as clear-cut as it used to be.[5] Photography changed it all in such a way that, according to Roland Barthes, a photo in a strange way represents an un-coded message.[6] As a matter of fact, when looking at a photo of a pipe we all in our verbal descriptions admit 'it is a pipe'. It is we who commit treachery towards the image—or to use Gerhard Jaritz's explanation: 'Using verbal descriptions of pictorial sources (or also original objects), we only rarely have the opportunity to deal with anything like the original wording of the source of full-text. We are creating our own text'.[7]

The development of photography and the establishment of history and art history as scientific occupations go hand in hand. When in 1839 the French government bought the rights to the daguerreotype process, the purpose was to support scientific research. Photographers were sent to Egypt to make 'real' copies of the hieroglyphs. We still use photographs as a mimetic or at least an acceptable equivalent to the original image; as a matter of fact, the plates in the present volume are based on this assumption. But things have changed. Today we know that even Robert Capa composed 'fakes': the falling man from the Spanish Civil War is not a dying republican soldier. Nobody believes in photography any longer. Benetton made the final post-modern showdown with

---

[5] Brendan Cassidy, 'Introduction, Texts, and Audiences', in *Iconography at the Crossroads*, ed. by Brendan Cassidy (Princeton: Index of Christian Art, Princeton University, 1993), pp. 3–15.

[6] Roland Barthes, 'Rhétorique de l'image', *Communications*, 4 (1964), 40–51.

[7] Gerhard Jaritz, *Images. A Primer of Computer-Supported Analysis with Kleio IAS* (St Katharinen: Max-Planck-Institut für Geschichte, 1993), p. 16.

the mimetic representational power of the most realistic visual medium, photography. Furthermore, the simulation of a painting in three-dimensional (3-D) space strikes a blow against the ascendancy of photorealism in computer rendering. Simon Niedenthal demonstrates this by colliding a painting by Antonello da Messina, 'St Jerome in his Study', with the most recent rendering technology and suggesting the use of radiosity processing to check a 2-D representation against a 3-D structure.

The development of landscape and portrait painting gradually moved art away from iconography. The invention of photography marked a culmination of this movement. The final exposure of the 'treachery' of images has questioned the mimetic aspect. In a way these movements create a point of departure for modern research in pictures. With the loss of iconography and the mimetic aspect of realism in all kinds of pictures (dare I call it a pre-iconographic level of an image?) we are free to turn to the images of the past with new eyes. Is this what Erwin Panofsky meant when at the end of his life he gave up iconology? And is it not fair to think that the same situation has forced Irving Lavin to say that he sometimes thinks iconography is an invention of the devil?[8] Many of the articles in this volume demonstrate a marginalization of traditional iconographic studies and introduce not so conventional visual codes. Norbert Schnitzler's concern is significant for many of the articles when he demonstrates the mutual stimulations that combine new juridical concepts like 'deterrence' with corresponding concepts of representation. Is he elaborating another iconography or does he work at a new iconological level? None of the articles deals with the mimetic aspect as a documentary.[9]

The post-World War situation with the decline of the colonial powers has erased (art) historical explanations based on a centre-periphery theory. In the modern world there are no real centres of cultural or art historical activities. Finally the Internet has shown us an absolute decentralization of culture and information.[10] Hundred of thousands of images put on the Internet on equal terms make it almost impossible to point to specific artistic centres of the past. Such experiences are reflected in Michael Camille's essay 'At the sign of the "Spinning Sow": The "other" Chartres and images of everyday life of the

---

[8] Irving Lavin, 'Iconography as a Humanistic Discipline ("Iconography at the Crossroads")', in *Iconography at the Crossroads*, ed. by Brendan Cassidy (Princeton: Index of Christian Art, Princeton University, 1993), pp. 33, 38.

[9] Cf. Keith Moxey, 'Reading the "Reality Effect" ', in *Pictura quasi fictura. Die Rolle des Bildes in der Erforschung von Alltag und Sachkultur der Mittelalters und der frühen Neuzeit*, ed. by Gerhard Jaritz (Vienna: Verlag der österreichischen Akademie der Wissenschaften, 1996), pp. 15–21.

[10] Axel Bolvig, 'Ars longa—vita brevis', in *Medium Aevum Quotidianum,* ed. by Gerhard Jaritz (Krems: Gesellschaft zur Erforschung der materiellen Kultur des Mittelalters, 1998), pp. 7–20.

medieval street'. The famous cathedral of Chartres is not necessarily the only centre of the city. Its art is not the only one worthy of research. The preoccupation with so-called 'marginal' images has been so intense during the last decades that Jean Wirth treats the subject in an overall discussion of the research into the marginal figures of manuscripts from Emile Mâle's negation of meaning to Sharon Davenport's reading a spiritual meaning into every example.

After Marcel Duchamp's 'Ready Mades' there can be no real distinction between high art and low art or non-art. In ' "Primitive paintings: the visual world of populus rusticus', Helena Edgren writes: 'The primitive paintings still suffer from the label of "second-rate art" that they received a hundred years ago, and consequently they have not been able to compete with finer paintings for the attention of art historians'. Now the competition is vigorous. Michael Camille's 'Spinning Sow' and Axel Bolvig's 'Wooden Shoes' have nothing to do with art with a capital A.

Another questioning of the traditional preoccupation with the intentional meanings of an image, be they those of the artist or the donor, has been—it is my conviction—inspired by the modern world's use of pictures. No contemporary visual media can survive without reflecting on 'what the spectator sees'.[11] Could and should the spectator see and experience one and only one intentional meaning? Anna Nilsén reflects on conditions of visual communication in her article 'Man and picture: on the function of wall paintings in medieval churches': '. . . the interiors of the churches were too dark for the whole body of paintings to be identified by the congregation'.

Since the establishment of the technique of printing, historians have had access to huge amounts of written source material. This is one of the explanations why most historians fastened themselves in linguistic irons. Since Leopold Ranke, historical methodology has bound itself to the Gutenberg Galaxy.[12] In her article, Lena Liepe, an art historian, notes that 'after all, it is not the image itself that interests the historian'.[13] Today the situation has turned around 180 degrees. You can write a history of world art in one volume but you can only print a small selection of the works of art. In this new millennium—in principle—you can store millions of pictures on huge hard disks but nobody will have time or energy to read about each single object. Image databases offer

---

[11] The expression refers to Richard Wollheim, 'What the Spectator Sees', in *Visual Theory: Painting and Interpretation*, ed. by N. Bryson, M. A. Holly, and K. Moxey (Cambridge: Polity Press in association with Basil Blackwell, 1991), pp. 101–50.

[12] Axel Bolvig, 'Zur Kritik digitalisierender Geschichtsproduzenten', in *Electronic Filing, Registration, and Communication of Visual Historical Data, Abstracts for Round Table no 34 of the 18th International Congress of Historical Sciences*, ed. by Axel Bolvig (Göttingen: Max-Planck-Institut für Geschichte, 1995), pp. 1–7.

[13] Cf. Keith Moxey, *The Practice of Theory. Poststructuralism, Cultural Politics, and Art History* (Ithaca and London: Cornell University Press, 1994).

possibilities for comparative analysis of historical image information.[14] Several of the present articles deal with the use of image databases. Jörgen van den Berg demonstrates the new potentiality of ICONCLASS as a common indexing system within a digitized world. Jérôme Baschet argues for an 'iconographie sérielle' which is 'indispensable pour faire apparaître l'épaisseur historique et la complexité des phénomènes, dès lors qu'on la conçoit . . . comme la production de gammes de variations, au sein d'environnements complexes et mouvants'. Gerhard Jaritz shows how the database Real brings new light to visual phenomena such as cleanliness and men's hairstyles. In the image database we are confronted with connections of the qualitative and the quantitative, opening up possibilities of searching for patterns, their role, rules, and connotations. Axel Bolvig uses the database of Danish wall paintings to demonstrate that in the pictorial world wooden shoes were not used by peasants but by evil people and devils, and that they connote rebellion.

The growing acceptance of a unique and individual visual meaning independent of the linearity of linguistics is stressed by Lena Liepe when writing that 'the main potential of images as historical sources lies precisely in their visual formation'. Ulla Haastrup demonstrates the historical power of images. She challenges the historians' positivistic belief in the superiority of written material when using images as evidence of the existence of Jews in medieval Denmark in spite of written silence. Søren Kaspersen in his 'Framing history with salvation' indicates a medieval, politically tinted, connotative use of visual language in detailed programs. With three different examples Frank Colson, Jean Colson, Ross Parry, and Andrew Sawyer demonstrate a superiority of the image. 'When we are considering power (to use Bryson's phrase) "not as a monolith, but as a swarm of points traversing social stratifications and individual persons",[15] it appears to be (in these three examples at least) the image that thrives as a representational framework'. This acknowledged superiority of image to word is behind Francis Haskell's article on J. Huizinga showing that *The Autumn of the Middle Ages* is 'the first major work of history to have been inspired, both directly and self-confessedly, by visual sources'.

An established acceptance of images as invaluable material in our understanding of the past stresses another treachery of the image. We do not look at the same pictures as did our forefathers. The content of a text is the same whether it is written by hand or printed in Palatino or in Times. This means that we can copy a text without changing the content. But we cannot copy an

[14] Gerhard Jaritz, 'Comparative Analysis of Historical Image Information', in *Electronic Filing, Registration, and Communication of Visual Historical Data* (as note 12), pp. 29–33.

[15] N. Bryson, 'Semiology and Visual Interpretation', in *Visual Theory: Painting and Interpretation* (as note 11), pp. 61–73 (p. 71).

image—we create a new image with a resemblance to the original.[16] Each individual picture is the result of an inevitable connection between form and content. A change in the former involves a change in the latter. Therefore we are forced to reconsider the physical conditions of pictures. Rolf-Jürgen Grote and Annette Hornschuch write about the use of IT and the need for interdisciplinary research in 'Innovative hybride graphische Systeme zur Denkmalüberwachung':

> Selbstverständlich können die im Verlauf der Forschungsprojekte entwickelten oder geplanten rechnergestützten Verfahren der Visualisierung und Dokumentation zunächst nur vorläufige Interpretationshilfen geben. Sie sind als Service-Leistungen aufzufassen, die einem interdisziplinären Untersuchungsteam den Einstieg in vertiefende Zustands- und Schadenserfassungen erleichtern und erste Hinweise für Konservierungs- und Restaurierungsmaßnahmen ermöglichen.

The title of Phillip Lindley's article is significant and explains why research in images is such a broad-spectrum project: 'The Lincoln CD-ROM Project: history, theory, conservation, and images'. The chief objective of the Lincoln Project was to document the evolution of conservation and the progress of conservation work. The intention behind this volume is to demonstrate an interrelated fan of approaches to understanding the visual world of the past.

To stress the diversified but exiting instability of visual communication I cannot resist quoting *Against Art and Artists* by Jean Gimpel. As its struggle against the Reformation developed, Rome decided to use art as a means of action against Protestant heresy. Art and artists were to be indoctrinated, and their work supervised. In 1573, Paolo Veronese was summoned to appear before the Holy Office because of his *Last Supper*. He had continued to paint religious subjects, ignoring the instructions of the Council of Trent. Into his picture he had introduced all kinds of human and animal figures, all of which the Holy Office considered incompatible with the gravity of the subject.

> *Inquisitor*: Does it seem to you proper in a painting of the Last Supper of our Lord to represent fools, drunken Germans, dwarfs and other trifles?
>
> *Veronese*: No.
>
> *Inquisitor*: Why did you do it?
>
> *Veronese*: I did it with the idea that these people were outside the room where the supper was taking place.
>
> *Inquisitor*: Do you know that in Germany and other places infected with heresy they are in the habit of using various paintings full of low subjects and similar inventions to tear to pieces, vilify and make fun of the things of the Holy Catholic Church, in order to teach false doctrine to foolish and ignorant people?
>
> *Veronese*: The Commission was to decorate the picture as I thought fit. It is large

[16] Søren Kjørup, 'Billedkommunikation', in *Visuel Kommunikation*, vol. 1, ed. by Bent Fausing and Peter Larsen (Copenhagen: Medusa, 1980), pp. 58–82.

> and can hold many figures. . . . If there is space left in a picture I decorate it with invented figures. . . . We painters claim the license that poets and madmen claim.

The inquisitors were not satisfied with Veronese's explanation. They ruled that within three months he must correct and amend his picture.

Paolo Veronese did not correct his picture. He changed the title. The *Last Supper* became *The Feast in the House of Levi.*[17]

Who is treacherous towards images? In my opinion the many possible answers lie in a new *Iconology*.

---

[17] Jean Gimpel, *Against Art and Artists*, rev. edn (Edinburgh: Polygon, 1991), pp. 55–56. This is a translation of the original French, *Contre l'art et les artistes, ou la naissance d'une religion* (Paris: Seuil, 1968).

Images and History

Art and history: the legacy of Johan Huizinga

† FRANCIS HASKELL *

The present reputation of Johan Huizinga is a curious one. His masterpiece, *The Autumn of the Middle Ages*, remains in print, as it has done more or less ever since it first appeared over seventy years ago,[1] and a casual glance at paperback bookshops in the U.K., France, Italy, and Germany suggests that foreign translations are still in strong demand (can one say the same of any other major historical work of our century?); in his native Netherlands a new research institute has just been named after him and, on a recent visit to Amsterdam, I got the impression that just about half the student population there was engaged in investigating some aspect of his achievement; and any current book or article which refers to him, invariably, and as a matter of course, attaches the adjective 'great' to his name. And yet scarcely a single modern scholar accepts either the methodology or the conclusions on which his reputation is based. Above all, as far as I can see, no art historian now agrees with the central tenet of his book to the effect that the magnificent art of fifteenth-century Flanders—the art of Jan van Eyck and Rogier van der Weyden—represents not an innovative 'Renaissance' but an autumnal, if ostentatious, decline from the Middle Ages. Just how that art did emerge remains very controversial, but Huizinga's view has either been explicitly rejected—as

* Sadly, Francis Haskell died before he was able to revise this essay; minor emendments have been made by the editors with the assistance of Nicholas Penny.

[1] I will be referring throughout this article to the new, complete English translation of the book by Rodney J. Payton and Ulrich Mammitzsch, published by The University of Chicago Press in 1996, despite the fact that, as I have written in *The New York Review of Books* (4 April 1996), very occasionally the English version produced by F. Hopman (London: E. Arnold, 1924), under Huizinga's supervision, does seem to incorporate new ideas which are of real value.

by the distinguished connoisseur of Northern Art, Horst Gerson, in an otherwise appreciative appraisal[2]—or (more usually) totally ignored.[3] By contrast, Panofsky in a note in his *Early Netherlandish Painting*, which, ever since its publication in 1955 has been recognized as constituting a milestone in studies of the period, does refer with respect to Huizinga's achievement.

Nevertheless, one would not realize that at least one theory in that book—a theory of crucial importance to Panofsky—may well have been suggested to him by a reading of Huizinga. Indeed, perhaps this was not something that Panofsky himself would have acknowledged. The theory I have in mind is, significantly, just the one in *Early Netherlandish Painting*, which has been most trenchantly criticized and ultimately dismissed by art historians: the theory of 'concealed or disguised symbolism'. As is well known, Panofsky argues that the conquest of natural appearances by Jan van Eyck and some of his contemporaries was so effective that it carried with it the supreme risk of destroying what had hitherto been the principal purpose of a picture: 'to instruct, arouse pious emotions and awaken memories'.[4] A painting such as Jan van Eyck's *Portrait of Giovanni (?) Arnolfini and his Wife*, in the National Gallery in London (fig. 1, plate 1), might be thought of as devoid of meaning in that sense,[5] and a way had therefore to be found of reconciling 'the new naturalism with a thousand years of Christian tradition'. That way was to be the conscious application of disguised symbolic interpretations 'to each and every object, man-made or natural'. Thus when we look at van Eyck's *Lucca Madonna* in Frankfurt (fig. 2, plate 2) we—and still less fifteenth-century spectators—are not invited to be awe-struck by the apparently natural positioning of the Virgin and Child seated under a three-dimensional canopy in a simply furnished room around which we could find our way without difficulty, in contrast to the stylized and artificial conventions adopted by Flemish artists in the depiction of similar scenes a generation or so earlier, such as Broederlam's *Annunciation and Visitation* in Dijon (fig. 3). Panofsky emphasizes instead the significance of the candlestick which

---

[2] H. Gerson, 'Huizinga und Kunstgeschichte', in *Johan Huizinga 1872–1972*, papers delivered to the Johan Huizinga conference, Groningen 11–15 December 1972, ed. by W. R. H. Koops, E. H. Kossmann, and Gees van den Plaat (The Hague: Nijhoff, 1973), pp. 207–22.

[3] See, for instance, Jan Bialostocki, *L'art du XVe siècle, des Parler à Durer* (Paris: LGF, 1993).

[4] Erwin Panofsky, *Early Netherlandish Painting* (Cambridge, MA: Harvard University Press, 1955), p. 141. For Panofsky's reference to Huizinga, see p. 74, n. 2.

[5] See *National Gallery Catalogues: The Fifteenth-Century Netherlandish Schools*, ed. by Lorne Campbell (London: National Gallery Publications, 1999), pp. 174–211.

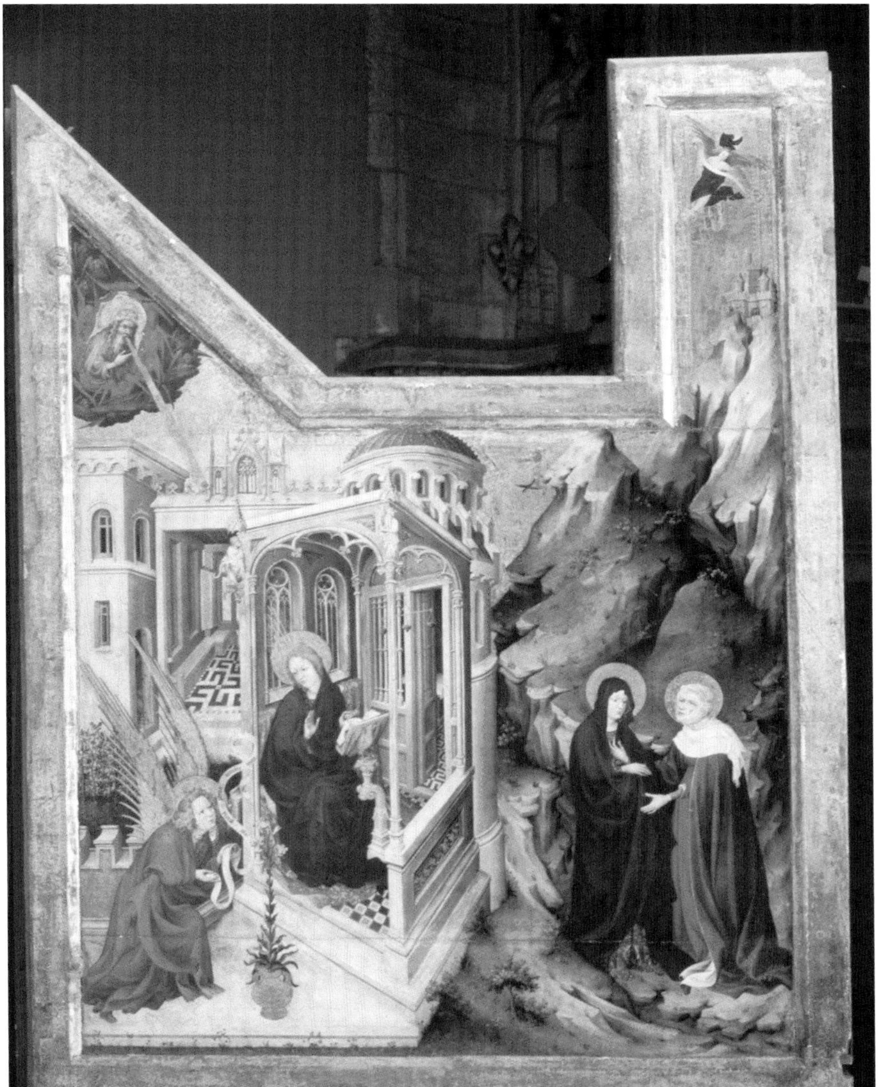

Fig. 3. 'Annunciation and Visitation', Melchior Broederlam. Tempera on wood, 167 x 125 cm. Musée des Beaux-Arts, Dijon. © Musée des Beaux-Arts, Dijon

supposedly denotes the Virgin (who supports her child as the candlestick supports the candle); of the glass carafe and the basin, which serve for 'an indoors substitute for the most typical symbols of the Virgin's purity 'the fountain of gardens' and 'well of living waters' of The Song of Songs'; and of the four lions on the armrests of the Virgin's throne which 'bring to mind' the Throne of Solomon, as described in The Book of Kings; and so on.[6] The effect of all this is to neutralize the impact of van Eyck's vivid and real novelty and to make the painting appear far more 'medieval' than it strikes us at first sight. Indeed, Panofsky points out that van Eyck is still making use—though on a far more systematic and sophisticated basis—of the same type of symbolism that Broederlam had earlier employed in his *Annunciation*, where, for instance, the three windows on the cornice allude to The Trinity and the circular structure behind the Virgin's shrine has been designed to look like a tower because this was a recognized symbol of chastity.[7]

The case that van Eyck was not the 'realist', and hence 'progressive', painter so admired by the nineteenth century had, of course, been made very forcefully by Huizinga, who had stressed, again and again, the overriding importance of symbolism in his art and in that of his contemporaries—a symbolism that had by now lost its original significance and served only 'to give concrete shape to every conception. Every thought seeks expression in an image, but in this image it solidifies, and becomes rigid'.[8] For Huizinga, this feature of fifteenth-century Flemish art had been characteristic of the decline of an overripe civilization rather than of the lusty birth of a new one. Panofsky's conclusion is not, of course, the same as this, but its implications do seem to me to be close enough to it to warrant the hypothesis that the two could have been related—and I was delighted to come across the suggestion made by Gerson (who was writing at a time when the concept of 'disguised symbolism' was still generally accepted) that Huizinga would have been gladdened by Panofsky's theory had he been able to know of it.[9] When reading Panofsky's emphasis on the intellectually designed, rather than realistically observed, features of van Eyck's *Virgin and Child* in Frankfurt, and similar pictures elsewhere, I cannot help recalling that Huizinga had repeatedly claimed that the *horror vacui*, the over-elaborate detail, the exaggerated finish in the paintings of van Eyck and his contemporaries signified an end, rather than a beginning—often magically beautiful, but sometimes pompous and artificial. Well before Panofsky had singled out the deliberately

---

[6] Panofsky (as in note 4), pp. 137, 143–44.

[7] *Ibid.*, p. 132.

[8] For the following analysis of Huizinga, see (where not otherwise indicated) Francis Haskell, *History and its Images* (New Haven: Yale University Press, 1993), pp. 468–95.

[9] See Gerson (as in note 2), p. 212.

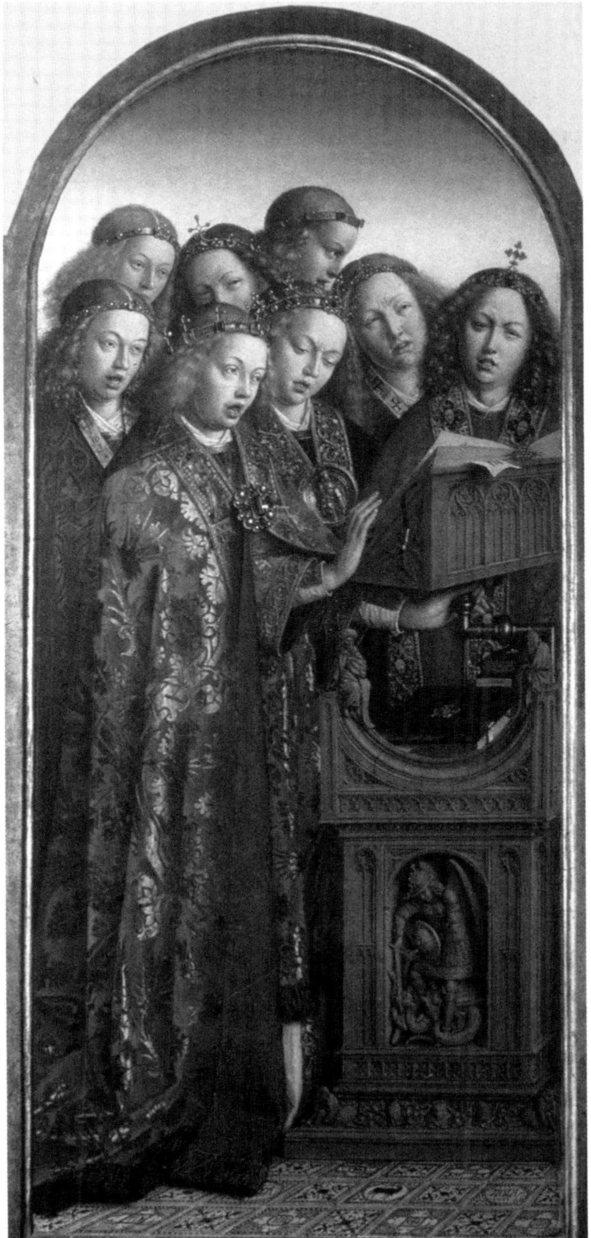

Fig. 4. 'Singing angels', Jan van Eyck. The Ghent altarpiece. Oil on panel. Cathedral of St Bavo, Gent. © Cathedral of St Bavo, Gent

archaizing and contrived elements in the *Virgin and Child* in Frankfurt, Huizinga had warned his readers not to be misled by the Singing Angels in the Gent altarpiece (fig. 4) who appear to be so straightforwardly and freshly rendered: 'the heavy garments, all dark red and gold with sparkling gems, the overly emphasized, distorted face, the somewhat pedantic ornaments of the music stand—all are the painterly equivalent of the dazzling bombast of the literary Burgundian court style'.[10]

A few words of Otto Pächt's polemical review of *Early Netherlandish Painting* silently demolish the principal thesis behind the great works of both Huizinga and Panofsky: 'While it is arguable whether one should start the history of Italian Renaissance painting with Giotto or with Masaccio, no doubts are permissible as to where the caesura between the Middle Ages and modern times has to be made in Northern painting'[11]—for it is, of course, precisely the sowing of such doubts that characterizes the works of both these cultural historians.

Cultural historians working outside the field of painting have been just as sceptical (perhaps even more) of Huizinga's views. In particular, a number of distinguished Italian scholars, of whom the most conspicuous is probably Eugenio Garin, have barely been able to conceal their resentment beneath a thin veneer of guarded respect, and it has been plausibly argued that this hostility may have been aroused by a feeling of disquiet that Huizinga's concentration on northern Europe (disenchanted though it was) may have distracted attention from the achievements of the Italian Renaissance as celebrated by Burckhardt—the more so as it was the North that was to play a more influential role than Italy in the creation of the modern world.[12]

Within the last few years, two important English studies have gone out of their way to dispute Huizinga's claim—perhaps the most influential of all his claims—that by the fifteenth century the notion of chivalry, with its attendant enthusiasm for tournaments and displays of the most ritualized yet extravagant nature, had lost its original purpose of training virtuous warriors to defend Christianity and had sunk into morally meaningless prodigality, and dreamlike evasion of reality. On the contrary, we are now told, the tournament still retained its value as a preparation for actual warfare, and in any case the nostalgia for the chivalric values of three hundred years earlier—a nostalgia which, it is admitted, certainly does pervade Burgundian court culture—served to uphold those values

---

[10] Huizinga (as note 1), p. 342.

[11] See *The Burlington Magazine* (1958), 275.

[12] Alberto Varvaro, 'Riconsiderando l'Autunno del Medioevo', in *Filosofia e storia della cultura. Studi in onore di Fulvio Tessitore*, ed. by G. Cacciatore, M. Martirano, and E. Massimilaa (Naples: Morano, 1998), pp. 785–97.

against later distortions of them.[13]

My reading of modern literature on the religious beliefs and practices of the time is too scanty for me to judge whether Huizinga's view that they too had become sterile and artificial still commands respect, but I do know that he has been criticized in this field also and that he has certainly been made to pay dearly for the hostages that he offered to fortune by once admitting that he had made no serious reference to Joan of Arc on the grounds that she would have upset the balance of *The Autumn of the Middle Ages.*

Most surprising and devastating of all, perhaps, are the couple of paragraphs which in 1941 the fine French historian Lucien Febvre devoted to undermining the very basis of Huizinga's approach—surprising both because Febvre expressed such warm admiration for the book which, he complained, had been so 'prosaically' translated as 'Déclin du moyen âge' and because, only a year later, he had echoed so closely some of the opening phrases of *The Autumn of the Middle Ages* in his own masterpiece, *Le Problème de l'incroyance au XVIe siècle—la religion de Rabelais.* Thus Huizinga states:

> When the world was half a thousand years younger all events had much sharper outlines than now. The distance between sadness and joy, between good and bad fortune, seemed to be much greater than for us... Just as the contrast between summer and winter was stronger than in our present lives, so was the difference between light and dark, quiet and noise....[14]

If we now turn to Febvre we find:

> Let us conjure up François Rabelais's contemporaries—their violence and capriciousness, their inability to resist surface impressions, their extraordinary changes of mood, their astonishing quickness to anger, to take offence, to draw the sword and then kiss and make up [. . .]. These are the natural products of a life full of contrasts, much sharper than we can imagine: the contrast of day and night, unknown to us in our electrically lit homes; the contrast of winter and summer, tempered for us in normal times by a thousand devices, whereas they were subjected to the seasons' rigours and necessities practically without letup, for weeks and months at a time. . . .[15]

Yet despite this homage to the great Dutch historian Febvre questions the very notion of singling out some particular sentiment—the violent oscillation, for instance, between cruelty and tenderness, extreme hatred and extreme goodness,

---

[13] Malcolm Vale, *War and Chivalry* (London: Duckworth. 1981); Maurice Keen, 'Huizinga, Kilgour and the Decline of Chivalry', in *Medievalia et Humanistica*, new series, no. 8 (Cambridge, 1977), pp. 1–20.

[14] Huizinga (as note 1), pp. 1–2.

[15] Lucien Febvre, *The Problem of Unbelief in the Sixteenth Century—The Religion of Rabelais*, trans. by Beatrice Gottlieb (Cambridge, MA: Harvard University Press, 1982), p. 99.

which exudes 'the mixed smell of blood and roses'—as having been characteristic of the decline of the Middle Ages. Cannot the same sentiment be detected just as clearly at the dawn of the Middle Ages—or, indeed, at the dawn of modern times?[16]

Some recent writers have indeed gone much further than this. Thus in a subtle and admirable study of the imagery associated with the early years of François 1er of France, the French art historian Anne-Marie Lecoq quite often finds Huizinga's concepts relevant to her discussion, despite the fact that the subtitle of her book contains the phrase *l'aube de la Renaissance*, which seems to pose a deliberate challenge to the *Autumn of the Middle Ages*. On one occasion she even claims that Huizinga's analysis of a popular feature of decaying Burgundian rhetoric—the use of 'reverse symbolism' whereby 'the lower does not point to the higher, but rather the higher to the lower, since, in the mind of the inventor, the earthly things that he intends to glorify with some heavenly ornamentation are foremost'—is more applicable to the court of Henri IV early in the seventeenth century than to that of François 1er in the sixteenth.[17] The case against Huizinga is thus formidable: and yet he lives.

Are we to assume that this is because he belongs with those great, imaginative and self-confident pattern-makers whom we associate mainly, but not exclusively, with the nineteenth century: men such as Burckhardt and Taine and the anthropologist Sir James Frazer and (dare I say it?) Marx and Freud, who have—often with spellbinding virtuosity—constructed syntheses, whose inner consistency continues to mesmerize us even after the experts have convincingly proved to us that they are frayed at the edges and often decayed at the core? To some extent, this is certainly true of the work of Huizinga. And it is also all too easy to understand why, ever since 1914, Europeans and Americans should, however reluctantly, be particularly attracted by the poignant spectacle of a decaying but flashy culture—especially when that spectacle is evoked with incomparable poetry, as Dutch colleagues assure us is the case of *The Autumn of the Middle Ages* in the original.

And yet the survival of the book depends on much more varied causes than that, and I want to devote the remainder of this essay to the two features of Huizinga's work that strike me as still being both original and challenging—and to show, incidentally, how both of them have indeed also been challenged.

The Autumn of the Middle Ages is, I believe, the first major work of history to have been inspired, both directly and self-confessedly, by visual sources—and here I must at once apologize for the need I will frequently have to succumb to

---

[16] Lucien Febvre, 'Comment reconstituer la vie affective d'autrefois? La sensibilité et l'histoire', *Annales d'Histoire Sociale,* 111 (1941), reprinted in *Combats pour l'histoire* (Paris: A. Colin, 1953), pp. 221–38 (pp. 226–27).

[17] Anne-Marie Lecoq, *François Ier imaginaire: Symbolique & politique à l'aube de la Renaissance française* (Paris: Macula, 1987), p. 353 and elsewhere.

from now on: that is, to draw on a recent book of my own—*History and its Images*—that tries to explore the strengths and weaknesses of the use of such sources by writers ever since the Renaissance. For it is, of course, true that, long before Huizinga, much historical writing had, to a greater or lesser extent, been significantly affected by responses to the visual arts. In 1864, Hippolyte Taine had planned 'to study Italian history by making use of painting for my documentation instead of written sources', perhaps aware of the fact that some ten years earlier John Ruskin had already claimed to do just that in *The Stones of Venice*. I wish that I knew enough about Huizinga's development to discover whether or not he had (as seems likely) read this astonishing and perverse masterpiece and, if so, whether he remembered from it the brief, but eloquent, passage in which Ruskin recalls visiting Venice before the days of the railway and being so 'entranced by the visionary charm of a scene so beautiful and so strange' that he feared running the risk of forgetting that the past of the city had been marked by dark cruelty and fear and that the evidence of art could therefore be misleading. Above all, I would like to know whether Huizinga was acquainted with a famous aphorism of Ruskin's that seems to me to encapsulate much of the methodology that was to serve him for *The Autumn of the Middle Ages*: 'Great nations write their autobiographies in three manuscripts: the book of their deeds, the book of their words, and the book of their art. Not one of these books can be understood unless we read the two others; but of the three, the only quite trustworthy one is the last'. For reasons that will later become obvious I want to draw particular attention to a few words of that phrase: 'Not one of these books can be understood unless we read the two others': we will return to their implications.

The Stones of Venice can, however, hardly be described as a work of history, however great its influence on the writing of history may or may not have been, and we must turn now to the explanation provided by Huizinga himself of the inspiration for his own spiritually akin, but far more coherent, masterpiece. Writing in the very last years of his life he tells us that although he had, as a child, been fascinated by the Middle Ages and, as a student, by the visual arts, in later years his professional interests had moved to the remote field of ancient Indian theology and literature until, in 1902, he paid a visit to the remarkable exhibition of Flemish Primitives held that year in Bruges. Some five years or so later, on a Sunday afternoon between 1906 and 1909, probably 1907, 'when my wife's time was taken up by looking after the young children', it occurred to him, in a flash, while walking through the countryside, 'that the late Middle Ages were not the herald of something new that was to come, but the fading away of something that had already passed. This thought, if it can be called a thought, revolved above all around the art of the van Eycks and their contemporaries, which considerably occupied my mind at that time' and which was generally being interpreted as the dawn of a Northern Renaissance. 'My perception was directly opposed to this. Some years passed, however, before I began to work it out . . . [and] I began in 1910 to read as much as possible of the Burgundian and French historians of the period. . .'.

It is the chronology of these stages that I want to stress. If we are to trust Huizinga, he saw the early Flemish pictures in 1902, reacted against the prevailing view of them in 1907, and only in 1910 began to read the literature of the time, which—nine years later—led to *The Autumn of the Middle Ages*. In other words it was the *visual* source that stimulated his interest in the *written* ones—and not the other way round. I emphasize this as strongly as I can, because in a very famous and enthralling lecture (at which I had the honour to be chairman and which was subsequently published as book called *In Search of Cultural History*) Ernst Gombrich argued in 1967 that instead of starting 'from the impression [that] van Eyck's paintings made on him', Huizinga 'took the opposite line. He simply knew too many facts about the age of van Eyck to find it easy to square his impression of his pictures with [what he knew of the culture]. He felt he had rather to re-interpret the style of the painter' so that van Eyck's realism 'could no longer be seen as a harbinger of a new age; his jewel-like richness and his accumulation of detail were rather an expression of the same late Gothic spirit that was also manifested much less appealingly in the prolix writings of the period which nobody but specialists read any more'.

But if Huizinga is telling the truth about his development—and I cannot see why we should doubt that he is—it was only *after* he had had the perception (whether valid or not is another matter) that Flemish painting was affected, over-refined, and fussy that he followed up the literary sources and chronicles which led him to conclude that the whole period was one of decline. It would therefore naturally be of interest to examine for ourselves just what were the pictures that made this impression on him at the decisive Exhibition of 1902—and, to some extent, we can do this thanks to surviving catalogues, descriptions and photographic records. It would be pedantic, absurd in fact, to pursue this line of enquiry too far, because quite obviously he had plenty of later opportunities to see Flemish pictures elsewhere, but we are all the same entitled to believe that the first, overpowering, revelation came to him at the Bruges Exhibition, so that it is worth noting that only one certain, and incidentally very small, work was to be seen there by the artist who is now usually called Robert Campin and recognized as one of the founders of the new Flemish painting—an artist whose domestic, almost ungainly, realism conveys so very different an image from the delicate but luxurious elegance of van Eyck. And although as many as seventeen pictures were attributed to Rogier van der Weyden in the catalogue, it was agreed that in none of these cases was the attribution wholly convincing, while it was in any case not possible to borrow from Spain his large and dramatic *Deposition from the Cross* (now in the Prado), which exemplifies just that boldness of conception and originality of design that Huizinga professed himself unable to discover in the art of the period. There were, on the other hand, two

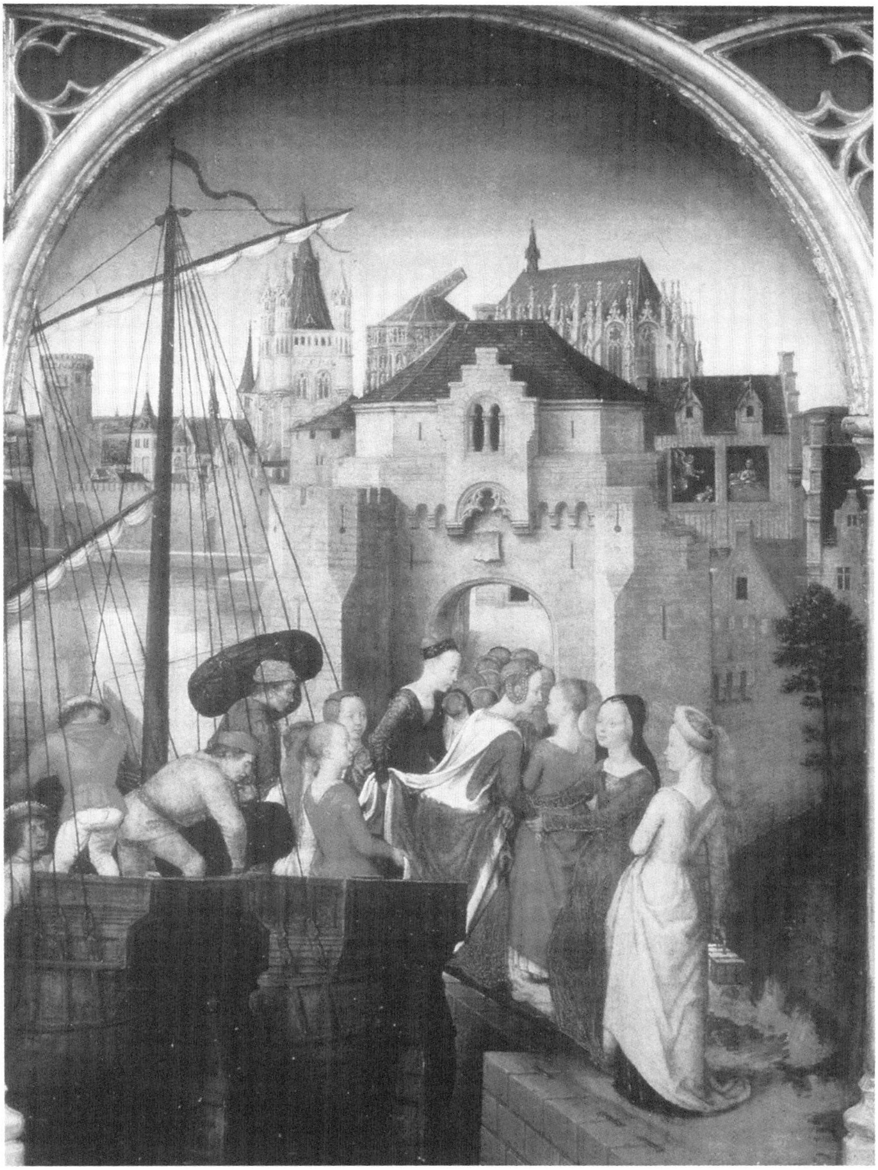

Fig. 5. 'Shrine of St Ursula', Hans Memling, detail. Wood, 37.5 x 30 cm. Bruges Groeninge Museum. © Groeninge Museum, Bruges

wings of an altarpiece showing no fewer than eight scenes from the legend of the martyrdom of St Ursula (fig. 5) by an anonymous master of the second half of the fifteenth century who had at one time been thought to be Memling and more recently (for easily understandable reasons) has been considered to be a miniaturist from Bruges working on a larger scale than the one he was accustomed to. In fact, I get the impression that although the stars of the Exhibition were van Eyck, Memling, and Gerard David, it was appealing but relatively minor pictures of this sort, combining picturesque and fanciful architecture with eminently pretty, though slightly gawky and awkward, figures engaged in scenes of ceremony and cruelty—pictures of which there were large numbers—that would have been most apparent to visitors to the Exhibition. Indeed, by far the most famous of the many genuine Memlings to be seen there was the small shrine in the form of a tabernacle depicting episodes from the same legend, painted in the spirit of a chivalrous fairy story of the very kind which plays so prominent a part in Huizinga's conception of the Middle Ages. It is, therefore, tempting to suggest that he was so struck by works of this nature that he hardly bothered to look at the numerous portraits by Memling that were also present and that appear to represent sober, devout, God-fearing merchants who created the riches needed for the exotic pastimes and costumes of court life but who are of no interest to the author of *The Autumn of the Middle Ages*. More in keeping with the spirit of that book was a large and horrifying picture by Gerard David of the *Flaying of the Unjust Judge* (in Groningen) which, although he does not mention it, must surely have helped to stimulate Huizinga's evocation of the atrocious tortures and executions freely carried out in the Low Countries during the fifteenth century. Similarly, although he does not refer to Hieronymous Bosch (and, in other writings, tends to play down his importance), who was represented by a handful of paintings (two or three of which were authentic), it is hard not to see his so-called 'diableries' as a formative influence on Huizinga's view of the period as credulous, perversely child-like and ultimately detestable.

It is thus not unreasonable to take Huizinga at his word when he tells us that he first formed an impression of Flemish and Burgundian civilization of the fifteenth century as unbalanced, neurotic, cruel, and fanciful on the basis of the pictures that he suddenly came across at the Bruges Exhibition in 1902.

But if this rescues Huizinga from one of the traps into which Gombrich claims he had fallen, it may seem to thrust him still more vigorously into the other—the fallacy, that is, of adopting the Hegelian viewpoint whereby if the nature of the art cannot be deduced comfortably from 'the spirit of the age' in general, then at least that 'spirit of the age' can itself be deduced from the nature of the art. It is a reproach that has quite often been made against Huizinga both explicitly and implicitly—most unsparingly (and misguidedly), I believe, by another even more encyclopaedic historian of the Middle Ages, the German Ernst Robert Curtius—an historian of literature and a philologist, who had little if any interest in the visual arts, but who in many other ways was rather similar to Huizinga. Both were conservative and pessimistic by instinct, disgusted as well as horrified by the twentieth century—yet (understandably) reluctant to commit themselves too far in view of the certain dangers to which such outright opposition would have led—and, above all, both men were at home with the whole of European civilization: along with Panofsky among the very last of their kind. I used the phrase that 'I believe' that Curtius had Huizinga in mind when indulging in rather a muddled outburst in the first chapter of his *European Literature and the Latin Middle Ages* although this is not explicit, and he was certainly even more concerned to correct the influence of Wölfflin,[18] Curtius stigmatized the concept of 'art history as a super discipline' and insisted that:

> literature has different forms of movement, of growth, of continuity, from art. It possesses a freedom which is denied to art [. . .] with the literature of all times and peoples I can have a direct, intimate, and engrossing vital relationship, with art not. Works of art I have to contemplate in museums. The book is more real than the picture. [. . .] To understand Pindar's poems requires severe mental effort—to understand the Parthenon frieze does not. The same relation obtains between Dante and the cathedrals, and so on. Knowing pictures is easy compared with knowing books. Now if it is possible to learn the 'essence of Gothic' from the cathedrals, one need no longer read Dante. . . .

One of the more surprising features about this very questionable statement is that Huizinga himself seems to have anticipated—and to have shared—some of the anxieties that gave rise to it. As early as 1919—well before Curtius—he himself pointed out that:

> our perception [today] of former times, our historical organ, so to say, is more and more becoming visual. [. . .] The change of our ideas about the Middle Ages is due less to a weakening of the romantic sense than to the substitution of artistic for intellectual appreciation.

And by 1940—at much the same time as Curtius—he was deploring the fact that 'as more and more visual material for the appreciation of the past became quite generally available, so thinking and writing about the past fell into increasing neglect'. It is true that he does not mention the fact that it was he himself who, more than any other historian, had been (unwittingly) responsible for stimulating such a 'one-sided aesthetic view' of the past, but it is also true that no-one less than he deserved Curtius's reproach (if, indeed, it was directed at him) of forgetting that 'there are essential differences between the book and the picture'.

On the contrary. One of the reasons that makes it difficult to admire the approach of most later historians to visual evidence lies precisely in the fact that

---

[18] See Ernst Robert Curtius, *European Literature and the Latin Middle Ages*, trans. from German by Willard R. Trask (Princeton: Princeton University Press, 1990), Chapter 1, especially pp. 11–16.

none of them seems to have taken sufficient account of some of the weaknesses of his own methodology pointed out by Huizinga and of the dichotomy between art and literature outlined by Curtius. It was, after all, Huizinga himself, and not one of his critics, who emphasized how very limited was the material available to the historian who wished primarily to understand the past on the basis of visual evidence—an awareness, incidentally, that makes it all the more astonishing that he paid almost no attention whatsoever to tapestries and miniatures. None of the recorded bathing and hunting scenes by Jan van Eyck or Rogier van der Weyden had survived—let alone the elaborate costumes and ephemeral decorations of the time: in contrast, written records of absolutely every kind were to be found in abundance. It was Huizinga also who analysed with a subtlety worthy of Lessing (even if not always convincingly) the differing expressive possibilities open to the artist and the writer in the Middle Ages. Love, he argued for instance, could not be depicted adequately in fifteenth-century painting or miniatures, because it always appeared as hieratic, solemn, artificial—whereas we know from surviving literature that the sentiment itself certainly existed. That said, it is only through painting that we learn that people could respond to the effects of light breaking through darkness or the freshness of the countryside in spring, because the literary conventions were too contrived to allow for the expression of such feelings.

And it is through this sort of analysis that Huizinga reaches a conclusion of absolutely fundamental importance for anyone interested in cultural history:

> It is a general phenomenon that the idea which works of art give us of an epoch is far more serene and happy than that which we glean in reading its chronicles, documents, or even literature. Plastic art does not lament. [. . .] [Hence] the vision of an epoch resulting from the contemplation of works of art is always incomplete, always too favourable, and therefore fallacious.[19]

I doubt if I could work up much enthusiasm for any historian aiming to make use of visual evidence (as so many historians now claim that they do) who did not, at the very least, ponder or, or challenge, this penetrating axiom—for it is, of course, open to challenge—and it brings me to what seems the central issue in my discussion of why we should continue to take Huizinga very seriously today. For in certain fundamental ways he differed radically from those great creative historians and systematizers to whom I compared him a little time ago. Unlike them, Huizinga was always aware of the potential weaknesses in his own approach. He was tempted by the notion of an all-embracing Hegelian synthesis—what cultural historian is not?—but he could not stifle his doubts about its validity in the face of conflicting testimony. I read in a book review recently that it is now fashionable for scholarly books to shun conclusions and to end on a note of enquiry. I was dismayed by this comment, partly because I had

---

[19] *The Waning of the Middle Ages* (New York: Doubleday Anchor, 1954), pp. 242–43.

thought that, as I grew older, I myself had developed this procedure in the light of the experience of a lifetime—and it is always disconcerting to discover that one's apparently original and deeply pondered contributions to scholarship are, in fact, merely the consequences of fashion. I do not, in any case, believe that Huizinga thought of his book in this way, but I do believe that, fashionably or not, we can approach it in such a spirit if we choose to. His Dutch critics—and he has some pretty ferocious ones[20]—have been scathing about his timidity, the tentative nature of his aesthetic involvement, his vacillations, and his reluctance to commit himself forcefully enough. I must confess that it is partly these very weaknesses—if that is what they are—that help to keep *The Autumn of the Middle Ages* so stimulating for me. In 1905, many years before he had even begun to think of embarking on that masterpiece, Huizinga delivered his inaugural lecture at the University of Groningen and chose as its title 'The aesthetic element in historical thought'. In it he argued that it is through images that we can best approach the past. He pointed to the example of Michelet in perfecting this method and told a story from Michelet's history of the French Revolution that has haunted me ever since I first came across it. Long after the revolution a young man asked the aged Merlin de Thionville how he had brought himself to condemn Robespierre. The old man seemed to be regretting what he had done and then suddenly he arose brusquely: 'Robespierre', he said, 'Robespierre. If you had seen *his green eyes*, you, too, would have condemned him as I did'. For Huizinga also, the image came first, enabling us to see the past 'more lucidly, more sharply and more colourfully—*in short, more historically*', but this was only a first stage, and in *The Autumn of the Middle Ages* he was able to create a book which demonstrates, with incomparably evocative power but also with incomparable critical insight, just what further structures can be built on foundations whose intrinsic nature would still repay the most serious investigation.

[20] See especially Pieter Geyl, 'Huizinga as Accuser of his Age', reprinted in *Encounters in History* (London: Collins, 1963).

Images and the historian[*]

JEAN-CLAUDE SCHMITT

A growing number of historians have for some years now been taking an interest in art and in the image, an area of research traditionally reserved for 'art historians'. This development in the historian's craft has very clearly had consequences for both disciplines. It has widened the historian's field of study, obliging him to reflect on objects and on values—in particular aesthetic values—which he has hitherto not been wont to take into account. It has in turn obliged art historians to think about the achievements and the future course of their own discipline, and about the social dimension of works of art: moving, one might say, in the opposite direction from that taken by the historians in response to their new requirements. It is now accepted that collaboration is not only desirable but necessary; this present volume is but one example of the trend. What remain to be laid down are some precise guidelines, to ensure that successful collaboration bears fruit. Three such guidelines seem to me to stand out as vital:

1. we must first adopt a historiographical perspective, and ask the proper questions concerning the developments which have both hindered and made possible the rapprochement of our two disciplines;
2. we must agree on the methodology to apply to the analysis of images;

[*] Translated into English by Brian J. Levy. The original first appeared as 'L'historien et les images', in *Der Blick auf die Bilder. Kunstgeschichte und Geschichte im Gespräch*, ed. by Otto Gerhard Oexle, Max-Planck-Institut für Geschichte (Göttingen: Wallstein, 1997), pp. 9-51.

3. we must outline the historical problems and issues relating to the role accorded to the image in social activities.[1]

Historiography

Francis Haskell has recently reminded us of the important part played ever since the Renaissance by images, from ancient coinage to paintings hanging in museums, in historians' reconstruction of the past.[2] His monograph does not really develop the theoretical aspect of his subject, nor does he take account of all the latest developments in historical research; it is, however, an extremely rich work and reveals very well indeed how historians, from the beginnings of their discipline, have hesitated between three possible standpoints.

Some have sought (or indeed still seek) to find in images a more or less faithful representation—and thus more or less acceptable to historical scholarship—of social *realia*, whether it be the portrayal of warfare (the scenes in the Bayeux Tapestry, for example), of agricultural techniques (drawn from illustrated calendars in manuscripts), or medieval domestic interiors (based on certain Nativity scenes). It cannot be denied that some at least of these images are of documentary relevance; however, this direct appropriation of images by some historians tells us nothing of the images themselves, of their *raison d'être*, or, above all, of the far more complex nature of the whole process of 'representation'.[3] It is dangerous self-deception to assume that for people in the past (or, for that matter, for us today) a sense of what was 'real' could exist independently of their attitudes as performers on the social stage, or of the way in which they might portray it in their works. The problem with this 'positivist' approach is that it gives the illusion that all art (at least until the arrival of abstract art) has a referential function, quite distinct from its other possible functions, and thus capable of being isolated by the historian. To be sure, an image is

[1] I am here adopting the point of view of a social historian who, for the past decade and in company with other historians and art historians, has been reflecting on the status and functions of the image in medieval culture, under the aegis of the Western Medieval Historical Anthropology Group at the Paris École des Hautes Études en Sciences Sociales. This research project has been essentially a collective one; my gratitude is due to my co-researchers, friends, and colleagues J. Baschet, J.-Cl. Bonne, A. Debert, and M. Pastoureau.

[2] Francis Haskell, *History and its Images. Art and the Interpretation of the Past* (New Haven and London: Yale University Press, 1993).

[3] A survey of recent scholarship in this area may be found in Jean-Claude Schmitt, 'Représentations', in *Georges Duby. L'écriture de l'Histoire*, ed. by Claudie Duhamel-Amado and Guy Lobrichon, Bibliothèque du Moyen Age, 6 (Brussels: De Boeck–Université, 1996), pp. 267–78.

always the image of something; but it is this fact that may delude us into thinking that we merely have to state what the image represents in order to say everything about its representation. In any case, this is beside the point; time and again, the images themselves are perfectly capable of reminding us that their function is less that of 'representing' an outside reality than of adapting this reality to their own particular mode.[4] For the historian, it should be a matter less of isolating and of 'reading' the contents of an image than of appreciating first and foremost that image in its totality: form and structure, functions and functioning.

For other historians, art bears witness to a Zeitgeist on which, by analogy with the styles familiar to art history, they bestow the names 'Romanesque', 'Gothic', 'Flamboyant' or 'Baroque'. They do not, however, take the trouble to analyse any actual works; generally speaking, they barely look at them. Francis Haskell calls them 'philosophers' (as opposed to 'antiquarians') and has gone so far as to include among their number Jules Michelet, Jacob Burckhard, and Johan Huizinga. As far as the latter is concerned, he notes that he very rarely ever turns to a work of art to depict a specific aspect of medieval society, with the exception of Chapter Nine of *The Autumn of the Middle Ages*, devoted to 'the vision of Death'. While praising Huizinga for having been in his opinion the last great historian to make a major contribution to the subject of history and its images, and for recognizing that through the image we can see the past 'more lucidly, more sharply and more colourfully, in short more historically', Haskell criticizes him for reverting in the final analysis to the traditional prejudice of devaluing the importance of images, compared with texts, because 'works of literature offer one more criterion than do works of art: they make it possible for us to appreciate the spirit as well as the form'.

The most common attitude has surely consisted, above all, of one long process of avoidance, between history (social, political, and even cultural) and art history, with each enjoying divergent lines of development. This avoidance is not fortuitous. It has its roots in the privileged position of the tongue, of speech, over all the other symbolic functions of mankind. It stems from the constitution of history as a 'literary' discipline in the eighteenth century, and as a positive science in the nineteenth, with pride of place given to written documents, judged to be more objective and reliable than pictures.

In exactly the same way as positivist history, based on 'the text', was able to align itself with archaeology, whose irrefutably objective foundations were laid down by the very material nature of the objects and inscriptions studied, so art history, all preoccupied with the appreciation of 'masterpieces', styles, and

---

[4] The ability of images, particularly in the modern period, to signify that the only reality they portray is that of representation has recently been studied by Victor I. Stoichita, *L'Instauration du tableau. Métapeinture à l'aube des Temps modernes* (Paris: Klincksieck, 1993); and by Klaus Krüger, 'Der Blick ins Innere des Bildes. Aesthetische Illusion bei Gerhard Richter', *Pantheon*, 53 (1995), 149–66.

artists, found itself comfortably associated with philosophy, its mission being to determine 'Beauty', in all its timelessness. As a result, in the 1888 inaugural lecture of his Archaeology course, Charles Diehl was able to draw a distinction between philosophy and art history on the one hand, with their seeking after the 'laws' governing universal aesthetics, and, on the other hand, history and archaeology, standing shoulder to shoulder and studying 'facts'. On art historians, he said: 'An ideal of supreme beauty serves as their yardstick when they come to study and to judge every age's particular ideal of beauty'. While 'art history is the close, and inseparable, kin of philosophy and aesthetics', in contrast 'archaeology is linked to history, and is its indispensable and utterly reliable adjunct'.[5]

A little later, following on from Alois Riegl (*Stilfragen*, 1893), Heinrich Wölfflin (*Kunstgeschichtliche Grundbegriffe*, 1915), and Henri Focillon (*La vie des formes*, 1934), the priority given by art historians to form and its *sui generis* development could only serve to widen still more the gulf between their artistic Heavenly Spheres and the (as it were) down-to-earth preoccupations of social and political history. Art history had its own 'cycles' (from the Classical to the Baroque), quite independent of the chronology of reigns or social systems. 'Styles' were simply a matter of 'schools', 'workshops', or 'influences' —even of 'national traditions'[6]—and there was hardly any attempt to break out of the closed province of art history.[7]

For anyone seeking to do more to link artistic development with that of society as a whole, such a relationship could only be achieved in a metaphorical or reductionist sense. Thus, Emile Mâle, stating once and for all that thirteenth-century religious art (with the exception of 'purely decorative work', which he deliberately discarded from his field of study, on the grounds of its lack of 'symbolic meaning')[8] could be compared to a 'book', their aim being to make Church teaching visually manifest, particularly to the illiterate masses. From this standpoint he was able to distinguish levels of meaning and function, by analogy with the *Speculum* of Vincent of Beauvais: the Mirror of Nature, the Mirror of

---

[5] Cited by Jean Hubert, 'Archéologie médiévale', in *L'Histoire et ses méthodes*, ed. by Charles Samaran (Paris: Gallimard – Pléïade, 1961), pp. 275–328 (317–20).

[6] In some cases, this involved all the ideological drift only too well illustrated in nineteenth-century history. See the frank study by Eric Michaud, 'Nord-Sud (Du nationalisme et du racisme en histoire de l'art. Une anthologie)', *Critique*, no. 586 (March 1996), 163–87.

[7] Louis Pressouyre, 'Histoire de l'art et iconographie', in *L'Histoire médiévale en France. Bilan et perspectives*, Société des Historiens Médiévistes de l'Enseignement Supérieur; edited by Michel Balard; with a preface by Georges Duby (Paris: Le Seuil, 1991), pp. 247–68.

[8] Emile Mâle, *L'art religieux du XIIIe siècle en France* (Paris: Armand Colin, 1898; new edn., Paris: Le Livre de Poche, 1948), p. 24, n. 5.

Science, the Mirror of Moral Instruction, and the Mirror of History.

Nowadays we can see the obvious conceptual limitations of such a project: an entire literate culture cannot be seen through images, any more than the image can be reduced to just a reflection of culture. In its time, however, this enterprise proved highly tempting to those contemporary historians who were conscious that art was an important card to play in general cultural history, yet who (by virtue of their training as historians) felt ill-equipped to embark upon such a study. Emile Mâle's synthesis at least seemed to deal with medieval art in categorical terms which they found intelligible.

Marc Bloch, for example, referred to Mâle when he made his own suggestions concerning the parallel development of society and contemporary artistic achievements. This great historian's ambiguous attitude towards medieval art has recently been well noted by Ulrich Raulff.[9] On the one hand, history, above all rural history, was for him a science of observation, to be carried out by means of maps, plots, and aerial photography, which he had learned to use during the Great War. He also took a close interest in Lefebvre des Noëttes's research on the Bayeux Tapestry, relating to the history of military costume. On the other hand, Marc Bloch might be considered representative of that type of French intelligentsia who have been accused of being less than sensitive to visual stimuli.[10] However that may be, Bloch effectively confesses his lack of competence, in those pages of his 1939 *La société féodale* devoted to 'Façons de sentir et de penser', in which—and here is where he cites Emile Mâle—he stresses the need for the historian to look into society's 'expression plastique', but hesitates himself to set out on such a hazardous path.[11] Nonetheless, for his projected 1933–34 collection of essays, he had envisaged grouping a number of items under the rubric 'Images et imagination collective', which would have included *inter alia* his fine article on 'La vie d'outre-tombe du roi Salomon', originally published in 1925, a year after *Les rois thaumaturges*.[12] In both article and monograph, Bloch amply demonstrates his skill in looking very closely at images and in understanding their ideological impact, and he even sketches a comparative history of Western Christian and Byzantine images. But he went no

---

[9] Ulrich Raulff, *Ein Historiker im 20. Jahrhundert: Marc Bloch* (Frankfurt am Main: Fischer, 1995), p. 93.

[10] This is the theory put forward by Martin Jay, *Downcast Eyes. The Denigration of Vision in Twentieth-Century French Thought* (Berkeley: University of California Press, 1993).

[11] See Jean-Claude Schmitt, 'Façons de sentir et de penser. Un tableau de la civilisation ou une histoire-problème?', in *Marc Bloch aujourd'hui. Histoire comparée et sciences sociales*, ed. by Hartmut Atsma and André Burguière (Paris: École des Hautes Études en Sciences Sociales, 1990), pp. 407–18 (408).

[12] This proposed collection, containing this article, has at long last been published: Marc Bloch, *Histoire et historiens. Textes réunis par Etienne Bloch* (Paris: Armand Colin, 1995), see in particular pp. 167–90.

further down this path, nor did he really pursue the ethno-historical approach illustrated by his book. In both cases markers were laid down, but medievalists were only later to follow them.

The harmful effect of the lack of communication between the developing disciplines of history and the history of art respectively may be well measured by the fact that, at this precise time when Marc Bloch was wishing devoutly for a proper analytical use of images by historians, art history, first in Germany, then in Great Britain and the U.S.A. (with Aby Warburg and his successors, headed by Fritz Saxl and Erwin Panofsky), was undergoing an unprecedented conceptual sea-change, but one which took a long time to influence the preoccupations and methods of historians. It would appear that Marc Bloch himself failed to note this transformation in the fields of theory and methodology.[13]

However, our modern retrospective judgement of the Warburg heritage and of the New History born in France with the setting-up of the Annales School, does enable us to appreciate the extent to which intellectual projects, albeit belonging to different cultural and linguistic traditions, were sufficiently analogous as to allow for future collaboration. Still, such collaboration was by no means automatic: disciplinary conservatism, and the legitimate priority accorded by historians to other matters (in particular, in the fields of economic and demographic history), have for a long time had the opposite effect of keeping problems and issues apart, instead of enabling them to come together. In another area, however, in the current configuration between human and social sciences, some concepts—despite their long-standing definitions—have shown themselves to be highly heuristic, and highly efficacious.

Such is the case of the concept of 'symbolic form', which Erwin Panofsky borrowed from the philosophy of Ernst Cassirer and applied historically to the question of plane perspective.[14] Panofsky postulated a decisive break with the history of styles, which was supposed to offer very little by way of interest to the social historian. He rejected the deduction that plane perspective stemmed from the subjective psycho-physiological experience of vision: on the contrary, he stressed the absolute abstraction of the nature of its twin constituent principles (the vanishing-point to infinity, and the homogeneity of the field of representation). He also saw the origins of the discovery of perspective in the context of advances across the range of intellectual history (in optics and mathematics), rather than in the single field of art history; and finally, he showed the effects of perspective in turn on the rationalisation of subjective sight, including the

[13] This fact makes Haskell's point (*History and its Images* (as in note 2), p. 8 and n. 1, p. 496) that the Annales School did not as a whole pay much attention to the importance of art for the historian. All this was to change for a later generation, as witness the work of Georges Duby, for example.

[14] Erwin Panofsky, *La perspective comme forme symbolique et autres essais. Précédé de 'La question de la perspective', par Marisa Dalai Emiliani* (Paris: Minuit, 1975).

extreme visionary experience of mystics. In this way Erwin Panofsky made an essential contribution to the promotion of perspective as a subject of the 'general history' which informs all our current efforts. The aim of this 'general history', so ardently desired by Michel Foucault, is to articulate all the various 'symbolic forms' governing the functions of a society at any given period.

This is precisely the way in which Warburg's notion of 'Kulturwissenschaft' broke with the concept of a 'cultural history' still linked (even for Karl Lamprecht) to the ideas of progress and evolution, or to a strictly national framework.[15] In its origins at least, it really had nothing about it of the purely intellectual history, which it would become for Panofsky, in whose hands it would tend towards a reduction of the 'iconological' element and towards a study of those intellectual traditions which would enable all a work's multiple meanings to be deciphered. Initially, the notion took in the various aspects of a society's 'Weltanschauung': all 'the issues of social history and social psychology, of society and politics'.[16] It is impossible not to recognize here some common features with the twentieth-century's other great landmark in the field of historiography: the contemporary, but totally (or mainly) independent work of the Annales School.

One of the most famous projects, and one which indeed engaged all the attention of the Annales historians, was Erwin Panofsky's attempt to incorporate in one single explanation the principles of Gothic architecture and Scholasticism.[17] His point of view is structural and relational, seeking to uncover, in two contemporary, but otherwise apparently heterogeneous phenomena—the University disputation and the system of Gothic vaulting—common principles of clarification and conciliation of opposing forces. This attempt is, however, open to criticism, for being still organized around the idea of a basic parallelism between the various forms of human thought: figurative and mythic, architectural and philosophical. In a 'general history', there does not always have to be harmony between the different 'symbolic forms' or the different 'languages' of a given society: there may also be contradictions between them, or even conflict, in historical circumstances where unity will always be a problematic factor.[18] The problems of the specificity of art, and of the sometimes conflicting relations

---

[15] See Otto Gerhard Oexle, in the Introduction to *Memoria als Kultur*, ed. idem (Göttingen: Vandenhoeck & Ruprecht, 1995), p. 25.

[16] Michael Diers, 'Mnemosyne oder das Gedächtnis der Bilder. Über Aby Warburg', in ibid., pp. 79–94 (87).

[17] Erwin Panofsky, *Architecture gothique et pensée scolastique, précédé de l'Abbé Suger de Saint-Denis. Traduction et postface de Pierre Bourdieu*, 2nd edn (Paris: Minuit, 1967).

[18] See Hubert Danisch, 'Art (Histoire de l')', in *La Nouvelle Histoire*, ed. by Jacques Le Goff, Roger Chartier, and Jacques Revel (Paris: Retz-C.E.P.L., 1978), pp. 68–77.

between the different 'symbolic forms' of a single society, should be at the very forefront of the work of the 'image historian'.

Methodology

Our historian is thus faced with the double challenge of analysing art both in its own right *and* in its dynamic relationship with the society which produced it. The work, in France, of someone like Pierre Francastel, a sociologist of art (hostile to all pseudo-sociology) and a meticulous analyst of figurative thought, and, in the United States, of Meyer Shapiro, a highly perceptive specialist in the field of Romanesque art,[19] seems to me to be particularly illuminating for the present-day historian.

For the medievalist, almost always working on images which are explicitly, or at least implicitly, in a relationship with a text (first and foremost, the Biblical text), an essential task is to bring out the specificity of the illustrated work, and to draw from it all possible inferences. The structures of the fixed image (the only kind of image available to Western civilisation until the invention of cinematography) and of language are totally different. The former strikes the eye simultaneously in all its constituent parts, even if it subsequently calls for a longer period of 'decipherment' and of comparison with other, analogous but older images. It constructs its own space or, as Francastel would put it, its own constituent system of figures and places. Language, however, written or spoken, extends over time, from the duration of the sentence to that of the whole discourse, while creating the illusion that its meaning has imprinted itself instantly upon our minds. Francastel has observed this very acutely:

> The words which issue from our lips over a period of time form a snare, leading us to assume that the thoughts they contain are on the contrary unified and simultaneous. The snare of images which have appeared fixed throughout the centuries is to evoke within us a combination of perception, knowledge and idealized imaginings which only sporadically go together. That is why the mechanisms of language and pictorial representation cannot be geared together.[20]

The respective specificity of image and language rules out any possibility of the former being thought of as merely 'illustrating' a text, even in the case of a miniature painted facing the text and in direct relationship with its sense or meaning. Text conveys the signified temporally, via a succession of words; image ensures, in spatial terms, the emergence of a 'figurative thought' which is

---

[19] Meyer Shapiro, *Words and Pictures. On the Literal and Symbolic in the Illustration of a Text* (The Hague and Paris: Mouton, 1973).

[20] Pierre Francastel, *La figure et le lieu. L'ordre visuel du Quattrocento* (Paris: Gallimard, 1967), p. 351.

totally different. Besides, the construction of the image's space and the way the figures relate to each other are never neutral: at one and the same time, they express, and produce, a classification of values, hierarchies and ideological choices.

In Panofskian terms, an image's meaning stems in the first instance from iconography (in the strict sense of the word): in a single manuscript such as the Gospels of Otto III, a portrait of the king in majesty analogous to that of Christ in Majesty is full of significance, both for the medieval representation of kingship and for that of the Divine (figs. 1 and 2).[21] But no less important is the way in which the structuring of the image may explicitly link these elements. For example, in the 1511 Ansbach Retable, the fact that God the Father, operating the press which crushes his Son, is wearing the same tiara as Pope Gregory the Great, who—symmetrically opposed to him in relation to the suffering Christ—is collecting the hosts coming out of the press, means that the image suddenly becomes (in its historical context) a very meaningful summary of an entire ideological programme, by bringing together the mystery of the Incarnation, the dogma of the Trinity, and the sacrament of the Eucharist, and above all by asserting the legitimacy of pontifical authority confronted with the first throes of the Protestant Reformation (fig. 3, plate 3).[22] Analysis of an image must therefore take into account, as well as iconographical motifs, all the relationships governing its structure and characteristic of modes of representation specific to a given culture and period. The following are some principles to aid such analysis:

1. 'In-depth study'. One should be aware of the stratification of the scene, from the background, which in miniatures sometimes consists of a gold-leaf ground, to the figures placed in the 'foreground': the first to strike one's eye, often seeming larger than the others, completely visible from top to toe, and, within the value-system set up by the image, enjoying a privileged position over the figures 'taking up the rear' and partially concealed by them. In just such a way, the illuminated initials of a manuscript of Gratian's *Decretum* play on the characters' size and posture (sitting, standing), on the choice and brightness of the colours of their clothing, and above all on their position 'in front of' or 'behind' the letter framing these figures. All this may suggest a social hierarchy by no means indicated explicitly in the text itself (fig. 4).[23]

---

[21] Munich, Bayerische Staatsbibliothek, MS. Clm 4453, fols 24 and 34^{v}.

[22] *Le Pressoir mystique. Actes du colloque de Recloses (27 mai 1989)*, ed. by Danièle Alexandre-Bidon (Paris: Cerf, 1990), p. 4 (Church of St Gumbert, Ansbach Retable, *c.* 1511, school of Dürer).

[23] Baltimore, The Walters Art Gallery, MS. W. 133, fol. 123 (Gratian, *Decretum*, Paris or Northern France, *c.* 1300). Cf. Jean-Claude Schmitt, 'Le miroir du canoniste. Les images et le texte dans un manuscrit médiéval', *Annales E.S.C.*, 48 (1993), 1471–95.

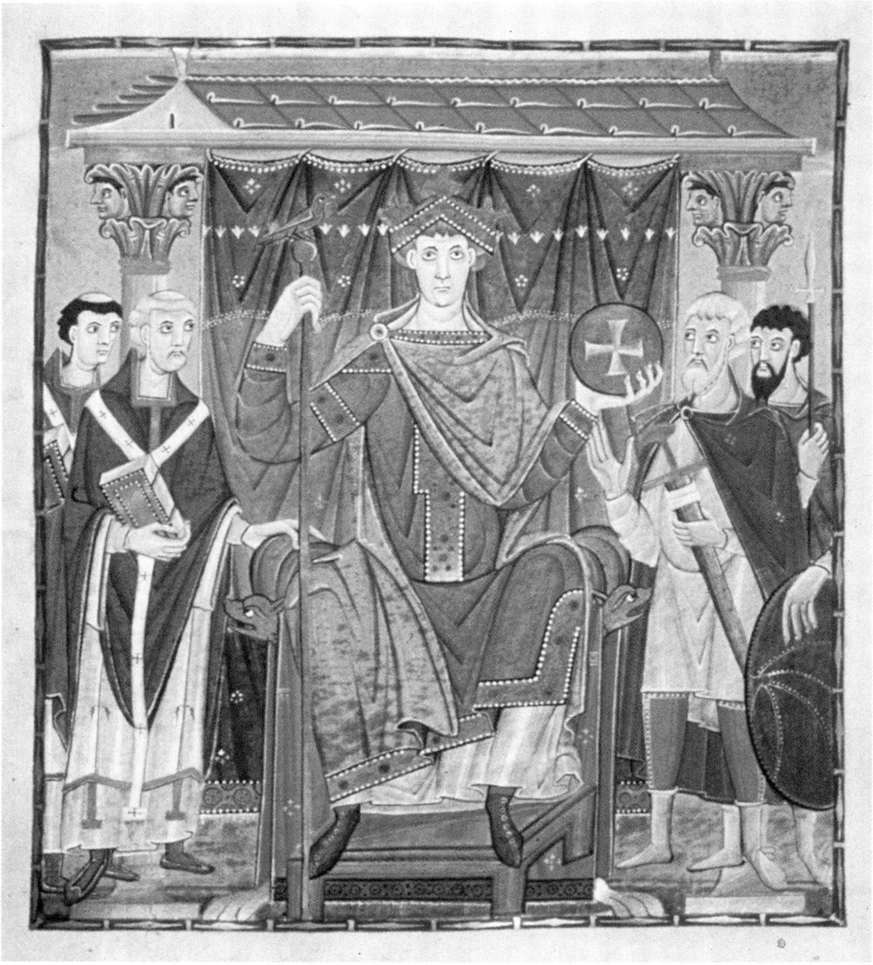

Fig. 1. Gospels of Otto III: majesty of kingship. Munich, Bayer. Staatsbibliothek, MS. Clm 4453, fol. 24ʳ. © Bayer. Staatsbibliothek, Munich

2. The image should also be considered as an 'inscribed surface', with a set of hierarchies, both vertical (ascending or descending) and horizontal (from right or from left: from the point of view normally of the image, but sometimes of the spectator). There is above all a sense of compartmentalisation, of rhythm, and of internal dynamics, achieved by means of representational features (such as architectural motifs contributing to the organisation of the image, as well as setting each scene within a formal

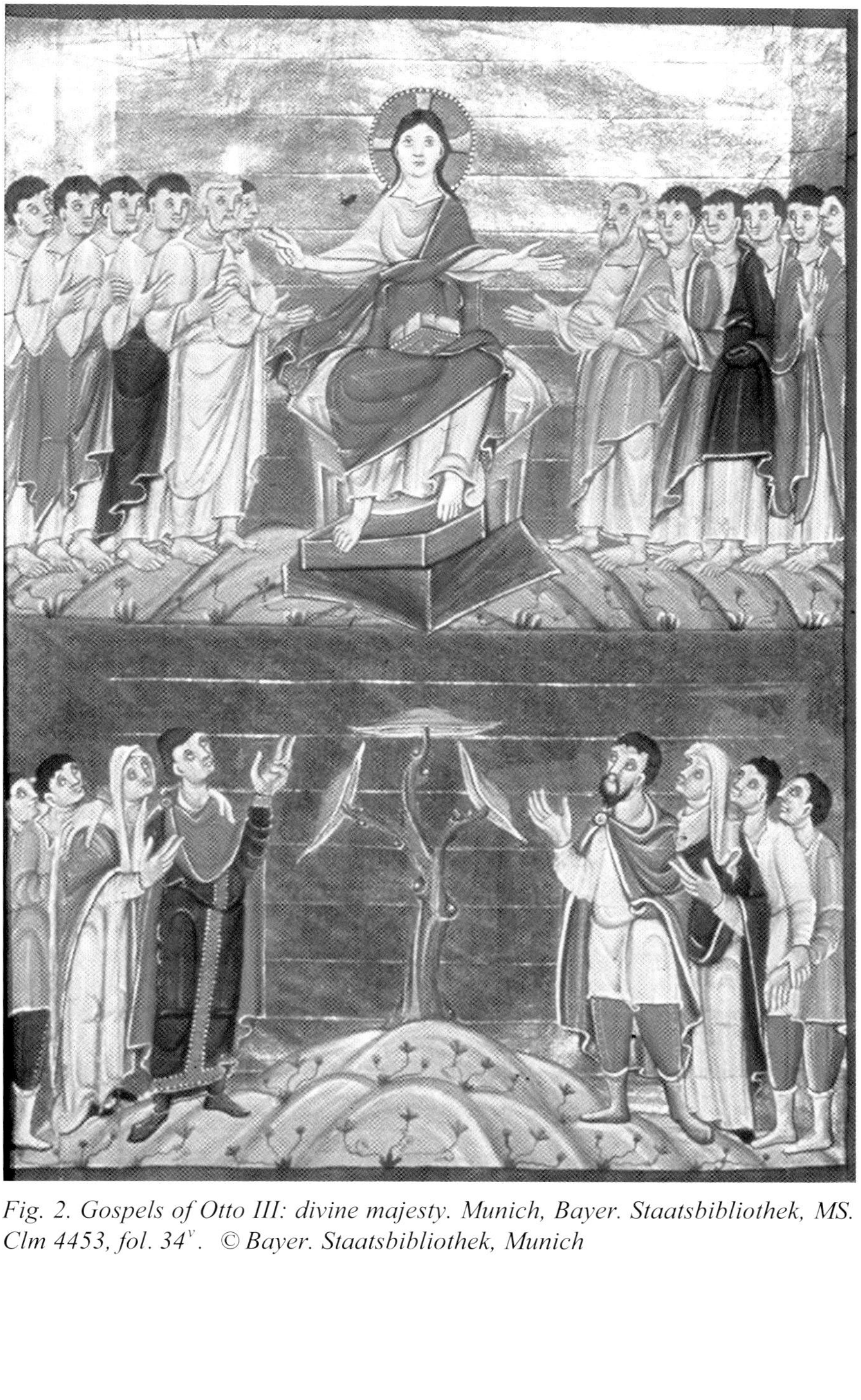

Fig. 2. Gospels of Otto III: divine majesty. Munich, Bayer. Staatsbibliothek, MS. Clm 4453, fol. 34ᵛ.

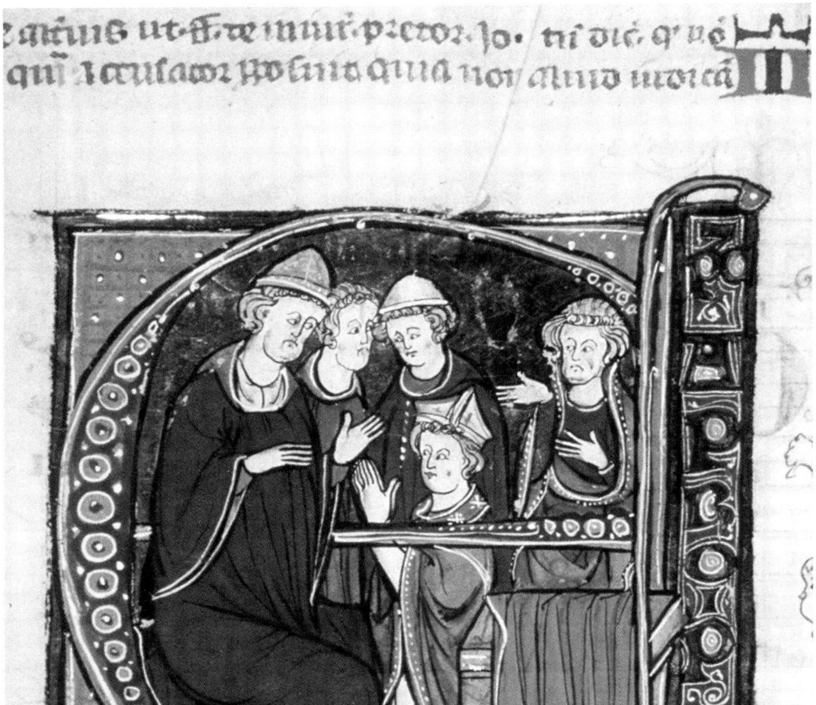

Fig. 4. Decretum Gratiani, decorated initial: the dominant figure of the canonist. Baltimore, The Walters Art Gallery, MS. W. 133, fol. 123. © The Walters Art Gallery, Baltimore

frame), and also of the colour scheme allotted to each image and to the whole work in which it appears. In the miniatures (and we may assume that the same was true with wall-paintings and polychrome church sculpture), these colours excel in producing alternating, chiasmic, echoing, and repeat effects which give the image its dynamic quality and provide a visual link between certain figures. They also impart a degree of temporality to the representational space, where appropriate, stressing a narrative line. The linked sequence of scenes from Genesis in the St Louis Psalter does not simply represent a faithful 'illustration' of the *historia* as present in Holy Writ but is achieved through a continual repetition, from one image to another, of lines, forms, and colours suggesting the continuity of the narrative itself (figs. 5 and 6).[24]

3. Representational figures, ornamental motifs, forms, and colours acquire full meaning only when considered in relationship: their relative positions; contrasting or comparative features; the distance separating them; or else the ways in which they come together, are juxtaposed, or even blend one with the other. A single figure may be a composite, a dreamlike meld of several, otherwise distinct figures, so as to express, through the contradiction of posture or movement, the dialectic of the artist's aim and meaning.[25] The attempts made from the twelfth century onwards to achieve a suitable representation of the logical paradox of the Trinity, by combining the unity of Divine Essence ('Three-in-One-ness') with the necessary distinction of the three personae ('Threefold-ness'), provide ample evidence of the power and creativity of medieval 'figurative thought'. In fact, we can detect a hesitation, mainly between two logically opposed patterns: three distinct and matching figures (the triandrous pattern),[26] and three figures fused together (the 'Throne of Grace') (fig. 7).[27]
4. No image is ever completely present in isolation. It often forms part of a series: for instance, of full-folio miniatures in a single Psalter manuscript, or of historiated initials commencing each Life in an illuminated manuscript of the *Golden Legend*, or each *causa* in a manuscript of Gratian's *Decretum*.

---

[24] Paris, BnF, ms. lat. 10,525, fols 13^{v} and 14^{r} (St Louis Psalter, Paris, mid-thirteenth century).

[25] See, for example, the fusion within the historiated initial of the two figures of Jacob, one dreaming, the other wrestling with the angel, in Oxford, All Souls College, MS. 6, fol. 96^{r} (Amesbury Psalter, thirteenth century). Cf. Jean-Claude Schmitt, 'La culture de l'*imago*', *Annales. Histoire, Sciences sociales,* 51 (1996), 3–36 (p. 8, fig. 1).

[26] Paris, BnF, ms. esp. 353, fol. 13 (*Bréviaire d'Amour*, fourteenth century).

[27] Cambridge, Trinity College, MS. B. II. 4, fol. 119 (Psalter, thirteenth century). Cf. François Boespflug and Yolanta Zaluska, 'Le dogme trinitaire et l'essor de l'iconographie en Occident de l'époque carolingienne au IVe Concile de Latran (1215)', *Cahiers de Civilisation Médiévale*, 37 (1994), 181–240, illus.

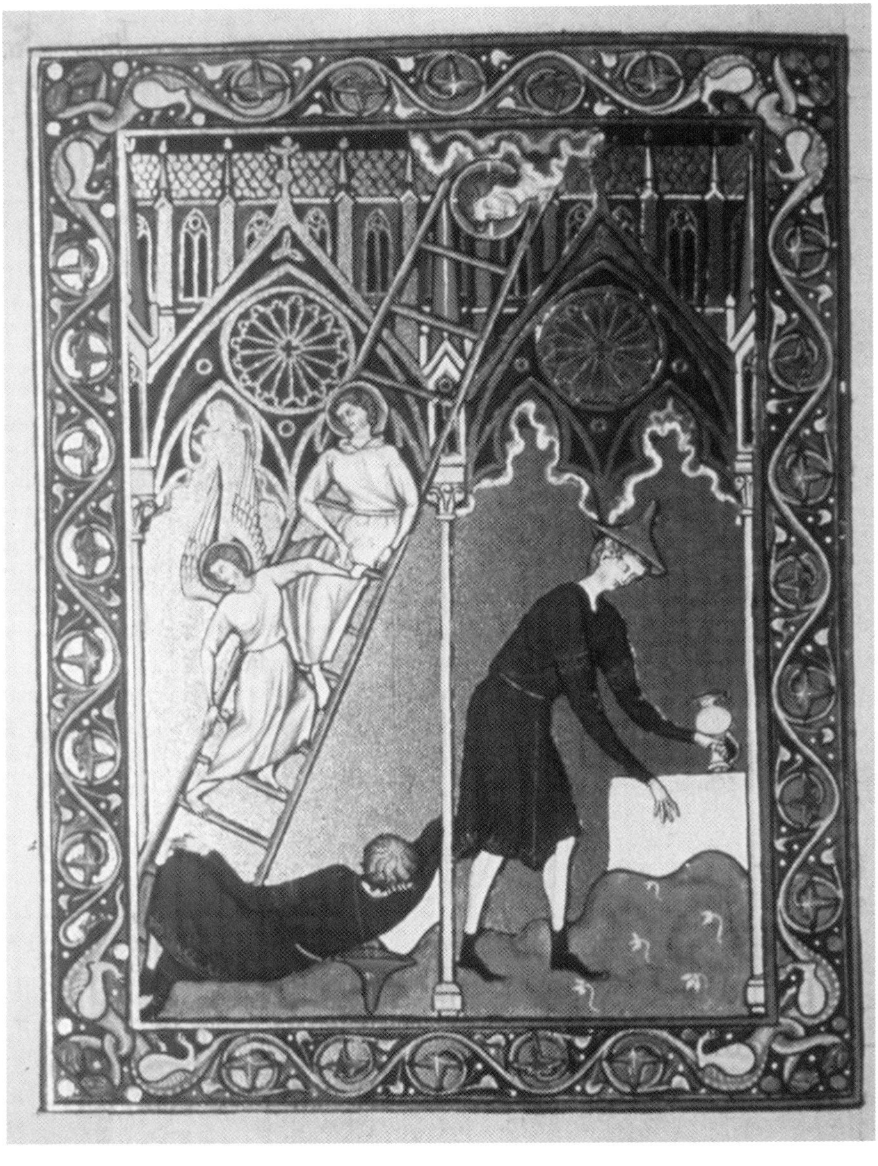

Fig. 5. St Louis's Psalter: Jacob's ladder, and the anointing of the stone of Bethel. Paris, Bibliothèque nationale de France, ms. lat. 10525, fol. 13ᵛ. © Bibliothèque nationale de France, Paris

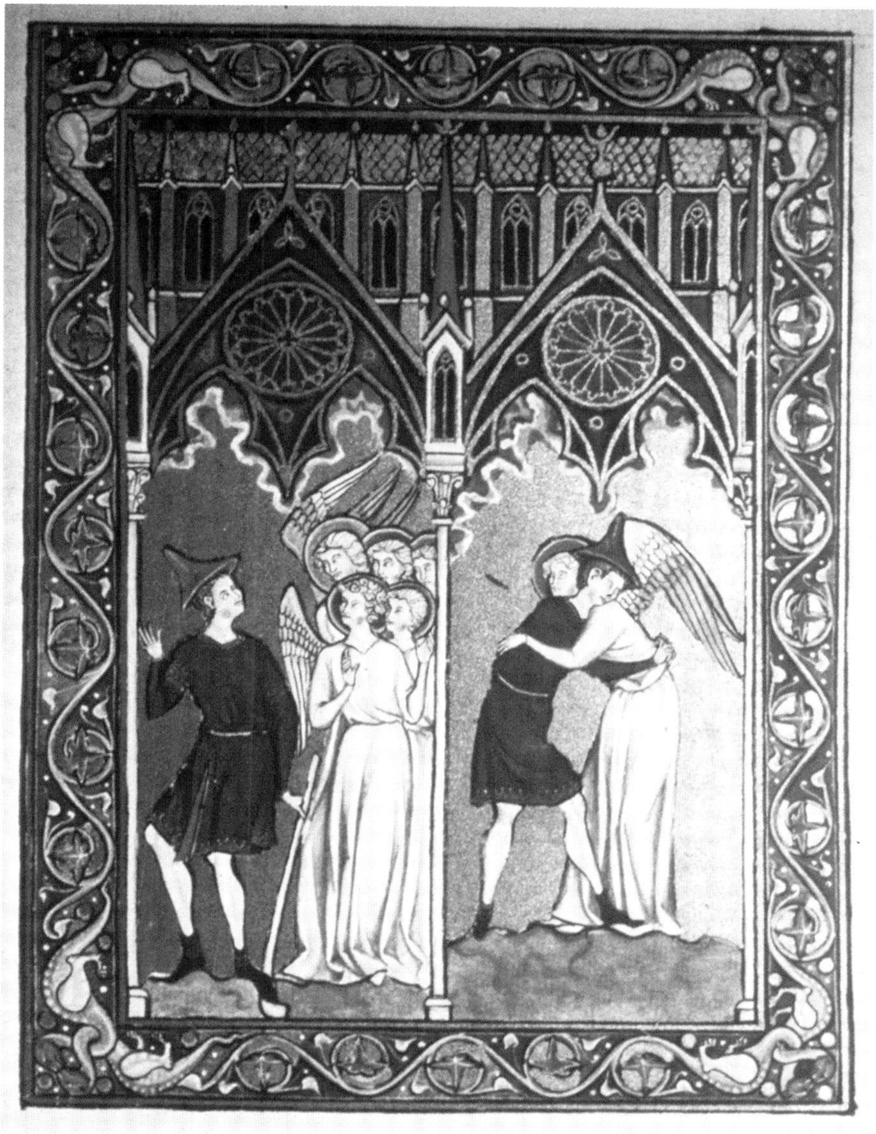

Fig. 6. St Louis's Psalter: Jacob's meeting with the angel, and Jacob wrestling with the angel. Paris, Bibliothèque nationale de France, ms. lat. 10525, fol. 14ʳ.

The only truly meaningful work is perhaps that of the entire series: isolating one image will always be arbitrary, and misguided.

5. An 'original' series of this kind must be distinguished from those 'constructed' by the historian, based on iconographical, formal, structural, thematic, or chronological criteria. The possibilities of constructing such series, and above all of cross-referencing them, are infinite: for example, a chronological series of Romanesque sculpted tympana can be created; this may then be cross-indexed with one of Last Judgement scenes, not only in sculpture but also in manuscript illustrations and wall-paintings. Or again, a series of representations of Abraham's Bosom can be tailored, as exhaustively as possible, to reflect an historical anthropologist's study of 'Divine parentage';[28] or one may concentrate on structure, seeking out all the graphic examples of a right–left division which may correspond to a crucial ideological patterning in medieval society.[29]
6. It is all the more imperative to think hard, and now, about the principles of the construction of iconographical series, because the facilities of IT documentation (via computers and digital images) are on the point of transforming utterly our conditions of scholarly research and our opportunities of gaining access to material; this offers the possibility, through the cross-indexing of image-selection criteria, of creating unlimited numbers of new, and virtually complete archives. But these technological developments raise as many new theoretical problems as they offer unheard-of practical possibilities.[30]
7. Finally, a crucial point must be made: an image does not simply express some cultural, religious or ideological 'signified', deemed to exist well before or beyond this particular artistic expression. On the contrary, it is the image itself which creates this element, just as we perceive it: creates it by its very structure, form, and social effect. In other words, any analysis of a work of art, of its form and structure, is inseparable from a study of its functions. There must be unbroken continuity between analytical research and historical interpretation.[31]

---

[28] Jérôme Baschet, 'Inventivité et sérialité des images médiévales. Pour une approche iconographique élargie', *Annales. Histoire, Sciences sociales,* 51 (1996), 93–134.

[29] Jean-Claude Bonne, *L'art roman de face et de profil. Le tympan de Conques* (Paris: Le Sycomore, 1984).

[30] Over the past few years, several different systems of image-indexing have been proposed. Our own suggestion has at least the merit of simplicity: *Thésaurus des images médiévales* (published by the Groupe d'Anthropologie Historique de l'Occident Médiéval, Paris, 1996).

[31] On these points, see *L'image. Fonctions et usages des images dans l'Occident médiéval*, ed. by Jérôme Baschet and Jean-Claude Schmitt (Paris: Le Léopard d'Or, 1996).

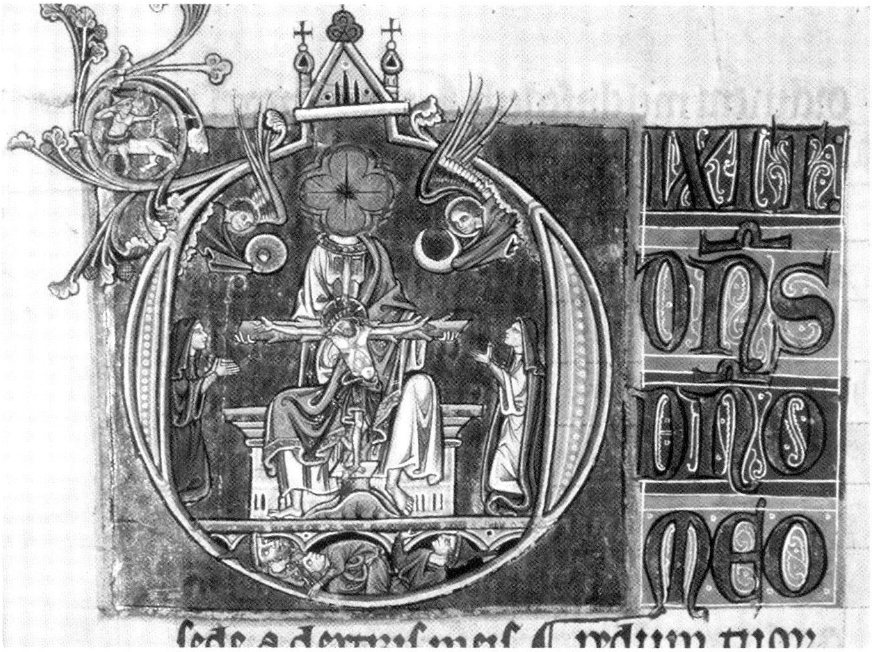

Fig. 7. Psalter (thirteenth century): the throne of grace. Cambridge, Trinity College, MS. B. 11.4, fol. 119. © Trinity College, Cambridge

History

Hans Belting makes a distinction, in Western tradition, between a medieval 'age' of the image and its ritual and religious uses ('Bild und Kult'), and an age of 'art' ('Zeitalter der Kunst') which dawned in the third decade of the fourteenth century in Flanders and Italy and which is marked, notably, by 'the invention of painting'.[32] The idea of the 'Bild', as he uses the term, operates on two different levels. First the historical level, the author appearing to deny any aesthetic intent in images created 'before the artistic era'. And second, the historiographical level: Belting states that social and cultural historians (of all periods) talk nowadays of 'images', in order to treat them as they would other documents with which they are familiar, and to distinguish their approach from that of 'art

[32] Hans Belting, *Bild und Kult. Eine Geschichte des Bildes vor dem Zeitalter der Kunst* (Munich: C. H. Beck, 1990); Hans Belting and Christiane Kruse, *Die Erfindung des Gemäldes. Das erste Jahrhundert der niederländischen Malerei* (Munich: Hirmer, 1994).

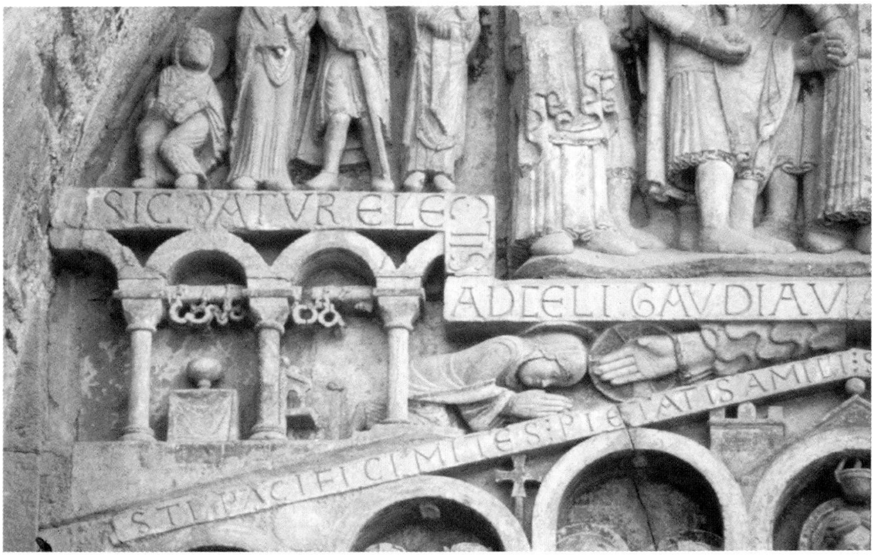

Fig. 8. Conques, Abbey Church of Sainte-Foy, tympanum (detail): St Foy in her church, prostrate before the hand of God

historians' mainly concerned with identifying workshops, dating works, and recognising styles.

Hans Belting has solid reasons for categorising, if not all then at least a large number of, medieval images by their 'cultic', religious function. This feature certainly does distinguish them from modern easel painting and its continually developing aesthetic and secular functions. But one should not be too categorical: not all medieval images were 'cult' objects (in the sense that the enthroned statue of St Foy at Conques or the 'Veronica' cloth undoubtedly were). One must also distinguish between a whole range of different 'cultic' items. At Conques, for instance, the sculpted tympanum at the very entrance to the abbey church very probably did play a part in the veneration of the famous statue-reliquary of St Foy preserved in the choir. The figure of St Foy in fact appears on this tympanum, prostrate before the Hand of God as though she has just left her throne in the body of the church, which is also depicted in the sculpture, as are the chains hanging from the capitals under the vaults, left as *ex-voto* offerings by miraculously-cured pilgrims (fig. 8). The tympanum thus invited those who were ready to proceed into the building to prepare themselves for the imminent vision of the *Majestas*, by having them anticipate (but without yet actually revealing it) the miraculous treasure they had come to 'adore'. As a result, carved on the tympanum and in her own tri-dimensional Majesty, the saint was present in two images, which played complementary yet very different roles in the development of her cult. If we turn to the frescoes in Italian courts of law, these were associated not with any 'cult' in the religious sense of the word but with civic ceremonies : at Siena, for example, justice was dispensed beneath the painted representation of Good and Bad Government. Conversely, not all modern images manage to escape the clutches of various sacred or profane 'cults'; nowadays, a visit to a museum or to a major art exhibition often takes the form of a ritual act, to which social pressure lends a note of obligation.

Over and above all this, however, if we deny medieval images the status of 'art' ('Kunst'), we are faced with many difficulties. Costly material, expensive labour, glittering gold, gemstones, and colours, and an item's manifest beauty would all combine simultaneously to exalt the glory of God and the prestige of a rich and powerful sponsor. All these qualities would enhance the aesthetic value of the work, which was considered inseparable from its religious or social functions.[33] Therefore, one should not make a distinction between 'cult' and 'art' but, rather, note how the one takes on the attributes of the other and is thereby fulfilled. Clearly, one of the most difficult, and urgent tasks allotted to modern historians and art historians is to understand the aesthetic function of works (insofar as they may be considered 'works of art') as part and parcel of their historical significance: be it in a 'cultic', political, legal, or ideological context).[34]

In actual fact, it is very difficult to see how the three terms set out in Belting's thesis can line up in a one-to-one relationship: one given period, one type of image, one exclusive function. In every period there are many types of images, each one with many possible functions.

That is why I also wish to retain the word *image* when referring to the Middle Ages, not to distinguish it from 'art' but, rather, to restore to it all its meanings and to group together the three components of the medieval *imago*: the world of material images (*imagines*); that of the imagination (*imaginatio*), composed of mental, oniric, and poetic images; and finally that of anthropology and Christian theology, founded on the concept of Man created *ad imaginem Dei* and promised salvation through the Incarnation of Christ *imago Patris*. If one only considers one of these aspects, one will inevitably end up with a warped and incomplete

---

[33] Meyer Schapiro, 'On the aesthetic attitude in Romanesque Art', in his *Romanesque Art* (New York and London: Thames and Hudson, 1977), pp. 1–27.

[34] On this point, see the recent work by Jean-Claude Bonne: 'Pensée de l'art et pensée théologique dans les écrits de Suger', in *Artistes et philosophes: éducateurs?*, ed. by Christian Descamps (Paris: Centre Georges Pompidou, 1994), pp. 13–50; 'Formes et fonctions de l'ornemental dans l'art médiéval (VIIe–XIIe siècle)', in *L'image* (as in note 31), pp. 206–49; and 'Les ornements de l'histoire (à propos de l'ivoire carolingien de saint Rémi)', *Annales. Histoire, Sciences sociales,* 51 (1996), 37–70.

view of the history of the medieval image. The common task of historians and art historians must be to study '*imago* als Kultur'.[35]

We can thus agree with Belting when he observes that our acceptance of the word *image* has coincided with the widening by historians of a field of study traditionally reserved for art historians. From now on, this should be our common aim: to situate images within the overall context of 'social imagination', with all its factors of power and memory,[36] without in any way rejecting the specific contribution made by art historians to our knowledge of artistic works and traditions.

To achieve this, we are fortunately not lacking in conceptual equipment. Thanks (again) to Aby Warburg, we no longer separate the study of a work's function from the analysis of its structure. Pierre Francastel expressed very similar ideas when he compared the representational structures, with their respective functions, of the Giotto frescoes in the Upper Church at Assisi, and Duccio's 'Maestà' in Siena: 'Here again, function has dictated the composition and the systematic ordering of the constituent parts'.[37] In the relationship between an image's form and function, we can see the expression of the aims and objectives of the artist, of the sponsor-patron, and of the entire social group responsible for the work's creation; and this work enshrines, from the very outset, the attitudes of the person or persons to whom it was addressed, and the uses (liturgical, for example) to which the image was put. Not only should the type of image be taken into account, but also the place for which it was intended (very different from the museum or library where it is often to be found today), its possible mobility (whether, for instance, it could have been carried in a procession), and also the 'interactive performance' between the figures within the image exchanging glances with each other and with the spectators in the world outside.

Similarly, the thoughts of someone like Michel Foucault teach us that no image is first and foremost a simple 'document' for the historian (any more in fact than is a charter or a chronicle).[38] Nor is it a 'monument' reserved for the art

---

[35] See Jean-Claude Schmitt, 'La culture de l'imago' (as in note 25). p. 4.

[36] Andrea von Hülsen-Esch, 'Zur Konstituierung des Juristenstandes durch Memoria: Die bildliche Repräsentation des Giovanni da Legnano', in Oexle, *Memoria als Kultur* (as in note 15), pp. 185–206.

[37] Francastel (as in n. 20), p. 195.

[38] Michel Foucault, *L'archéologie du savoir* (Paris: Gallimard, 1969), p. 13. Foucault sees a link between the appraisal of a document and a projected 'general history' along the lines of the 'Kulturwissenschaft' discussed above. My own idea of applying the notion of 'document-cum-monument' to medieval images owes much to Jérôme Baschet's 'Les images: des objets pour l'historien?', in *Le Moyen Age aujourd'hui: trois regards contemporains sur le moyen âge: histoire, théologie, cinéma: actes de la rencontre de*

historian! It is for both of them, and in every detail, a 'document-cum-monument', providing information about the historical circumstances of its production and simultaneously revealing itself as a statement of religious faith or as a proclamation of social prestige. Every image aims visibly at becoming a 'receptacle of memory', a *monumentum*, all the more so since memory itself, the individual *memoria* as defined by St Augustine at the dawn of Christian culture,[39] and also the collective *memoria*, in all its social and cultural dimensions, consists above all of 'images'.[40] All this may easily be recognized (just to take one prestigious example) in the miniatures—replete with the affirmation of dynastic glory but still overseen by God, to Whom they are equally offered—of Henry the Lion's Gospels (fig. 9, plate 4). Here once more, following the Ottonian model which we have already seen (figs. 1 and 2) and responding to the depiction of political sovereignty at the very moment of its divine legitimization—coronation by the hand of God—we find, on the facing folio, the glorious manifestation of divine Majesty (fig. 10, plate 5).[41]

The historian must right from the start study a work in all the synchronic depth of its social, cultural, and ideological underpinnings. But he must also compose a history, take account of diachronic movement, tackle the delicate question of the division into periods, propose a chronology. We have already seen how highly unsatisfactory metaphorical references to a succession of styles may appear: 'Romanesque', 'Gothic', etc., and yet, conversely, an attempt to tack upon art a chronology based purely on matters of social history may equally lead us to underestimate the rhythmical patterns of evolution which are very

---

Cerisy-la-Salle, juillet 1991, ed. by Jacques Le Goff and Guy Lobrichon (Paris: Le Léopard d'Or, 1998).

39 Augustine, *Confessions*, X, 8: '[. . .] in the vast halls of my memory, where are stored the treasures of all those innumerable images that entered by the gateway of my senses [. . .]'. See also the very interesting case (as regards the relationship between memory and image) of the monk Arnold of St Emmeran, cited by Patrick J. Geary, *Phantoms of Remembrance. Memory and Oblivion at the End of the First Millennium* (Princeton: Princeton University Press, 1994), pp. 16–19, and 159.

40 See, in Oexle, *Memoria als Kultur* (as in note 15), as well as the above-cited piece by A. von Hülsen-Esch (as in note 36): Bernhard Jussen, '*Dolor* und *Memoria*. Trauerriten, gemalte Trauer und soziale Ordnungen im späten Mittelalter', pp. 207–52; and Martial Staub, 'Memoria im Dienst von Gemeinwohl und Öffentlichkeit. Stiftungspraxis und kultureller Wandel in Nürnberg um 1500', pp. 285–334.

41 Otto Gerhard Oexle, 'Das Evangeliar Heinrichs des Lõwen als geschichtliches Denkmal', in *Das Evangeliar Heinrichs des Löwen. Kommentar zum Faksimile*, ed. by Dietrich Kötzsche (Frankfurt am Main: Insel Verlag, 1989), pp. 9–27; and Joachim M. Plotzek, in *Heinrich der Löwe und seine Zeit. Herrschaft und Repräsentation der Welfen 1125–1235. Katalog der Ausstellung, Braunschweig 1995*, ed. by Jochen Luckhardt and Franz Niehoff, I (Munich: Hirmer, 1995), pp. 206–10.

much part of images and their uses. A good example of these difficulties is given by the first volume of the *Histoire artistique de l'Europe*, devoted to the Middle Ages and edited by Georges Duby.[42] Duby puts forward a chronology of Western images which, after an initial five-hundred-year block (from the fifth to the tenth century), suddenly becomes refined and subdivided into far shorter phases, with precise dating: 960–1160, 1160–1320, 1320–1400. The terms of reference for each of these periods are perfectly justifiable. And yet the individual essays which follow, signed by a galaxy of art historians, specialists in Ottonian manuscript illustrations, Romanesque façades, English alabasters, church treasuries, enamels, stained-glass windows, funerary sculptures, and many other items, do not really take much account of the chronological frame laid down from the outset. The point is that chronology is never a simple matter; it is not necessarily the same for all products of a given society: there is no real reason why the art of stained glass should develop at the same pace as, say, a noble lineage. In these circumstances we should conceive of historical time as a *system* of various chronological strands, with advances in one sector being counter-balanced by sluggish development in another. The integration of art history in our projected 'total' cultural history should result in some far more complex divisions into periods than historians and art historians have independently been used to.

This view of historical time as a multiple and contradictory entity must necessarily precede any consideration of the function of images. Once he is prepared to side-step his discipline's traditional questions, and strive towards a better understanding of the relationship set up between his objects and their social context, the art historian will find himself, quite naturally, blending two chronologies: that of the evolution of styles, and that of the evolution of society. This was Millard Meiss's working hypothesis when he started out on his study of Florentine and Siennese painting after the Black Death:[43] what could have been the impact of the epidemic (which in a few months carried off more than half of the population of those wealthy cities) on the art of this period? In fact, counter to all expectations, the Plague left no trace on Tuscan painting, except perhaps in the negative sense, as a horror that may certainly not have been unspeakable (since writers and chroniclers, headed by Boccaccio, did speak of it), but was unpaintable, and so was excluded by the artists. Above all, however, Meiss's research has allowed us to uncover the 'fundamental anachronism of painting

[42] *Le Moyen Age*, ed. by Georges Duby, in *Histoire artistique de l'Europe*, ed. by Georges Duby and Michel Laclotte (Paris: Seuil, 1995). Apart from Duby himself, twenty-six specialists from five different European countries collaborated on this work.

[43] Millard Meiss, *Painting in Florence and Siena after the Black Death* (Princeton: Princeton University Press, 1951); translated into French, with a preface by Georges Didi-Huberman, as *La peinture à Florence et à Sienne après la Peste Noire. Les arts, la religion, la société au milieu du XIVe siècle* (Paris: Hazan, 1994).

and its subject-matter', in the words of Georges Didi-Huberman, who has shown that the image of the Triumph of Death (beginning with the great fresco of Buffalmacco, in the Campo Santo at Pisa) actually predates the Black Death. The 'event' of the Black Death was not the cause of an evolution in painting and its themes; any cause is to be sought earlier, more deeply-rooted in the structural development of mental and religious images of the Hereafter and of the fate awaiting people after death.[44]

The matter of connecting images to their contemporary social background is also a prerequisite to a further field of research, nowadays still largely uncultivated, but one which Marc Bloch had already declared to be an essential goal of new historical studies: comparative history. Images and attitudes towards images in different societies represent for me one of the best means of observing the divergent courses of development followed by neighbouring civilisations, stemming sometimes from common roots. Christian image-culture gradually defined itself in opposition to the 'idols' of classical antiquity, which were considered all the more shamefully evil for the powerful fascination which they still exerted.[45] It also had to justify itself in the face of Judaism's proscription of the graven image, while at the same time reiterating its affinity with the Old Testament and the Ten Commandments. Finally, in the course of the Middle Ages, Western Christendom and the Greek Church found themselves in radical opposition over the matter of religious images, their formal characteristics, their ritual uses and their theoretical underpinnings.

Byzantium moved from the most violent iconoclasm to the most fervent iconolatry; this contrastive history led to a theology of the icon (with John the Damascene, Theodore of Studion, and Nicephore the Patriarch) which has known no equivalent in the West. In the long term, these icons have become characterized by a relatively conservative formalism, explainable by the fact that they are seen to bear, in their very matter, the imprint of divine emanation. Their beauty is no independent quality: it is that of the invisible Power manifest in them; and the wondrous stories of their divinely-inspired creation has quite overshadowed the act of the artist who painted them.

In the Western Church, on the other hand, the history of the image has been both calmer and more inventive: it has barely strayed at all from the *via media* laid down by Gregory the Great, and the waves of iconoclasm (towards 600, at the beginning of the ninth century, at times of medieval

---

[44] Jérôme Baschet, *Les Justices de l'au-delà, Les représentations de l'enfer en France et en Italie (XIIe–XVe siecle)* (Rome: École Française de Rome, 1993), p. 293; and 'Image et événement: l'art sans la peste (1340–1400)', in *La pesta nera: dati di una realtà ed elementi di una interpretazione* (Spoleto: Centro di Studi sul alto Medio Evo, 1994), pp. 25–47.

[45] Michael Camille, *The Gothic Idol. Ideology and Image-Making in Medieval Art* (Cambridge: Cambridge University Press, 1989).

heresy, and finally during the Protestant Reformation) have always been of limited effect. But then the Latin churchmen never developed a 'theology of the image' comparable in depth and subtlety to Greek icon theology. On the other hand, despite the heavy influence of religious tradition, the diversity, creativity, and sheer inventiveness of Western iconography contrast sharply, and utterly, with Orthodox formalism.[46] This made it easier to recognize the artist's autonomy, and from an early date.

The Romanian art historian Daniel Barbu seems to me to have perfectly defined the formal differences between Western and Eastern art, and their dual effect, both on the social level (regarding the status of the artist) and on the political level (concerning in each case the relationship between image and religious or secular authority). Taking as his point of departure the state of the West in the Carolingian period, he writes:

> The *Libri Carolini* lay down, even if only on a theoretical level, a certain degree of autonomy for the creator of religious images, vis-à-vis the authority of the Church. It is this autonomy which is perhaps responsible for the inventiveness which distinguished Western artists from Byzantine painters, and also for the highly diverse and restless treatment of forms which was to lend such vigour to the art of the Christian West throughout the Middle Ages. The Church failed right from the start to include the visual domain within the purlieu of its authority. Since it had not been considered a *res sacra*, the image acquired a secular and professional status which was always prohibited in Byzantium, where religious painting remained essentially the responsibility of the clergy. In the West, because the art of image-making was not duty-bound to follow prototypes controlled and 'managed' by the ecclesiastical hierarchy, it became almost free-thinking once in the presence of its own criterion of truth: beauty. This was a sensitive concept of beauty, no longer to be justified purely by its being the reflection of something intelligible. It is at this very precise point that might be traced the very obvious divergence of the Byzantine tradition and the flourishing art of the West.[47]

Going on to point to the status of the Byzantine image in the context of ritual icon veneration, Barbu goes on to state: 'The control of the Byzantine church over the visual arts does not always conceal its close links with the operation of Imperial authority'.[48]

The comparative approach should not merely set out to study the formal make-up of images, or style, or the actual chronology of artistic traditions. As the above references have shown, it must also bear in mind the religious, liturgical,

---

[46] Jean-Claude Schmitt, 'L'Occident, Nicée II et les images du VIIIe au XIIIe siècle', in *Nicée II, 787–1987. Douze siècles d'images religieuses*, ed. François Boespflug and Nicolas Lossky (Paris: Cerf, 1987), pp. 271–301.

[47] Daniel Barbu, 'L'image byzantine': production et usage', *Annales.Histoire, Sciences sociales*, 51 (1996), 71–92 (74–75).

[48] Ibid., p. 79.

and political functions of images, and even more generally the social and ideological contexts of their creation and reception. Byzantine icons and Western images draw on very different modes of social governance. In the East, the 'war on images' was in all respects a political matter. Iconoclasm was decreed in the eighth century by the Emperor, for whom it was an opportunity to assert his prerogatives (to an unprecedented degree) in the spiritual domain. Yet it is a fact that it also marked the beginning of the waning of his power, as the clerics began to prepare their revenge. For them the only legitimate priest-king, the new Melchisedech, was Christ, who had said, 'My kingdom is not of this world'. In opposition to the Old Testament models put forward by the Imperial party of iconoclasts, the Patriarch and those monks in favour of icons cited the inspiring example of the New Testament and the legitimacy of the Church of Christ and its sacred images, the cult of which was renewed with unprecedented pomp.[49] Nothing equivalent ever took place in the West, even when Charlemagne had the 'Libri Carolini' drawn up against Pope Hadrian I's desire to extend the cult of images into the Frankish Empire. Constantine's dream of a mingling of powers did not survive an early separation of *regnum* and *sacerdotium*. The figure of Melchisedech priest-king of Salem (Genesis 14. 18–20) did not become dominant in Western political ideology, with the exception of some supporters of the German Emperor: his presence was restricted to the typological symbolism of Christ and the Eucharist.[50] The 'separation of powers', which was in the long term to remain a characteristic feature of all Western culture, was very formally codified under Gregory VII. Admittedly, at this precise period, from the eleventh century onwards, some Western images (called 'objects of worship' or 'devotional') were recognized as enshrining a sacrality and a miraculous power unthinkable two hundred and fifty years earlier, at the time of the 'Libri Carolini'. But this combined power and sacrality—and one thinks, for example, of the cult of the Veronica, promoted by the papacy throughout Western Christendom at the beginning of the thirteenth century—only affected the institutional Church and religious attitudes, or at the very most the religious apanage and protocol of the political power, without the latter's legitimacy ever becoming dependent upon it. Neither the nature nor the exercising of imperial or royal power was ever bound up with the denial or affirmation of the power of holy images. Heretics and (later on) Reformers would indeed set about religious

[49] Gilbert Dagron, *Empereur et prêtre. Étude sur le 'césaro-papisme' byzantin* (Paris: Gallimard, 1996).

[50] See 'Melchisedech', in *Lexikon der christlichen Ikonographie*, III (Freiburg im Breisgau: Herder, 1971), cols 241–42, with particular reference to Nicholas of Verdun's retable at Klosterneuburg: Melchisedech, wearing the Imperial crown, is offering up on an altar the sacrifice of Host and Chalice. For opposing examples of resistance to the political use of the figure, in Western 'Mirrors of Princes', see Jacques Le Goff, *Saint Louis* (Paris: Gallimard, 1996), pp. 127, 405, 578.

images:[51] in so doing, they would certainly shake the Church hierarchy to its foundations and disturb the public weal, but were never able to threaten the legitimacy of political authority.

Western images, with the most diverse forms and functions, were able to flourish in the Middle Ages in two distinct domains of society and culture. This separation proved the guarantee of their relative freedom and of their unparalleled development. In Western Christendom, religious images were constrained neither by any 'theology of the icon' nor by the power, which in the Eastern Empire a holy monarch might wield over icons, either to destroy them or to venerate them. As for profane images (ranging from the frescoes in local Italian courtrooms to portraits of fifteenth-century princes or merchants), these very early on bore the stamp of a degree of autonomy, from which crucible modern art and modern artists would finally emerge, fully emancipated.

---

[51] Horst Bredekamp, *Kunst als Medium sozialer Konflikte. Bilderkämpfe von der Spätantike bis zur Hussitenrevolution* (Frankfurt am Main: Suhrkamp, 1975); Olivier Christin, *Une révolution symbolique. L'iconoclasme huguenot et la reconstruction catholique* (Paris: Minuit, 1991).

Nostalgia for the real: the troubled relation of art history to visual culture

KEITH MOXEY

'When the real is no longer what it used to be, nostalgia assumes its full meaning'.[1]

One of the persistent features of art theoretical writing in the last twenty years has been the concern of a number of critics to insist on the 'end of art', the 'end of art history', and the 'end of aesthetics'. Motivated by a variety of critical perspectives, such critics all address the grand narrative of 'art' afforded by Hegelian philosophy. Some believe that we live at the end of the process Hegel described, according to which art is to be viewed as the materialization of the 'spirit', the principle of enlightenment, as it makes its way through time. Following Hegel, Arthur Danto, for example, argues that the age of art is over because the 'spirit' has transcended its materialization in artistic production and has assumed wholly intellectual form as philosophy.[2] While acknowledging that artistic creation continues unabated, Danto insists that art is no longer the place where the transhistorical drive toward self-consciousness is realized. The teleological thrust of artistic modernism has ended. The narrative whereby the various modernist movements bore a dialectical relationship to one

[1] Jean Baudrillard, 'The Precession of Simulacra', in *Simulations*, trans. by Paul Foss, Paul Patton and Philip Beitschman, Semiotext(e) 12 (New York: Semiotext(e), 1983).

[2] Arthur Danto, 'The End of Art', in *The Philosophical Disenfranchisement of Art* (New York: Columbia University Press, 1986), pp. 81–115; idem, 'Three Decades After the End of Art', in *After the End of Art: Contemporary Art and the Pale of History* (Princeton: Princeton University Press, 1997), pp. 21–39.

another, so that in contradicting its predecessor each new initiative sublated that which came before into its own nature, has reached its conclusion. The unveiling of Andy Warhol's 'Brillo Box' in 1964 introduced a note of irony that rendered the process complete:

> For the past century, art has been drawing toward a philosophical self-consciousness, and this has been tacitly understood to mean that artists must produce art that embodies the philosophical essence of art. We now can see that this was a wrong understanding, and with a clearer understanding comes the recognition that there is no further direction for the history of art to take. It can be anything artists and patrons want it to be.[3]

Other critics, such as Hans Belting, also follow Hegel in the conviction that not only art but also art history has ended.[4] Just as artistic production has lost its internal necessity, so the principle of form, or style, on which a history of art could be distinguished from other forms of historical interpretation, no longer serves as a guarantee of its autonomy. The collapse of the idea of style as the unifying concern of the history of art has led to a proliferation of different histories of art, each pursuing a different agenda:

> The more the inner unity of the history of art understood as an autonomous discipline failed, the more it dispersed itself into the surrounding context of culture and society in which it was thought to be included. The struggle about method lost its sharpness, and the histories replaced one compelling art history with several, indeed many, art histories, which exist peacefully alongside each other like the different directions of contemporary art.[5]

For Douglas Crimp, it is the rise of the museum that sealed the fate of universalist aesthetics. Associating Hegel's notion of the 'end of art' with the historical rise of the museum, Crimp argues that art's institutionalization, its confinement in the museum under the aegis of an idealist theory of aesthetics, served to remove it from the context of everyday life.[6] The idea of art's autonomy, its alleged universal value, is effectively responsible for its demise. While art continues to be produced, its autonomous status ensures that it cannot be an agent in everyday cultural and social interactions. The birth of the museum deprived art of its social significance, guaranteeing that it could only occupy a marginal position in the life of culture.

---

[3] Danto (as in note 2), p. 36.

[4] Hans Belting, *The End of Art History*, trans. by Christopher Wood (Chicago: University of Chicago Press, 1987); idem, *Das Ende der Kunstgeschichte: Ein Revision nach zehn Jahren* (Munich: Prestel, 1994).

[5] Belting (as in note 4), p. 22 (my translation).

[6] Douglas Crimp, *On the Museum's Ruins* (Cambridge, MA: MIT Press, 1993).

> Once materialized within the museum, idealist aesthetics could be expected to neutralize the possibility of art as revolutionary praxis or resistance. The effective removal of art from its direct engagement in social life, the creation of an 'autonomous' realm for art, became the museum's mission, and it was against this that radical forms of modernist theory and practice were directed.[7]

Finally, in a context far removed from art theory, the entire Western conception of art and history has been challenged by a new awareness of the way in which it is compromised by the existence of different cultures which either have no cultural equivalents or whose potential equivalents are so radically different as to be incommensurable. In his book *Time and The Other*, Johannes Fabian points out that in the context of colonialism, Western modernism, with its obsession with teleology and evolution, effectively discredited and marginalized notions of time held by non-Western societies. Post-colonial politics reminds us of the Eurocentric bias of modernist ideology. Modernist claims to universality can no longer be substantiated in an age that recognizes the value of cultural otherness. Just as modernist, or historicist, time once invalidated the time of other cultures, so our awareness of the legitimacy of different systems serves to undermine the Western project.[8] In these circumstances, it is clear that there is nothing self-evident about the concepts, 'art', 'art history', and 'aesthetics'. Far from belonging to the order of things, they have been shown to be cultural constructions that are bound to the times and places of their creation.

It is no coincidence that these various hypotheses should have been advanced in the context of the poststructuralist challenge to the signifying power of language, and to the master narratives on which the myth of modernism was based. The death of art, art history, and aesthetics can be viewed as a metaphor of the broader epistemological crisis inaugurated by deconstruction. In his essay, *The Parergon*, Derrida argued that in 'The Critique of Judgement' Kant's attempt to distinguish art from other cultural artefacts on the basis of a posited universal human response depended upon the construction of aesthetic value rather than upon its discovery.[9] Derrida suggested that, say, in distinguishing a picture from its frame, ascribing aesthetic significance to one and not to the other, Kant discerned universal values in a distinction that was in fact culturally ordained and therefore particular and local.

---

[7] Ibid., p. 303.

[8] Johannes Fabian, *Time and The Other: How Anthropology Makes Its Object* (New York: Columbia University Press, 1983).

[9] See Jacques Derrida, *The Truth in Painting*, trans. by Geoff Bennington and Ian McLeod (Chicago: University of Chicago Press, 1987), pp. 17–147; also David Rodowick, 'Impure Mimesis, or the End of the Aesthetic', in *Deconstruction and the Spatial Arts: Art, Media, Architecture*, ed. by Peter Brunette and David Wills (Cambridge: Cambridge University Press, 1994), pp. 96–117.

A failure to distinguish the study of art from the study of other kinds of images is often used as a criticism of the new field of academic inquiry known as 'visual studies' or 'visual culture'. In this essay, I shall attempt to argue that the animus directed against this new form of cultural analysis is misplaced. Rather than view the rise of the study of varied and often popular forms of image production—one in which art is included in a spectrum of other kinds of visual products—as a potential threat to art as an institution, I would claim that the value of these visual juxtapositions lies in comparing and contrasting the ways in which the study of each genre, say painting, television, or advertising, makes use of different theories and methods in the making of meaning. While this view relativizes the study of art, suggesting that it is just one among many forms of visual production, it recognizes the ethical and political concerns that motivate its students. The study of 'visual culture' insists that there is nothing 'natural' or 'universal' about claims to aesthetic value. The importance of the study of art, as opposed to other kinds of images, lies in defining the particular significance attached to the idea of aesthetic value in different cultures at different moments in time.[10]

In viewing art from this perspective, in rendering it susceptible to comparison with other forms of visual imagery and the ways in which they have been understood, the study of 'visual culture' must acknowledge an agenda of its own. That agenda, I would maintain, is inextricably linked to the history of poststructuralism. Basing itself on a recognition of the role of subjectivity in the pursuit of objectivity, a recognition that established fields of study are the record of an 'archaeology' of discourse, visual studies are often concerned with the way in which the objects of study reveal the ethical and political commitments of those who study them.

W. J. T. Mitchell, who is perhaps most responsible for the way the term 'visual culture' is currently employed, envisions visual culture as a field of study, a focus for the varied interests of scholars working in many disciplines from a number of different points of view. As a member of a faculty group at the University of Chicago, Mitchell helped develop both a rationale and a syllabus for a yearlong academic course in the subject.[11] Regarding visual culture's relation to art history, Mitchell writes:

---

[10] The continued use of the term *art* in this essay, particularly in contrast to something called *non-art*, should be regarded as a means by which to refer to a changing form of cultural discourse that deals with artefacts for which philosophical, religious, and/or political claims are advanced, which are considered part of the heritage of the nation-states, and which play a role in the capitalist commodities market.

[11] W. J. T. Mitchell, 'What is Visual Culture?', in *Meaning in the Visual Arts: Views from the Outside: A Centennial Commemoration of Erwin Panofsky* (1892–1968), ed. by Irving Lavin (Princeton: Institute for Advanced Study, 1995), pp. 207–17.

> From the standpoint of a general field of visual culture, art history can no longer rely on received notions of beauty or aesthetic significance to define its proper object of study. The realm of the vernacular and popular imagery clearly has to be reckoned with and the notion of aesthetic hierarchy, of masterpieces and the genius of the artist have to be re-described as historical constructions specific to various cultural place-times.[12]

If the distinction between art and visual artefact is to be seen as a cultural construction rather than as a cultural 'given', then what kinds of imagery is visual culture to address? On this point Mitchell is far less specific:

> The point of a course in visual culture, in short, would be to provide students with a set of critical tools for the investigation of human visuality, not to transmit a specific body of information or values. If the questions and debates are posed frankly, as the very substance of the course rather than as something already settled, then information, values, and exposure to the finest productions of visual culture will inevitably follow.[13]

Such a definition appears to beg the question. The world of images is so vast as to necessitate a frame. Having already dismissed 'received notions of beauty or aesthetic significance', it is difficult to understand his invocation of the idea of quality, his reference to 'the finest productions of visual culture', as the grounds for determining the content of the course. While Mitchell's reluctance to suggest a frame for the study of visual culture might be regarded as providing a useful flexibility for a field of study that has yet to locate itself historically, that reluctance must also be regarded as a theoretical weakness.[14]

A more important drawback to Mitchell's proposed course is its ambition to provide students with 'a set of critical tools for the investigation of human visuality'. This sentiment, which echoes the goals of traditional art appreciation courses that aspire to enable students to 'learn to look', suggests that there might be a simple set of concepts, a toolbox, with which the rich and complex world of visual experience might be understood.[15] If visual culture is not to be reduced to the

---

[12] Ibid., p. 210.

[13] Ibid., pp. 207–17.

[14] It is a weakness shared by certain other publications on the subject of 'visual culture', which, in celebrating the heterogeneity of the potential subjects to be addressed, fail to address the necessity to offer a focus, an agenda, or a rationale for the enterprise. See, for example, *Visual Culture*, ed. by Chris Jenks (London: Routledge, 1995), which includes essays on topics as diverse as advertising, visual reporting, contemporary art, the visual experience of the city, fascist imagery, television and so forth.

[15] The formalist ideology of Joshua Taylor's famous *Learning to Look* (Chicago: University of Chicago Press, 1957) has been usefully contextualized by Linda Seidel and Katherine Taylor in their account of the social and cultural agendas that have determined the status and function of 'art' at the institution for which Taylor's course was designed.

study of art on the basis of a universal notion of aesthetic significance, why should its potential be foreclosed by assuming that there is a universal epistemological basis for the enterprise?

Rather than reduce the analysis of visual culture to a single set of principles, it seems to me that the point of the academic study of images is the recognition of their heterogeneity, the different circumstances of their production, and the variety of cultural and social functions they serve. It is precisely because the interpretative paraphernalia, the heuristic strategies, used in the elucidation of different traditions of visual production are so radically different from one another that each form of investigation has much to gain from a familiarity with the others. This, in fact, is the underlying logic behind the structure of at least one of several university programmes that have adopted 'visual studies' as their title. In the graduate programme instituted at the Univ. of Rochester in the late 1980s for instance, studies in 'Visual and Cultural Studies' consist of a variety of discipline-based requirements.[16] Students can take courses in art history, film, or popular culture, without sacrificing the specificity of the interpretive traditions associated with the study of each form of cultural discourse. Their exposure to different methodological traditions enables them to inform their own interpretations with an awareness of a broad range of different points of view. For example, in the study of art history, they are capable of drawing upon theories and methods familiar to them from their study of, say, film or television.

More importantly perhaps, an awareness of the ideological diversity implicit in the various fields that concern them, the sensitivity of students to the way in which the production of knowledge manifests the circumstances in which it takes place, as well as the interests of those involved, affords them insight into the changing nature of their own cultural activity. In being asked to familiarize themselves with the traditions that animate each discipline, students have an opportunity to analyse and deconstruct the philosophical attitudes and cultural values that have informed the frame constructed around those disciplines at different moments in time. Recognition of the shifting and unstable nature of disciplinary discourses, the way in which they have responded to changing historical circumstances, enables them to evaluate the parameters within which the disciplines currently operate. The awareness that disciplines are not frozen in time, that there is nothing foundational about the methodological differences that distinguish them from one another, empowers those who study visual culture to cross disciplinary boundaries with creative and productive results. If there is nothing sacred about the way in which a

---

See Linda Seidel and Katherine Taylor, *Looking to Learn: Visual Pedagogy at the University of Chicago* (Chicago: University of Chicago Press, 1998).

[16] For a discussion of the aims of this project, see Scott Heller, 'Visual Images Replace Text as Focal Point for Many Scholars', *Chronicle of Higher Education* (19 July 1996), Appendix I. The Rochester programme has inspired a similar enterprise at the University of California, Irvine.

subject has been studied in the past, then there is nothing to prevent it from being viewed from a different perspective in the future.

Needless to say, the rise of visual culture as a subject of academic interest has not gone unchallenged. Ironically enough, that challenge has come both from scholars familiar with and sympathetic to poststructuralist thought, as well as from those dedicated to the preservation of the status quo. While the tendency to blur the distinction between art and non-art contains within it an implicit rejection of the idea of universal aesthetic value that has been the traditional basis of art historical studies, it also seems to have offended critics identified with new approaches to interpretation in the visual arts, including those who have explicitly rejected the idea of the humanist subject on which traditional claims for aesthetics are made.

In 1996, the journal *October* circulated a questionnaire to a number of academics who could be identified as broadly interested in the study of images, including art historians, students of film, and of visuality in general, soliciting their views regarding the visual culture initiative. The questionnaire betrayed the suspicion of its framers: namely, that the establishment of this new field was an unfortunate development, which catered to the exploitative interests of late capitalism. Since such a claim is clearly not self-evident, it is worth examining in some detail. Question three reads: 'It has been suggested that the precondition for visual studies is an interdisciplinary rubric in a newly wrought conception of the visual as disembodied image, re-created in the virtual spaces of sign-exchange and phantasmatic projection. Further, if this new paradigm of the image originally developed in the intersection between psychoanalytic and media discourses, it has now assumed a role independent of specific media. As a corollary, the suggestion is that visual studies are helping, in its own modest, academic way, to produce subjects for the next stage of globalized capital'.[17]

Who was it that made this suggestion? Who said what to whom, when, and where, and what did they mean by it? The disembodied voice of the text affords no clue to these queries. The potential respondent who seeks to react to these assertions is placed at a disadvantage. What, for example, is meant by, '. . . the precondition for visual studies is an interdisciplinary rubric in a newly wrought conception of the visual as disembodied image'? If this is meant to suggest that visual studies seek to separate the image from the rest of the cultural production that surrounds it, nothing could be further from the truth. The point of visual studies, as I see it, is to locate the image in the midst of the meaning-making processes that constitute its cultural environment. Such a definition means, for example, that visual studies deliberately ignores those guarantees that have

[17] *October*, 77 (1996), 25. For responses to the issues raised by this questionnaire, see Douglas Crimp, 'Getting the Warhol We Deserve: Cultural Studies and Queer Studies', *Social Text* (1999), and Irit Rogoff, 'Studying Visual Culture', in *The Visual Culture Reader*, ed. by Nicholas Mirzoeff (London: Routledge, 1998), pp. 14–26.

traditionally been sought by scholars interested in preserving the autonomy of art. One of the assumptions underlying visual studies, I believe, is that the image is saturated with the word. Visual sign systems are inextricably bound up with linguistic and other codes that characterize a particular culture at a particular historical moment.

Question three's suggestion, namely, that a poststructuralist approach to the study of the image—one that implies that aesthetic value is culturally constructed rather than foundational, is a manifestation of the economic characteristic of late capitalism—is hard to follow. Here the inspiration seems to be Fredric Jameson's influential argument concerning postmodernism.[18] Jameson subscribes to an evolutionary view of history according to which postmodernism necessarily follows modernism because its culture is the product of the late capitalist economy. While such an understanding views history as a teleological movement through time, in Jameson's case this is not a Hegelian model but a Marxist one; the engine of history is not the passage of the spirit but the class struggle. According to Jameson, theoretical critiques of the 'grand narrative' of Western history offered by Marxist thought are to be viewed as symptoms of a particular historical moment. Criticism of totalizing theories of history, in this case the Marxist view, is considered a manifestation of the post-modern condition, rather than as a challenge to a traditional conception of history. On this view, the Marxist understanding of history is not to be questioned because it is impossible to think outside it. History is regarded as the real circumstance of human existence, rather than as a particular philosophical outlook. Jameson's Marxism is necessarily a metaphilosophy, one that must encompass all other philosophical systems while refusing to recognize that it is one itself. This very lack of self-reflexivity, however, this naturalization of the grounds of historical thought (the foundation of modernism as a literary and artistic movement), is what visual studies seek to challenge.

Based on a Derridean philosophy of language, one that insists that language is the home of metaphysics and that meaning is only constructed out of its absence, visual studies focuses first and foremost on the frame within which meaning is produced. Rather than subscribe to a theory that reduces theoretical innovation to the ideological 'superstructure' of a culture whose shape is determined by its economic 'base', visual studies insists that despite the cultural forces that necessarily condition consciousness, human action is far from predictable. In the absence of the kind of totality posited by Jamesonian theory, it is the very conflicts of cultural discourse, its heteroglossia, which ensures that the principle of agency cannot be overlooked in cultural analysis. In the wake of poststructuralism, a set of theories that emphasized the indeterminacy of

---

[18] See Fredric Jameson, *Postmodernism or The Cultural Logic of Late Capitalism* (Durham, NC: Duke University Press, 1991), and more recently, *The Cultural Turn: Selected Workings on the Postmodern* (London: Verso, 1998).

meaning and our inability to know the world, Jameson supports one of the more traditional of the grand narratives of history, namely Marx's claim to understand the relation of human beings to the real circumstances of their existence. In this situation, not only his theory of culture but also the attack on visual studies that is based upon it seems to constitute a kind of 'nostalgia for the real'.

Hal Foster, who also contributed an essay to the same issue of *October*, took a negative stance toward the idea of visual culture, arguing that it implied a move from '*art* to *visual* and from *history* to *culture*'.[19] Taking the second set of binaries first, Foster claims that visual culture participates in what he calls an 'ethnographic turn'. By this he means that in recognizing that positionality matters in the production of discourse—that knowledge is inflected by the interests of those responsible for its articulation—visual culture is in danger of compromising traditional (i.e., Marxist) conceptions of history. 'For in the ethnographic model one moves horizontally, from site to site across social space, more than vertically, in a discourse inscribed with an historicity, a responsibility of form, of its own. In this way, the shift from history to culture may promote, in art as well as in criticism, a posthistorical reduction as often as a multihistorical complication'.[20]

Foster thus opposes diachrony to synchrony, arguing that the latter gains at the expense of the former. Recognition of the spatiality of culture, of the multitude of subject positions that animate it, is regarded as inimical to chronology. If the differences among subject positions are sufficiently radical, then it becomes impossible to agree upon a single version of the historical events. Foster's misgivings, however, are misplaced. In dispensing with the grand narratives that hitherto have animated our conception of history, visual culture does not propose foregoing a philosophy of history. It is not time that is under attack by those who wish to study visual culture, for it is the interaction of the principles of time and space to which this field of investigation is dedicated. If the Hegelian and Marxist narratives are abandoned, then it becomes possible to rethink history from the perspective of cultural difference. Far from being a reductive development, such a move opens up the study of history to make its narratives potentially far richer and more interesting. In other words, 'multihistorical complication', the possibility of telling an historical narrative from a variety of points of view, cannot be identified with 'posthistorical reduction', the alleged collapse of history attributed to the challenge of its grand narratives, without appearing paradoxical.

In replacing *art* with the concept of the term *visual*, Foster claims that visual culture foregoes the potential inherent in the concept of art's autonomy. Invoking 'subjection', as autonomy's 'other', he argues that without autonomy, art is

---

[19] Hal Foster, 'The Archive Without Museums', *October*, 77 (1996), 97–119 (p. 104).

[20] Ibid., pp. 104–05.

capable of being 'reduced' to the merely visual. In an argument reminiscent of Adorno's view of art as a locus of resistance to capitalist culture, Foster writes:

> Enlightenment thinkers like Kant proclaimed autonomy in order to wrest institutions away from the 'ancien régime', art historians like Riegl to resist deterministic accounts of art, modernists from Manet to Judd to challenge the priority of iconographic texts, the necessity of illustrational meaning, the imperialism of the mass media, the overburdening of art with voluntaristic politics, and so on. Like essentialism, autonomy is a bad word, but it may not always be a bad strategy: call it *strategic autonomy*.[21]

It is no accident, of course, that Foster's last phrase, 'strategic autonomy', should echo Gayatri Spivak's 'strategic essentialism'.[22] Like Spivak's conception of essentialism as something that can be either relative or absolute according to political circumstance, so the idea of 'strategic autonomy' both relativizes and asserts the autonomy of art at the same time. In Foster's case, the assertion of the autonomy of art is a political gesture (one that is historically determined and subjectively freighted), meant to stave off the threat to art that is posed by the visual. For Foster, this is an either/or situation; either art is autonomous, or it disappears into the visual.

Against Foster, I would argue that the binary oppositions 'autonomy/subjection', 'art/visual', are, in fact, uncalled for. Rather than insist on the primacy of art in relation to other forms of cultural imagery, why not simply recognize its distinctiveness? Why not view art as one of the many kinds of imagery that constitute visual culture? Rather than see art dissolved into other forms of imagery that surround it, it is in the interest of visual culture to recognize it as a distinct form of visual creativity, one possessed of an historiographic tradition of its own. Indeed, the point of visual culture would be not only to recognize the different genres of image production that characterises a particular culture, but also to insist that their unique qualities call for distinct approaches to their interpretation.

If, as I have been arguing, the notion of art is not necessarily to be regarded as opposed to the idea of 'visual culture', if it is possible to conceive of art as a particular circumscribed form of cultural discourse, one distinguished or bracketed off from other forms of cultural interaction, how then might we define the breadth and scope of the field of imagery the new field of study might address? One quick way to reduce the new enterprise to absurdity would be to suggest that it should be open to a consideration of *all* forms of cultural imagery, ranging from digital and electronic images to comic strips, without making qualitative distinctions between them. The rationale for including or excluding

---

[21] Ibid., pp. 118–19.

[22] Gayatri Spivak, 'Subaltern Studies: Deconstructing Historiography', in *In Other Worlds: Essays in Cultural Politics* (New York: Routledge, 1988), pp. 197–221.

different genres of image production under the rubric 'visual culture' will clearly depend on historical circumstances, educational needs and political considerations.

In current circumstances, I believe that one of the most powerful reasons for including the study of art along with non-art lies in the acknowledgement of the collapse of foundationalist theories of knowledge. 'Visual culture' opens doors to the production of knowledge from a variety of different subject positions. It fosters forms of interpretation inspired by feminism, queer studies, and postcolonialism. Rather than seek consensus, it benefits from the radical disagreement among different styles of interpretation. The heteroglossia that characterizes the operations of visual studies is regarded as a positive and dynamic aspect of its activities. The pursuit of differing styles of interpretation under the aegis of 'visual culture' means that the particular interests associated with each form of knowledge production are hard to miss. Since it is no longer possible to suggest that knowledge is 'disinterested', the alterity of the juxtaposed voices inevitably will draw attention to the cultural agenda that informs the enterprise. Each form of argumentation can afford to foreground rather than conceal its political affiliations.

Current theoretical assumptions concerning knowledge production suggest that it is in difference rather than in sameness that the strongest contributions to the humanities are likely to be made. Each discipline has an opportunity to expand its repertoire of interpretative methodologies in relation to those around it, and it is in the interstices between disciplines that the greatest insights regarding the structure of our knowledge, as well as our need to pursue it, are likely to be derived.

Image Databases and History

Pourquoi élaborer des bases de données d'image? Propositions pour une iconographie sérielle

JÉRÔME BASCHET

Aujourd'hui, la nécessité de constituer des bases de données d'images est de plus en plus clairement ressentie par les chercheurs. Les initiatives et réalisations se sont multipliées au cours de la décennie écoulée, promues soit par des institutions de recherche, soit, souvent aussi, par des chercheurs individuels, à la fois soucieux de valoriser les matériaux mis à jour par leurs propres travaux et désireux de contribuer à la constitution des outils documentaires dont ils ressentent le besoin.[1] Ce rôle important joué par les chercheurs, qui détournent ainsi une part du temps normalement voué au travail scientifique proprement dit, peut s'interpréter à la fois négativement, comme signe d'une certaine inertie des institutions, et positivement, dans la mesure où la constitution

[1] Parmi bien d'autres exemples, on citera pour le premier cas la base de données des manuscrits enluminés des Bibliothèques publiques de France, entrepris par l'Institut de Recherche et d'Histoire des Textes (C.N.R.S., Orléans), et pour le second le projet PREALP, consacré aux peintures murales alpines et mené par Dominique Rigaux, ou encore le projet *Fons Sacra*, consacré à l'iconographie des fonts baptismaux européens, lancé par Harriet Sonne. Il existe évidemment de nombreuses situations intermédiaires (ne serait-ce que parce qu'une initiative individuelle doit, pour réussir, trouver des soutiens institutionnels). Parmi de nombreux exemples, on citera, la base de données consacrée aux peintures murales danoises, dirigée par Axel Bolvig (cf. A. Bolvig, 'Danish Wall Paintings—An Introduction', *Medium Aevum Quotidianum*, 39 (1998), 7–8, numéro consacré à cette base de données), ou encore les vidéodisques des manuscrits enluminés de la Bibliothèque Vaticane, à la réalisation desquels j'ai pris part (trois vidéodisques réalisés en collaboration entre la Bibliothèque Vaticane, l'École française de Rome et l'École des Hautes Études en Sciences Sociales, et disponibles depuis 1994).

des outils documentaires s'articule ainsi directement aux besoins de la recherche. Quoi qu'il en soit, on ne peut que se réjouir des progrès accumulés durant ces dernières années, des réalisations déja accomplies et des projets en cours, tout en regrettant les retards pris et en remarquant que la situation actuelle est encore très loin de correspondre aux possibilités ouvertes par les développements techniques.[2]

Au-delà du bilan des années écoulées et du diagnostic sur la situation présente, il convient de s'interroger plus attentivement sur les objectifs et les perspectives scientifiques de tels investissements, sur leur nécessité et leurs conséquences, sur les relations entre ces nouveaux moyens documentaires et la modalités de la recherche dans le domaine des images médiévales. On ne reviendra pas ici sur les principes qui, selon nous, devraient guider l'établissement des bases de données,[3] et on s'efforcera seulement d'analyser leur effet pour la recherche. A cet égard, il serait évidemment fort réducteur de limiter les bienfaits des bases de données à un simple gain de temps, à la facilité plus grande avec laquelle elles permettent de disposer des images nécessaires à une enquête particulière. Faire valoir l'augmentation du nombre des oeuvres mises à la disposition des chercheurs paraît également insuffisant. De même que la photographie a modifié la pratique traditionnelle de l'histoire de l'art en facilitant et multipliant les comparaisons possibles, on soutiendra qu'aujourd'hui la possibilité d'accéder et de 'manipuler' des stocks d'images considérables (et à terme la totalité des oeuvres conservées) doit entraîner dans la pratique de la recherche des modifications non seulement quantitatives mais aussi qualitatives.

Ce sont précisément les transformations des méthodes d'analyse des oeuvres, induites par les nouvelles techniques, qui nous semblent appeler réflexion et discussion. On proposera ici une contribution à ce débat collectif, en défendant la proposition d'une *iconographie sérielle*. Cette expression suggère d'emblée une dimension quantitative (à la mesure des masses d'images sous lesquels les historiens et les historiens d'art peuvent craindre d'être bientôt ensevelis . . .). Pourtant, l'iconographie sérielle ne se préoccupe pas seulement de grands

---

[2] L'un des principaux regrets tient à la sous-utilisation de l'Index of Christian Art de Princeton, qui reste pourtant le plus ample outil de recherche documentaire concernant les images médiévales. On peut ici incriminer la lenteur de son informatisation et la restriction de ses implantations. Il est tout à fait anormal que cet instrument de travail ne soit pas systématiquement utilisé par les chercheurs concernés par l'image médiévale.

[3] Je m'en suis expliqué ailleurs, à la fois théoriquement ('Les vidéodisques des manuscrits de la Bibliothèque vaticane et la réalisation d'une base de données iconographique', *Arte medievale*, 1 (1992), 199–205, et 'Remarques sur l'indexation iconographique. L'expérience des vidéodisques des manuscrits de la Bibliothèque Vaticane', *Mélanges de l'École française de Rome, Moyen Age*, 106 (1994), 179–88), et pratiquement, par la mise au point collective du *Thésaurus des images médiévales*, éds. Groupe d'Anthropologie Historique de l'Occident Médiéval, CRH-EHESS (Paris, 1993).

nombres, qu'il suffirait de gérer par d'habiles recours statistiques. S'appuyant sur une analyse de la nature et du mode de fonctionnement des images médiévales, l'iconographie sérielle place au centre de la réflexion l'articulation du traitement quantitatif et de l'analyse qualitative. Elle prend pour objet des *gammes de variations*, incluant régularités massives et combinatoire des variantes, exploration du champ de possibilités figuratives et radicalité des coups d'éclats. En faisant apparaître des séries de transformations, l'analyse sérielle peut tout à la fois traiter des productions massives et restituer à chaque oeuvre sa singularité. Ce faisant, non seulement elle contribue à une nouvelle perception de l'iconographie médiévale, qu'on ne saurait analyser en termes de stéréotypes codifiés ou de modèles passivement reproduits, mais elle prend part aussi à un débat qui traverse l'ensemble du champ des sciences sociales, en quête de méthodes permettant d'articuler l'individuel et le collectif, le particulier et le général.[4]

Inventivité de l'art médiéval

Afin de fonder la pertinence d'une approche sérielle, il importe, en préalable, de mettre en question le préjugé encore courant selon lequel les images médiévales relèveraient d'un art stéréotypé, presque figé, et de surcroît obligé à reproduire passivement la doctrine de l'Eglise. On soutiendra au contraire que le Moyen Age occidental, surtout à partir du IXe et plus nettement encore du XIe siècle, est une période de liberté particulièrement grande pour les images et de profusion iconographique exceptionnellement intense.[5] L'approche sérielle doit alors être conçue en relation avec la reconnaissance de cette extrême inventivité. La conception d'un art stéréotypé, dogmatique, épaulée par la vieille idée de l'image comme Bible des illettrés, correspond particulièrement à la vision transmise par Emile Mâle.[6] Pour ce dernier, l'art, soumis à l'Eglise et au dogme, 'traduit la

---

[4] Le texte qui suit reprend (à quelques légères modifications près) la seconde partie de 'Inventivité et sérialité des images médiévales. Pour une approche iconographique élargie', *Annales. Histoire, Sciences sociales*, 51 (1996), 93–133. En ce qui concerne la notion d'iconographie, on renvoie à la première partie de cet article.

[5] On parlera de liberté de l'art (ou des images), plutôt que de liberté de l'artiste, pour ne pas préjuger du statut de ces derniers, ni mésestimer le rôle des commanditaires. Ce que l'on veut mettre en évidence concerne l'inventivité des oeuvres elles-mêmes. Enfin, il est clair que cette liberté ne saurait être comparée aux conditions de création des artistes des XIXe et XXe siècles. Voir R. Berliner, 'The Freedom of Medieval Art', *Gazette des Beaux-Arts*, 28 (1945), 263–88.

[6] Pour la critique de cette notion, je renvoie à mon article 'Introduction: l'image-objet', dans *L'image. Fonctions et usages des images dans l'occident médiéval*, éds. J. Baschet et J.-C. Schmitt (Paris: Cahiers du Léopard d'Or, 1996), pp. 7–26.

pensée des docteurs', reproduit 'tout de que les théologiens, les encyclopédistes, les interprètes de la Bible ont dit d'essentiel'.[7] Expression d'une pensée structurée, encyclopédique, l'art—en particulier celui du XIIIe siècle—constitue un ensemble unifié; il repose sur l'usage d'un language codifié, normatif, conventionnel.[8] Il est donc possible d'en traiter comme d'une réalité homogène: 'nous le considérons comme un tout vivant, un ensemble achevé'.[9] L'art exprime *le* discours de l'Eglise, et c'est pourquoi il est possible de tenir *un* discours sur l'art de cette époque.

Dans *L'image médiévale*, Jean Wirth a reformulé de façon neuve et stimulante le projet d'Emile Mâle d'une saisie globale de l'art et de l'iconographie du Moyen Age.[10] Concernant la question du caractère codifié de l'art médiéval, sa position est ambiguë. D'un côté, il souligne que l'iconographie n'est pas le décalque de la théologie, et peut même la contredire. Il traque avec prédilection tout ce qui déborde des types iconographiques courants: les hybridations, les traits originaux, et même l'inconvenance, et souligne 'la prodigieuse inventivité de l'art religieux'. Pourtant, l'hypothèse centrale du livre, attribuant un caractère logique à l'image, réintroduit des caractères de codification et de systématicité qui autorisent à parler de l'*image médiévale* (au singulier).[11] Il est significatif que Jean Wirth reprenne, pour souligner le caractère logique de l'iconographie médiévale, l'exemple des nimbes, déjà invoqué par Emile Mâle.[12] Sans doute en complique-t-il la présentation; mais il demeure qu'il surestime le caractère logique et systématique du fonctionnement du nimbe dans l'art médiéval (négligence de certaines formes, ni circulaires, ni carrées, ou encore des degrés d'ornementation; non prise en compte du fonctionnement syntaxique du nimbe).[13] Plus largement, tout en partageant l'idée d'une extrême inventivité de

---

[7] Emile Mâle, *L'art religieux du* XIIIe *siècle en France. Etude sur l'iconographie du Moyen Age et sur ses sources d'inspiration* (Paris, 1898 ; 8e éd., 1948), p. 13 et p. 351: 'Ici, comme partout ailleurs, les artistes du XIIIe siècle furent les interprètes dociles des théologiens'.

[8] L'art médiéval, 'écriture sacrée', se rapproche du fonctionnement du langage verbal: ses signes 'sont de véritables hiéroglyphes: l'art et l'écriture se confondent', ibid., p. 31.

[9] (cf. note 7), p. 15. Ceci se traduit dans l'étude concrète, par exemple lorsque E. Mâle traite de l'Enfance du Christ, en faisant comme s'il existait un cycle type, reproduit à l'identique dans toutes les oeuvres (p. 353).

[10] J. Wirth, *L'image médiévale. Naissance et développements,* VIe–XVe *siècle* (Paris: Klincksieck, 1989), pp. 18–23.

[11] Pour une critique de cette conception, et en particulier des références à la logique, cf. J.-C. Bonne, 'A la recherche des images médiévales', *Annales E.S.C.*, 2 (1991), 353–73.

[12] Wirth (cf. note 10), pp. 23–25; Mâle (cf. note 7), p. 30.

[13] Ainsi, l'aspect syntaxique conduit très souvent à réserver le nimbe pour le personnage principal, comme le Christ, et à l'exclure pour les autres (les apôtres

l'art médiéval, on préfère attribuer à ce dernier un degré de systématicité moindre, ce qui conduit à faire le constat d'une diversité plus considérable encore que ne le suggère Jean Wirth.[14]

Mais qu'est-ce qui autorise cette 'liberté' de l'art, dès lors que l'on n'oublie nullement l'intervention des commanditaires, ni non plus le rôle de l'Eglise qui fait peser sur la société une domination idéologique puissante? Le plus important ici est de souligner que l'Eglise médiévale n'est pas un corps homogène, mais qu'elle est au contraire, comme la société tout entière, parcourue de tensions et animée de contradictions parfois intenses. La doctrine n'est pas davantage *une*. Elle évolue, fait l'objet de débats, donne lieu à des conflits y compris au sein de l'orthodoxie (Immaculée Conception, Pauvreté . . .). Elle se module depuis la haute spéculation des théologiens, jusqu'aux oeuvres de divulgation, en passant par ses mises en actes liturgiques et théâtrales, ou encore ses expressions dévotionnelles et mystiques. Les discours cléricaux intègrent des traditions d'abord étrangères à la doctrine, qui peuvent ensuite en faire pleinement partie, ou rester marginales (apocryphes, légendes, conceptions folkloriques . . .).

D'autre part, l'Occident médiéval—à la différence du domaine byzantin—se caractérise par une faible intervention normative des clercs dans le domaine des images. Du moins est-ce le cas après la fin de la Querelle des images,[15] et à l'exception de quelques tendances limitatives, par exemple chez saint Bernard. Certes, les clercs rappellent, en particulier dans les traités liturgiques, les fonctions des images et évoquent parfois certaines significations des thèmes principaux.[16] Mais rares sont les interventions visant à fixer, à corriger ou à condamner les modes de représentations. De fait, on constate une mobilité

---

notamment), sans qu'il soit pour autant question de remettre en cause la sainteté de ces derniers (exemples dans les mosaïques de Monreale). Dans certaines oeuvres, un même personnage apparaissant plusieurs fois, peut être, selon les cas, nimbé ou non. Un traitement exhaustif de la figuration des nimbes montrerait à quel point il est difficile de réduire les images, même sur un point aussi élémentaire, à une codification stricte et homogène.

[14] L'analyse des représentations de l'âme fournit un autre exemple où le désir de systématicité conduit à réduire l'iconographie à des codes beaucoup trop simplifiés; cf. J. Wirth, 'L'apparition du surnaturel dans l'art du Moyen Age', dans *L'image et la production du sacré*, éds. F. Dunand, J.-M. Speser et J. Wirth (Paris, 1991), pp. 139–64, et mes remarques dans 'Anima', dans *Enciclopedia dell'arte medievale* (Rome, 1991), pp. 804–15.

[15] Y. Christe a souligné que les choix occidentaux inspirés par les milieux carolingiens a permis de libérer l'art chrétien occidental 'de trop fortes contraintes doctrinales', cf. 'L'émergence d'une théorie de l'image dans le prolongement de Rm 1,20 du IXe au XIIe siècle en Occident', dans *Nicée* II. *Douze siècles d'images religieuses*, éds. F. Boespflug et N. Lossky (Paris, 1987), p. 304.

[16] Baschet, 'Introduction: l'image-objet' (cf. note 6).

figurative, qui contraste de manière saisissante avec la stabilité beaucoup plus grande des formules dans l'art byzantin. Cette 'liberté' de l'art est même admise théoriquement, comme en témoignent les reprises du *Dictum Horatii*, notamment dans le *Rationale divinorum officiorum* de Guillaume Durand.[17]

Enfin, les attitudes critiques de quelques clercs, condamnant certains types iconographiques, illustrent a contrario l'existence de cette marge de manoeuvre de la création figurative. Elles montrent que les images opèrent parfois sur les franges de l'orthodoxie, créant des représentations qui tantôt apparaissent licites et tantôt inadmissibles. Parmi d'autres exemples, on rappellera l'intervention d'Antonin de Florence contre les Annonciations montrant l'enfant Jésus, déjà formé, descendant vers la Vierge, ou encore celle de Gerson condamnant les statues des Vierges ouvrantes.[18] Mais, pour le Moyen Age, de telles critiques constituent des points de vue, certes éminents, mais qui n'ont pas force de décision officielle, doctrinale ou disciplinaire.[19]

Plus largement, c'est l'analyse des thèmes iconographiques qui doit fonder l'idée d'une inventivité de l'art médiéval (comme on le verra plus loin). De nombreux thèmes iconographiques n'ont pas à proprement parler d'équivalent textuel. Ainsi, l'Arbre de Jessé a certes des sources scripturaires, qui légitiment cette figuration (Is 11). Mais l'image constitue une élaboration originale, synthétique, assurant une présence massive à une mise en jeu spécifique et visuellement puissante d'un énoncé relatif à la filiation du Rédempteur, aux rapports entre l'humain et le divin et au rôle qu'y tient l'Eglise.[20] Autre exemple: la figuration

---

17 '*Pictoribus atque poetis/ Quidlibet audendi semper fuit aequa potestas*', cf. A. Chastel, 'Le *Dictum Horatii quidlibet audendi potestas et les artistes* (XIIIe–XVIe *siècle)*', repris dans *Fables, formes, figures*, 1 (Paris, 1978), pp. 363–76. Outre la formule horatienne, Guillaume Durand indique que les peintres représentent les scènes bibliques 'à leur convenance' (*Sed et diversae hystoriae tam novi quam veteris testamenti pro voluntate pictorum depinguntur*, cité par A. Chastel, p. 366).

18 On ne peut développer ici ni l'analyse de ces images ni celle des protestations qu'elles suscitent. Sur le premier exemple, voir les remarques (qu'on ne partage pas entièrement) de J. Wirth, 'L'apparition du surnaturel' (cf. note 14), pp. 148–52. Sur les Vierges ouvrantes, cf. G. Radler, *Die Schreinmadonna "Vierge ouvrante"* (Francfort, 1990).

19 Il en va autrement à partir du Concile de Trente, lorsque le contrôle clérical sur les images tend à se renforcer; et le traité de Molanus est l'expression de cette nécessité nouvelle, Molanaus, *Traité des saintes images*, éds. François Boespflug, Olivier Christin et Benoît Tassel (Paris, 1996). Voir aussi la condamnation pontificale de certains types trinitaires, aux XVIIè et XVIIIè siècles, analysée par F. Boespflug, *Dieu dans l'art* (Paris, 1984).

20 Sur ce thème, cf. A. Guerreau-Jalabert, 'La Vierge, l'Arbre de Jessé et l'ordre chrétien de la parenté', dans *Marie. Le culte de la Vierge dans la société médiévale*, éds. D. Iogna-Prat, E. Palazzo and D. Russo (Paris, 1996), pp. 137–70.

des types trinitaires, dans leur variété, illustre à quel point la complexité et les contradictions de la doctrine chrétienne ouvrent largement le spectre des possibilités figuratives.[21] Ainsi, loin du constat d'un art homogène, décalque passif de la doctrine de l'Eglise, la vitalité et le dynamisme de la pensée chrétienne, au sein d'une société complexe, confèrent à la création figurative une large marge de manoeuvre. L'analyse sérielle se doit de prendre en compte (et même de rendre compte de) cette grande inventivité.

Les types de séries

L'analyse iconographique ne saurait se fonder sur des images isolées. S'il est vrai que les images pensent, on doit ajouter qu''elles se pensent entre elles'.[22] L'étude des séries est par conséquent une nécessité, ne serait-ce que parce qu'elle est la condition de l'apprentissage du voir, de cette 'difficile conversion de la vision' dont parle Otto Pächt.[23] La confrontation des images d'une même série est indispensable à l'analyse de la signification de chacune d'elle, tant il est vrai qu'il n'y a de sens que par différence, ou plutôt dans une dialectique des régularités et des écarts.[24] Enfin, une part importante de la signification d'une oeuvre se trouve dans son rapport avec d'autres, ou pour le dire avec Hubert Damisch, 'ce qui importe est moins ce qu'une oeuvre d'art représente que ce qu'elle transforme'.[25]

Trois espèces principales de séries peuvent être distinguées: l'ensemble d'images produit par l'oeuvre elle-même; le *corpus* thématique construit par le chercheur; les hyperthèmes, réseaux complexes également élaborés par le chercheur. S'agissant du premier aspect, on rappelera que les images médiévales sont rarement conçues de façon isolée (contrairement à ce que produit le tableau). Elles s'inscrivent généralement dans un lieu ou sur un objet, au sein duquel se forme un complexe d'images. Ainsi, dans la série des miniatures et des lettres qui ornent un manuscrit, le sens ne peut se construire qu'à travers

---

[21] Cf. F. Boespflug and Y. Zaluska, 'Le dogme trinitaire et l'essor de son iconographie en Occident de l'époque carolingienne au IVe Concile de Latran', *Cahiers de civilisation médiévale*, 37 (1994), 181–240.

[22] H. Damisch, 'La peinture prise au mot', *Critique*, 370 (1978), 289 (reprennant ici la formule de C. Lévi-Strauss concernant les mythes).

[23] O. Pächt, *Questions de méthode en histoire de l'art*, trad. frse (Paris, 1994), p. 40.

[24] Sur ce modèle de la connaissance, inspiré par la linguistique, cf. C. Lévi-Strauss, lorsqu'il indique que l'objet de l'ethnologie est moins les sociétés elles-mêmes que 'les écarts différentiels' entre elles; *Anthropologie structurale* (Paris, 1957 ; réimpr. 1974), p. 384.

[25] H. Damisch, *Le Jugement de Pâris. Iconologie analytique* 1 (Paris, 1993), p. 168.

l'analyse des constantes et des singularités, des échos entre les images, des processus de transformation qui accompagnent la lecture du livre.[26] Dans le cas des cycles monumentaux, l'analyse doit faire intervenir d'autres paramètres spécifiques, afin de rendre compte d'un 'lieu d'images' (régularités narratives, associations thématiques entre les scènes, relations entre les images et leurs lieux d'inscription, perçus tant dans leur valeur symbolique que dans leur fonction liturgique).[27]

L'importance fondamentale de cet aspect de la recherche ne saurait être mise en doute, mais la nature du présent exposé conduit à insister surtout ici sur le second type de séries. A côté des réseaux d'images constitués par l'oeuvre, l'historien doit aussi construire des séries d'images appartenant à des objets différents, dans des lieux et des temps délimités de façon précise. C'est du reste une démarche constitutive de l'histoire de l'art classique, interessée principalement par les phénomènes stylistiques: Otto Pächt a insisté sur le caractère génétique de l'histoire de l'art, qui vise à inscrire chaque oeuvre dans le processus du devenir des formes artistiques. Elle doit donc construire des 'séries généalogiques au sein desquelles chaque oeuvre trouve sa place et son sens.[28]

Toutefois, on admettra que la recherche de 'modèles', largement pratiquée par l'histoire de l'art, s'est souvent fourvoyée, en particulier lorsqu'elle pense la production figurative de façon passive, en terme d''influence'. Cette démarche, obnubilée par la recherche des similitudes, conduit généralement à négliger les différences entre l'oeuvre et ses antécédents, alors que celles-ci sont au moins aussi importantes que les points communs. Elle s'interdit ainsi de saisir le processus de transformation, qui devrait pourtant être au coeur de l'approche sérielle.

On ne saurait pour autant oublier que l'art médiéval, et plus largement la culture médiévale, fonctionne sur la reconnaissance d'une forte valeur de traditionnalité. Le prestige d'une oeuvre dépend souvent de sa révérence à l'égard d'un prototype vénérable, ce qui n'empêche pas l'artiste de l'adapter, de le transformer sous couvert de cette marque d'hommage. Herbert Kessler a bien souligné que cette traditionnalité de l'art devait être pensé, non sous la catégorie passive de modèle, mais à l'aide de la notion active de 'citation' (soit une forme

---

[26] Cf. un cas de métamorphose réglée et de progression sérielle, analysé par J. Hamburger, *The Rothschild Canticles. Art and Mysticism in Flanders and the Rhineland circa 1300* (New Haven: Yale U.P., 1990). Dans une étude à venir, H. Kessler élabore, à propos des miniatures de la *Bible de Vivien*, un modèle particulièrement subtil de fonctionnement du manuscrit.

[27] Je me permets de renvoyer sur ces aspects à mon livre *Lieu sacré, lieu d'images. Les fresques de Bominaco (Abruzzes, 1263). Thèmes, parcours, fonctions* (Paris-Rome: La Découverte—École française de Rome, 1991).

[28] Pächt, *Questions de méthode* (cf. note 23), notamment p. 163.

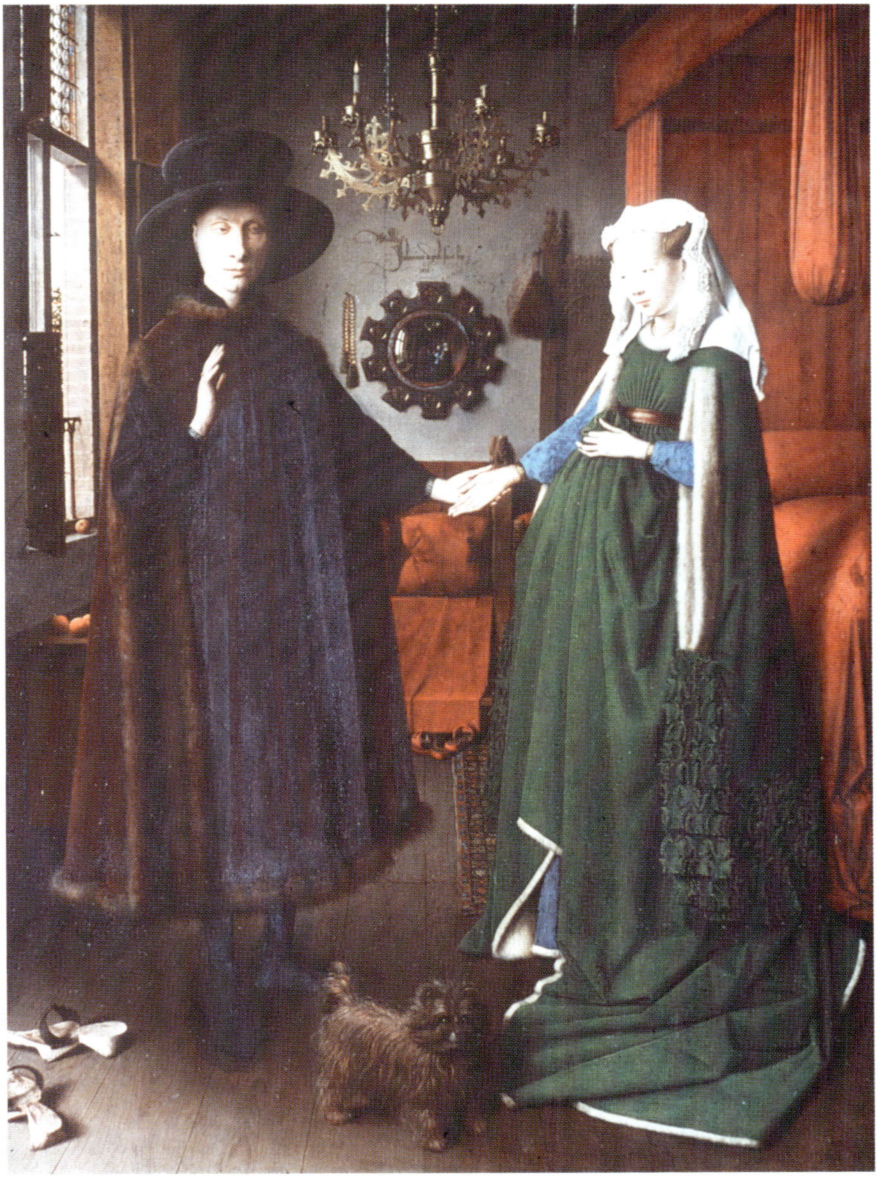

Plate 1: 'Arnolfini and his wife', Jan van Eyck. 1434. Oil on oak, 81.8 x 59.7 cm. National Gallery, London. NG 186.

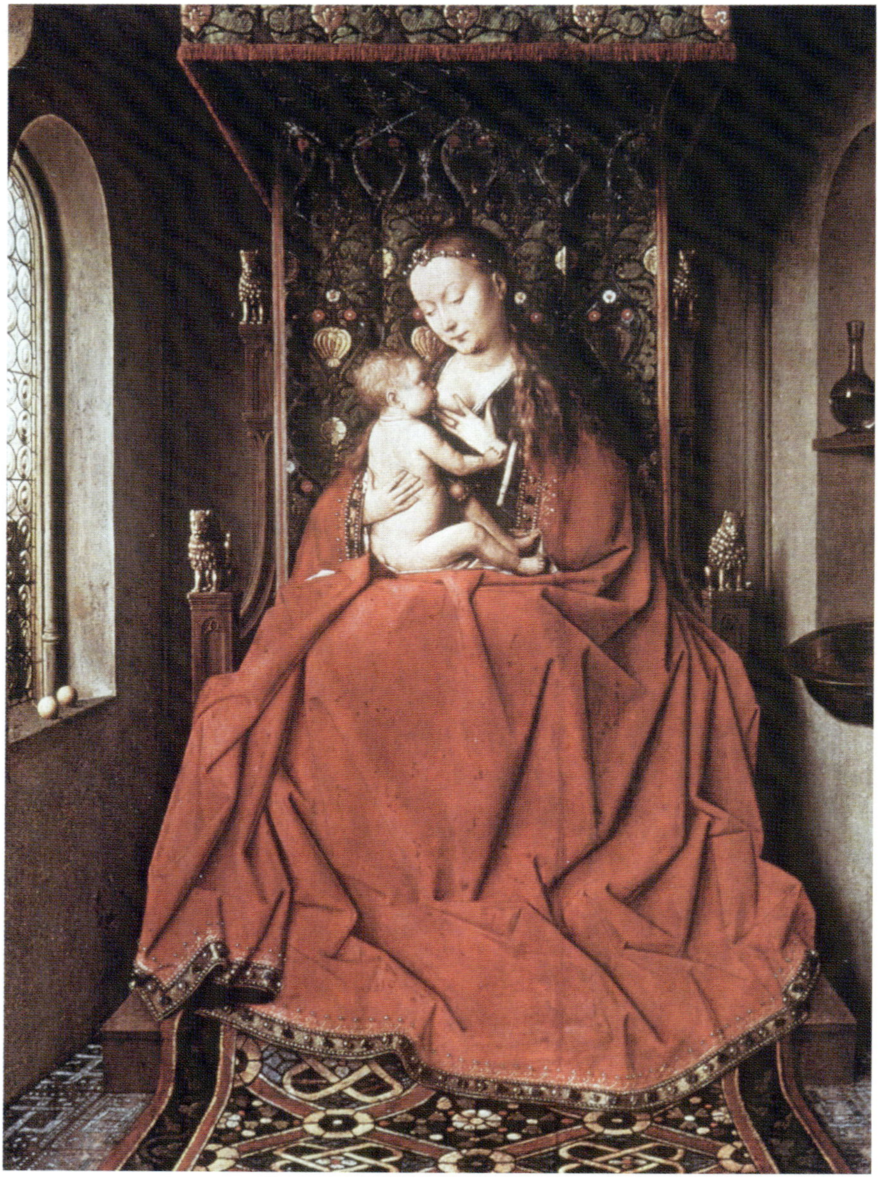

Plate 2: 'Lucca Madonna', Jan van Eyck. c. 1436. Oil on wood, 65.5 x 49.5 cm. Städelsches Kunstinstitut, Frankfurt.

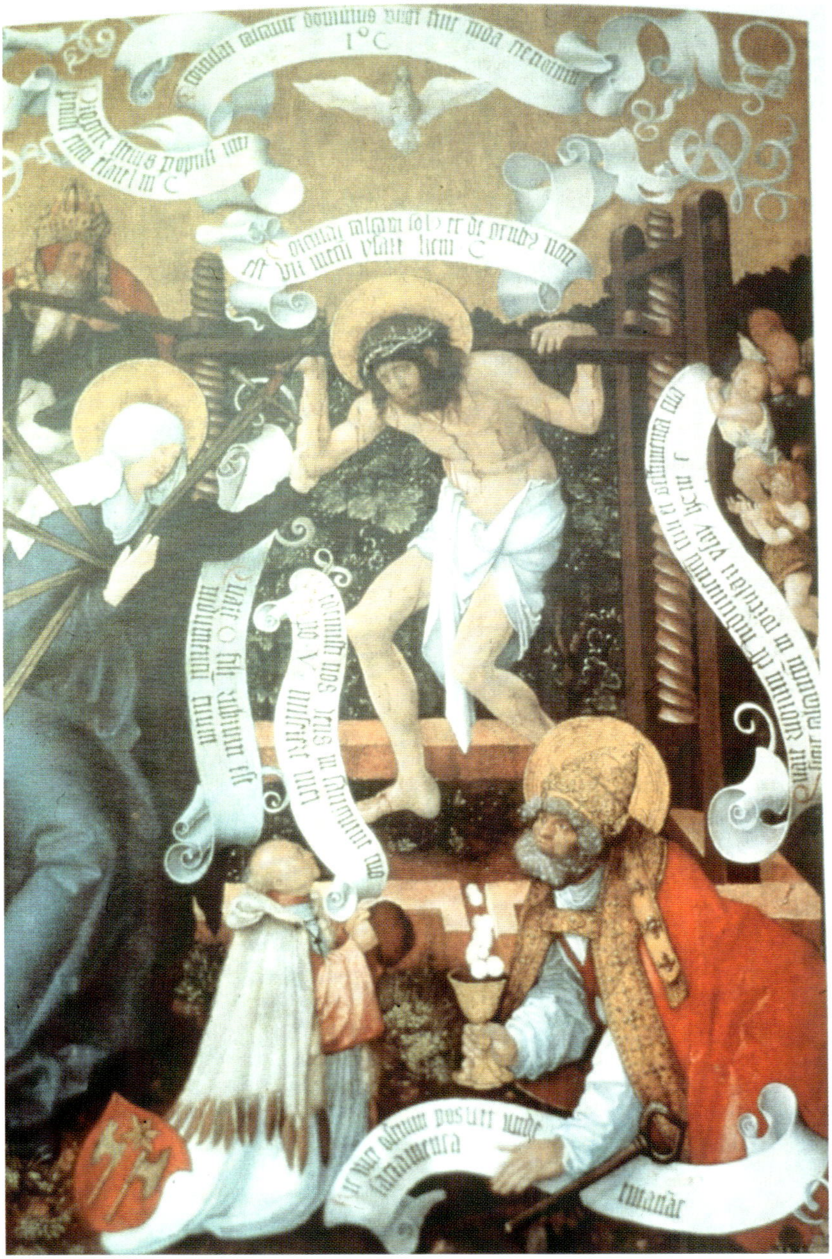

Plate 3: The mystical press (c. 1511): the image of the pope echoing that of God the Father.

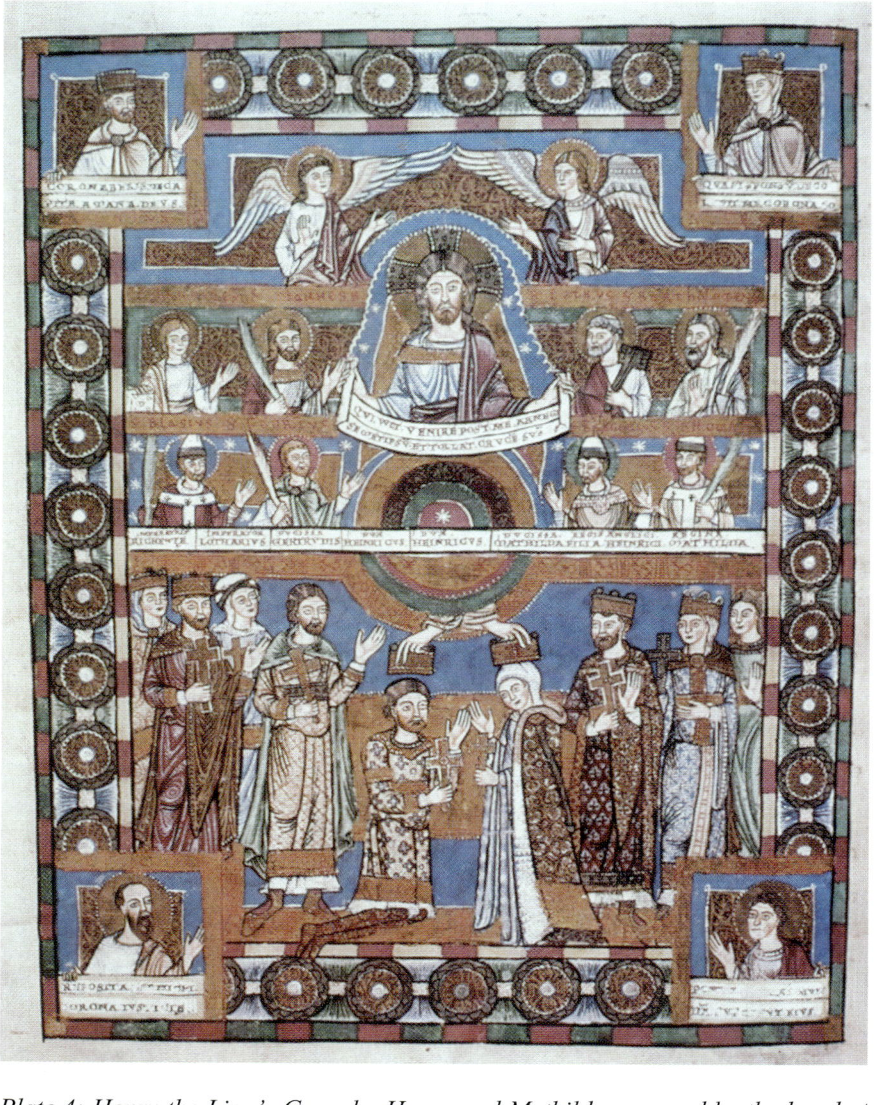

Plate 4: Henry the Lion's Gospels: Henry and Mathilda crowned by the hand of God. Wolfenbüttel, Herzog August Bibliothek, MS. Guelf. 105, Noviss. 2°, fol. 171^{v}.

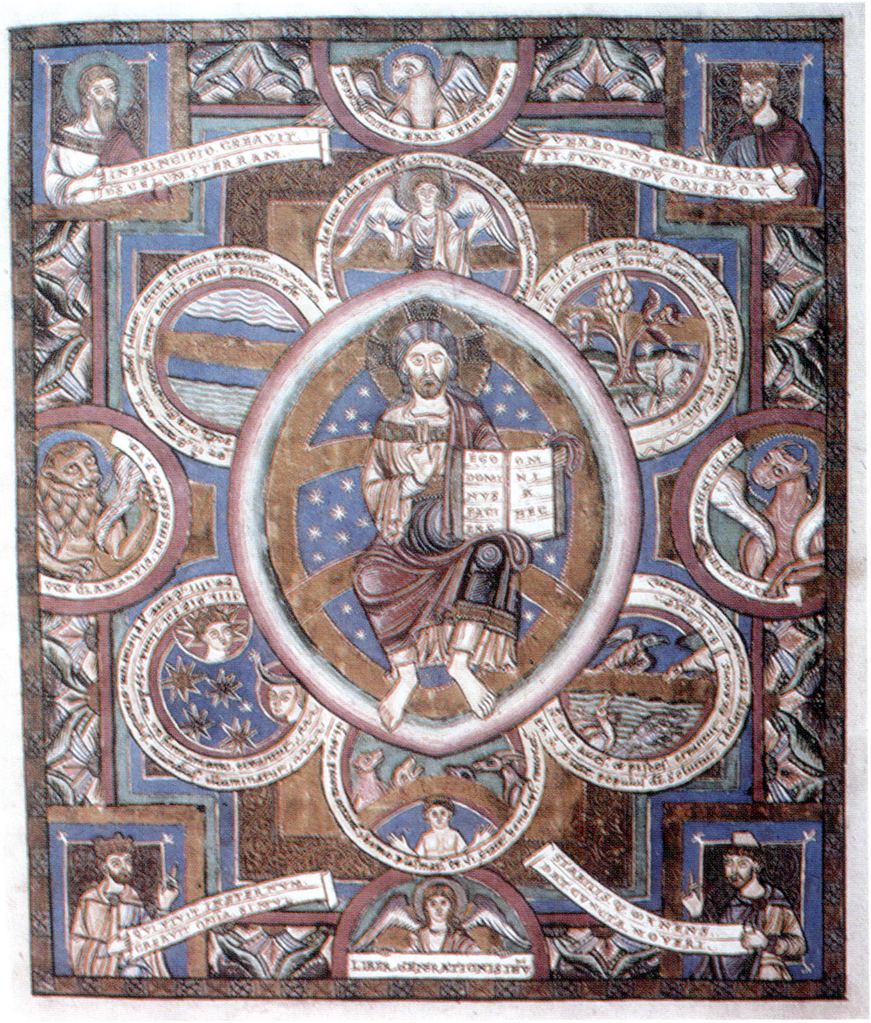

Plate 5: Henry the Lion's Gospels: divine majesty and the creation of the world. Wolfenbüttel, Herzog August Bibliothek, MS. Guelf. 105, Noviss. 2°, fol. 172^r^.

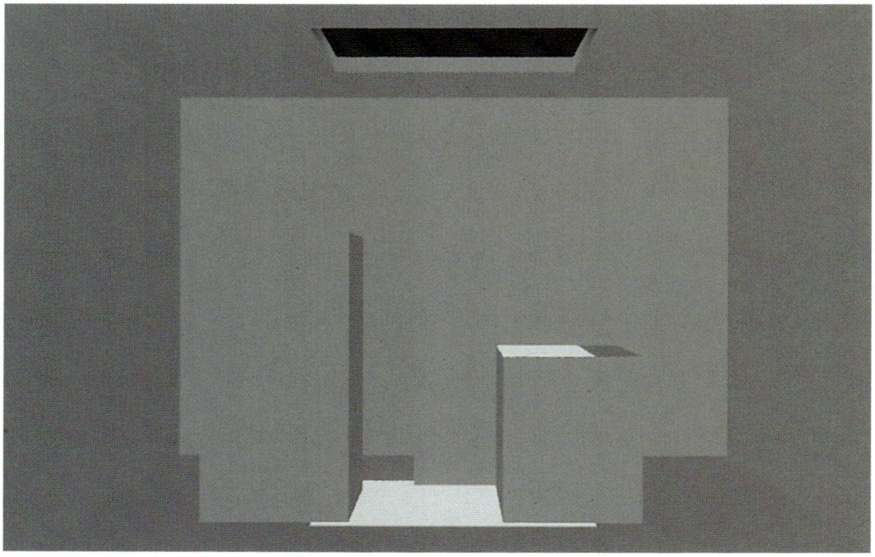

Plate 6: Cornell box, default lighting.

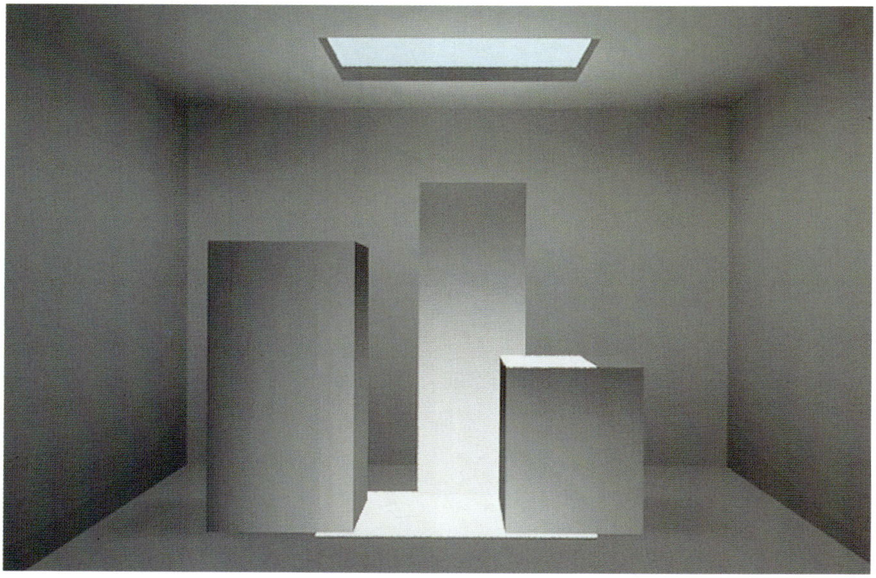

Plate 7: Cornell box, raytraced rendering.

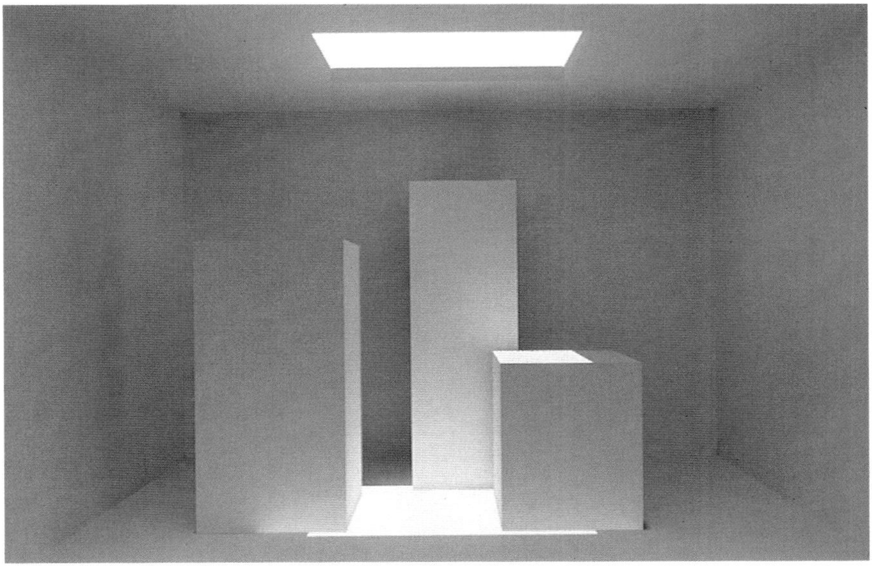

Plate 8: Cornell box, radiosity rendering.

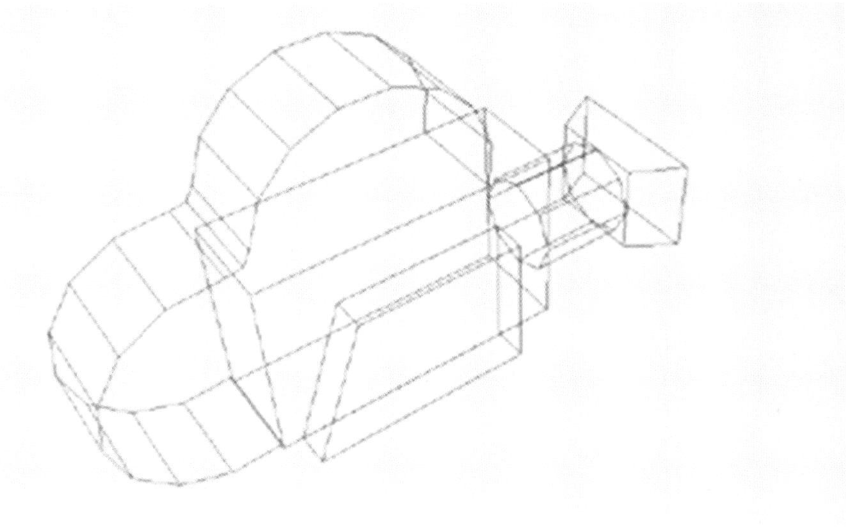

Plate 9: Maya camera icon.

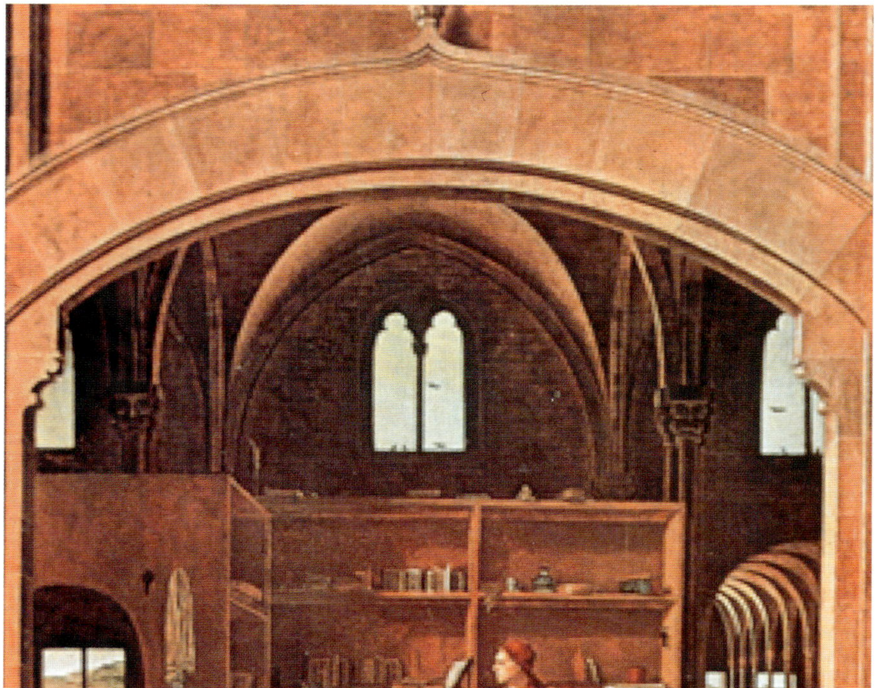

Plate 10: 'St Jerome in his study', Antonello da Messina, c. *1450.*

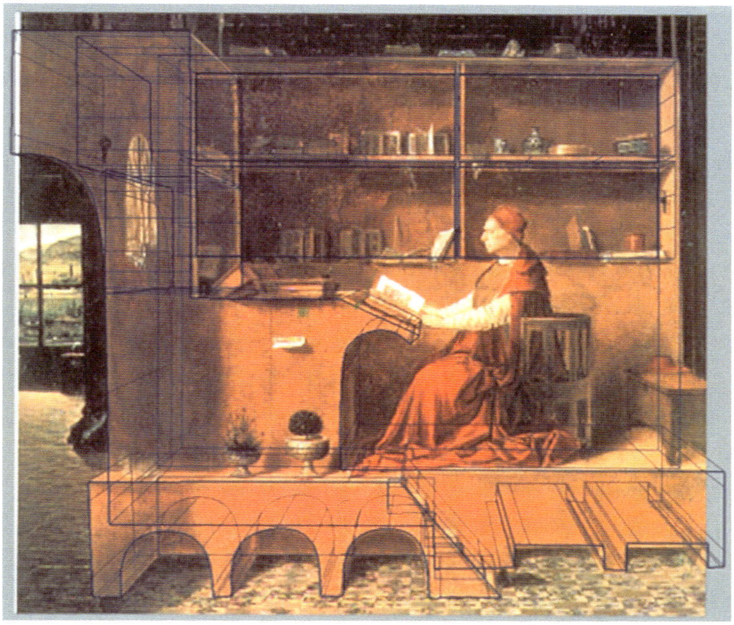

Plate 11: Wireframe.

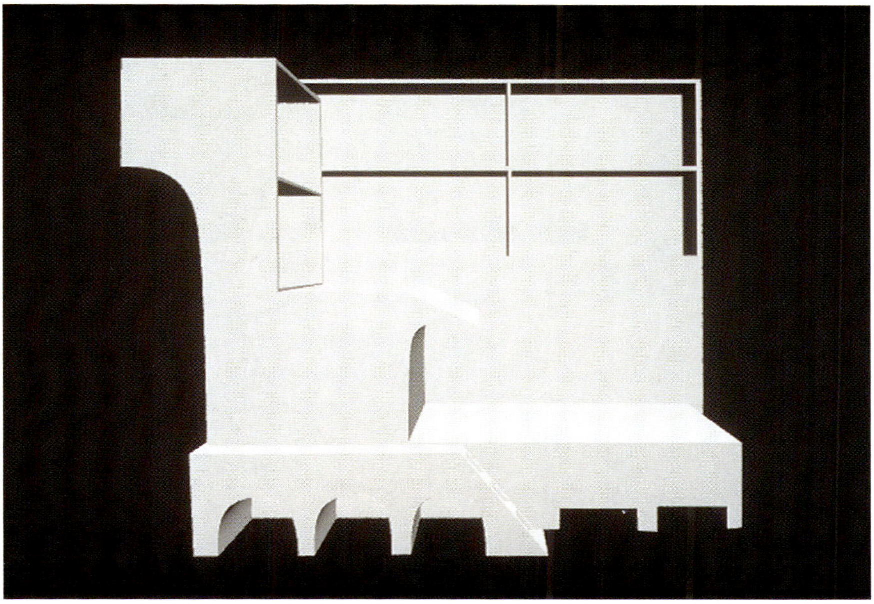

Plate 12: Untextured three-dimensional form.

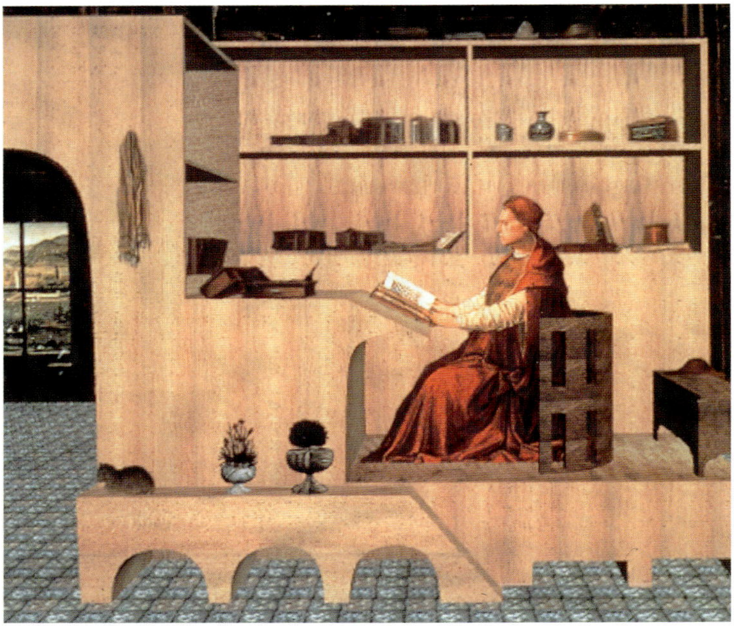

Plate 13: Default light and textures, no shading.

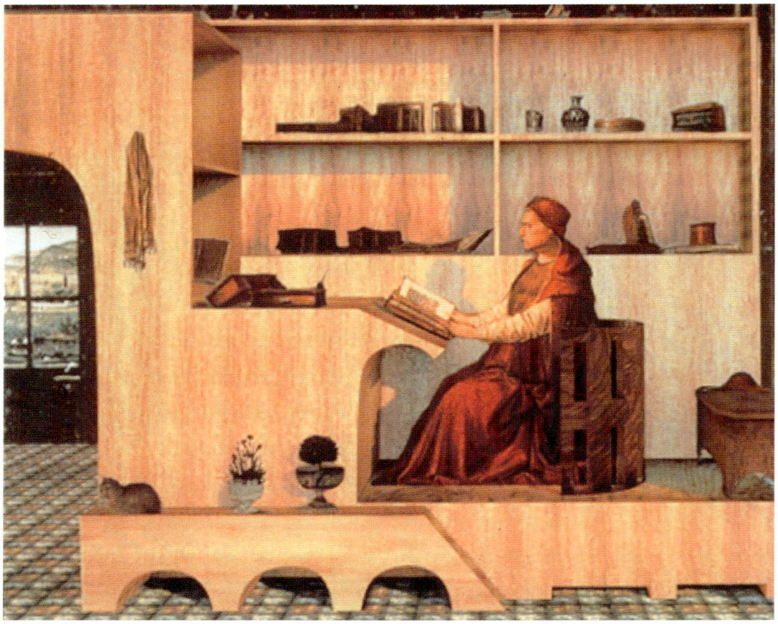

Plate 14: Jerome.

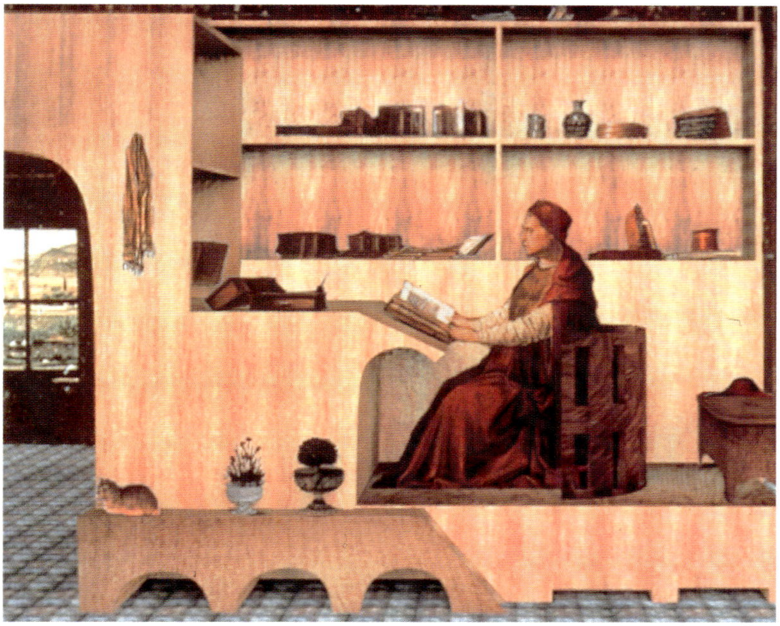

Plate 15: Jerome.

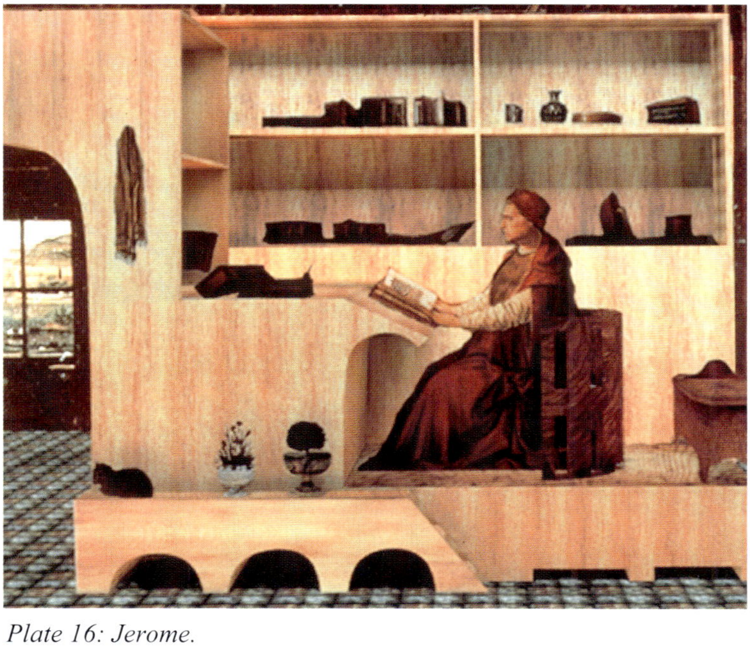

Plate 16: Jerome.

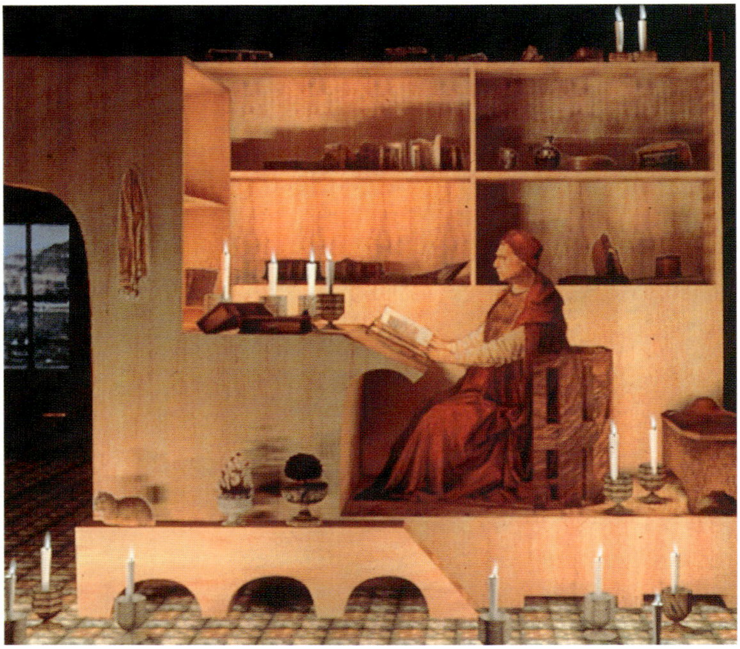

Plate 17: Jerome.

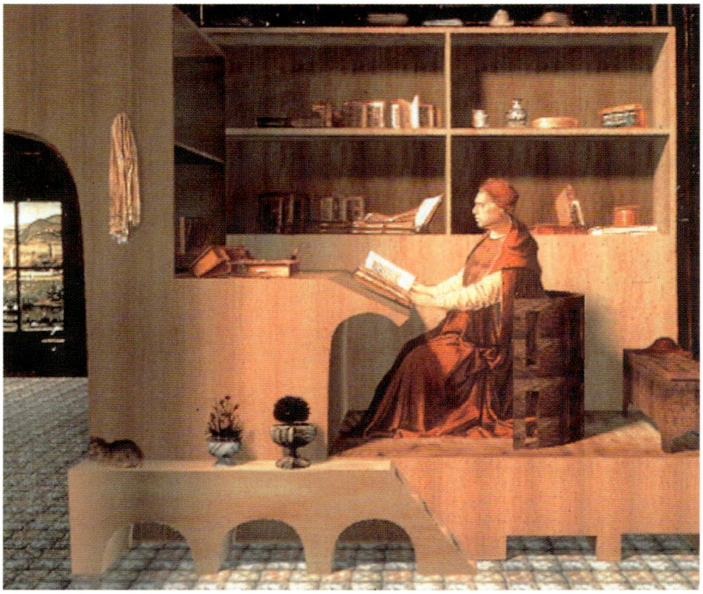

Plate 18: Jerome.

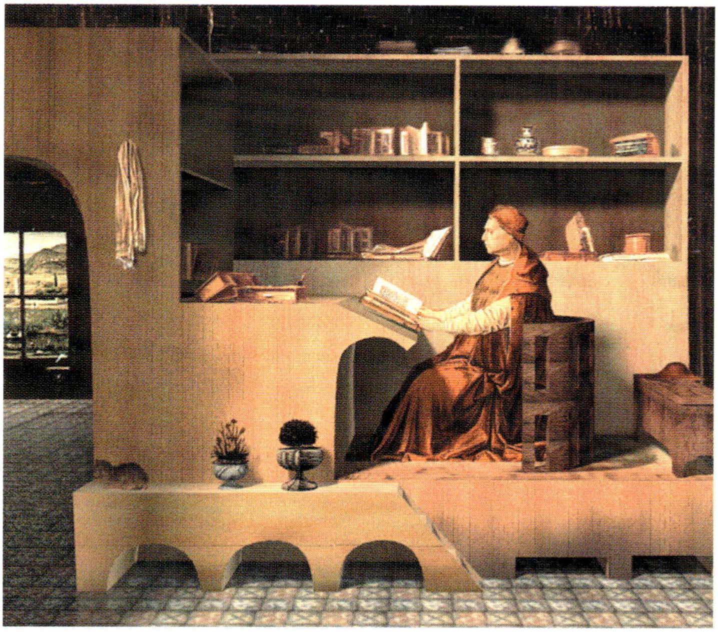

Plate 19: Jerome.

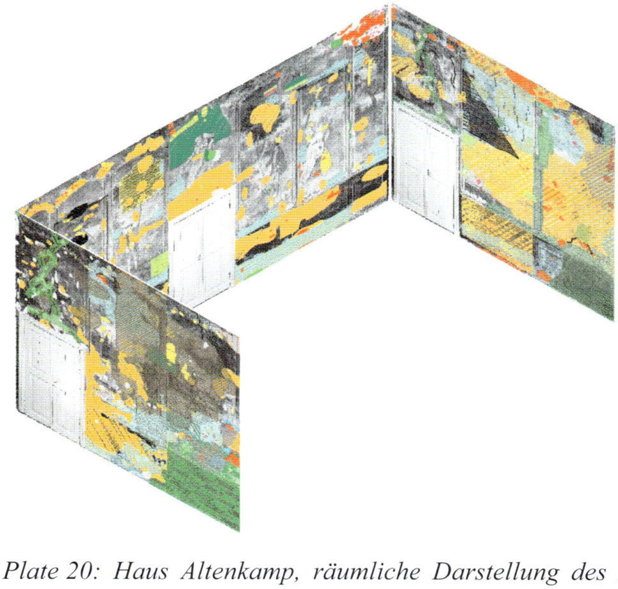

Plate 20: Haus Altenkamp, räumliche Darstellung des Entrées überlagert mit Schadenskartierung, Ansicht von Nordwesten.

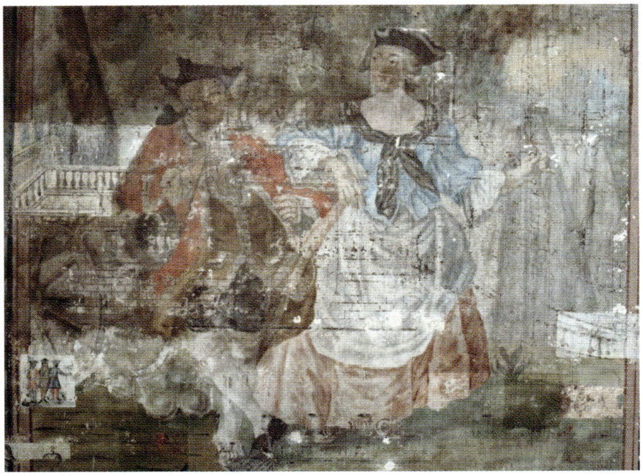

Plate 21: Haus Altenkamp, Entrée, Wandmalerei-Ausschnitt der Südwand, Überlagerung der Farbauszüge. Das Farbbild wurde aus den schwarz/weißen Spektralbildern berechnet. Durch Kalibrierung des fotografischen Prozesses läßt sich so eine langzeitstabile, rekonstruierbare colormetrische Abbildung realisieren.

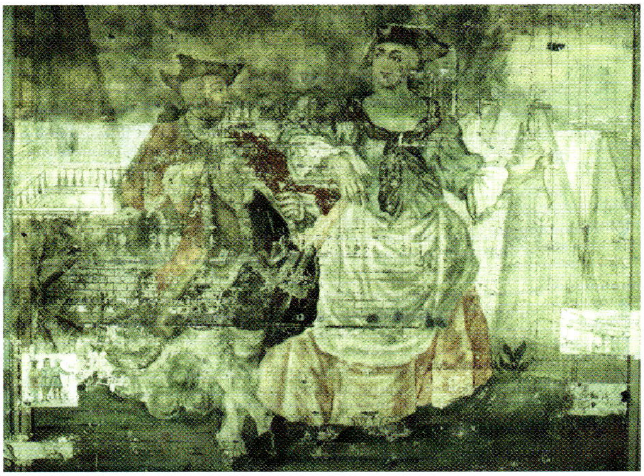

Plate 22: Das Thermobild setzt sich aus 4 Einzelbildern zusammen. Vom Objekt reflektierte Strahlungen im Bereich zwischen 8 und 14 mm wurden registriert. Die Abbildung zeigt Kältebrücken an den Seiten der Wände (Anschluß zur Außenwand bzw. zu unbeheizten Nachbarräumen). Der wärmere (grüne) Bereich in Bildmitte weist darauf hin, daß durch einen offenen Kamin im Nachbarraum Wärme abgesogen wird.

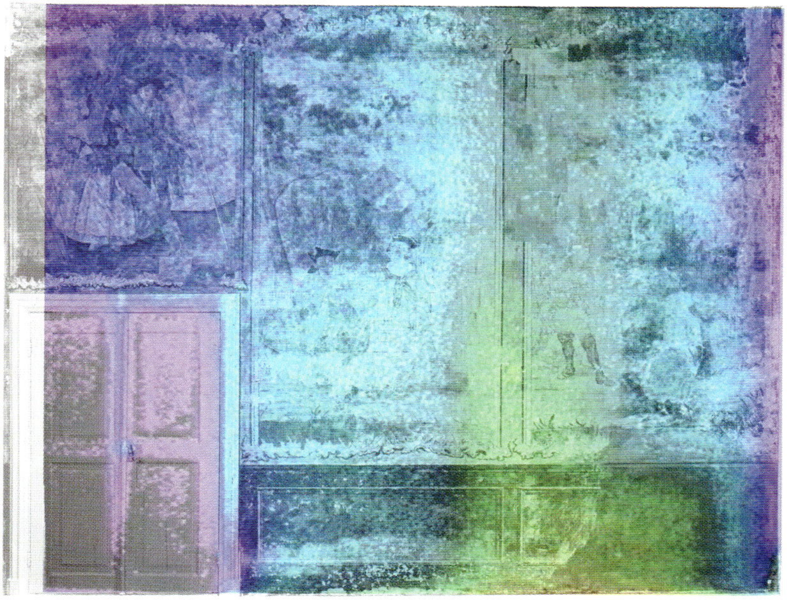

Plate 23: Haus Altenkamp, Entrée, Thermobild der Südwand, überlagert mit Schadenskartierung.

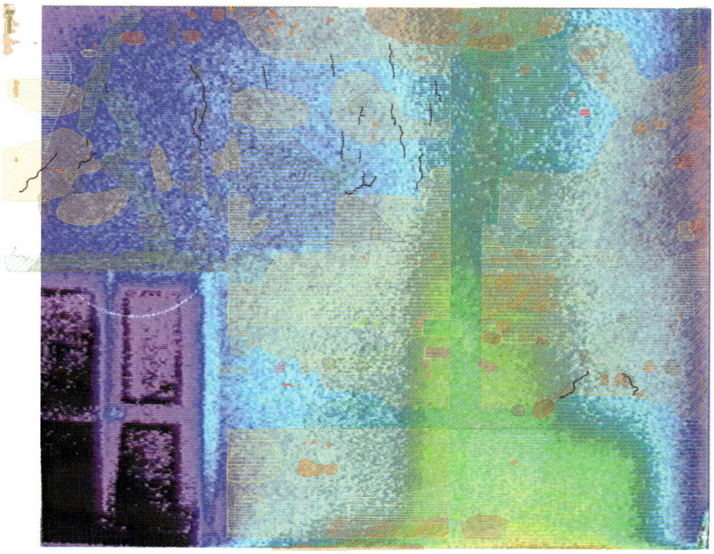

Plate 24: Die Überlagerung korreliert die Schadenskartierung mit bauphysikalischen Aussagen.

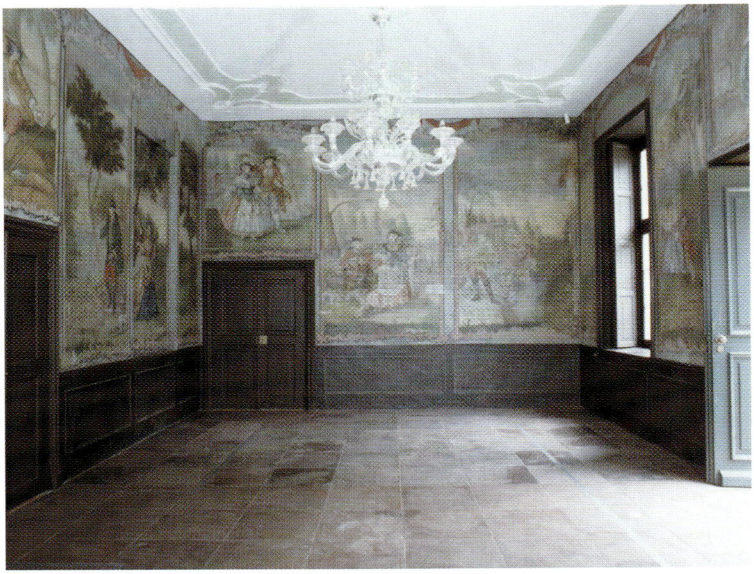

Plate 25: Haus Altenkamp, Entrée, nach der Restaurierung.

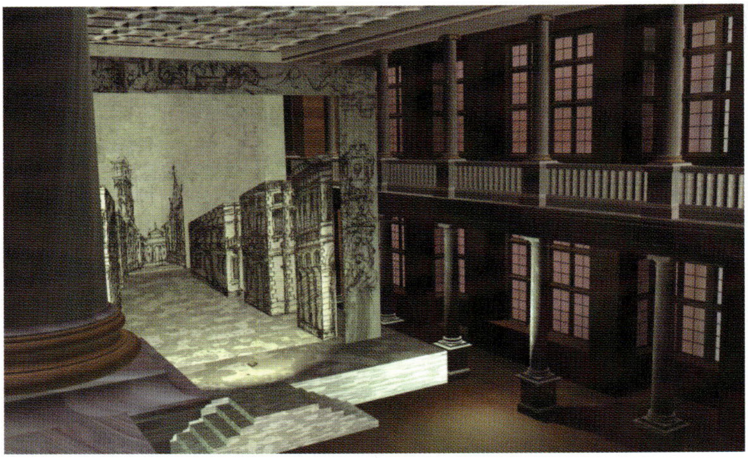

*Plate 26: Representation of a view from the west balcony of the first Jacobean Banqueting House (*c. *1607–1619) looking towards Inigo Jones' scenery for* The Vision of Delight *(1617). Computer-generated model, Ross Parry, 1999. Details from Inigo Jones, 'A Street in Perspective' and 'Proscenium and Hunt Scene', Devonshire Collection, Chatsworth.*

d'intertextualité).[29] Il importe en outre d'analyser l'enjeu de telles citations.[30] la référence à une tradition peut porter une valeur idéologique, constituer une revendication politique (ainsi la reprise par les rois normands de modèles byzantins impériaux),[31] indiquer une dépendance institutionnelle (s'agissant de la diffusion des modèles romains),[32] ou un désir de Réforme spirituelle et ecclésiologique (à travers la citation de modèles paléochrétiens.[33] Enfin, on suggèrera que la tradition artistique est peut-être, paradoxalement, l'un des facteurs qui contribuent à la liberté de l'image: le caractère vénérable attaché à cette tradition, dont les hommes de l'art sont en partie les dépositaires, est un paramètre important dans le processus conduisant à l'oeuvre finale, à côté de la volonté du commanditaire et éventuellement des références textuelles obligées.

Construire une série

Bien que l'approche sérielle concerne également les approches stylistiques ou formelles, c'est surtout aux séries iconographiques qu'on s'intéressera ici, et en particulier aux séries quantitativement amples.[34] Dans les conditions actuelles de la recherche, construire des séries rassemblant la totalité des sources conservées reste une tâche inaccessible. Aboutir au résultat le plus satisfaisant possible demande encore un investissement en temps (et parfois en argent) considérable. En dépit d'instruments précieux, au premier rang desquels l'indispensable *Index*

---

[29] H. L. Kessler, 'The State of Medieval Art History', *The Art Bulletin*, 70 (1988), notamment p. 176.

[30] On tiendra compte de la gradation existant entre des oeuvres plus fortes, plus innovatives, et d'autres plus imprégnées de formules établies, parfois produites de façon répétitive (mais admettant néanmoins des variations infimes, et rarement analysables comme simple reproduction).

[31] E. Kitzinger, 'The Gregorian Reform and the Visual Art: a Problem of Method', *Transactions of the Royal Historical Society*, 22 (1972), 87–102.

[32] Kessler, 'The State of Medieval Art History' (cf. note 29), pp. 176–78.

[33] H. Toubert, 'Le renouveau paléochrétien à Rome au début du XIIᵉ siècle', repris dans *Un art dirigé. Réforme grégorienne et iconographie* (Paris, 1990).

[34] D'autres séries, pour être plus restreintes, n'en sont pas moins dignes d'intérêt. Ainsi, dans *Le Jugement de Pâris* (cf. note 25), H. Damisch suit, à travers une série d'oeuvres exceptionnelles, les métamorphoses d'un modèle de l'Antiquité jusqu'à Picasso, en passant par Raphaël et Manet. Il y définit son objet comme 'tresse', plutôt que comme série, pour en souligner le caractère imbriqué, excluant 'tout principe d'explication linéaire' (p. 221). Il y a là un cas assez différent de ce que les images médiévales nous donnent généralement à travailler: une série de chefs-d'oeuvre qui se pensent les uns les autres, et non un ample *corpus* d'objets présentant entre eux une gamme de relations beaucoup plus variée.

of Christian Art de Princeton, l'état actuel des outils de recherches documentaires (bases de données, iconothèques, catalogues des manuscrits enluminés, corpus des oeuvres monumentales, banques d'images, CD-Rom, serveurs internet . . .), reste très insatisfaisant en dépit des progrès accomplis, et limite malheureusement la portée de la démarche sérielle. On ne peut donc qu'insister sur la nécessité d'accélérer la réalisation d'outils dont la recherche a besoin et que les techniques modernes permettent de produire. Outre leur vertu première de recherche documentaire, ces outils, permettant une visualisation rapide des images concernées, favorisent les rapprochements, les confrontations et les croisements entre tous les fils de cet écheveau que constitue la production visuelle médiévale. Ils sont les vecteurs privilégiés de l'approche sérielle. Ils doivent tout à la fois la servir et l'encourager.

Construire une série d'images suppose, dans une première étape, de rassembler, par tous les moyens disponibles, un *corpus* aussi exhaustif que possible. Une étude iconographique qui ne reposerait pas sur la prise en compte de toutes les oeuvres pertinentes accessibles serait sinon illégitime, du moins fragile. Mais construire une série, c'est ensuite, à rebours, dissocier, fragmenter la masse des documents obtenus. Car le *corpus* rassemblé est constitué d'éléments fortement hétérogènes, qui ne se laissent pas traiter au sein d'un ensemble unifié.

La distinction par support (manuscrits enluminés, sculpture, peinture murale, vitrail, orfèvrerie . . .) s'impose pour deux ordres de raison. Chaque technique possède ses règles et ses procédés formels propres, jouant de la valeur et des possibilités plastiques des matériaux utilisés, et des formats mis en oeuvre. Surtout, la distinction par support impose de considérer les types d'objets ou les lieux architecturaux auxquels sont liées les images. Elle fait intervenir les usages des images-objets, les relations éventuelles entre thèmes représentés et fonctions des objets, ainsi que les modalités de visibilité et de réception.[35]

La distinction selon les contextes thématiques est, dans certains cas au moins, indispensable. En effet, l'analyse doit procéder différemment selon qu'elle a pour objet un *thème* iconographique ou un *motif* iconographique. Un thème, comme l'Annonciation ou la Remise des tables de la Loi à Moïse, constitue une unité structurale élémentaire possédant une cohérence propre, pouvant faire l'objet d'une scène spécifique, notamment dans une miniature, une lettre ornée

---

[35] Enfin, ces distinctions permettent d'évaluer l'importance accordée au thème concerné—laquelle se mesure moins aux dimensions et à la visibilité de l'oeuvre qu'au degré de sacralité de l'objet ou du lieu auquel l'image est attachée. Cette dernière question prend une acuité particulière pour les motifs négatifs, comme l'enfer ou le diable, dont l'intégration dans un objet ou un lieu chargé de sacralité est hautement problématique; je renvoie à mon article 'L'enfer en son lieu: rôle fonctionnel et dynamisation de l'espace cultuel', dans *Luoghi sacri e spazi della santità*, éds. S. Boesch-Gajano et L. Scaraffia (Turin, 1990), pp. 551–63.

ou un cycle mural.[36] En revanche, on appelle motif iconographique un élément constituant d'un thème. Il en va ainsi de l'enfer qui, pour l'essentiel, apparaît à l'intérieur d'ensembles plus complexes, comme le Jugement dernier, la Parabole de Lazare ou la Chute des anges.[37] La distinction entre thèmes et motifs est indispensable, même si elle n'est pas rigoureusement étanche. Conformément au principe structural de prééminence des relations sur les éléments constituants, on ne saurait aborder un motif iconographique sans une analyse globale du thème dans lesquels il s'insère. C'est le seul moyen de mesurer l'importance du motif, de saisir sa fonction dans un ensemble cohérent, et par conséquent d'atteindre un point pertinent de signification.

Les distinctions selon les temps et les lieux sont également importantes. Une étude de la répartition chronologique (à la fois globale, et en tenant compte des distinctions par thèmes et par supports) fait apparaître des phénomènes décisifs pour l'étude historique. Elle permet de distinguer le nouveau du traditionnel, d'identifier la période d'apparition du thème ou du motif étudié, de préciser ses rythmes de développement, et éventuellement de déclin,[38] et enfin de saisir les évolutions et les variations géographiques de ses modes de représentations.

En outre, la fragmentation du corpus doit être poussée à l'extrême, dès lors que chaque oeuvre singulière constitue un cas particulier, intégrant le thème étudié dans une série d'images spécifique, en rapport avec un objet unique et dans un contexte chaque fois particulier. Il ne saurait, en principe, y avoir d'étude sérielle sans une approche structurale de chaque oeuvre singulière appartenant à la série. Approche structurale et étude sérielle sont totalement et intimement entremêlées. Chaque image doit même être située au croisement de multiples séries (série dans l'oeuvre, environnement de celle-ci, séries thématiques, traditions formelles . . .). Chaque série étant elle-même complexe et non-linéaire, c'est une sorte de sphère de relations qu'il faut dessiner autour de

---

[36] Ce qui n'exclut pas que le thème soit intégré dans une série constituant un ensemble structural plus ample. En outre, de même qu'un personnage peut synthétiser plusieurs identités différentes, une unité thématique peut condenser différents thèmes, et notamment plusieurs moments généralement dissociés.

[37] Le fait qu'un motif puisse être parfois représenté de façon indépendante, devenant ainsi un thème à lui seul, n'invalide pas la distinction proposée. Un tel processus d'autonomisation doit au contraire être analysé comme un phénomène d'une grande portée.

[38] L'étude du développement quantitatif d'un thème devrait tenir compte non de valeurs absolues, mais de valeurs relatives référées au nombre global d'images produites (ou disons conservées). Il faut donc prendre en considération la forte croissance de la production d'images, entre XIè et XVè siècle. En ce sens, le développement régulier d'un thème au cours de cette période est difficilement interprétable. En revanche, un déclin quantitatif n'en prend que plus de relief.

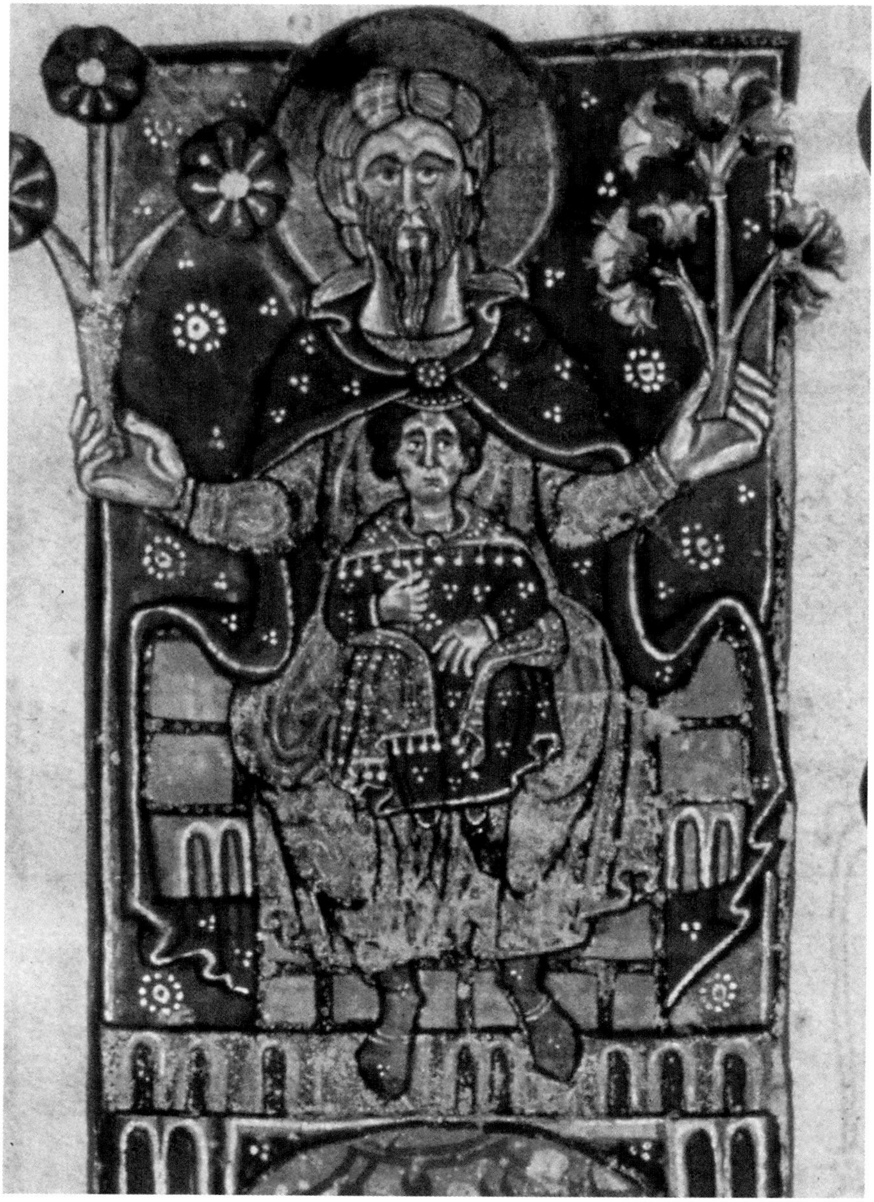

Fig. 1. Evangéliaire, Bibliothèque vaticane, ms. Vat. lat. 39, fol. 58, 'Lazare dans le Sein d'Abraham' (troisième quart du XIIIe siècle). © Biblioteca apostolica vaticana

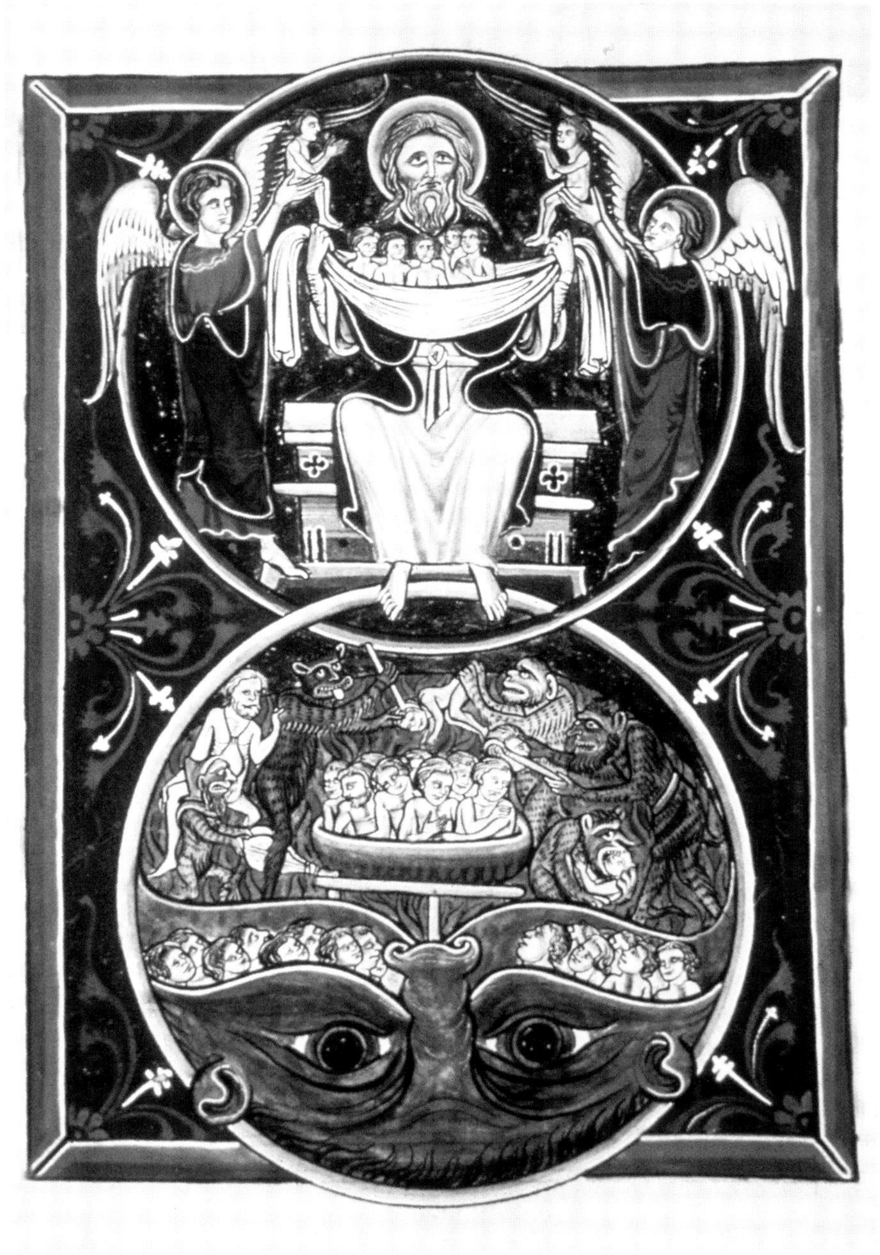

Fig. 2. Psautier de Blanche de Castille, Paris, Arsenal, ms. 1186, fol. 171, 'le Sein d'Abraham et l'enfer' (c. *1225). © Bibliothèque nationale de France, Paris*

chaque image singulière. L'enjeu et la difficulté de l'étude iconographique consistent à faire tenir ensemble l'approche sérielle et l'étude structurale des oeuvres singulières; elle doit pratiquer d'incessants allers-et-retours entre ces deux démarches.

Au total, le caractère fortement hétérogène des éléments constitutifs d'une série iconographique aboutit à un fractionnement extrême de celle-ci. En matière d'images, le sériel est un faux quantitatif. Il semble n'appeler que des traitements mathématiques frustes. Il impose de compter les occurrences en fonction des paramètres retenus, mais de façon nécessairement très approximative (notamment en raison des incertitudes de datation), avec pour seul objectif raisonnable d'évaluer et de comparer des ordres de grandeur. Les études iconographiques doivent apprendre à compter plus qu'elle ne font généralement, et à considérer l'importance quantitative des phénomènes étudiés. Pourtant, il semble généralement prématuré de plaider pour un véritable traitement statistique, en raison des marges d'incertitudes, des facteurs d'hétérogénéité et de la faiblesse des masses concernées.[39]

Analyser une gamme sérielle

L'approche sérielle vise à cerner régularités, variations, singularités et exceptions. Dans une première démarche, un classement typologique est souvent nécessaire et permet de faire apparaître des constantes. On peut ainsi, par exemple, distinguer parmi les représentations du sein d'Abraham trois types formels principaux, selon que le patriarche rassemble les élus entre ses bras (fig. 1), dans un linge (fig. 2) ou dans un pan de son vêtement (fig. 3).[40] Mais l'analyse sérielle ne peut s'en tenir à

[39] Un véritable traitement statistique peut être envisagé dans quelques cas privilégiés, concernant un motif simple, très fréquent, ou pour lequel les facteurs d'hétérogénéité jouent un rôle moindre qu'à l'habitude. Les cas déjà évoqués des représentations de l'âme ou du nimbe pourraient être de bons exemples de séries analysables statistiquement. Voir aussi les traitement quantitatifs réalisés à partir de la base de donnée des peintures murales danoises, J. J. Borrild, 'Medieval Danish Wall Paintings. An Internet Database', *Medium aevum quotidianum* (cf. note 1), pp. 21–36.

[40] Respectivement: Evangiles, Bibliothèque vaticane, Vat. lat. 39, f. 58 (Italie du Nord, troisième quart XIIIe siècle); Psautier de Blanche de Castille, Paris, Arsenal MS. 1186, f. 171^{v} (Paris, vers 1225); Légendier dominicain, Oxford, Keble College, MS. 49, f. 239 (Ratisbonne, vers 1270). Ces trois oeuvres relèvent de contextes thématiques différents: Jugement dernier, Parabole de Lazare, sein d'Abraham isolé en rapport avec la fête des morts. Sur le sein d'Abraham, figuration du lieu paradisiaque promis aux élus, je renvoie à une première esquisse dans 'Medieval Abraham: Between Fleshly Patriarch and Divine Father', *Modern Language Notes*, 108 (1993), 738–58, ainsi qu'à *Le Sein du Père. Abraham et la paternité dans l'Occident médiéval* (Paris: Gallimard, 2000).

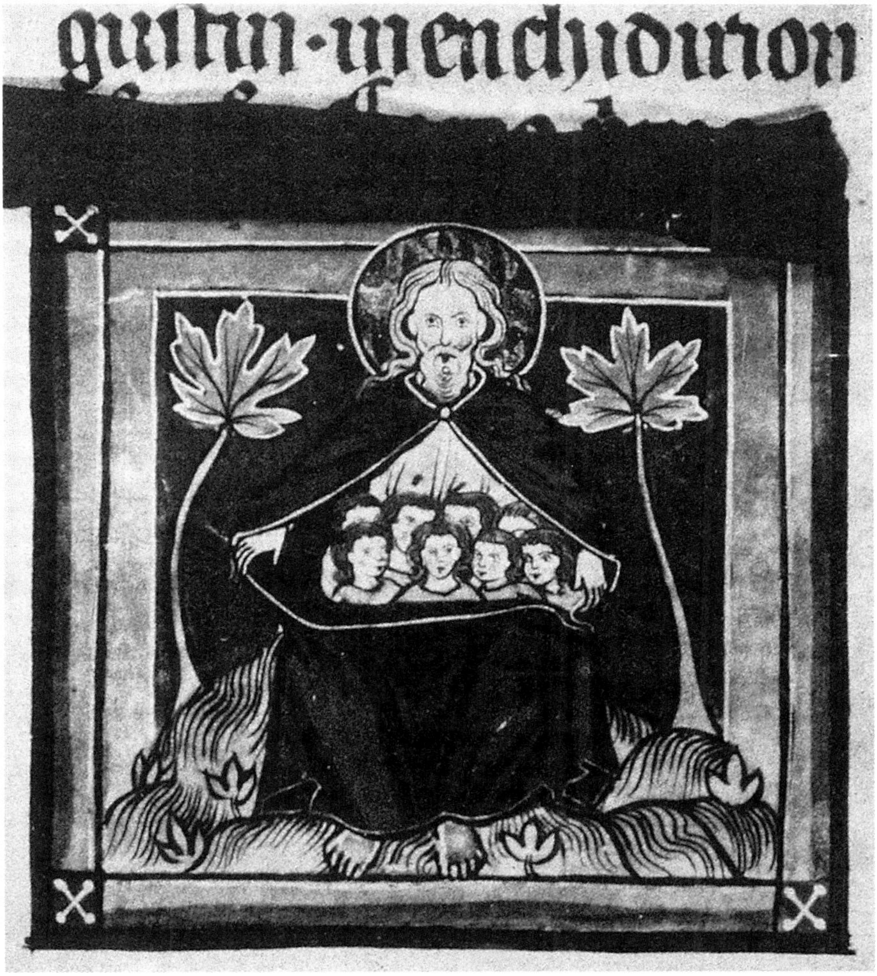

3. Légendier dominicain, Oxford, Keble College, MS. 49, fol. 239: 'le Sein d'Abraham' (c. *1270). © Keble College Library, Oxford*

de telles classifications, qui semblent reproduire une notion de 'type iconographique' rigidement fixé, qui doit être regardée avec méfiance. L'approche sérielle montre au contraire qu'il n'existe que des *gammes de réponses.*[41] Dans le cas du sein d'Abraham, l'analyse des trois grands ensembles définis fait apparaître,

[41] On pense ici à la notion de multiplicité, précisée par Deleuze, à partir de l'oeuvre de Foucault, G. Deleuze, *Foucault* (Paris, 1986), pp. 11–30; M. Foucault, *L'archéologie du savoir* (Paris, 1969).

ici les variations des formes du linge, leur dégré de concavité, les effets ainsi produits, là la façon de tenir les élus, enfin les modalités et le degré plus ou moins intense d'inclusion dans le manteau. A un premier regard, la typologie met en évidence des constantes, tandis que l'analyse sérielle vise à intégrer, dans la régularité d'une série, la singularité de chaque oeuvre, qui combine des réponses particulières à un ensemble d'options possibles, et qui noue un réseau propre de tensions et de contradictions. En articulant régularité et variations, à travers la construction de gammes, on entend sortir de la dualité de l'original et du banal, du singulier et du répétitif, critiquée par Michel Foucault.[42] On espère ainsi approcher ce qu'il y a d'actif à l'intérieur de séries que l'on refuse de tenir pour des types iconographiques constants.[43]

En conséquence, ce n'est pas nécessairement dans les chefs-d'oeuvre que l'analyse iconographique trouve le plus de profit, même si ceux-ci sont parfois d'une richesse qu'on aurait tort de mépriser. Se détourner des oeuvres majeures ne signifie nullement que l'approche sérielle a pour vertu principale de faire apparaître des constantes qui pourraient sembler à l'historien plus révélatrices que les singularités. Car l'approche sérielle permet aussi de repérer, dans des oeuvres apparemment assez banales, des variations qui, tout en étant discrètes, s'avèrent pour l'analyse iconographique d'une grande portée. Plus largement encore, la démarche sérielle montre que, au sein d'une gamme de variations, il n'y a pas de régularités sans ondoiement des possibilités de transformations. Les régularités sont 'en alerte'; l'inventivité vient se nicher dans les micro-déplacements, dans les décalages infimes.

La série se donne comme une exploration quasi-systématique d'un champ de possibilités. Ces *champs de possibilités*, objets spécifiques de l'approche sérielle, ne sont pas infinis, mais ils sont d'une ampleur généralement surprenante. Ce n'est pas l'effet d'une pure liberté du créateur ou d'une simple mécanique combinatoire, mais plutôt la conséquence du caractère hétérogène des oeuvres qui constituent la série. Les variations de matériaux, de localisation, de format, d'usage, d'environnement, d'époque, de relation avec les traditions figuratives (etc.) contribuent à faire varier la mise en oeuvre d'un ensemble thématique. L'hétérogénéité des oeuvres, faisant jouer l'élément iconographique observé, est comme le kaléïdoscope qui permet à l'historien d'explorer les multiples facettes de son objet. La gamme sérielle est le champ expérimental mettant à l'épreuve la régularité et la variabilité de l'objet.

[42] Foucault, *L'archéologie du savoir* (cf. note 41), pp. 184–94.

[43] Le banal lui-même est actif: 'la régularité n'est pas moins opérante, n'est pas moins efficace et active, dans une banalité que dans une formation insolite' (cf. note 41), p. 189. Dire que 'tout le champ énonciatif est à la fois régulier et en alerte: il est sans sommeil', p. 191, c'est aussi reconnaître que la régularité des énoncés n'est jamais une pure identité, une simple reproduction.

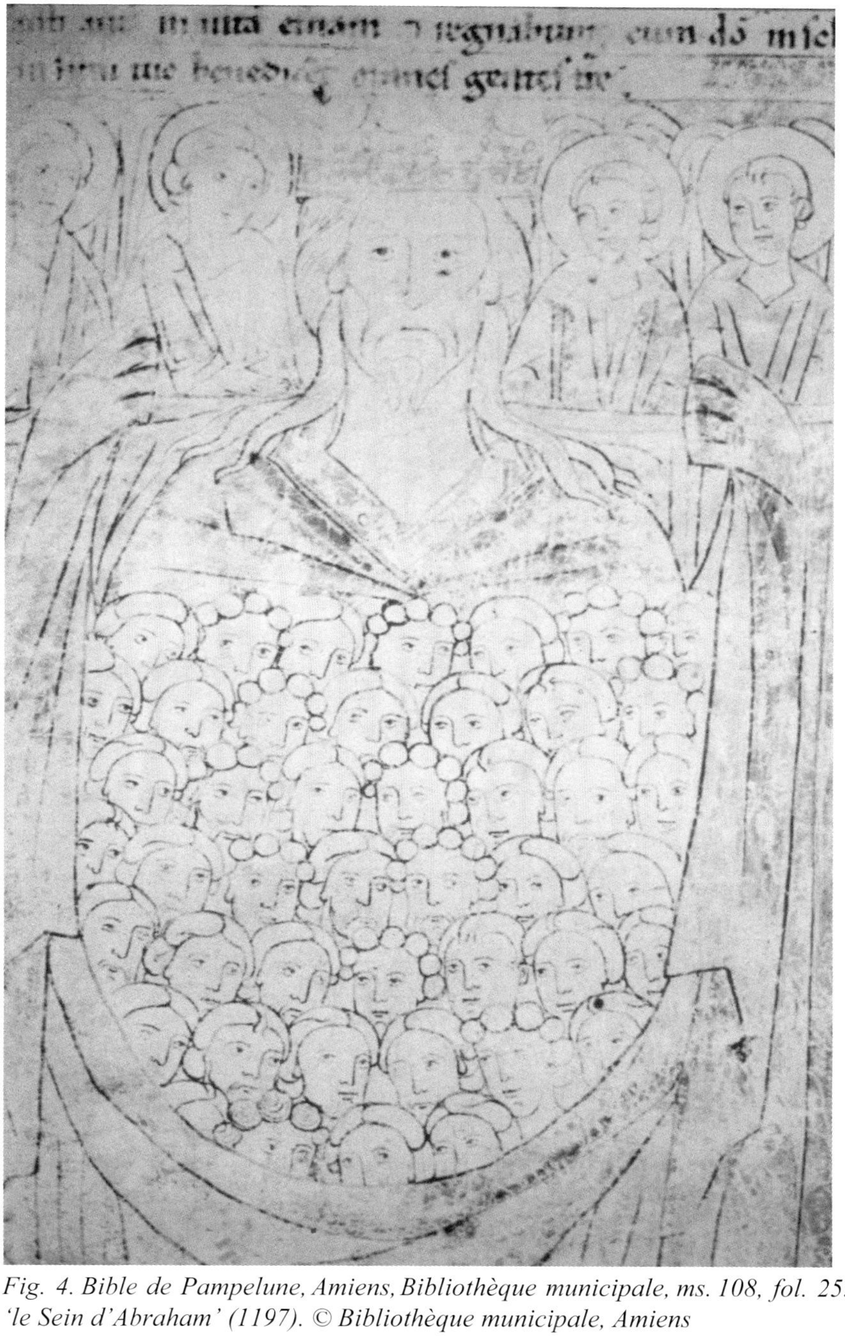

Fig. 4. Bible de Pampelune, Amiens, Bibliothèque municipale, ms. 108, fol. 255^{v}, 'le Sein d'Abraham' (1197). © Bibliothèque municipale, Amiens

Outre les gammes de variations, l'étude sérielle fait considération des cas les plus radicaux, en ayant soin d'en distinguer plusieurs espèces. Certaines s'inscrivent aux points extrêmes d'une gamme de variations. Dans le cas du sein d'Abraham, il s'agit notamment des images qui poussent le plus loin l'inclusion des élus dans le corps-vêtement du patriarche (fig. 4).[44] Sujets de prédilection de l'analyse, de telles images semblent révèler, plus clairement que les autres, la dynamique à l'oeuvre dans la gamme sérielle. D'autres cas singuliers se placent plutôt en marge des séries. Ainsi, les hybridations iconographiques constituent une intersection entre deux séries. Lorsque, dans une image du Trône-de-Grâce, le corps du crucifié disparaît à l'intérieur du manteau du Père (fig. 5),[45] il s'opère un croisement entre deux types trinitaires, le Trône-de-Grâce et la Paternité divine, qui montre le Fils tenu *in sinu patris* (Jn 1, 18, entendu ici au sens de 'dans le pli du Père'; fig. 9).[46] Il s'agit là d'une solution exceptionnelle, qui relève de cette exploration systématique des possibles à laquelle l'étude sérielle nous fait assister.[47]

Enfin, on qualifie d''images-limites' les oeuvres exceptionnelles qui se singularisent par leur radicalité au sein de leur série, et s'aventurent parfois jusqu'aux marges de l'orthodoxie. Une des plus célebres est la Quinité de Winchester, qui a jadis retenu l'attention de E. Kantorowicz.[48] On évoquera ici l'exemple du Jugement dernier du Camposanto de Pise.[49] L'oeuvre est singulière, à la fois

---

[44] Bible de Pampelune, Amiens, Bibliothèque municipale, ms. 108, f. 255 v (Pampelune, 1197).

[45] Psautier de Stephen de Derby, Oxford, Bodleian Lib., MS. Rawlinson G. 185, f. 97 (milieu XIVe siècle).

[46] Sur ce thème, cf. *infra*. Le terme d'hybridation utilisé par J. Wirth (cf. note 10, pp. 16–17), convient bien dans un tel cas, concernant la jonction de deux types iconographiques. Mieux peut-être qu'au cas de la Judith-Salomé étudiée par J. Wirth: en effet, une figure ambivalente constitue la somme des deux figures initiales (A + B); le résultat d'une hybridation tient de A et de B, sans être entièrement ni A ni B.

[47] Lorsqu'un élément ou une fonction caractéristique d'un personnage glisse vers une autre figure, on parlera plutôt de transfert iconographique. C'est le cas au XVe siècle, lorsque le linge contenant les élus n'est plus tenu par Abraham, mais par la figure paternelle du Trône-de-Grâce: soit une image du *sinus trinitatis*. Un tel phénomène peut révéler des relations, notamment d'homologie, entre les figures concernées, comme ici entre Abraham et Dieu le Père. Sur ce type iconographique, voir (avec quelques réserves); P. Sheingorn, 'The Bosom of Abraham Trinity: A Late Medieval All Saints Image', dans *England in the 15th Century. Proceedings of the 1986 Harlaxton Symposium*, éd. D. Williams (Londres, 1987), pp. 273–85.

[48] E. Kantorowicz, 'The Quinity of Winchester', *The Art Bulletin*, 29 (1947), 73–85; et J. Kidd, 'The Quinity of Winchester Revisited', *Studies in Iconography*, 7–8 (1981–82), 21–32.

[49] Je renvoie à mon travail *Les justices de l'au-delà. Les représentations de l'enfer en*

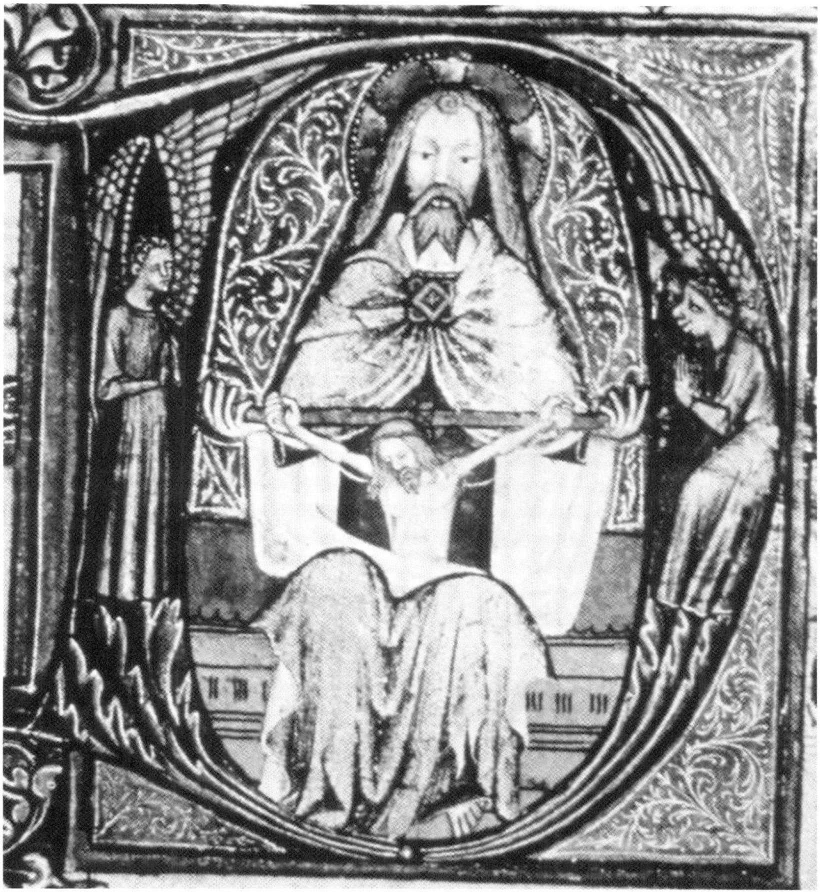

Fig. 5. Psautier de Stephan de Derby, Oxford, Bodleian Library, MS. Rawlinson G. 185, fol. 97, 'le Crucifié dans le Sein du Père' (milieu xive siècle).

parce qu'elle cristallise une mutation décisive dans l'histoire des représentations infernales, mais aussi par certains aspects d'une telle radicalité qu'ils restent sans postérité. Ainsi, la Vierge quitte sa position habituelle d'intercession pour prendre place à côté du Christ, dans une mandorle identique à celle de son Fils. La figuration d'un tel couple judiciaire est un phénomène extraordinaire, bien éloigné des indications scripturaires et de toute la tradition théologique et figurative relative au Jugement dernier. On doit en donner une interprétation

---

France et en Italie (*XIIe–XVe siècles*), Bibliothèque des Écoles Françaises d'Athènes et de Rome, 279 (Rome, 1993).

multiforme, par référence à la stucture exceptionnellement bipolaire de l'oeuvre (Jugement d'un côté, enfer de l'autre), en rapport avec l'essor du culte de la Vierge, ou encore en termes politiques (ralliement de Pise au camp guelfe dans les années 1330, qui fait de la figure mariale un enjeu civico-ecclésial majeur). On songe également à la dualité Justice (qui condamne)/Miséricorde (qui pardonne), habituellement fondue dans la seule figure du Christ, mais qui apparaît ici, de façon clivée, à travers le couple Vierge/Christ. A cet égard, cette image révèle une tension, entre le désir de miséricorde qui anime une 'religion d'amour' et l'affirmation d'une exigence de châtiment, qui travaille en profondeur le christianisme médiéval.[50]

Voilà bien l'enjeu de ces images-limites et de tous les types d'oeuvres exceptionnelles dont il vient d'être question. Il s'agit de parvenir à articuler de façon satisfaisante les régularités sérielles et les cas extrêmes. L'historien serait bien aise de pouvoir attribuer aux images extrêmes une capacité à révéler des contradictions que les oeuvres plus courantes tiennent généralement masquées. Elles seraient ainsi comme les porte-voix de la majorité silencieuse des images. Mais la prudence s'impose: à faire parler une oeuvre pour toutes les autres, on risque de prêter à la série une homogénéité qu'elle ne possède pas. Or, il convient de souligner que l'image extrême s'inscrit dans un moment précis et exprime les tensions d'un contexte singulier (comme le revirement politique de Pise, lors de la réalisation des fresques de Buffalmacco). C'est dans un second temps seulement, et en procédant par recoupements, que l'on peut éventuellement attribuer à l'image extrême une valeur plus large. La compréhension conjointe des gammes sérielles et des images exceptionnelles impose d'articuler le local et le général. Il s'agit d'analyser, dans ses dynamiques historiques, un champ de possibilités où jouent ensemble le singulier et le régulier, l'extrême radicalité des coups d'éclats et la palpitation tranquille des modestes variantes.

Vers l'étude des hyperthèmes

On veut enfin évoquer l'étude des réseaux formés par un ensemble de thèmes iconographiques—ce que l'on désignera sous le nom d''hyperthème', c'est-à-dire un réseau formé par un ensemble coordonné de plusieurs thème iconographiques. Au total, on aura marqué trois paliers dans l'analyse iconographique: les motifs (constituants élémentaires d'une organisation thématique), les thèmes, les hyperthèmes (jonction de plusieurs unités thématiques). Une fois encore, ces distinctions ne doivent pas être appliquées de façon trop rigide, car l'étude peut

---

[50] Les représentations de Satan s'aventurent également parfois jusqu'aux marges de l'orthodoxie, en prennant un tour quasi dualiste; je renvoie à 'Satan, prince de l'enfer: le développement de sa puissance dans l'iconographie italienne (XIIIe–XVe siècle)', dans *L'autunno del diavolo*, éds. É. Corsini et E. Costa (Milan, 1990), pp. 383–96.

associer plusieurs niveaux, et certains hyperthèmes peuvent être constitués à la fois de thèmes et de motifs. D'autre part, on note que l'étude d'un motif—comme l'enfer, la bouche, ou les anges—et celle d'un hyperthème, sont l'une et l'autre transthématiques, obligeant à prendre en examen plusieurs thèmes. Néanmoins, la triple distinction proposée n'est pas inutile: la difficulté dans l'analyse d'un motif tient aux conditions d'extraction d'un élément commun appartenant à des unités structurales distinctes, tandis que l'étude d'un hyperthème vise à saisir les relations entre des unités structurales cohérentes.[51]

Le projet d'une approche hyperthématique évoque la démarche de Jean Wirth qui, dans *L'image médiévale*, tente de mettre en évidence 'un système iconographique', 'un réseau de relations qui produit du sens par sa logique propre'.[52] Sans vouloir forcer la pensée de Jean Wirth, qui reconnaît les limites de l'entreprise, il semble bien que sa visée (son désir) le pousse, en accord avec l'hypothèse d'un fonctionnement logique de l'image, vers la recherche d'une unité structurale globale de l'iconographie médiévale (du moins à chacune des époques considérées). Or, une telle perspective risque de surestimer la systématicité de l'objet étudié, et de laisser échapper une part de la spécificité des images singulières (peut-être aussi parce qu'elle néglige parfois d'en construire les séries aussi complètement que possible). Pour le dire avec J.-C. Bonne, en matière d'iconographie, 'il y a *du* systématique mais certainement pas *un* système, des réseaux thématiques et même des réseaux de réseaux (des rhizomes) que les oeuvres tissent entre elles mais certainement pas *un* réseau des réseaux qui puisse être suturé de bout en bout'.[53] C'est pourquoi l'étude des hyperthèmes se place à un niveau de globalité inférieur à celui que vise Jean Wirth. On se propose en effet d'inclure dans le projet iconographique l'étude de réseaux de thèmes, sans pour autant supposer qu'ils forment des systèmes parfaitement cohérents, logiques, et en excluant la visée d'un système global de

---

[51] Ajoutons cependant que l'étude d'un motif peut tendre vers celle d'une formation hyperthématique. En effet, comme on l'a dit, elle suppose nécessairement l'analyse de la structure d'ensemble dans laquelle s'inscrit le motif, de sorte que l'étude de ce dernier, dans la totalité de ses contextes thématiques, revient d'une certaine façon—mais plus ou moins nettement selon les cas—à mettre en relation tous les thèmes concernés.

[52] *L'image* (cf. note 10), p. 230 ('Il existe en somme un système iconographique. . . . On a essayé d'évaluer son degré d'autonomie et le jeu complexe des initiatives qui le fondent. Il reste à voir jusqu'à quel point il se structure logiquement pour produire ses propres significations'), et pp. 231–33 et 261.

[53] 'A la recheche' (cf. note 11), pp. 371–72. Il en va de même que de la société selon Lévi-Strauss: il y a du structurel, des structures, mais elle n'est pas une structure, ni même une série de structures homologues. Elle est 'un ordre des ordres': un réseau de structures, unies par des relations extrêmement complexes, et qui toutes ensemble ne suffisent encore pas à rendre compte de la totalité d'une société (*Anthropologie structurale* (cf. note 24), ch. XV–XVI, notamment pp. 390–92).

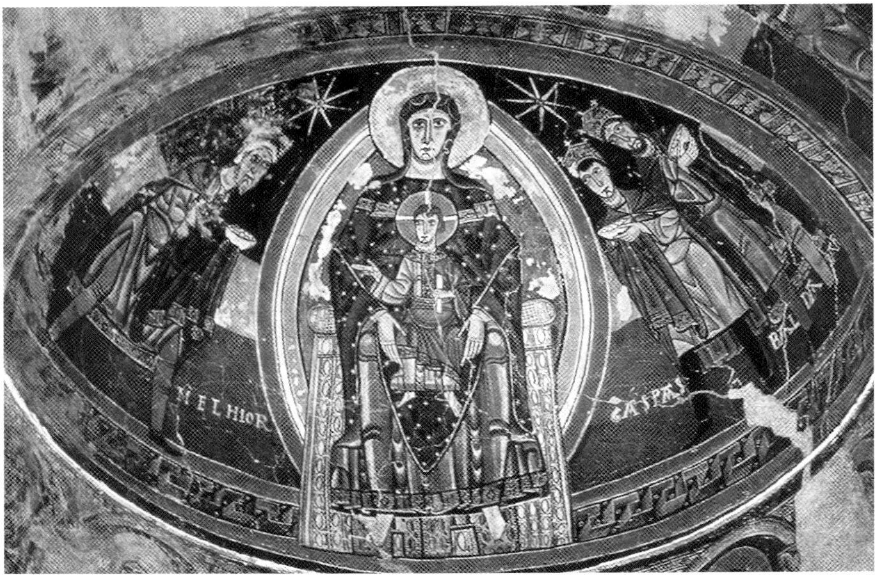

Fig. 6. Santa Maria de Tahull, fresque absidiale (conservée au Musée d'Art de Catalogne, Barcelone), 'Vierge à l'enfant et adoration des mages' (xiie siècle).

l'iconographie des périodes considérées.

Rappelons d'abord que les mises en relation de thèmes relèvent d'une pratique omniprésente dans la culture chrétienne médiévale: correspondances typologiques entre les deux Testaments, mises en relation d'événements multiples par la liturgie. D'autre part, les cycles figuratifs, en particulier dans les peintures murales, sont, à travers les échos, les parallèles ou les oppositions qu'ils tissent, des outils à penser les relations entre les thèmes iconographiques.[54] L'exégèse et l'iconographie se donnent elles-mêmes comme pensée de l'interthématicité. L'étude des hyperthèmes peut s'appuyer sur ces caractères; elle s'inscrit dans le prolongement de ce constat, mais pousse au-delà de ce que les oeuvres singulières formulent explicitement.

---

[54] Cf. *Lieu sacré, lieu d'images* (cf. note 27). Aux exemples déjà évoqués, on ajoutera le vis-à-vis fréquent (établi par exemple à la Martorana de Palerme) entre la Nativité montrant le Christ enfant dans les bras de sa mère et la Dormition où l'âme-enfant de la Vierge est cette fois dans les bras de son Fils. Il y a là, explicitée par l'oeuvre elle-même, un lien structural d'inversion entre deux thèmes iconographiques, qui produit une signification nouvelle, irréductible à la somme de celle des deux thèmes isolés.

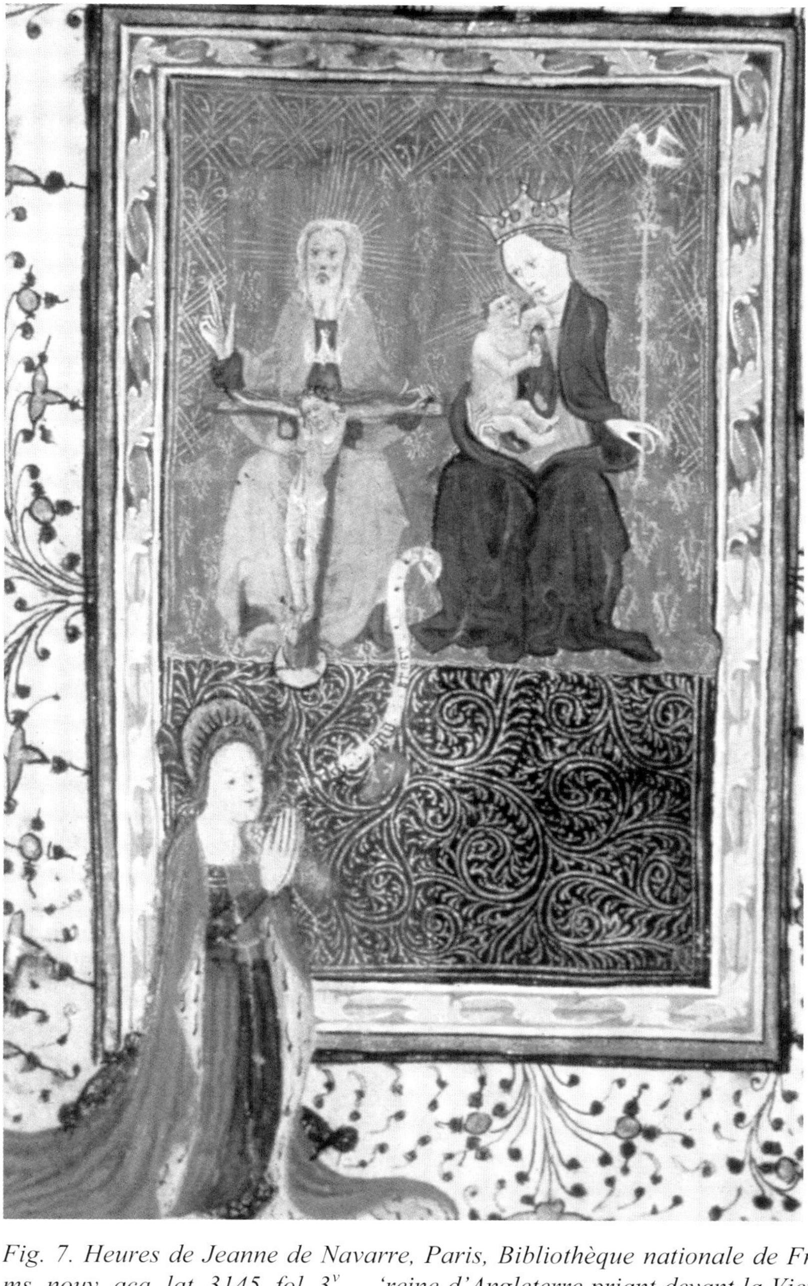

Fig. 7. Heures de Jeanne de Navarre, Paris, Bibliothèque nationale de France, ms. nouv. acq. lat. 3145, fol. 3ᵛ, 'reine d'Angleterre priant devant la Vierge à l'enfant et le Trône-de-Grâce'. © Bibliothèque nationale de France, Paris

Pour illustrer ce qu'est un hyperthème,[55] j'évoquerai le cas dont je poursuis actuellement l'étude, étant entendu que ce qu'on dira ici, de façon sommaire, ne peut valoir comme démonstration quant aux significations mises en jeu, mais seulement à titre de prétexte permettant d'esquisser quelques remarques méthodologiques. L'hyperthème considéré concerne les représentations de la parenté divine (c'est-à-dire l'ensemble des liens pensés en termes de consanguinité ou d'alliance, unissant les figures surnaturelles, ou celles-ci et les hommes, ainsi que les liens de parenté spirituelle entre les hommes, qui sont en rapport étroit avec les précédents). Sont ainsi englobées, entre autres, les figurations de la Trinité, les relations entre Vierge et Trinité, entre Vierge et Christ (filiation réciproque et alliance), ou les figurations de la *Mater Ecclesia* (dans ses relations avec le Christ et avec les fidèles).

A l'intérieur de cette configuration, on peut délimiter un sous-ensemble, qui constitue également un hyperthème et dont la présentation sera plus aisée. Cet hyperthème est le paradigme dérivant de l'expression 'dans le sein de' (*in sinu* . . .), qui s'avère être un opérateur de conjonctions particulièrement fécond. Il regroupe des éléments se caractérisant à la fois par l'expression d'un lien de filiation et par la représentation d'un personnage principal tenant une (ou des) figure(s) dans son sein, c'est à dire entre ses bras, dans un linge ou dans son vêtement, conformément au champ de significations ouvert par le terme *sinus*.[56] Autour du sein d'Abraham déjà évoqué, on voit se dessiner une constellation de thèmes, dont les principaux sont: le type trinitaire de la Paternité divine, la Vierge à l'enfant, certaines figurations rares de l'Ecclesia, des représentations généalogiques, ainsi que, dans une certaine mesure, la Vierge au Manteau.

L'analyse peut porter, d'abord, sur les relations des thèmes pris deux à deux (qu'on ne peut toutes expliciter ici). Ceci est particulièrement difficile si l'on veut tenir compte de tous les facteurs, notamment chronologique et quantitatif, et éviter de réduire chaque thème à un type simple, alors qu'il constitue au contraire une (ou plusieurs) gamme(s) de variantes. Partons de la Vierge à l'enfant, le thème quantitativement le plus développé de notre paradigme—et plus largement de tout l'art médiéval (avec la Crucifixion). La similitude formelle est forte (fig. 6), tant avec la Paternité divine qu'avec le Sein d'Abraham (du moins avec l'un de ses trois types formels), au point qu'on peut attribuer à la Vierge à l'enfant un statut de référent, ayant probablement joué un rôle dans le développement des deux thèmes mentionnés, autour de l'an mil.

---

[55] Autre exemple: les Repas du Christ (huit thèmes, outre la Cène), étudiés par D. Rigaux, dans une perspective sérielle, parfois vigoureusement quantitative, et soulignant l'intérêt d'une approche comparée de ces thèmes; D. Rigaux, *A la table du Seigneur. L'Eucharistie chez les Primitifs italiens. 1250–1497* (Paris, 1989).

[56] L'hyperthème est construit sur la base d'un *motif* commun, associé à des figures différentes. C'est bien toutefois le réseau des thèmes, pris dans leur globalité, qu'il s'agit d'étudier.

Mais, loin d'être la reprise passive d'un modèle, le transfert d'un schéma formel, qui ne peut se produire que s'il est pertinent dans son nouveau contexte, est hautement signifiant. La figuration d'un même mode de relation à l'égard du Christ, mais glissant d'un emploi concernant sa Mère à un autre, mettant en scène son Père céleste, constitue l'indice d'un relation forte à l'intérieur de l'hyperthème étudié. Au reste, d'autres éléments confirment l'homologie, de plus en plus marquée au cours du Moyen Age, entre la relation Père/Christ et la relation Vierge/Christ. Cette équivalence constitue une relation structurale forte, sensible par exemple dans les dispositifs visuels qui mettent en parallèle Trône-de-Grâce et Vierge à l'enfant (fig. 7).[57]

Entre certaines représentations du sein d'Abraham et de la Paternité divine,[58] les ressemblances vont parfois jusqu'au décalque formel, bien que, prises globalement, les deux séries soient loin de se recouvrir strictement (fig. 8–9).[59] Le rapprochement est aussi thématique: il s'agit dans les deux cas d'exprimer un rapport de paternité, d'une nature assez proche (spirituelle ou divine), ce qui est d'autant plus net que ces deux images paternelles, Dieu et Abraham, sont parfois fondues en une figure ambivalente. La relation entre ces deux thèmes permet de saisir un jeu complexe de rapprochements et de différenciations. L'écart entre les deux thèmes est mis en évidence par l'analyse globale des deux séries, ainsi que par l'examen des cas où ils se trouvent associés au sein d'une même oeuvre, comme au tympan de Soria (fig. 8). L'enjeu de cette différenciation est fondamental: il s'agit de souligner l'écart entre la filiation intratrinitaire du Père au Fils (une filiation égalitaire, non-hiérarchique et sans rapport de génération, qui inverse radicalement les données de la filiation charnelle) et la filiation surnaturelle des chrétiens (à l'égard d'Abraham et de Dieu). La conjonction des similitudes et des écarts souligne que ces deux relations sont en partie homologiques (d'où le lien de germanité entre le Christ et les chrétiens), mais en

---

[57] Heures de Jeanne de Navarre, Paris, BnF, ms. n. acq. fr. 3145, f. 3ᵛ (miniature anglaise, ajoutée au début XVᵉ siècle). Même dispositif dans l'Evangéliaire d'Italie du Nord, déjà cité, Bibliothèque vaticane, Vat. lat. 39, f. 171ᵛ–172. C'est surtout à partir du XIIIᵉ siècle que les théologiens soulignent l'équivalence du sacrifice de la Mère avec celui du Père (Bonaventure, dans ce contexte, indique 'Mater per omnia conformis est Patri', In *Lib. Sententiarum*, 1, 48, 2; cité, avec d'autres textes, par T. Dobrzeniecki, 'Medieval Sources of the Pietà', *Bulletin du Musée National de Varsovie*, 8 (1967), 5–24).

[58] Sur ce thème, voir en dernier lieu, F. Boespflug et Y. Zaluska, 'Le dogme trinitaire' (cf. note 21), pp. 197–202.

[59] Tympan de l'église Santo Domingo, à Soria, Castille, fin XIIᵉ siècle; Décrétales, Bibliothèque Vaticane, Vat. lat. 1389, f. 4 (Bologne, première moitié XIVᵉ siècle). Certaines formes d'inclusion sont utilisées pour l'un des thèmes mais exclues pour l'autre. Ainsi, l'usage du linge, dominant dans le cas du sein d'Abraham, n'apparaît jamais dans la Paternité divine, signe probable d'une volonté de différencier les deux thèmes.

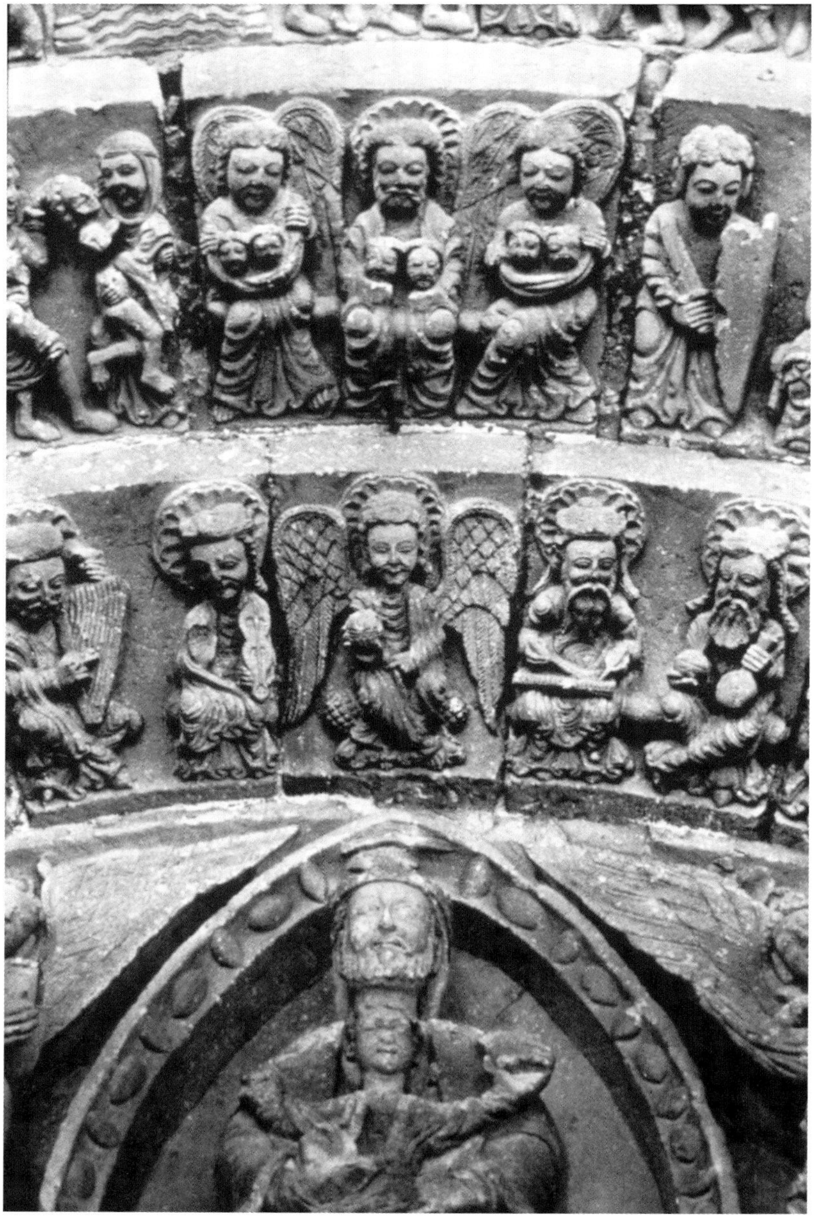

Fig. 8. Soria, Santo Domingo, portail, au tympan: 'le Fils dans le Sein du Père', au centre de la seconde voussure: les élus dans le Sein des Patriarches (vers 1200). © Author

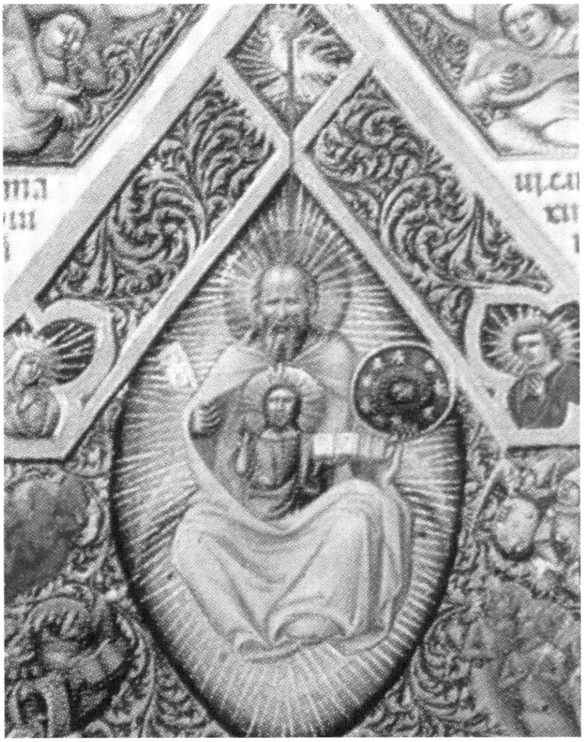

Fig. 9. Décrétales, Bibliothèque vaticane, Vat. lat. 1389, fol. 4, 'le Fils dans le Sein du Père' (première moitié du XIVè siècle). © Biblioteca apostolica vaticana

partie seulement (les théologiens concevant, dans ce contexte, les hommes comme fils adoptifs de Dieu, tandis que le Christ seul est Fils véritable). On a ici un cas de relation complexe associant, de façon nécessaire, homologie et écart.

La relation entre Sein d'Abraham et Vierge au Manteau permet d'illustrer un autre type de rapport (fig. 10).[60] Cette fois, le rapprochement formel est limité, puisque les fidèles sont, dans ce dernier thème, rassemblés, non *in sinu* mais sous le manteau de la Vierge (remarquons toutefois que la différence d'échelle entre le personnage principal et ceux qu'il rassemble contre lui est de même nature). Pourtant, le lien thématique est puissant: sein d'Abraham et Vierge au manteau expriment tous deux, quoique dans des contextes généralement différents, l'appartenance des fidèles à la communauté ecclésiale. Dans les deux cas, ce lien

[60] Fribourg, cathédrale, contrefort Sud, XIVè siècle. Sur ce thème, cf. P. Perdrizet, *La Vierge de miséricorde* (Paris, 1908); V. Sussman, 'Maria mit dem Schutzmantel', *Marburger Jahrbuch für Kunstwissenschaft*, 5 (1929), 285–351.

est figuré par la réunion à une figure parentale unique (*Abraham pater omnium credentium; Maria mater omnium*), par la fusion dans un groupe et par l'inclusion dans un corps-vêtement. Abraham dans son rôle de réceptacle céleste des justes et Marie dans sa fonction de protectrice des vivants et des morts, symbolisant l'un et l'autre la communauté ecclésiale, se trouvent donc en position équivalente. Au reste, cette relation se trouve confirmée par des convergences exceptionnelles. C'est le cas lorsque la Vierge au Manteau apparaît dans le Jugement dernier, ce qui nous rapproche du contexte paradisiaque caractéristique du sein d'Abraham (fig. 11);[61] inversement, il peut arriver que ce dernier prenne un forme si singulière que l'on soit tenté de le qualifier d''Abraham au Manteau'.[62] Là encore, les cas les plus singuliers de la gamme sérielle favorisent les connexions interthématiques.

Mais un décalage chronologique existe entre les deux thèmes: la Vierge au Manteau apparaît dans la seconde moitié du XIIIè siècle, pour se développer seulement au siècle suivant, lorsque le temps fort de figuration du sein d'Abraham s'achève et fait place à un progressif déclin. Sans conclure à un remplacement d'un thème par l'autre (car leurs fonctions ne sont pas strictement assimilables), on peut cependant avancer l'idée d'un relai objectif (et progressif) de l'un par l'autre. On a donc à faire cette fois à une équivalence forte, mais visuellement peu explicitée, entre deux thèmes se succédant chronologiquement.

Par ailleurs, l'étude hyperthématique doit prendre en compte les relations entre les éléments considérés et ceux qui fonctionnent à leur égard dans un rapport d'opposition. Dans le cas du sein d'Abraham, deux éléments antithétiques se présentent. En tant que figuration paradisiaque, le sein d'Abraham ne peut être compris sans considérer en regard les représentations infernales, d'autant que les échos formels soit avec la gueule d'enfer, soit avec la marmite où cuisent les damnés sont souvent très explicites (fig. 2). L'expression d'une incorporation, d'une inclusion dans une forme suggérant une intériorité rassurante, caractéristique du sein d'Abraham, prend plus de force encore lorsqu'elle est confrontée à des images de dévoration qui se fixent sur le seuil, sur l'ouverture corporelle, dans son aspect le plus angoissant. D'autre part, on peut établir un lien structural entre sein d'Abraham et sacrifice d'Abraham.[63] Cette association révèle les deux faces de la figure du patriarche: d'un côté, le

---

[61] *Heures de Marie de Bohun*, Copenhague, B.R., Thott. 547, 4°, f. 32^{v} (Angleterre, *c.* 1380–95).

[62] Psautier, Munich, Staatsbibl., Clm 2641 (plat de reliure, Ratisbonne, *c.* 1250): dans ce Jugement dernier, le manteau d'Abraham, figuré en buste, s'élargit vers le bas et recouvre les élus (on peut s'en faire une idée en isolant mentalement la partie supérieure de la miniature de la figure 3, réalisée dans le même milieu).

[63] Ce lien est établi par plusieurs oeuvres, qui placent ces deux éléments en vis-à-vis, par rapport à l'axe médian (par exemple tympan roman de Saint-Michel-de-Lescure, près d'Albi, ou autel d'or de Lisbjerg, conservé au Musée national de Copenhague).

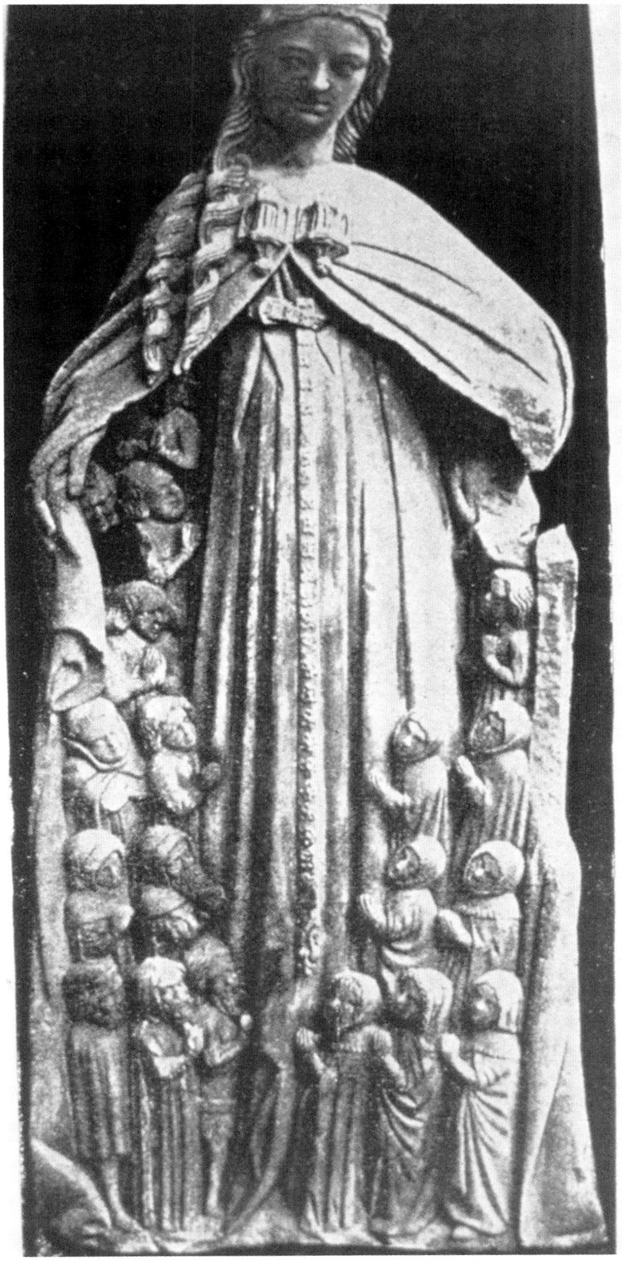

Fig. 10. Fribourg, Cathédrale, contrefort, 'la Vierge au manteau', xive siècle. © Author

père protecteur qui rassemble avec bienveillance sa progéniture contre lui; de l'autre, le père terrible, manifestant la cruauté de la Loi divine et prêt à trancher la gorge de son fils. Outre cette évocation clivée de la figure paternelle, on remarquera la logique de cette mise en relation. C'est en effet par l'épreuve du sacrifice qu'Abraham devient définitivement père d'une multitude (Gn 22), c'est-à-dire, dans la relecture chrétienne, père de tous les élus qu'il est précisément destiné à réunir au paradis, dans son sein. L'analyse d'un hyperthème ne saurait donc négliger ces 'antithèmes', ou plus largement les relations d'opposition qui donnent leur plein relief aux motifs étudiés.[64]

Enfin, au-delà des relations entre les thèmes pris deux à deux, l'analyse de l'hyperthème peut tenter d'articuler l'ensemble de ces liens. Sans s'y engager ici, on indiquera que cette démarche a permis de mieux cerner la position à la fois stratégique et ambiguë du sein d'Abraham. Admettons, dans les monothéïsmes, une organisation selon deux axes: l'un paternel, centré sur le sacrifice (Père-Fils, Abraham-Isaac), l'autre maternel (l'Eglise), définissant la communauté.[65] Il est remarquable que l'étude hyperthématique fasse apparaître le sein d'Abraham, à travers ses liens avec la Paternité divine et avec la Vierge au Manteau, précisément à l'intersection de ces deux axes. En effet, Abraham est en position d'équivalence structurale tant avec la Vierge-Eglise qu'avec Dieu le Père. On peut ainsi mieux rendre compte de l'articulation de la fonction maternelle et de la fonction paternelle dans l'image du sein d'Abraham, placé à la jonction de la conception d'un Dieu-Père et d'une communauté-Mère.

En dépit du caractère encore expérimental de la démarche évoquée, on peut dégager de cet exemple quelques indications générales. D'abord, on se gardera de préjuger du dégré de systématicité de l'hyperthème étudié. Celui-ci doit au contraire demeurer toujours en question, du fait de la complexité de chaque thème, mise en évidence par l'analyse sérielle, et de la diversité des relations susceptibles d'unir les thèmes entre eux. Ainsi, on a pu faire apparaître des types de rapports de nature différente: transfert de modèles formels, possibilités de comparaisons partielles mais aidant à saisir la spécificité de chaque thème, cohérences structurales, soit par opposition ou inversion, soit par équivalence (en distinguant coexistence et substitution dans la chronologie), soit par un jeu complexe de rapprochements et d'écarts. Encore ces relations ne sont-elles le plus souvent que partielles, s'appliquant rarement à la totalité des séries thématiques considérées. Les relations mises en évidence sont fluctuantes, indécises et hétérogènes quant à leur nature et à leur intensité (tout comme les

64 D'autres formes de relations antithétiques peuvent être analysées: dans le cas Nativité du Christ/Dormition de la Vierge (qui se réfère également au paradigme de *sinus*), il s'agit plutôt d'un effet de chiasme (cf. note 54).

65 Voir les remarques de G. Rosolato, 'La communauté constituée en tant que fonction maternelle', dans son recueil d'articles *Pour une psychanalyse exploratrice dans la culture* (Paris: Presses universitaires de France, 1993), pp. 287–301.

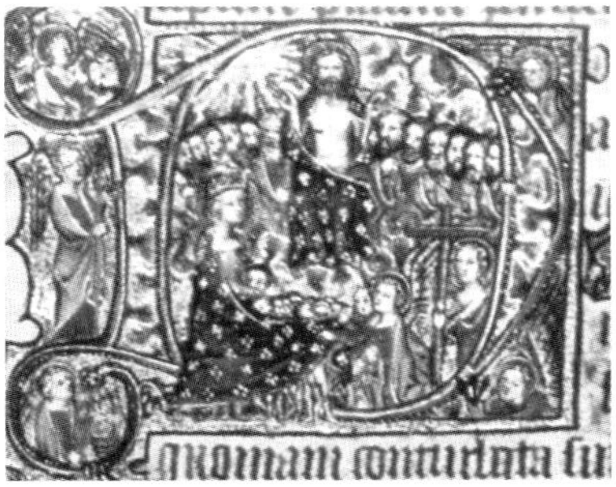

Fig. 11. Heures de Marie de Bohun, Copenhague, Bibliothèque royale, Thott. 547, 4°, fol. 32ᵛ, 'la Vierge au manteau protégeant les élus lors du Jugement dernier' (c. *1380–95). © Kongelige Bibliotek, Copenhagen*

thèmes eux-mêmes, notamment par leur poids quantitatif). Ainsi, s'il peut être possible de faire apparaître, dans un hyperthème, certaines relations structurales, on ne saurait dire, du moins a priori, que l'hyperthème lui-même constitue une structure. Il s'agit plutôt d'un réseau de relations complexes, chacune devant être pensée dans sa singularité. Cependant, en dégageant des connexions, des glissements, des homologies et des écarts, l'hyperthème apparaît comme l'un des cadres pertinents de l'approche iconographique. Il permet de sortir du fractionnement dominant de la recherche actuelle, sans pour autant postuler une systématicité incompatible avec le fonctionnement des gammes sérielles.

Conclusion

Les études iconographiques, au sens défini ici, ont de beaux jours devant elles. L'approche des hyperthèmes peut ouvrir des perspectives nouvelles; celle des motifs est presque sans limite, à la mesure de l'élargissement du questionnement des disciplines historiques. Même dans le domaine des thèmes iconographiques, pourtant plus traditionnel, beaucoup reste à faire, et on est surpris du nombre considérable de thèmes qui n'ont pas fait l'objet d'une étude satisfaisante. Ainsi, le renouvellement des problématiques et des méthodes découvre, pour l'approche iconographique, un champ immense à explorer. C'est à cette aventure que doivent contribuer les nouveaux moyens documentaires que, tous, nous appelons de nos voeux et à la constitution desquels nous nous efforçons de contribuer.

On insistera, pour finir, sur la nécessité d'articuler l'inventivité et la sérialité des images médiévales. La reconnaissance de l'inventivité et de la liberté des images (dans les limites qu'il convient d'assigner à ce terme) donne un sens à l'approche historique. Celle-ci n'a de portée qu'à condition de reconnaître que les images sont un lieu spécifique de mise en jeu des rapports sociaux et d'expérimentation des représentations du monde. De plus, par l'exploration systématique des thèmes, mise en évidence par l'approche sérielle, elles révèlent certains aspects d'énoncés fondamentaux, qui, ailleurs, apparaissent sous d'autres angles et sous d'autres lumières. L'approche sérielle est indispensable pour faire apparaître l'épaisseur historique et la complexité des phénomènes, dès lors qu'on la conçoit, non comme le repérage de types fixes dans un corpus homogène, mais comme la production de gammes de variations, au sein d'environnements complexes et mouvants. L'approche sérielle permet alors d'articuler le singulier et le général, l'inventivité et la traditionnalité. C'est dans cette perspective, croit-on, que l'iconographie peut contribuer à une approche historique—mais problématiquement historique—des images médiévales. Et c'est à cela aussi que peuvent contribuer les bases de données d'images, conçues non seulement comme instruments documentaires, mais aussi comme supports matériels d'un renouveau des méthodes d'analyse.

Image and word: systematic research into the relations between image and word in Dutch culture (1500–1800)

JÖRGEN VAN DEN BERG, HANS BRANDHORST, AND PETER VAN HUISSTEDE

Making a repertory of Dutch printers' and publishers' devices has been a long-term effort in an era marked by the short-term financing of academic projects. It started in 1983 and, working on it intermittently, it took until 1999 to reach a stage where its results can be published in the form of a catalogue + CD-ROM. The printers' devices project is essentially a spin-off or 'by-product' of the Short-Title Catalogue Netherlands (STCN); its collection is thus destined to grow as more material is gathered while STCN progresses. Over time the original purpose of the project has gradually changed, from preparing a mere bibliographical tool to compiling a corpus of images that presents a valuable source for the history of visual culture.

In order to enable users to study the cultural and historical context of printers' devices, not only did we make very detailed descriptions of the images with the Iconclass system but we also studied these images and the mottoes against the background of other sources, such as emblem books, Erasmus's *Adagiorum chiliades*, and illustrated title pages. Several of these sources and essays on the context they share with devices will be published separately.

In this essay we discuss some of the features of the catalogue, published both as a book and as a CD-ROM.[1] After a brief introduction to the phenomenon of

[1] P. van Huisstede and J. P. J. Brandhorst, *Dutch Printers' Devices 15th–17th Century, a Catalogue with CD-ROM*, 3 vols. (Nieuwkoop: De Graaf Publishers, 1999).

printers' devices, we describe a few editorial and technical issues facing editors who answer the challenge to publish this amount of data both electronically and in print.

Recurrent Usage and the Arrangement of Devices

For many years after 1657, when Joannes Maire ceased to print and publish books in Leiden, several variants of his well-known device—a man digging with a spade in a landscape below the motto *Fac et spera*—continued to be used by other printers and publishers. One of these variants, number 0223 (fig. 1), was used by Maire in 1642 and 1652, and again in 1654 in a book printed for Lowijs Elzevier. However, it also adorned the title pages of at least eight editions available from the shop of another Leiden printer and bookseller, Pieter van der Aa, in the years between 1686 and 1690. It was furthermore found on eight editions published by Frederik Haaring in the period 1688–98. Moreover, between 1668 and 1697 the same variant was associated with at least six other names: Johannes van Bilderbeeck, Anthony Schouten, Cornelis Driehuysen, Abraham Gogat, Jacobus Moukee, and Leonardus Strick. Although it could perhaps be established who actually owned this small wood-block after 1657, we can safely predict that the history of its ownership will be a complicated one.

From the late sixteenth century onwards, a device showing a personification of the Christian, in particular the Calvinist, religion, was used throughout Europe by many Protestant printers and booksellers. In the northern Netherlands during the seventeenth century alone, some twenty variants of this device were produced, ultimately deriving from an illustrated poem and emblem by Theodore de Bèze. On title pages it occurs in combination with the names of at least twenty different printers and booksellers. The oldest Dutch variant, number 0742 (fig. 2), was used in Delft by Bruyn Harmensz. Schinckel in 1593. Without its typeset motto, *Religio Christiana*, it appears in several Schinckel editions from 1601 to 1603. After Schinckel, the block was associated with Jacob Lenaertsz. Meyn, Jan Jacobs Palensteyn, and, finally, in 1634, with Volchard Jansz. Camerlingh, all of whom were active in Enkhuizen.

Another variant of the same device, number 0387 (fig. 3), was first used by Gerrit Jansz. Arensteyn in 1634. More than half a century later we still come across the same block: in 1697 Jacob Claus had it printed on the title page of his edition of the works of Hans Engelbrecht van Brunswijk. No matter what historiographical issues this varied pattern of usage may suggest, it first of all alerts an editor to the problem of how to arrange his material. On the more than 16,000 title pages in our photocopy archives we have identified the prints of some 2,000 different blocks and plates. So every block was printed an average of eight times. On average too, every block has been associated with at least two different printers or booksellers, leaving us with well over 4,000 instances of a

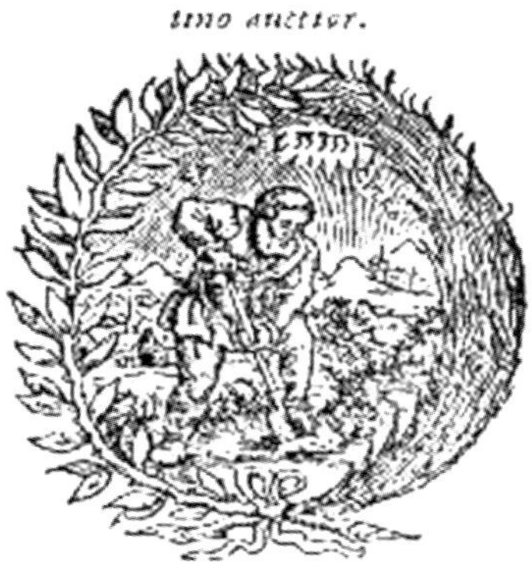

Fig. 1. Device number 0223. © Institute of Information and Computing Sciences, Utrecht University

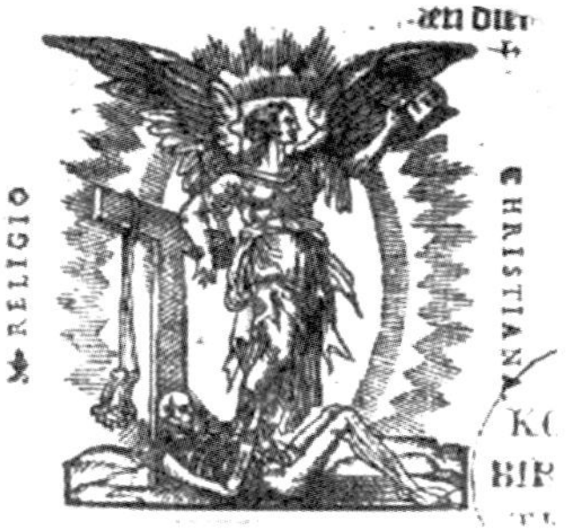

Fig. 2. Device number 0742. © Institute of Information and Computing Sciences, Utrecht University

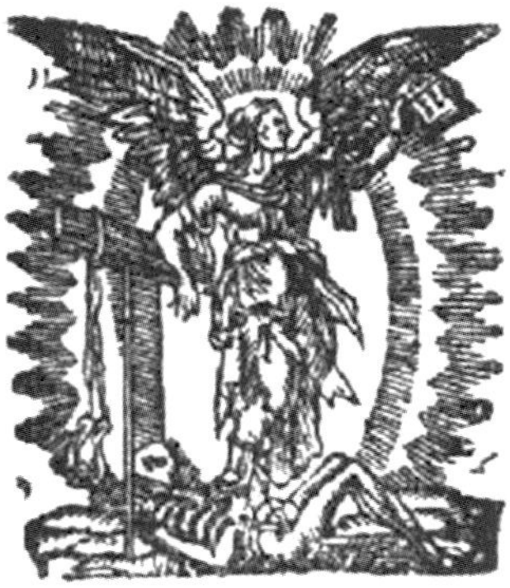

Fig. 3. Device number 0387. © Institute of Information and Computing Sciences, Utrecht University

block linked to a name or a combination of names. The association of devices with different names naturally poses some problems, for a catalogue—like this one—is arranged alphabetically according to the names of printers and publishers. Most essentially it brings out the problems of redundancy (a device may be used repeatedly by different printers, which leads to multiple entries for the same device) and of attribution (when two names are associated with a device, where should one put it in the catalogue?).

Even though a device may seem to begin its life as a personal invention, appearances can be deceptive, due to lack of information or historical coincidence. In Dordrecht, in 1622, the printer Dirck van Vreeswijck used for the first time the device number 0284 (fig. 4), which conceals a pun on his last name. The picture shows Joseph fleeing Potiphar's wife. Its motto *Quantum quisque timet, tantum fugit* contains Latin words for both halves of Vreeswijck's name: *timere* can be translated in Dutch as *vrezen* [to fear], while *fugere* [to flee] can be translated as *wijken*. However, already in 1621, and also in Dordrecht, this device had been used for van Haemstede's martyrology published by Joris Waters, Zacharias Jochimsz, and François Boels. To be sure, the appearance of the device in this publication could very well indicate that the actual printer was Dirck van Vreeswijck, but our prime source, the book at hand, is silent on this question.

How careful we must be when inferring the ownership of a device from internal evidence like an obvious pun on someone's name can be shown with many examples. An instructive one is that of device 0453 (fig. 5). If the only occurrence of this block was in a book published by Philippus Bonus in Leiden in 1673, we might be tempted to conclude that this device was originally designed as a pun on his latinized surname. Bonus, then, would be not a translation of the Dutch name 'de Goede' but a rather more trivial latinisation of the name 'Boon'. The word *boon* is the Dutch equivalent of the Latin *faba* [bean] . . . said to have flourished in the motto of 0453: *Dum stabant pisae sic viguere fabae*. Although this could very well be the pun Bonus intended, his device was actually an *objet trouvé* rather than an *inventio*, because the block originally was the device of the chamber of rhetoric 'De Jonge Batavieren'. Jan Philipsz. van Steenwegen used it for them on a play by P. Nootmans in 1629. In the same year Jan Pietersz. Waelpot printed another play by Nootmans with the same device, and Abraham Waelpot used it in 1652 and 1659.

It will be clear, even from these few examples, that reconstructing the ownership or usage sequence of a device can be a puzzling affair. Internal indications may be misleading, while the consecutive, or even simultaneous, association of different names with a device can hide a Gordian knot of historical realities. To cut the knot we decided on the separate inclusion of every instance of a device's use. In practice this means that a separate section of the catalogue is devoted to every owner—or rather user—of a block. We also state for every user in which years he or she actually used it, and how often it was used per year. By thus mirroring the recurrent use of a block, the catalogue provides the reader

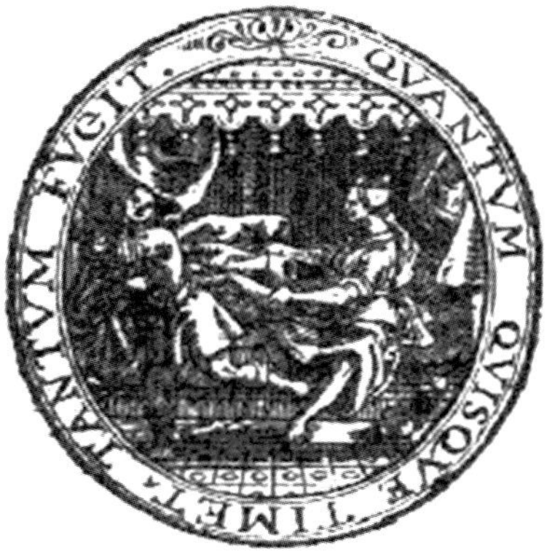

Fig. 4. Device number 0284. © Institute of Information and Computing Sciences, Utrecht University

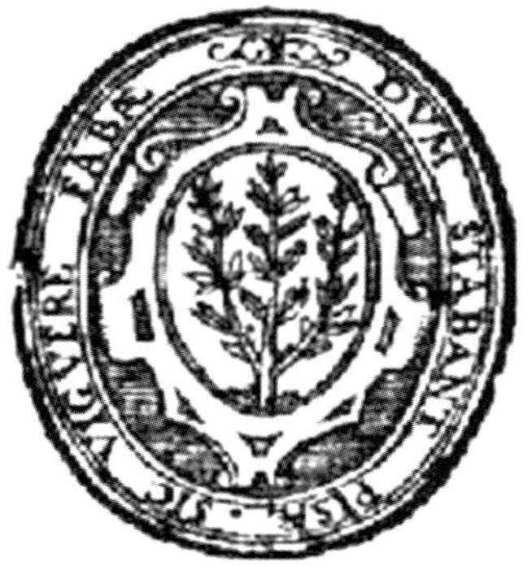

Fig. 5. Device number 0453. © Institute of Information and Computing Sciences, Utrecht University

with a better opportunity for critical assessment of our data than a more polished state of our attributions would have done. This strategy has produced catalogue entries that will occasionally raise the eyebrows of some bibliographers, because we may deliberately ignore what seems so obvious, as with Vreeswijck's device. This will be most evident in cases in which a bookseller's name is joined to a device that is actually the device of the printer, while the printer's name is not mentioned anywhere in the book; or cases in which, vice versa, the printer's name is combined with the bookseller's device. In all instances of this kind the device has been catalogued under the name found in the book. Still, even though this approach is aimed at preventing premature attributions, we cannot altogether avoid attributions. Nor did we want to avoid them. Whenever more than one name is found in a book, be it on its title page or in a colophon, we had to decide under which primary name the device would actually be presented. Some of these decisions are completely arbitrary, but the usage of devices and internal evidence about the names of printers, streets, and shops may provide information on which to found an attribution. Whenever available, the STCN data on addresses and shop signs are provided with the catalogue entries.

How Devices Were Selected

Ex literarum studiis immortalitatem acquiri . . . 'To reach immortality through the study of letters'. While some wishful thinking and commercial interest are mixed with this humanistic creed, printers and booksellers throughout Europe sincerely believed in it and gave vent to their beliefs by means of their devices. In the northern Netherlands we come across several variants of the device. The motto may be abbreviated to *Studiis immortalitatem acquirimus*, paraphrased as *Literae immortalitatem pariunt* or played with as in *Vita sine litteris mors est.* The main connotations of the imagery accompanying these statements are immortality and fame, visualised either by a phoenix, a personification of Fame, a Triton trumpeting on a shell, or Minerva, alone or with Mercury. Such a widespread sentiment cannot be traced to a single source. At best we may try to establish which literary and/or visual expressions were comparatively successful in disseminating it. It will hardly come as a surprise that, judging by the number of devices inspired by its motto and its imagery, one of the popular expressions of the theme was an emblem by Andreas Alciatus.

Alciatus's book of emblems certainly was not the only book of moral instructions, proverbial expressions and attractive imagery that printers and booksellers explored in their search for an attractive device. Emblems and devices invented by Claude Paradin, Paolo Giovio, Roemer Visscher, Hadrianus Junius, Jacob Cats, to name but a few; adages collected by Erasmus; quotable phrases from classical sources such as Vergil and Seneca; and, of course, biblical citations—all could be exploited by book producers who wished to make a statement about their religious convictions or to demonstrate the quality of their education and their business.

Sometimes devices testify to a ready knowledge of these sources and a high level of inventiveness in adapting a source to the particular situation of a printer or bookseller. Devices of this type can be found in the catalogue under names like Corverius, van Waesberge, van der Wouw, Wachtendonck, Cloppenburgh, Ravesteyn, and Brandt. Sometimes, however, devices are simply ornamental. They may also be a simple 'Hausmarke', or limit themselves to a decorative play with their owner's initials, or use the arms of an academic, cultural, or political organisation. Devices of this kind can be found under Allardus Gauter, Gheraert Leeu, Marten Gerbrantsz, or Pieter van der Slaart.

The simple fact that the arms of a city or a university, emblems from a widespread emblem book, images from shop signs, or someone's initials could all be turned into a device shows that any effort at defining what a printers' device *is* would be irrelevant, because it is the *use* that makes the device. This explains why other visual elements—tail-pieces, title vignettes, marginal illustrations, or initials—were sometimes included in the catalogue as well. The criterion of usage proved an acceptable guide in deciding on the inclusion of devices in the present corpus. Perhaps users may find it was applied too liberally, but even then the criterion remains unambiguous and clear.

Slightly less self-evident is the history of the corpus upon which this catalogue is based. When data collecting started, some fifteen years ago, the ambition was almost exclusively bibliographical, as the initiative came from the STCN. The STCN is the Dutch bibliography covering the period from the first Dutch products of the printing-press to the year 1800. In its database the user will eventually find all books published to that date within the present borders of the Netherlands as well as all books printed in Dutch abroad. Between 1982 and 1997 the Dutch holdings 1540–1700 in the Koninklijke Bibliotheek (KB) and the university libraries of Amsterdam and Leiden were described. In 1997 the collection 1540–1800 of the university library in Utrecht was taken in hand, while work on the eighteenth-century holdings of the KB has been in progress since 1995. Also, Dutch editions from the period 1622–1700 in the British Library are being processed both for the STCN and for a future volume in the British Library's catalogue series. At the moment the STCN amounts to circa 80,000 descriptions. The estimate is that it will eventually contain some 300,000 titles.

The STCN is accessible from many Dutch libraries, but it can also be consulted from home or office by users with Internet access to the KB or any other institution providing a connection to PICA's Online Retrieval System (ORS) and Open Library Network (OBN). Recently, it has also become accessible worldwide through the Hand Press Book Database (HPB) established by the Consortium of European Research Libraries (CERL).

The STCN's original assumption was that an informal photocopy archive of the devices of printers and publishers with access to their iconography could be useful as a tool for the identification of printers and booksellers. And it was. However, the *systematic* collection of large quantities of pictorial material is somewhat of a *terra incognita* even for most art historians. Obviously, it took some time for the team of bibliographers to develop criteria for the selection of the imagery found on title pages, since not every picture found there is a printer's or a publisher's device. Once or twice, during that process, a device may have escaped notice. Conversely, sometimes a picture has been archived, which—it has been decided, on closer inspection—is not an actual device.

The presence of a printers' or publisher's device is always mentioned in the bibliographical descriptions of the STCN, and this information can be used for retrieval when consulting the database through the aforementioned Online Retrieval System or the Open Library Network. In early 1999 the STCN database contained some 17,000 references to printers' devices. Since this figure includes references to material that has been left out of the present catalogue, for example eighteenth-century editions, it closely matches our own count of circa 16,000 prints. So, even though a complete comparison of the two lists of references is simply not feasible, we are confident that only rarely will a device have completely slipped through the net. Despite incidental or, rather, accidental divergences, the devices project is completely dependent on STCN for its material, so all devices included in our catalogue and dated between 1540 and 1700 were found in the libraries whose collections were indexed by STCN: the Koninklijke Bibliotheek, the university library of Amsterdam, and the university library of Leiden. Devices from Utrecht's university library and the British Library—both of which are still incompletely catalogued—are not included here. Nor are devices included of printers or publishers who started their business after 1700. Devices dated before 1540 were included on the basis of secondary publications, particularly from those that provide reproductions of this material, such as Nijhoff's *L'Art typographique*[2] and Juchhoff's *Drucker- und Verlegerzeichen des XV. Jahrhunderts.*[3] The information about the usage of the devices from the period before 1540 is not based on personal inspection but is derived from these older published sources, once or twice supplemented from the STCN database.

The Elements of an Entry

The Utrecht printer Abraham van Herwijck associated himself with his Old Testament namesake and chose as his device a picture of Abraham about to sacrifice Isaac. Another Abraham, namely Abraham van Blancken, used a device showing some moles burrowing into a hill. His choice, at first sight surprising, is at least partly explained by his address, the Molsteegh—'Mole Alley'—in Amsterdam. A third one, Abraham Biestkens, also of Amsterdam, referred to the 'church under the cross' by way of his device, which shows a lily surrounded by thorny shrubs. His choice of device is directly related to the name of his shop and the sign with which it was adorned: '*De Lelye onder de doornen*'. All kinds of associations, whether simple or very intricate, could stimulate the invention of a device.

The names of streets and shops can help us to understand the choice of device. We are grateful for the Koninklijke Bibliotheek for permission to include the

[2] W. Nijhoff, *L'art typographique dans les Pays-bas pendant les années 1500 à 1540: reproductino en facsimile des caractères typographiques, marques d'imprimeurs, gravures sur bois et autres ornements employés pendant cette période*, 3 vols. (The Hague: Nijhoff, 1926–35).

[3] R. Juchhoff, *Drucker- und Verlegerzeichen des XV. Jahrhunderts in den Niederlanden, England, Spanien, Böhmen, Mähren und Polen* (Munich: Verlag der münchner Drucke, 1927).

information on location and shops, which has been collected while STCN built its thesaurus of printers and publishers, their places and years of activity, addresses, and shop signs. Together, these data are the core of each record created for the devices used by individual printers. Sometimes a note, usually about some form of co-operation or certain family relationships, has been added.

The STCN project is scheduled to continue for quite a number of years. During the last four years the rate at which new material was added to the on-line database has even accelerated. Our biographical information, though ultimately deriving from this database, had to be 'frozen' at some point, and then adapted to the format of our own files. This implies that it dates back to the start of the final editing, the beginning of 1998. Divergencies between the data of this study and the data the STCN is offering on-line can usually be explained by this time gap.[4] Users are advised to consult the STCN on-line data if they want to make absolutely sure that they have the fullest and most recent information.

The main elements (entries in the database) that have been detailed by the study are:

Device number [Number]

The device numbers, although randomly assigned, are meaningful since they are the unique identifiers of blocks and plates. They can be employed to retrieve all instances of the use of a particular block. The user can do this either by consulting the printed concordance—device number to printer—or by searching the CD-ROM by device number.

Iconography 1: Free text description

A free text description has been created of every block. Although it may seem redundant to classify the pictorial elements of iconographical interest with Iconclass as well as to describe them in prose, these two components of an entry are actually complementary. A reproduction needs to be accompanied by a description of its subject. The systematic classification of subject matter is a prerequisite for building a systematic index of the iconography of the devices. Wherever necessary, the description explains the general relationship between the distinct iconographic elements to which an Iconclass notation is assigned.

A feature of the textual descriptions, intended to serve those who do not read Dutch, is the inclusion of the Dutch translations of those words that hint at the

[4] The same holds, obviously, for any publication based on STCN-data of a more recent date than ours. As a matter of fact STCN editors J. A. Gruys and Jan Bos are preparing a printed publication of all the addresses and shop signs.

name of a printer, or his address or shop sign. Often these puns are pretty obvious, because the keywords are present in the motto and/or name, e.g. Cloppenburgh's *Siet ick sta aen die deure ende cloppe* illustrated with a man knocking [*kloppend*] on the door of a castle [*burcht*]. Sometimes it is helpful to know the Dutch translation of an English word. When a printer named Bot uses a picture of a flounder for his device it is useful to know that 'bot' is also a Dutch word for flounder. On the CD-ROM the full text of the descriptions is made searchable in the Keyword picklist, with its accompanying KWIC index.

Iconography 2: Iconclass notations [ICO]

This article is not a suitable place to explain at length what is Iconclass. A more extensive explanation of the Iconclass system is to be found in the CD-ROM's helpfile on Iconclass. Information is also made available on-line, on the Iconclass website (http://iconclass/let.uu.nl) at Utrecht University. Moreover, a substantial number of catalogues using Iconclass, both on paper and on CD-ROM, has been published during the last decade or so, exposing a wide audience to the system.

However, since vocabularies are generally used according to rules that are specific to a project, a few remarks are in order about the way we have applied Iconclass to the printers' devices. This holds even more strongly as the research of our Image & Word project has considerably affected our views on the iconography of the devices. In this project several types of sources—selected emblem books, printers' devices, occasional engravings, title pages, Erasmian texts—are digitized and connected through hyperlinks; their text is transcribed and SGML-tagged[5] to facilitate the hyperlinking; and their iconography is indexed with Iconclass. And because historiographical studies are written in the same electronic format, we can hyperlink comments and source texts. Thanks to this project, which has embedded our research on printers' devices for a decade now, we have gained a better grip on the contents of a number of important emblem books and texts such as Erasmus's *Adagiorum chiliades*.

Being better informed about what we like to call 'the emblematic game', we have included much detail in our iconographic encoding of the devices and also added many Iconclass notations on the basis of our interpretation of the mottoes. A few examples should clarify this approach and thus give an idea about the kind of iconographic data that have been recorded.

The first device mentioned in this introduction was number 0223, originally used by Joannes Maire. In spite of its apparent simplicity, any description of its subject matter will of course depend on the purpose and the frame of mind of the indexer. However, there will not be much debate about the fact that it shows a

[5] Standard Generalized Markup Language.

man digging with a spade in a hilly landscape. Over his head we read *Fac et spera* as well as the name of God in the shape of a Jahweh tetragram. Men digging with spades occur in more than fifty different printers' devices, while the Latin roots 'spe–' and 'labor–' are to be found in more than seventy. Whatever the implications of these numbers may be, they make it unlikely that a man digging in a landscape with a text such as 'work and hope' above him, is just a realistic depiction of the hard labour of a seventeenth-century peasant. Without speculating about the wider context or deeper meaning, we feel justified in assuming that anyone researching the imagery of Labour or Hope could be interested in a picture such as this. Therefore our description includes these more abstract concepts.

Thus Maire's device is indexed with the following Iconclass notations:

46A170 Labour;
5(+12) Abstract Ideas and Concepts—an abstract concept represented by a male figure; and
56D1(+3) Hope; 'Speranza', 'Speranza delle fatiche' (Ripa)—symbolical representation of concept.

Of course it is also to be found with those notations that describe the man digging with a spade, the landscape with hills, the olive-and palm-branch framing the scene, or the tetragram from which a radiance emanates:

11C13 tetragram (in Roman or Hebrew script)—symbol of God the Father;
22C31 radiance emanating from persons or things;
25G3(OLIVE-TREE)(+22) olive-tree: branch, stick;
25G3(PALM-TREE)(+22) palm-tree: branch, stick;
25H11 mountains; and
47I122 digging with a spade—soil cultivation.

On the CD-ROM it is explained—and demonstrated in action—that the hierarchical organisation of Iconclass also ensures retrieval of this picture through keywords such as 'God', 'Christian religion', 'symbol', 'supernatural light', 'ray of light', 'soil', 'farmer', 'cultivation', 'agriculture', 'spade', and many more.

A small detail of the picture that could easily go unnoticed is the bird on a branch facing the man (fig. 6). While this could be seen as a naturalistic addition—e.g. a small bird waiting for the seeds that will be sown shortly—it can also be read as the visual counterpart of the motto's exhortation to hope. Exploration of the emblem books that we have indexed in much the same way as these devices, informs us that the crow can be the attribute of Hope—*corvix, avis tributa spei*. As such it is included in the various *picturae* of Alciatus's emblem *In simulacrum Spei* [the imagery of Hope], and commented on by humanists such as Claude Mignault. It is the bird's call—*cras, cras*—that triggers the association, because in Latin this call means 'tomorrow, tomorrow'. . . .

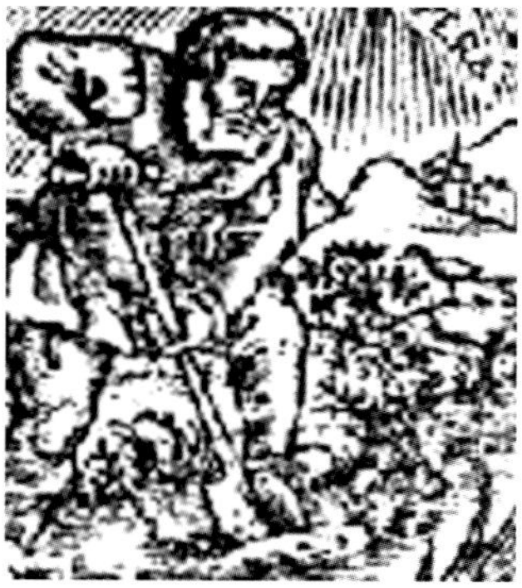

Fig. 6. Detail of device number 0223. © Institute of Information and Computing Sciences, Utrecht University

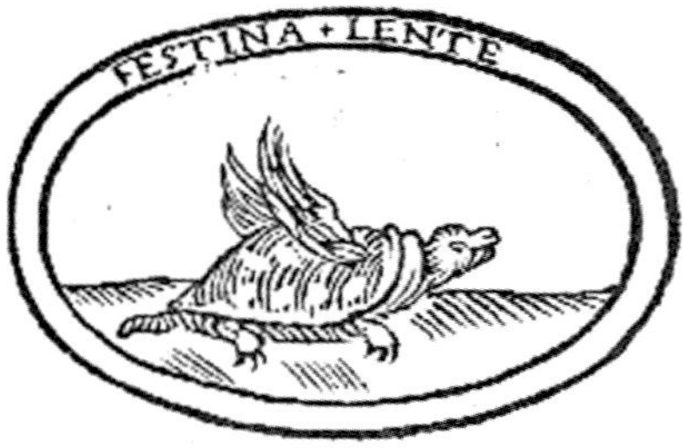

Fig. 7. Device number 1312. © Institute of Information and Computing sciences, Utrecht University

Needless to say, it remains a question whether the inventor of the device or its contemporary observers would have connected it to this little piece of ornithological lore, dating back to antiquity. These reservations, however, do not diminish the potential usefulness of our encoding of the picture with the aforementioned notation 56D1(+3) and with the concept:

> 25F32(CROW)(+1) song-birds (with NAME)—animals used symbolically.

Our interpretation of the bird's presence, which occurs in 25 out of 28 versions of the device found to date, may be wrong. Nonetheless, given the modest position of our description in the historiographical argument about the picture's meaning—it is nothing but a first step—no harm is done.

In much the same manner, the picture of a turtle with wings (fig. 7) accompanied by the motto *Festina lente* [make haste slowly] is encoded with the notations for the opposing speeds of motion—slowness and haste—which are at the heart of the device's meaning:

51M1(+3) Fast Motion—symbolical representation of concept; and
51MM1(+3) Slow Motion—symbolical representation of concept.

Moreover, we include references to emblem books, the *Adages* of Erasmus, and to other literature as well, wherever we think this would constitute a helpful hint to the user. Thus the following concepts are added to the description of the winged turtle:

83(ERASMUS, Adagiorum chiliades II i 1) specific works of literature (with AUTHOR, Title); and
86(FESTINA LENTE) proverbs, sayings, etc. (with TEXT).

Two things should be clearly understood about this enrichment of the iconographic description. References to literature such as the *Adagiorum chiliades* or an emblem book do not imply that we think we have identified *the* source of a device. In some cases devices are indeed straightforward copies of emblems. More often, however, the ideas expressed by an emblem, and the visual and literary means used in the process, are adapted to the situation of a new user and to the message he or she wants to communicate. The cultural substratum on which the emblematic game is played is far too complex and the information about the genesis of specific devices too sparse to tolerate a reductivist approach. As a matter of fact, of the possible relations between devices and emblems, the straightforward 'model-copy' relation is not the most instructive.

In much the same vein, a word of warning is in order about the symbolic interpretations, of which the identification of a crow as the attribute of Hope is an example. The potential for conveying meaning, even of 'simple' iconographic elements such as crows and turtles, is by no means exhausted once we have identified one of their aspects. The corpus of printers' devices itself provides the means of countering such simplistic assumptions, as it shows that turtles could also be used to express independence: carrying their house on their back, they are self-sufficient animals that are *overal thuys* [anywhere at home]. Furthermore, their Dutch name 'schildpad' could stimulate the imagination in a direct way, as is illustrated by the device of Amelis Jansz. van Paddenburgh, which shows a turtle in the foreground with a castle [*burcht*] in the distance. As lack of speed also characterises snails, it is not surprising that they too could advertise a printers' claim that his work did not suffer from error-producing haste.

The gist of what has been said here about the status of our references to abstract ideas and emblem literature through Iconclass codes also applies to the part of the codes identifying biblical sources. There too, mottoes play an important role when we have to decide the usefulness and accuracy of a reference to a particular text. One example should suffice to illustrate this: a device that exists in more than a dozen variants shows an open book encircled by a quotation from Joshua 1:8: *Laet het Boeck deser Wet van uwen monde niet comen* [this book of the law must ever be on your lips]. Whether or not the open book of the device should be identified with 'this book of the law' is not the main issue here. What is important is that applying the most appropriate Iconclass concept '71E51 Joshua communicating with God (in general)' could suggest that the biblical hero himself is depicted rather than the content of his communication with God. The reason we decided to assign possibly confusing notations to a device like this is that, properly warned in this introduction, users may still benefit from these references.

It may seem an odd thing to say, after having assigned more than 20,000 Iconclass notations to the corpus, but given our limited systematic access to the iconographic and textual details of sources such as emblem books, there still is much room for improvement and expansion. Our descriptions, it cannot be emphasised enough, may suffice to awaken the historical opponent, but not to put him to rest.

Mottoes [MOT]

Mottoes of printers' devices are not only interesting in their own right but also important for other reasons. They help us understand the iconography of a device. But a motto may also clarify why a particular theme was chosen by a particular person. When Cleopas and Peter realise they have been talking to Jesus on the way to Emmaus, they say, according to Luke: *nonne cor nostrum ardens erat in nobis dum loqueretur in via* [did we not feel our hearts on fire as he talked with us on the road]. The Dutch translation of the phrase *ardens erat* contains the root 'brand', which gave Marten Jansz. Brandt a reason to choose this theme for his device. This would seem to be confirmed by the fact that Jacob de Meester, who used the same subject a few years before Brandt, quoted Matthew 18:20—*waerder twee of drie in miin naem vergadert ziin*—instead of Luke.

Mottoes may, furthermore, help us to distinguish variants of a device, for example because of variant spellings. Whenever it was considered appropriate or useful, the motto of a device would be exploited to improve or expand the iconographic description, as we explained above. Literal transcription of the mottoes, preserving orthographical variations and upper and lower case, are included to help identify blocks. Normalised versions of the mottoes were included too on the CD-ROM, to ensure easy retrieval of basically identical text.

Initials and monograms [INI]

Under this heading we have gathered the initials of printers, booksellers, draughtsmen, and woodcutters. Whenever it seemed possible to assign initials or a monogram to a bookseller or printer, we have done so, taking into account that our chances of correctly identifying the letters hidden in an ornate monogram depend on the number of times it is used by the same printer. In such monograms you often see what you know.

Systematic research to identify the artists' signatures was beyond the scope of this catalogue. Suggestions of that nature are mostly traditional and intended to allow the easy retrieval of pictures with identical initials or monograms.[6] Notwithstanding the moderate status of devices, they will supplement what is known about the oeuvre of artists such as the van Sichems and the Serwouters.

Years and frequency of use [RAN]

An important addition to the types of information brought together in the pilot study is the survey of a device's use by a particular printer or bookseller. For every user of a device we have recorded in which years he or she employed it and how often it was used per year. These are the years that are included in the picklists *Start date* and *Latest date* of the CD-ROM's central search facility.

Images

The illustrations of devices have been digitized with a flatbed scanner. All scans—some of photographs, some of photocopies—were made at the same, moderate, resolution of 200 dpi. In the printed catalogue the images are presented at a fixed size. The full-size images can be found on the CD-ROM, where one can check them against a fixed scale.

The Catalogue as a Book and as a CD-ROM

In the past century, important repertories have been compiled of the printers' devices of France, England, Germany, Switzerland, Spain, Italy, and, most recently, Belgium. No such repertory existed for the Netherlands, in spite of its being one of Europe's major centres of book production. To be sure, a survey of devices from the Low Countries had been included in the fourth volume of the *Bibliotheca Belgica*,[7] and many devices were reproduced in Briels's study about the migration of printers and publishers from the southern to the northern

[6] These will be found on the CD-ROM via the item Expert Search of the Search menu. In Expert Search you should consult the picklist IN2 Initials (explained).

[7] *Bibliotheca Belgica. Bibliographie générale des Pays-Bas. Fondée par Ferdinand van der Haeghen*, rééditée sous la dir. de Marie-Thérèse Lenger, 7 vols. (Brussels: Editions Culture et Civilisation, 1964–75). See especially vol. IV, pp. 60–208: '*Marques Typographiques*'.

Netherlands in the late sixteenth and early seventeenth century.[8] The devices of the Elzeviers were listed and reproduced by Rahir,[9] and various essays were devoted to the devices of specific printers or publishers. Occasionally, devices were discussed in thematic studies such as that of Simoni[10] about verbal and visual puns in Dutch devices or that of Nielson[11] about Latin mottoes on Dutch devices. However, no attempt at a comprehensive survey of Dutch devices had been made. Given the intimidating fact that by now 'only' 80,000 of an estimated total of 300,000 editions have been catalogued by STCN, a complete catalogue of Dutch devices cannot be expected for many years to come. Still, enough material has been collected now to warrant a publication.

While its foreign predecessors differ among themselves in scope, method, and ambition, our survey, a latecomer in the field, is characterised by a feature that sets it apart from all of them. Publishing the repertory both as a book and in an electronic form is symptomatic of the central role computerisation has played in most stages of the research and of the editorial process. Not only is our selection of material dependent on the computerised catalogue of the STCN project but also the wish to hyperlink the sources we are bringing together in our Image & Word project requires them to be transformed into electronic documents, and to be enriched with some form of markup. We do think this process would deserve a detailed treatment, but here we must limit ourselves to those aspects which have had an immediate effect on the form and content of the present publication.

When we began to prepare our data for publication we decided to make the results of our research available as a printed book and in an electronic format. For technical and editorial reasons, CD-ROM was chosen as the medium. The CD-ROM included with the book provides an environment tailored for fast and flexible querying and offers quite a number of options to compare the results of queries. However, we are well aware that the use of a CD-ROM is connected to the life cycle of the operating system it is made for, and we can be sure that a

---

[8] J. G. C. A. Briels, *Zuidnederlandse boekdrukkers en boekverkopers in de Republiek der Verenigde Nederlanden omstreeks 1570–1630* (Nieuwkoop: B. de Graaf, 1974).

[9] E. Rahir, *Catalogue d'une collection unique de volumes imprimés par les Elzevier et divers typographes hollandais du 17ᵉ siècle* (Paris: Damascène Morgand, 1896). See especially pp. 419–66: 'Fleurons et marques typographiques des Elzevier de Leyde et des Elzevier d'Amsterdam—Principaux fleurons et marques typographiques de diverses officines de Hollande du XVIIᵉ siècle dont les productions se joignent à la collection Elzevirienne'.

[10] A. E. C. Simoni, 'Bearwood, Tree, Flatfish & Co: some punning Dutch devices', in *Festschrift Hellinga, Forty-three Studies in Bibliography presented to Prof. Dr. Wytze Hellinga on the occasion of his retirement from the chair of Neophilology in the University of Amsterdam at the end of the year 1978* (Amsterdam: Nico Israel, 1980), pp. 447–66.

[11] A. C. Nielson, *Latijnse Zinspreuken op Nederlandse Boekmerken* (Amsterdam: Ellerman Harms, 1952).

printed book will outlive that. Moreover, computers, let alone CD-ROMs, still are not used by every researcher potentially interested in the subject. In other words, there are several arguments to add a printed catalogue of Dutch material to other recent ones, such as the survey of Italian devices by Giusseppina Zappella[12] and that of southern Netherlandish devices by Frank Vandeweghe and Bart Op de Beeck.[13]

A multi-purpose datastore

The concept of exploiting the same data for multiple purposes may sound rather trivial. Is that not precisely what computers allow you to do? Still, when a file should behave correctly in an SGML / XML environment but should also be easily converted to HTML; when it should print as though it was typeset with a desktop publishing program but do so without forcing the editor to arrange the layout of some 1,600 pages with 3,500 illustrations page by page; when it should be converted into a database with indices but remain open for corrections until the evening before the final conversion—then the concept becomes slightly more ambitious and deserves some comment.

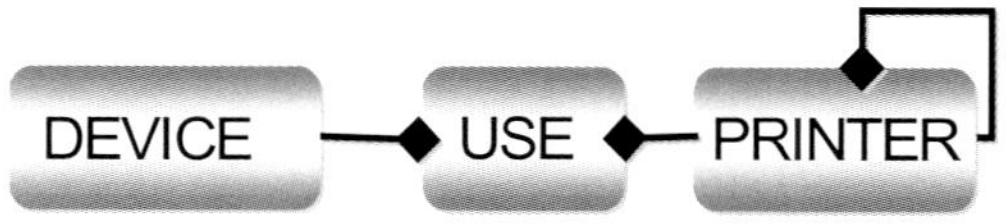

Conceptual Datamodel

The complex relationship of printers or booksellers with the devices they used to sign and uniquely identify their book production can be described logically as a 'many to many' relationship between the entity 'device' and the entity 'printer'. This relationship is actually even more complex since printers or booksellers worked together and used in different 'joint ventures' the same or new devices. Sometimes devices were even merged into one new presentation of symbols and concepts of the original devices. So the entity 'printer' has a recursive relationship with itself. This observation is crucial for designing the logical structure of the datastore that has to hold all the data as well as for the interaction design of the software.

[12] G. Zappella, *Le marche dei tipografi e degli editori italiani del Cinquecento. Repertorio di figure, simboli e sogetti e dei relativi motti*, vol. 1: *Testo*, vol. 2: *Tavole*, Editrice Bibliografica (Milan: Editrice Bibliografica, 1986).

[13] F. Vandeweghe and B. Op de Beeck, *Drukkersmerken uit de 15de en 16de eeuw binnen de grenzen van het huidige België* (Nieuwkoop: B. de Graaf, 1993).

SGML for structure and semantics

The CD-ROM, the printed catalogue as well as the hypertext system all derive from a single file datastore that reflects the above-mentioned structure. It consists of records that still preserve the data format but are now expressed in a so-called 'tagged format' file, using SGML markup for its overall structure and semantics. A (simplified) sample looks like this:

```
<PRINTER>
    <THES>
        <VNM> Frederik Haaring</VNM>
        <PL1> Leiden</PL1>
        <JA1> 1688–1712</JA1>
        <PL2> Amsterdam</PL2>
        <NJA2> 1710</NJA2>
    </THES>
    <STCN>
        <OCC> bookseller, 1688–1700</OCC>
        <ADR> Kloksteeg (in de), 1692; Raapenburg, op de Hoek van de
        Nonnesteeg nevens de Academie ('t), 1694–1699</ADR>
    </STCN>
    <DM>
        <NUM> 0017</NUM>
        <TXT> A man digging with a spade, in a landscape; Jahweh-tetragram; a
        laurel-branch and a palm-branch as frame</TXT>
        <NOT> 11C13; 22C31; 25F32(CROW)(+1); 25G3(OLIVE-TREE)(+22);
        . . . </NOT>
        <SP1> FAC ET SPERA</SP1>
        <SP2> Fac et spera</SP2>
        <RAN> 1690(1); 1693(1); 1695(1); 1696(1) </RAN>
    </DM>
    <DM>
        <NUM> 0182</NUM>
        <TXT> Rocky coast with beacon-light, pillars of Hercules, the sun as a
        face, ships, banderole with inscription</TXT>
        <NOT> 24A6; 25H131; 25H23241; 46C24(+63); . . .</NOT>
        <SP1> INTELLIGENTIBUS</SP1>
        <SP2> Intelligentibus</SP2>
        <RAN> 1693(1) </RAN>
    </DM>
</PRINTER>
```

(Indentation for readability only)

The SGML elements <THES>, <STCN>, and <DM> function as containers for the information in the form of 'tagged data'. They contain basic 'chunks' of information about the printers and devices. These 'chunks' are hierarchically

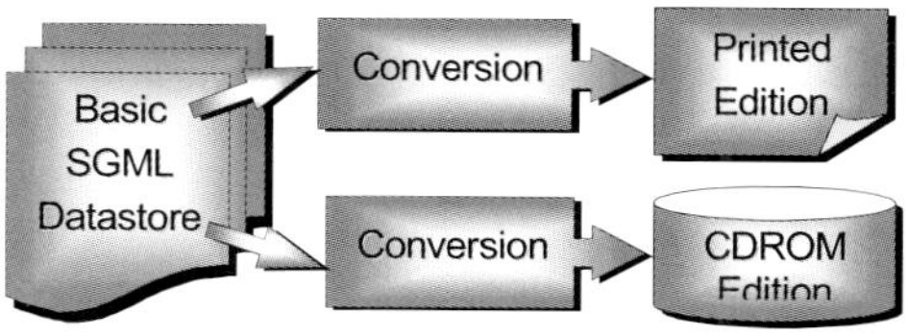

subordinated to the <PRINTER> element. The contents of the <THES>, <STCN>, and <DM> elements are as follows:

> < THES>: preferred and variant name of the printer, places and dates of activity; based on the thesaurus compiled by Gruys and De Wolf;
> <STCN>: professions, addresses, and shopsigns, if any; data derived from the holdings of the STCN database; and
> <DM>: information found on title page and in colophon, to which a description of the device is added.

A small, dedicated document type definition (DTD) was written to be able to check the file with an SGML parser. The strength of the SGML application lies in the ease with which the separate 'chunks' of structured textual data can be manipulated. This is especially convenient if new information, e.g. information originating from the STCN database, necessitates moving the description of a device to a different printer. Since <DM>-elements always contain the data we saw on (the photocopy of) title pages and colophons, attributions become immediately identifiable as such: a title page may carry two or more names, but the information is stored under only one of them.

For the book-production, the file was imported into an Inmagic database to generate all indices and check its content. The original file, again, is filtered through a pipe of small programs with the help of tools such as *Sed*, *Awk*, and *Python*. At the end of the pipeline a full-blown SGML file is generated. This file is transformed into a regular \LaTeX\ file using software based upon the model of the linuxdoc project. \LaTeX\ is used to typeset the book because the core of the catalogue consists of about 3,500 images, each with a corresponding description. Typesetting this amount of material page by page would have been a very cumbersome process, and time spent on it would have seriously reduced the time available for checking and refining the data.

The issue here is precisely the one Leslie Lamport described in *\LaTeX\ A Document Preparation System*: the time spent on typesetting material should be infinitesimal compared to the time spent on collecting it. This resulted in a three-volume, 1600 page catalogue organised into sections as follows:

Heading

- Name of the printer or bookseller
- Location: city (cities) and date(s) of activity
- Profession(s): professional specialization [printer, bookseller, etcetera]

- Address(es), shop sign(s), and notes

Device entries:

- The number of the device
- A textual description of the device
- ICO: the ICONCLASS notations used for the systematic classification of iconography;
- INI: initials that are visible on the device;
- MOT: the transcription of the motto of the device;
- RAN: the range of the use of the device by the printer or bookseller. Format: a year

For the design of the CD-ROM the conceptual datamodel was used to logically bind all the data of the different entities. For that purpose the basic SGML datastore was converted to a multi-table physical datastructure that is optimized for querying. This means that the data were finally organised in a way that allowed for redundancy if it helped to speed up the process of selecting and browsing the data or if it improved the ease of use of the CD-ROM application. The tabular data were imported in a proprietary database manager that handles all the physical data-manipulation. In the final application, the user is presented with indices on all the attributes of the three conceptual entities: printer, device, and use.

Device attributes	
NUM	Unique ID number of devices (identical to printed edition)
TXT	Free text description of device
NOT	Iconclass notations
SP1	Literal transcription of motto (case preserved)
SP2	Normalized transcription of motto [biblical location added]
SPL	Language(s) of the motto
IN1	Initials of printers, booksellers, artists
IN2	Initials interpreted (for artists: traditional interpretation)
OPM	Notes
Printer & bookseller attributes	
KEY	Unique ID number of printers & booksellers
ASDN	Preferred name, arranged by last name
VAR	Variant orthography, pseudonyms, etc.
VNM	Preferred name starting with first name
COMB	Names (more than one on title page and/or in colophon)
DRU	Preferred name, arranged by last name, no brackets
OCC	Occupations and specific qualifications
UIT	Shop signs
ADR	Addresses, usually street names
PLC	Name(s) of city/cities where shops were located
YEAR	Period(s) during which shops were active
OPM	Notes

Use attributes

KEY	Unique ID number of printers & booksellers
NUM	Unique ID number of devices (identical to printed edition)
RAN	Years in which a device was used

The software design of the CD-ROM application (proprietary to our Institute for Information Science) is conforming to the successful and well-proven concepts that have been implemented for the DISKUS series (in June 1999 more than 16 different titles). The interaction design allows a gradual refinement of user interactivity to access the overwhelming amount of data. It offers different styles for novices and experts to formulate queries.

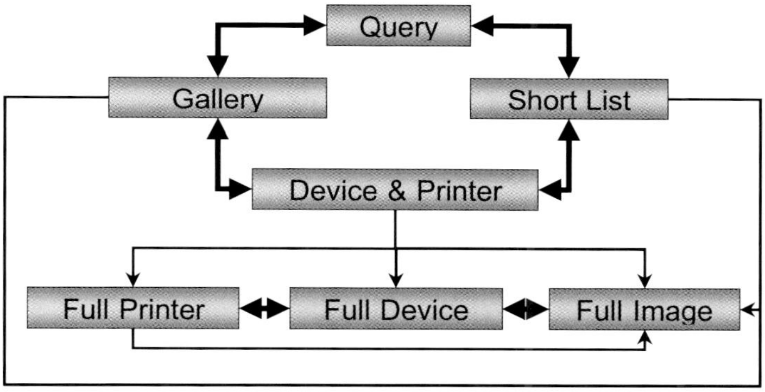

Query formulation

The interface of the Printers' devices CD-ROM presents the user first with a screen where a query can be formulated by choosing from different 'TABs' and picklists. The different 'TABs' represent the entities Printers & Booksellers and Devices and give access to the main attributes in associated picklists. In those cases where single words were derived from phrases, a KWIC index (KeyWords In Context) is available for even more detailed selection. Selection criteria can be combined with Boolean logic for complex query construction.

In expert mode the user is given additional access to all original fields (more than 20 different attributes). The user can browse through the systematic classification scheme of the full ICONCLASS hierarchy (potentially 24,000 different concepts) and can search with ICONCLASS keywords (potentially more than 18.000).

Browsing the selection

The results are presented in different layouts that coincide with different ways of scanning large amounts of data visually. One is a *gallery* with thumbnail images (imagescan only), and the second is a *short list* of selected devices, containing a thumbnail image and a basic description.

Single-entry browsing

A third way of looking at the results is by browsing single entries from the selection presented in hyper-document style: thumbnail image + related printer(s) + intermediate description and with hyperlinks to full data of printer(s), device and image.

Web of full printer & device data

From the different presentations of the query results, one can easily jump within the underlying complex relational web of printers and devices. This web has a hyper-document style of presentation and interaction:

full text with hyperlinks, multiple fonts, hotspots, inline buttons and icons;

multiple and resizable windows (the physical screensize of the monitor is the only limitation); and

all data in detail presented.

What started as a query to limit the amount of results ends in a non-limitative web of related documents about devices, printers, booksellers, woodcutters, et cetera. The user certainly does not have restricted access to this domain.

Back to the Future

To ensure they can be read in the future and on different types of computers, the data are kept in an ASCII file with SGML markup describing its structure and content. But longevity and portability are not the only arguments for choosing an SGML file as our primary method of storing information. A very important additional reason is that as an SGML file it can also function as part of the larger corpus of documents that is gradually built up as our Image & Word project progresses.

This corpus consists of both primary sources and historiographical essays that are to be made available electronically and that are interconnected through a hypertext linking structure. Among the sources that so far have been transcribed in full, marked up, and indexed iconographically are editions of Andreas Alciatus, *Emblematum libellus*, Hadrianus Junius, *Emblemata*, Paolo Giovio, *Dialogo dell'imprese militari et amorose*, Gabriele Simeoni, *Imprese heroiche et morali*, Claude Paradin, *Devises heroïques*, Johannes Sambucus, *Emblemata*, Geoffrey Whitney, *A Choice of Emblemes and other devises*, Joost van den Vondel, *Toonneel des menschelikken levens of de vernieuwde Gulden Winkel*, and Jan Moerman, *Microcosmos*. In several cases more than one edition of a text has been transcribed.

In addition to these emblem books a transcription was made of the 1730 edition of Friedrich Roth-Scholz, *Thesaurus Symbolorum ac Emblematum*, a survey of devices of European printers and booksellers, with an extensive commentary and also a short essay on printers' devices by Claude Mignault.

In a sense the title of Roth-Scholz's survey suggests a central topic we are dealing with in our own essays: the printers' device as a case of 'applied emblematics'. Central notions in the emblematic game are concepts that are also pivotal in a key text such as Erasmus's *De duplici copia verborum ac rerum*: richness, association, adaptation, imitation, paraphrase, interpretation, emulation, *loci communes*, etc. The rich and complex relations between texts, concepts, and images, caused by their continuous ordering and re-ordering, irresistibly call to mind the image of a web. Seen against the background of the Internet hype, this metaphor may appear to be a platitude. Yet, the hierarchical organisation and web-like linking structure of both Iconclass and SGML make them eminently suitable for tracing the meandering structure of early modern thought and artistic invention. Thus we consider electronic documents combining both instruments to be the natural habitat for the essays we are presently preparing. The subjects we shall deal with include: the relationship between emblems and devices, Dutch devices in a wider European perspective, Rubens's painting *The Ship of State* in the light of emblems and devices, the topography of bookselling and printing using addresses and shop signs, the meaning of trees in printers' devices, and the imagery of Labour.

The idea that book production is a laborious process has been illustrated in devices since the early stages of the printing business. One cannot help but wonder why.

Six St Jeromes: notes on the technology and uses of computer lighting simulations

SIMON NIEDENTHAL

I would like to begin with a quotation from St Bonaventure: 'Light is the substantial form of bodies; by their greater or lesser participation in light, [bodies] acquire the truth and dignity of their being'.[1] By 'bodies', Bonaventure refers not to our physical being but, rather, to matter itself; his argument takes place in the context of the great medieval metaphysics of light. In a similar vein, Robert Grosseteste begins *De Luce*, his thirteenth-century treatise on light, with the assertion that:

> Light of its very nature diffuses itself in every direction in such a way that a point of light will produce instantaneously a sphere of light, unless some opaque object stands in the way. [. . .] Corporeity [that is, the capacity of matter to take form and occupy space], therefore, is either light itself or the agent which performs the aforementioned operation and introduces dimensions into matter in virtue of its participation in light.[2]

Light is portrayed by both theologians as the mechanism by which the cosmic x, y and z axes are defined, the first of a number of intriguing echoes of medieval thought on light and optics that one encounters in digital image synthesis.

In a less metaphysical sense, an understanding of the power of light to define things underlies foundational lighting curricula everywhere (including my own). A quick survey of some notable photographs demonstrates the way in which

---

[1] Umberto Eco, *The Aesthetics of Thomas Aquinas* (Cambridge, MA: Harvard University Press, 1988), p. 110.

[2] Ibid.

light and value are central to the perception of pictorial form, surface qualities, space, and volume. Qualities of light, moreover, have the capacity to wield emotional influence through association with primal visual needs. And as with all visual experience, what we see and the way we think about light is informed by cultural traditions. As sensory phenomenon and interpretative touchstone, light yields to both scientific and cultural analysis, and serves as a useful starting point for a consideration of new applications of digital technologies to the subjects of art and architectural history.

In his seminal work *The Reconfigured Eye*, William J. Mitchell traces the development of digital image synthesis from simplest to most complex techniques, with reference to corresponding changes that occurred in painting during the Italian Renaissance and afterwards. His opening argument establishes a dialogue between photography and painting, two media with differing manners of engaging value and representing light effects. 'Synthetic-shading procedures' Mitchell writes, 'are used to develop perspective views into closer approximations to—even simulations of—photographs. (Thus they are closely analogous to the procedures Renaissance artists employed to convert line cartoons into tonal and coloured paintings)'.[3] The process of creating a digital image based on a 3D scene begins with the fashioning of a wire-frame model to express the physical boundaries of surfaces and objects. In the early days of digital image generation, the boundaries were denoted as a list of vertices in 3D Cartesian space, though now we have become accustomed to manipulating wire-frame models through interfaces as graphical representations. Once the objects and spaces of a scene have been modelled, surface characteristics are associated with each formal element, light qualities and positions are specified, and the scene is rendered. The rendering program takes into account the geometry, surface qualities, and lights of a scene and renders a two dimensional representation of that scene from a given viewpoint.

Mitchell goes on to explore digital image rendering from simple flat shading to the most complex radiosity calculations, referring along the way to artists as diverse as Reynolds, Vermeer and Paul Gauguin. The easiest way to render a surface in the computer is to simply specify a single colour for each point on the surface, but over time rendering algorithms have been refined to allow the calculation of shading and light effects of progressively greater complexity and fidelity to visual experience. One conceptual breakthrough was the development of ray-tracing. The rationale for ray-tracing is that while there are billions of light photons bouncing around in any visual environment, the ones that really matter are those that enter the eye.[4] In the ray-tracing process a virtual picture

[3] William J. Mitchell, *The Reconfigured Eye* (Cambridge, MA: MIT Press, 1992), p. 137.

[4] This insight is taken from the Lightscape Visualization System Getting Started, pp. 1–7.

plane composed of a grid of pixels is defined, and a ray is traced from an eye point through each pixel into the scene until it reaches a surface. The light environment informs the surface characteristics of each point, and the resulting hue is used to colour the pixel. This process continues until all pixels in the grid have been coloured. Ray-tracing is, as Mitchell points out, analogous to the way in which a perspective is constructed, and he quotes Leonardo:

> 'Obtain a piece of glass as large as a half sheet of royal folio paper and fasten this securely in front of your eyes, that is, between your eye and the thing you want to portray. Next, position yourself with your eye at a distance of two-thirds of a braccio from the glass and fix your head with a device so that you cannot move at all. Then close or cover one eye, and with the brush or a piece of finely ground red chalk mark on the glass what you can see beyond it'. Thus each ray [Mitchell continues] in the viewing pyramid projects a colour from a point in the scene to a point on the picture plane. . . .[5]

Besides the similarities to perspective construction, the process of projecting rays from the eye to a surface beyond is reminiscent of Euclid's theory of vision, which was considered viable at least until the optical work of Al-Hazan, though popular long into the medieval period.[6]

Although ray-traced renderings allow the simulation of more sophisticated visual phenomena, such as accurate reflections and refraction, the products of this sort of rendering still lack a sense of the real presence of light. Specifically, the interreflection and colour bleed from one surface to another are not calculated. In a room like the one in which I write this sentence, we could say that there are areas of direct illumination, where lights are shining directly on surfaces, and other areas of indirect illumination that are lit by the light bouncing from surfaces. The indirect illumination is not calculated in a ray-traced image. Practically speaking, simulating accurate light presence in a ray-traced image calls for a procedure that combines a photographic process—involving setting lights within the software—with one in which areas of light and dark value are applied directly to surfaces in a manner more analogous to painting. In the words of the old cinematographer's saw, 'if you can't paint with light, light with paint'.

So, following Mitchell's lead, I have rendered a simple scene using techniques of progressively greater complexity (fig. 1, plate 6). This is a simulation of a room with a skylight and several cubes in it, rendered under default lighting. Default lighting in *Alias* is the computer graphics equivalent of Grosseteste's formless universe. Anyone who has looked at light for a while can play around for a few minutes and produce something that demonstrates a more convincing impression of light in the environment (fig. 2, plate 7). The Phong shading

---

[5] Mitchell (as in note 3), p. 139.

[6] David Park, *The Fire Within the Eye: A Historical Essay on the Nature and Meaning of Light* (Princeton: Princeton University Press, 1997), p. 78.

algorithm appears complex, yet it renders a fraction of the effects of light in a real space. In fact, it is so limited a model that I had to paint many of the subtle shadows and gradations in this figure directly on the surfaces, rather than rely upon the algorithm's inadequate simulation of surface-to-surface interreflection.

The advent of radiosity rendering—which models light behaviour much more accurately than other rendering modes—signals a major advance in the capabilities of computer simulation (fig. 3, plate 8). Radiosity rendering derives originally from methods developed by thermal engineers in the 1960s to simulate heat transfer between surfaces, as a means of designing jet engines, among other things. In the mid-1980s, computer scientists at Cornell University began to apply these techniques to the modelling of light with the computer. Radiosity calculations are based upon the principle of conservation of energy. When light is introduced into an environment, it illuminates some surfaces directly, and, depending on surface characteristics, some of the light is absorbed and the rest reflected back into the environment. Most current renderers do not calculate the contribution of surface-to-surface interreflection to the illumination in a scene. Radiosity software models interreflection by creating a mesh which stores the illumination values associated with each surface. After distributing energy from the light sources, the algorithm checks each surface and determines which has the most energy to reflect back into the environment. The progressive distribution of light energy continues until all of the energy in the environment has been absorbed, or until the process is stopped.

Architectural historians eager to simulate unbuilt or destroyed buildings have seized upon rendering technologies of greater sophistication, and examples abound of reconstructions of everything from Frank Lloyd Wright buildings to the castle of Mad King Ludwig of Bavaria.[7] Notable works that have pioneered the use of radiosity rendering technology in an architectural context include Kent Larson's 1993 simulation of Louis Kahn's unbuilt Hurva synagogue.[8] Larson's most recent work continues the exploration of light and surface in Kahn's unbuilt projects for Scripps at La Jolla.[9] Also beautifully realised is MIT colleague Takahiko Nagakura's visualisation of Terragni's unbuilt Danteum.[10] These projects are not the rule, however, for although computer-generated images have become commonplace in recent years, just as commonplace is the absence of rich and compelling illumination qualities and surface definition.

---

[7] B. J. Novitsky, 'Reconstructing Lost Architecture', *Computer Graphics World* (December 1998), 25. See also the April 1999 issue of *CGW*.

[8] Vincent Scully, 'A Virtual Landmark', *Progressive Architecture* (September 1993), 80–87.

[9] Kent Larson, *Louis I. Kahn: Unbuilt Masterworks* (New York: Monacelli Press, 2000).

[10] These images are taken from the 1998 Siggraph reel.

Mitchell's contention that the development of techniques of digital imaging is analogous to painting procedures is both encouraging and problematic: encouraging because it suggests that processes we are currently engaged in can be informed by art history; problematic because it fails to address significant differences between digital and analogue. Making precise distinctions is central to thinking critically about media, yet we continually witness the bleeding of art terminology into the realm of the digital. Early on I was struck by the way in which filmic and photographic concepts were embedded in software. Consider, for example, the camera icon from Maya software (fig. 4, plate 9). But the analogies in software go far beyond the photographic. In computer graphics we refer to renderings, we employ software called Painter and Piranesi, and, while waiting for an action to be performed, my laptop executes a little version of the Mona Lisa instead of showing the usual clock face. Another amusing example of the intersection of painting vocabulary and interface design is the creation icon in 3D Studio Max, a hand with a spark at the fingertip that is a cross between Adam's creation in the Sistine Chapel and ET. But anyone who has performed a task as elementary as 'drawing' a curve in a 3D package understands just how limited are the analogies between digital and other media. I always think of defining a c.v. curve as being more like an abstract type of wood bending, of applying forces to a ductile material and editing the points until the desired profile has been achieved. Any notion of the gestural component of drawing pretty much goes out the window in 3D software.

The construction of painting space in a digital medium is one means of exploring Mitchell's painting/rendering analogy, and, in fact, the last few years have seen a number of examples. Though the simulation of a painting in 3D space is often seen as striking a blow against the ascendancy of photorealism in computer rendering, some projects seek a wider scope, including 'Rouen Revisited' by Paul Debevec at the University of California. The Rouen project uses Monet's 30 or so canvases of the cathedral as well as historical and contemporary photos, to allow a viewer to reconstruct the front façade from any number of possible viewpoints at any time of day or season. Debevec describes his project as follows:

> Fascinated by the play of light and atmosphere over the Gothic church, Monet systematically painted the cathedral at different times of day, from slightly different angles, and in varied weather conditions. Each painting, quickly executed, offers a glimpse into a narrow slice of time and mood. We are interested in widening these slices. . . .[11]

[11] From Paul Debevec's Home Page, alberti.cs.berkeley.edu/~debevec/. Another project involving the 3D reconstruction of a painting space is the stomach-churning fly-through of Van Gogh's Yellow Room on the artmuseum.net web site: www.artmuseum.net/vangogh/3dloginpage.asp

While this project undoubtedly advances the technology of image generation, it raises questions about the uses of digital construction. Architecture at least aspires to three dimensions in its built form. There are many reasons that the Kahn and Terragni projects, for example, remained unbuilt—often financial ones—but there is still something to be learned about the modulation of light that can be usefully approximated by computer simulation. Construction of painted architectural space is a bit more problematic. After all, a painting is quite content to remain in two dimensions.

I would argue that 3D simulation of painting space is useful when it goes beyond merely expanding the subject to another dimension and instead adds an additional facet to our understanding of the work at hand. Applying photo-realistic simulations of light behaviour to a painting can serve, for example, as a means of throwing the painter's value choices into relief. Thus the tasks of the 'Six St Jeromes' project: first, to reconstruct some of the intellectual context of a painting, and, second, to rethink the dangers, uses, and legitimate pleasures of this sort of simulation. The goal of this project as it was initially conceived was to put Mitchell's thesis to the test, to collide a fifteenth-century painting with the most recent rendering technology, and to see what emerges.

Antonello da Messina's 'St Jerome in his Study' (National Gallery, London) dates from somewhere between 1450 and 1475 (fig. 5, plate 10); there seems to be some uncertainty as to whether the painting represents Antonello's early work, or was produced during his later stay in Venice.[12] The French novelist Georges Perec, who kept a print of the painting on his wall, nicely grasped the snug bookishness of the study. 'The whole space' Perec writes,

> is organized around the piece of furniture (and the whole of the piece of furniture is organized around the book). The glacial architecture of the church (the bareness of the tiling, the hostility of the piers) has been cancelled out. Its perspective and its vertical lines have ceased to delimit the site simply of an ineffable faith; they are there solely to lend scale to the piece of furniture, to enable it to be inscribed. Surrounded by the uninhabitable, the study defines a domesticated space inhabited with serenity by cats, books and men.[13]

The St Jerome painting offers itself for several reasons. First, because da Messina was among the first Italian artists to work with oil paints and glazes, and the new materials allowed him a greater range of tonal and light effects. He was also active in a period in which the changes documented by Mitchell were becoming fully felt. Moreover, the painting responds well to conceptions of light in the art theory of da Messina's contemporaries like da Vinci.

---

[12] Cf. N. Little, 'A Note on the Date of London "St Jerome in his Study" by Antonello da Messina', *Arte Veneta* (1976), 154–55.

[13] Georges Perec, *Species of Spaces and Other Essays* (New York: Penguin, 1997), p. 86.

The project began with the construction of a wireframe model of St Jerome's study, corresponding to the perspective of the painting (figs. 6 and 7, plates 11 and 12). A preliminary shaded version of the scene with default lighting and basic texturing (fig. 8, plate 13) was brought into Lightscape software for radiosity processing. Once the model was set up in an environment that roughly corresponds to the illumination qualities in the painting, it became possible to begin a quick series of 'what if?' renderings: what would it look like if sunlight was coming from the other side? (fig. 9, plate 14). What if the light coming in the doorway was very cool and flat? (fig. 10, plate 15). What if soft light was coming in exclusively from the clerestory windows above? (fig. 11, plate 16). What if Jerome decided to burn the midnight oil? (fig.12, plate 17).

At this point it struck me that I had achieved only a sort of inverse appreciation of the light of the painting. That is, none of my variations seemed as satisfying as the light in the original. So in my fifth and sixth versions of St Jerome I attempted to reconstruct the lighting environment suggested by the painting (fig.13, plate 18), and used whatever techniques necessary to replicate the values on the surfaces (fig. 14, plate 19). In doing so, I learned that the painting manifests a close relationship to theories on painting and light of near contemporaries like da Vinci. The painting exhibits, of course, a wonderful chiaroscuro, as defined by Leonardo:

> The first intention of the painter is to make a flat surface display a body as if separated from this [picture] plane, and he who most surpasses others in this skill deserves most praise. This accomplishment, with which the science of painting is crowned, arises from light and shade, or as we may say chiaroscuro.[14]

Further, the treatment of the saint's face echoes other writings of Leonardo on the rendering of facial form:

> The utmost grace in the shadows and the lights is added to the faces of those who sit in the darkened doorways of their dwellings. Then the eye of the beholder observes the shaded part of the face thrown into deeper shade by the shadows from the aforesaid dwellings, and sees brightness added to the illuminated part of the face by the radiance of the atmosphere. Because of such increases in the shadows and light the face acquires great relief. . . .[15]

Besides his 'St Jerome', Antonello's portraits also frequently demonstrate this strategy. In his treatise on light in Renaissance theories of art, Moshe Barasch distinguishes two schools of thought on the concept of illumination. In the first, a 'functional' conception, the major task of light is to illuminate bodies and render them visible, while the function of shadows is to produce relief and the semblance of corporeality. The second approach emphasises the relation of light

---

[14] Mitchell (as in note 3), p. 139.

[15] Ibid, p. 143.

to contents and themes.[16] 'St Jerome in his Study' responds to both of these conceptions. Close scrutiny reveals careful delineation of the form of the desk, apparent in the touches on the panel that do not reference the suggested light environment—gradations, for example, where one surface meets another. And as we have seen, the treatment of Jerome's face echoes da Vinci's advice on how to make a body emerge from the picture plane. But the presence of light in the painting also references iconographic themes. In her study of the painting, Penny Howell Jolly notes the presence of Marian symbolism and the similarities of the Jerome painting to an Annunciation. 'Like Mary at the Annunciation', Jolly writes, 'Jerome is bathed in a celestial light and visited by a divine presence'.[17]

Ultimately this project suggests possible uses for radiosity rendering as a tool of art scholarship. One could use computer simulation and radiosity processing to check a 2D representation against a 3D structure upon which it was based, to help visualise the behaviour of light and simulate the space of unbuilt or lost projects, to aid in the process of conservation or historic preservation, or to study the illumination environment of works of art. This is especially useful in cases where the conditions of illumination in a space have altered over time.

As a field of study in itself, however, computer-generated light has barely been explored. One good critical touchstone to apply to the generation of new digital projects is the question: could this project have been done if the computer did not exist?[18] Could it even have been thought of? One thing that sets computer simulations apart from light in real space is the light algorithm itself, and gaining an understanding of computer-generated light calls us to contemplate the differences between the algorithm and real light behaviour. For example, one unique quality of light produced by algorithm is that the algorithm can be reversed: if the intensity of a source in most 3D packages is set to a negative number, the source extracts light from the scene. 'The light that shineth in darkness' becomes 'the light that shineth darkness', inverting the process with which I opened this paper: 'Light of its very nature diffuses itself in every direction in such a way that a point of light will produce instantaneously a sphere of light'. . . . The capacity to simulate the inverse of light behaviour—to create spheres of darkness—is clearly one path to explore with algorithmic light, and offers the possibility of new modes of spatial visualisation that philosophers like Grosseteste could never have conceived.

---

16 Moshe Barasch, *Light and Colour in the Italian Renaissance Theory of Art* (New York: New York University Press, 1978), pp. xi–xiii.

17 Penny Howell Jolly, 'Antonello da Messina's St Jerome in his Study', *Art Bulletin*, 65 (June 1983), 252. Jolly's argument is based upon a reading of Jerome's Epistle 22 to Eustochium, in which Jerome counsels imitation of Mary as the basis for conduct.

18 I am indebted to an editorial by John Lansdown in *Leonardo Magazine* (1998) for this test.

The Lincoln CD-ROM Project: history, theory, conservation, and images

PHILLIP LINDLEY

The last two decades have seen paradigm shifts within Art History. Two are of particular relevance here. First is the macro-theoretical reconfiguration of the academic discipline of Art History, for the subject's intellectual boundaries have been challenged and redefined by a generation impatient with inherited assumptions about the nature of Art and the tasks of the art-historian.[1] Whilst art historians have sought to include wider fields of visual culture within their study, so have other academic disciplines also begun to deploy visual imagery as evidential material with increased sophistication; now, art historians often need to understand and adopt *their* methodologies. Inevitably, given the relatively small numbers of art historians and the increasingly wide spheres of their activity, this has led to some changes in the core methodologies that define art history. Medievalist art-historians today sometimes seem to have more in common theoretically with historians and archaeologists working in the same period than they do with other art-historians working in later chronological areas. The second transformation is technologically driven: the digitization of texts and imagery has permitted new types of questions to be posed (and answered), as texts and images can be readily accessed, analysed, and manipulated. The project with which I am here concerned stands at the intersection of these two paradigm shifts.

John Larson, the consultant conservator to the Dean and Chapter of Lincoln

---

[1] E. Fernie, *Art History and its Methods: A Critical Anthology* (London: Phaidon, 1995), provides a helpful introduction to the vast literature on the subject. See also *The New Art History*, ed. by A. L. Rees and F. Borzello (London: Camden Press, 1986).

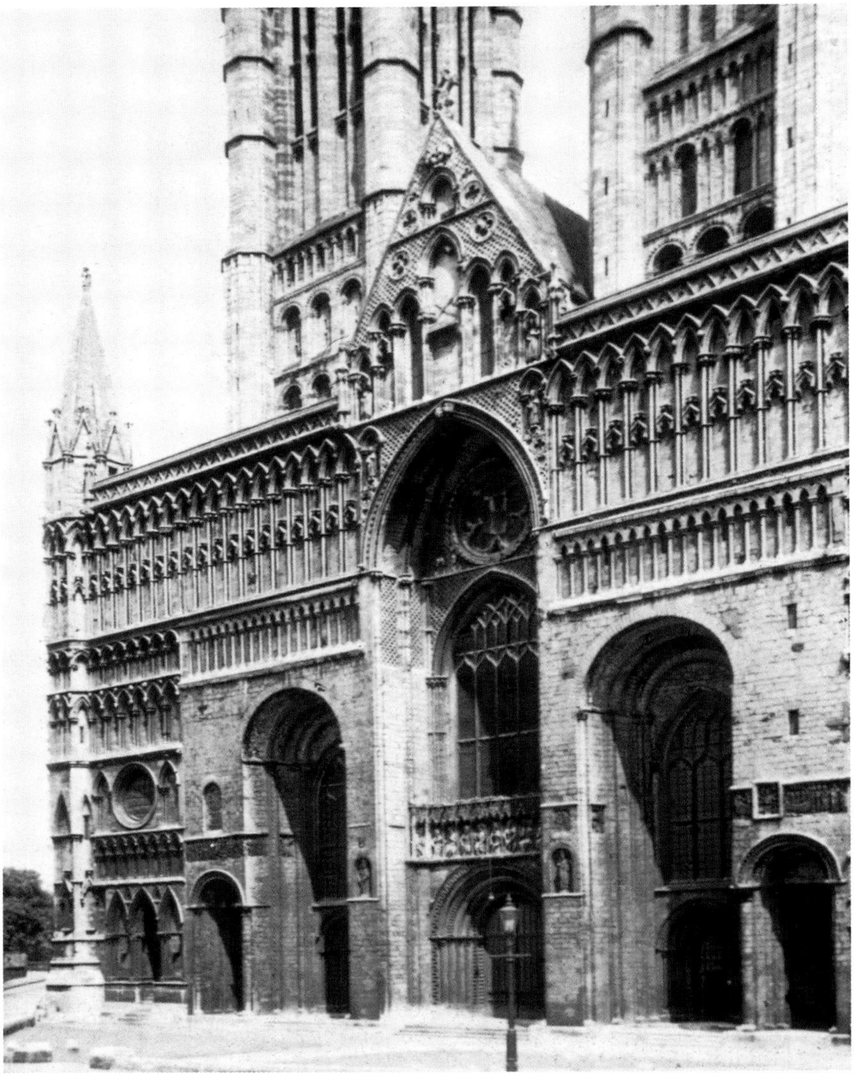

Fig. 1. The west front, Lincoln Cathedral . © National Buildings Record, London

during work on the celebrated Romanesque sculptural frieze of the cathedral's west façade (fig.1), first discussed with me the project of producing a multimedia archive of the conservation policies and work on CD-ROM in 1991–92. Two years later we were actually able to begin (January 1994). A CD-ROM is a finished product, analogous to the book, and is imbricated within the historical moment in which it was produced. This seemed important to us, given that the aim was to produce a conservation archive that would inform future debate about the conservation policies and practices which should be adopted at Lincoln and elsewhere. The choice of CD-ROM rather than WWW can also be a profound drawback because five-year-old designs look astonishingly outdated and seem slow and crude, but the medium permits a firm navigational line to be plotted, at the expense of the iterative de-privileged possibilities of the web. Moreover, six years ago it was not clear to us how the web was going to develop.

The chief objective of the Lincoln project was, then, to document the evolution of conservation policy and the progress of conservation work on the Romanesque frieze sculptures. The conservation programme has been highly contentious, with at times vitriolic debate about the methodologies to be employed for cleaning the sculpture and—when it became clear that some sculptures were in too fragile a condition to return to the façade—about the nature of their replacements and where and how the removed panels should be displayed. These issues were complicated by a weighty debate about whether architectural sculpture should ever be removed from its context and about how the meaning or meanings of the sculpture were and are affected by their placement. It has been well said that 'the history of conservation, which is rarely written, is an integral part of conservation studies', and the Lincoln CD is intended to play an important role in future conservation debate.[2]

The sculpted frieze was, at the start of the current conservation campaign, in a perilous state, a point first raised in 1976 by the doyen of Romanesque sculpture studies in England, Professor George Zarnecki. Some major losses had already occurred this century, and there is no doubt at all that without conservation there would have been further, and potentially catastrophic, structural failures. A detailed survey of the frieze took place in 1984, and the consulting architects reported on several options in 1986. A great deal of work took place in the next few years, and test cleaning started in 1987, with a major symposium convened in 1988 to debate the future conservation strategies.[3] Work on cleaning and conserving four panels began in 1989.

The CD documents the evolution of policy and the progress of conservation at Lincoln, in minute detail, up until 1994. It charts the investigations into the potential of modern technology—for instance the widely used 'airbrasive' machines—to clean the reliefs, to conserve them, and to replicate them. There

---

[2] C. V. Horie, *Materials for Conservation: Organic Consolidants, Adhesives and Coatings* (Oxford: Butterworth-Heinemann, 1987), p. vi. For an introduction to the project as originally planned, see P. Lindley and D. Emmony, 'The Romanesque Frieze of Lincoln Cathedral: Information Technology, Conservation and Archiving', *Local Historian*, 24 (1994), 83–90.

[3] See *The Romanesque Frieze and its Spectator*, ed. by D. Kahn (London: Harvey Miller, 1992).

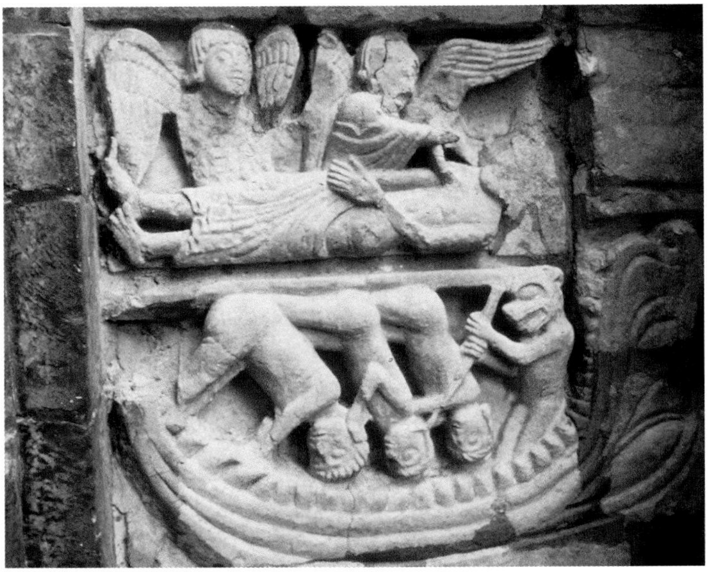

Fig. 2. 'The Death of Lazarus and Dives and his companions in Hell' (panel 8, according to Professor Zarnecki's numbering system) after 1987 cleaning. © The Dean & Chapter of Lincoln

was also considerable interest in the use of lasers to scan, clean and replicate sculpture at Lincoln.[4] The CD should therefore be of immediate relevance to the conservation, and specialist art-historical, communities. By making all this documentation available, the Dean and Chapter have demonstrated a unique and remarkable readiness to provide public access—for the first time for any English Cathedral (indeed, probably for any historic building)—to the entire process of conservation and policy formation.

A number of decisions have been taken at Lincoln, which will undoubtedly be controversial once the scaffolding has been removed. The replacement of original panels (fig.2) with modern carvings which are not 'archaeologically exact' will certainly be contentious. Modern 'copy' carvings of the panels, based on the removed originals, include reconstructions of lost details, to make the meaning of the sculptures clearer; but the 'recreation' of lost sections of reliefs, whether or not there is scholarly input into the appearance of the finished work, is problematic when much of the rest of the frieze comprises damaged originals

[4] For a convenient introduction to the subject, see now *Laser Cleaning in Conservation: An Introduction*, ed. by M. Cooper (Oxford: Butterworth-Heinemann, 1998). For the debate about conservation methods in general, see *Sculpture Conservation: Preservation or Interference?* ed. by P. Lindley (Aldershot: Scolar Press, 1997).

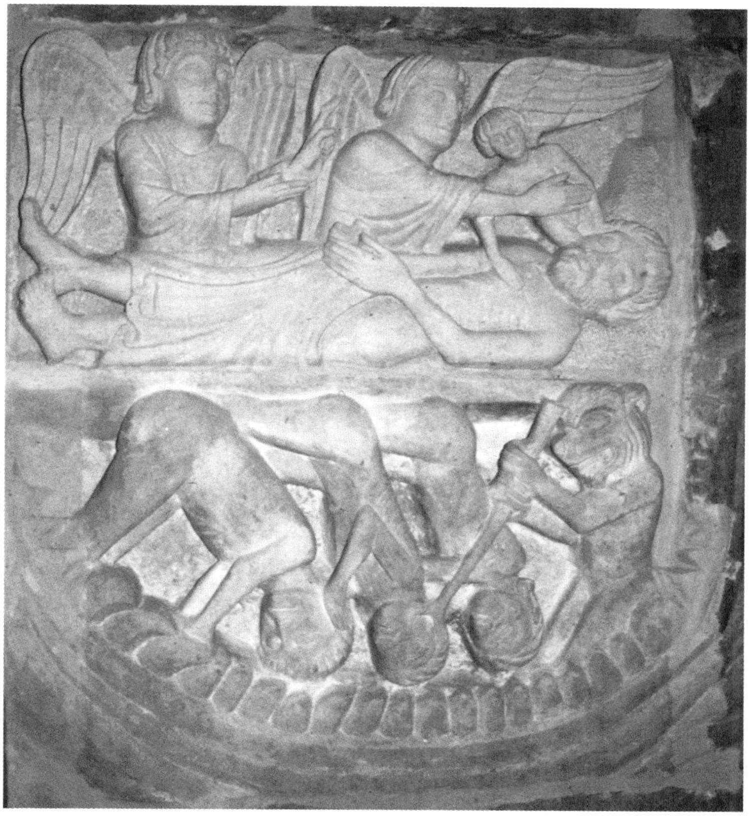

Fig. 3. 'The Death of Lazarus' block has been copied, and missing detail (e.g. the soul of Lazarus) supplied by the sculptor John Roberts. The lower block of 'Dives . . . in Hell' is also a copy carving. © *Author*

(fig. 3).[5] However, the current policy differs from the late eighteenth-century one, which resulted in a replacement panel for one of the series of 'Torments': it is more 'scholarly', and the damaged originals are being retained (fig. 4).

A research assistant, Mrs Ellen Pawley, began work in January 1994, her job being to work systematically through all the works archives at Lincoln Cathedral relating to the conservation of the Romanesque sculpture of the west front (there was, at that time, no full-time archivist for the works department), to digitize all the material and to arrange it in chronological order for publication on CD-ROM. The assembling, transcription, and digitizing of the conservation archive

[5] This point is noted in the report by John Larson, dated January 1992 and accessed from the CD's Conservation Archive, p. 55.

and every aspect of the Information Technology design were her responsibility in 1994 and 1995–96.[6] There was to be no interpretation of the evidence, which was to be assembled purely as an archive: in other words the principle of separating records from analysis was to be respected. However, in 1997 the conservation team at Lincoln imposed certain new requirements, the chief one being that although the conservation archive is still arranged as a chronological sequence (the work of Ellen Pawley) as originally planned, an introductory summary of the documentary evidence has been provided at the 'top level' of the archive. The basic point that interpretation should be distinguished from the archival evidence has not thereby been entirely abrogated, for it will throughout be possible to check my summaries against the contents of the documents themselves. Paradoxically, perhaps, the process of bringing the project to completion has imbued in me a certain scepticism about the relationship of written archives to what actually took place. It has also become clear how many decisions are made informally and are never officially recorded at all.

In order to make the conservation archive more accessible to non-specialist users, there are four brief introductory 'tours'. It should be stressed, though, that there is a profound difference between the conservation archive on the one hand and the 'tours' on the other. The conservation archive is as close as we can make it to an objective summary of all pertinent documents provided by the Dean and Chapter's conservation team, together with the complete documents themselves. The interpretative tours, on the other hand, necessarily contain my personal views and will undoubtedly need to be modified in the light of the future research. The tours comprise an introduction; a guide to the city, castle, and minster (providing an introduction to the history of Lincoln from Roman times, an account of the Castle and of the foundation of the diocese and building of the cathedral); a description of the architectural location of the frieze in the west façade of the minster; a descriptive analysis of the iconography of the frieze; and, finally, a discussion of the date and style of the sculptures, examining archaeological, structural, and stylistic matters. These tours cumulatively provide an introduction to the conservation archive itself. The archive contains a 67-page 'top-level' guide to the contents and the substantial documentary material of all kinds made available to us. It includes detailed reports by a variety of specialists commissioned by the Dean and Chapter over the years. The process of writing an introduction to these documents made it possible to compare the different assumptions of these specialists, and it becomes evident that only a holistic approach, combining the methodologies and employing all the studies of the various specialists, will satisfactorily resolve some of the outstanding questions about the frieze. In other words, the possible uses of the multimedia archive go beyond its immediate objectives, to enable new questions to be asked and,

[6] Although the design has been upgraded by Ms Kate Boardman in 1998–99, the design is essentially that fixed in 1994–95.

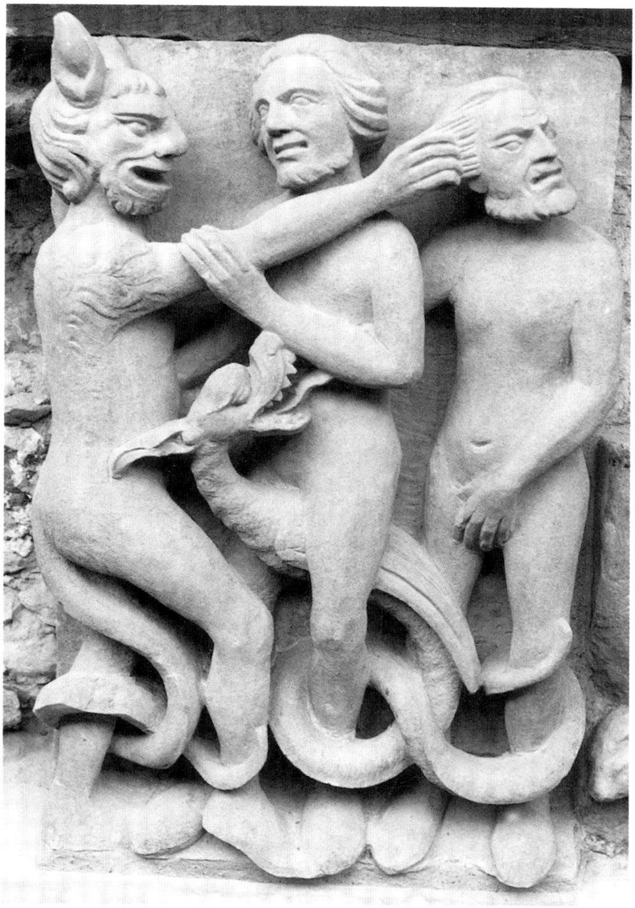

Fig. 4. Eighteenth-century 'Torments' panel after recent conservation. © Central Photographic Unit, University of Leicester

sometimes, answered. One current debate, on the date of the frieze, may illustrate this point.

Anyone writing on the Romanesque sculpture of Lincoln Cathedral is fortunate to be able to draw on the work of George Zarnecki, whose studies serve as our starting-point. Professor Zarnecki first wrote a pamphlet on the sculpture in 1963, a work which he twice revised in the 1970s and extensively revised and augmented in 1988, taking account of the work of others, most notably that of Professor Eric Fernie and Dr Richard Gem.[7] There has also been important work

[7] G. Zarnecki, *Romanesque Lincoln: The Sculpture of the Cathedral* (Lincoln:

by John Larson who was for a time responsible for the conservation programme as consultant to the Dean and Chapter.[8] Recent archaeological investigations have also led to radical new reappraisals of the frieze, together with equally dramatic new interpretations of the architectural context in which they belong.[9]

The west front of Lincoln Cathedral is the work of several different periods and styles. The central section of the west end was built by Bishop Remigius of Fécamp, who was appointed by the Conqueror to the country's largest see, at Dorchester-on-Thames in 1067. A council at Windsor decreed the removal of episcopal sees to large towns, and in 1072–73 Remigius moved his see to Lincoln, the site of a Norman castle built by William the Conqueror in an area enclosed by the old Roman town walls. The reasons for the removal of the see from the extreme south of the diocese to the extreme north were partly strategic (its military significance had already been grasped by the Romans), partly economic (Lincoln was a wealthy and important trading city with excellent waterborne connections with the east coast), and partly a rebuttal of the Archbishop of York's claim to a part of the diocese.

Henry of Huntingdon, who was a schoolboy in Lincoln at the end of the twelfth century, records that the church had been established in a trading area, at the top of the hill, next to the castle. Writing *c* 1129–33, he describes how Bishop Remigius:

> bought lands in the upper city itself, next to the castle which was distinguished by its very strong towers, he constructed a strong church in that strong place, a beautiful church in that beautiful place, dedicated to the Virgin of Virgins; it was to be both agreeable to the servants of God and also, as suited the times, invincible to enemies.[10]

Honywood Press, 1988), p. 8 and note 1. The first booklet was entitled *Romanesque Sculpture at Lincoln Cathedral* and was published in the Lincoln Minster pamphlets series. See also E. Fernie, 'Alexander's Frieze on Lincoln Minster', *Lincolnshire History and Archaeology*, 12 (1977), 19–28 and R. Gem, 'Lincoln Minster: Ecclesia Pulchra, Ecclesia Fortis', in *Medieval Art and Architecture at Lincoln Cathedral*. BAACT, 8 (Leeds, 1986), pp. 9–28.

[8] J. Larson, 'The Lincoln Frieze: A Problem of Conservation and Historical Investigation', in *Romanesque: Stone Sculpture from Medieval England*, ed. by B. Heywood (Leeds: Henry Moore Sculpture Trust, 1993), pp. 28–34.

[9] J. Baily, 'Lincoln Cathedral. Progress on the Romanesque Frieze', *Church Building*, 33 (1995), 16–21. Baily deploys evidence derived from Professor Lawrence Butler's unpublished report, now contained in the CD-ROM. A startling new interpretation of Bishop Remigius's 'façade' is contained in D. Stocker and A. Vince, 'The Early Norman Castle at Lincoln and a Re-evaluation of the Original West Tower of Lincoln Cathedral', *Medieval Archaeology*, 41 (1997), 223–33.

[10] *Henry of Huntingdon, Historia Anglorum*, London: Rolls Series, VI, 41, ed. by T. Arnold, p. 212; the translation is that of Gem (as in note 7), p. 9. For Henry see also the

Henry ought to know what he was talking about: he had spent his early years in the household of Bishop Robert Bloet, then became archdeacon of Huntingdon and started to write his 'Historia' at the request of Bishop Alexander the Magnificent, a work that occupied him on and off till his death in 1155.

The recent publication of Stocker and Vince's view that the west end of the cathedral was conceived as a keep containing the bishop's hall, rather than as a church façade, mean that interpretation of the structure has become very controversial. Whatever the original status of the western end of Remigius's cathedral (and even its dating is unclear now), all that apparently survives above ground of his great cathedral is the remains of the west front, damaged and palimpsested by later additions. It has a Triumphal Arch format: a major arch flanked by two smaller recesses with flanking niches (the effect was changed when the top of the central arch was removed in the mid-thirteenth century). The west front was certainly wider than the aisles of Remigius's cathedral, and it may have marked a development towards the screen façade. It seems to have been very plain, even austere in architectural design, the decoration being confined essentially to the window openings, string course, and the capitals, a very much simplified version of Corinthian. (The original entrance doorways have been removed, and there is no evidence of what they originally looked like.) It seems also to have been militarily defensible and was indeed used as a military base in the 1140s.[11]

Until the time of Bishop Alexander, the third Bishop of Lincoln, 1123–48, there appear to have been no major changes to Remigius's church. Professor Zarnecki has argued, however, that under Bishop Alexander there were four major operations on the west façade:

1. The heightening of the walls of the façade towards the west, south and north and their decoration with intersecting arches (figs. 5 and 6).
2. The building of the western towers (these, in their upper parts, now have fourteenth-century additions made by John de Welbourn, *c.* 1360–80, who also inserted the Gallery of Kings in the façade).

The other two operations Bishop Alexander is credited with undertaking are of particular relevance here. These are:

3. The insertion of three new doorways into the west façade.
4. The addition of a frieze of imagery below the string course.

Both of these works have been damaged by later changes to the façade. First, a large and extremely inventive mid-thirteenth century window was inserted above

Dictionary of National Biography, s.n.

[11] *The Historia Novella by William of Malmesbury*, ed. and trans. by K. R. Potter (London: Nelson, 1955), p. 48. For the context, see also Gem (as in note 7), p. 10.

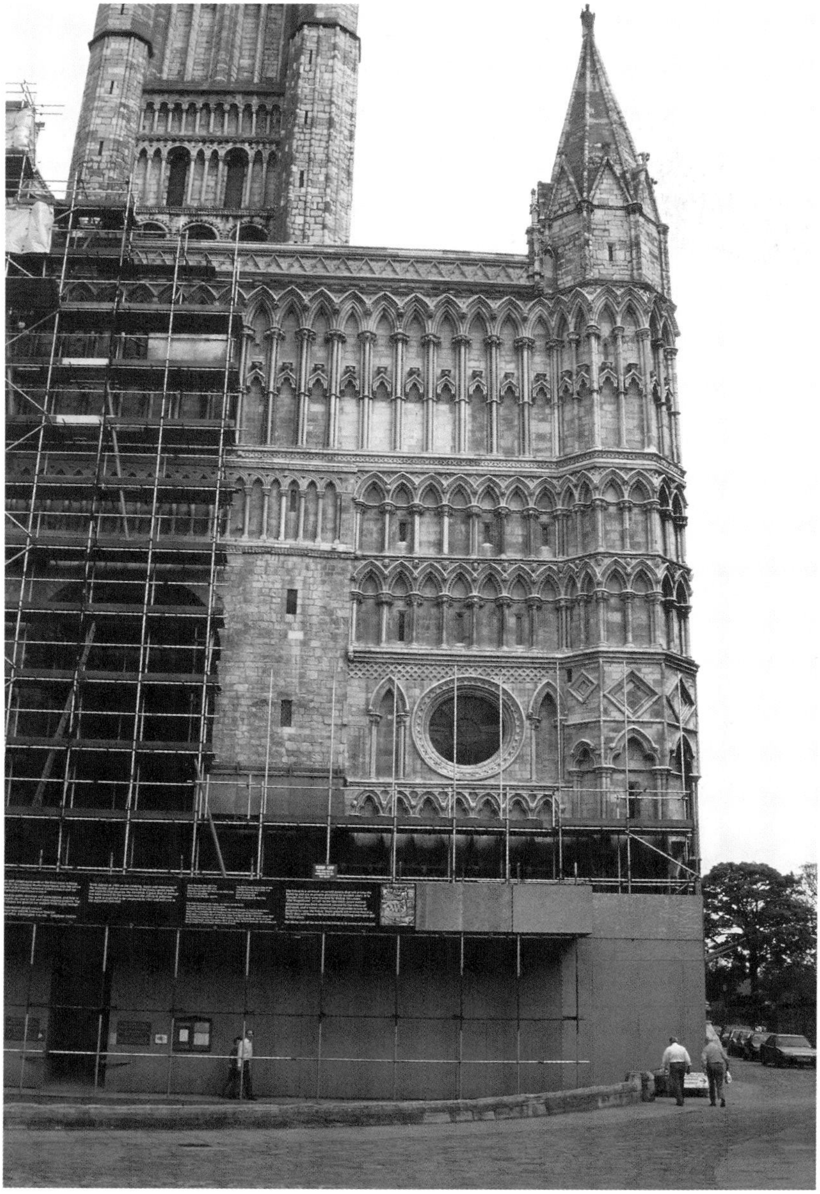

Fig. 5. South side of west façade of Lincoln Cathedral in 1994. To the right of the scaffolding in this photograph is bishop Remigius's work. Immediately above it are the intersecting arches ascribed to Bishop Alexander. The massive extension to the right and above dates from the thirteenth century. © Author.

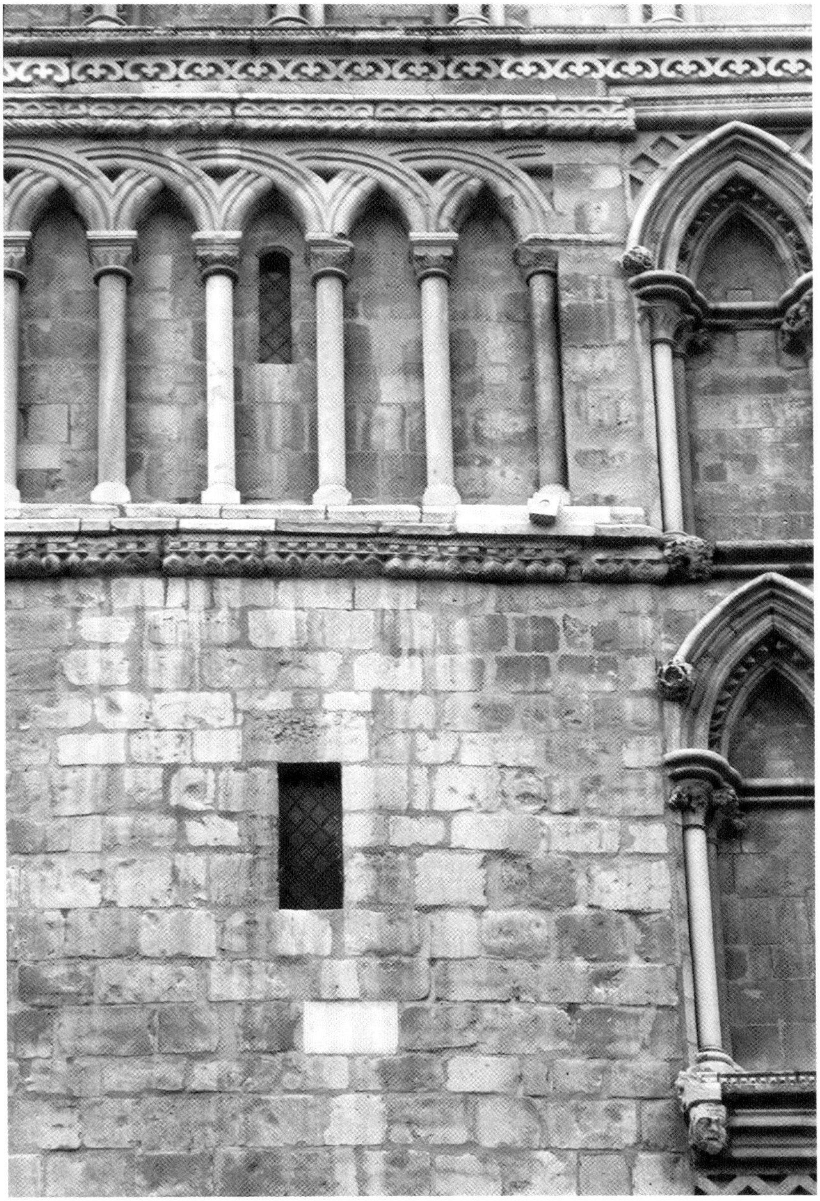

Fig. 6. Detail of the above. This shows Bishop Remigius's work with the intersecting arches ascribed to Bishop Alexander above. To the right one can just see the beginning of the thirteenth-century extension to the façade. © *Author.*

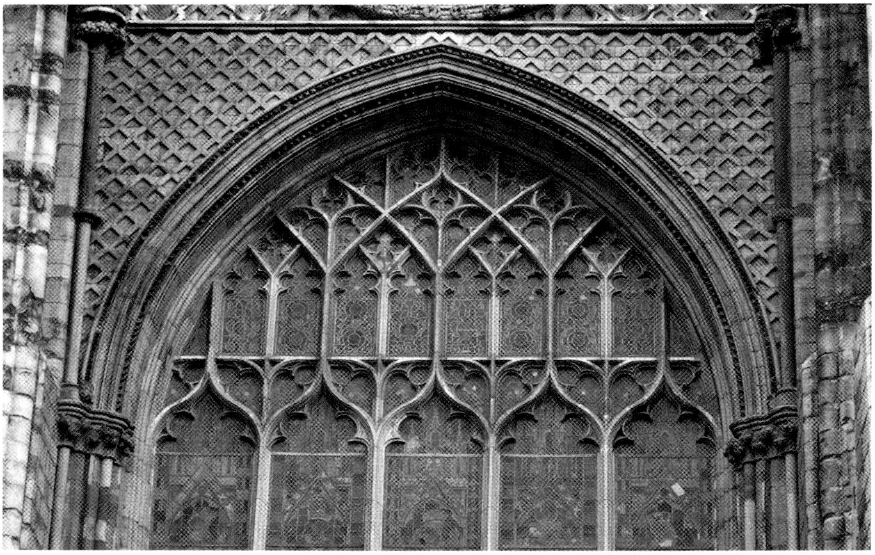

Fig. 7. Perpendicular-style window inserted by John de Welburn, in the fourteenth century, into the framework of a thirteenth-century one. © *Author*

the central doorway, almost certainly in conjunction with other major works, the massive extension to the Romanesque façade and, behind these extensions, the additions of the Morning Chapel on the north and Consistory Court on the south.[12] Then, under John de Welbourn, probably in the 1370s, three new windows were inserted, the central one sweeping away its Gothic predecessor (fig. 7). The two lateral ones will have effaced the frieze panels at this level and, even more damagingly, the splendid cycle of English monarchs was intruded above the central doorway, completely destroying whatever Romanesque sculpture was in this location. Deliberate iconoclasm at the Reformation and later restorations have also affected the frieze.[13]

It is an unhappy fact that there is no unequivocal evidence for the dating of Alexander's alterations to the west front of the church. The date and attribution of this work has to be argued primarily from stylistic evidence. It is widely agreed that Zarnecki's analysis of the doorways (fig. 8) proves their indebtedness to Abbot Suger's work at Saint-Denis.[14] *All* the stylistic evidence,

---

[12] G. Russell, 'The Thirteenth-Century West Window of Lincoln Cathedral', in *Medieval Art and Architecture at Lincoln Cathedral* (as in note 7), pp. 83–89.

[13] T. Cocke, 'The Architectural History of Lincoln Cathedral from the Dissolution to the Twentieth-Century', in ibid., pp. 148–57. See, too, idem, 'James Essex, Cathedral Restorer', *Architectural History*, 18 (1975), 12–22.

[14] Zarnecki (as in note 7), p. 32.

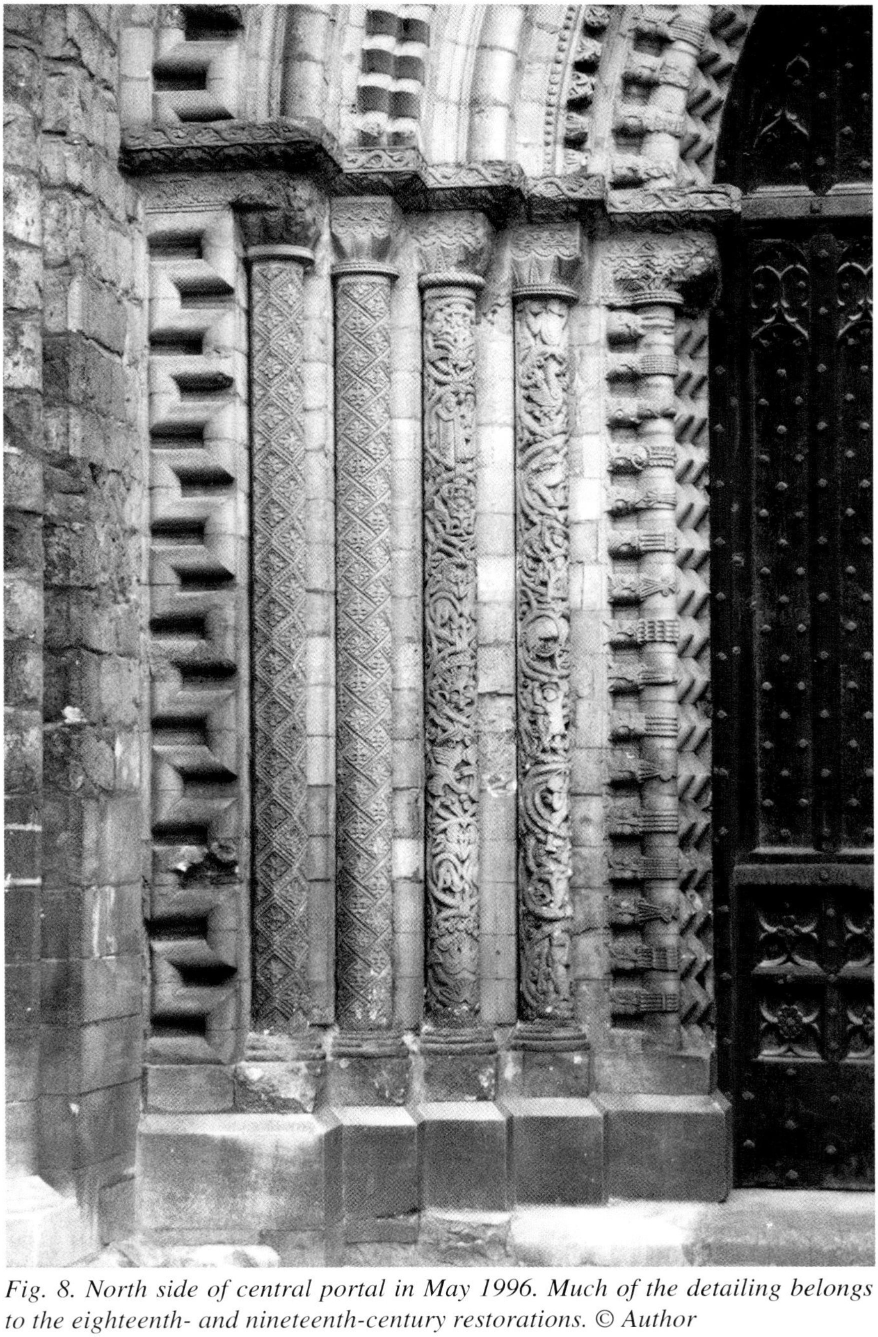

Fig. 8. North side of central portal in May 1996. Much of the detailing belongs to the eighteenth- and nineteenth-century restorations. © Author

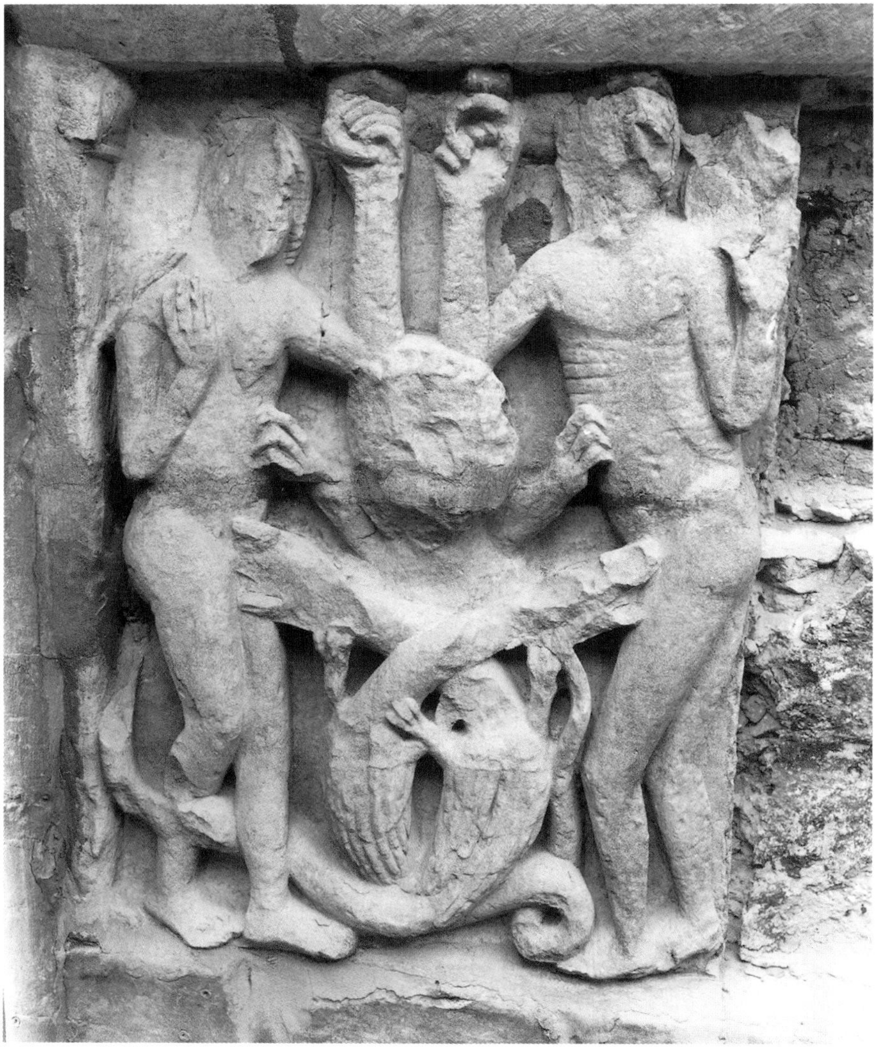

Fig. 9. The panel showing the punishment of Lust from the 'Torments' sequence on the north side of the façade, revealing the join between the panels of stone: the large dark mark above the shoulder of the right-hand figure is from the grouting treatment, designed to reinforce the west front, and carried out in the 1920s (see R. S. Godfrey, Lincoln Cathedral *, Lincoln 1930, for this process). © Central Photographic Unit, University of Leicester.*

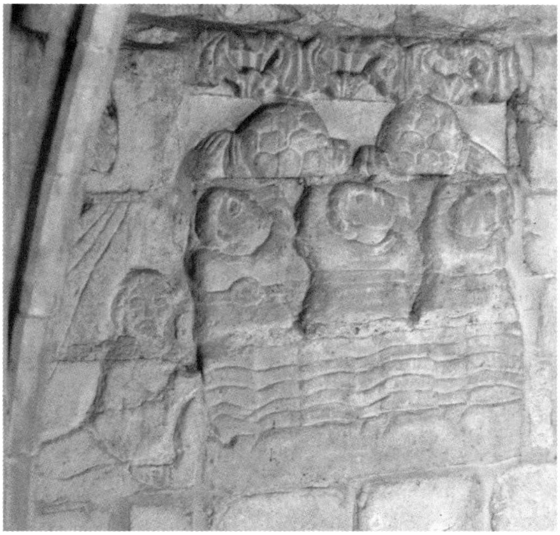

Fig. 10. 'The Deluge' and 'Giants' (panels 16 and 17) in the Ringers' Chapel. The sculptures are unfinished and out of narrative sequence. They are carved on three horizontal pieces of stone each. © Author

particularly that which relates the portal detailing to Abbot Suger's Saint-Denis, indicates a terminus post quem of 1140 for them.

One interesting feature of these lavish doorways is the lack of any sculpted tympana, something at odds with their stylistically up-to-date French-influenced features. A possible reason for this absence is that Alexander had decided to confine the main iconographic thrust of the west front to a series of frieze panels at a higher level. The general iconographic scheme on the south is devoted to Old Testament scenes and on the north to New Testament parables and an expanded Last Judgement (though not all the scenes read in the same direction in the latter series). The narrative order is usually assumed to read out from the centre to the sides, but the loss of the most important parts, over the central doorways, makes any overall reconstruction tentative to say the least.[15]

Recent analysis of the stone types has revealed that Zarnecki was wrong in assuming that the panels were carved from the same material as the surrounding ashlar—in fact, those that have been analysed seem to have been usually carved

---

[15] Ibid., chapters 5 and 6. For a challenge to his reading, see C. Frugoni, 'Modène-Lincoln: un voyage manqué', *Etudes et Lettres* (1985), 25–52. Professor Zarnecki has kindly sent me a copy of his yet unpublished paper delivered in 1996, in which he convincingly rebuts her arguments. I had come to similar conclusions in my CD-ROM text.

on end-bedded Ancaster stone blocks quarried some 20 miles away[16]—but he was surely right in dating the frieze to the same period as the doorways. There are detailed similarities: the foliage of the 'Adam and Cain' panel, for instance, is very like that of the north doorway capitals, and a lion on a colonette now ex situ is like those on the 'Daniel' panel.[17]

Professor Zarnecki argued that the panels were carved in a shop probably in the cathedral precincts, where generally two or more stones were dressed to shape in preparation for carving, the divisions within scenes generally being horizontal (fig. 9).[18] This was not an invariable rule: the punishment of 'Avarice' (panel 3, following Zarnecki's numbering system), for instance, is carved on a single panel; exceptionally the panels in the Ringers' chapel (the 'Deluge' (panel 16) and 'Giants' (panel 17)) are carved onto three horizontal stones (fig. 10). Very importantly, these last panels are both unfinished and in the wrong narrative place, which indicates that there was a major disturbance to the frieze before it was put in place.[19] Professor Zarnecki has shown that the present placing of 'Noah Building the Ark' (panel 13) (fig. 11) exposes the left edge of the two slabs on which the relief is carved and could only have been the result of a change of plan. Moreover colonettes with capitals are carved at the left side of 'Noah building the Ark' (fig. 12) and on the right-hand side of 'God's covenant with Noah' (panel 15) showing that they were intended to open and close the continuous stretch of Noah narratives. The scene of 'God instructing Noah to build the Ark' (panel 12) was intended to be placed further back in the recess, separated from the first in the continuous narrative series by the respond. Then came 'Noah building the Ark' and a lost or unexecuted scene such as 'Noah putting the animals into the Ark' (so long as it were a narrow panel). Then would have come the 'Deluge' (panel 16) and the 'Ark on the waters'. This is to assume that the sculptors worked to a brief which required them to fill the space where there was an opening in the front, which is now filled by the 'Daniel' panel (panel 14), placed totally out of sequence. Zarnecki argues that it was moved here in the 1240s when the new Gothic window was inserted.[20]

---

16 Panel number 3, 'Avarice', seems to have been carved in Lincoln limestone, as is the frame of the 'Daniel' relief. The unpublished petrotrographical report, by D. P. Jefferson (1991), is in the CD-ROM. An earlier report (1988), by R. Sanderson, is also in the CD-ROM.

17 Zarnecki (as in note 7), plates 37 and 38.

18 Ibid., pp. 36–37.

19 Fernie (as in note 7), pp. 25–26.

20 Zarnecki (as in note 7), pp. 55–58. He further argues that, originally, over scenes of the 'Creation' and 'Fall' was a large composition featuring a 'Tree of Jesse' on one side and 'Daniel' on the other, flanking a 'Coronation of the Virgin'. Fragments of 'Christ in Majesty' and 'St. Paul' found in 1832, he believes, were originally associated with the frieze above the north doorway.

Recently a good deal of criticism has been levelled at Zarnecki's account of the frieze. Almost all this evidence has resulted from the conservation campaign, which thus far has been confined to the northern panels. Zarnecki argued that five courses of the masonry from Remigius's front were cut away for the reception of the frieze.[21] It has been pointed out that more of the scenes than he had allowed for were partially cut onto the pre-existing ashlar of the front. This tended to indicate they were sculpted partially, at least, in situ: this is particularly clear in the case of 'The Death of Lazarus' and 'Dives in Hell' (panel 8), where the Hell Mouth is continued onto the ashlar (fig. 2). John Larson suggested that the 'Feast of Dives' (panel 7) was a fragment of a larger panel, which had been here reused.[22] He also argues that the 'Harrowing of Hell' (panel 4) and 'Elect in Heaven' (panel 5) are original to Remigius's façade, and thus apparently favours an eleventh-century date for them.[23] He demonstrated that at the corner, at the junction of the 'Harrowing of Hell' and the 'Elect in Heaven', the blocks of stone overlapped, showing that they could only have been carved in situ (fig. 13).[24] In the case of the 'Feast of Dives', the scene is continued onto the drip-course or 'lintel' (this is not the ashlar of the front but inserted Ancaster material, according to Dr. Jefferson) and one block, at the bottom left, is part of the ashlar. 'Abraham's Bosom' (panel 6) (fig. 14) also has parts carved on blocks of ashlar (the two on the lower right).

There are clearly enormous stylistic variations in the panels, and several different hands can be detected. The stylistic distinctions between 'Abraham's Bosom' on the north side and 'Adam and Cain' (panel 10) (fig. 15) on the south, for instance, are so great that it has been asked whether such differences can be accommodated within a stylistic frame of just a few years.[25] An important but still unpublished report by Professor Lawrence Butler in July 1993 argued, on the basis of his investigation of the mortar behind four panels which had been removed and two which were still in situ though with side elevations exposed—'the eighteenth-century panel' 3a; 'Avarice' (panel 3); 'Sodomy' (panel 2); 'Harrowing of Hell' (panel 4); 'Feast of Dives' (panel 7); 'Death of Lazarus' and 'Dives in Hell' (panel 8)—that the panels, core, and surrounding stones were all part of one building operation. One implication is either that the carvers, if they were twelfth-century craftsmen, were working on pre-existing panels which had

---

[21] Ibid., p. 37.

[22] Larson (as in note 8), p. 31.

[23] Ibid., p. 33

[24] This had already been noted by Zarnecki (as in note 7), p. 38.

[25] Larson (as in note 8), p. 33, citing also earlier commentators who viewed the reliefs as Anglo-Saxon in origin.

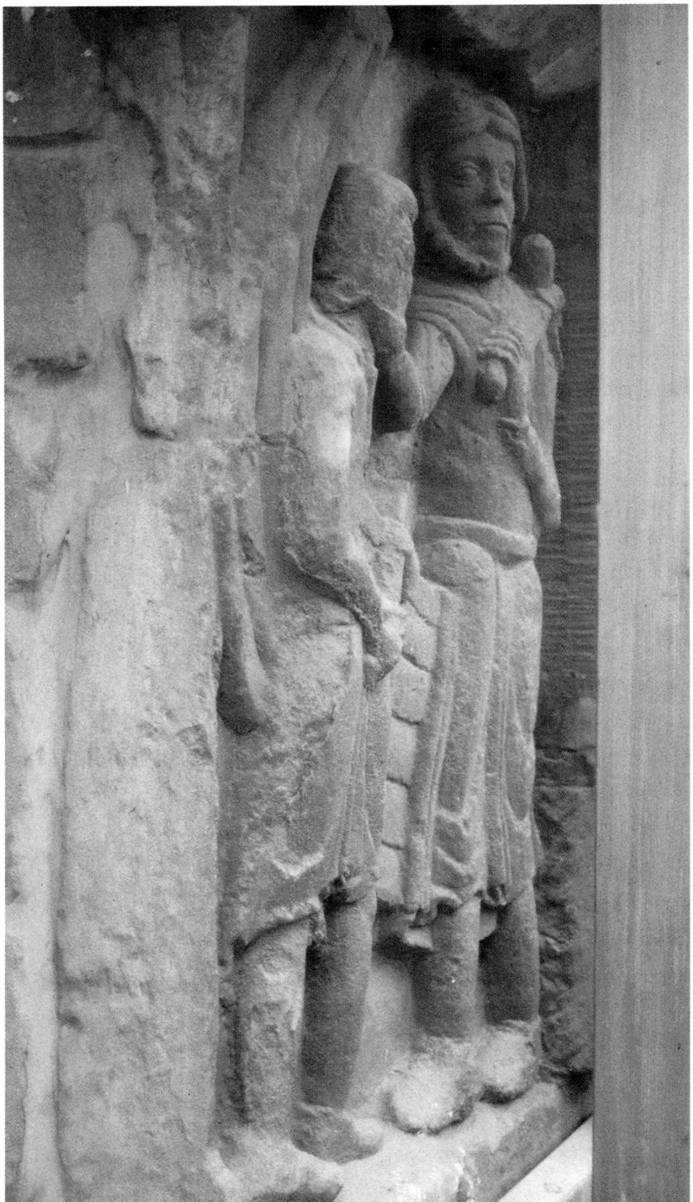

Fig. 11. View of left-hand side of 'Noah building the Ark' (panel 15) (photo taken in 1996), revealing the exposed side of the slab. © Author.

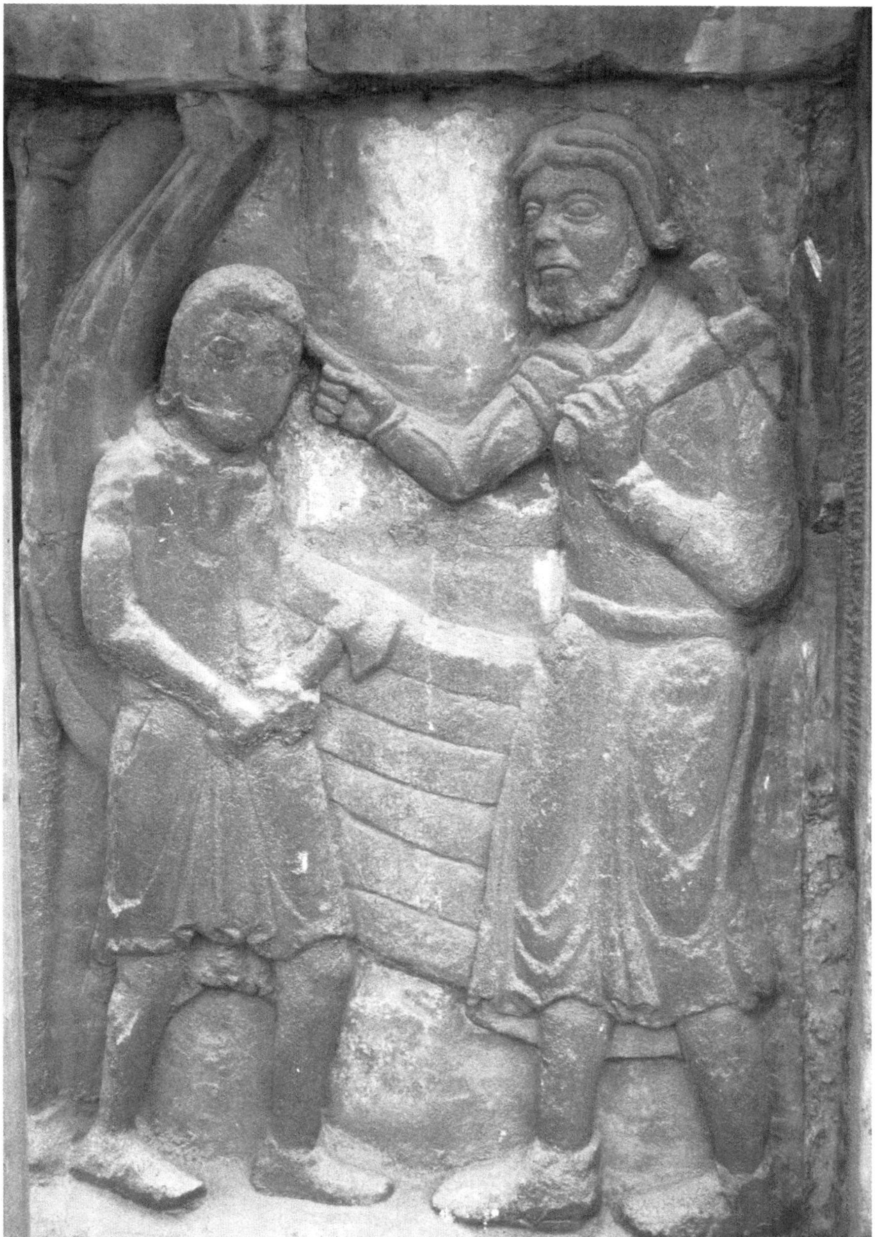

Fig. 12. Frontal view of 'Noah building the Ark' (panel 15), showing colonette and capital on its left-hand side (photo taken in 1994). © Author

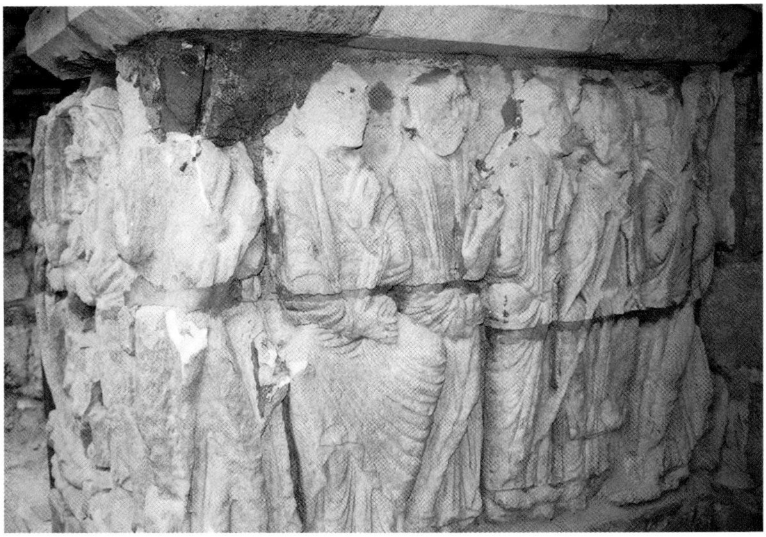

Fig. 13. Junction between 'The Harrowing of Hell' and 'The Elect in Heaven' (panels 4 and 5), showing that figures from both scenes are carved onto the same corner blocks. © Author

been placed in this location by Remigius's workmen,[26] or that the work of inserting the panels was much more extensive than has been supposed. Although Professor Butler did not pursue the argument further, Dr John Baily recently suggested that the panels may even have been collected over a long period, perhaps by Remigius as well as Alexander, 'by sending carvers they discovered on their travels back to Lincoln with a commission to cut some panels'.[27]

Much more investigative work must take place before such issues can be resolved: does the composition and consistency of the mortar behind the reliefs *really* indicate the latter were all put in place in the same period that the façade was built? Professor Butler's report inadvertently provides evidence that mortar changes between 1090 and 1140 cannot confidently be discriminated because he assumes, following Professor Zarnecki, that the top, 'lintel', block of the 'Feast of Dives' (panel 7), showing architectural canopies, was originally the string course of Remigius's façade (fig. 16). 'There is no difference in the fawn mortar,

---

[26] There is, of course, Anglo-Saxon precedent for architectural frieze sculpture: see M. Biddle, 'A Late Saxon Frieze from the Old Minster', *Antiquaries Journal*, 46 (1966), 329–32; D. Kahn, 'Anglo-Saxon and Early Romanesque Frieze Sculpture in England', in *The Romanesque Frieze and its Spectator* (as in note 3), pp. 61–74.

[27] J. Baily, 'Lincoln Cathedral: Progress on the Romanesque Frieze', *Church Building*, 33 (1995), 20.

which attached [the lintel] to the core', he comments, 'from that which attached the stones of the course above, the stones of the panel and the stones of the base course below'. Jefferson's petrological analysis, also in the CD-ROM's conservation archive, argues that this lintel is a replacement for a section of original string course and he believes it was inserted at the same time as the panels below it.[28]

The evidence of an interpretative mistake made by the sculptor responsible for carving a single block of ashlar at the bottom left of panel 7 (fig. 16) also suggests that the Ancaster panels were insertions. The sculptor carved draperies of one of Dives' companions when the block should have been carved as part of the tablecloth: this suggests that the sculptor responsible for the rest of the relief did not carve this ashlar block. The Ancaster panels were probably, then, insertions, with the ashlar subsequently carved by another sculptor in situ. Had *all* the relief been carved in situ, no such mistakes would have taken place. It anyway seems rather unlikely that the large blocks of end-bedded Ancaster stone on which the reliefs are carved could have been built into the façade during Bishop Remigius's construction of the west front rather than inserted during Bishop Alexander's episcopate (fig. 1). Modern architectural and archaeological analyses of Remigius's building have stressed its plainness and military air: it seems improbable that it also featured, or was planned to feature, a sculptural programme, the only possible reason for the placing of the Ancaster slabs. Whatever the case, it is clear that further technical analysis is essential, on the southern run of panels, to help resolve such questions. Updated versions of the CD-ROM should incorporate this new research.

It is possible that the putative historical context of the carving of the reliefs can explain their stylistic and iconographic anomalies. It seems unlikely that the panels were put in place whilst Bishop Alexander was still alive, for it is difficult to believe that the patron would tolerate such changes as were introduced when the Ringers' Chapel reliefs were left out of their proper narrative place.[29] The fact that the latter sculptures were also left unfinished suggests that they were simply inserted in a hurry, with little concern for narrative coherence. Historical evidence provides a context both for Bishop Alexander's commissioning of the works and for the failure to install them in his lifetime. Between Bishop Alexander's appointment in 1123 and 1139, the bishop with his cousin, Nigel, Bishop of Ely (1133–67), and his uncle, Roger, Bishop of Salisbury (1107–39),

---

[28] 'It appears more likely that a lintel made of oolite was inserted beneath the window for the full width of the panel, prior to the removal of the ashlar where the panel was to be inserted. This lintel could then have been carved in situ'.

[29] Cf. Zarnecki (as in note 7), p. 58: 'One is bound to say that the evident muddle in the present order of the southern section of the frieze strongly suggests that the original team of sculptors left before completing their work and that the reliefs were put up by masons unequal to the task'; Fernie (as in note 7), p. 27.

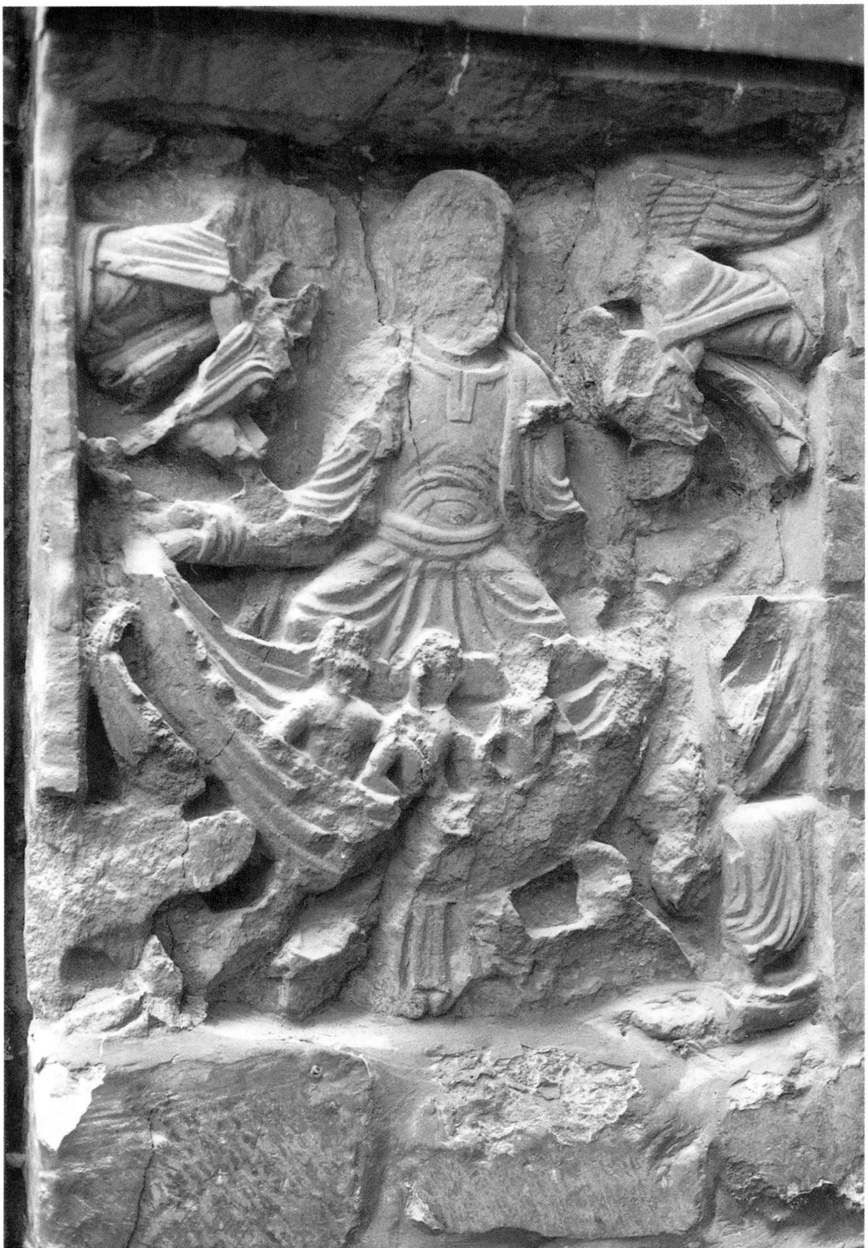

Fig. 14. 'Abraham's Bosom' (panel 6). Note that part of the scene (lower right hand side) is carved onto the ashlar of the west front. © Author

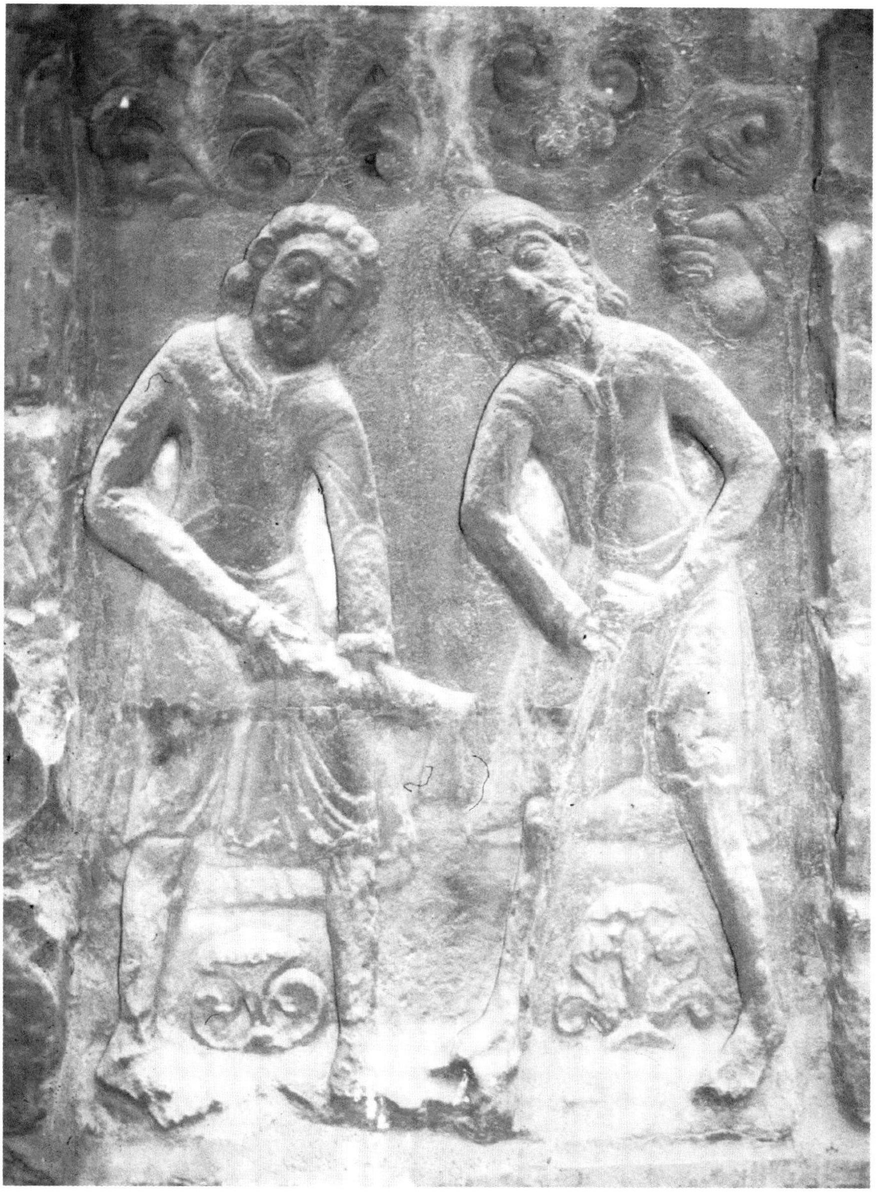

Fig. 15. 'Adam and Cain' (panel 10). © Author

were enormously powerful figures at court. Stephen's accession at the end of 1135 was greatly aided by Bishop Roger's procurement of the treasury on his behalf.[30] The trio acquired considerable power, which collapsed when in 1139 they were all arrested. The contemporary author of the 'Gesta Stephani' portrayed Alexander and his kinsmen as bishops who 'went back [. . .] humble and downcast, stripped of their empty and ostentatious splendour, to hold their church property in a manner which befits a churchman'. Before, Alexander had been a great builder of castles, now he began to found religious houses, all in the period 1139–41.[31]

In the complicated period of the anarchy, when so many magnates changed allegiance to protect or enhance their own interests, Alexander was soon given an opportunity to re-establish himself in King Stephen's favour. Around Christmas 1140, the keep of Lincoln castle was seized by Ranulph Earl of Chester and his half brother William of Roumare. Alexander reported the action to Stephen. Stephen marched on Lincoln where he was received by the bishop and invested the castle. According to William of Malmesbury the king 'made a castle of the church of the blessed Mother of God in Lincoln' [Ecclesiam beate Dei genetricis de Lindocolino incastelaverat] (a phrase used of other churches at the time e.g. Bridlington), but Ranulph escaped, joined Stephen's other opponents, marched on Lincoln, took the king prisoner, and sacked the city on 2 February 1141.[32] Lincoln was again the scene of warfare in 1144, though this time, apparently, the cathedral was not used. It seems possible, then, that Bishop Alexander's work on embellishing the cathedral will postdate 1141 and might even follow 1144. This would allow only four years until his death in 1148, and given that he was abroad in 1144 and 1147, it is highly probable that the frieze sculptures were not completed at the time of his death but were hastily inserted into the façade with some parts carved in situ under his successor, Bishop Robert Bloet. Thus the difficult historical circumstances of Bishop Alexander's last decade and his death perhaps before the reliefs were finished suggests that there were already major discontinuities and disruptions to the original frieze programme when it was first put in place: it was never finished in accordance with the patron's wishes. Such an hypothesis, of course, is wholly in accord with Professor Zarnecki's stylistic analysis of the reliefs. Although the middle of a

---

30 A. G. Dyson, 'The Monastic Patronage of Bishop Alexander of Lincoln', *Journal of Ecclesiastical History*, 26 (1975), 1–24 (p. 2).

31 Ibid., p. 3.

32 Bishop Alexander, who had celebrated mass for the royal army, followed the lead of Bishop Henry of Blois and joined Matilda's court at Winchester. In September 1141 the king's party exchanged Earl Robert of Gloucester, who had been captured by them, for the king. See also P. Dalton, 'In Neutro Latere: The armed neutrality of Ranulf II Earl of Chester in King Stephen's reign', in *Anglo-Norman Studies, XIV, Proceedings of the Battle Conference*, ed. by M. Chibnall (Woodbridge: Boydell Press, 1992), pp. 38–59.

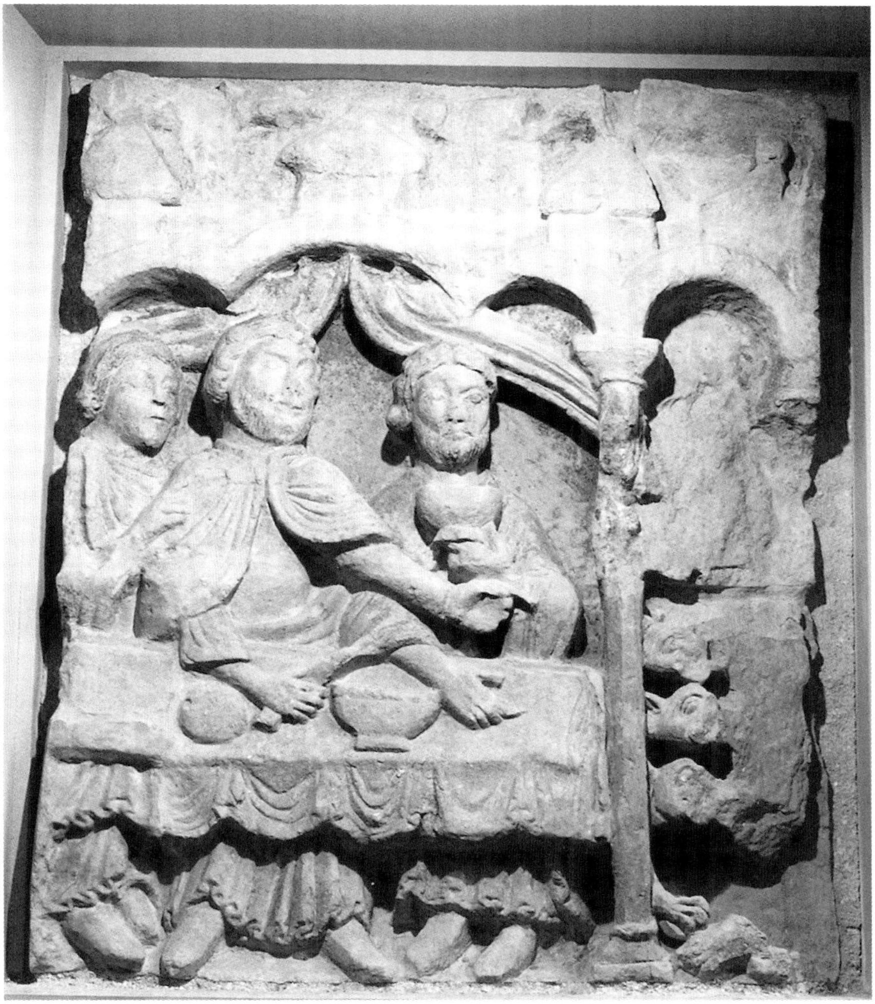

Fig. 16. 'The Feast of Dives' (panel 7) after conservation and removal from the west façade, now on exhibition in the cathedral. The top block of stone, showing architectural detailing of the canopy, is not the same ashlar as the façade masonry, but is an Ancaster stone of the same type that was used for the inserted panels carved by the sculptors (the bottom left stone in this photograph is a copy because the ashlar masonry of the façade onto which the detail was originally carved was impossible to remove with the rest of the scene). © Central Photographic Unit, University of Leicester.

major campaign of research and conservation is perhaps not the best time to advance theories about the date of the reliefs, it is to be hoped that the ready accessibility of all the information on CD-ROM will soon facilitate many new contributions to the debates about the Lincoln frieze.

The successful completion of the Lincoln CD raises some interesting general issues for the future. It is, as the Lincoln project indicates, technically possible to design a 'shell' into which textual information and imagery can be integrated for other major conservation projects. If the archive's design is agreed in advance, the difficulties of retrospective archiving experienced at Lincoln would be obviated. When large volumes of state and private money are being devoted to conservation schemes, should it not be an automatic requirement that all this information is digitally archived? Any archive—whether issued on CD or on the Web—should contain all pertinent pre-conservation reports and policy decisions as well as an archive of the work which actually takes place, so that a relatively complete archaeological record is available for the future. Not only will this automatically democratize the often secretive decision-making of unelected quangos but also it will make huge volumes of information available to historians and will ensure that later treatments are easier to decide upon: past failures and successes will have been carefully documented. Conservation theory—which is far from sophisticated—will have the potential for major advances on the basis of huge volumes of data. Now is the time to insist that it should be state policy that every conservation project which receives major state finances should be digitally archived as a prerequisite of such funding.

Innovative hybride graphische Systeme zur Denkmalüberwachung und -verwaltung am Beispiel historischer Wandmalereien—Ein Erfahrungsbericht

ROLF-JÜRGEN GROTE AND ANNETTE HORNSCHUCH

1. Die Datenbank der mittelalterlichen Wandmalereien in Niedersachsen—Servicemöglichkeit für Denkmalpflege und Kulturwissenschaft

Historische Wand- und Deckenmalereien sind wichtige Belege unseres Kulturerbes. Das schmückende Ausmalen von Räumen war in allen Kulturen und Epochen ein wesentlicher Bestandteil der Raumgestaltung. In anschaulicher Weise können sie kulturelle Werte und Normen vermitteln. Als beredte Zeugen ihrer Entstehungszeit spiegeln sie kulturelle Entwicklungen wider und geben Auskunft über Wandlungen oder Konstanten von Sitte, Moral, Religion, Weltanschauung, Kunstempfinden und Geschmack im Laufe der Zeiten. Außerdem können sie eine Chronologie von Handwerks- und Technologiegeschichte aufzeigen.

Niedersachsen hat einen Bestand von mehr als 250 bedeutenden Raumausmalungen allein des Mittelalters. Inzwischen konnte er im Rahmen einer rechnergestützten Inventarisierung flächendeckend nach Verbreitung und Altersschichtung, den wichtigsten Schäden und den kunsthistorischen Inhalten erfaßt und ausgewertet werden.[1] Die Endstufe wird ein Corpus-Werk mit einem ent-

---

[1] R.-J. Grote, H. Glashoff und D. Pandlowsky, 'Die Erfassung der mittelalterlichen Wandmalereien in Niedersachsen—Ein Projekt zum Schutz einer gefährdeten Kunstgattung',

sprechenden Schadensatlas bilden.[2]

Um rasch zu ersten Ergebnissen zu kommen, wurde interaktiv zwischen Dokumentaren und Denkmalpflegern eine auf die wesentlichen Informationen reduzierte Version einer praxisorientierten Datenbank entwickelt.[3] Sie ist iterativ ausbaufähig und setzt sich aus folgenden Bausteinen zusammen:

1. Gebäudebezogene Daten (Eigentümer, Ansprechpartner, Heizung, Material, Gebäudeschäden usw).
2. Stichwortartige Beschreibung der ikonographischen Zusammenhänge (Auswertung der Darstellungen nach dem kunsthistorischen Klassifikationssystem ICONCLASS der Niederländischen Akademie der Wissenschaften).
3. Lokalisierung der einzelnen Malereien im Gebäude mit grafischer Orientierung durch Verteilungsskizzen.
4. Restauratorische Bestands- und Zustandserfassung der Wandmalereien (Angaben zu Maltechnik, Konservierung, Restaurierung usw).
5. Arbeitsfotos nach normiertem Fotoplan als visuelle Hilfe.

Berichte zur Denkmalpflege in Niedersachsen, 14.2 (1994), ss. 81–83; R.-J. Grote, H. Glashoff und D. Pandlowsky, 'Die EDV-gestützte Erfassung der mittelalterlichen Wandmalereien in Niedersachsen—Ein Projekt zum Schutz einer gefährdeten Kunstgattung', in *Der Kaiserdom in Königslutter. Ein Kulturdenkmal auf dem Prüfstand. Interdisziplinäre Service-Leistungen der Denkmalpflege an einem national bedeutenden Kunstwerk*, Arbeitshefte zur Denkmalpflege in Niedersachsen. 14 (Hannover, 1996; im folgenden zitiert als: *Kaiserdom in Königslutter*), ss. 98–101; vgl. außerdem in diesem Zusammenhang: K. Dobrat und U. Paehlke, *Mittelalterliche Wand- und Deckenmalerei in Niedersachsen—eine annotierte Bibliographie* (Dipl.-Arb.), Fachhochschule für Bibliothekswesen, Information und Dokumentation (Fh. BID) (Hannover, 1989); *Konzept und Realisierung einer Objekt-Datenbank der mittelalterlichen Wandmalereien Niedersachsens* (Faltblatt Fh. BID. Objekt-Datenbank im Bibliotheks-, Informations- und Dokumentationswesen) (Hannover, 1990); A. Seiberlich: *Probleme ikonographischer Klassifikation am Beispiel mittelalterlicher Wandmalereien Niedersachsens* (Dipl.-Arb.) (Fh. BID. Hannover, 1991); S. Weber, *Mittelalterliche Wandmalerei: Literaturbericht zu Fragen der Maltechnik und des mikrobiellen Befalls* (Dipl.-Arb.) (Fh. BID. Hannover, 1990).

[2] Für großzügige Unterstützung und Förderung des Projektes sei der Stiftung Niedersachsen ganz herzlich gedankt. Als erster Einstieg in die Materie entstand gemeinsam mit der Fh. BID die Diplomarbeit von C. Schladenhaufen, *Conception et réalisation d'un programme d'exploitation d'une base de données, developpée sous dBASE III+* (Rapport de stage Univ. Claude Bernard Lyon I, 1991); außerdem: R.-J. Grote, *Wandmalereien—Probleme ihrer Bestands- und Zustandserfassung*. Vortrag gehalten anläßlich Alte Kirche Idensen—Internationales kunsthistorisches Symposium in Wunstorf, am 21.11.1991.

[3] A. Hilpüsch, *Konzept und Realisierung einer Datenbank mittelalterlicher Wandmalereien Niedersachsens* (Dipl.-Arb.), Fh. IuK Hannover (Hannover, 1995) (inzwischen kontinuierlich den aktuellen Erfordernissen der Denkmalpflegepraxis angepaßt).

6. Literaturzitate nach DIN 1505 mit Annotationen zu gebäude- und gemälderelevanten Aussagen.

Über ein Recherche-Modul ist es möglich, differenzierte inhaltliche Fragestellungen für die ständige Denkmalpflegepraxis zu beantworten.[4] Mögliche Suchfragen aus der Vielfalt kunstwissenschaftlicher und denkmalpflegerischer Problemstellungen könnten beispielsweise folgendermaßen lauten:

1. In welchen Kulturdenkmalen des Landkreises Hildesheim existieren mittelalterliche Wandmalereien?
2. Auf welchen niedersächsischen Wandmalereien des 14. Jahrhunderts wird die Geburt Christi dargestellt?
3. Welche Wandmalereien im Braunschweiger Dom weisen Schäden durch Algen oder Salzbelastung auf?

Selbstverständlich lassen sich mit den erläuterten Recherche-Möglichkeiten nicht nur kunsthistorische Fragestellung beantworten. Bei voller Ausschöpfung des Entwicklungspotentials lassen sich darüber hinaus eine Fülle aus der Denkmalpflegepraxis kommender Probleme lösen bis hin zu einem objektbezogenen Monitoringsystem für Maßnahmen der Wartung und Qualitätskontrolle oder—mit Blick auf den Gesamtbestand niedersächsischer Wandmalereien—einem flächendeckenden Schadensatlas im Rahmen eines Denkmalerhaltungsplanes.

Das Modellprojekt wurde übrigens so angelegt, daß sich entsprechende praxisorientierte Hilfen auch für andere wichtige Kulturdenkmale—wie z.B. Altäre—daraus ableiten lassen könnten.

Wegen erheblicher Finanzierungsprobleme ist trotz des vorhandenen knowhows das große Entwicklungspotential dieses wichtigen Arbeitsinstrumentes zur Zeit allerdings nur ansatzweise ausgeschöpft.

2. Rechnergestützte Denkmalinformationssysteme für historische Wandmalereien

2.1 Problemstellung

Wegen immer knapper werdender Resourcen müssen auch bei der Betreuung des einzelnen Kulturdenkmals Personal und Fördermittel noch effizienter eingesetzt werden, ohne daß Service-Leistungen und Bearbeitungsgüte darunter leiden. Wie dieses Ziel zu erreichen ist—und welche positiven Lösungsmöglichkeiten bereits bestehen—, läßt sich an den Wandmalereien als besonders problematischer

[4] F. Papendorf und R.-J. Grote, 'Servicemöglichkeiten der Denkmalpflege—Datenbank der mittelalterlichen Wandmalereien in Niedersachsen', *Berichte zur Denkmalpflege in Niedersachsen*, 17.2 (1997), ss. 97–100.

Kunstgattung beispielhaft darstellen.[5]

Auch Kulturgüter in Innenräumen wie historische Wandmalereien sind vielfältigsten Schadensfaktoren ausgesetzt.[6] Um die komplexen Wirkungsmechanismen für Therapie- und Wartungskonzepte zu erfassen, zu interpretieren und zu quantifizieren, ist eine methodisch abgesicherte Arbeits- und Dokumentationssystematik dringend erforderlich (wobei unter 'Dokumentation' die 'planmäßige Sammlung, Ordnung und Nutzbarmachung von Dokumenten und Daten' zu verstehen ist).[7] Da die bisherigen Verfahren bei der Bearbeitung komplexer Fragestellungen erkennbar an Grenzen gestoßen sind, bilden rechnergestützte Arbeitshilfen inzwischen innovative Schwerpunkte auf internationaler Ebene.[8]

---

[5] Vgl. z. B.: *Historische Technologie und Konservierung von Wandmalerei*, Vortragstexte der dritten Fach- und Fortbildungstagung der Fachklasse Konservierung und Restaurierung (Schule für Gestaltung. Bern, 5. und 6. November 1984. Bern, 1985); *Schäden an Wandmalereien und ihre Ursachen. Ein Forschungsprojekt des Bundesministers für Forschung und Technologie. Aktuelle Vorberichte zu den ersten interdisziplinären Befunden*, Arbeitshefte zur Denkmalpflege in Niedersachsen. 8 (Hannover, 1990; im folgenden zitiert als: *Schäden an Wandmalereien*); *Forschungsprojekt Wandmalerei-Schäden. Ein Förderprojekt des Bundesministers für Forschung und Technologie. Schlußbericht zu den interdisziplinären Befunden*, Arbeitshefte zur Denkmalpflege in Niedersachsen. 11 (Hannover, 1994; im folgenden zitiert als: *Forschungsprojekt Wandmalereischäden*); *Kaiserdom in Königslutter*.

[6] Vgl. z. B.: S. Fitz, 'Metallkorrosion in Innenräumen', in *Materialkorrosion durch Luftverunreinigung*, Tagung Köln, 17.–19.10.1984 (VDI-Kommission Reinhaltung der Luft. Düsseldorf, 1985), ss. 83–94 (VDI-Berichte. 530); S. Fitz, E. Fitz-Ulrich, G. Frenzel, R. Krüger, H. Kühn und E. Schmidt, *Die Einwirkungen von Luftverunreinigungen auf ausgewählte Kunstwerke mittelalterlicher Glasmalerei* (Berlin, 1984); D. Camuffo und A. Bernardi, 'Microclimate-induced weathering on the Sistine Chapel', *European Cultural Heritage. Newsletter on Research* 2.1 (Jan. 1988), ss. 36–42; D. Camuffo und A. Bernardi, *Analisi microclimatica al Cenacolo Vinciano*, Bolletino Geofisico 14.3 (Dic. 1991); D. R. Fuchs und J. Leissner, *Environmental monitoring using Glass Sensors: Relevant Features for small-scale mapping at Monuments*, 3rd International Conference on Non Destructive Testing (Viterbo, 1992).

[7] H. Glashoff, 'Möglichkeiten der Datenorganisation und Wissenschaftsdokumentation am Beispiel des Pilotprojektes "Wandmalerei-Schäden und ihre Ursachen" ', *Restaurierung von Kulturdenkmalen. Beispiele aus der niedersächsischen Denkmalpflege* (Berichte zur Denkmalpflege in Niedersachsen. Beih. 2) (Hameln, 1989), ss. 21.

[8] Inzwischen ist es gelungen, wichtige Einzelprobleme einer Lösung zuzuführen. Dies hat z. B. das Kolloquium ‚Denkmalpflege und computerunterstützte Dokumentation und Information' in Stuttgart, 1.–2.12.1992, beispielhaft gezeigt. Vgl. hierzu: *Denkmalpflege und computergestützte Dokumentation und Information*, Dokumentation der Tagung des Deutschen Nationalkomitees für Denkmalschutz in Zusammenarbeit mit der Vereinigung der Landesdenkmalpfleger in der Bundesrepublik Deutschland und dem Informationszentrum RAUM und BAU der Fraunhofer-Gesellschaft 1. und 2. Dezember 1992 in Stuttgart (Schriftenreihe des Deutschen Nationalkomitees für Denkmalschutz. 44).

Bei historischen Kulturgütern verhält es sich wie in der Medizin: Auch bei ihnen hängt die Therapie ganz entscheidend von einer sorgfältigen Anamnese und Diagnose ab – irreparable Langzeitschäden sind die Folgeerscheinungen von Maßnahmen, die mangelhaft eingeleitet und weitergeführt worden sind.

Historische Wandmalereien sind komplizierte Verbundsysteme. In der Regel gestalten sich Konzipierung und Durchführung einer systematischen Maßnahmenkette bei der Objektbetreuung daher außerordentlich schwierig. Es muß das spezifische Schadenspotential des jeweiligen Kulturdenkmals, seiner Umgebung und seiner Umwelteinflüsse berücksichtigt werden. Dabei sind sehr heterogene Informationen zu erfassen, auszuwerten, zu vernetzen und nach Interpretation in Therapiekonzepte umzusetzen.

Die wichtigsten Informationsträger sind:

1. visuelle Informationen: Fotos, Bestandspläne, Kartierungsunterlagen usw.
2. Textinformationen: Zum Bau, zu den Wandmalereien, zur Phänomen-

---

Anregende Impulse vermittelten die Fachtagungen 1993 und 1994 des Rheinischen Amts für Denkmalpflege zum Thema: EDV in der Denkmalpflege (vgl. dazu auch: 'Tagungsbericht, Pulheim—Abtei Brauweiler. Fachtagung: EDV in der Denkmalpflege', *Denkmalpflege im Rheinland* Nr. 2. (1994), ss. 65–72. Wichtige Vorarbeiten leistete 1990 unter anderem auch die Arbeitsgruppe ‚Bestandsaufnahme' des BMFT-Verbundprojektes 'Steinzerfall'. Vgl. außerdem: *Dokumentation in der Restaurierung. Akten der Vorträge der Tagung in Bregenz 23.–25. November 1989* (Salzburg, 1994); *Bestandserfassung und Bestandsanalyse an Kulturdenkmalen. 1. Fortbildungsveranstaltung für Restauratoren am 5. März 1993 in Hannover*, Niedersächsisches Landesverwaltungsamt—Institut für Denkmalpflege. Materialien zur Fort- und Weiterbildung.1 (Hannover 1993). Für die Bearbeitung von Kulturgut, vor allem historischer Bausubstanz, sind statistische Erklärungsmodelle (Cluster- und Faktorenanalysen) eine wichtige Interpretationshilfe. Führend auf diesem Gebiet ist das Laboratoire de Recherche des Monuments Historiques, Paris. Als visuelle Hilfe bei der Bearbeitung der bedeutenden Wandmalereien in der Franziskanerkirche von Arezzo (Kapellenausmalung von 1452–1466 durch Piero della Francesca) wurde mit gutem Erfolg ein rechnergestütztes Kartierungsverfahren mit einer modifizierten Standardsoftware eingesetzt, das praxisoptimiert ist (den Herren Drs. Mauro Matteini und Arcangelo Moles, die dem Verfasser eine Demonstration am Objekt ermöglichten, sei an dieser Stelle nochmals herzlich gedankt). Vgl. auch St. Casciu, G. Centauro und M. Chimenti, 'Neue EDV-gestützte Verfahren im Praxiseinsatz—Arezzo (Italien), Franziskanerkirche', in *Kaiserdom in Königslutter*, ss. 113–17; G. Centauro und M. Maffioli, *Un progretto per Piero della Francesca* (Firenze, 1989). Außerdem: S. Beck, C. Temme und H. Rademacher, 'Facility Management als Werkzeug für die Denkmalpflege', in *Kaiserdom in Königslutter*, ss. 88–91; R.-J. Grote, 'Objektdokumentation? Innovative Arbeitshilfen für die Denkmalpflege—EDV und historische Wandmalereien', in *Kaiserdom in Königslutter*, ss. 82–87; H. Gutscher und E. Favre-Bulle, 'EDV-gestützte Dokumentation eines interdisziplinären Restaurierungsprojektes: Die Wandmalereien in der Cluniazenserkirche Romainmôtier (Schweiz)', in *Kaiserdom in Königslutter*, ss. 106–12.

kartierung und zu Analysedaten.
3. Analysedaten.

Die Schwierigkeit besteht vor allem darin, daß zahlreiche Informationsträger zueinander in Beziehung gesetzt und vernetzt werden müssen, wobei eine große Zahl von Interaktionen möglich ist, die eigentlich nur EDV-gestützt[9] oder mathematisch-statistisch (wie z.B. durch Cluster- und Faktorenanalysen)[10] ausgewertet werden können:

1. Interaktion der Informationsträger zum Raum.
2. Exakte Zuordnung der Informationsträger zu der zeitlichen Komponente: Die einzelnen Bearbeitungsstufen müssen—vor allem auch bezogen auf frühere Maßnahmen—im Zeitkontinuum multitemporal vergleichbar sein, denn die denkmalpflegerische Betreuung von Wandmalereien ist ein nie endender zyklischer Prozeß. Dessen wichtigste Phasen (Anamnese—Diagnose—Therapie—Monitoring—Qualitätskontrolle) münden schließlich wieder in neue Erhaltungsmaßnahmen—sofern nicht primäre Schadensursachen ermittelt und ausgeschaltet worden sind.
3. Die jeweilige Dokumentation muß daher auf die gleiche Art gewonnen werden, um die Vergleichbarkeit der Daten zu gewährleisten.
4. Schließlich müssen die Interdependenz der Schadensphänomene selbst und deren dynamische Abläufe erfaßt und für Therapiekonzepte sinnvoll miteinander in Verbindung gebracht werden.

2.2 Lösungsmöglichkeiten

Der Einsatz der in den letzten Jahren rasch weiterentwickelten innovativen

---

[9] Erste Erfahrungsberichte über entsprechende Praxisanwendungen des Niedersächsischen Landesamtes für Denkmalpflege u. a. bei R.-J. Grote, V. Stelzer und G. Weinzierl, 'EDV-gestützte Zustandserfassung und Dokumentation', *Bautenschutz und Bausanierung*, 14.8 (1991), ss. 46–49; R.-J. Grote und V. Stelzer, 'Innovative Verfahren bei der Restaurierung von Kulturdenkmalen' in ‚Berichte über die Tätigkeit der Bau- und Kunstdenkmalpflege in den Jahren 1989–1990', *Niedersächsische Denkmalpflege* 14 (Hameln, 1992), ss. 36–44 (im folgenden zitiert als *Niedersächsische Denkmalpflege*); R.-J. Grote, V. Stelzer und G. Weinzierl, 'Zustandserfassung: Der Geschichte auf der Spur. Ein EDV-gestütztes Verfahren für historische Baudenkmäler,' *Bausubstanz*, 8.10 (1992), ss. 30–33; H. Glashoff, 'Dokumentation und Datenmanagement', in *Forschungsprojekt Wandmalereischäden*, ss. 34–36; R.-J. Grote, 'EDV-gestützte Hilfen für die Bestandserfassung und Zustandsanalyse bei Schäden an Kulturdenkmalen', ebd. ss. 37–40.

[10] H. Glashoff, 'Analytisch-statistische Interpretationshilfen zur Ursachenforschung von Schäden an historischen Wandgemälden', in *Niedersächsische Denkmalpflege*, 14, ss. 45–53.

Techniken und Verfahren, wie z. B. Bilddatenverarbeitung, Multispektralanalyse, CAD und computergestützte Datenvisualisierungs- und Verwaltungstechniken, ermöglicht in vielen Belangen eine sinnvolle Anwendung in der Denkmalpflegepraxis. Im Vordergrund müssen dabei die Möglichkeiten einer straff geplanten, interaktiven Maßnahmenkette bei der Objektbearbeitung stehen. Der Einsatz der Datenverarbeitung bietet die große Chance einer effektiven Verknüpfung so verschiedenartiger Datenträger wie Kartierungen, Textinformationen und Bilder, Messungen und Analysen, um die dringend erforderliche Verbesserung der Zeitabläufe sowie der Bearbeitungsgüte zu erreichen.

Im Rahmen verschiedener Forschungsprojekte[11] sind im Niedersächsischen Landesamt für Denkmalpflege (NLD) die Grundlagen für ein mehrdimensionales, bildbasierendes (rechnergestütztes) Informationssystem geschaffen worden, das gleichermaßen innovative Lösungen für die effiziente Bearbeitung des einzelnen Kulturdenkmals und erste positive Ansätze für einen flächendeckenden Schadensatlas mit kunsthistorischen Beschreibungen für die multidisziplinäre Auswertung enthält. Im Praxiseinsatz konnten inzwischen vielfältige Erfahrungen und weiterführende Anregungen gesammelt werden. Dabei ergab sich als wichtigstes Fazit, daß ein verbindliches Standardverfahren der Objektbearbeitung nicht realisierbar ist, sondern die Dokumentationsmethodik dem spezifischen Anforderungsprofil des jeweiligen Kulturdenkmals adaptiert werden muß.

2.2.1 Der Braunschweiger Dom und die Stiftskirche in Königslutter

Als exemplarische Belege können unter anderem die Bestands- und Zustandserfassung der bedeutenden Wandmalereien in der Stiftskirche von Königslutter und der Domkirche in Braunschweig gelten: Kulturdenkmale, deren außerordentlich umfangreiche Ausmalungszyklen eine sehr unterschiedliche Schadensproblematik und Restaurierungsgeschichte aufweisen.

---

[11] Vgl. die entsprechenden Themenschwerpunkte in: *Schäden an Wandmalereien*, sowie: *Forschungsprojekt Wandmalereischäden*; außerdem Anmerkung 9 und R.-J. Grote und P. Königfeld, 'Die Stiftskirche in Königslutter und ihre Ausmalung—Erhaltungsplanungen für ein gefährdetes Kulturdenkmal', *Niedersächsische Denkmalpflege*, 15, ss. 81–94. (Die Methodenplanung wurde während des DBU-Vorprojektes zum Modellvorhaben Stiftskirche Königslutter im Rahmen der innovativen Fortschreibung des Projektantrages inzwischen konzeptionell aktualisiert. Vgl. dort S. Beck und C. Temme, *Möglichkeiten der (EDV-gestützten) Kartierung als ein Teilbereich der Dokumentation bei der Bearbeitung von Objekten*, Report (Hannover: Niedersächsisches Landesamt für Denkmalpflege, 1996); D. Pandlowsky, *Innovative Möglichkeiten der EDV-gestützten Daten- und Bildspeicherung*, Report (Hannover: Niedersächsisches Landesamt für Denkmalpflege, 1996).

Als erster Einstieg wurde bei beiden eine generalisierende Schadenserfassung gewählt. Die angewandten Verfahren unterscheiden sich wegen der objektspezifischen Gegebenheiten jedoch erheblich: In Braunschweig eine Fotodokumentation auf CD-ROM mit rechnergestützter Suche nach restauratorisch-naturwissenschaftlichen und kunsthistorischen Fragestellungen[12]—in Königslutter dagegen eine konventionelle "händische" Phänomenkartierung in Verbindung mit einem (bilddaten-basierten) 3D-Raummodell, das nach entsprechender Praxisoptimierung vor allem der Visualisierung von Wandmalereischäden in Korrelation mit den bauimmanenten Schadensagentien sowie möglicher Umweltbelastungsfaktoren dienen soll.[13]

Die vom NLD konzipierte Arbeitssystematik ist konsequent auf die spezifische Problematik des Ausmalungsprogrammes im Braunschweiger Dom mit dem Ziel maximaler Arbeitseffizienz zur Kostendämpfung abgestimmt. Bereits im Vorfeld der Konzepterstellung gemeinsam mit dem zuständigen Stadtkirchenbauamt durchgeführte Kosten-Nutzenanalysen erwiesen die gewählte Lösung als optimal.

Wesentliches Kennzeichen ist der modulare Aufbau: Die Erfassungssystematik kann als Ganzes oder auch nur in einzelnen Bausteinen zum Einsatz

---

[12] R.-J. Grote, H. Glashoff, G. Drescher und D. Pandlowsky, 'Die Wandmalereien im südlichen Querhaus des Braunschweiger Doms—aktuelle Befunde und ihre Dokumentation', *Berichte zur Denkmalpflege in Niedersachsen*, 15.3–4 (1995), ss. 109–15; R.-J. Grote, H. Glashoff und D. Pandlowsky, 'Arbeitsökonomie und Kosteneffizienz als Grundlagen denkmalpflegerischer Zielplanung: Die Wandmalereien im Braunschweiger Dom', in *Kaiserdom in Königslutter*, ss. 92–97. Für großzügige Unterstützung und Förderung seien der Richard Borek Stiftung, dem Braunschweigischen Vereinigten Kloster- und Studienfonds sowie der Domstiftung gedankt, die in Verbindung mit erheblichen Bundes- und Landesmitteln die Durchführung des Projekts ermöglichten. Ganz herzlich bedanken möchte sich der Verfasser auch bei Herrn Dipl.-Ing Norbert Koch sowie Frau Karin Kautzer-Lehmann vom Stadtkirchenbauamt, die über Finanzierungsplanung, örtliche Bauleitung und Koordination aller Beteiligten hinaus mit mannigfachem fachlichen Rat und vielseitiger Hilfestellung ganz erheblich zum Gelingen des Projektes beigetragen haben. Schließlich sei an dieser Stelle dem interdisziplinären Team für die konstruktive Zusammenarbeit im Rahmen der Projektarbeit Dank gesagt.

[13] Ebd. S. Beck, E. Behrens, D. Pandlowsky und C. Temme, 'Maßnahmenbegleitende Dokumentation—Entwicklung eines Orientierungssystems', *Kaiserdom in Königslutter*, ss. 14–19; J. Heckes, A. Hornschuch und P. Haferland, 'Möglichkeiten der Bilddatenverarbeitung, Visualisierungen und Kartierungen auf der Grundlage von Photos mit Standardsoftware', *Kaiserdom in Königslutter*, ss. 118–21. Der Deutschen Bundesstiftung Umwelt und dem Braunschweigischen Vereinigten Kloster- und Studienfonds sei an dieser Stelle nochmals herzlich gedankt, die mit erheblichen Fördermitteln das interdisziplinäre Projekt ermöglicht haben. Dank gilt aber auch der Kirchengemeinde und allen übrigen Helfern und Team-Mitgliedern, die mit Rat und Unterstützung zum Gelingen der Untersuchungen beigetragen haben.

kommen. Zur Verknüpfung der verschiedenen Datenträger wurde die Datenverarbeitung so einfach wie möglich konzipiert und praxisoptimiert. Besonderer Wert wurde darauf gelegt, daß der Zugriff auch auf bewährte "händische" Verfahren jederzeit möglich ist.

Im Braunschweiger Dom handelt es sich um eine restauratorische Schnellerfassung des sehr umfangreichen Wandmalereibestandes und seiner wichtigsten Schadensparameter. Sie soll einer anschließenden interdisziplinären Bearbeitung die Konzentration auf objektrelevante Schadensbereiche ermöglichen. Korrespondierend mit der Befunderhebung durch szenenbezogene 'Checklisten' wurde als visuelles Medium eine systematische Reihenfotografie gewählt, wobei es sich um mehrere hundert Einzelszenen handelt.

Ihre Einzelsequenzen wurden auf Photo-CD überführt und können mit einer einfachen Datenbank phänomen- und themenbezogen angesteuert werden (Shoebox Photo-Access für Windows/PhotoEdge für Windows). Parallel dazu wurde ein "händisches" Ablagesystem der "Ortho-Fotos" nach Einzelszenen geschaffen. Auch ihnen ist die entsprechende "Checkliste" (also die Erfassungsmaske) des Restaurators jeweils zugeordnet.

In einer zweiten Bearbeitungsphase wurden die Befunde auf Übersichtszeichnungen (layer auf Transparentfolien) übertragen und zusammenfassend im szenischen Kontext visualisiert. Damit ist es möglich, die Schadensverteilung und andere objektrelevante Phänomene wie z. B. den Anteil der Originalsubstanz an Wandmalerei mit dem Komplexitätsgrad der Schäden quantifizierend in einem ersten Überblick zu erfassen und zu korrelieren.

Cluster- und Faktorenanalysen (Algorithmus nach WARD, Euklidische Distanz, Software SYSTAT) dienten als statistische Auswertungshilfen, um die dominanten Schadensbereiche aus den sekundären herauszufiltern und damit später den gezielten Einsatz eines interdisziplinären Untersuchungsteams zu ermöglichen.

2.2.2 Forschungsprojekt 'Wandmalerei-Schäden'

Auch im Rahmen des vom Bundesminister für Forschung und Technologie finanzierten Forschungsprojektes "Wandmalerei-Schäden" wurde eine innovative Arbeits- und Dokumentationssystematik realisiert (die allerdings inzwischen erheblich verfeinert und praxisoptimiert worden ist).[14] Dabei konnten ver-

---

[14] Siehe auch VDI-Richtlinie 3798 ,Untersuchung und Behandlung von immissionsgeschädigten Werkstoffen insbesondere bei kulturhistorischen Objekten'; P. W. Mirwald, 'Erhebungen, Situationsstudien und Handlungsorganisation im Kooperationsverbund aller an Untersuchungen und Erhaltungsmaßnahmen am Baudenkmal beteiligten Stellen', *Bautenschutz und Bausanierung*, Sonderh (1989), ss. 16–20; H. Glashoff, 'Möglichkeiten der Datenorganisation und Wissenschaftsdokumentation am

schiedene EDV-gestützte Verfahren piloterprobt werden. Ziel war die Entwicklung eines ganzheitlichen modularen Denkmalinformationssystems, das den jeweiligen objektspezifischen Gegebenheiten flexibel angepaßt werden kann.

Der Projektverlauf war geprägt von der Bewältigung einer übergroßen Fülle heterogener Daten. Dies zeigte sich z.B. schon bei ganz normalen restauratorischen oder naturwissenschaftlichen Phänomenkartierungen[15]—wobei die "Kartierung" allerdings nur als Modul des umfassenderen Denkmalinformationssystems aufzufassen ist. Als wichtige visuelle interdisziplinäre Erkennungs- und Entscheidungshilfe durch Schichtung von Transparentfolien in Kartierebenen (layer) konzipiert, war bei komplexen Schadensbereichen die beabsichtigte Ablesbarkeit mit herkömmlichen Verfahren in der Regel nicht mehr zu bewältigen.

Es ergab sich daher zunehmend, daß die Entwicklung rechnergestützter Verfahren zur Bewältigung der bei der Erfassung, Analyse und Dokumentation der Wandmalereischäden progressiv wachsenden Datenfülle unabdingbar war.

Beispiel des Pilotprojektes "Wandmalereischäden und ihre Ursachen" ', in *Restaurierung von Kulturdenkmalen* (Berichte zur Denkmalpflege in Niedersachsen. Beih. 2: Hannover, 1989), ss. 21–24; S. Beck, U. Geruschkat und H. Glashoff, 'Foto und Raumkoordinate als Hilfsmittel der Befunddokumentation', in *Schäden an Wandmalereien*, ss. 16–18; H. Glashoff, 'Dokumentation und Datenmanagement', in *Forschungsprojekt Wandmalerei-Schäden*, ss. 35–36.

[15] Speziell zum Kartieren und anderen visuellen Arbeitshilfen vgl. B. Fitzner und R. Kownatzki, 'Kartierung und empirische Klassifizierung der Verwitterungsformen und Verwitterungsmerkmale von Natursteinen an geschädigten Bauwerkspartien', *Bautenschutz und Bausanierung*, Sonderh (1989), ss. 21–25; B. Fitzner und R. Kownatzki, 'Bauwerkskartierung', *Der Freiberufliche Restaurator*, H. 4. 1990, ss. 25–40; 'Die Dokumentation in der Bestandsaufnahme—Untersuchung, Bewertung und Restaurierung denkmalpflegerischer Objekte', Bericht der Arbeitsgruppe 'Bestandsaufnahme' des BMFT-Projekts, Steinzerfall', *Bautenschutz und Bausanierung*, Sonderh (1990); ferner: H. F. Reichwald, 'Möglichkeiten der zerstörungsfreien Voruntersuchung am Beispiel der ottonischen Wandmalereien in St. Georg Reichenau-Oberzell', in *Historische Technologie und Konservierung von Wandmalereien* (Bern, 1985), ss. 106–31; G. Drescher und M. K. Jensen, 'Schadenskartierungen. Fallbeispiel Ev.-ref. Kirche in Krummhörn-Eilsum', in *Forschungsprojekt Wandmalerei-Schäden*, ss. 88–92; vgl. auch H. P. Autenrieth und P. Turek, 'Modelle für eine grafische Inventarisation mittelalterlicher Wandmalereien', in *Schäden an Wandmalereien*, ss. 27–32; S. Beck, 'Computer Aided-Design (CAD) als Arbeitsmittel', *Niedersächsische Denkmalpflege*, 14, ss. 53–62; U. Geruschkat und H. Glashoff, 'Visuelle Objektdokumentation', in *Schäden an Wandmalereien*, s. 15; T. Trapp, 'Optische Methoden der Schadenserfassung', in *Forschungsprojekt Wandmalereischäden*, ss. 45–48; S. Beck, 'Die Kartierung als Mittel der Bestandsaufnahme', in *Forschungsprojekt Wandmalerei-Schäden*, ss. 41–44; D. Gadesmann und P. Königfeld, 'Möglichkeiten einer "einfachen Phänomenkartierung" als Grundlage der Schadensanalyse-Schloßkapelle in Celle', in *Kaiserdom Königslutter*, ss. 102–05; zum aktuellen Entwicklungsstand vgl. z. B. den Beitrag von Jürgen Heckes et al. Anm. 13.

Das Denkmalinformationssystem wurde an ausgewählten Objekten bzw. Objektbereichen erfolgreich piloterprobt. Eine Einsatzoptimierung konnte allerdings nicht mehr erfolgen, da inzwischen das Forschungsprojekt seinen Abschluß gefunden hatte.

Da bei denkmalpflegerischen Maßnahmen viele Beobachtungen, Untersuchungen und Messungen durchzuführen sind, erwies sich die Einführung eines definierten dreidimensionalen Koordinatensystems in Verbindung mit einer relationalen Datenbank als sinnvoll. Die exakte Zuordnung der vielfältigen interdisziplinären Aktivitäten zu Koordinaten ermöglichte eine gemeinsame Basis für die spätere Auswertung, Dokumentation und Archivierung.

Die Erfassung des Baudenkmals erfolgte innen und außen dreidimensional über Tachymetrie. Markante Meßpunkte, die das Baudenkmal in seiner Geometrie beschreiben, wurden in Fotos eingetragen. Somit war eine eindeutige Identifizierung der Punkte bei der nachfolgenden Rekonstruktion durch CAD gegeben. Bei Bedarf können über das CAD-System Längs- und Querschnitte sowie 3D-Gittermodelle erzeugt werden.

Als Grundlage für die anschließende Kartierung von Zuständen und Schadensbereichen dienten herkömmliche Fotografien. Bei Wandmalereien ist es dringend erforderlich, daß diese Einzelbilder zusammenhängende Gemäldepartien erfassen. Sie sollen möglichst frontal zur Wand aufgenommen werden, um starke Verzerrungen zu vermeiden. Durch Überdeckung der Einzelbilder wurde ein 'Fotomosaik' zusammengefügt. So war es möglich, alle Bereiche des Baudenkmals lückenlos abzubilden.

Die Einzelbilder wurden sodann nach ihren Koordinaten erfaßt und den dreidimensionalen Raumkoordinaten des Baudenkmals zugeordnet. Über fotogrammetrische Stereoaufnahmen der Wandpartien konnten die Ecken und Mitten der Einzelbilder dreidimensional bestimmt werden. Dabei dienten die über die Vermessung (Tachymetrie) aufgenommenen Punkte als Paßpunkte für die Fotogrammetrie. Damit war der Bezug zwischen den zweidimensionalen Bildkoordinaten und den dreidimensionalen Raumkoordinaten hergestellt und jeder Punkt eindeutig lokalisierbar.

Für die Zustands- und Schadenserfassung wurden im Projektverlauf verschiedene Verfahren getestet. Im Vordergrund stand die Erarbeitung EDV-gestützter Kartierungsunterlagen als Grundlage für weiterführende Auswertungen.

Zunächst wurden videografische Aufnahmen erstellt, digital aufbereitet und als Einzelbilder auf einem Laptopbildschirm dargestellt. Eine entsprechende Software sollte die Phänomenkartierung direkt vor der Wandmalerei auf den Hintergrundbildern des Laptops ermöglichen. Wegen der technischen Grenzen des Laptops wurde die Realisierung dieses Vorhabens allerdings dann zurückgestellt.

Als Alternativlösung wurde versucht, ein eigenständiges Kartierungsprogramm zu entwickeln, das auf kalibrierten, nicht digital vorliegenden Einzelfotos basierte. Dabei fehlte allerdings der direkte Bezug von Bearbeitungsfläche und Kartierung: Das Foto liegt separat auf einem Digitalisiertablett, während die

Kartierung isoliert und ohne bildlichen Bezug auf dem Bildschirm erscheint. Ein weiterer Nachteil bestand in den hohen Entwicklungskosten einer speziellen Kartierungssoftware, die menuegesteuert auch von Computerlaien angewendet werden kann.

Daher erschien es sinnvoll, bereits auf dem Markt erhältliche CAD-Standardsoftware entsprechend den spezifischen Anforderungen zu modifizieren und anzuwenden. Auch dabei wurde ein auf dem Digitalisiertablett liegendes, kalibriertes—möglichst orthogonales—Einzelfoto als Kartierungsunterlage verwendet. Als Orientierungshilfen wurden Strichzeichnungen des entsprechenden Fotos erstellt und auf den Bildschirm eingeblendet, um eine Lokalisierung der zu kartierenden Phänomene zu ermöglichen. Als großer Vorteil erwies sich die Flexibilität des Verfahrens: Die Kartierungen lassen sich entweder konventionell vor Ort anfertigen und anschließend stationär weiterbearbeiten oder unmittelbar am Objekt in den Laptop eingeben.

Die erfaßten Bildinformationen wurden über eine Schnittstelle in einer relationalen Datenbank abgelegt und verwaltet. Die Datenbank korrelierte die Eintragungen der Zustands- oder Schadensphänomenerfassung sowie der textlichen Beschreibung miteinander, da sie über das Koordinatensystem miteinander verbunden sind. Fotos, Videoaufnahmen usw. können leicht über die Datenbank diesen Eintragungen zugeordnet werden. Dadurch war sowohl ein schnelles Auffinden aller gespeicherten Dokumente wie auch ein jederzeitiges Reproduzieren der Informationen und eine erleichterte Kommunikation mit anderen Projektteilnehmern, aber auch ein langfristiges, einheitliches und sicheres Abspeichern der Informationen gegeben. Bei zusätzlichem Ablegen der Fotos auf langzeitspeichernde Bildplatten könnten diese Fotoinformationen zu jedem beliebigen Befund und zu jedem späteren Zeitpunkt wieder auf dem Bildschirm dargestellt werden. Damit ließe sich in Form eines späteren Monitoring eine Langzeit-Zustands-/Schadensbeobachtung durchführen.

2.2.3 Fotografische/visuelle Bestandserfassung in Haus Altenkamp

Problemstellung und Auswahl der Bearbeitungstechniken

Wegen der großen kunst- und kulturgeschichtlichen Bedeutung der Wandmalereien werden zusätzlich zu den konventionellen Verfahren der Bestands- und Zustandserfassung/Dokumentation weitere innovative Lösungen piloterprobt, die qualifiziertere Erkenntnisse und Entscheidungshilfen ermöglichen. Ein Bearbeitungsschwerpunkt ist daher der Einsatz der Bilddatenverarbeitung zur Schadensfeststellung und als Monitoringsystem in Verbindung mit multispektralen Aufnahme- und Auswertungstechniken. Angelehnt an Verfahren aus der Fernerkundung, die bereits seit geraumer Zeit multispektral zerlegte Bilddaten von Satellitensystemen zur Flächendetektion, -überwachung und kartie-

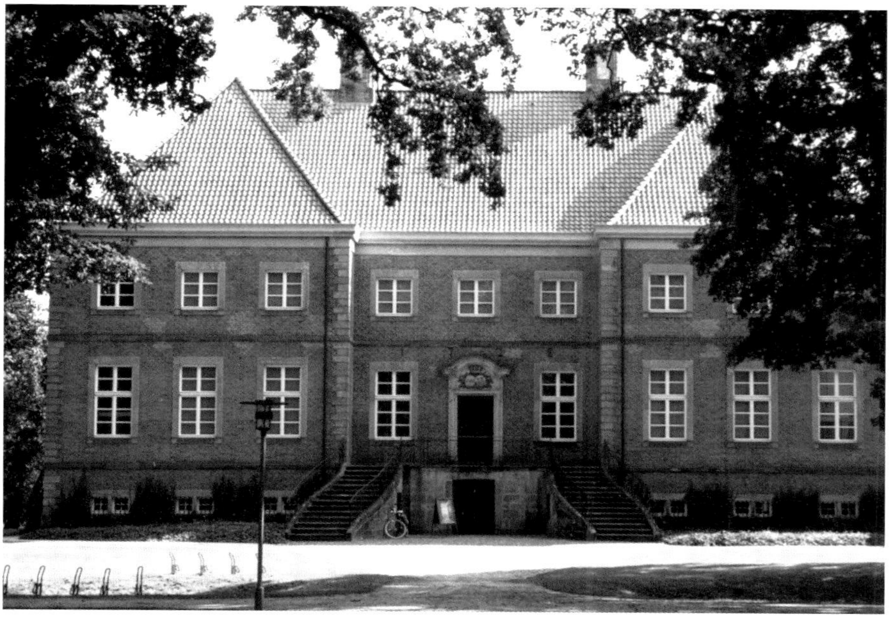

Fig. 1. Haus Altenkamp, Ansicht von Westen. © Landesamt für Denkmalpflege, Hannover

rung nutzt, konnten an Ausmalungsbeispielen (Stiftskirche Königslutter[16] und Herrenhaus Altenkamp [fig. 1, 10, plate 25][17]) entsprechende Verfahren zur Phänomenerkennung zielgerichtet modifiziert und eingesetzt werden. Eine Kombination aus analogen fotografischen Aufnahmeverfahren und digitalen Bearbeitungstechniken sollte an diesen Beispielen eine Arbeitsmethodik aufzeigen, die einerseits optimierte Daten für eine manuelle Kartierung liefert, darüber hinaus jedoch die Bilddaten in einem Monitoringsystem verwaltet. So können zum Beispiel die multispektralen Bildfolgen eines Motives durch Mustererkennungsalgorithmen ausgewertet und nach Schadensbildern abgefragt werden. Wurden an einer Wandmalerei zum Beispiel in der Vergangenheit Ausmalungsbereiche nachbearbeitet oder restauriert, so kann eine komplexe Analyse der Aufnahmen dies dokumentieren, obwohl für das unbewaffnete menschliche Auge keine Veränderungen feststellbar sind. Eine a priori Analyse von Schäden zur Vorbereitung restauratorischer Maßnahmen wird so ermöglicht.

---

[16] Vgl. Heckes et al. Anm. 13.

[17] Herrn Jürgen Heckes, Deutsches Bergbau-Museum/Forschungsbereich Informationssysteme, sowie Herrn Maro Moskopp, Luftbild Eifel seien an dieser Stelle für mannigfachen fachlichen Rat und vielseitige Hilfestellung ganz herzlich gedankt.

Einleitung

"Unser so beschäftigtes Jahrhundert hat selten Zeit zum Lesen, immer aber Zeit zum Sehen" (Theophile Gautier, 1858).

Eventuell beeinflußt durch diese Erkenntnis hat das technologisierte 20. Jahrhundert zahlreiche 'Seh-Hilfen' in Form von fotografischen Abbildungstechniken geschaffen. Eine gezielte Auswahl dieser Techniken, abgestimmt auf die Möglichkeiten der digitalen Datenverarbeitung, führt in einigen Wissenschaftsbereichen sogar dazu, daß Computer gut genug sehen können, um den Menschen ablesbare Antworten auf spezielle Fragestellungen geben zu können.

Als ein Beispiel seien die Geowissenschaften zu nennen, die seit geraumer Zeit multispektral zerlegte Bilddaten von Satellitensystemen zur Flächendetektion, -überwachung und -kartierung nutzen.[18] Speziell entwickelte Bildverarbeitungsalgorithemen können hierbei durch zielorientierte Kombinationen der Eingabe-Bildddaten neue leicht interpretierbare Ergebnisse schaffen.[19]

Motiviert durch diese positiven Ergebnisse wurden neben der konventionellen Dokumentation der Wandmalereien am Beispiel des Entrées des Hauses Altenkamp innovative Ansätze einer erweiterten fotografischen Abbildungsserie zur besseren Unterstützung und Rationalisierung der restauratorischen Arbeiten verfolgt.

Erweiterte fotografische Dokumentation der Wandmalereimotive

Vor allen weiteren Maßnahmen wurden die Wandmalereimotive flächendeckend mit einer Mittelformat-Fachkamera auf Schwarz/Weiß Film abgebildet. Gemäß einer im Vorfeld erstellten Einteilungsmatrix wurden Ausschnittvergrößerungen sämtlicher Bildszenen als Basis für eine manuelle Kartierung angefertigt (fig. 2, plate 20).

Zusätzliche photogrammetrische Meßbilder und eine geringe Anzahl von geodätisch bestimmten Meßpunkten stellten eine geometrische Grundlage für die Herstellung von maßstäblichen digitalen Kartierungsunterlagen dar.[20]

Mit dem Ziel einer annähernd wertneutralen fotografischen Farbaufzeichnung wurden die Wandmalereien durch RGB-Farbauszüge (Rot, Grün, Blau) abgebildet. Diese werden durch Absorptionsfilter realisiert, die nur den Spektralanteil ihrer Eigenfarbe passieren lassen. Die Farbauszüge werden sequentiell auf Schwarz/Weiß Film belichtet und können durch additive Farbmischung der Primärfarben zu Reproduktionszwecken zu einem Farbbild zusammengesetzt werden (fig. 3, plate 21). Diese, gegenüber der herkömmlichen Mehrschichtenfarbfilm-Belichtung aufwendige, jedoch seriösere Art der Farbaufzeichnung erfordert die Einhaltung und Kontrolle verschiedener Aufnahmeparameter, die ständig eine Anpassung auf den jeweiligen Stand der Entwicklung im fotografisch-technischen Bereich verlangen.

---

[18] *Manual of Remote Sensing*, 1 & 2 (American Society of Photogrammetry, 1983).

[19] M. Kappas, *Fernerkundung nah gebracht* (Bonn, 1994).

[20] Vgl. Heckes et al. Anm. 13.

Der Hauptvorteil dieses Verfahrens besteht jedoch darin, daß unkontrollierte Farbvermischungseffekte, die bei der konventionellen Farbabbildung unvermeidbar sind, nahezu ausgeschlossen werden können.[21]

Zur Normierung und Kontrolle der Aufnahmeserien wurde jeweils ein durch spektrale Messung erfaßtes Testobjekt aus 4 Graufeldern in jede Aufnahme integriert.

Für ausgewählte Testflächen mit typischen Schadensphänomenen wurden für eine erweiterte Differenzierung der spektralen Eigenschaften der Wandmalerei Zwischenkanäle im sichtbaren Bereich (Cyan und Orange) und in den angrenzenden nicht sichtbaren Bereichen (Ultraviolett und Infrarot) installiert (fig. 4). Diese Zusatzkanäle sind eine wertvolle und unverzichtbare Hilfe zur Aufdeckung minimaler unterschiedlicher spektraler Reize, die jedoch den gleichen Farbeindruck auslösen. Multitemporale normierte Multispektral-Aufnahmen könnten so z.B. das Verblassen der Farbe oder Retuschen deutlich sichtbar machen.

Eine Wiederholung der Aufnahmeserien im Haus Altenkamp ist nach Abschluß der Restaurierungsarbeiten vorgesehen.

Digitale Dokumentation

Als Basis für eine digitale Befundkartierung wurden die fotografischen analogen Abbildungen durch einen kontrollierten Scanvorgang gerastert. Der Feinheitsgrad der Digitalisierung wurde so gewählt, daß Flächen mit einer Auflösung von 1 mm^2 wiedergegeben wurden. Zur Schaffung eines einheitlichen Bezugsystemes wurden die Bilder eines spektralen Bandes digital entzerrt und zu einem Bildplan montiert. Auf diesen Plan wurden anschließend die weiteren Bänder pixelgenau eingepaßt.

Gleichzeitig bildet dieser Bildplan die Grundlage für die Einarbeitung der manuellen Kartierung, die auf Kopien der Bildpläne durch Umfahren der Schadensmerkmale mit Farbstiften durchgeführt wurde. Die digitalen Kartierungen wurden nach Regeln, wie sie aus Geographischen Informationssystemen[22] bekannt sind, geometrisch und thematisch strukturiert und mit einem geeigneten CAD-Programm digitalisiert (fig. 5). Sämtliche Elemente der manuellen Kartierungsfolien wurden in Form von Flächenelementen übertragen und durch Definition der Umgrenzungslinien durch geschlossene Polylinien gezeichnet. Die visuelle Differenzierung fest eingrenzbarer und nicht eingrenzbarer Bereiche erfolgte über unterschiedliche Linientypen. Die Visualisierung der Befunde innerhalb einer Kartierungsthematik wurde durch variierende Schraffuren differenziert. Innerhalb des digitalen Informationssystemes werden die Bereiche durch eindeutige numerische Identifikationen verwaltet, die, gesteuert durch

---

[21] H. Frieser, *Photographische Informationsaufzeichnung* (München, Wien, London, New York, 1975).

[22] R. Bill und D. Fritsch, *Grundlagen der Geo-Informationssysteme* (Heidelberg, 1994).

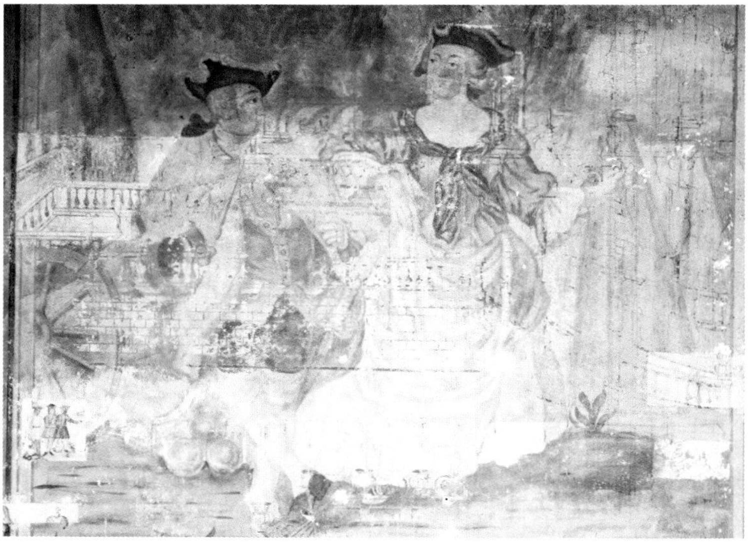

Fig. 4. Haus Altenkamp, Entrée, Wandmalerei-Ausschnitt der Südwand, UV-Fluoreszenz-Aufnahme. © Landesamt für Denkmalpflege, Hannover

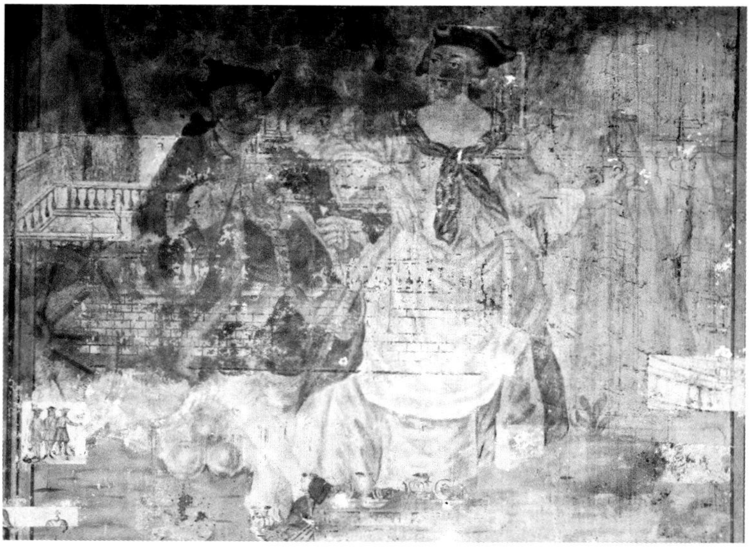

Fig. 5. Das Bild entsteht durch Beleuchtung mit 320-380 nm und durch Filterung mit 440-660 nm. Die Verwendung unterschiedlicher Farben bei früheren Restaurierungen der linken Figur wird deutlich sichtbar. © Landesamt für Denkmalpflege, Hannover

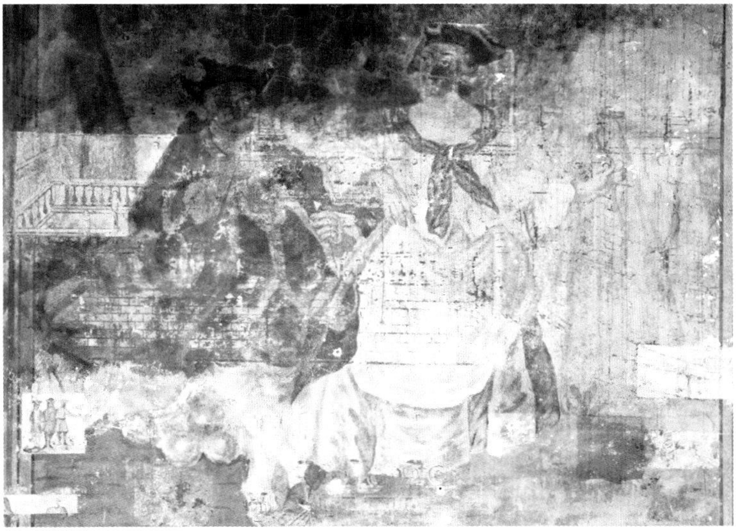

Fig. 6. Haus Altenkamp, Entrée, Bildplan der Südwand, überlagert mit Thermobild. © Landesamt für Denkmalpflege, Hannover

Datenbankabfragen, numerische und statistische Auswertungen über das Schadenspotenial durchführen können.

Für eine integrale Objekterfassung, die auch räumliche Komponenten wie z.B. Raumklima berücksichtigt, können die Daten auch 3-dimensional bearbeitet werden (fig. 6).

Neben der Übertragung der Ergebnisse der konventionellen manuellen Kartierung vor Ort wurde unter Einbeziehung der digital aufbereiteten multispektralen Bildserien die Möglichkeit der stationären digitalen Kartierung—einer Kartierung ohne ständigem Zugang zum Objekt, ausschließlich anhand der Bilddaten—erprobt.

Zusammenfassend ist nach Abschluß der interdisziplinären Arbeiten festzuhalten:

1. Die multispektrale Aufnahmetechnik ermöglicht eine gute Visualisierung vorhandener Schadensbilder. Alle kartierten Schadensbilder konnten in den Bildern lokalisiert werden. Eine Vielzahl von Schäden kann einfacher, genauer und schneller in Bildern kartiert werden als manuell vor Ort (figs. 7, 8, 9, plates 22, 23, 24).
2. Die manuelle Kartierung kann nur eine erste Übersicht der Schäden darstellen. Eine Detailkartierung ist mit Bildverarbeitungstechniken wirtschaftlicher zu lösen.
3. Eine langfristige, platzsparende Archivierung der digitalen Kartierung ist nach heutigem Stand der Technik möglich. Der Zugriff und die

Reproduzierbarkeit der Ergebnisse bleibt dabei stets gewährleistet.

4. Im Rahmen eines langfristigen Wartungskonzeptes können bei zielgerichteter Weiterentwicklung Kartierungen ohne die "Handschrift" wechselnder Bearbeiter realisiert werden.

Computergestützte automatisierte Dokumentation

Als Fernziel der multispektralen Datenerfassung und Auswertung wurde versucht, ein typisches Schadensbild durch automatisches Bildverstehen zu erkennen. Die Bilder werden hierbei aufgrund ihrer Rasterung als eine Vielzahl von Flächenelementen aufgefaßt, wobei partiell unterschiedliche physikalische Eigenschaften des abgebildeten Objektes durch variierende Reflexionen in den spektralen Bändern aufgeschlüsselt werden. Somit ergeben sich pro Flächeneinheit mehrere Meßwerte, die zu einem n-dimensionalen Punkt zusammengefaßt werden. Durch mathematische Ähnlichkeitsbetrachtungen der N-Tupel können so Punktmengen (Cluster) gebildet werden.

Eine Definition der Auswerteschlüssel und ihrer mathematischen Definition, einhergehend mit der Interpretation der maschinell erkannten Flächen, wird sich nur durch enge interdisziplinäre Zusammenarbeit von restauratorisch, fototechnisch und naturwissenschaftlich geschulten Fachleuten erfolgreich realisieren lassen.

Obwohl der Aufwand zur Objektabbildung durch multispektrale Aufnahmeserien zunächst nicht unerheblich ist, kann diese Vorgehensweise thematische Kartierungen ohne menschliches Eingreifen ermöglichen. Die Objektinformationen müssen dazu in relevanten spektralen Bereichen optimiert erschlossen werden, wobei die technische Realisierung der spektralen Bänder stets innerhalb eines vertretbaren technischen Aufwandes bleiben muß. Ein großer Vorteil der Objektdokumentation durch die erweiterten fotografischen Aufnahmen besteht bereits heute schon darin, daß durch Einzelbetrachtung, aber besonders auch durch Synergieeffekte bei der digitalen Kombination von spektralen Bändern Schadensphänomene deutlicher sichtbar werden.

Somit kann die Multispektralauswertung eine Methode der Zustandserfassung werden, die in Teilen stationär durchgeführt werden kann und Kosten, z.B. für Gerüstzeiten, minimieren könnte.

Ein weiterer Vorteil besteht in der Möglichkeit der direkten digitalen Kartierung ohne den Umweg des 'Abzeichnens' der manuellen Kartierung.

Ein bereits bestehendes Schadensglossar wird zu einer Dokumentationsvereinheitlichung führen; es ermöglicht, das Schadenspotential eines Einzelobjektes—aber auch das von verschiedenen Objekten—im zeitlichen Verlauf zu vergleichen.

3. Ergebnisse

Die Modellversuche erbrachten zahlreiche Anregungen, die als Bestandteile EDV-gestützter Verfahren bereits im Vorfeld wichtiger Restaurierungen in die Praxis überführt werden sollten. In allen Projekten des NLD hat sich nachdrücklich gezeigt, daß vor jeder wissenschaftlich fundierten Untersuchung zunächst eine generalisierende Analyse des Baues und aller auf ihn einwirkenden, meist sehr heterogenen Schadensfaktoren unerläßlich ist ("integrale Objekterfassung"). Erst nach dieser langfristig zu terminierenden Vorlaufphase ist es sinnvoll, ein interdisziplinäres Untersuchungsteam gezielt an das Baudenkmal heranzuführen und die erheblichen personellen, apparativen und finanziellen Bindungen effektiv zu strukturieren.

Folgende wichtige Bearbeitungsschritte wurden inzwischen realisiert bzw. befinden sich im Projektstadium:

1. Vollständige geometrisch und farblich richtige Abbildung der Wandmalereien und ihrer Schäden als Grundlage für die händische interdisziplinäre Schadenskartierung sowie als Basis für die digitale rechnergestützte Weiterbearbeitung zu einem entsprechenden Denkmalinformationssystem.
2. Das Denkmalinformationssystem ist modular aufgebaut: Es kann geometrische Informationen, Bilder und Textinformationen speichern und verarbeiten. Es wird für die aktuelle Bestands- und Zustandserfassung sowie für alle weiteren Bearbeitungsschritte dringend benötigt. Die Einarbeitung und das Abrufen der Daten erfolgt rechnergestützt unter Einsatz von layer-Bildung, ihre Ablage über Fenstertechnik in einer relationalen Datenbank.
3. Die Kartierung von Zustandsmerkmalen am Objekt erfolgt nicht mehr wie bisher von Hand (z.B. mit Buntstiften auf Transparentpapier über einem Foto), sondern direkt am Rechner, wobei ein beliebig wählbarer Bildausschnitt der Wandmalerei als Hintergrundinformation auf dem Bildschirm erscheint. Vor diesem Hintergrundbild können dann direkt auf dem Bildschirm mit einer entsprechenden Software bestimmte Bildinhalte interpretiert und markiert werden. Über Legenden und speziell zu erstellende Menues sollen die erfaßten Zustandsmerkmale mit Kennungen versehen und in Ebenentechnik (layers) rechnerintern abgespeichert werden. Auf diese Weise können in einem nachfolgenden Schritt verschiedene Zustandsmerkmale miteinander korreliert werden. Es werden damit Interpretationshilfen für eine interdisziplinäre Ursachenforschung der verschiedenen beteiligten Fachleute und erste Hinweise auf Schadensursachen gegeben. Außerdem lassen sich die rechnergestützt erfaßten Kartierungsdaten über Raumkoordinaten einem 3D-Modell zuordnen und in Verbindung mit einer Datenbank langfristig

und mit schnellem Zugriff abspeichern.

4. Das bisher entwickelte Verfahren der Zustandskartierung und Dokumentation, das modulartig aufgebaut ist und dessen Komponenten—dem objektspezifischen Anforderungsprofil entsprechend—austauschbar bzw. entbehrlich sind, kann zu einem integralen System der Objekterfassung ausgebaut werden, um im Rahmen einer Erstdiagnose generalisierende Analysen des Objektes mit allen auf dieses einwirkenden, meist sehr heterogenen Merkmalen und Schadensfaktoren durchführen zu können. Dazu sollen als weitere Module generalisierende Detektionsverfahren zur Erfassung der flächenhaften Verteilung z. B. von Mauerfeuchte, Salzen, Temperaturparametern usw. am Objekt und im Raum (Thermografie, Elektrowiderstands- und Kapazitätsmessungen, Elektromagnetische Reflexion (EMR), Radar- und Seismikverfahren usw.) eingesetzt werden, um damit ggf. aktive und inaktive Schadenszonen herauszuarbeiten.
5. Die wichtigsten Parameter der gewonnenen Daten könnten in ein vereinfachtes, über CAD erstelltes 3D-Gittermodell oder über ein durch Bilddatenbearbeitung generiertes 3D-Modell überführt werden. Damit lassen sich anschaulich Bereiche mit Schadenshäufungen relativ genau in ihrer räumlichen Verteilung erkennen und auch ggf. 'Altschäden' (durch Akten-, Archivauswertungen, Altfotos) mit den aktuellen Befunden korrelieren. In Verbindung mit dem 3D-Modell können vor allem bei komplexen mehrräumigen Bauwerken sämtliche zu einem Objekt gehörende Informationen raumweise strukturiert ('Raumbuch') abgelegt werden.
6. Nach einer ersten Schadenserfassung ('Phänomenkartierung') und flächenhaft angelegten interdisziplinären Tastuntersuchungen sollen an schadensrelevanten Referenzflächen analytisch-statistische Interpretationshilfen zur Ursachenforschung von Schäden (Faktoren- und Clusteranalysen[23]) angewendet werden. Sie sollen eine Trennung von dominierenden und zufälligen Symptomen an potentiellen Schadensstellen erreichen und damit eine Entwicklung von Strategien einleiten, außerdem die Beobachtungen und Analysen zunächst auf ein nötiges Minimum reduzieren. Somit wäre es möglich, den analytischen Aufwand vor Ort erheblich zu straffen und trotzdem erste Hinweise auf Schadensursachen zu geben, typische Symptomkombinationen/Interaktionsketten modellhaft aufzuzeigen und damit das Erarbeiten von Interpretationshilfen für die interdisziplinäre Ursachenforschung zu erleichtern.
7. Insgesamt dient die systematisch strukturierte Maßnahmenkette einer fundierten Grundlagenermittlung und damit der effektiven Ausführungsplanung und -überwachung bis hin zur Qualitätskontrolle.

[23] Vgl. Glashoff Anm. 10.

4. Zusammenfassung

Insgesamt bilden die zum Teil innovativen rechnergestützten Verfahren des NLD der Anamnese und Schadenserstdiagnose sowie Dokumentation ein integrales System, dessen Komponenten—dem objektspezifischen Anforderungsprofil entsprechend—austauschbar bzw. entbehrlich sind. Der Schwerpunkt bei wichtigen Kulturdenkmalen sollte jedoch auf einer ganzheitlichen Anwendung liegen.

Selbstverständlich können die im Verlauf der Forschungsprojekte entwickelten oder geplanten rechnergestützten Verfahren der Visualisierung und Dokumentation zunächst nur vorläufige Interpretationshilfen geben. Sie sind als Service-Leistungen aufzufassen, die einem interdisziplinären Untersuchungsteam den Einstieg in vertiefende Zustands- und Schadenserfassungen erleichtern und erste Hinweise für Konservierungs- und Restaurierungsmaßnahmen ermöglichen. In diesem Zusammenhang könnten die entsprechenden Verfahren der Schadenserstdiagnose—in einer zweiten Bearbeitungsstufe vor allem auf objektrelevante Referenzflächen konzentriert—zunehmend an Bedeutung gewinnen. Dabei muß jedoch immer im Vordergrund stehen: mit möglichst geringem finanziellen und dokumentarischen Aufwand komplexe Datenstrukturen schnell und präzise zu erfassen, zu korrelieren, zu einem Therapie- und Wartungskonzept auszuwerten sowie—unter dem Gesichtspunkt multitemporaler Reproduzierbarkeit für qualitätssichernde Monitoringmaßnahmen—langfristig abzuspeichern. Dabei sollten nach Möglichkeit selbstverständlich auch die bewährten 'händischen' Verfahren mit einer schrittweisen Überführung in rechnergestützte Hilfen der Bestandserfassung und -sicherung zum Einsatz kommen. Daß eine ständige Pflege und Aktualisierung dieser hochentwickelten Arbeitsinstrumente durch gründlich ausgebildetes, nach mehrjähriger Erfahrung mit den spezifischen Erfordernissen der Denkmalpflegepraxis vertrautes Fachpersonal—wie diplomierte Dokumentare—eigentlich ein zwingendes Erfordernis ist, sei an dieser Stelle als selbstverständliche Grundvoraussetzung nachdrücklich betont.

Cutting off the king's head: images and the (dis)location of power

Frank Colson, Jean Colson, Ross Parry, and Andrew Sawyer

Imagining the Past

Today, it seems unquestionable that the privileging of text within our histories has denied us certain stories and certain views of the past. Allowing text to be the stuff of substance, and image merely that of illustration, has impoverished our models of distant historical places and moments. Culturally conditioned and technologically limited to building the past from and with words—with all the structural constraints therein—we have been limited (or so we now believe) as to the shapes and patterns we can conceive and demonstrate. It is arguable that the complexities of power in the historical contexts we are engaged in analysing cannot be fully grasped when restricted to one medium.

This is a multi-authored essay representing the work of four individuals, of different formations, but all engaged by the proximity of images and power. Moreover, the work exemplified in the case studies discussed here could not have been done without an active engagement with digital technology—they have been enabled by the use of Kleio Image Analysis System, an Open Hypermedia environment, and Computer Aided Design. But our engagement is led by our theoretical and historiographical perspective; and whilst that perspective has been broadened and developed by these technologies, it was not shaped by them. Therefore, outside the footnotes, technology as such will not be mentioned again.

Imaging Power

The emergence of the novel and puissant Dutch Republic from the medieval Low Countries in the last quarter of the sixteenth century, stands as our first example: the textualization of its political theory never achieved the impact of Machiavelli, Bodin or Hobbes—indeed its most elegant theorist, Johannes Althusius (1557–1638)—and the terms and concepts he used—is practically forgotten.[1] Yet the republic did see the outpouring of a large body of historical and political prints or cartoons, some 2000 surviving for the period 1588–1632.[2] Beyond the meticulous cataloguing of the early collectors these 'diagrammatic' prints have not been studied systematically in the way that, for instance, 'textual' pamphlets have been analysed.[3] Intimately connected, as they are, with the political life of a novel and potent polity, they compose a significant source—a pivotal source if we agree with Moxey's argument that 'the social values expressed by the visual sign systems of these media cannot be distinguished from some underlying reality that they are assumed to "reflect" ', but that 'to all intents and purposes, these systems *constituted* the society whose values they articulated'.[4]

We reach a similar conclusion when we turn our gaze to late nineteenth-century Brazil—what many, indeed, would refer to as another great early modern Republic. What we may—cautiously—call 'A total history of Brazil' has not yet been written because (again) historians have restricted themselves to

---

[1] Johannes Althusius, *Politica methodice digesta* (1603, enlarged version 1610 and 1614). A Westphalian, Althusius (1557–1638) was Syndic of Emden, a town not technically part of the Republic, but garrisoned by the Dutch, to whom his work was dedicated. The work is now most accessible to the English reader in abridged form in F. S. Carney, *The Politics of Johannes Althusius (*London: Eyre and Spottiswoode, 1965). In his introduction to Carney's work, J. Friedrich described the *Politica* as 'a culmination of medieval social thought and a watershed of modern political ideas' (p. xix). However, many of Althusius' terms (such as 'symbiosis' and 'consociato') are not now part of the political lexicon.

[2] The period covered by our research into Dutch prints is set within the famous Eighty Years' War of 1568–1648 in which the Dutch won their independence.

[3] The catalogues of F. Muller, *De Nederlandsche Geschiedenis in platen. Beredeneerde beschrijving van Nederlandsche historieplaten, zinneprenten en historische kaart*en, 4 vols (first published Amsterdam, 1863–82; reprint Amsterdam: N. Israel, 1970); and G. van Rijn, *Katalogus der historie- spot- en zinneprinten betrekkelijk de geschiedenis van Nederlanden, verzameld door Atlas van Stolk*, 10 vols (Amsterdam, 1895–1933) include most of the prints of the period. Recently, Horst and Tanis in *Images of Discord* (Grand Rapids: Eerdmans, 1993) have raised the profile of the prints.

[4] K. Moxey, *Peasants, Warriors and Wives* (Chicago: University of Chicago Press, 1989), p. 131.

textual sources. Not merely in the sense that (as in many parts of early modern Europe) to be literate was to be a tiny segment of society—adult, male, rich and white, but rather that though prolific, laws, reportage and formal debate (i.e. textual representations), simply codified one particular version of politics and culture. The privileged—in Brazil at least—the *public* rather than the *private* realm; the *public* events of legislative debate, the *public* war between stated interest, and they set aside the intense and all-pervasive *private* violence of privilege and deference—a significant strand in the configuration of power.

What is clear is that within both of these stories of 'early modern' polities, our enduring proclivity to text has both limited our interpretation and shaped our presentation of the past. Yet what is just as true is that those historiographical communities that are bringing images in from the margins (literally and metaphorically) are producing edifying, relevant, and credible new takes on the past. Within, for example, the studies of early seventeenth-century England, the formulaic portraits of Jacobean and Caroline culture are now emerging as embodiments and acts—rather than just ornaments and depictions—of the Jacobean and Caroline elites.[5] Similarly, the lavish scenery designs of the opulent royal festivals of King James I of England are, today, approached as components of—rather than simply backdrops to—the ideology of absolute monarchy.[6] Likewise, due to the widening of our, as it were, evidential franchise, the architectural façades and building styles of the English Renaissance stand, today, less as mere stages for, and more as active engagements with, the political fracture of the time.[7] In fact, within this new multi-format—dare one say 'multi-media'—historiography, to consider the temporary images of (for example) civic pageantry more as technologies of power, and less as insubstantial ephemera, seems not only possible but necessary.[8]

---

[5] For an accomplished study of one such portrait, see Ellen Chirelstein, 'Lady Elizabeth Pope: The Heraldic Body', in *Renaissance Bodies: The Human Figure in English Culture c. 1540–1660*, ed. by Lucy Gent and Nigel Llewellyn (London: Reaktion, 1990), pp. 36–59. The most sensitive and informed analysis of early Stuart portraiture is John Peacock, 'The Politics of Portraiture', in *Culture and Politics in Early Stuart England*, ed. by Kevin Sharpe and Peter Lake (Basingstoke: Macmillan, 1994), pp. 199–229. For a more panoptic take on the subject, see David Howarth's very accessible *Images of Rule: Art and Politics in the English Renaissance, 1485–1649* (Basingstoke: Macmillan, 1997).

[6] In this respect the work of Stephen Orgel has been instructive. See his 'The Royal Theatre and the Role of King', in *Patronage in the Renaissance Court*, ed. by Guy Fitch Lytel and Stephen Orgel (Princeton: Princeton University Press, 1981), pp. 261–73; as well as his important earlier work, *The Illusion of Power: Political Theatre in the English Renaissance* (Berkeley: University of California Press, 1975).

[7] See Tim Mowl and Brian Earnshaw, *Architecture Without Kings: The Rise of Puritan Classicism Under Cromwell* (Manchester: Manchester University Press, 1995).

[8] For a close examination of the cultural influences within one such arch used in

But what the recent historiography of early Stuart England also demonstrates is that more than just increasing the quantity of meaningful evidence available to us, images, in fact, provide levers and conduits, glimpses and echoes of discourses that are simply not as accessible in our other documents. This argument, about theory but developed from an engagement with the remaining artefacts, or sources, of three different milieu, can be provided with a nexus by considering one particular (though, admittedly, rather complex) discourse—the discourse of 'power'. With particular reference to those three 'early modern' polities already mentioned, we argue for the existence of a potent bond between the nature of power and the nature of images. And that, perhaps, the story of power is—occasionally—one best found within and told through images.

Our definition of 'power', here, is, of course, crucial. The 'power' (that we are suggesting synchronizes so adroitly to the nature of images) is that as described by Michel Foucault—specifically as laid out in his 1976 essay on the subject. Echoing (if not a confessed subscriber to) the parameters of post-structuralism, Foucauldian power is net-like and dynamic, not hierarchical and stable. Rather than centralized it is diffuse, shifting rather than static. Polysemic, polyvalent, and ubiquitous, Foucauldian power is a constant interplay of inter-relationships, a continuing struggle, an-ongoing negotiation within which every definition (by speech, by thought, by gesture, by text, and, yes, by image) is a moment of—and cause for—the reconfiguration of power itself. In this conceptualization, individuals do not 'exercise' power, but are themselves the points of its manifestation. Foucault, however, appends a caveat: we are not conditioned to think of power in this way. Modern political theory, he explains, has inherited and bound itself to the 'Leviathan' of sovereignty—and a notion of an ordered, concentric, and descending power, even if the actual figure or body of the sovereign itself is no longer there. The Foucauldian challenge, therefore, is for us to 'Cut off the King's Head' within our conceptions of power—and, consequently, unfix and de-gravitate that presumed 'centre'.[9]

James' triumphal entry into London, see Gervase Hood, 'A Netherlandic Triumphal Arch for James I', in *Across the Narrow Seas: Studies in the History and Bibliography of Britain and the Low Countries Presented to Anna E. C. Simoni*, ed. by Susan Roach (London: The British Library, 1991), pp. 67–82. For the text of the procession in which the arches were used, see Thomas Dekker and Ben Jonson, *The Magnificent Entertainment Given to King James, Queen Anne his wife, and Henry Frederick the prince, upon the day of His Majesty's triumphant passage (from the Tower) through his Honourable City (and Chamber) of London, being the 15. of March. 1603*, as reproduced in *Jacobean Civic Pageants*, ed. by Richard Dutton (Keele: Ryburn Publishing, 1995), pp. 19–115.

[9] 'Truth and Power: Interview with Alessandro Fontano and Pasquale Pasquino', trans. by P. Patton and M. Morris, in M. Foucault, *Power, Truth, Strategy* (Sydney: Feral Publications, 1979), pp. 29–48 (p. 38). For Foucault's thinking on power in the context

And this is our point: the structure of meaning (the discourse) created by this act of theoretical regicide creates a system of meaning web-like, topographic, where (freed from the chain of hierarchy) anything can connect to a plethora of others. In other words, Foucault's notions of power—notions that resist hierarchical, centralized systems of authority—would seem to be more readily and more substantively visualized, and more intuitively understood in and through images. Or (to state the corollary), text is a system whereby symbols are arranged linearly and sequentially within a (consequent) hierarchical structure; i.e., the very antithesis of Foucauldian power. Consequently, the frame of reference/referents which represents and demonstrates the complex interconnecticity—the topography—of modern theories of power, might be, we suppose, the image. (Text is but a sub-set of Image, the latter explicitly promoting and encouraging more than one view.) Or put another way: though we understand text is in itself 'power', we suspect 'power' may be *diagrammed* more readily and more effectively than it can be *textualized*.

Diagramming the Dutch Republic

Our own observations tell us that practitioners of power politics are aware of the significance of gesture, of 'power dressing', of all that is encompassed by the word image. Similarly, in the past, power was often manifested through media other than the word. Moreover, some forms of power—physical forms—simply cannot be described with words (one cannot describe the electrical system that transfers power around a car or a building: one diagrams it). And there are certainly some historical cultures that seem to expound this. For instance, John Montias has demonstrated that the Dutch Republic was saturated with images.[10] That such an image-conscious society included a vigorous brand of political imagery (closely connected with its rejection of Habsburg rule and its Republic's burgeoning power) may not be unconnected. The Republic was wired for a discourse of diagrammed power in the way that today's information societies are wired for Information Technology.

---

of a wider debate, see S. Lukes, *Power* (Oxford: Basil Blackwell, 1986), and for a context admirably free of postmodern jargon, see S. R. Clegg, *Frameworks of Power* (London: Newbury Park; New Delhi: Sage, 1989). Anybody who doubts that our conceptions of power are shaped by this 'sovereign' construct might take up Microsoft's PowerPoint software, set to diagram an organization; they will find it practically impossible to create anything but 'top down' structures, presumably because those who specified the software could conceive of nothing else.

[10] J. M. Montias' major work was *Artists and Artisans in Delft* (Princeton: Princeton University Press, 1982), which demonstrated the quantities of paintings and prints, which could be found in almost all homes in Delft in the early seventeenth century.

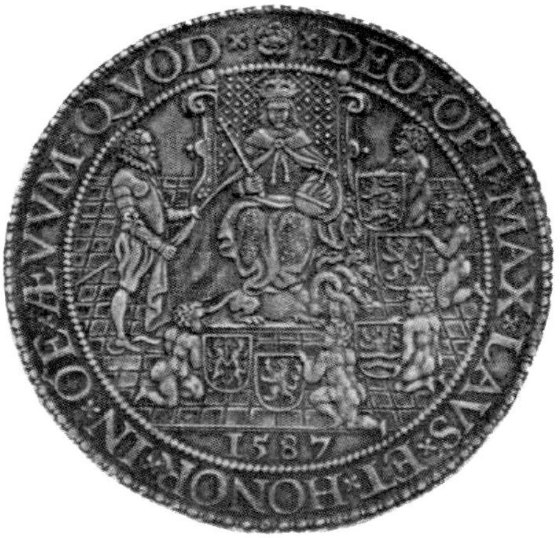

Fig. 1. 'Penning' dated 1588: from H. E. Greve, De Tijd van den Tachtigjarigen Oorlog in Beeld *(Amsterdam: Uitgevers-Maatschappy "Elsevier", 1908), p. 67*

The Dutch, who had thrown out the man who would be king in the Abjuration of 1581 (their own, as it were, Foucauldian moment in the redefinition of power), established a polity defined by constant negotiation: a definition far closer to Foucault's concept than that defined by a trajectory that includes Bodin, Hobbes, and sovereign power.[11] And it is perhaps significant that, in the work of Johannes Althusius, we find analyses of the polity carried out in an ascending manner—as Foucault argued we should. This form-giving power of this dynamic, imbalanced state could be comprehended more clearly if we could graphically contrast a 'sovereign' view of the Dutch situation with a domestic counterpart. Fortunately, due to the involvement of the English in the developing maelstrom in the Low Countries, we have English observations from the period. A pictorial example may be seen in a coin produced by the partisans of the English Earl of Leicester, sent to aid the Dutch in 1585 (fig. 1); we see their situation depicted sovereignly, with Elizabeth of England, Leicester, an apocalyptic beast, and the provinces kneeling at the monarch's feet in supplication. The Latin text translates: 'To the best and greatest God be praise and honour forever, because . . .' and then the text ends, the rest (i.e., the reason for the praise) only being expressible in the image within.[12] In short, here it is

[11] The classic work is F. H. Hinsley, *Sovereignty*, 2nd edn (Cambridge: Cambridge University Press, 1986). He traces the trajectory Bodin-Henry VIII-Hobbes, and regards sovereignty as he defined it as the pinnacle of political theory.

[12] The reverse shows clerical figures, seven in all, who appear to be falling. They can be distinguished by their dress as, at the lowest point, the pope (losing his grip on a

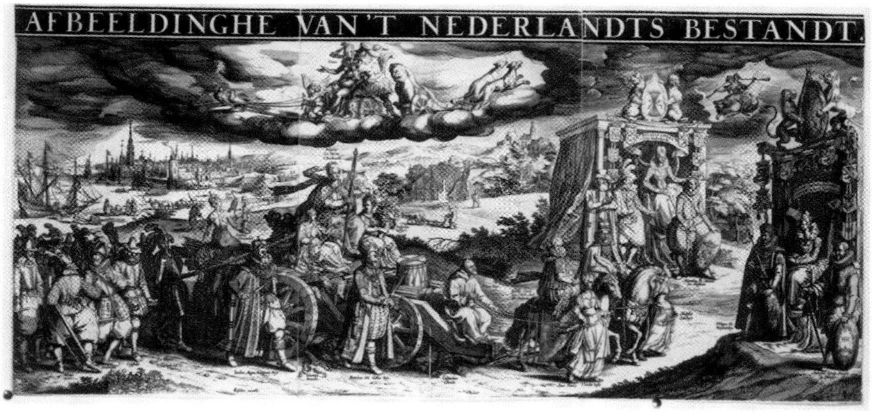

Fig. 2. C. J. Visscher, 'Afbeelding van 't Nederlandts Bestandt' [Image of the Netherlands Truce], c. *1609. FM1267. Reproduced by permission of the Rijksprentenkabinet, Rijksmuseum, Amsterdam*

only an image that can express the coin's message. And that message can be simply diagrammed or described in hierarchical terms.

In contrast to this hierarchic image, far more complex 'diagrams' flourished among the political prints of the Republic. An example can be seen in a depiction of the truce negotiations of the early 1600s, Muller's print number S1267c (fig. 2).[13] 'Reading' it primarily as a political diagram, we see, from the left, military forces in confusion at the end of the fighting, a great carriage representing the truce, aided by the monarchs of England and France, led by allegorical figures and the Archdukes, and carrying Peace and other virtuous characters. It is steered by Johan Ney, a Jesuit and the Habsburg negotiator of the Truce. It heads towards a sunlit region—indicated stage right, as it were, rather than illustrated—between two booths, representing the Independent Netherlands and the Habsburg Netherlands. Clearly much could be said about such an image. The point here, however, is that dynamic, shifting patterns and

---

monstrance and a chalice), followed by a group consisting of a cardinal, two monks, two bishops, and possibly a Jesuit. Above, the Tetragrammaton is shown in a cloud from which lightning strikes the clerics. The text reads QVEM DEVS CONFICIET SPIRITV ORIS SVI. 'Whom the Lord shall consume with the spirit of his mouth'. II Thess. 2. 8 The coin is attributed to the Earl of Leicester, or rather his partisans in the Netherlands, in major coin catalogues (e.g., E. Hawkins, A. W. Franks, H. A. Grueber, *Medallic Illustrations of the History of Great Britain and Ireland to the Death of George II*, vol. I (London: British Museum, 1885), p. 139, their no. 99).

[13] *Afbeelding van't Nederlandts Bestandt* [Image of the Netherlands Truce], *c.* 1609, C. J. Visscher. FM1267. An allegorical print about the Twelve Years of Truce 1609–21.

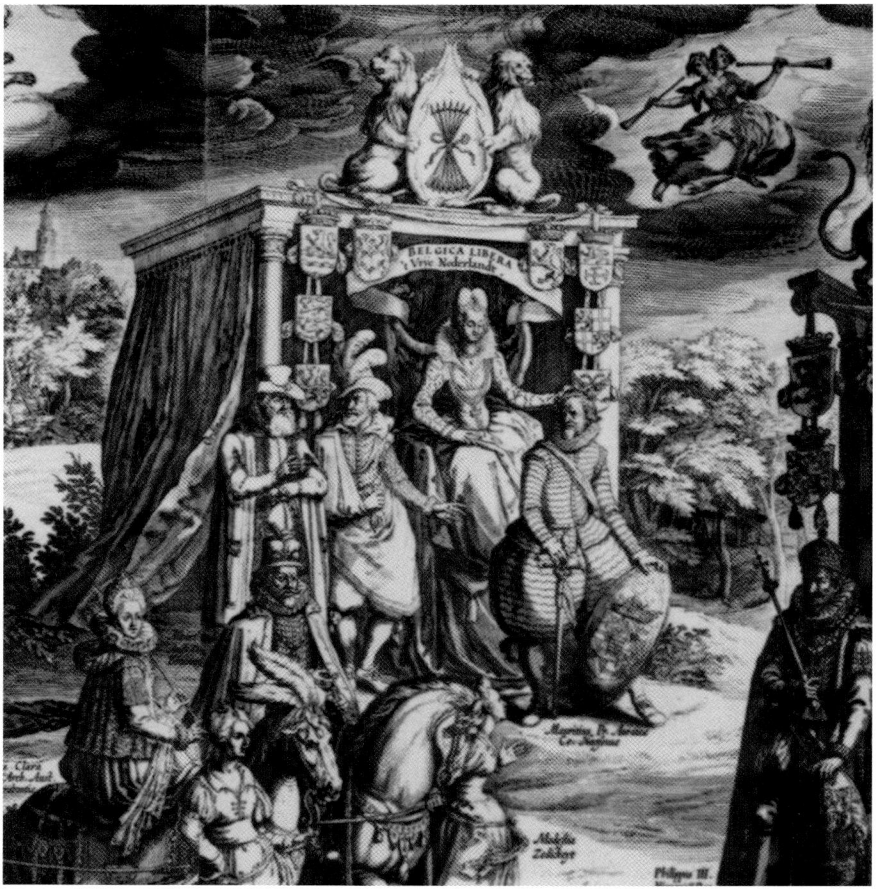

Fig. 3. Detail, 'Afbeelding van 't Nederlandts Bestandt' [Image of the Netherlands Truce], c. 1609. FM1267. Reproduced by permission of the Rijksprentenkabinet, Rijksmuseum, Amsterdam

networks of power are diagrammed. For example, in one detail (fig. 3) a cameo represents the Independent Netherlands. The intense debate within the Republic occasioned by the negotiations is graphically projected: the Netherlands maid gestures to Maurits, the Dutch commander on her left; to her right, the gestures and glances of the figures representing the States General are, likewise, there to be noted. This scene stands as a microcosm of the entire image, alive with debate, negotiation and movement. Here—in interplay, interconnecity, diffusion—is Foucault's concept of power diagrammed.

Moreover, if we take each 'element' of Leicester's image—crown, throne, monarch, and kneeling figures, naked in supplication—and analyse a sample of

Dutch imagery for the same elements,[14] it can be demonstrated that such elements were mostly portrayed in a negative fashion, rarely neutrally, and only on some occasions with any positive connotations. Thus the discourse projected by Leicester was, it seems, quite inappropriate to his circumstances as Governor General in the Netherlands from 1585 to 1588. It is in imagery, more than in major canonical texts, that the constant negotiation implicit in the 'un-centralized' and disaggregated manifestation of power that structured the nascent Dutch State is most strikingly obvious.

Picturing Brazil's República

However it is not just the non-sovereign inter-relations of power of the Dutch Republic that seem to sharpen when viewed pictorially. For when we turn to our other Republican example, we likewise find a discourse of power that was—and needs to be—recalled through images. For instance: it is hardly surprising that scholars attempting to examine the extraordinary events of the period 1868–1910 (generally regarded as the founding years of contemporary Brazil) should have wrestled with the fact that though slavery ended and the Republic emerged, the structure of social relationships inherited from the colonial era was retained. Brazil has continued as a society characterized by social apartheid. In 1883 a political slogan proclaimed 'Brazil is coffee, coffee is the "Negro", the "Negro" is Brazil'. But by 1900 the 'Negro' was forgotten, coffee was hegemonic: the 'Negro' was emphatically not Brazil? In fact, South America's premier power, centre of one of the world's most lucrative trades, a continental polity, entered into a crippled existence in the twentieth century—one from which it has not recovered. Hitherto the reasons for this have remained obscure. Until, we think about the nature of power, because scholars have failed to take on board the dynamic, net-like, diffuse nature of power in this continental polity. Indeed, however sophisticated such statements as 'the structure collapsed in May 1888' (when the Abolition Law was approved by the Legislature)[15] and 'revolution of Abolition' might appear at first glance, they have become simple tributes to the

[14] Kleio IAS enables each element of each image to be registered for searching and data retrieval, down to a very detailed level if required, by the use of textual image descriptions linked to digital representations of the prints themselves. Thus, for example, if during research the gesture of kneeling is found to be of significance, all the scenes showing such a pose or gesture can be called, viewed, and referenced.

[15] Seymour Drescher, 'Brazilian Abolition in Comparative Perspective', *Hispanic American Historical Review* (August, 1988), 429–60 (p. 459). Drescher develops the useful notion of an hierarchical regime of notables (p. 458), 'demoralized' by the mass mobilization of the crisis of 1886–88. He notes that the transition from slavery has barely been discussed.

tactical ability of oligarchs.[16] They do not examine the threat to private absolute authority explicit during the final years of the struggle to end slavery. Because—and this is the crucial point—they fail to confront the fact that power in Brazil remained neither hierarchical nor stable. Such approaches, therefore, do not enable us easily to understand either the fragility of the state in twentieth-century Brazil nor the continuation of its colonial heritage as social apartheid. In short, the intrinsic poverty of textual sources that deal with the public rather than the private limits their explanatory value in explaining change in a dynamic structure, because they do not enable scholars to cross the door from public to private. Scholars of Brazil have been aware of this, and the last decade has seen increasing recourse to the work of literary critics' expressions of 'misplaced' [*fora de lugar*][17] and to the anthropologist's sense of the public place as incessant war.[18] But, exciting as these are as idealizations, they have only the most limited power as explanation, because they operate at the wrong remove. Though contextualizations, they do not enable us to describe in the most approximate fashion the extraordinary impact of 1887–89 on the future course of Brazilian history. Such models do not, for example, explain the extraordinary sense of alienation felt by army officers against the rule of merchants and lawyers—'frock coats'—nor the extraordinary influence of foreign ideas—casting a long shadow over the twentieth century. They allude to but do not elucidate the

[16] Jacob Gorender's *A escravidão reabilitada* (São Paulo: Ática, 1990) discusses the recent historiography of 1887–88 as that of an 'abolitionist revolution', pp. 133–38. Gorender correctly identifies the role of slaveocrat leaders in a transition which would be 'slow, gradual and secure', p. 146, and notes scholarly attention given to the perception of the 'faithful slave' during the crisis of 1887–88; Lilia Schwarcz, *Retrato em branco e negro. Jornais, escravos e cidadãos em São Paulo no final do século XIX* (São Paulo: Companhia das Letras, 1987).

[17] Roberto Schwarz, *Misplaced Ideas. Essays on Brazilian: Culture* (London: Verso, 1992), especially 'Misplaced Ideas. Literature and Society in Late Nineteenth Century Brazil', pp. 19–32 (original title: 'As idéias fora de lugar' [misplaced] *Estudos Cebra* (1973), 3).

[18] Roberto A. da Matta, *A Casa & a Rua. Espaco, cidadania, mulher e morte no Brasil* (São Paolo: Editora Basiliense, 1985), especially pp. 71–102. Da Matta's House [Casa] and street [Rua] are basic dynamic opposites within the web of relationships described by Foucault. The Brazilian anthropologist's essay, 'For an Anthropology of the Brazilian Tradition' or 'A Virtude esta no Meio', in *The Brazilian Puzzle. Culture on the Borderlands of the Western World*, ed. by David J. Hess and Roberto A. da Matta (New York: Columbia University Press, 1995), pp. 270–93, argues (p. 276) that 'we will not advance towards significant understanding of Brazilian and Latin American reality if we do not discover the deep relations between the impersonal commands of law (conceived as a function of 'individuals') and 'friends' (a universe governed by the implicit and personalized rules of parentela (the extended family structure on which social influence is based)).

extraordinary gulf between the tenacious belief in modernity that is the public doctrine of state organizations and the brute power of private privilege that remains untouched by law. They take little account of the way in which men perceived that in 1887–88 the war between private privilege and general security that had surfaced in the 1830s had suddenly re-surfaced and the savage nature of private power again lay exposed. Most of all, they do not address the central debate of the time: the ownership of progress and science—the pervasive heritage of the French Revolution: and the acute and specific threat of 'degeneration' that haunted the political elite of the age. Using text we might as historians describe the words of the proclamation of abolition as a 'tersely worded death warrant for a collapsing structure', *but* we cannot easily understand its *aftermath*—text gives rise to the sense of political relationships which remain ill defined, hence 'misplaced'.

Therefore, in order to understand this sense of the 'misplaced', other forms of expression have to be brought to the argument,[19] for example images—in this case, specifically mass-produced cartoon images. For though it was only the poet and the novelist who could venture beyond the public to the livid intimacies of private power, it was only the cartoonist who had the medium through which to represent these complex discourses.[20] Acknowledged fictions have their uses, but even literary giants such as Machado de Assis, writer, newspaper columnist, and in 1888 a well-placed clerk in the Ministry of Agriculture could only obliquely refer to the 'absolute oligarchy' in a minor publication—their novels amply describing the effect of its existence. Nevertheless his column in the leading newspaper, the *Gazeta* provides the vital bridge, a sense of the 'vie quotidienne', which allows the historian to move towards a fuller explanation, one which includes the argument of images and their role in explaining the political

---

[19] Pereira Barreto: 'On the one side are the abolitionists, riding on a sentimental rhetoric and armed with a revolutionary metaphysics, on the other side are the landowners, silent and humiliated, in the attitude of those who meditate upon their guilt or meditate an impossible revenge' (quoted from Paula Beiguelman, *Teoria Acão no Pensamento Abolicionista*, vol. I of *Formação Política do Brasil* [São Paulo: Livraria Pioneira, 1967], p. 159).

[20] Not simply because cartoons were so diffused, but because images play such a large role in the discussion of the complex grammar of encompassment and passages between 'this world' and the 'other world' [da Matta, p. 276]. The open hypermedia environment, Microcosm, allows individual links and associations to be catalogued and classified according to the various perceptions of contemporary viewers and latter-day scholars alike. The flexibility of the environment enables the identification of critical components of the various images and their referents, limiting allusion and inference while clarifying arguments. Frank Colson, 'Case Study C. Hypermedia Database Management Systems: Microcosm as a Research Tool', in *Databases in Historical Research*, ed. by Charles Harvey and Jon Press (London: Macmillan, 1996), pp. 69–71.

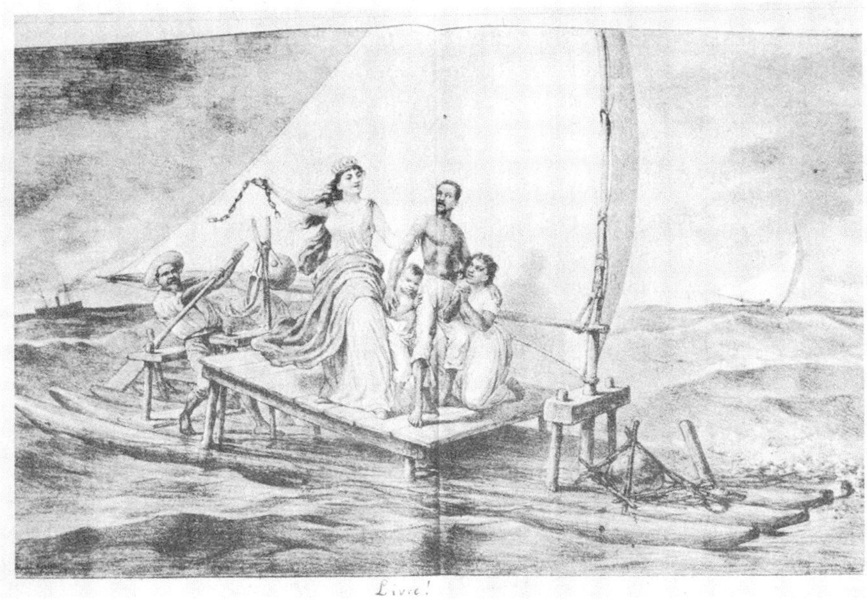

Fig. 4. 'Livre', Revista Illustrada *, Rio de Janeiro, 14 October 1884*

topography of everyday life.[21]

The day-to-day chronicle of official political life in late nineteenth-century Brazil was, by early modern standards, extraordinarily amply documented. Some thirty newspapers and periodicals followed and created daily life in Rio de Janeiro, capital of the Empire. Sheer plethora is daunting enough, and the study of the page is rewarding. It is however crucial to note that, thanks to French influence and the advent of a market among the urban elites, the period witnessed the remarkable flowering of the political cartoon. Systematic cataloguing of the cartoons for Rio at least is complete and some editions of the long run of the *Brasil Illustrada*, edited by Angelo Agostini, have been reproduced in facsimile. A prolific caricaturist, Agostini's understanding of the intricate topography of power has meant that his work has long been used by scholars to enliven their accounts. Evoking currents of political life, the caricatures are brilliant, strident, yet building a subtle vocabulary of power—typified by the cartoon 'free' [*livre*] published in 1883

[21] Arguably the greatest of all Portuguese-language novelists, author of nine novels and more than two hundred short stories (1839–1908). For his political allusion, see Machado de Assis, *Bons Dias! Crônicas (1888–89), edicão, introducão e notas de John Gledson* (São Paulo: Editora Hucitec, 1990), pp. 13–14.

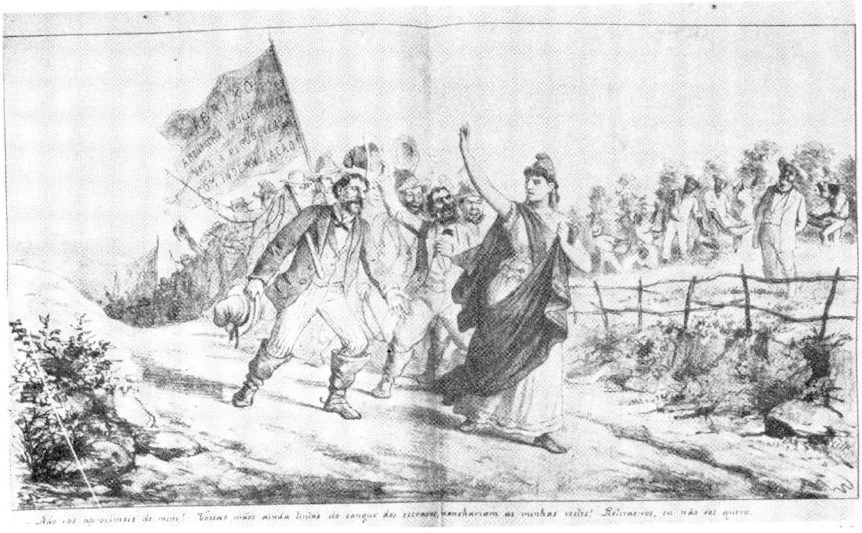

Fig. 5. 'Não vos aproximeis de mim! Vossas mãos ainda tintas de sangue dos escravos manchariam as minhas vistas! Retirae-vos, tu não vos quero.' Revista Illustrada *15 June 1888 [original orthography]*

(fig. 4).[22] Yet they have not been 'read'—perhaps because they allude to that constant negotiation that remained a hallmark of political life under Empire and (after 1889) the Republic or, more prosaically, because historians have found it difficult to collate the visual clues projected by these images. The sense of concealed brutalities that the limits of such negotiation between had been reached in 1888 is nowhere more powerfully expressed than in another cartoon 'The Republic courted by the ex-proprietors of slaves' published only a few days after the abolition act had been signed.[23] The fact that the cartoons would be

[22] 'Livre'—depicting a *jangada* [raft] commonly used as a lighter to ship goods over the reefs of Ceará to ocean-going steamships. In 1884 the *jangadeiros* [lightermen] refused to transport slaves for sale in neighbouring Maranhão or the Southeast. Agostini depicted their leader Nascimento steering a raft carrying a slave family and the figure of 'liberty'. The depiction of the family, and the figure of 'liberty' contrast richly with stereotypical views. From R. Maghalães Jr., *Deodoro. A Espada contra o Império* (São Paolo: Companhia Editora nacional, 1957), vol. I, facing p. 192.

[23] The radical press, led by the *Cidade do Rio* on 25 May wrote that 'we have notices from the interior that various ex-slave owners have refused to obey the law and have informed their captives that they can only leave their lands or receive a salary once they have received a letter of manumission from the Regent'. The cartoon was criticized in the press on 18 June. It has been reproduced in Maghalães Jr (as in note 22), p. 348.

posted up in country Venda and city cafes, corner kiosks, or coffee-houses (available to the millions of illiterates) determined that they would inhabit a world of invocations and votives. Indeed, the appeal to 'modernity' in its French allusions, by 1888 well known to viewers, makes this image a vital evocation of the crisis which broke as slavery collapsed.

This image is part of an historical moment when sovereign power was disaggregated—when the link between the crown (supreme mediator) and its natural supporters was fractured. It depicts a procession of ex-slave-owners dressed in traditional country garb (arguably similar to slave-catchers) following a tattered banner reading 'Down with the Abolitionist Monarchy—Long Live the Republic with Compensation' (fig. 5). Here República unleaves the ruptured discourse of power (or, as one radical put it, the bestialization of the people) which characterized 1888–89. Published within weeks of the proclamation of abolition on 13 May, and much discussed in the Press (for Agostini had long campaigned in the abolitionist cause), the cartoon works at many levels. República epitomizes the civic virtues of a Robespierre, her robes, the cap and the tricolour rosette, and the stance, denoting purity, right, and reason, liberty and progress. With her foot forward on the march of Progress we are asked to wonder whether she will allow her purity to be stained by those who pursue her to other more bestial ends. Her protests are vehement and proud: 'Do not come near to me! Your hands are still red with the blood of slaves. You will stain my robes. Leave me! I do not want you!' But the ex-slaveowners remain insistent. They will choose 'revolution' (even the French Revolution's tricolour) rather than face the hierarchical polity. For the planters seek to expropriate Progress and divorce it from liberty. Their campaign flag demands 'compensation' for the slaves they have lately owned and dressed. Their eyes are avid, their intention evil. The days when the cartoon was being sold in Rio were ones in which the Press was dragging example after example of planters refusing to release their slaves, imprisoning and whipping them, to the attention of the authorities, who often looked the other way. The depiction of ex-slaveowners as harbingers of unreason and bent on the prostitution if not subversion of the Republic was a powerful one. Fear and avidity characterize the image of the planters, as they face a world in which authority does not appear to be theirs alone. For months, abolitionist agitation had begun to isolate planters from traditional support among the free poor and local propertied, as well as administrative organizations, which they had long controlled. By late 1887 slaves were not simply resisting planters, but also were running off the plantations and receiving support from clandestine and increasingly vociferous abolitionists. As early as November 1886 the Imperial government had refused to arm local militia (the National Guard) to prevent the militarization of the plantations. By October 1887 units of the army refused to return slaves to their owners. The Church, long a supporter of the status quo, finally abandoned the planters in late 1887, leaving their authority to rest on the degree to which they could informally organize local violence. Their private 'rights' to govern their Ashantis with complete impunity seemed in 1887–88 to have been usurped, by the government they expected to own.

Their desperation and pursuit of unreason so evident in the piercing and distraught impression of the 'archetypical' planters is quite remarkably documented. Since the abolition of the lash in late 1886 they had petitioned the Crown for guarantees of their property, for protection against a population of vagrants.[24] In May and June 1888 the abolitionist Press reported numerous threats made by ex-proprietors to the freedmen on their plantations. Yet that unreason is evidenced not merely by the visual contrast to the secular sanctity of República but also by the picture of workers (blacks and whites alike) gathering in a coffee crop widely documented to be one of the largest on record. The bemused expression on the face of the overseer indicated that the procession of planters is not really concerned with the crop, still less with slaves and their families, but is concerned with the business of recovering the web of connections and patronage which were, as far as the planters were concerned, the essence of the state. The demand for immediate compensation is not merely a literal assault on the Republic of reason and purity but also a reassertion that Progress shall be impelled by savage dominion rather than law.

In effect, what these images capture and diagram is the extent of the social rupture that emerged in 1887–88, when a Crown, ruling by hereditary right and through established laws, clashed with provinces and their historic liberties, as well as proprietors who regarded themselves as having absolute dominion over their lands. Scholars have noted that the 'absolute oligarchy' immediately emerged as ally of the Republic, and many ex-slaveowners profited from the years of high prices commanded by coffee. But most have failed to appreciate the extent to which many felt that the mobilization of the free population in support of abolition that occurred in 1887 presaged a loss of control over their private local societies. The motifs of freedom characterized by the stance of the liberated slaves in Ceará in 1884 were widely diffused. By mid-1888 few would disagree that abolition had been won by the slaves themselves, with explicit support from several different segments of society and the 'golden law' of 13 May 1888 was (like so many previous reforms) a simple act of 'public security'. After the trauma of March–May 1888, planters were desperate to reconquer local hegemonies—hence the apparently irrational flight to the Federal Republic. The irony, therefore, that a regime of secular purity and order would protect the privacy of the lash was not lost to a contemporary reader of this and other images. Similarly, the depiction of the planters in the procession in traditional

[24] *'Fuga de escravos em Campinas': discursos pronunciados no senado pelo Exmo Sr. Barão de Cotegipe (Presidente do Conselho e Ministro de Estrangeiros)* (Rio de Janeiro: Imprensa Nacional, 1887), pp. 16–19. The speeches of the Council President addressed the issues raised by these petitions, sent to Parliament from May 1887, to abolition.

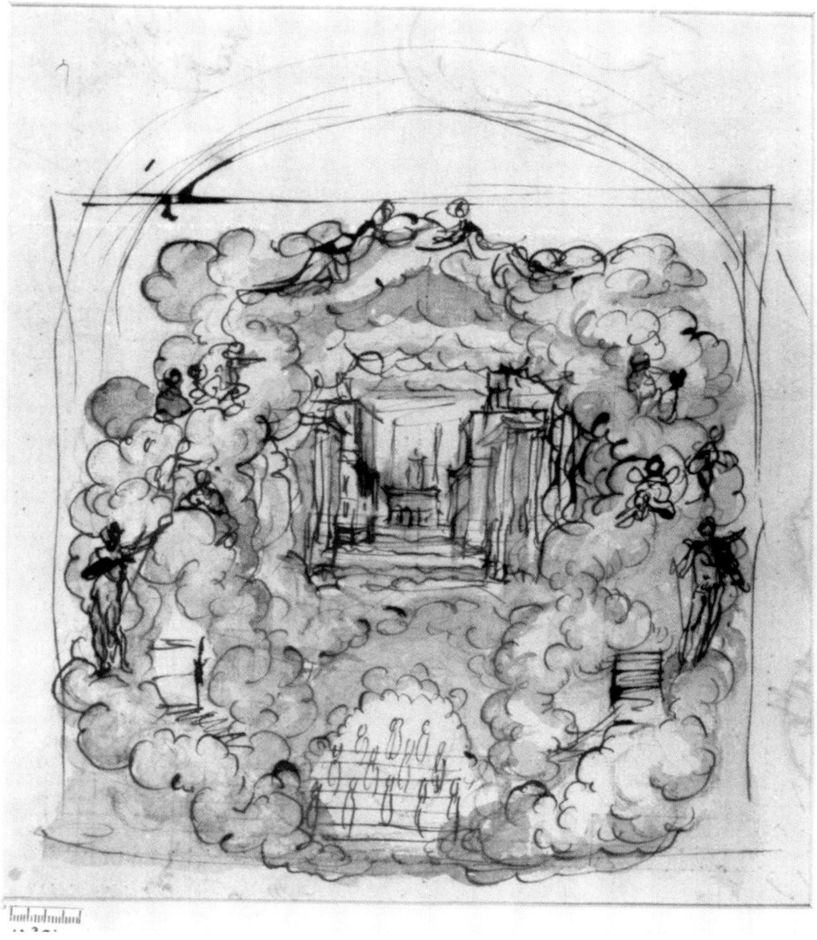

Fig. 6. Inigo Jones, 'Pallas of Perfection', Devonshire Collection, Chatsworth. Reproduced by permission of the Duke of Devonshire and the Chatsworth Settlement Trustees. © Photographic Survey, Courtauld Institute of Art, London

rough country garb (compared, at least, to the overseer), is no casual act—by early 1888 some of the planters who controlled the largest and most industrialized establishments already had freed their slaves. Angelo Agostini's layered image of June 1888 has, therefore, captured the moment of disruption which brought about the invocation of Order and the Republic by those whose legitimacy was that of custom and brute force. It points to forms of power which most regimes—including the Dutch Republic—have been unable to do little more than mitigate.

Mapping English Sovereignty

It was a similar struggle over (and appropriation of) the agents of 'progress' that characterizes our third and final example—the illusionary images of the English court masque. The court masques were exclusive royal entertainment performed before the king, his family, and his court as well as any (invited) visiting dignitaries. Though Elizabeth I (in the sixteenth century) and Lord Protector Oliver Cromwell (in the middle of the seventeenth century) enjoyed similar sorts of festivals, the English masque was almost entirely confined to a short history from 1605 to 1640. In content they were a combination of music, poetry, visual effect, dance, and song; 'pictures with light and motion' claimed the polymath Inigo Jones, designer of most of the shows.[25] Usually taking place on the evening of Twelfth Night or at Shrovetide (or, occasionally, at times of court wedding), these were lavish, conspicuously expensive events in the royal calendar, taking several hours to perform (sometimes, evidently, to the tedium of king and courtiers alike)[26] and, more times than not, staged in the royal Banqueting House at Whitehall.[27] The masques were a complex blend of indulgent frivolity and

[25] Jones offered this description in the text of the 1632 masque *Tempe Restored* (lines 49–50); reproduced in Stephen Orgel and Roy Strong, *Inigo Jones: The Theatre of the Stuart Court*, 2 vols (London: Sotheby Parke Bernet; and Berkeley: University of California Press, 1973), vol. II, pp. 479–504.

[26] 'Why don't they dance?' the king was reported to have called out at one eventful masque in 1618, 'What did they bring me here for?' See Orazio Busino's full account in *Calendar of State Papers: Venetian, 1617–19*, 24 January 1618, 'Anglipotrida', pp. 110–14. The original MS is in the archive of St Mark's, Venice (CLVII, cod. MCXXII. fols 72–75).

[27] In contrast to that of its successor (still standing on Whitehall today), there is little extant evidence relating to the first Jacobean Banqueting House. A sketch by Elizabethan architect Robert Smythson from *c.* 1609 (British Architectural Library, RIBA, London) provides an impression of the groundplot of the site. Similarly, Andrew Kerwyn's accounts relating to royal works at the time of Banqueting House's construction (a protracted process from 1604 to 1610) proffers valuable clues as to the building's internal and external design; see 'Declared Accounts of the Pipe and Audit Office, Works and Buildings', Public Record Office, London, E 351 / 3240–43. Consequently, studies of the space have been few and far between. See: Per Palme, *The Triumph of Peace: A Study of the Whitehall Banqueting House* (London: Thames and Hudson, 1957), pp. 1–5 and 115–18; *Dramatic Records in the Declared Accounts of the Office of Works 1560–1640*, The Malone Society Collections, vol. 10, ed. by R. F. Hill and F. P. Wilson (London: Malone Society, 1977), pp. xvi–xvii; and most recently—and most usefully—*The History of the*

state solemnity, sober didactics, and cutting satire. And, invariably, they turned upon an epiphanic moment where discord and antic movement were transformed into political order, serene spiritual and intellectual harmony. Throughout, the masquing space served (in a metonymic rather than metaphoric way) as a microcosm of the kingdom—with the sovereign central, pivotal, and privileged.

An image that shows well the stylized illusionary vista that was presented before the king is Jones's preparatory sketch (fig. 6) for a scenery design from *c.* 1618–19. The drawing, made in pen and brown ink washed with warm grey, was used, most likely, for the performance of George Chapman's *Masque of the Twelve Months*, the last festival, in fact, to be performed in the Banqueting House before an accidental fire destroyed it in January 1619.[28] Reporting on the entertainment, a contemporaneous diplomatic despatch gives us an indication of how this two-dimensional image was realized—in performance—as three-dimensional scenery:

> . . . at the foot of the room opposite his Majesty a curtain which hid all the wall at that end was let drop, revealing a perspective with very lovely ornaments which stood in the air between the ceiling of the room and the solarium. In it were seated all the lords of the masque, in the most beautiful order. By means of a hidden device it descended very, very gently down to the ground. Behind this perspective, in proportion as the lords' seat descended, and at their backs, there were seen in another perspective castles, towers, palaces, rooms and pictures in foreshortening. In truth it seemed to me that I had never seen anything that gave more cause for wonder. . . .[29]

The account makes clear that this image—like so many of Jones's masque designs before and after it—exploited the visual and spatial implications of

---

King's Works , ed. by H. M. Colvin (London: Her Majesty's Stationery Office, 1982) IV:II, pp. 322–24.

[28] A persuasive case was made for the connection between this drawing and Chapman's masque in a paper by Martin Butler entitled 'A re-identified Chapman masque and the Jacobean response to European crisis', delivered at *Texts and Cultural Change: History, Politics and Interpretation, 1520–1660*, The Reading Literature and History Conference, 16–19 July 1995. However, David Lindley, in his 'Select Chronology of Stuart Masques', makes no mention of the masque. Instead, the masque for 1619 is cited as Thomas Middleton, *The Masque of Heroes*; see his *Court Masques* (Oxford and New York: Oxford University Press, 1995), pp. xxvii–xxviii. Similarly, Stephen Orgel and Roy Strong's 'Calendar' in their *Inigo Jones* (as in note 25), vol. I, pp. 85–87, makes no reference to Middleton or to Chapman in respect to a 1618/9 masque. Their only relevant entry is for a 'Lost Masque for Prince Charles' for 1619.

[29] G. B. Gabalence's diplomatic dispatch of 12 February 1619 reproduced in J. Orrell, 'The London Court Stage in the Savoy Correspondence', *Theatre Research International*, 4 (1978–79), 84–85.

linear perspective to fix the king as primal spectator, as 'Britain's glorious eye'.[30] The geometrical construct of linear perspective, of course, privileges one eye in space—especially when that perspectival effect is the receding flats of a theatrical scene. The prospect of a street scene in perspective, for example, such as that which opened Ben Jonson's masque *The Vision of Delight* in 1617, was only aligned to the king's point of view. In contrast, a spectator positioned up in the balcony (see fig. 7, plate 26), askew to the stage, would have been presented with a very different (awry) arrangement of scenic objects—intentionally, explicitly, didactically.

But as well as underscoring the notion of the English king's unique acuity,[31] Jones's image also connected to discourses of stoic learning and civic instruction, of 'royal education and right'.[32] For this image of the 'Pallas of Perfection' (Jones usefully labelling his drawing on the far left of the paper) can also be read as a visual mnemonic of state-sanctioned discourse. Indeed, by 1618 it was something of a convention to present before the king and his court abstract themes and values rendered into (seemingly) substantive architectural form. From the 'Temple of Peace' (in 1604) to 'The Throne of Beauty' (in 1605) and from the 'House of Fame' (in 1609) to the 'House of Chivalry' (in 1610) and the 'House of Honour' (in 1614), the scenery of the English court masque repeatedly used images of buildings as analogues of complex thought. Drawing upon the medieval and early modern traditions of artificial memory, as well as the practice of contemplating and presenting conceptual space as physical space,[33] the 'Pallas of Perfection' brought (to use the words of one Elizabethan

---

[30] Thomas Campion, *Lord Hay's Masque* (1607), line 374, as reproduced in Orgel and Strong, *Inigo Jones* (as in note 25), vol. I, p. 119.

[31] See Ross Parry, 'The Careful Watchman: James I, didacticism and the perspectival organization of space', in *Disziplinierung im Alltag des Mittelalters und der frühen Neuzeit*, Veröffentlichungen des Instituts für Realienkunde des Mittelalters und der frühen Neuzeit 17, ed. by Gerhard Jaritz (Vienna: Der Österreichischen Akademie der Wissenschaften, 1999), pp. 275–97.

[32] The line is from Ben Jonson's masque *Pleasure Reconciled to Virtue*, performed in the Banqueting House on Twelfth Night 1618. As the young Prince Charles descends 'The hill of knowledge', a song calls for the figure of Atlas to allow men to 'read' the lines and signs of royal education, in both the spectacle itself (performed to, and centred upon King James) and the presence of Charles as one of the masques. Orgel and Strong, *Inigo Jones* (as in note 25), vol. I, pp. 285–88.

[33] See, for instance, the four treatises written as dialogue between a master and scholar on the importance of knowledge and science (and especially astronomy and the 'spheres') that make up Robert Record's, *Castle of Knowledge* (1556). Similarly, for a later text that describes—at length—the elements of the world using the metaphors of 'a magnificent house' ('heaven is the roofe; . . . the Moone and Starres, night Lamps; severall regions, severall roomes; . . . the earth, the floor, the sea a mote; the surface of the earth, an

mnemotechnician) 'a multitude into one'.[34] It provided an immediate, accessible and memorable diagram of a unified and ordered realm. It mapped, in a sense, the *shape* of Jacobean power.

Therefore, though just a preliminary sketch, implicit within this image is Jacobean monarchy in all its complexities. The early seventeenth century was, after all, a moment of massive epistemic change, at which a medieval court stared steadfast into the face of modernity. In this respect the 'Pallas of Perfection' represents an appropriation by the monarchical culture of the resurgent visual technologies of linear perspective that were empowering the eye of the Renaissance individual. Likewise, it denotes a moment when the technologies of visual mnemonics that were empowering the mind of early-modern learners was brought, judiciously, into close association with monarchical culture, particularly James I's cultural role as royal pedagogue, God's proxy as the 'sorest and sharpest schoolmaster'.[35] In this regard, Jones's image is a complex, layered diagram of power, within which the agents that could have promoted the sovereignty of the individual have instead been spun to promote the individuality of the sovereign. 'The Pallas of Perfection' (and the other scenes like it) relates a system of power at a time of epistemic rupture—a system of power reduced to an accessible, immediate, and intuitive representation. A lasting image born from ephemera, Jones's design can be read as a visual construction of the political reality of early Stuart England. And yet, significantly, it is also a construction (on privileged sight and mnemonic shape) that is difficult to replicate in text.

---

embroydered carpet'), see Samuel Purchas, *The Kings Tower and Triumphant Arch of London. A Sermon preached at Paul Crosse, 5 August 1622* (London: W. Stansby, Henry Fetherstone, 1623), pp. 25–27. Likewise for an author conceiving the act of faith as an architectural project, see Robert Barrell, *The Spiritual Architecture, or The balance of Gods Sanctuary to discerne the weight and solidity of a true and sincere, from the Leuiti, and varitie of a flase and counterfeit prefession of Christianity . . . a Sermon preached at Pauls Cross 16. November 1623* (London: Augustine Matthews and John Norton, 1624).

[34] See Thomas Fulwood's *The Castel of Memorie: wherein is conteyned the restoring, augmenting and conserving of the Memorye and Remembraunce, with the safest remedies and the best preceptes thereunto in any wise appetieyning . . .* (London: Rouland Hall, dwelling in Gutter lane, at the sign of the half eagle and the key, 1562), Chapter 6.

[35] James I, *The Trew Law of Free Monarchies: or The Reciprock and Mutuall duetie betwixt a free King and his naturall Sujects*, as reproduced in *King James VI and I: Political Writings*, ed. by Johann P. Sommerville (Cambridge: Cambridge University Press, 1994), pp. 62–84 (p. 83).

Conclusion

What perhaps examples such as the cartoon of Brazil's *República*, or the print of the Dutch truce negotiations, or even the design for a Jacobean masquing scene show, is that 'ruptured' discourses of power can sometimes be discerned more effectively through non-textual sources. When we are considering power (to use Bryson's phrase) 'not as a monolith, but as a swarm of points traversing social stratifications and individual persons',[36] it appears to be (in these three examples at least) the *image* that thrives as a representational framework. For Jacobean England it served as a cogent mnemonic; for revolutionary Brazil it served as the space of private discourse; and for the early republican Low Countries it manifested and projected a radical but workable alternative to the world of absolutist, sovereign powers envisaged by Bodin and Hobbes.

Furthermore, when we are confronted with moments when this diffuse location of power is itself dislocated—whether we call that moment epistemic change, or 'out of placeness'—it is the structure (or, indeed, the lack of structure—the 'potentiality') within the format of the image that seems to lend itself so ideally to the discourse. It is there in the polyvalency of the Dutch prints. It is there in the self-conscious fissures of the Jacobean festival designs. And it is captured in the layered networks of meaning within the cartoons carried by the Brazilian Press. In short Images would seem to convey a *structure of meaning* more applicable, and more responsive, to *structures of power*, even (or maybe *especially*) at moments of dislocation—whether that dislocation was seen as perilous, or indicative, or functionally apt in the circumstances where it was recognized.

Now that History has promoted its images from secondary illustration to primary evidence (from scenery to protagonist), it is perhaps time to explore how in this new leading role it can allow us to see very different stories of the past. And, particularly with regards to these 'Diagrams of Power'—as *Net* rather than *Hierarchy*, *Texture* rather than *Text*—it does seem that there is some evidence to suggest that there are stories that cannot be told with words alone. Through the lens of 'text'—in our sources and in our publications—the past has all too easily become an ordered, fixed, hierarchical place. With the kaleidoscope of 'image' (above all the digital image) we now look to a past of movement and interplay.

[36] N. Bryson, 'Semiology and Visual Interpretation', in *Visual Theory. Painting and Interpretation*, ed. by N. Bryson, M. A. Holly, and K. Moxey (Cambridge and Oxford: Polity Press, 1991), pp. 61–73 (p. 71).

'Serra ex ferro'—'Serra ex vitro':[1] medieval history—computers—image messages reconsidered

GERHARD JARITZ

The discourses initiated, determined, and influenced by the contents and messages of images are about depicted actions, persons, objects etc. In this respect, there is certainly no basic difference between images and the representations of spoken or written text. In our, the historians', constructions, we clearly always have to be mindful of these factors and contexts. Of particular interest are those fields and aspects that are discussed regularly and intensively in our sources. There, we are confronted with connections of the qualitative and the quantitative, opening the possibility to search for patterns, their role, rules

[1] Thomas Aquinas, *Summa Theologiae*, I, q. 39, a. 8: 'Quilibet autem artifex intendit suo opere dispositionem optimam inducere non simpliciter, sed per comparationem ad finem. Et si talis dispositio habet secum adiunctum aliquem defectum, artifex non curat, sicut artifex, qui facit serram ad secandum, facit eam ex ferro, ut sit idonea ad secandum; nec curat eam facere ex vitro, quae est pulchrior materia, quia talis pulchritudo est impedimentum finis' [Every artist strives to put the best arrangement into his work - not the best in absolute terms, but the best in relation to his aim. If such a composition involves some adverse effect, the artist does not worry about this. If, for example, the artist is making a saw for cutting, he makes it of iron, because iron is suitable for the purpose, and he does not dream to make it of glass, which is a more beautiful material, for such beauty is in conflict with the aim]; see Władysław Tatarkiewicz, *History of Aesthetics*, II: *Medieval Aesthetics* (The Hague and Paris, and Warszawa: Mouton and PWN, 1970), p. 262.

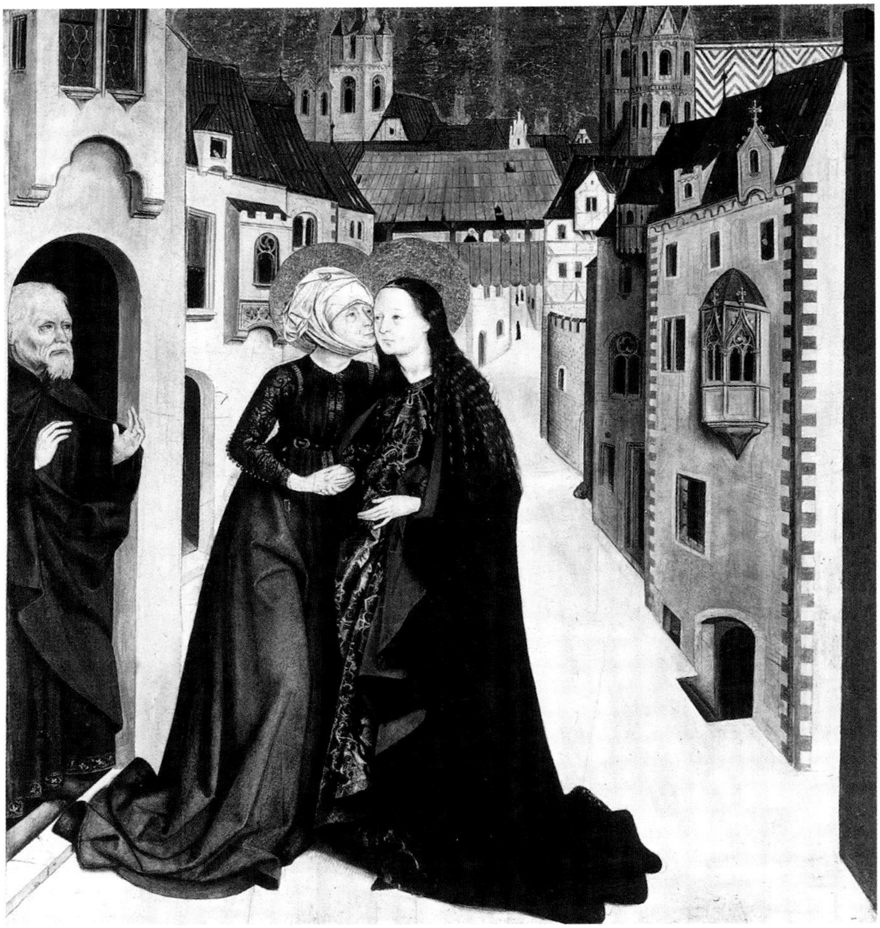

Fig. 1. 'Visitation of the Virgin', Master of the Schottenaltar, panel painting, Austrian, 1469/1480. Vienna, Schottenstift. The idealized paved and clean street in Vienna is appropriate to the 'Visitation of the Virgin'. © Institut für Realienkunde des Mittelalters und der frühen Neuzeit, Krems.

and raising connotations.

When using pictures for such types of analysis, we certainly have to be conscious of the fact that we are dealing with various levels of the 'reality of images',[2] just as we have to be alert when using written or any other source

[2] Concerning late medieval images, see Keith Moxey, 'Reading the 'Reality Effect', in *Pictura quasi fictura. Die Rolle des Bildes in der Sachkultur des Mittelalters und der frühen Neuzeit*, ed. by Gerhard Jaritz, Forschungen des Instituts für Realienkunde des

material. When, for instance, we analyse medieval visual sources, we have to be aware that the 'reality of images' and this 'reality of contexts' influenced the medieval perception of information by the pictures' beholders, just as they, albeit in another way, influence our own perception.

In order for the message to be apprehended, the contents and contexts have to be proper and purposeful ones. The qualities have to be appropriate to the objects, to the depicted persons, to the actions. The saw has to be made out of iron, as Thomas Aquinas stressed in the thirteenth century; the painter cannot make it out of glass, the more beautiful material, such beauty being in conflict with the aim, for only an iron saw can convey the act of sawing.

There is always a need for the beholder to have a suitable means to recognize the message—something that we already find in the well-known example from the *Libri Carolini* (end of the eighth century). This concerns two identical pictures of a beautiful woman: one represents the Virgin Mary, the other represents Venus. The first is to be venerated, the latter discarded.[3] The painter provided the beholders with the solution, with a clearly recognizable sign for those who were able to read and to understand: one picture received the caption 'Virgin Mary'; the other received the caption 'Venus'. In this example it was the

---

Mittelalters und der frühen Neuzeit. Diskussionen und Materialien, 1 (Vienna: Verlag der Österreichischen Akademie der Wissenschaften, 1996), pp. 15–22; Gerhard Jaritz, ''Et est ymago ficta non veritas'. Sackultur und Bilder des späten Mittelalters', in *ibidem*, pp. 9–13; idem, *Zwischen Augenblick und Ewigkeit. Einführung in die Alltagsgeschichte des Mittelalters* (Vienna: Böhlau, 1989), pp. 71–92.

[3] *Libri Carolini* IV, 16: 'Offerentur cuilibet eorum qui imagines adorant . . . duarum feminarum pulchrarum imagines, superscriptione carentes, quas ille parvipendens abjicit, abjectasque quolibet in loco jacere permittit, dicit ille quis: Una illarum sanctae Mariae imago est, abjici non debet; altera Veneris, quae omnino abjicienda est, vertit se ad pictorem quaerens ab eo, quia in omnibus simillimae sunt, quae illarum sanctae Mariae imago sit, vel quae Veneris? Ille huic dat superscriptionem sanctae Mariae, illi vero superscriptionem Veneris: ista quia superscriptionem Dei genitricis habet, erigitur, honoratur, osculatur; illa quia inscriptionem Veneris, dejicitur, exprobatur, exsecratur; pari utraeque sunt figura, paribus coloribus, paribusque factae materiis, superscriptione tantum distant' [A man who venerates pictures was shown two pictures of beautiful women without any captions, which someone had thrown away, caring little for them. Someone said to him: one of these is a picture of the Virgin Mary and should not be thrown away, and the other is of Venus, and should at all costs be thrown away. The man turned to the artist and asked him which one was the picture of Mary, and which one was of Venus, for they were completely alike. The painter supplied one picture with the caption: The Virgin Mary, and the other with the caption: Venus. The picture with the caption: Mother of God, was elevated, venerated, and kissed, and the other, because it had the caption: Venus, was maligned, scorned and cursed, although both were equal in shape and colour, and were made of identical material, and differed only in caption]; see Tatarkiewicz (as in note 1), p. 100.

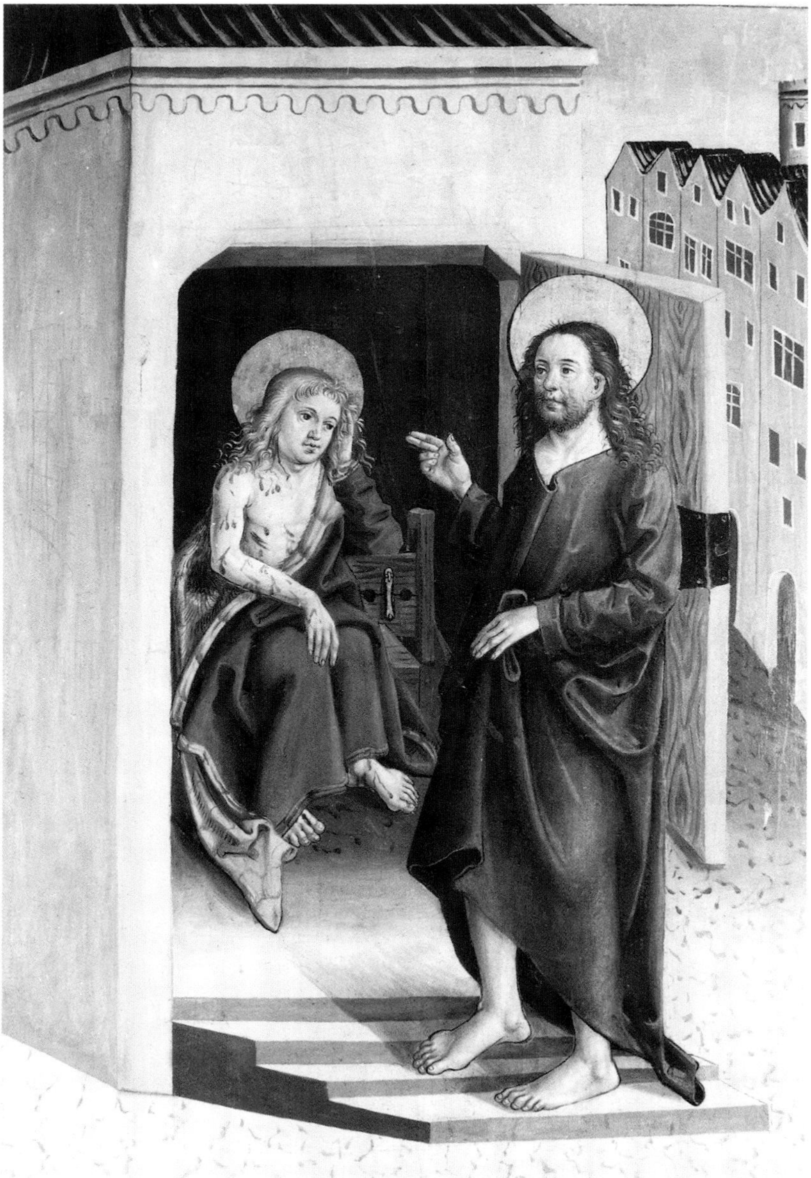

Fig. 2. 'Christ Visiting St George in Prison', panel painting, 1516. Spišská Sobota (Slovakia), parish church. The idealized paved and clean urban streets is appropriate to 'Christ Visiting Saint George in Prison'. © Institut für Realienkunde des Mittelalters und der frühen Neuzeit, Krems

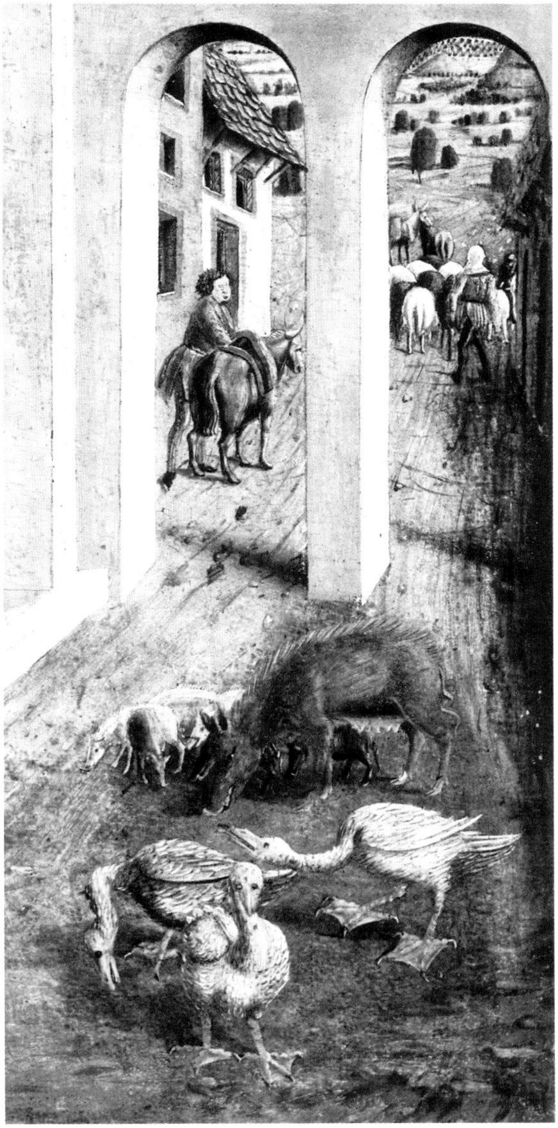

Fig. 3. 'The Dream of St Joseph', Friedrich Pacher, (detail: the hard road to Egypt), panel painting, Tirol, before 1500. Innsbruck, Landesmuseum Ferdinandeum. The negative model of a bad and dirty road is appropriate to the 'Dream of Saint Joseph' suggesting that they start the difficult 'Flight to Egypt'. © Institut für Realienkunde des Mittelalters und der frühen Neuzeit, Krems

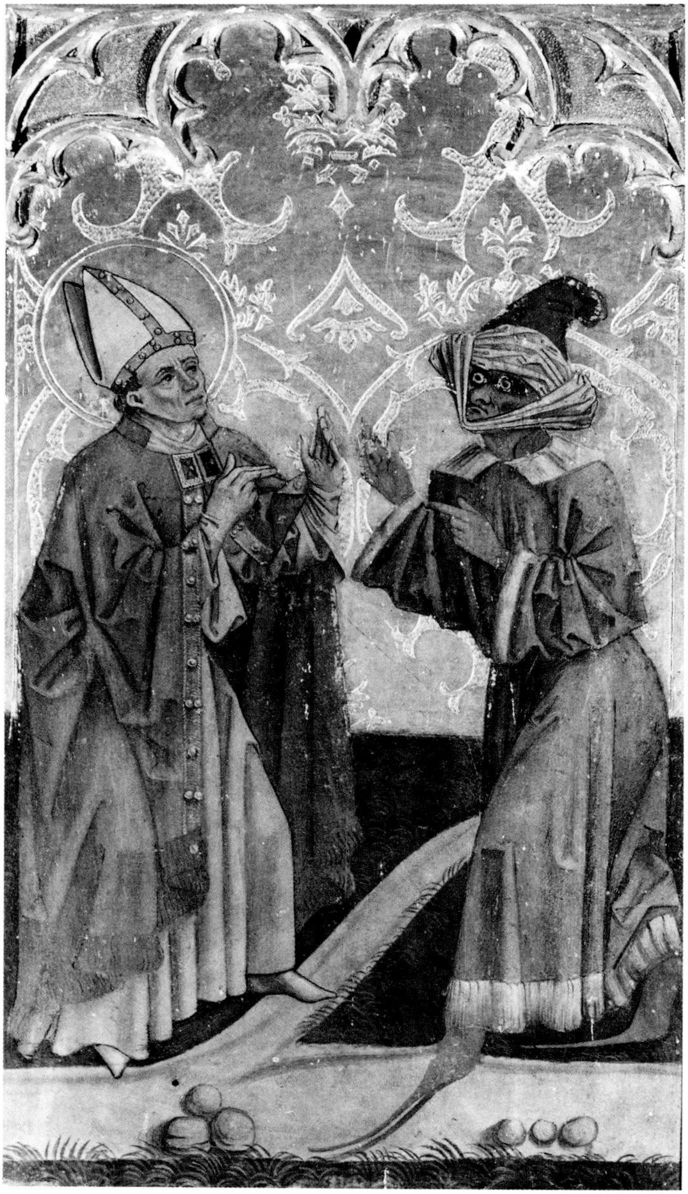

Fig. 4. 'The Temptation of St Martin by the Disguised Devil', panel painting, before 1500. Göflan (Südtirol), parish church. The ground is strewn with stones. © Institut für Realienkunde des Mittelalters und der frühen Neuzeit, Krems

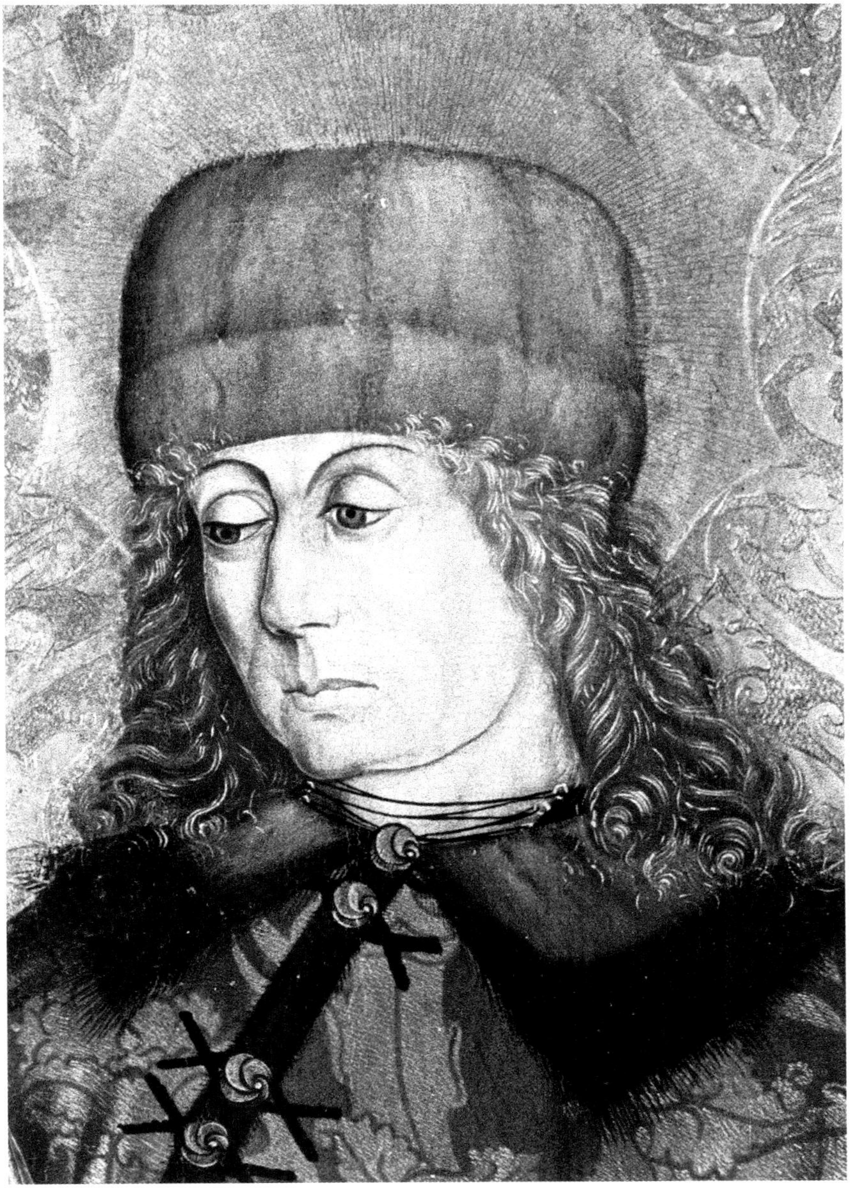

Fig. 5. 'St Florian and St Sebastian' (detail: Emperor Frederick III as St Sebastian), panel painting, Styrian, c. *1480. Obdach (Steiermark), church of the hospital. The long and curled hairstyle of Emperor Frederick III. © Institut für Realienkunde des Mittelalters und der frühen Neuzeit, Krems, Austria*

caption that counted; the caption 'Venus' created the image of Venus for those who could read or who were told; the caption 'Virgin Mary' turned the second image into the Mother of God. In other cases, however, it is the presented form and quality of the actual contents of the pictures that creates the recognition. But always some kind or type of context of the signs in different levels plays the important role—as also for our own analyses.

Let us come back to the discourse initiated and influenced by images, and let us concentrate on intensity, regularity, and the particular connotation offered by the contents: this combination of the qualitative and the quantitative. For our studies and our search for relevant patterns, computer-supported image analysis has proved particularly useful. Some Central European groups of images and their interpretation may serve as examples. The basis for analysis is about 20,000 late-medieval images,[4] described in a very detailed, structured, and standardized way that are available in a Κλειω-database,[5] thus making text–image links possible in different variants.[6] The issues of visual representation that we are interested in are those that often play a decisive role in late-medieval written evidence dealing with aspects of daily life and material culture. As examples we will deal with streets and roads and their quality and cleanliness;[7] male hairdressing;[8] other material signs of the outward appearance of social groups,

---

[4] These images are integrated in the database REAL of the 'Institut für Realienkunde des Mittelalters und der frühen Neuzeit' of the Austrian Academy of Arts and Sciences. See Gerhard Jaritz, *Everyday Life in the Middle Ages and Digital Image Analysis* (1995): http://rubens.anu.edu.au/chart/jaritz.html; idem, 'Computergestützte Bildanalysen in der Geschichte mittelalterlichen Alltags', *Österreich in Geschichte und Literatur*, 39 (1995), 156–61. Parts of the contents of REAL are available on: http://www.imareal.oeaw.ac.at.

[5] Concerning Κλειω, see Manfred Thaller, Κλειω. *A Database System* (St Katharinen: Scripta Mercatura Verlag, 1993); Matthew Woollard and Peter Denley, *Source-Oriented Data Processing for Historians: A Tutorial for kleio* (St Katharinen: Scripta Mercatura Verlag, 1993); see also http://www.gwdg.de/kleio/ and http://gilgamesch.hki.uni-koeln.de/develop/site/. With regard to Κλειω-image analysis, see Gerhard Jaritz, *Images. A Primer of Computer-Supported Image Analysis with kleio IAS* (St Katharinen: Scripta Mercatura Verlag, 1993); see also idem, 'Medieval History and Digital Image Processing', *Schede Umanistiche. Rivista semestrale dell'Archivo Umanistico Rinascimantela Bolognese*, nuova serie (1998), 201–09.

[6] See Gerhard Jaritz. *Bound Images: Encoding and Analysis* (1995): http://www.uky.edu/~kiernan/DL/jaritz.html.

[7] On medieval streets and roads, see, e.g., Jean-Pierre Leguay, *La rue au moyen âge* (Rennes: Ouest France, 1984); Lynn Thorndike, 'Sanitation, Baths, and Street-Cleaning in the Middle Ages and Renaissance', *Speculum* 3 (1928), 192–203.

[8] See Jean Loubier, 'Das Ideal der männlichen Schönheit bei den altfranzösischen Dichtern des XII und XIII Jahrhunderts' [Phil. Diss. Friedrichs-Universität Halle Wittenberg] (Halle a. S., 1890), pp. 44–56; Oskar Voigt, 'Das Ideal der Schönheit und

such as pointed shoes,[9] and the image of peasantry.[10] They here will be used as examples to show the general possibilities and uses of visual sign language from the fourteenth to the beginning of the sixteenth century.[11] For this, they also can be seen as important individual sources of information for a history of mentalities of the late Middle Ages.[12]

The quality of streets and roads regularly played an important role in a variety of late medieval written sources, particularly those of urban areas: there are distinct references in laws, craftsman contracts, donations, account books, chronicles, travel accounts, etc. The poor quality of medieval roads is still a stereotype in today's historical presentation of the Middle Ages, particularly the one taught in schools. But in the many late-medieval discussions about roads, their cleanliness, the contrast between paved and unpaved, and between easy and difficult travel over them are all of critical importance. And it seems to be quite obvious that images in their contexts also deal with such questions and problems and use them to mediate a variety of different messages.[13]

On the one hand, we are confronted with the image of the highly idealized urban street conforming to every requirement as to cleanliness, of top quality,

---

Hässlichkeit in den altfranzösischen chansons de geste' (Phil. Diss., Universität Marburg, 1891), pp. 34–36; Gerhard Jaritz, 'Young, Rich, and Beautiful. The Visualization of Male Beauty in the Late Middle Ages', in *The Man of Many Devices, Who Wandered Full Many Ways. Festschrift in Honor of János M. Bak*, ed. by Balázs Nagy and Marcell Sebők (Budapest: Central European University Press, 1999), p. 63.

[9] See Gerhard Jaritz, 'Schnabelschuh und Hörnerhaube oder: Bild, Sachkultur und Kontextualisierung', in *8. Österreichischer Kunsthistorikertag. Vergangenheit in der Gegenwart—Gegenwart in der Kunstgeschichte?*, Kunsthistoriker 11/12, 1994/1995 (Vienna: Österreichischer Kunsthistorikerverband, 1996), pp. 8–12.

[10] See, generally, Gerhard Jaritz, 'The Material Culture of the Peasantry in the Late Middle Ages: "Image" and "Reality"', in *Agriculture in the Middle Ages. Technology, Practice, and Representation*, ed. by Del Sweeney (Philadelphia: University of Pennsylvania Press, 1995), pp. 163–88.

[11] Concerning the literary sign language of dress, see Gabriele Raudszus, *Die Zeichensprache der Kleidung. Untersuchungen zur Symbolik des Gewandes in der deutschen Epik des Mittelalters*, Ordo. Studien zur Literatur und Gesellschaft des Mittelalters und der frühen Neuzeit, I (Hildesheim: Olms, 1985).

[12] See Axel Bolvig, 'Images of Late Medieval 'Daily Life'. A History of Mentalities', *Medium Aevum Quotidianum*, 39 (1998), 94–111.

[13] See Gerhard Jaritz, 'Umweltbewältigung. Der Beitrag der Geschichtswissenschaften', in *Umweltbewältigung. Die historische Perspektive*, ed. by Gerhard Jaritz and Verena Winiwarter (Bielefeld: Verlag für Regionalgeschichte, 1994), pp. 14–16 and errata; idem, 'Alltag in der Stadt des 15. und 16. Jahrhunderts', in *Alltagserfahrungen in der Geschichte Österreichs*, ed. by Ernst Bruckmüller (Vienna: ÖBV Pädagogischer Verlag, 1998), pp. 52–55.

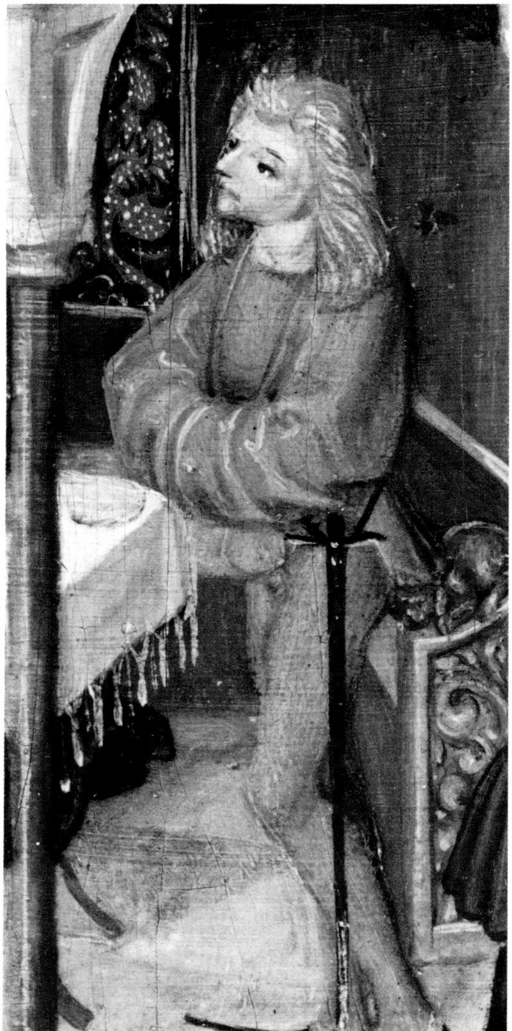

Fig. 6. 'Parable of Dives and Lazarus' (detail: the servant of Dives), panel painting, Upper Rhine, end of the fifteenth century. St. Paul im Lavanttal (Kärnten), collections of the Benedictine monastery. The long and curled hairstyle of the servant of Dives. © Institut für Realienkunde des Mittelalters und der frühen Neuzeit, Krems

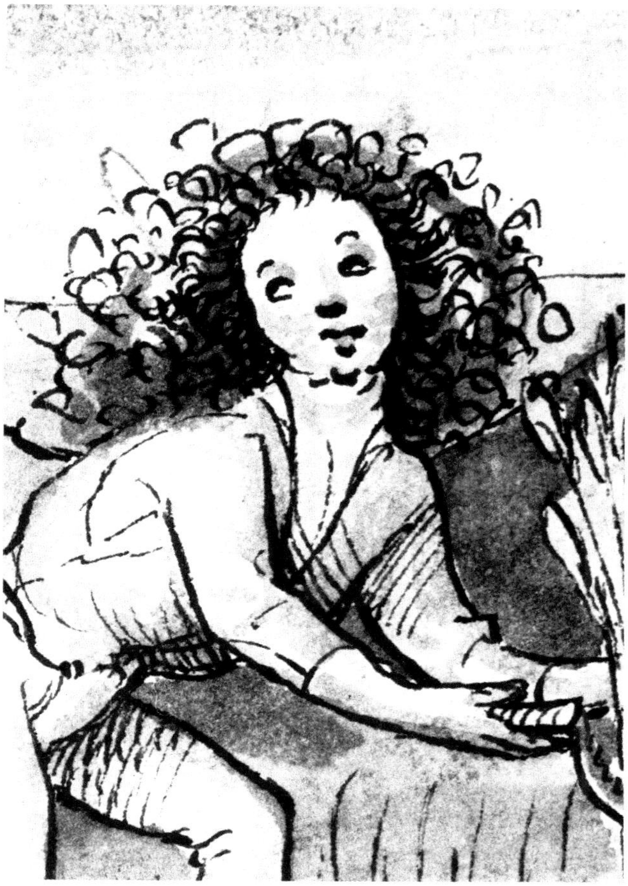

Fig. 7. 'Labours of the Months', month of August (detail: hairstyle of an 'improper' peasant), ink drawing, South German, 1475. Vienna, Österreich. Nationalbibliothek, MS. 3085, fol. 5r. The chaotic curly hair of an 'improper' peasant. © Institut für Realienkunde des Mittelalters und der frühen Neuzeit, Krems

and in excellent condition with a good standard of pavement. For example, the particular religious event of the 'Visitation of the Virgin' (fig. 1) is integrated into a depiction of the community for which the image was produced: in this case Vienna.[14] The representation of the street follows two patterns of ideali-

[14] See Heinrich Ferenczy, *Das Schottenstift und seine Kunstwerke* (Vienna: Orac, 1980), p. 194; Walther Brauneis, 'Beitrag zur mittelalterlichen Topographie der Stadt Wien', *Österreichische Zeitschrift für Kunst und Denkmalpflege*, 27 (1973), 121–31.

zation, that of one's own town and one of a highly important religious action. This ideal of one's own community need not necessarily be a 'real' image, but may obviously just be a type. Such an example, for instance, may be seen in a representation of 'Christ Visiting Saint George in Prison', out of a winged altarpiece in today's Slovakia (fig. 2). Again, the paved and clean streets play a relevant role in the idealization of action and place.[15]

On the other hand, a contrasting image of roads may be recognized in cases where a generally negative connotation should be mediated. This is, for instance, particularly true of the flight of the Holy Family into Egypt. One typical example is a representation of the 'Dream of St Joseph', in which the angel appears and tells him that he and his family should flee (fig. 3). It shows the very bad, dirty, and hard road to Egypt, a road on which animals forage for food. Bad roads, paths, and squares may also turn up in connection with other negative connotations that images should mediate. One of these examples is the 'Temptation of St Martin by the Disguised Devil' showing the ground strewn with stones (fig. 4).[16]

Religious messages, therefore, obviously use a language of signs that is based soundly on the practical experience and knowledge of the beholders. In this case that language is based on regular discussion about an important material aspect of everyday life: streets and roads. The contrasts in their quality are the means of providing the audience with auxiliary information to reinforce religious and spiritual messages. In order to apprehend such results, it is useful to employ the above-mentioned text–image databases and analyse them qualitatively and quantitatively with regard to contents and contexts. This means, for instance, searching the databases for the topics and contents of late-medieval works of art, where streets and roads are described verbally as well-paved or clean, or where there are descriptions of dirt, stones, puddles, or foraging animals in the context of streets. A comparison of the results of these two queries shows 'message-bound contrasts', of which a few examples have been selected above.

Another example may be taken with regard to aspects of the outward appearance of people. For the whole of the Middle Ages, the image of beautiful males followed a certain pattern.[17] One of the key indicators was their long and curled hair of fair or light brown colour.[18] Such hair was also used to represent the actual inner qualities of these beautiful, rich, and young males, or other men closely connected to them. In images, it was typically used for rulers (fig. 5), rich and socially important men, their servants (fig. 6), angels, or the apostle John the

---

[15] See Libuše Cidlinská, *Gotické krídlové oltáre na Slovensku* [Gothic winged altarpieces in Slovakia] (Bratislava: Tartan, 1989), p. 82.

[16] As in note 13.

[17] See Gerhard Jaritz, 'Young, Rich, and Beautiful' (as in note 8), pp. 61–77.

[18] As in note 8.

Evangelist.[19] Other groups of lower status in the social hierarchy of medieval society do not have this type of hair. If such men wear long and curled fair hair in images, they may obviously be connected with patterns of the 'world upside-down'.[20] This becomes very clear, for instance, in the obviously satirical and also didactic illuminations of a South German manuscript of 1475, representing the Labours of the Months. There, the peasants have a coiffure that by no means fits their role and social position (fig. 7), but the depiction also shows that they were not quite successful in their attempt to overturn the order of the world; their curls look rather chaotic.[21] These Labours of the Months, therefore, show proper peasants' work done in the proper season. But parts of the outward appearance of the persons doing this work obviously do not correspond to their social status and function. In a humorous and satirical way, the pictures seem to represent the attempt of peasants to rise in the social hierarchy by changing aspects of their outward appearance. This is a topos that we find regularly, particularly in medieval literary sources.[22] The peasants try to adopt the hairstyle of the nobility but are not really able to do so. Thus, such images or texts mediate not only humour and satire to their audience but also a moral: Look what happens to peasants who act like this; one laughs at them, so be careful that something similar does not happen to you, if you try to leave your proper place in the social order.

Late-medieval pictures also operate in a similar way with regard to specific items of dress. Amongst the most discussed pieces of clothing in the late Middle

---

[19] See *Gotik in der Steiermark. Katalog der Landesausstellung Stift St Lambrecht* (Graz: Styria, 1978), p. 135; Jaritz, 'Young, Rich and Beautiful' (as in note 8), pp. 64–65.

[20] Concerning the motive of the 'world upside-down' generally, see, e.g., Hedwig Kenner, *Das Phänomen der verkehrten Welt in der griechisch-römischen Antike* (Klagenfurt: Geschichtsverein für Kärnten, 1970); Roger Chartier and Dominique Julia, 'Die verkehrte Welt', in *Die unvollendete Vergangenheit und die Macht der Welt-auslegung*, ed. by Roger Chartier (Berlin: Wagenbach, 1989), pp. 73–82; Helmut Hundsbichler, 'Im Zeichen der 'verkehrten Welt', in *Symbole des Alltags—Alltag der Symbole*, ed. by. Gertrud Blaschitz, et al. (Graz: Akademische Druck- und Verlagsanstalt, 1992), pp. 555–70; Christa Grössinger, *The World Upside-Down. English Misericords* (London: Harvey Miller, 1997).

[21] Jaritz, 'Young, Rich, and Beautiful' (as in note 8), p. 65.

[22] See, e.g., Helga Schüppert, 'Der Bauer in der deutschen Literatur des Spätmittelalters', in *Bäuerliche Sachkultur des Spätmittelalters*, Sitzungsberichte der Österreichischen Akademie der Wissenschaften, phil.-hist. Klasse, 439 (Vienna: Verlag der Österreichischen Akademie der Wissenschaften, 1984), pp. 125–76; Herman Braet, ''A thing most brutish': The Image of the Rustic in Old French Literature', in *Agriculture in the Middle Ages. Technology, Practice, and Representation*, ed. by Del Sweeney (Philadelphia: University of Pennsylvania Press, 1995), pp. 191–204.

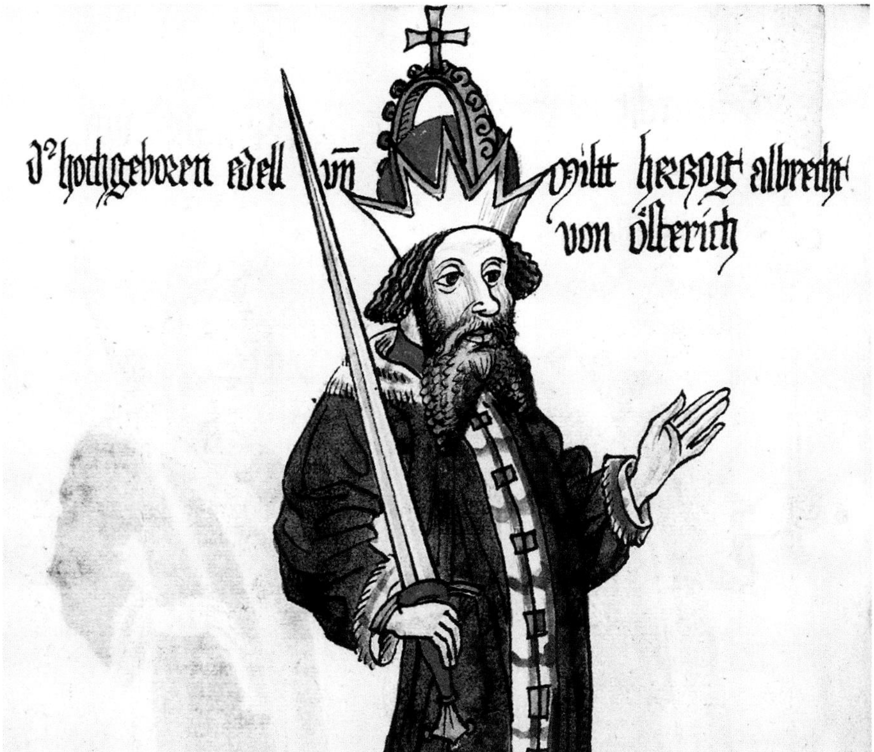

Fig. 8. 'Duke Albrecht of Austria', ink drawing, Tirol, last quarter of the fifteenth century. Vienna, Österreich. Nationalbibl., MS. s. n. 12820, fol. 40^{v}. The pointed shoes of Duke Albrecht of Austria. © Institut für Realienkunde des Mittelalters und der frühen Neuzeit, Krems

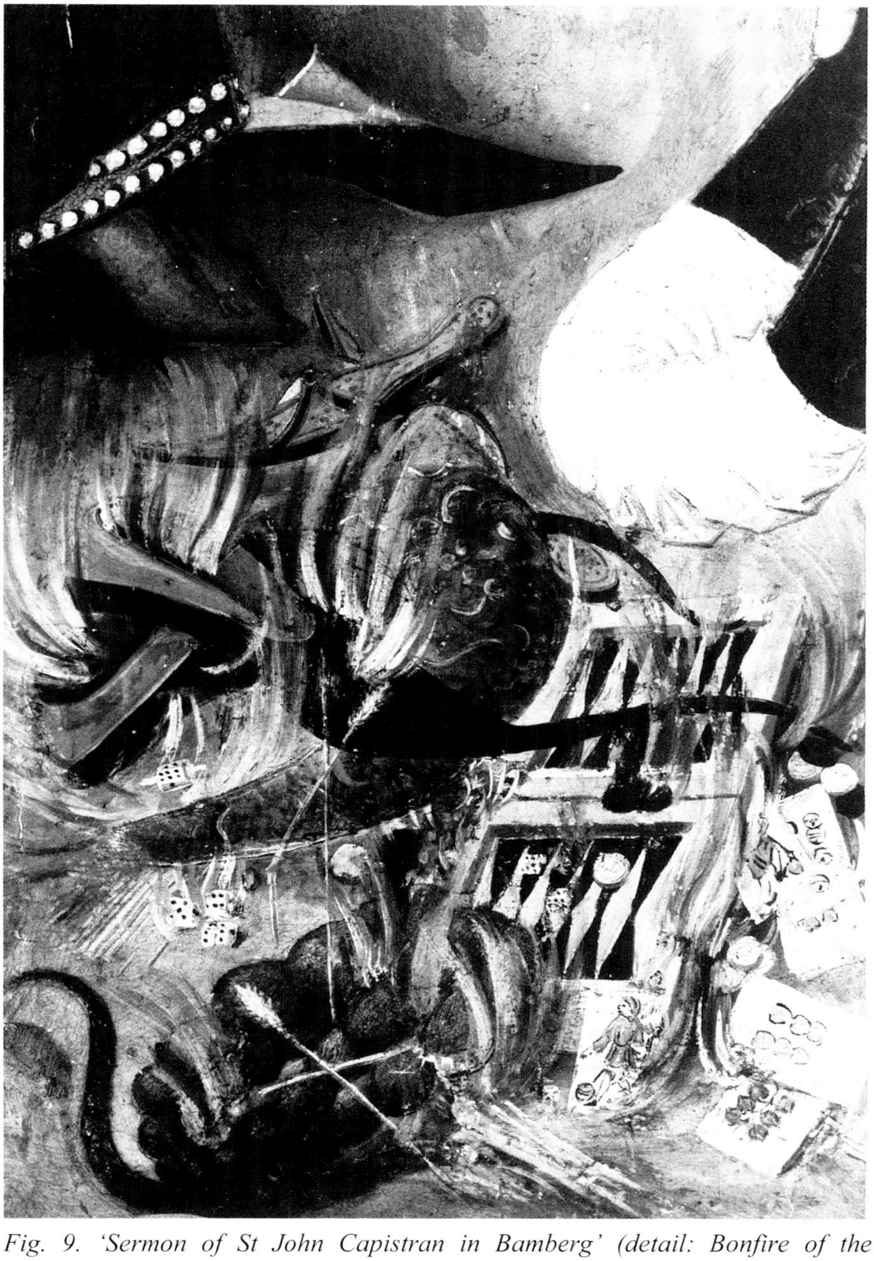

Fig. 9. 'Sermon of St John Capistran in Bamberg' (detail: Bonfire of the Vanities), panel painting, c. 1470. Bamberg (Germany), Staatsgalerie. Pointed shoes are burnt as an object of the Vanities. © Institut für Realienkunde des Mittelalters und der frühen Neuzeit, Krems

Ages were pointed shoes.[23] Throughout Europe, particularly around the mid-fourteenth and mid-fifteenth century, sumptuary laws and sermons deal with them, especially prohibiting or criticizing town-dwellers' wearing of them; chronicles regularly report problems that occur for men who use them. They are to be seen as a sign of superbia for large parts of late-medieval society. If one analyses pictorial sources from the period, one comes across a pattern similar to what we have seen when examining male hairstyles. Pointed shoes seem to have been very fashionable and legitimate for people of the upper classes, such as rulers (fig. 8) or noblemen, and again their servants (fig. 6).[24] All of them seem to have been allowed and privileged to wear them as a sign to show their exceptionally high status or their close connection to such persons. This clearly emerges from written as well as pictorial evidence. Conversely, pointed shoes are regularly used in images to represent negative connotations for specific lower class people, particularly persons such as tormentors of saints or other enemies of order and faith (see fig. 4). An example closer to practical life is represented in an image of the Bonfire of the Vanities initiated by a sermon of St John Capistran in Bamberg (fig. 9). Here, pointed shoes are shown as one of the objects of superbia to be destroyed.

Thus, on the one hand, a concentration on individual objects and details of the outer appearance of persons is enhanced by these new computer-supported approaches.[25] On the other hand, the complete and general appearance (i.e., the sum total of signs) of the individuals depicted may also be analyzed. An interesting example is again the use of the 'image of peasants' as a positive or as a negative model.[26] The typical legitimate working dress of peasants consists of the undyed, knee-long, coarse woollen tunic; they wear simple shoes or boots, or are barefoot. In that manner, they may be depicted publicly and didactically to

---

[23] As in note 9.

[24] Concerning obvious problems, also occurring for members of the nobility, cf. the well-known 'Berner Twingherrenstreit' in the 1470s. See Leo Zehnder, *Volkskundliches aus der älteren schweizerischen Chronistik* [Schriften der Schweizerischen Gesellschaft für Volkskunde, 60] (Basel: Krebs, and Bonn: Habelt, 1976), pp. 81–83; Gerhard Jaritz, 'Kleidung und Prestige–Konkurrenz. Unterschiedliche Identitäten in der städtischen Gesellschaft unter Normierungszwängen', *Saeculum*, 44 (1993), 16–17.

[25] See, generally, Gerhard Jaritz, ' "Seiden Päntel an den Knien" oder: Die Hoffart liegt im Detail', in *Ut populus ad historiam trahatur. Festgabe für Herwig Ebner zum 60. Geburtstag*, ed. by Gerhard Dienes, et al. (Graz: Leykam, 1988), pp. 63–74.

[26] This use of peasants as a positive and negative model can also occur at the same time in the same source; see Jaritz, 'The Material Culture of the Peasantry' (as in note 10), pp. 165–66; *Quellen zur Geschichte des Bauernstandes im Mittelalter*, ed. by Günther Franz [Freiherr vom Stein-Gedächtnisausgabe, 31] (Darmstadt: Wissenschaftliche Buchgesellschaft, 1974), pp. 548–52.

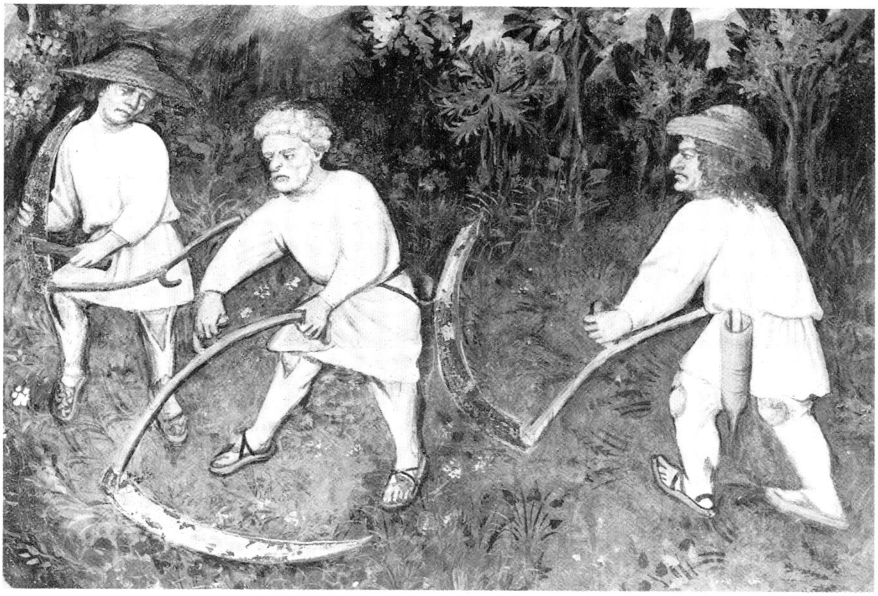

Fig. 10. 'Labours of the Months', month of July (detail: peasants at mowing and hay-making), wall-painting, c. *1400. Trento, Castello Buonconsiglio, Torre d'Aquila. The ideal outer appearance of a field-working peasant. © Institut für Realienkunde des Mittelalters und der frühen Neuzeit, Krems*

show their positive function in medieval society (fig. 10).[27] The peasants are doing the right work at the right time in the right way, and they are correctly dressed. They are a positive model for the whole of society. But peasants can certainly also function as a negative model; as we have seen, they may be used as an object to demonstrate satirically, and also didactically, the wrong way of behaving. This might be the case in a representation of the Last Judgement (fig. 11). There, the sinful peasant is clearly clad in dress that certainly does not fit his work and status: doublet, hose, codpiece, and duckbill-shoes. His negative inner state is visualized by his outer appearance. The peasants, whom we mentioned before, with their chaotic curled hair, make the same point (see fig. 7). They wear doublets and hose that are pointed at the feet, again a type of dress that certainly does not belong to rural fieldwork (fig. 12). The image's

[27] See Nicolò Rasmo, *The Frescoes at the Torre Aquila in Trento* (Rovereto: Manfrini, 1962); Gerhard Jaritz, 'Lebensbilder? Die mittelalterlichen Fresken aus dem Adlerturm von Trento (Trient)', in *Das andere Mittelalter. Emotionen, Rituale und Kontraste* (Krems: Kunst-Halle Krems, 1992), pp. 127–33.

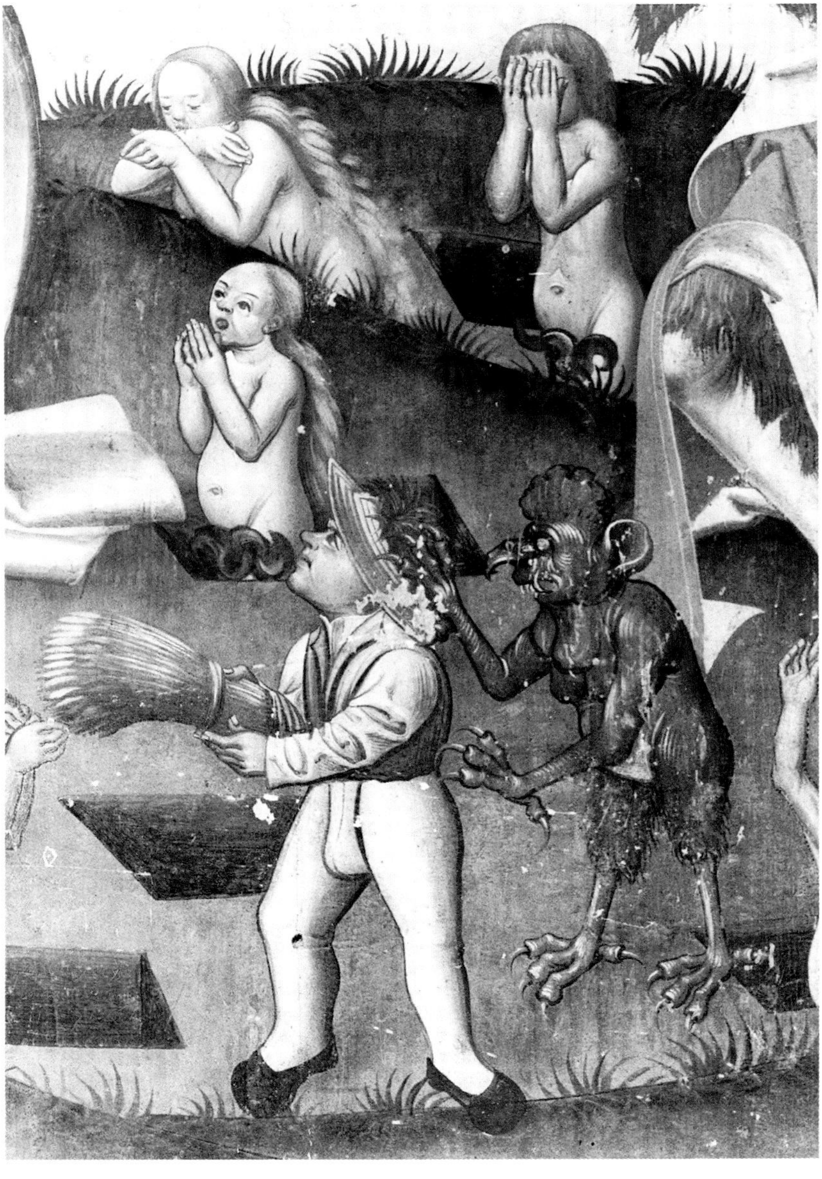

Fig. 11. 'Last Judgement' (detail: the devil grips a peasant), panel painting, Schnatterpeck-workshop, first quarter of the sixteenth century. Kortsch (Süd-Tirol), trustee church. The 'improper' peasant gripped by the devil on Judgement Day. © Institut für Realienkunde des Mittelalters und der frühen Neuzeit, Krems

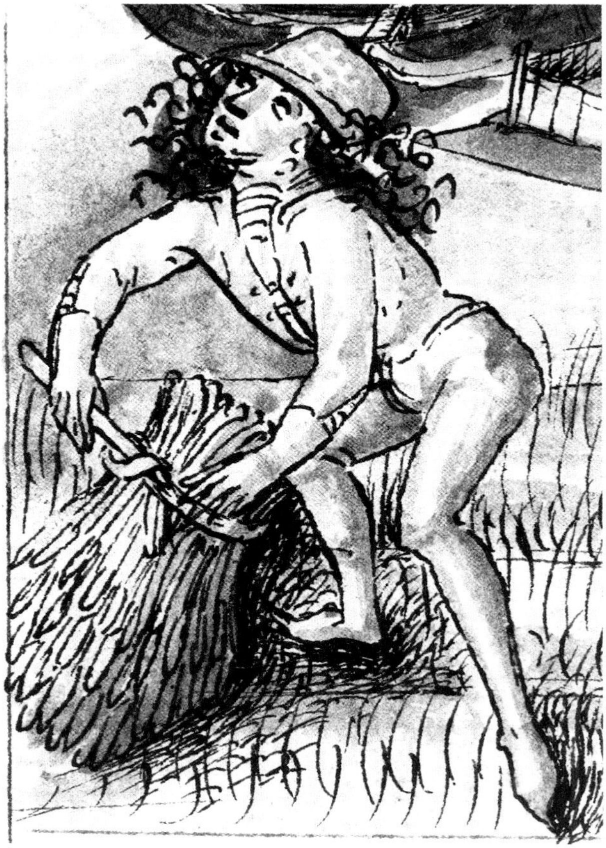

Fig. 12. 'Labours of the Months', month of August (detail: one of the 'improper' field-working peasants), ink drawing, South German, 1475. Vienna, Österreich. Nationalbibliothek, MS. 3085, fol. 5ʳ. 'Improper' outer appearance of a field-working peasant. © Institut für Realienkunde des Mittelalters und der frühen Neuzeit, Krems

message can only have been meant comically and satirically and, thus, also didactically and with a moralizing intention.[28] They are not proper peasants any more.

[28] For the satirical-didactic treatment of peasants in late medieval and early modern art generally, see, e.g., Hans-Joachim Raupp, *Bauernsatiren. Entstehung und Entwicklung des bäuerlichen Genres in der deutschen und niederländischen Kunst, ca. 1470–1570* (Niederzier: Lukassen, 1986); Keith Moxey, *Peasants, Warriors and Wives. Popular Imagery in the Reformation* (Chicago: University of Chicago Press, 1989), pp. 35-66.

The 'contrasting' image messages used painted material objects and phenomena that belonged to everyday knowledge and experience in the late Middle Ages. They have been analyzed through the use of a large database of digitalized images, linked with detailed, standardized, and highly structured image descriptions. It is not the 'realities' of medieval roads, of hairstyle, of pointed shoes, or of peasants' dress that are important, but the messages intended to be mediated by these painted examples. The application of computer-supported methods to apprehend these patterns has been mentioned at the beginning of this contribution but not dealt with extensively. With the help of selected examples, this article intended rather to discuss some trends in the development of the aims of (art) historical research in dealing with the source evidence of late medieval images. An awareness of the relation among—and the context of—the images' contents, their patterns, and intended messages has started to play an important role in medieval studies. The computer-supported methods are very suitable for this type of analysis, and by using them, some of the purposes of analysis have themselves been modified and developed; comparative research into the 'texts' of image representations in a qualitative and quantitative way has increased, becoming more sophisticated and refined.

It has definitely been one of the major successes of computer-supported (image) analysis in the historical disciplines during the recent years that many scholars are now so familiar with it that it no longer seems necessary to place a strong emphasis on explaining or describing it in detail. Most of the currently available methods using computer-supported image analysis have been explored extensively; their theoretical background has often been clarified. As we have reached this point, we have become much more able to concentrate on our specific historical research interests.

Quantitative image analysis: the Painter of wooden shoes

AXEL BOLVIG

Introduction

The preceding two decades have witnessed a fundamental change in historians' access to new source material.[1] The digital revolution has created facilities for storing huge amounts of images, the results of which we have now begun to see. Images constitute a growing part of the material for research—and presentation too—deployed by medievalists.[2] The digital revolution may result in a paradigmatic change in our understanding of the Middle Ages and in the presentation of our research. Working with images—qualitatively and quantitatively—we need to establish new methods of analysis and interpretation.

Art history is a discipline that concentrates on images, but art historical research traditionally has excluded many different kinds of imagery from its field of operation. Art historians are facing an expansion of their research material as well as the necessity for a new methodology to take over from that of the Warburg School. Late in his life Erwin Panofsky gave up the term *iconology* and Irvin Lavin confessed that sometimes he thought iconography was an invention of the devil.[3] These two statements form a good starting point for art historians to

---

[1] François Garnier, *L'âne a la lyre. Sottisier d'iconographie médiévale* (Paris: Le Léopard d'Or, 1988), p. 27.

[2] Gerhard Jaritz, 'Images. A Primer of Computer-Supported Analysis with Kleio IAS', *Halbgraue Reihe zur historischen Fachinformatik*, 22 (1993), pp. 11–14.

[3] Irving Lavin, 'Iconography as a Humanistic Discipline', in *Iconography at the Crossroads*, ed. by Brendan Cassidy (Princeton: Princeton University Press, 1993),

elaborate on a new methodology, and within the preceding decades we have witnessed an intense and fruitful discussion concerning new approaches to images and new definitions of what is art.[4]

Historical methods are firmly based on working with texts and the whole apparatus for research has been based on and around the written word. At the time when Nieburg, Ranke, Seignobos, and their followers elaborated on a scientific historical methodology, images could be reproduced only in black and white copies as woodcuts or engravings.[5] In a way, pictorial source material did not exist for the fathers of the historical sciences, or, if it did, then only to a limited extent. 'Following the recovery in the fifteenth century of so much ancient literature, written records came to monopolize the sources on which they drew'.[6] Consequently they turned towards philology. In a sense, they represent the same attitude towards images expressed by Gregory the Great and the many erudite medieval scholars who thought—or at least wrote—that images are the Bible of the illiterate. So why use visual source material when you are able to read a text?[7] Until the present, historians have hesitated to fashion new methods that deal with pictures.[8] Of course we shall not completely give up the terms: Tradition/Überreste or Document/Monument, but the binding of history to philology was invented by the devil. In the years to come he will be defeated.[9]

Easy access to thousands of images changes the way research can take place and, consequently, also the contents of that research. One hundred years ago, access to images required travel. Art could be experienced almost exclusively in

---

pp. 33, 38.

[4] The list of contributions from Baschet and Baxandall to Warnke and Wirth is impressive. As a matter of fact there is a need for a bibliography on this subject matter.

[5] William M. Ivins, Jr., *Prints and Visual Communication* (Cambridge, MA: MIT Press, 1978).

[6] Francis Haskell, *History and its Images. Art and the Interpretation of the Past* (New Haven: Yale University Press, 1993), p. 2.

[7] The Danish founder of a scientific historical methodology, Kristian Erslev, published in 1911 a book *Historisk Teknik*, which is still in use at the universities. In the book he only once refers to an image, namely the depiction of green horses on the Bayeux tapestry. He states that we do not believe that horses were green in the eleventh century! Concerning the lack of a methodology among Danish historians towards visual material see Axel Bolvig, 'Med passende ændringer', in *Sølv og salte*, ed. by Tove Hansen (Copenhagen: Rhodos, 1990), pp. 225–37.

[8] Rainer Wohlfeil, 'Methodische Reflexionen zur Historischen Bildkunde', in *Zeitschrift für Historische Forschung*, Beiheft 12 (1991), pp. 17–35.

[9] Concerning the relationship between history and art history see Jérôme Baschet, 'Les images: des objets pour l'historien?', in *Le Moyen Age aujourd'hui. Actes de la rencontre de Cerisy-la-Salle*, ed. by J. Le Goff and G. Lobrichon, Cahiers du Léopard d'Or, 7 (Paris: Le Léopard d'Or, 1997), pp. 101–35.

museums and churches, particularly cathedrals. The museums and a number of the cathedrals were situated in the most important cultural centres of Europe. The subjects of research were therefore centralized and reflected the purchasing policy of the great museums. Very often, art-historical research was concentrated on rather small numbers of subjects, which were defined as Fine Art. Historians very seldom visited museums in order to research.

The experiences of the visitors to museums and cathedrals were only fixed on their retinas. Many art historians of the nineteenth century developed an outstanding visual mnemonics, but still it was an unstable means of storing visual information. From that personal image-store, art historians might retrieve many examples with forms and contents from artworks experienced years ago pertinent to the subjects of their current investigations. Checking and modifying hypothetical connections required another trip to museums and cathedrals perhaps far away from the subject of investigation. The result was often arbitrary and naturally dependent on the museums and cathedrals actually visited by the investigator.[10]

Later, the situation was improved by a growing number of illustrations in printed editions. The available visual material began to grow and is still growing. For a long time, it was still a matter of access to relevant printed material and of what material has or has not been actually printed. A subject that was made the object of massive printed reproduction tended to become a centripetal force for explanation of artistic imitation and influence. Theories of artistic influence and migration of style grew dependent on what was printed and accessible. During recent decades, the visual history of the past is most often the history of slides and reproductions.[11]

Today, the accessibility of visual material is growing rapidly. The establishment of huge image databases is an expanding undertaking in numerous institutions. The computer revolution has embraced the visual side of the past. In the future, art history will have to expand its field of research to new kinds of images, and historians will be forced to include images as a vital source material. The accessibility of images will turn history and art history upside down. Today, you can write about medieval art in one volume, but you still can print only a very limited selection of the works of art. In future, you will—in principle—be able to gather pictures of all the medieval artefacts you like on huge hard disks and browse through thousands of images. But nobody will have the energy and

---

[10] Regarding connoisseurship, see Jaynie Anderson, *Collecting Connoisseurship and the Art Market in Risorgimento Italy. Giovanni Morelli's Letters to Giovanni Melli and Pietro Zavaritt (1866–1872)* (Venice: Instituto veneto di scienze, lettere ed arti, 1999) [Dr. Phillip Lindley has kindly drawn my attention to this book].

[11] Charles S. Rhyne, 'Computer Images for Research, Teaching and Publication in Art History and Related Disciplines,' *Visual Resources* 12 (1996), pp. 19–51 (p. 25).

time to read about this enormous body of images.[12]

The rapid diffusion of the Internet is facilitating easy access to widespread visual source material.[13] Among other things, the Internet will erode traditional nation-bound research and presentation. The construction of the Internet rests on a kind of equality among the thousands of individual websites and, consequently, also among the growing number of image databases.[14] There is no centre on the Net and therefore no periphery. Looking for similarities between pictures or eventual models of your object of investigation will take you in many directions and not to a specific centre for artistic creativity and innovation. Centre-periphery theories are homeless in cyberspace. They are replaced by intercultural and interactive structures that cannot avoid influencing our medieval studies. The question of individual authorship will become less important.[15] In conjunction with a growth of research in visual history we shall witness a corresponding growth of interdisciplinary research that will not work within and accept today's national frontiers.

The computer revolution involves new ways of defining an image. An image manifests itself in or is presented by means of physical material. This implies that it has a physical demarcation in proportion to something that is not a picture. The cropping or the frame sets the limit. Of course a painting can hold several individual subordinate motifs but the frame sets a limit to the contents and the extent of the visual message. With the invention of photography, cropping has had a growing importance to the definition of an image.[16] This development has reached its peak with the digitalization process. Cut-and-paste functions are indispensable tools when working with computer-supported research in pictures.[17] By these means we, as users, create our own images, and each of us produces an individual verbal definition and description. The process of transcribing visual information to a linguistic system is twofold. It is based on conventions—that is, iconography in a broad definition—and it is based on

---

[12] Axel Bolvig, 'Ars longa—vita brevis', *Medium aevum quotidianum* 39 (1998), pp. 9–20 (15).

[13] Rhyne (as in note 11).

[14] A collection of more than five hundred links to web-sites with medieval images is to be found on www.kalkmalerier.dk/links.

[15] Cf. Ivan Gaskell, 'History of Images', in *New Perspectives on Historical Writing*, ed. by Peter Burke (University Park: Pennsylvania State University Press, 1993), pp. 168–92.

[16] Harold Evans, *Pictures on a Page* (London: William Heinemann, 1978), pp. 203–36.

[17] Charles S. Rhyne, 'Images as Evidence in Art History and Related Disciplines', in *Museums and the Web*, ed. by David Bearman and Jennifer Trant (Pittsburgh: Archives & Museum Informatics, 1997), pp. 347–61.

analogy, which also itself is based on coded systems that by analogy refer to an outside world. Having no grammar or linearity, an image is an open system that cannot by itself present a precise amount of information.[18] Consequently, each scanning and, even more, each cutting-out of details requires new definitions that can vary ad infinitum. Defining or indexing these new digital images is a huge problem in the establishment of image bases but contrariwise also gives the researcher new opportunities to create relevant source material and to bring together visual information from a variety of pictures.

The definition of an image, then, is bound to its framing and/or cropping and cutting.[19] With wall paintings, the problem is that there is no material frame in a traditional sense. An oil painting has a frame, which does not belong to the image. A wall painting needs no frame, as the material of which it consists is the same as the surrounding walls.[20] Consequently the building itself, the architecture, constitutes the frame, within which many individual iconographic or analogue motifs can be traced. When dealing with wall paintings, you always make a selection based not on framed subjects but on iconographic definitions or the recurrence of motifs, be it the Crucifixion, Saint Laurence, the heavenly Castle, or a wooden shoe. The selected subject may receive a new 'identity', but it still belongs to the totality of the architectural interior.[21]

The above-mentioned considerations will, in the following section, be exemplified by the inclusion of the image base with Danish wall paintings, which is accessible on the Internet on www.kalkmalerier.dk/.[22]

Danish Wall Paintings: Alternative Images

In some twenty churches situated in the district of Southeast Funen and the island of Langeland, we find vault decorations that do not fit traditional iconography or our understanding of artistic expression. It is a matter of a very strange,

---

[18] Susanne K. Langer, *Philosophy in a New Key. A Study in the Symbolism of Reason, Rite and Art* (Cambridge, MA: Harvard University Press, 1942); Roland Barthes, 'Rhétorique de l'image', in *Communications*, 4 (1964), pp. 40–51.

[19] Gerhard Jaritz, 'Comparative Analysis of Historical Image Information', in *Electronic Filing, Registration and Communication of Visual Historical Data*, ed. by Axel Bolvig (Göttingen: Max-Planck-Institut für Geschichte, 1995), pp. 29–33.

[20] Sometimes we find painted frames. This goes especially for pictures of St Christopher. Still the painted frame belongs to the total decoration of the church.

[21] Axel Bolvig, 'Hæc pictura completa fuit—Om kalkmalerier og rammer', in *Hikuin*, ed. by Annedorte Vad (forthcoming).

[22] Jesper Jerne Borrild, 'Medieval Danish Wall Paintings—an Internet Database', in *Medium aevum quotidianum*, 39 (as in note 12), pp. 21–36.

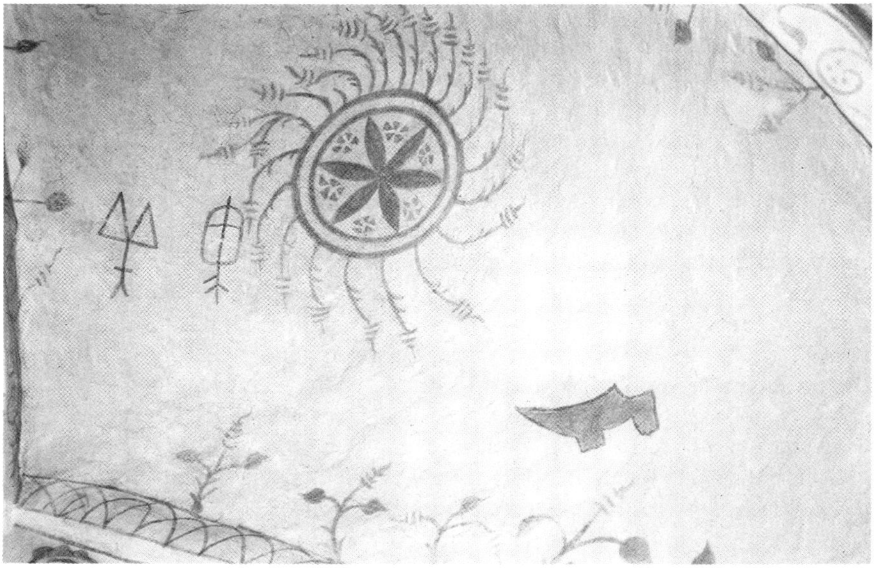

Fig. 1. Gudme church. Wall painting, 'wooden shoe'. 1488. © Author

perhaps 'primitive', and certainly alternative imagery.[23] Traditional indexing of these paintings based on conventional iconography or visual analogy is difficult. The churches were decorated during the last three decades of the fifteenth century by an artist or a workshop that has been named the Painter of Wooden Shoes ('træskomaleren'). The name has been given because the workshop has painted one or more wooden shoes, among the peculiar imagery and ornamentation, in most of the churches (fig. 1).[24]

The painted wooden shoes are not framed in any way, so even if they possess their own connotations they cannot be treated as if they were isolated from the rest of the decorations in the churches. They belong to an imagery consisting of strange and grotesque figures and birds, almost abstract configurations, with very few traditional religious subjects. All the configurations appear as isolated motifs, but none of them have painted frames to give them an explicitly individual existence. They belong to one 'picture', that is to say the whole decoration within the church. All the picture's information must be interpreted on the level of the 'reality' of the image and not of the 'reality' of actual life.[25] The depicted wooden shoes must be evaluated in their context.

---

[23] www.kalkmalerier.dk—search: HMJ in arkivnr.

[24] www.kalkmalerier.dk—search: HMJ-152 (Gudme).

[25] Jaritz (as in note 2), p. 16.

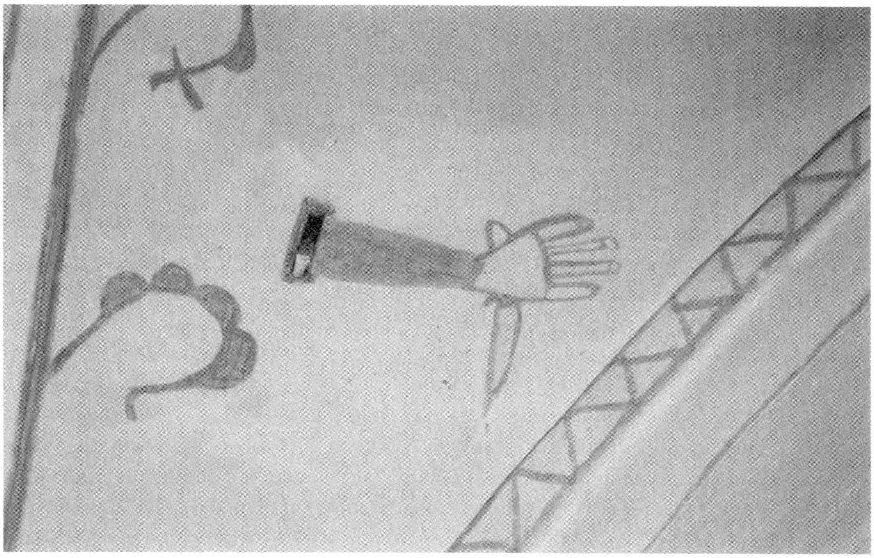

Fig. 2. Ørbæk church. Wall painting, 'hand with a knife'. 1490. © Author

In Ørbæk church the Painter of Wooden Shoes has depicted an arm stretching out of one of the built-in holes in a vault. The hand is holding a pointed knife (fig. 2).[26] What does that mean? What are the traditional connotations of a knife? In the long history of mankind, the knife has always been *the* murder weapon of the ordinary man. Today we talk about 'die Dolchstoss Legende', referring to the German army being stabbed in the back by the civilian population during the First World War. The Night of the Long Knives refers to Hitler's execution of many of the S. A. leadership without trial. When forced to retire in 1908, the Danish Prime Minister J. C. Christensen said that he was 'stabbed in the back'. Since 1808 the expression 'they are at daggers drawn' has meant unbridled hostility. 'Mack the Knife' is a famous scoundrel in one of the plays by Bertold Brecht. The Serbian ultra-nationalist Vuk Draskovic published in 1982 a book entitled 'The Knife', in which the knife symbolizes the Muslims, the ugly and dangerous enemy. Looking farther back in history we see that the knife always has been connected to negative and deadly conceptions. Lady Macbeth says 'Give me the daggers: the sleeping and the dead are but as pictures. . .'.[27] The Danish king Erik Klipping was murdered in 1286; the annals write that the

---

[26] www.kalkmalerier.dk—search: HMJ-125 (Ørbæk).

[27] William Shakespeare, *Macbeth*, act. II, scene 1 (murder of Duncan, king of Scotland).

king's body had fifty-six wounds.[28] In another source we read: 'In the year 1286 king Erik, son of Christopher of pious memory, died on St Cecilia's night, caused by the knives of the impious, terribly murdered by his own men in his own bed'.[29] According to the written material, murderous knives belong to the impious.

In the wall paintings, too, the knife occurs as a negatively connoted tool, a tool for murdering, wounding, and cutting. The Circumcision of the child Jesus, which is the first step on his bloody story of salvation, is performed with a knife.[30] The executioners skin St Bartholomew with knives,[31] and the breasts of St Catharine are cut off with knives.[32] Of course the knife is the most practical tool to be used for these purposes—what else should they use?—but it hurts the victims. It is being used for torture. The fatal function of the knife can be seen in depictions of the deadly sin *Ira*—Anger. In Jørlunde church a visualization of the seven deadly sins was painted around 1510. Anger is depicted as a murderer with a knife.[33] In Fanefjord church there is a depiction of Joab stabbing Abner from behind with a knife: it is a betrayal, just as is the kiss of Judas.[34] In Vigersted church a juggler is playing with and throwing two pointed knives. The dress accentuating his body and the proximity of a woman performing a lascivious dance classify the juggler as the opposite of established social groupings.[35]

In contrast, the killing performed by professional soldiers by order of the

---

[28] 'Annales Ryenses', *Danmarks middelalderlige annaler* (Selskabet for udgivelse af kilder til dansk historie, 1980), p. 175: 'Rex E[ricus] occisus est in lecto in nocte sancte Cecilie a suis, quos maxime dilexerat, inflictis sibi ulneribus DVI'.

[29] *Libri datici Lundenses, Lund domkapitels gavebøger* (Selskabet for udgivelse af Kilder til dansk Historie, 1973), p. 296: 'Anno incarnacionis M.CC.LXXX.VI. rex Ericus, pie recordacionis Chrisofori regis quondam filius, pugionibus impiorum occubit in nocte beate Cecilie a suis in proprio lecto crudelissime trucidatus'.

[30] www.kalkmalerier.dk —search: sh/46, 14/139 (Tingsted).

[31] www.kalkmalerier.dk—search: 20/72 (Tyvelse).

[32] www.kalkmalerier.dk—search: 12/57 (Århus Cathedral).

[33] www.kalkmalerier.dk—search: 16/19 (Jørlunde); *Danmarks Kirker, Frederiksborg amt*, 1975, pp. 2259–60; in some woodcuts in *Pèlerinage de la vie humaine* the vice Treachery is depicted with a pointed knife in her hands: see Michael Camille, 'Reading the Printed Image', in *Printing the Written Word. The Social History of Books circa 1450–1520*, ed. by Sandra Hindman (Ithaca and London: Cornell University Press, 1991), pp. 259–91.

[34] www.kalkmalerier.dk—search: 12/19 (Fanefjord); Ulla Haastrup, 'Danske kalkmalerier 1500–1536', in *Danske kalkmalerier 1500–1536*, ed. by Ulla Haastrup (Copenhagen: Nationalmuseet, 1992), pp. 37–38.

[35] www.kalkmalerier.dk—search: 22/198 (Vigersted).

authorities in the Massacre of the Innocents normally is performed with swords.[36] And Abraham uses not a knife, of course, but a sword to sacrifice his son Isaac.[37] Real heroes fight each other with lances or swords, never with knives.[38] I need not mention that St Martin cuts his coat with a sword, even if a knife would be more useful.[39] And in the Agony, St Peter is armed with a sword, which he uses to cut off the ear of Malchus.[40] Of course a holy man cannot use a knife to attack a soldier, even if he might have had one in his belt.

The knife, therefore, generally has murderous connotations, and such connotations must be attached to the knife in the hand stretching out of the hole in Ørum church. This knife is not the only one depicted in the church. On a painting—now whitewashed over—could be seen a very strange person putting a pointed knife into the anus of a devil or a monster in order to tap fluids into a jug.[41] In this motif the knife is used to exploit the devil or Evil itself. In Allesø church the Painter of Wooden Shoes has depicted another hand holding a knife.[42] In Ryslinge church the same workshop presented a grossly caricatured male person equipped with knives at both his hips.[43] The knife depicted by the Painter of Wooden Shoes in these parish churches is loaded with dangerous, murderous and rebellious connotations. How does the negative knife correspond to the rest of the decorations?

Historians and art historians have had difficulty relating to the imagery of the Painter of Wooden Shoes. 'For a modern viewer they are not easily understood'.[44] It makes you wonder how they ever came to be accepted as a suitable decoration in the church.[45]

> Grotesque masks with a fool's cap and hands that grasp a rib or a knife might be considered as a reflection of an extremely baroque caprice which combined with images marked by dark superstition and horror gives you an insight into emotional life of the late Middle Ages seen from its most glaring sides.[46]

---

[36] www.kalkmalerier.dk—search: barnemord*.

[37] www.kalkmalerier.dk—search: 22/27 (Glesborg).

[38] www.kalkmalerier.dk—search: 15/33 (Dronninglund).

[39] www.kalkmalerier.dk—search: 30-3/79 (Tuse).

[40] www.kalkmalerier.dk—search: Tilfangetagelse; John 18.10 writes that Peter drew his sword.

[41] www.kalkmalerier.dk—search: HMJ-123 (Ørbæk).

[42] www.kalkmalerier.dk—search: HMJ-219 (Allesø).

[43] www.kalkmalerier.dk—search: HMJ-32 (Ryslinge).

[44] *Danske kalkmalerier 1475–1500*, ed. by Ulla Haastrup (Copenhagen: Nationalmuseet, 1991), p. 46.

[45] Hans J. Frederiksen, 'Troens kunst', in *Ny dansk kunsthistorie*, vol. 1 (1999), p. 217.

[46] Egmont Lind, *Report to the National Museum*, quotation from Lise Gotfredsen, 'Nogle sære billeder', in *ICO*, nos 3–4 (1977), p. 20.

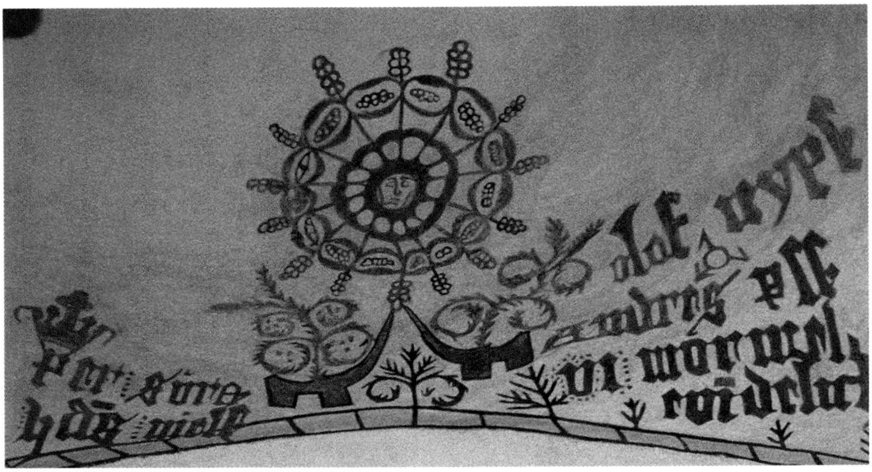

Fig. 3. Stege church. Wall painting, 'two wooden shoes'. 1494. © *Author*

Another scholar, Lise Godtfredsen, concludes that the painter was psychotic—maybe schizophrenic, 'which means that we must be content with not being able in a satisfactory way to interpret his images. It also means that we no longer need to spend time researching them to find a deeper theological meaning. Their logic eludes daylight and our senses'.[47]

Nevertheless, researchers have thrown themselves into interpreting the decorations of the Painter of Wooden Shoes. Ulla Haastrup writes that these primitive decorations performed by bricklayers become meaningful representations of symbols of the course of the year with its ecclesiastical festive days and secular calendar entries. She suggests that the many depicted wooden shoes, rather than being emblems, must be regarded as symbols. She asks if a wooden shoe symbolizes an artisan because workers used this special footwear.[48] Henrik M. Jansen has written a book about the Painter of Wooden Shoes, which offers a broad survey of decoration campaigns of this workshop.[49] Leif Søndergaard takes a standpoint opposite to Lise Godtfredsen's. While she thinks that the images in Ørbæk church were painted by a psychotic person, Leif Søndergaard is convinced that they stem from the thoughts and beliefs of ordinary artisans in the countryside in the late fifteenth century. This means that they possess logic and are meaningful, but in a different way from images made by professional painters. He concludes that most such wall paintings in churches decorated by

[47] Gotfredsen (as in note 46), p. 28.

[48] *Danske kalkmalerier 1475–1500* (as in note 44), pp. 30–31.

[49] Henrik M. Jansen, *Træskomaleren—Et fynsk kalkmaleriværksted i 1400-tallet* (Svendborg: Svendborg & Omegns Museum, 1991).

the Painter of Wooden Shoes are intended to protect the vaulting against demonic forces from outside: they are apotropaic.[50] The database of Danish wall paintings offers an opportunity for quantitative comparison, and querying the database about wooden shoes provides you with another answer. In the relatively few images that depict artisans, we never find a wooden shoe worn by them.[51] One might believe that peasants wore wooden shoes, but this is not the case. Peasants are depicted in the First Labour and the Legend of the Fast Growing Seed. A search of these subjects reveals no wooden shoes at all.[52] In the Dance of Death the peasant does not wear wooden shoes.[53] And neither do the two hunchbacked peasants in the Dominican monastery at Århus.[54] We get the same negative result when making a query on shepherds in the database.[55] In the depiction of the Prayer of the Rich and the Poor Man, neither man is wearing wooden shoes.[56] Apparently all the above-mentioned social groups wore a kind of leather shoe; certainly not wooden shoes.[57]

The wooden shoes depicted by the Painter of Wooden Shoes and the few other equivalent depictions are not designed as an ordinary foot-shaped piece of footwear. Normally they have high wedges and long pointed toes (fig. 3).[58] They

---

50 Leif Søndergaard, 'En håndværkers tro og tanker—om kalkmalerierne i Ørbæk kirke', *Årbog for Svendborg & Omegns Museum 1995* (1996), pp. 55–65; Leif Søndergaard, 'Magiske tegn, figurer og formler i senmiddelalderlige kalkmalerier', in *Billeder i middelalderen. Kalkmalerier og altertavler*, ed. by Bisgaard, Nyberg, and Søndergaard (Odense: Odense Universitetsforlag, 1999), pp. 165–216.

51 www.kalkmalerier.dk—search: 16/147 (Åstrup); 22/199 (Vigersted); sh/598 (Kirkerup); 11/90 (Tved); 15/6, 15/8, 15/9 (Sulsted); Gislinge, reproduced in Niels M. Saxtorph, *Danmarks kalkmalerier* (Copenhagen: Politikens Forlag, 1986), p. 92; Tirsted, reproduced in Axel Bolvig, *Dagligliv i middelalderen* (Copenhagen: Gyldendal, 1979), p. 30.

52 www.kalkmalerier.dk—search: 20/150 (Hyllested); 12/180 (Lyngby); 14/141 (Tingsted); 14/112 (Tågerup); 30-3/62 (Tuse); 17/57 (Keldby); 14/44 (Reerslev); sh/316 (Gjerrild); 32-3/73 (Elmelunde); 17/130 (Lem).

53 www.kalkmalerier.dk—search: ko136 (Nørre Alslev).

54 www.kalkmalerier.dk—search: 11/125 (Århus Dominican monastery).

55 www.kalkmalerier.dk—search: sh/358 (Reerslev); 30-3/53 (Tuse); 9/34 (Mørkøv).

56 www.kalkmalerier.dk—search: fattig*.

57 The publication of the comprehensive excavations in Svendborg, close to the territory of the Painter of Wooden Shoes, mentions a large number of leather shoes but no wooden shoes; see Willy Groenman-van Waateringe, *Leather from Medieval Svendborg* (Odense: Odense University Press, 1988). The same can be said of the huge collections of shoes at the museums of Coventry; see Susan Thomas, *Medieval Footwear from Coventry* (Coventry: Coventry Museum, 1980). Encyclopaedia Britannica informs us under the reference 'sabot' that wooden shoes are used by peasants in France and the Netherlands, www.eb.com:180/cgi-bin/g?DocF=micro/515/84.html.

58 www.kalkmalerier.dk—search: HMJ-104 (Vindinge); HMJ-107 (Frørup); 17/67

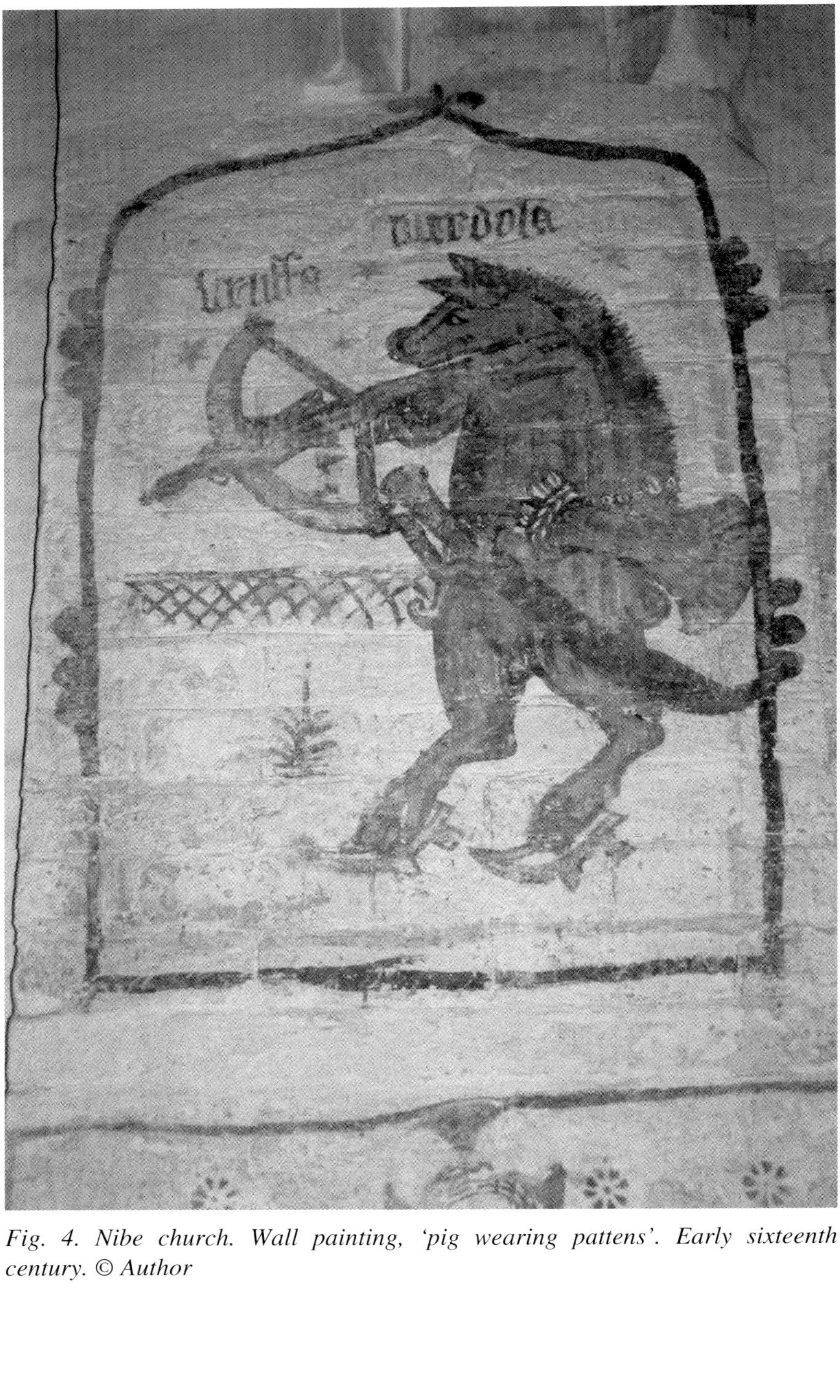

Fig. 4. Nibe church. Wall painting, 'pig wearing pattens'. Early sixteenth century. © Author

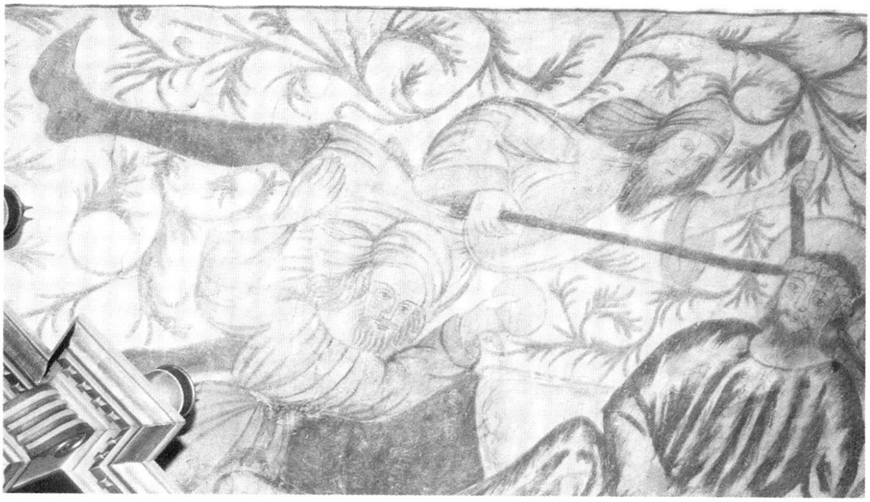

Fig. 5. Gislev church. Wall painting, 'Crowning of Thorns', detail. c. *1520.* © *Author*

connote the dangerousness of pointed objects exactly as does the knife.

A search in the database on wooden shoe ('træsko') reveals quite another picture of the figures using this footwear.[59] In the chapel of The Three Magi at Roskilde Cathedral, the youngest of the kings is depicted as an extremely dressy young man.[60] He has long bright hair under his hat, which looks like a crown. His dress shows off his body. The sleeves are slit up to his upper arms. In the belt a pointed dagger is placed like a phallic symbol. On his feet are long elegant wooden shoes—'pattens'—with high wedges. This type of shoe functioned as an overshoe, which raised the person further above the dirty and muddy ground. The detailing of these wooden shoes followed the fashion of leather shoes.[61] It is not unusual that the youngest of the kings is sumptuously and provocatively dressed (which did not prevent guardians of morality all over Europe making sarcastic remarks about clothing that reveals the body).

Balthazar is not the only one to wear elegant pattens. Among the paintings in Nibe church we find a pig with a crossbow walking on its hind legs with an equivalent kind of wooden shoe (fig. 4).[62] In medieval imagery pigs are nega-

---

[59] www.kalkmalerier.dk—search: træsko in ting (the Danish characters can be replaced by * in the search field).

[60] www.kalkmalerier.dk—search: sh/188 (Roskilde Cathedral).

[61] Francis Grew and Margrethe de Neergaard, *Shoes and Patterns*, Medieval Finds from Excavations in London, 2 (London: HMSO 1988), pp. 91–101.

[62] Reproduced in Kurt Nielsen and Søren Skovfo, *Nibe kirke. Dens bygning,*

tively connoted.[63] The same type of shoe is to be found in Udbyneder.[64] Here it is worn by a devil, which at The Day of Judgement is chasing souls down to the Mouth of Hell. The devil's patten is worked out with a very long pointed toe. His other leg also is connected to wood: under his knee a wooden leg is fixed. In the Day of Judgement in Hørve church, a devil wears wooden shoes of a more ordinary kind on both feet.[65]

In Gislev church, one of the tormentors at the Crowning of Thorns wears wooden shoes (fig. 5), as does the tormentor at the whipping of Christ in the Post-Reformation paintings of Sulsted (fig. 6).[66] In Hyllested church, in a marginal image, a man fighting a woman is wearing wooden shoes. On an arcade pillar in Århus Cathedral we find a caricature of a lansquenet.[67] His head with a long pointed beard is placed on a long bird's neck. In his hands he is holding a sword and a halberd. He has lost one of his legs, which is replaced by a wooden leg. On the other foot he wears an elegant pointed wooden shoe. This caricature of a lansquenet, like the above-mentioned figures, represents the evil and the dangerous. All examples, therefore, of the use of wooden shoes, are negatively connoted, regardless of who is wearing them. In the imagery of medieval Danish wall paintings, the wooden shoe does not exist as the footwear of the ordinary man, either for work or for leisure. There seems to be no difference between pattens and ordinary wooden shoes within the 'reality' of the images.[68]

---

udsmykning og mennesker (Nibe: Nibe menighedsråd, 1995), p. 33.

[63] Frithiof Dahlby, *Symboler og tegn i den kristne kunst* (Copenhagen: J. Fr. Clausen, 1965), pp. 68 and 145; Dorthe Falcon Møller, *Music Aloft* (Copenhagen: Falcon, 1996), p. 99; see also Michael Camille, 'At the Sign of the Spinning Sow: The "Other" Chartres and Images of Everyday Life of the Medieval Street', in this volume.

[64] www.kalkmalerier.dk—search: 11/22 (Udbyneder).

[65] www.kalkmalerier.dk—search: 16/83 (Hørve).

[66] www.kalkmalerier.dk—search: sh/426 (Sulsted).

[67] www.kalkmalerier.dk—search: 66/68 (Århus Cathedral).

[68] The wooden shoe with high wedges (patten) was used as an overshoe for outdoor use. It is now and then depicted in Flemish painting where apparently it is impossible to find expressed any specific symbolic value. On a small altarpiece 'Christ carrying the Cross' *Kunsthistorisches Museum, Vienna. The Paintings* (London: Scala Books, 1997), p. 60, Hieronymus Bosch has a man near the cross wear pattens. It is difficult to say whether he represents Simon of Cyrene or an executioner; reproduced in Wolfgang Prohaska, *Kunsthistorisches Museum, Wien. The Paintings* (London: C. H. Beck/Scala Books, 1997), p. 60. In 'The Temptation of Saint Anthony' at Lisbon's Museo Nacional, Bosch depicts a strange figure who probably represents an evil messenger wearing pattens (Luís Afonso has kindly drawn my attention to this picture). On an altarpiece by Joos van Cleve (Kunsthistorisches Museum, Vienna), the Virgin Mary and the Jesus Child are seen together with Joseph, who has taken off one of his pattens, probably in respect for the holy child. In Jan Gossaert's 'St. Luke depicting The Virgin Mary with the Child', Luke

Jean-Claude Schmitt has written about the material and the symbolic realities in the Middle Ages with a starting-point in shoes. He refers to a story, a variant of the tale of the Jongleur de Notre-Dame, about a performer who for lack of money played a piece of music in honour of the representation of Jesus Christ at Volto Santo. The figure of Jesus gave his right shoe as a reward to the musician. Schmitt points to the fact that taking off a shoe indicates that you relinquish your possession of a woman or a field or that you convey your right to the one who

---

is kneeling at his drawing desk; he has taken off his pattens, apparently to show deference to Mary and her child; reproduced in Prohaska (op. cit.), p. 63. Taking off the pattens as a sign of deference is shown in several images. In Carlo Crivelli's 'The vision of the blessed Gabriel' (The National Gallery, London: NG 668), the saint is kneeling by the side of the Virgin Mary with the Child and has taken off his pattens. In Robert Campin's 'Merode altarpiece', the right wing is devoted to Joseph as a supplement to the central motif of the Annunciation. He is sitting in his workshop making a mousetrap. In all its realism Campin's painting is saturated with symbolism, and the mousetrap refers to St Augustine's statement that God had to make his appearance on earth in the shape of a human being in order to cheat the devil: 'The Lord's cross was the devil's mousetrap'. Under Joseph's long gown we see his left foot wearing a patten. Joseph, not showing deference but creating the symbolic devil's trap, keeps his wooden shoe on; reproduced in Jutta Held and Norbert Schneider, *Socialgeschichte der Malerei vom Spätmittelalter bis ins 20. Jahrhundert* (Cologne: DuMont, 1993), p. 25. In the 'Presentation in the Temple' (1450–1500) (The National Gallery, London: NG 706), Joseph is wearing beautiful pattens. In this scene he is not showing deference to the child and consequently he has not taken off his pattens. The most famous pair of pattens undoubtedly are those depicted in Jan van Eyck's 'The Betrothal of the Arnolfini' (The National Gallery, London). On the floor in front of Arnolfini lie his pattens with high wedges (see plate 1). They have long pointed toes like the pattens of Balthazar and the devil of Udbyneder. It seems obvious that he has taken off his overshoes, but their central position in the painting indicates that like St Luke he is showing deference to his fiancée. Arnolfini belonged to a wealthy milieu; drawing from the finds of excavations in London, Francis Grew and Margrethe de Neergaard state that especially during the late fourteenth century, pattens were worn in the City chiefly as a useful fashion accessory to protect the feet and the shoes of the well-to-do; see Grew and Neergaard (as in note 61), p. 91. In a wall painting by Domenico Di Bartolo in Santa Maria delle Scale, Siena (1443), a man is seen carrying a bier (?) wearing the same kind of wooden shoes; reproduced in Georges Duby, *An 1000 an 2000. Sur les traces de nos peurs* (Paris: Textuel, 1995), p. 35. All the above-mentioned representations of wooden shoes (pattens) differ from the pointed wooden shoes of the painter of Wooden Shoes. I dare say that the latter's wooden shoes (sabots) might contain a locally and socially delimited iconography of their own, but an iconography that anyhow connotes a widespread stratum of opposition and rebellion.

I have collected the above mentioned examples of depicted wooden shoes by travelling or looking in illustrated books and not by systematic research and certainly not—yet—by a search in image databases, which in the future without doubt will give me much more information to compare with the Danish material.

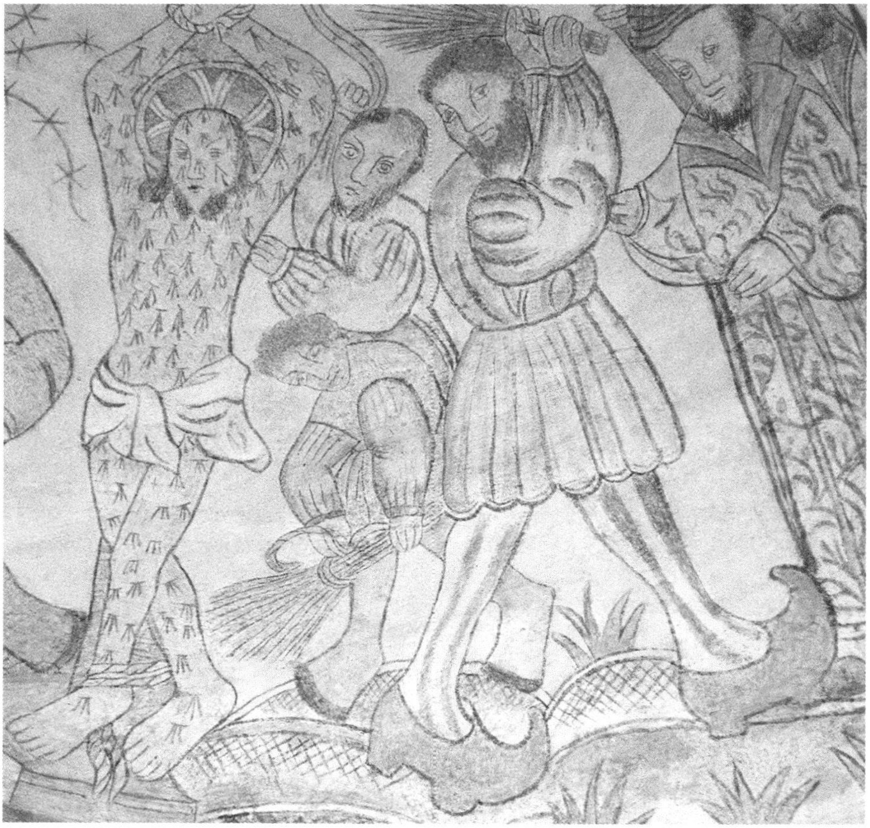

Fig. 6. Sulsted church. Wall painting, 'Whipping of Christ'. 1548. © Author

receives the shoe.[69] This notion connected to the shoe goes back to the book of Ruth in the Old Testament.[70] Whether there is a symbolic connection between this notion of shoes and the many depicted wooden shoes in the Danish churches I cannot say. It seems most likely, I think, that the connotations in the Danish paintings point in another direction.

---

[69] Jean-Claude Schmitt, 'Réalité materiélle et réalité symbolique. A propos du soulier de Christ', in *Pictura quasi fictura. Die Rolle des Bildes in der Erforshung von Alltag und Sachkultur des Mittelalters und der frühen Neuzeit*, ed. by Gerhard Jaritz (Vienna: Der österreichischen Akademie der Wissenschaften, 1996), pp. 73–85. The fact that Arnolfini has taken off his shoes at Van Eyck's Betrothal of the Arnolfini might be evaluated in this perspective, but apparently it does not make logical sense.

[70] Ruth 4.7–8.

The many wooden shoes associated with the Painter of Wooden Shoes are not at any rate depictions of the footwear of peasants and artisans. They cannot function as symbols of bricklayers. Their design does not fit an analogue depiction of a piece of footwear. As symbolic representations, the wooden shoes connote provocation (Balthazar, the lansquenet, and the pig), violence (the tormentors), and alternative forces in opposition to the mightiest ruler (the devil). As a symbol, the long pointed toe connotes the dangerous. The murderous knife in the hand sticking out of a hole in Ørbæk church is grouped with the pointed wooden shoes in connoting danger, provocation, and rebellion. In this connection it is important to note that the French word for wooden shoe is *sabot* and that *sabotage* means both the making of wooden shoes and vandalism. About 1300, *saboter* meant to thrust or to wound, and during the sixteenth century the word meant to shake, shock, or to torment.[71]

We do not know if there is a connection in meaning between French etymology and the iconography of Danish wall paintings, but the identical nature of the contents is remarkable. The rebellious significance hidden in these 'accidental' wooden shoes is underlined by the time of their execution, the years around 1500. Exactly during these decades Germany experienced violent peasants' rebellions that culminated in the 1520s. The revolutionary movement was named after its symbol of unity—a 'Bundschuh', which was the typical footwear of peasants in late medieval Germany. On their standards the peasants painted a shoe: the Bundschuh they wore themselves. The Bundschuh thus became the sign of rebellion.

At the same time as the Bundschuhbewegung, wooden shoes were painted in some twenty Danish churches gathered on southeast Funen and the surrounding islands, shoes that are depicted with a long pointed toe, which itself indicates rebellion. Shoes that in the imagery of the wall paintings are used by tormentors and devils. Shoes that can be found in decorations that deviate very much from traditional wall painting iconography. Faced with possible criticism from ecclesiastical authorities, the local peasants could answer: this is just an ordinary wooden shoe. But with René Magritte they would think: this is not a wooden shoe. With van Gogh they would feel that an image of a wooden shoe contains an infinity of meanings. Mutually they would know that the configurations on the vaults represent a sign of gathering, solidarity, resistance, and rebellion.

Martin Luther pinned his theses on church-doors as a natural place to disclose written communication. Inside the churches it was just as natural to communicate ideas and messages. The Painter of Wooden Shoes was not merely one

[71] O. Bloch and W. von Wartburg, *Dictionnaire étymologique de la langue française*, 8th edn (Paris: Presses universitaires de France, 1989), p. 567; A. Greimas, *Dictionnaire de l'ancien français*, 2nd revised edn (Paris: Larousse, 1980), p. 576. Jérôme Baschet has kindly given me this information. Paul Robert, *Dictionnaire alphabétique et analogique de la langue française*, 2nd edn, 9 vols (Paris: Le Robert, 1985), VIII, pp. 520–21.

psychotic person; as a matter of fact, the decoration of more than twenty churches during a couple of decades involves several painters. They all have in common the use of alternative iconography in opposition to traditional religious imagery. They use the depiction of a wooden shoe with high wedges and long pointed toes as a common sign.

The present use of the database results in a theory that wooden shoes only belong to negatively connoted figures and situations, never to artisans' or peasants' daily life. Do the depicted wooden shoes in this specific part of Denmark at this specific period of European history indicate the parishioners' wish to take over their local churches? Do we see a visualized rebellion against the established church? Or is the wooden shoe a sign of resistance directed towards the land-owning lords?

Images as Source Material

At the sign of the 'Spinning Sow': the 'other' Chartres and images of everyday life of the medieval street

† MICHAEL CAMILLE

The vast majority of people who visit Chartres, a short day-trip from Paris today, do so to see the world-famous Gothic cathedral with its superb twelfth- and thirteenth-century sculpture and stained glass. Modern interpreters of this building, beginning with Alphonse Didron in his 'Iconographie Chrétienne' of 1841, through Emile Mâle and down to the thousands of bibliographical entries listed in Van der Meulen's recent bibliographical survey, have made it into a great iconographic machine for the production of meanings.[1] Like all machines in the common science-fiction trope, this too becomes autonomous, not only outliving its creators but also 'taking over' the world, generating new interpretations in its increasing control of the Gothic imaginary. It has become a 'summa' in stone, educating the illiterate masses (today as well as in the past) in the basic truths of the Christian faith. Chartres Cathedral often is described as striving to contain everything in one vast encyclopaedia and microcosm: Old and New Testaments, past and future, body and spirit, virtue and vice, even 'low' as well as 'high' culture. The western complex includes not only the systematic order of the famous royal portal but also the statue of the ass playing the lyre carved at the base of the south tower. Michel Foucault argues that this insatiable yearning to encompass 'everything' results in the monument's

[1] Jan Van Der Meulen, *Chartres, Sources and Literary Interpretation, A Critical Biography* (Boston: Hall, 1989).

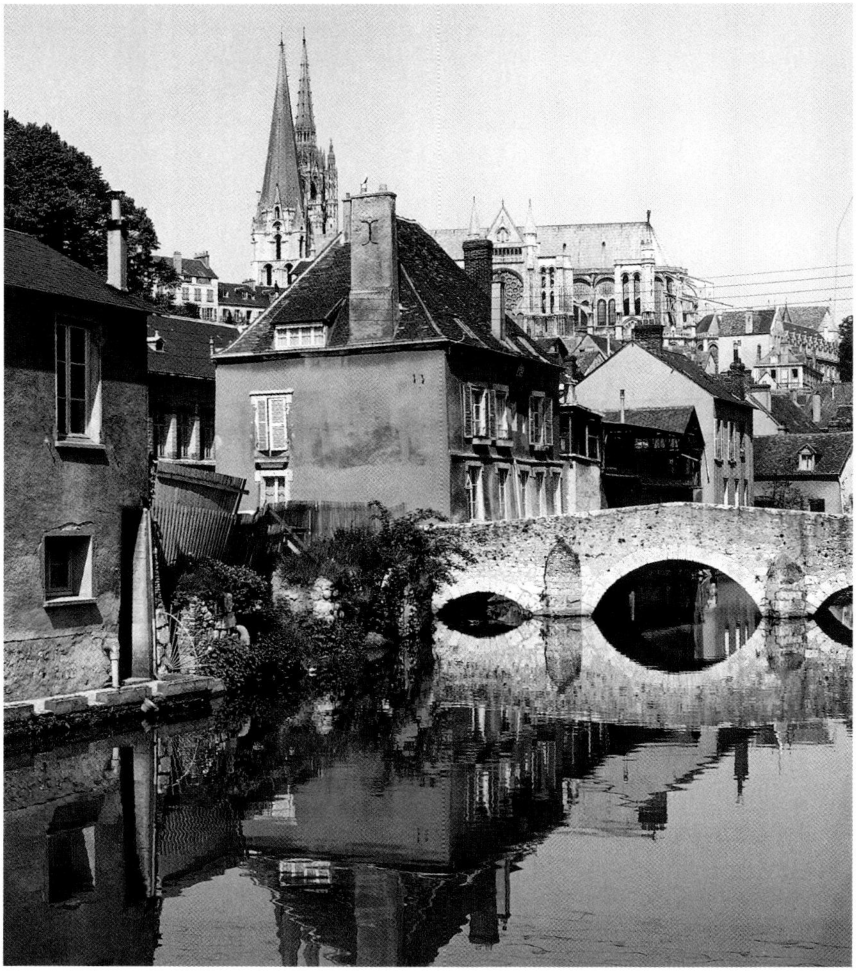

Fig. 1. Chartres. Distant view of the cathedral from the south east with 'Basse-Ville' in foreground. © Author

ultimate loss of meaning because of excess, a literal over-production of signification.[2] I would put this slightly differently: I would suggest that the cathedral manifests the desire to encompass and to structure official exegesis in opposition to the chaotic instability of the countless unofficial and indecipherable meanings that are projected onto it and that proliferate in the profane

[2] Michel Foucault, *Madness and Civilization*, trans. by Richard Howard (New York: Vintage Books, 1973), p. 18.

world it seeks, but fails, to exclude. This is its failure, because the proliferation of images pressing in from the outside ultimately prevent Chartres Cathedral from sustaining its isolated and separate place. However, it is also its triumph, since the boundaries of the sacred extend from its walls out into all spheres of the *socius* beyond.

In questioning why we still isolate the sacred from the profane as separate spheres in medieval culture, I shall be turning things upside down. I shall not discuss the contamination of the cathedral at the centre by 'popular' images from the outside, which is where one might want to begin with an image like that of the musical ass, but rather shall place the cathedral itself on the margins. I am going to talk instead about what I call the 'other' Chartres, hoping, in the process, to blur the image we might have of the cathedral as the spotless reflecting mirror of medieval society. This 'other' Chartres is not where clerics perform the liturgy and people confess, pray, and contemplate the next world. It is in this one, where they are born, puke, suck, play, work, eat, drink, defecate, breathe, sleep, and eventually die. It is the town itself, the Chartres of the marketplace, of the body, the mouth, the gut, and the anus, the 'material lower bodily stratum', as the Russian scholar Bakhtin termed it.[3] What was called the 'basse ville' or lower town contained both policed gates open to certain influxes of goods as well as sluices running out of it, waterways that flushed away the detritus and pollutants from the town's textile and tanning industries (fig. 1). These were the sites of entry and exit, the mouth and anus of this social body. The town in this sense embodied the 'high' and 'low' sacred/profane metaphor stretching steeply down below the walled enclosure of the holy city. During the Middle Ages, Chartres flourished as one of the largest and most active urban centres in northern France, especially its production and market in wine and cloth. In addition to the cathedral, the extant medieval architecture of Chartres includes a number of canonical residences with sculptural decoration that were inside the cloister, a wall that demarcated the ecclesiastical domain in the town and that was controlled by the bishop and chapter.[4] There are also important architectural remains from the town itself, most notably a group of wonderfully preserved timber-framed houses or 'maison de pans de bois' built during the fifteenth century. Timber-framed houses were crucial sites of sculptural decoration during the Middle Ages, a genre ignored by art historians today who

[3] Mikhail Bakhtin, *Rabelais and His World*, trans. by Hélène Iswolsky (Cambridge, MA: MIT Press, 1968), pp. 368–436.

[4] For the house opposite the cathedral with carvings of a pair of wrestlers and dice-players in the lunettes, see Yves Esquieu, *Quartier Cathédrale: une cité dans la ville* (Paris: Desclée de Brouwer, 1994), p. 96. For another interesting twelfth-century house, also probably a canonical residence, with monstrous human and animal figures carved in the lunettes, see A. Mayeux, 'Maison du XIIe siècle à Chartres', *Bulletin Monumental*, 79 (1920), 217–22.

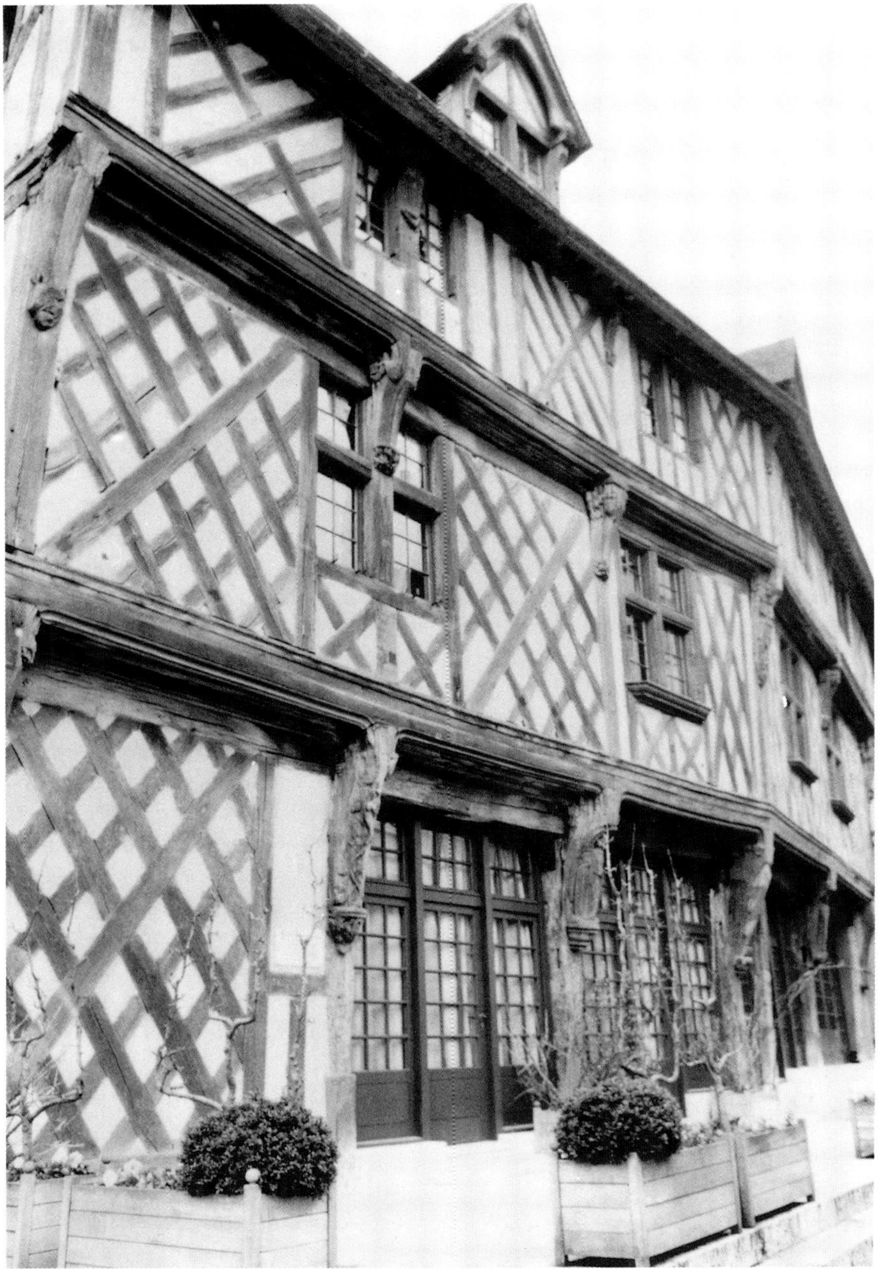

Fig. 2. Chartres, 'Maison du Saumon'. © Author

relegate these sculptures to the status of 'patrimoine folklorique' rather than admitting them to the status of 'art' proper.[5] One of these is the 'escalier de la Reine Berthe' containing numerous figural sculptures, but the one I want to focus on, just opposite the Hotel de Ville only a stone's throw from the south portal of the cathedral, is the building known as the 'Maison du Saumon' (fig. 2).

Named after the beautifully carved fish on the central console of the first storey, this three-storey, five-bay façade is divided by a series of sculpted figures, many now damaged beyond recognition. At the centre, flanking the great fish, are the angel and Mary of an Annunciation group much damaged during the Revolution.[6] As is usual in the other fifteenth-century houses I have examined with numerous sculpted elements, those which survive at Angers, Bourges, and various towns in Brittany, the sacred personages are placed on the lower storeys while the higher storeys are reserved for animal and satirical figures. As well as standing saints there are a number of animals carved on the façade in addition to the salmon: a butterfly and snail on a vine-leaf, for example. Most striking of all these wooden carved signs, however, is that on the far right of the second storey, diagonally adjacent to the watery sign that has given this house its name, the image of the 'truie qui file' or the spinning sow (fig. 3). The porcine creature is represented as a strange upside-down 'fileuse' or spinner. Lying on her back, she is busy working the spindle, which flies up in the corner, rather than dangling as it should from the long distaff, held in place by the belt that encircles the animal's plump body. This spinning equipment and even the belt to hold it in place can be paralleled in contemporary images of human female spinners, but before I come to analyse this aspect of the image I first want to establish some of the perimeters of pig-perception in fifteenth-century France.

---

[5] For French half-timbered houses in general, see: Camille Enlart, *Manuel d'archéologie française, II. Architecture civile et militaire* (Paris: Picard, 1904), pp. 185–88; R. Quenedey, *L'Habitation rouennaise* (Rouen: Lestringant, 1926; new ed. by Brionne, 1977); Pierre Garrigou Grandchamp, *Demeures médiévales: coeur de la Cité* (Paris: Desclée de Brouwer, 1994), pp. 118–203; Yves Esquieu, 'La maison médiévale urbaine en France: état de la recherche', *Bulletin Monumental*, 153 (1995), 109–41; and the most in-depth study yet undertaken of carvings located on houses on one site, by Daniel Leloup, *La Maison urbaine en Trégor aux XVe et XVIe siècles* (Rennes: Éditions Ouest-France, 1996).

[6] Roger Joly, *Histoire de Chartres* (Roanne: Horvath, 1982), p. 189; see also *Archives de la Commission des Monuments Historiques*, ed. by A. M. Baudot and A. Perrault, III (Paris, 1920), p. 10.

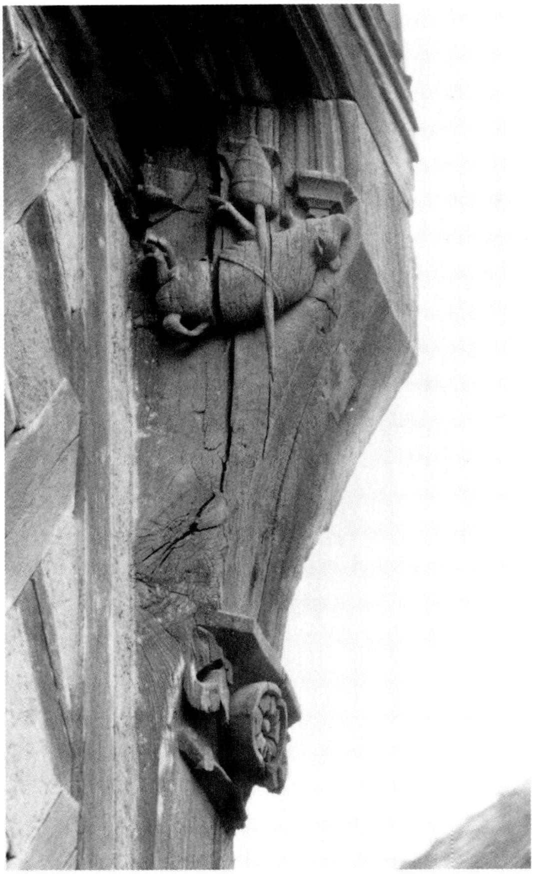

Fig. 3. Chartres, the 'Truie qui file' on the 'Maison du Saumon'. © Author

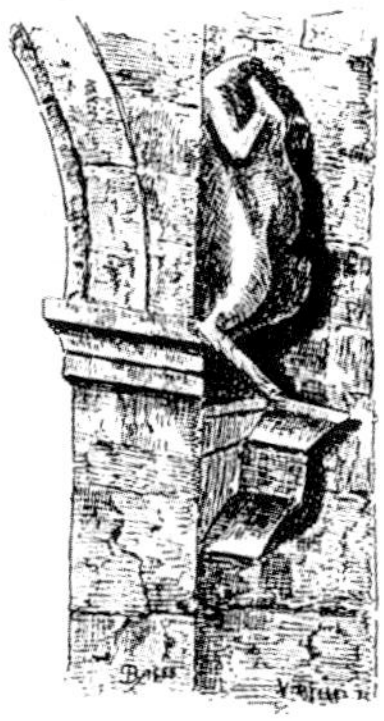

Fig. 4. The so-called 'Truie qui file' on the south tower of the cathedral, from L'Abbé Bulteau, Monographie de la Cathédrale de Chartres, *II (Chartres, 1888)*

Pig in the City

From medieval folktales and modern children's stories to the recent film 'Pig in the City', the myth of the urbane porker, the swine become socialite, the pig that leaves the filth of the farm for the swagger of city life, is a compelling myth articulating the deep-seated nature/culture contradiction. The very use of painted and sculpted animal images as both house signs and shop signs throughout the medieval urban space is an important aspect of this trajectory from countryside to city, making the question of what this pig is doing here especially significant.[7] The spinning sow is not a unique image, though this particular configuration with the sow upside down is, as we shall see, unusual. The image of the 'truie qui file' existed in many towns in medieval France. It is documented as a house sign at Dijon, Orléans, Rouen, Rheims, Sens, Troyes, and Paris.[8] Apart from a spinning sow carved on a house in Malestroit in Brittany, which will be discussed later in this paper, this one at Chartres is the only other medieval example I know—of what was a popular theme in house sculpture—to have survived to the present day. Compared to a theme such as the 'ass playing the lyre'—which, partly because it appears on the cathedral, has been the subject of numerous articles since the middle of the nineteenth century—there are very few studies of the spinning sow as an iconographical subject, an example of how we tend to prioritize ecclesiastical over non-ecclesiastical themes.[9]

---

[7] S. Roux, *Images des bêtes urbaines, milieux naturelles, espaces sociaux: Etudes offertes à Robert Delort* (Paris: Presses de l'Université de la Sorbonne, 1997), pp. 229–40.

[8] Albert Babeau, *Les Vieilles Enseignes de Troyes* (Troyes: P. Nouel, 1898), p. 21; Marie-Camille Patay, *Les Enseignes, emblèmes et inscriptions du vieil Orléans* (Orléans: H. Herluison, 1878), pp. 10–48; C. Porée, *Histoire des rues et des maisons de Sens* (Sens: Duchemin, 1920); and for Paris see Edouard Fournier, *Histoire des Enseignes de Paris revue et publiée par la Bibliophile Jacob* (Paris: E. Dentu, 1884), who discusses the 'truie qui file' on p. 115. For house signs in general in the Middle Ages, see E. de la Quérière, *Recherches historiques sur les enseignes de maisons particulières* (Paris: E. Didron, 1852) and Jean-Pierre Leguay, *La Rue au moyen âge* (Rennes: Éditions Ouest-France, 1984), pp. 104–10. The best illustrated discussion is Yves Papin, 'Les Enseignes médievales: un langage pittoresque et universel', *Archeologia*, 69 (1979), 37–42.

[9] For the meaning of the ass playing the lyre carved at Chartres, see the articles by Guy Villette listed in Van der Meulen (as in note 1), nos 710, 2068, 2069, as well as: Helen Adolf, 'The Ass and the Lyre', *Speculum*, 2 (1950), 49–57; Martin Vogel, *Onos lyras. Der Esel mit der Leier*, Schriftenreihe zu Grundfragen der Musik, 13–14 (Düsseldorf: Gesellschaft zur Forderung der systematischen Musikwissenschaft, 1973), vol. I, pp. 361–64; Alessandro Vitale-Brovarone, 'The Asinus Citharaaedus in the Literary and Iconographic Tradition of the Middle Ages', *Marche Romane*, 28 (1978), 125–29; M. de Meyer, *De Volks-en Kinderprent in de Nederlanden* (Antwerp and Amsterdam, 1962), p. 417; Wilfried Schouwink, *Der wilde Eber in Gottes Weinberg: Zur Darstellung des*

On the Chartres house the small sculpted figure of the pig fits perfectly into the triangular form of the spandrel-shaped bracket, and is quite visible from the street below, in a way that many marginal sculptures carved in stone on churches are not. Is there anything like this image on Chartres cathedral? On the base of the south tower is a group of incongruous animal performers. One of these is the already-mentioned theme of the ass playing the lyre carved on the south side of the southwest tower of the cathedral. This musical donkey is based upon Classical sources, and one of the few scholars to mention the spinning pig at Chartres has argued that, like the harping ass here, our spinning sow 'is based on a fable by Phaedrus'.[10] The Roman playwright's fable 'Asinus ad lyram' was known to medieval authors indirectly through a phrase in Boethius's *Consolation of Philosophy* but had entered vernacular proverbial discourse already by the twelfth century. The foolishness theme takes on a more specific Christian significance at this particular site. As an image of exclusion, it depicts the incongruity of lay people's vain attempts to perform the sacred themselves, for example, to read the Psalter. Paired with the image of the 'Ane qui vielle' is a much-damaged figure of an animal also up on its hind legs performing in human fashion, which, fascinatingly, many nineteenth-century scholars labelled the 'truie qui file' (fig. 4). In 1852 E. de la Quérière in his book *Recherches historiques sur les Enseignes des maisons particulières*, described this as the very same 'truie qui file' known in so many towns in France as a house sign. Even more influentially, in his 1888 monograph on the cathedral, Marcel J. Bulteau also described the vestiges of this statue as 'une quenouille, sa patte droite tenait le fil', probably projecting back onto the hardly legible statue on the cathedral an image he knew from the well-known local image in the town.[11] He saw it as a case of the contamination of the cathedral's symbolic structure by an extraneous and, in this case, inappropriate sign. However, here I disagree with scholars such as Van der Meulen who believe that meaning exists only where it has been inscribed by its medieval makers: the fact that many people in the nineteenth century saw and read this cathedral sculpture as the spinning sow, however erroneous this reading was, makes it part of the cumulative meanings adhering to the building and is just as relevant as those lingering on from the Middle Ages. In 1916 the Comte d'Armancourt presented a paper arguing that

---

Schweins in Literatur und Kunst des Mittelalters (Sigmaringen: Thorbeke, 1985); Nils-Arvid Bringeus, *Volkstümliche Bilderkunde* (Munich: Callewy, 1992), pp. 69–72; M. Pastoureau, 'L'homme et le porc: une histoire symbolique', in his *Couleurs, Images, Symboles* (Paris: Le Léopard d'Or, 1989), pp. 237–82; and *Mythologies du porc: Actes du colloque de Saint-Antoine-l'Abbaye (Isère)*, ed. by P. Walter (Grenoble: Millon, 1999), p. 263.

[10] Joly (as in note 6), p. 189.

[11] L'Abbé Bulteau, *Monographie de la Cathédrale de Chartres, II* (Chartres: Librairie R. Selleret, 1888), pp. 96–97; E. de la Quérière (as in note 8), p. 17.

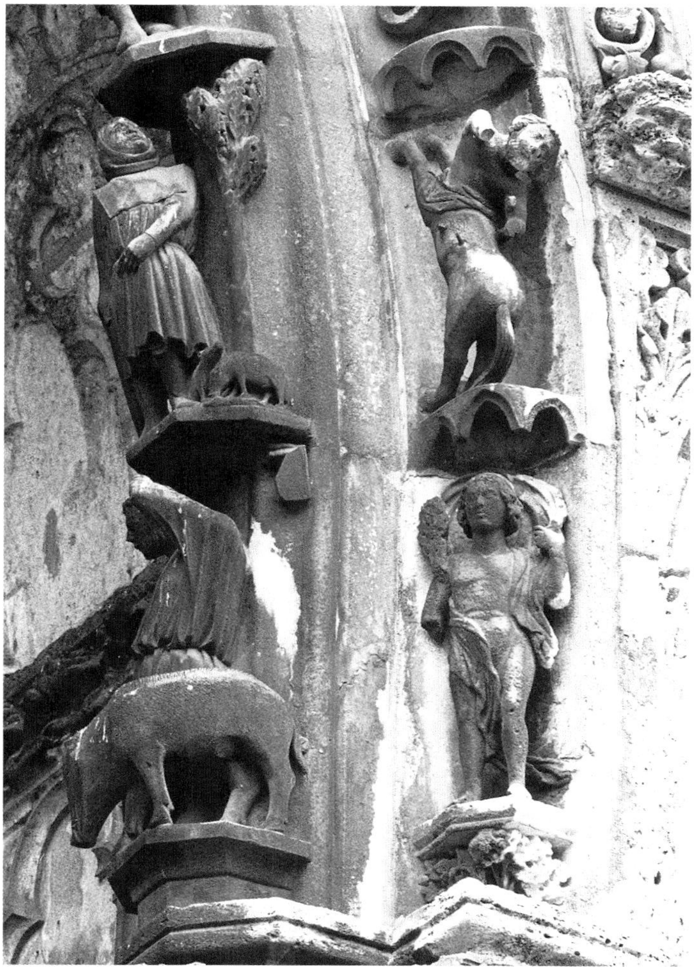

Fig. 5. Chartres Cathedral, North transept, right porch, right outer archivolts, 'December pig killing'. © James Austin

the so-called 'sow' indubitably displayed male genitals and that what was represented here was in fact another popular animal type: 'the wise dog which dances'.[12] The spinning sow then is one of the few things that did not appear

[12] Armancourt, *Société Archéologique de l'Eure-et-Loire*, 13 (1919), 413–16; see also Van Der Meulen (as in note 1), no. 2052; and Rüdiger Hoyer, *Notre Dame de Chartres, Der Westcomplex: Systematische Grundlagen der Bauarchäoligischen Analyse* (Frankfurt: Lang, 1991), Abb. 66, p. 91.

originally in the stone encyclopaedia of the cathedral. Its lack on the cathedral is made up for by its appearance in the marketplace.

Writing about medieval marginal sculpture, Nurith Kenaan-Kedar states that the images found carved on fifteenth-century French houses are taken from the traditional repertoire of themes already used for centuries in church corbels, like these figures at Chartres, as well as gargoyles.[13] Images such as the spinning sow, which occasionally appear in church contexts, are not the same, however, when they are placed on a civic building or house. For they are here linked to the life of the street rather than to the liturgy. The marketplace, which in Bakhtin's words was 'the centre of all that is unofficial enjoyed a certain extraterritoriality in a world of official order and official ideology, it always remained 'with the peo-ple" '.[14] When pigs appear in church sculpture, which they do quite rarely compared to other animals, it is usually as part of the calendrical cycle for December, as they do on the north transept, right porch sculptural archivolts of Chartres Cathedral (fig. 5). They refer to the sins of greed and lust as first defined by Clement of Alexandria, when they are shown being ridden by an ape or playing bagpipes. The pig had a long negative history in Christian art as 'an abomination', its uncleanness defined by Jewish dietary laws and by Christ casting out demons from a man into swine.[15] Most well known is the 'Judensau', carved at a number of cathedrals (but not at Chartres) and later popular in woodcuts, which shows the Jews suckling on the very creature they view as unclean.[16]

At the same time it would be also wrong to argue that the pig has a totally secular meaning on the house because it appears in a secular place, thereby separating the spheres of sacred and profane culture that in reality constantly overlapped. Writing about contemporary southern French communities from an anthropological perspective, Claudine Fabre-Vassas has written what is the most anthropologically complex account of the pig as sign in her book *The Singular Beast*. She makes the important point that 'the slaughter of the animal coincides with the rhythms of the destiny of Christ', making it a complex and volatile sign

[13] Nurith Kenaan-Kedar, *Marginal Sculpture in Medieval France: Towards the Deciphering of an Enigmatic Pictorial Language* (Aldershot: Scolar Press, 1995), pp. 134, 139, and 143.

[14] Bakhtin (as in note 3), pp. 153 ss.

[15] See: F. C. Sillar and R. M. Meyler, *The Symbolic Pig. An Anthology of Pigs in Literature and Art* (Edinburgh: Oliver and Boyd, 1961); Claude Gaignebet and J. Dominique Lajoux, *L'Art profane et religion populaire au moyen âge* (Paris: Presses universitaires de France, 1985), pp. 98–100; and Milo Kearney, *The Role of Swine Symbolism in Medieval Culture* (Lewiston: Mellen, 1996).

[16] See Isaiah Shachar, *The Judensau, A Medieval Anti-Jewish Motif and its History* (London: Warburg Institute, 1974).

of seasonal and pseudo-sacred authority in various communities.[17]

As signs, animals served a totally different function in the social imaginary than do their modern counterparts. Also, whereas in the countryside the pig was 'an important member of the family', once herded into cities their symbolic ambivalence turned more towards hate, not only because the pig's dung was now a nuisance on the street but also because the pig 'now stood as a sign of the gross immiseration of its fellow slum-dwellers'.[18] Precisely because they lived among poorer people, they might occasionally eat unattended babies, for which they were accused, tried, sometimes tortured, and then executed like human criminals. The monks of Saint-Geneviève ordered a pig to be publicly burned alive, and in 1403 another was imprisoned and had to pay room and board like other prisoners before its execution.[19]

The anthropologist Edmund Leach, in his study *Anthropological Aspects of Language: Animal Categories and Verbal Abuse*, views the pig as a particularly striking example of what he calls 'the intermediate category'—both man and animal, friendly and hostile.[20] The pig was associated with the outcast, the Jew, the prostitute, the leper. So why does it appear here? Peter Stallybrass and Allon White, in their ambitious attempt to 'sketch a theory of its *ambivalence*', describe the pig as an animal of the threshold, between the country and the city, the outside and the inside, the human and the animal.

> Not only did the pink pigmentation and apparent nakedness of the pig disturbingly resemble the flesh of European babies (thereby transgressing the man-animal opposition), but pigs were usually kept in peculiarly close proximity to the house and fed from the household's leftovers [. . .]. It is precisely the 'creature of the threshold' which becomes the object of fascination. Mixing faeces and food, human and animal, human skin and animal hide, the household and the farmyard and the field, the pig also lived to die—unlike sheep, cows and chickens, the pig was useful only to eat and proverbially, only became valuable when dead.[21]

---

[17] Claudine Fabre-Vassas, *The Singular Beast: Jews, Christians and the Pig*, trans. by Carol Volk (New York: Columbia University Press, 1997), p. 185.

[18] See Robert Delort, 'Les Animaux dans la ville occidentale à la fin du moyen âge', in *Villes, bonnes villes, cités et capitales: études d'histoire urbaine (*XIIe–XVII *siècle). Mélanges offerts à Bernard Chevalier*, ed. by Monique Bourin (Tours: Presses de l'Université, 1989), p. 345; F. Harrison, *Strange Land: The Countryside: Myth and Reality* (London: Sidgwick & Jackson, 1982), p. 61.

[19] E. P. Evans, *The Criminal Prosecution and Punishment of Animals* (London: Heinemann, 1906), pp. 140–44.

[20] Edmund Leach, 'Anthropological Aspects of Language: Animal Categories and Verbal Abuse', in *New Directions in the Study of Language*, ed. by E. H. Lenneberg (Cambridge, MA: MIT Press, 1964), pp. 23–63.

[21] Peter Stallybrass and Allon White, *The Politics and Poetics of Transgression*

They describe how 'the pig was duly celebrated as well as reviled', becoming 'the symbolic analogy of scapegoated groups and demonized "others" especially the Jews who were forced in some cities to perform races with pigs and be stoned'. The pig becomes 'a focus of what we call *displaced abjection*, the process whereby the "low" social groups turn their figurative and actual power, not against those in authority, but against those who are even "lower" (women, Jews, animals; particularly cats and pigs)'.[22] By eliding the Jew with the pig, the carnival crowd was producing a grotesque hybridization of terms expressly antithetical to each other according to the dietary rules of their victims, who, at carnival-time, would be excluded from the great pig-feast. For between December and March the killing of the family pig was a time of enormous rejoicing and festivity, incorporated into the liturgy of the 'cochonailles' when the community came together for the sacrificial death of the creature. The most important cluster of associations for the purposes—visible in calendar pages of many Flemish manuscripts showing the violent death of the pig in December, its hot blood caught by an old woman, and which kept folk alive through the winter—is the association between pigs and women.

Spinning Pigs and Women

The gender of this pig is made visible neither through her body nor through any teats, which in some examples show her suckling her young, but through what she does. Spinning was exclusively the work of women, practised by duchess and peasant alike and part of the traditional iconography of gender differentiation throughout the Middle Ages. While Adam delved out in the fields, 'Eve span' in the home, even while she tended her children.[23] Spinning their yarn simultaneously, they spun tales, and like the fates, time itself became associated with their unwinding actions. This feminine cultural space is described in the fifteenth-century French text *Les Evangiles des Quenouilles* or 'Distaff Gospels', a text that sets up exactly the same pseudo-sacred resonance that is at work in our image. The distaff was the woman's sceptre but also the weapon used to beat henpecked (another animal word used to articulate gender

(Ithaca: Cornell University Press, 1986), p. 47.

[22] Ibid, p. 53.

[23] See the excellent discussion by Francesca Canadé Sautman, 'La maturation du fil', in her *La Religion du quotidien: rites et croyances populaires de la fin du moyen âge* (Florence: Olschki, 1995), pp. 37–43; also Fouquart de Cambrai, Antoine du Val, and Jean d'Arras (attrib. to), *Les Évangiles des Quenouilles*, ed. by M. Jeay (Paris: Vrin–Presses de l'Université de Montréal, 1985); and Frances M. Biscoglo, 'Unspun Heroes: Iconography of the Spinning Woman in the Middle Ages', *Journal of Medieval and Renaissance Studies*, 25.2 (1995), 163–76.

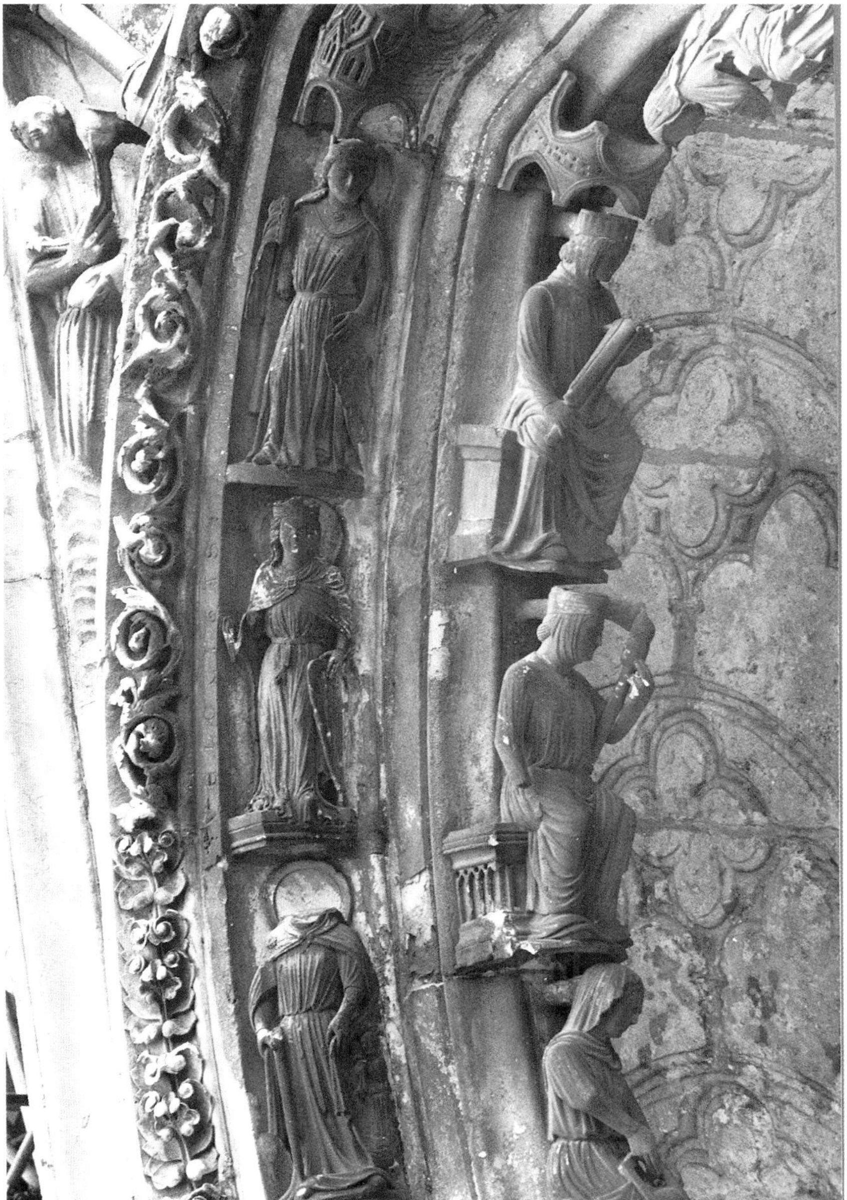

Fig. 6. Chartres Cathedral, North transept, left porch, left outer archivolts, 'Women carding and spinning'. © James Austin

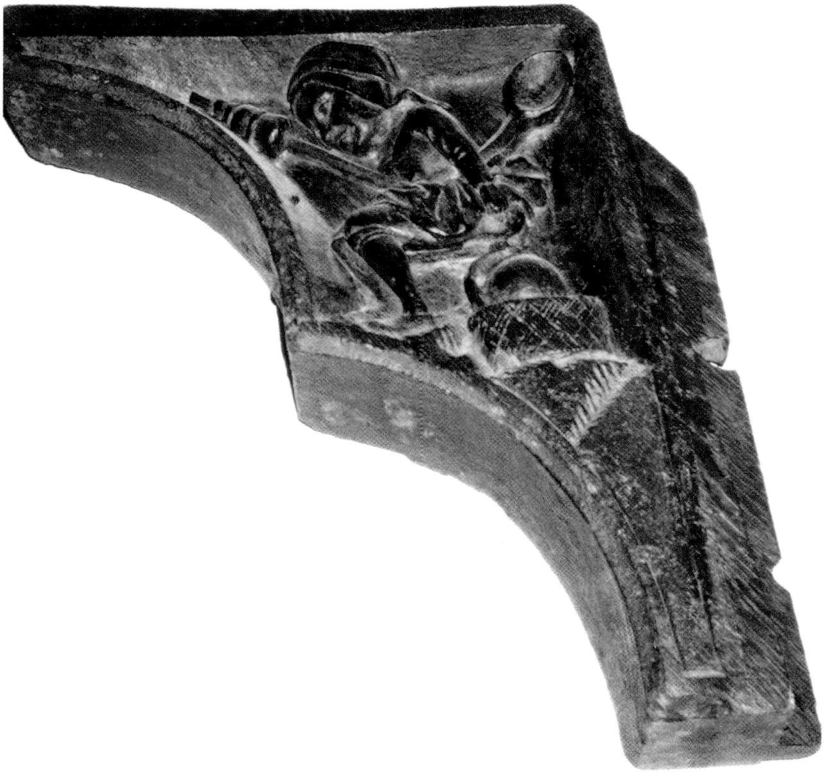

Fig. 7. 'Woman with distaff defecating'. Wooden 'aisselier' from an apothecary's shop. Late fifteenth century, Nantes, Musée Dobrée. © Author

relations) husbands. Therefore, when an image shows a man bearing the distaff it was of course to turn the world upside-down and give women rule. In practical rather than symbolic terms, the distaff (in French the 'quenouille') held the mass of raw wool fibres on top which had to be twisted and manipulated by the dextrous fingers of the female worker in order to produce yarn, wrapped around the dangling spindle (or 'fuseau' in French). The pig's cloven hoof of course is incapable of any such movement, a point emphasized in its delineation in the Chartres woodcarving. On the north portal of Chartres cathedral, women are carved in stone, spinning as exemplars of the active, as opposed to the contemplative, life; the latter are shown as women holding open books (fig. 6). This association was suggested by the liturgy.[24] In the realm of the street, the distaff

[24] For the spinning figures on the Chartres Cathedral north portal, see Adolf Katzenellenbogen, *The Sculptural Programs of Chartres Cathedral* (Baltimore: Johns

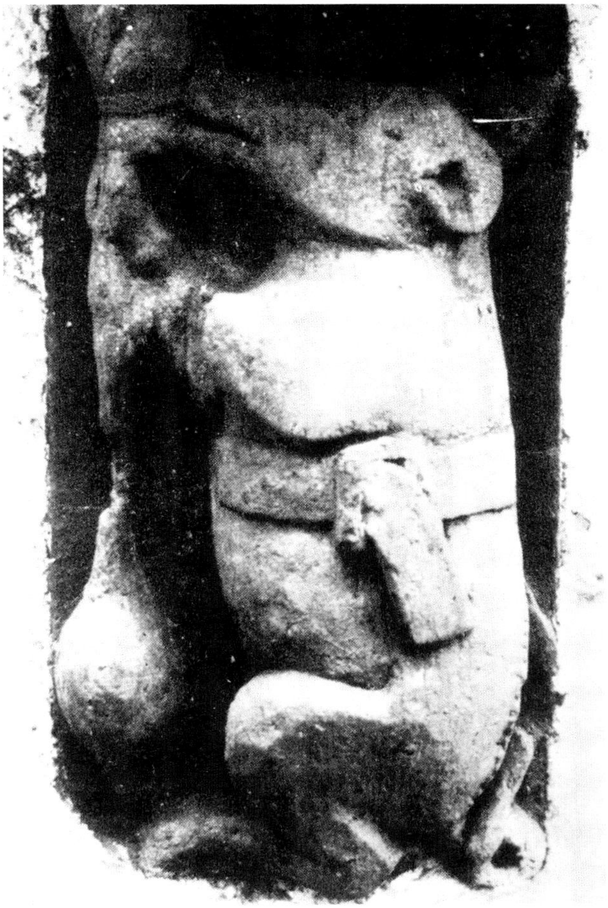

Fig. 8. 'Spinning sow'. Wood. Malestroit, Brittany. fifteenth century. © *Author*

appears as the woman's emblem in the lowest as well as the highest of realms: thus as she is carved squatting to defecate in a carving once placed on an apothecary's shop now in the Musée Dobré at Nantes (fig. 7).[25]

The other extant example of the spinning pig theme that I know of appears on a house at Malestroit in Brittany (fig. 8). Here the sow wears a similar belt but stands in an upright position like a human being. The spinning instruments being held in proper gravitational force allow the weight of the spindle to pull down

Hopkins University Press, 1959), p. 74.

[25] Dominique Costa, *Catalogue: Fascicule* I, *du* XIIe *au* XVIe *siècle, Musée Dobrée* (Nantes: Musée Dobrée, 1959), no. 192, p. 95.

the long twisted thread twisted by the fingers from the flax. She seems to be chewing on the flax held on top of her distaff, as the proverbial 'greedy pig'. In her excellent study of popular culture in late medieval France, which she calls 'la religion du quotidien', Francesca Sautman describes the image of the spinning sow in late medieval house signs as 'a sort of distorted spinner [. . .] in its place the porcine female spinner was impure, a carrier of leprosy like the menstruating woman'. She is the antithesis to the Virgin Mary carved below. The same contrast can be found on the page of a Rouen Book of Hours in which a prayer to the Virgin has a spinning sow painted in the lower margin.[26] In a fifteenth-century French herbal, the mother sow spins while a group of monkeys snatches her infant from its cradle (fig. 9). Having a world-turned-upside-down motif on the outer corner of the house façade is paralleled in a beautiful fifteenth-century house at Bourges, where the Annunciation is juxtaposed with a tiny inverted image of Marcoul the trickster showing his anus in a sign of male sexual and social power.[27] At Chartres the contrast is even more explicit between Mary and the porcine Eve, spinning her sickness and sexual sins in a morality that is social rather than ecclesiastical in nature. She is an antithesis to the Virgin Mary, whose robe-relic was the centre of the pilgrimage trade of the cathedral, a kind of gross anti-Virgin.

As Fabre-Vassas makes evident, the image of the sow had sexual overtones as well:

> The pig, like the child, thus lives in the maternal aura [. . .] the sow is the most irregular of females. The time is so short between its rhythmic cycles that [. . .] it forms the basis for the peasant's wariness: 'The sow is in heat all the time'.[28]

In Attic comedy, the pig is associated with the prostitute who was called a 'pig merchant'. The animal of the goddess Venus throughout the Middle Ages and the prostitutes of Southwark in London operated with a sign of a boar's head hung in front of their establishment. It is another chapter of my book, but this French stone sculpture now preserved at Wellesley College in the United States, and called 'Pigwoman with dog' in the catalogue of Gothic sculpture in American collections, is one of a small number of fourteenth-century brothel signs.[29] According to Varro the *porcus* was a 'nursery word' used by women to

[26] Paris, Bibliothèque nationale de France, ms. lat. 1178 fol. 35^{v}. 'Sancta Maria intercede pro nobis', cited in Sautman (as in note 23), p. 8.

[27] Michael Camille, 'Adam's House at Angers: Sculpture, Signs and Contrasts on the Medieval Street', in *Konstraste im Alltag des Mittelalters*, ed. by Gerhard Jaritz (Vienna: Verlag der österreichischen Akademie der Wissenschaften, 2000), pp. 143–78.

[28] Vassas (as in note 17), p. 108.

[29] Dorothy Gillerman, *Gothic Sculpture in America. I: The New England Museums* (New York: Garland, 1989), no. 195, pp. 250–51.

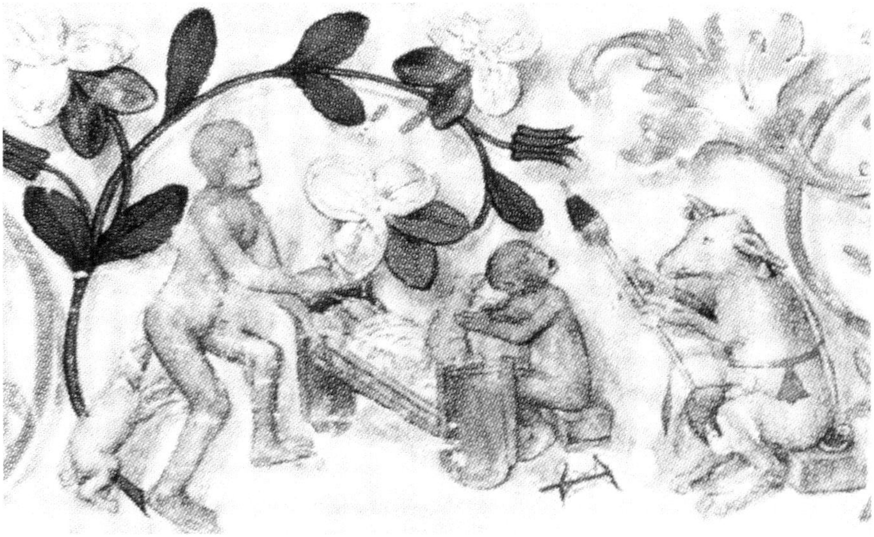

Fig. 9. 'Spinning sow and monkeys', Livre des simples médecines, *Paris Bibliothèque nationale de France, ms. fr. 9136, fol. 1. Late fifteenth century. © Bibliothèque nationale de France, Paris*

describe the pudenda of little girls. This woman, a pig from the waist down, offers the newcomer a drink and is being sucked in front, not by a dog but by another pig. Within the delicate Gothic gestures, this is a deeply misogynistic Gothic image.

Spinning was likewise loaded with erotic possibilities. Sautman describes how:

> although in the field of labour, spinning is an exclusively female task, its sexual symbolism was divided between the function of the 'quenouille' or 'distaff' which was 'female' and the 'fuseau' or spindle, which is masculine both as a noun and symbolically as that which the woman fondles with her hand. The act and its apparatus were implicated in a hot-bed of sexual double-entendres.

A contemporary poem among the 'Adevineux Amoureaux' describes a suggestive interchange between a man and a woman in which the lady appropriates the male 'fuseau' and he the female 'distaff', so that each offers the other the sexual organ they both desire. She offers her silver 'spindle': 'Je vous vens le fuseau d'argent? Vous avez le corps bel et gant'. He replies 'Lady, I will offer you the distaff/ I like to manipulate women, although especially those who have hairy nuts' ['Dame je vous vens la fusée/ Bien me semblez femme rusée/ Ailleurs avez escaillié noix'].[30] To spin also signified to create or give birth to a human being, adding a register of positive prosperity to the image.

[30] Sautman (as in note 23), pp. 41–42.

Like women, pigs were both celebrated and reviled in medieval culture. Although at Chartres Cathedral women were represented in images as the daughters of Eve, forever consigned to be secondary and sinful and always in danger of corrupting their own bodies and those of men with their sexual appetites, women in the city of Chartres played a considerable economic role. While they could not, of course, become canons in the cathedral, they could become leaders of important mercantile confraternities and groups such as the textile workers. Although marginal to the Church, women were fundamental to the growing market economy, as producers and consumers. In a recent discussion of the house and home as the domestic sphere of women, architectural historian Mark Wigley makes much of the metaphor of the body as a building. He cites the fourteenth-century Parisian physician Henri de Mondevile, who describes the body as a house, 'the house of the soul, which like any house can only be maintained as such by constant surveillance of its openings. The woman's body is seen as an inadequate enclosure because its boundaries are convoluted [. . .] turned inside-out'.[31] Peter Stallybrass has argued that 'the surveillance of women concentrated upon three specific areas: the mouth, chastity and the threshold of the house. These three areas were frequently collapsed into one another'.[32] Entrances and interiors are 'coded' female, especially churches, and even whole cities.[33] A wooden carving in the Stadhuis in Damme in Flanders shows a man looking up the anus of a vast sow, which is in fact a positive pun on the name of the waterway, the 'Zwyn', which connected Bruges to the sea.[34] If watery connections, as well as sacred and enclosed space, were coded feminine, as a number of studies have shown, the unexplored area of the street, I would argue, was masculine. However, as old prints depicting the Maison du Saumon in the early nineteenth century show, the space before this particular house often was filled with women, since it was the site of the flourishing fish market. In the modern imagination, fish, for a whole set of

[31] Mark Wigley, 'The Housing of Gender', in *Sexuality and Space*, ed. by Beatriz Colomina (New York: Princeton Architectural Press, 1992), pp. 337–55. For cities and gender, see Elizabeth Grosz, *Space, Time and Perversion: Essays on the Politics of Bodies* (London and New York: Routledge, 1995), pp. 103–11.

[32] Peter Stallybrass, 'Patriarchal Territories: The Body Enclosed', in *Rewriting the Renaissance. The Discourses of Sexual Difference in Early Modern Europe*, ed. by M. W. Ferguson (Chicago: University of Chicago Press, 1986), p. 126.

[33] A fundamental study is F. Choay, 'La ville et le domaine bâti comme corps', *Nouvelle revue de psychanalyse*, 8 (1974), 239–52; but see also the fascinating archaeological study by Roberta Gilchrist, 'Medieval Bodies in the Material World: Gender, Stigma and the Body', in *Framing Medieval Bodies*, ed. by Sara Kay and Miri Rubin (Manchester: Manchester University Press, 1994), pp. 43–61.

[34] L. Maeterlinck, *Le Genre satirique fantastique et licencieux dans la sculpture flamande et wallonne* (Paris : J. Schemit, 1910), p. 115 [fig. 68].

complex reasons, has become associated with women's bodies, but the gender mapping was different during the Middle Ages.

The Pig, the Fish and the Virgin

Medieval signs are linked to social functions. The reason for having the fish carved on the house (fig. 10) is not symbolic in the same way as the fish carved on the calendar of the north portal of Chartres Cathedral, a sign of the zodiac (fig. 11). This also was a sign linked to temporality, though not to the cycles of the year but to the actual selling of goods. The house was on the 'rue du Poisson-Doux', which was a centre for the selling of fresh-water fish throughout the Middle Ages. It was where merchants who brought mackerel and salmon from far afield sold their splendid specimens.[35] Compared to house signs, which were, for the most part, arbitrary in their signification, shop signs had to announce things for sale or services offered. Originally, merchants suspended the actual objects produced as signs: a loaf of bread for a baker, a 'plat à barbe' for the barber, or a pot on the end of a long pole for a potter. Throughout Europe, branches of vegetation had long been wound in a circle and suspended on a pole to indicate places where wine was sold, such as that visible in a fifteenth-century Parisian miniature.[36] These natural objects of decomposable material gradually came to be replaced by more permanent images. Shops were structured as an opening, the shutters coming down to form the counter or 'etal' while the top shutter or 'auvent' protected goods from sun and rain. The lack of literacy among the urban population is not, in my view, the main reason for names not being used. Instead, the way in which signs were organized articulated not personal identity but occupation and social position. Signs of métiers could be quasi-religious, such as roast-meat sellers using the sign of St Lawrence's grill and St Martin for inns, but most were based upon the similitude of service or goods sold, such as a shoe for a cobbler or a fish for a fishmonger as here.[37] The sign of the fish at Chartres would have been directly above barrels or panniers of real fish, rotting, smelling, and shining—perhaps some still squirming.

---

[35] Geneviève Aclocque, *Les Corporations, l'industrie et le commerce à Chartres du XIe siècle a la Révolution* (Paris: Picard, 1917), p. 181.

[36] For house signs, see Michael Camille, 'Signs in the City: Place, Power and Public Fantasy in Medieval Paris', in *Medieval Practices of Space*, ed. by M. Barbara Hanawalt and Michael Kobialka (Minneapolis: University of Minnesota Press, 2000), pp. 1–37; and the documents listed in Sautman (as in note 23), pp. 4–5; and Pierre Turpin, '"L'Escoive" ou "escouve" dans le language juridique et de la toponymie du Nord de la France', *Revue du Nord*, 22 (1936), 204–16.

[37] For St Lawrence, see Sautman (as in note 23), p. 3; and for a stone sign of a cobbler in Cordes, see Georges Duby, *Histoire de la France urbaine, II: la ville médiévale* (Paris: Seuil, 1980), p. 255.

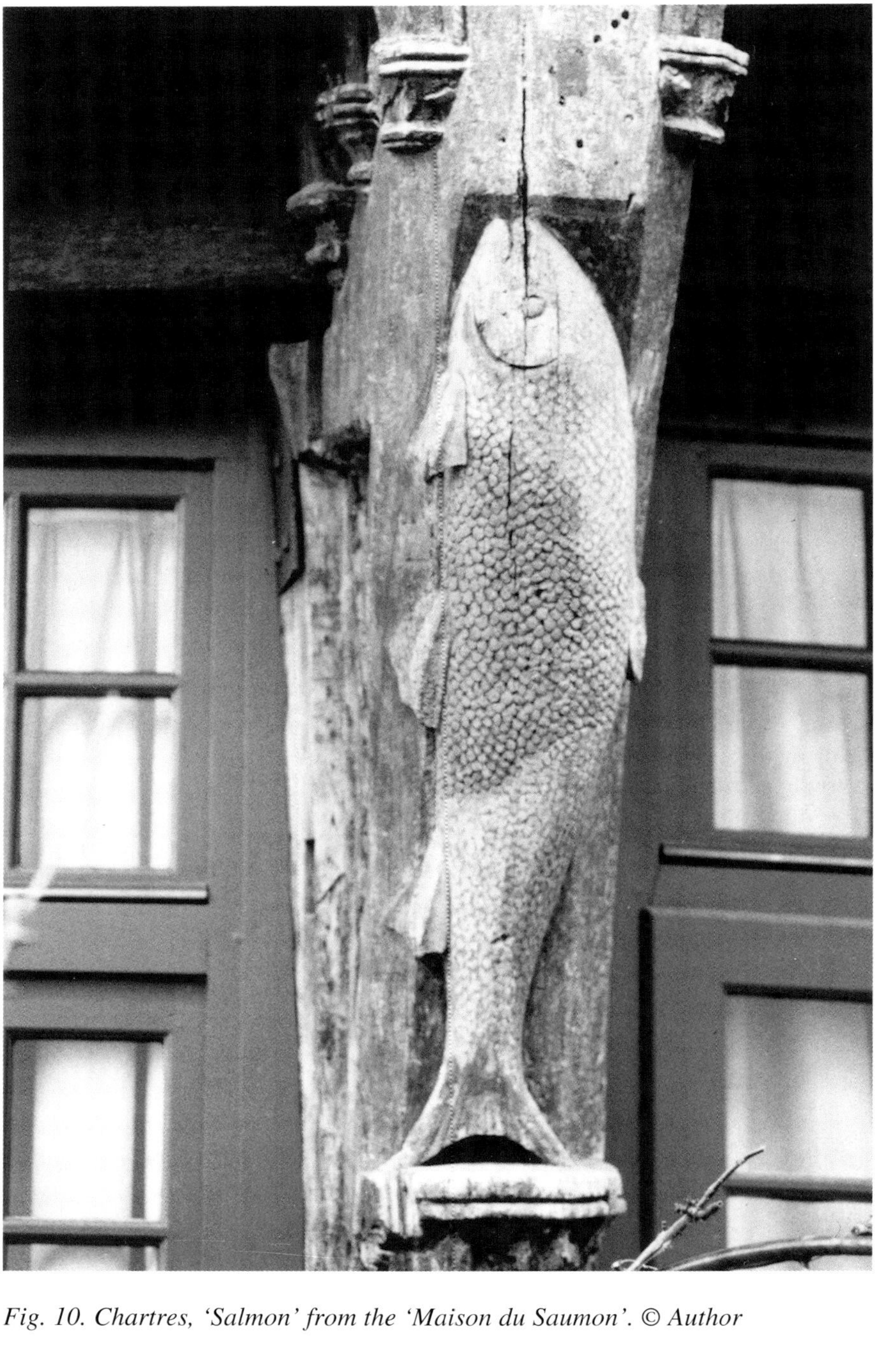

Fig. 10. Chartres, 'Salmon' from the 'Maison du Saumon'. © Author

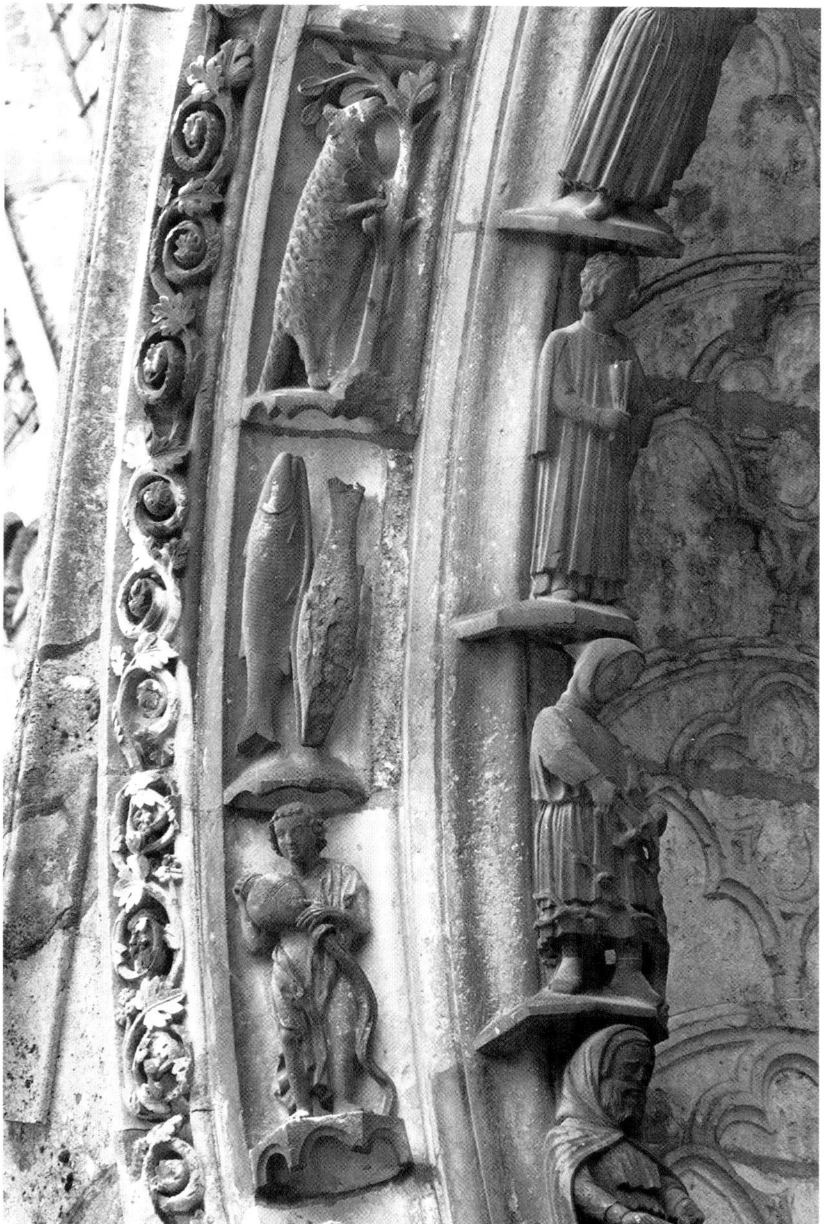

Fig. 11. Chartres Cathedral, North transept, right porch, left outer archivolts, Pisces. © James Austin

Something unusual about Chartres, which is significant for our image, is that in the fourteenth and fifteenth centuries, the selling of fish had been entirely concentrated in the hands of butchers. In 1147, the count of Chartres, Thibaut, had granted fish-sellers in Chartres a monopoly, but there was, as in all towns, great competition between the purveyors of Lenten and of non-Lenten fare.[38] Social conflicts between groups like meat-sellers and fish-sellers sometimes erupted in actual violence, and not only during Lenten and carnival celebrations when mock-battles between the two groups took place. The sign of the fishmongers is also multivalent and, like the sow, is linked to calendrical cycles and rituals in popular culture. The month of April (of course marked temporally by the sign of the fish, Pisces) also marked the resurrection of Christ, and the Lenten period leading up to it, being a time when fish as prescribed, was also the period of the 'Poisson d'avril'. This festive merrymaking in which young girls could choose new boyfriends has been linked etymologically to the word 'passion', since this is the period of spring rebirth and sexual growth. Many sixteenth-century texts play on the male 'mackerel', and one describes a young girl losing her virginity to a 'franc poison d'apvril'.[39] Perhaps this explains why this splendid scaly fish does not hang head down but has its head erect and upright in contrast to the pig that lies on its back. Once we realize that the fish is just as much an erotic sign as a sacred one, and that, like the adjacent sow, it articulates ritual and not just symbolic associations, we are in a position to understand just how rich a system of meanings was woven in the urban imaginary of the medieval street.

Although known in later sources as the 'maison du Saumon', this house in certain times or for particular communities took on the name of the 'Truie qui file'. We know of a number of houses that went under this name. The names of houses can change. One either suspects that the same visual sign, as it was worn and battered, perhaps less legible, was given a different designation. In this way a Parisian house called 'des trois chandeliers' in 1257 received a new sign till 1423 when it became the 'Cheval a louer'; but when it was referred to as 'des Sagittaires' in 1509 it may have been the same equestrian image which evoked a different name. The same is the case with the 'chastel' (1369) getting a new coat of paint and becoming the 'Château d'or' in 1613.[40] The proliferation of signs also meant that there was more than one sign of one subject. Paris had at last two houses of the spinning sow in the fifteenth century. A 'maison de l'Imaige Saint Jullien' existed on the Rue de la Juiverie, as well as on the rue Galande on the

---

[38] See Aclocque, *Les corporations*, p. 128; C. Billot, *Chartres à la fin du Moyen Age* (Paris: EHESS, 1987), p. 134.

[39] Sautman (as in note 23), p. 57.

[40] These examples are taken from the study of Parisian house signs by Adolphe Berty, 'Trois Ilots de la Cité', *Etudes archéologiques*, 12 (1855), 5–6.

left bank. His statue also graced the portal of the chapel of the hôpital Saint-Julien-des Ménétriers, where he served to embody the boundaries of a sanctified space. By contrast, the saint on the house stood in a different relation both to his divine prototype and to the viewer, who came towards it, not in pious contemplation, but crossed its path in everyday banal experience.[41] Such signs became the property of those they protected. Cities were divided according to different trades and their popular saint protectors. Signs like those of St Catherine or St Julian functioned in a totally different way in the space of the street than they would in a church. The most common sign in all medieval cities was that of the Virgin Mary. Not only was her image standing at every street corner but her carved figure also appeared as in this example integrated into scenes like the Annunciation. We should not regard such house signs as any less sacred than those images carved in wood on altars in churches. In 1418 a drunken Swiss soldier was not only publicly executed for attacking a corner statue of the Virgin in Paris but also burnt in effigy on the anniversary for years after.[42]

Images, art historians have realized in recent years, are not static representations of a pre-existing reality. They partake in that reality and often help construct it.[43] In terms of religious images, the liturgy is important, but for our image too we can discern in the scanty records of pig–human relations a series of rituals associated with this type of image. An example, once at no. 24 of the Marché aux Poirées in the Les Halles area of Paris, was an image of the spinning sow which was described as 'remarkable and more famous through the follies that the boys from the nearby shops performed there during Lent'. The source for this anecdote is Henri Sauval's *Histoire et Recherches des Antiquités de la ville de Paris* (1724), in which he goes on to describe it as 'un reste du paganisme' or relic of paganism.[44] This image of the sow was like that at Chartres, located on the rue des Poirées aux Halles, that is, on the building associated not with meat but with root vegetables. The fact that this ritual took place during Lent, the period of strict abstinence from any meat, is highly significant and chimes with those Lenten festivities surrounding the pig

[41] See Camille (as in note 36).

[42] Edouard Fournier, *Chroniques et Légendes des rues de Paris* (Paris: Dentu, 1893), pp. 364–65; illustrated in a 1633 engraving in Yvan Christ, *Eglises parisiennes actuelles et disparues* (Paris: Éditions Tel, 1947), p. 96; for this theme see also Edward Muir, 'The Virgin on the Street Corner: The Place of the Sacred in Italian Cities', in *Religion and Culture in the Renaissance and Reformation*, ed. by Steven E. Ozment, Sixteenth-Century Essays and Studies 11 (Kirksville, MO: Sixteenth-Century Journal Publishers, 1990), pp. 24–40.

[43] Michael Camille, *Mirror in Parchment: The Luttrell Psalter and the Making of Medieval England* (Chicago: University of Chicago Press, 1998).

[44] Henry Sauval, *Histoire et Recherches des Antiquités de la ville de Paris* (Paris, 1724), p. 57.

described in Fabre-Vassas. These included ritual battles between fishmongers and butchers on the morning of Holy Saturday.[45]

However, this image is more than a relic of paganism. It is known in other sources from the medieval period as one that took different forms in different communities. All involved the young men or 'bacheliers' of the community acting out a special semi-erotic relationship with the pig, either before or after its slaughter, and its being handed over to the women for the making of sausages, as a liminal sign of both danger and fecundity in the yearly cycle. These signs are folded into complex rituals of the sacred but they are primarily signs of commerce. An essential question of the Chartres image is why is the sow lying on its back? Is the pig dead? As soon as it is killed and the women collect the blood to make the blood sausages, it is scraped and hung upside down, and thus begins a complex of rituals dividing men and women, in which in some communities the youths steal the pig and play 'nocturnal games' with it, pretending to hide it from the rest of the population. A creature divided, the pig incarnates the sins of lechery and gluttony; demons take up residence within it. At the same time it is Christian flesh, endowed with a soul of blood, called upon to appear at the meals of Christmas and Easter.[46]

What all this suggests is that just like sacred images, these signs could also change over time as well as being linked to certain temporal rhythms and rituals. There may have been a play on words here as occurs in many medieval house signs such as 'Au Lion d'or'—'Au lit on Dort'. The verb 'filer' could indicate a pig doing something far more pig-like than spinning. A second example of the spinning pig known in Paris was also in a significantly charged mercantile site at no. 134 Rue Saint Antoine. This one is very well preserved in the Musée Carnavalet and probably dates from the early seventeenth century (fig. 12).[47] A low relief in terra cotta and wood, it was placed on the lintel of the first storey of a charcutier's shop. It shows the sow standing on her hind legs and with a belt around her waist to hold the distaff, just as in the Chartres example, although she manages to spin while at the same time suckle three piglets. This too has its legends, one of which relates it to a series of events involving an entertainer who is supposed to have dressed up an animal in women's clothing, an act that

---

[45] Vassas (as in note 17), p. 243.

[46] For the role of youth groups in extending the rites of the countryside into an urban setting see Robert Muchembled, *Popular Culture and Elite Culture in France 1400–1750*, trans. by Lydia Cochrane (Baton Rouge: Louisiana State University Press, 1986), pp. 165–69; and Nicole Pellegrin, 'Les Bachelleries: organisations et fêtes de la jeunesse dans le Centre-Ouest XVe–XVIIIe siècles', *Mémoires de la Société des Antiquaires de l'Ouest* 15 (1982), 73–86.

[47] Jean-Pierre Willesme, *Enseignes du Musée Carnavalet—Histoire de Paris* (Paris: Musée Carnavalet, 1996), no. 123, p. 79, which also describes the previous example from the Marché aux Poirées.

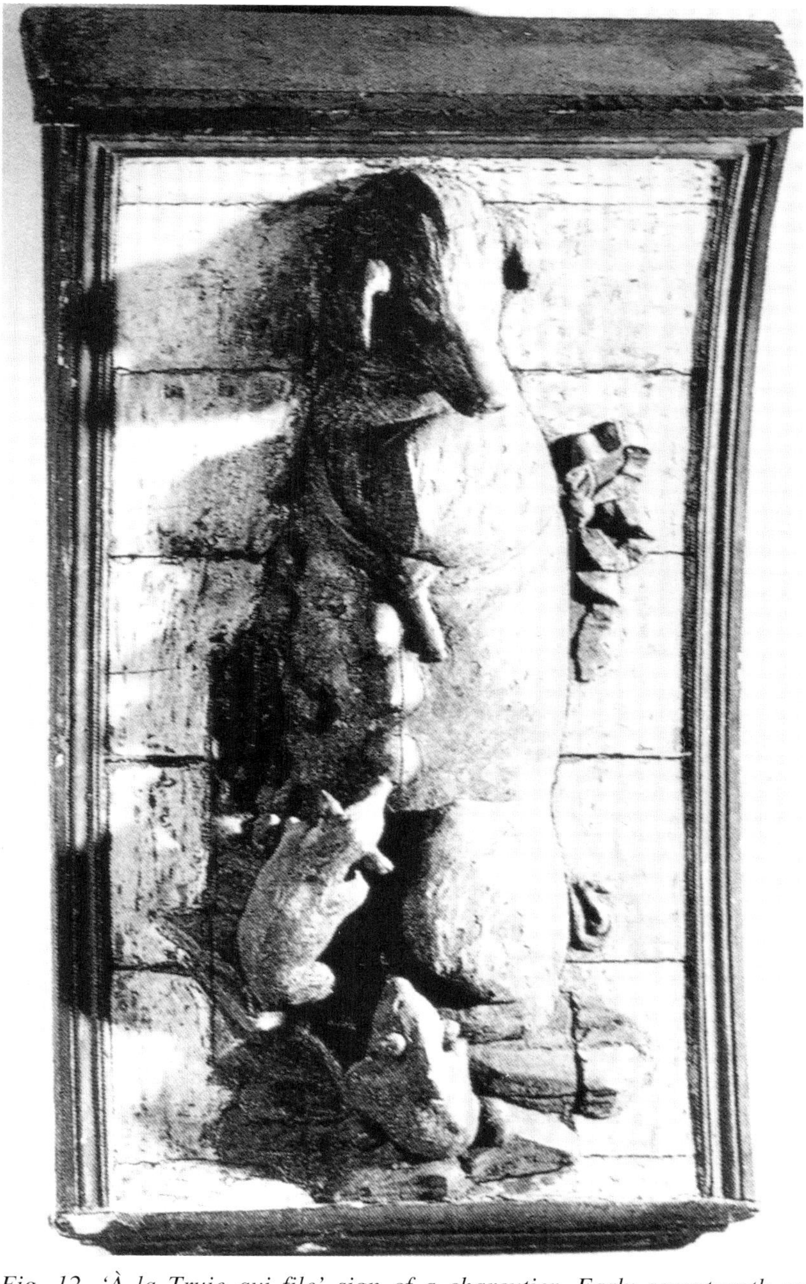

Fig. 12. 'À la Truie qui file' sign of a charcutier. Early seventeenth century. Paris, Musée Carnavalet. © Musée Carnavalet

eventually got him accused of witchcraft and burnt, along with his pig, at the stake.[48] This evidence also points to another register of negative associations of the pig with witchcraft: the capacities of women both to bewitch healthy valuable pigs with a glance of envy and to use them as demonic servants.

While the cathedral contains in its encyclopaedic 'summa' the various trades in the famous stained glass windows, where the fishmongers and indeed butchers both have their place, these are presented in narrative forms controlled by ecclesiastical prerogatives. As the late Jane Welch-Williams showed so brilliantly, they were not offerings made by the guilds to their church but signs of the appropriation of the mercantile by the Bishop and Chapter.[49] The signs we have been examining come from the people themselves. At first, it might seem in contrast to the ecclesiastical representations of the trades, which are clearly sacred signs. While this is true, it would not follow to argue, as scholars have since Bakhtin, that the culture of the Church was hegemonic and this mercantile world outside was free. We must resist the tendency to romanticize 'popular' art as the free-expression of the 'folk'. As Richard Sennet argues, 'The street bore the imprint of aggressive assertion, then, it was the space left over after people had asserted their rights and powers'.[50] The 'truie qui file', while being an image 'of the people' in Bakhtin's rather idealized sense of the term, is no less repressive, ideologically charged, and tyrannizing than the ass playing the lyre. It locates women in a particular place in the imaginary social order as ruthlessly as any sculpture of the vice of 'luxuria', but it does so in the space not of the sacred but of the street, with all its raucous noise and clamour. All this suggests that the image of the spinning sow held an ambivalent attraction for the people coming to the fish market at Chartres. It would have been, in a way, an antithetical image, embodying a series of both positive and negative associations, alimentary, social, and sexual many of them dealing with the status of women. If the cathedral represented her in the dichotomy of either Eve or Mary, this other building shelters a far more unstable and shifting series of signs.

For medieval people, stone was dead whereas wood was thought to be alive.[51]

---

[48] See: Fournier (as in note 8), p. 92; *Le Marais, mythe et réalité*, ed. by J.-P. Babelon (Paris: Picard, 1987), p. 255, who describes how 'l'enseigne pouvait venir d'une rumeur selon laquelle un montreur avait dressé une truie à filer, mais l'acte parut tellement extraordinaire qu'on le brûla avec sa truie Place de Grève, sous l'accusation de sorcellerie'.

[49] Jane Welch-Williams, *Bread, Wine and Money: The Windows of the Trades at Chartres Cathedral* (Chicago: University of Chicago Press, 1993).

[50] Richard Sennett, *Flesh and Stone: The Body and the City in Western Civilization* (New York: Faber, 1994), p. 193; and Jean-Pierre Leguay (as in note 8), pp. 98–110.

[51] M. Pastoureau, 'Introduction de la symbolique médiévale du bois', in his *L'Arbre: Histoire naturelle et symbolique de l'arbre, du bois et du fruit au moyen âge* (Paris: Le Léopard d'Or, 1993), p. 173.

Like the human body, it grew old and its flesh split and withered (notice the vertical split in our example) along with its significations. This sign is one of a number of representations carved in wood that I am working on for a larger project about this forgotten genre of street art in medieval France, including an enigmatic one from a now-demolished house once on the main street in Tours showing two women castrating a hybrid man (it was originally the corner post of a horse gelder's establishment), which has powerful resonances of gender. This should not surprise us. After all, the street was always a site of transaction and conflict rather than of transcendence and resolve. For this very reason, the images found on the medieval street refuse that myth of plenitude organized by the Church's system of signs. Always fractured, always spilling out into more multiple registers of meaning than can be contained under one rubric, the meaning of any street sign cannot be contained by a written text or verbal Logos. Unlike the cathedral, whose thousands of images are, by contrast, always in danger of multiplying into meaninglessness precisely because they are so over-determined, so ruled by the thrall of textuality, the more shifting significations of the street survive and prosper in the human imaginary through this flexibility of signification. Perhaps this is also why we in modernity have forgotten them and prefer to resurrect the eternal Logos from the dead stones of the cathedral rather than feel the pulse of everyday life through the living wood of the house.

In her analysis of the role of proverbs in sixteenth-century French culture, Natalie Zemon-Davis notes that they are often

> wide-ranging in metaphor and tone, inconsistent with one another and flexible [. . .], available for many different circumstances and for recommending different courses of action. Indeed, the meaning of any individual proverb might vary with the situation to which it was applied and the status of the speaker and listener.[52]

In the same way, the spinning sow as a 'proverbial' image functioned differently in the lexical and imaginary register than an 'official' image on the church's far more textualized apparatus. The 'Truie qui file' marked sites of multiple and shifting identities, places, and communities, not imposed from above but articulated from somewhere within the teeming multiplicity of the body politic itself.

There are enormous difficulties and dangers involved in any analysis and study of this material. With fewer than one percent of the images today extant of the hundreds that, as we know from documents once filled these urban spaces, a single image on one building like the 'Maison du Saumon' can too easily fill the aporia and become a kind of profane cathedral of the marketplace. A single image, like the spinning sow, comes to stand in for the hundreds of lost images that once surrounded it. Yet in terms of the issues raised in this present volume,

---

[52] Natalie Zemon-Davis, 'Proverbial Wisdom and Popular Errors', in her *Society and Culture in Early Modern France* (Stanford: Stanford University Press, 1975), p. 243.

what makes this material challenging for the researcher is that it demands a totally different Art History, flexible enough and anthropological enough to realize that visual signs work in history on A more complex level than traditional textual-iconographic and formal-aesthetic categories. Because of these difficulties, I have purposely avoided giving one uniform iconographic 'reading' of the image, to in any way limit the spilling out of meanings associated with the spinning sow in Chartres. That would be to undermine what I believe was its fruitful ambivalence as a sign on the street. Its meanings will not be better understood simply by using the Church Fathers or classical sources. Rather its context has to be sought within the complex notion of 'everyday life'. While some medieval historians—notably the Institut für Realienkunde at Krems, along with the French Annales school, notably the work of Jacques Le Goff and Jean-Claude Schmitt—have usefully incorporated this concept into their work, the Anglo-American tradition of Medieval Studies in which I work is deeply suspicious and dismissive of terms such as *everyday life*, *popular*, and even the term *folklore*.[53] While every stone of Chartres has been or will be decoded for its social, political, and historical significance, wooden 'vernacular' ones like the spinning sow only a few hundred yards away are left to rot heuristically, as indecipherable emblems of an irrecoverable popular.

Although I have been contrasting Chartres cathedral with what I have called the 'other' Chartres, what I hope to have shown is that these two sites are not mutually exclusive—one sacred the other profane, one a site of ritual and the other of the everyday. Images in both realms are highly ritualized products of culture whose meaning changes over time and is sometimes irrecoverably lost. The spinning pig, whether it articulates the power of women in rites of sexuality and fertility or their dangerous status as unclean and malefic, does so in relation not only to the Virgin Mary carved on the same house but also to all the images of the virgins that inhabited the city, including the cathedral. Where is this pig in the medieval imaginary of Chartres, excluded as it is from the salvific economy of the cathedral and the many other churches in the town, marginal as it is to this very house, but so crucial an aspect of people's lives?

---

[53] Jacques Le Goff, *Time, Work and Culture in the Middle Ages*, trans. by Arthur Goldhammer (Chicago: University of Chicago Press, 1980); Aron Gurevich, *Medieval Popular Culture: Problems of Belief and Perception* (Cambridge: Cambridge University Press, 1988); Peter Burke, 'Popular Culture Reconsidered', in *Mensch und Objekt im Mittelalter und in der Frühen Neuzeit*, ed. by Gerhard Jaritz (Vienna: Verlag der österreichischen Akademie der Wissenschaft, 1990), pp. 181–93; and the essays collected in *Symbole des Alltags Alltag der Symbole: Festschrift für Harry Kühnel zum 65. Geburtstag*, ed. by G. Blaschnitz, H. Hundsbichler, G. Jaritz, and E. Vavra (Graz: Akademische Druck, 1992). For the sceptical American position, see John Van Engen, 'The Christian Middle Ages as an Historiographical Problem', *American Historical Review* 91 (1986), 519–52.

Les marges à drôleries des manuscrits gothiques: problèmes de méthode

JEAN WIRTH

Dans la première moitié du XIIIe siècle se met en place un nouveau décor du manuscrit enluminé, la marge à drôleries. Des motifs profanes et humoristiques, très souvent animaliers, se multiplient à l'extérieur du texte et de son illustration, tantôt cantonnés dans des antennes émergeant de l'initiale, tantôt posés sur ces antennes ou flottant dans le bas de page. Après une série de tentatives, leur présentation se codifie vers 1250 dans les ateliers parisiens, en épousant une mise en page solidement organisée à partir de l'initiale. Elle évolue et se diversifie en restant très structurée dans les ateliers anglais, dans les villes du nord de la France et dans les Flandres. Vers 1300, le genre est adopté dans le sud de la France, en Espagne, en Allemagne et en Italie. A partir du milieu du XIVe siècle, les feuillages prolifèrent dans les marges des manuscrits parisiens et prennent la place des drôleries. Le genre est passé de mode. Il connaîtra cependant des *revivals* successifs jusqu'à la Renaissance.

La thématique des drôleries est d'abord empruntée à la chasse, à la danse, aux jeux, aux plaisirs galants; elle prend de plus en plus une dimension satirique incluant l'obscénité, l'anticléricalisme et même le blasphème, quel que soit par ailleurs l'ouvrage décoré. La majorité des manuscrits à drôlerie sont des psautiers et des livres d'heures, ce qui laisse tout d'abord perplexe. Face à l'idée préconçue d'un Moyen Âge confit en dévotion, dominé par des inquisiteurs qui auraient surveillé méticuleusement la production des livres, baignant *nolens volens* dans l'unanimisme d'une foi profonde et naïve, le phénomène est incompréhensible, mais tout compte fait secondaire. La plupart des chercheurs se sont longtemps contentés d'une remarque rapide pour signaler la présence de drôleries dans les manuscrits. Pourtant, d'autres domaines artistiques posaient des problèmes comparables et attiraient de temps à autre l'attention, ainsi l'oeuvre de Jérôme Bosch ou encore les miséricordes des stalles, tandis que la littérature en langue vulgaire donnait de la sensibilité médiévale une idée tout aussi contrastée, si l'on tenait compte d'oeuvres comme le *Roman de Renart* ou les fabliaux.

La redécouverte des drôleries médiévales commence au XIXe siècle. La caricature était alors un art de prédilection, de sorte que Wright, Champfleury, puis Maeterlinck se mirent à en faire l'histoire, avec une évidente sympathie pour l'humour médiéval.[1] Avec Emile Mâle commence timidement la discussion scientifique sur les marges à drôleries.[2] Après avoir réfuté les explications symboliques du décor animalier des églises gothiques données par Auber, Félicie d'Ayzac et même parfois par le Père Cahier, il introduit les drôleries des manuscrits liturgiques, pour réfuter l'objection que ces sujets n'auraient pas été tolérés par le clergé s'ils n'avaient eu un sens profond. Décrivant ensuite sommairement les marges de deux livres de prières (Paris, Bibliothèque Nationale de France, lat. 13260 et lat. 14284), il déclare: 'A quoi bon multiplier les exemples? Il est clair que de pareilles figures n'ont aucun rapport avec les Heures de la Vierge ou avec les Psaumes de la Pénitence qu'elles illustrent'. Il croit finalement pouvoir expliquer l'humour de ces oeuvres par la naïveté: 'La foi profonde donna à ces temps la gaieté, la sérénité de l'enfance'. Aussi, les drôleries sont-elles chastes: 'Au badinage des artistes il ne se mêla jamais ni indécence, ni ironie [. . .] Ce n'est qu'au XVe siècle qu'apparaît dans l'art ce réalisme un peu bas qui, à l'occasion, ne recule pas devant l'obscénité'.

Mâle semble vouloir clore le débat plutôt que le lancer. Mais, quel que soit son bien-fondé, l'idée que les drôleries n'ont pas de sens sera de plus en plus contredite au XXe siècle. Quant à l'affirmation qu'elles ne contiennent ni indécence, ni ironie, si elle est vraie de nombreux manuscrits parisiens, elle étonne à propos du livre d'heures lat. 14284, originaire de Thérouanne, dont l'auteur vient de louer la beauté. Il est en effet difficile de ne pas voir d'ironie dans la représentation de singes en clercs ou en évêques, dans une école de singes ou devant un chevalier effrayé par un escargot ou un lapin. On peut également se demander s'il est parfaitement décent de représenter un clerc se faisant surprendre en train de caresser une femme ou encore un évêque bénissant

---

[1] Th. Wright, *Histoire de la caricature et du grotesque dans la littérature et dans l'art* (Paris: Garnier frères, 1867) [trad. de: *A History of Caricature and Grotesque in Literature and Art* (Londres: Virtue Bros., 1865)]. Jules Fleury-Husson Champfleury, *Histoire de la caricature au moyen âge* (Paris: Dentu, [1870]). L. Maeterlinck, *Le genre satirique dans la peinture flamande* (Bruxelles: Van Oest, 1907).

[2] Emile Mâle, *L'art religieux du XIIIe siècle en France* (Paris: Armand Colin, 1987; 1ère éd. 1898), pp. 121–28.

un moine, un visage féminin sur le postérieur.[3]

Etat de la question

Des recherches plus poussées sur les drôleries se sont beaucoup fait attendre. Ni Dada, ni le surréalisme ne semblent avoir connu l'existence du genre, alors que l'oeuvre de Bosch recommençait à passionner. C'est dans une thèse allemande, celle de Marie Theres Bergenthal, que le genre est mis pour la première fois en relation avec la thématique littéraire du monde à l'envers et avec les *adynata*, les figures rhétoriques qui le décrivent.[4] En soi, le parallèle n'explique pas grand-chose, mais il montre que l'humour des enluminures marginales n'est pas un phénomène isolé. Surtout, il pose le problème du rapport entre les drôleries et des textes—fables, fatrasies, proverbes ou fabliaux—bien différents des prières qu'elles accompagnent le plus souvent.

Le lent démarrage de la recherche est d'abord dû à la difficulté d'accès du matériau. Encore aujourd'hui, rares sont les manuscrits publiés et on ne connaît souvent le décor marginal d'un manuscrit que par la reproduction d'un ou deux folios dans un catalogue. Aussi les travaux réalisés par Jurgis Baltrusaitis dans les années cinquante constituent-ils un exploit. Après avoir montré dans *Le Moyen Âge fantastique* ce que les drôleries devaient à la glyptique et aux monnaies romaines, il est parvenu, dans *Réveils et prodiges*, à brosser l'histoire du genre, en montrant sa constitution à partir d'un répertoire déjà existant dans l'art roman et persistant dans la périphérie—mais aussi au coeur—du monde gothique, puis en suivant son développement et ses mutations jusqu'à la Renaissance.[5] A ce jour, non seulement cette synthèse n'a pas été dépassée, mais personne n'a essayé de lui en substituer une autre. Pourtant, les travaux sur l'enluminure gothique se sont multipliés, la connaissance des ateliers, de leur localisation et de leur chronologie s'est beaucoup précisée. Par la force des choses, le travail de Baltrusaitis a vieilli.

Pas plus que Mâle, Baltrusaitis n'était enclin à chercher du symbolisme dans les drôleries, ni même à s'interroger longuement sur leur possible signification. C'est dans cette direction que se lança quelques années plus tard Lilian Randall, aux Etats-Unis où l'oeuvre de Panofsky avait mis ces études à l'ordre du jour et

---

[3] Paris, BnF, ms. lat. 14284, fol. 1^{v} (lapin et chevalier) 8 (singe en clerc), 23 (évêque bénissant), 31 (clerc et femme), 53^{v} (singe en évêque), 69^{v} (école des singes).

[4] Marie Theres Bergenthal, *Elemente der Drôlerie und ihre Beziehungen zur Literatur* (Berlin: Hohmann, 1934).

[5] Jurgis Baltrusaitis, *Le Moyen Âge fantastique. Antiquités et exotismes dans l'art gothique* (Paris: Flammarion, 1955; 2e éd. 1981), pp. 9–71. Idem, *Réveils et prodiges. Le gothique fantastique* (Paris: Armand Colin, 1960), en particulier pp. 70–76, 140–52, 196–234.

où Horst W. Janson venait de publier un admirable ouvrage sur l'iconographie du singe, faisant abondamment usage des marges enluminées.[6] Dès 1957, elle cherchait dans les *exempla*, les histoires amusantes dont les prédicateurs médiévaux truffaient leurs sermons, une source possible des drôleries.[7] Contrairement aux textes littéraires relatifs au monde à l'envers, les *exempla* donnent un signification morale aux motifs comiques. Ceux que cite Randall, comme l'histoire de Renart faisant le mort pour capturer les oiseaux, trouvent leurs équivalents visuels dans les marges. Le prédicateur peut utiliser l'histoire en faisant de Renart une figure du diable et lui donner ainsi un sens. Il reste à savoir si ce sens, qui n'est certainement pas inhérent à l'épisode, doit être reporté sur sa représentation dans les marges. L'auteur semble le croire.

Par ailleurs, Lilian Randall a compris la nécessité de rendre les marges plus accessibles à la recherche. En 1966 paraît *Images in the Margins of Gothic Manuscripts*, où l'auteur indexe par ordre alphabétique des sujets les décors marginaux de 238 manuscrits et publie 762 illustrations.[8] L'ouvrage donne enfin une image globale du genre et une bonne idée de sa richesse: il constitue une mine de renseignements et une base irremplaçable pour les recherches ultérieures. L'identification des sujets contient certes des erreurs et des imprécisions. A titre d'exemple, l'auteur ne fait pas la différence entre les clercs séculiers et les moines et qualifie curieusement d'abbés et d'abbesses les chanoines et les chanoinesses reconnaissables au port de l'aumusse. En dehors des cas où le terrier est représenté, les lapins sont qualifiés de lièvres. Mais, comme il faudrait une connaissance universelle du Moyen Âge et de la nature pour éviter toutes les fautes de ce genre, on ne peut que saluer l'érudition et la perspicacité qui dominent l'entreprise. Dans l'ensemble, les manuscrits sont identifiés aussi correctement que possible en fonction des connaissances alors disponibles. L'introduction ne fait pas l'histoire du genre, mais en fixe solidement les caractères généraux.

Sans manquer à la reconnaissance que suscite un tel travail, il faut en marquer les limites. Tout d'abord, les vérifications montrent que la collecte des informations a été conduite avec un soin inégal d'un manuscrit à un autre, souvent sur l'original, parfois sur de mauvais microfilms, voire sur des reproductions partielles du manuscrit. Bon nombre d'indications de folios sont fausses. De nombreuses confusions semblent s'être glissées entre la collecte des informations et l'impression de l'index. Il faut compter avec un taux d'erreurs ou

[6] H. W. Janson, *Apes and Ape Lore in the Middle Ages and the Renaissance* (Londres: Warburg Institute, 1952).

[7] L. M. C. Randall, 'Exempla as a Source of Gothic Marginal Illustration', *Art Bulletin*, 39 (1957), 97–107.

[8] L. M. C. Randall, *Images in the Margins of Gothic Manuscripts* (Berkeley: University of California Press, 1966).

d'omissions d'au moins 10%, de 50% environ pour certains manuscrits.[9] Surtout, la forme même de cet énorme index est déconcertante. En choisissant l'ordre alphabétique des sujets, l'auteur avait certainement en vue l'utilisation de la documentation par des chercheurs travaillant sur un thème iconographique, par exemple sur l'iconographie d'un animal particulier. Pour favoriser des travaux sur le décor du manuscrit, il aurait sans doute mieux valu faire le catalogue des sujets manuscrit par manuscrit et folio par folio, au lieu d'extraire les motifs de leur contexte. Pour tirer de l'index ce qui concerne un manuscrit particulier, il faut un travail considérable. L'ouvrage ne facilite pas l'étude de l'évolution du genre et de ses variations d'une région à l'autre. Il a peut-être même contribué à décourager ce genre de recherches.

Depuis la grande publication de Randall, Michael Camille est le seul auteur à avoir tenté une approche globale de la marge enluminée, dans un essai sur les marges du Moyen Âge au sens le plus large possible.[10] La marge de la page est mise en rapport, d'une part avec les emplacements comparables du décor architectural roman puis gothique, d'autre part avec la marginalité des personnages et des comportements représentés ou avec celle des langues vulgaires par rapport au latin. L'intuition fondamentale de l'ouvrage est intéressante. L'ordre hiérarchique de la page enluminée, la prédominance de son centre, réservé au texte et aux images qui l'illustrent, sur sa périphérie qui accueille toutes les fantaisies, justifie largement ce point de vue. Par ailleurs, l'absence d'inhibition de Camille et la vigueur de son vocabulaire lui permettent d'appeler un chat un chat et d'aborder franchement des sujets scabreux que ses prédécesseurs avaient ignorés par naïveté ou par pudibonderie. La gêne qu'on éprouve devant l'ouvrage (comme en témoigne le compte rendu assez dur de M. Hamburger)[11] vient surtout d'une démarche iconographique incertaine, parce que fondée sur une sociologie hâtive et sur une connaissance parfois approximative du matériau. Contentons-nous de deux exemples. En soulevant 'l'importante question de la différence des sexes' ou plutôt, selon le texte original, '*the important issue of gender*', l'auteur affirme que 'Les images que [les marges] contiennent sont essentiellement faites par des hommes et pour des hommes'.[12] Il serait plus opportun de noter, d'une part que nous ne connaissons absolument pas

[9] Parmi les manuscrits les plus mal étudiés se trouve le psautier-heures de Jean de Neuville (New York, Pierpont Morgan Library, MS. M. 730) dont plus de 90% des drôleries sont passées sous silence. Or ce manuscrit, datable entre 1243 et 1246, constitue l'un des moments essentiels dans le développement du genre.

[10] Michael Camille, *Images dans les marges. Aux limites de l'art médiéval* (Paris: Gallimard, 1997); trad. de: *Image on the Edge. The Margins of Medieval Art* (Londres: Reaktion, 1992).

[11] Cf. les observations de J. F. Hamburger, *Art Bulletin*, 75 (1993), 319–27.

[12] Camille (cf. note 10), pp. 170 et ss.

le pourcentage des enlumineurs de sexe féminin, d'autre part que les femmes prédominent largement parmi les destinataires des livres de prières à drôleries, en particulier de ceux qu'étudie Camille. Il n'est pas plus heureux d'affirmer à propos de la scatologie que 'les marges des manuscrits en sont littéralement pleines'.[13] Camille n'a sans doute pas regardé les mêmes manuscrits que Mâle ('Au badinage des artistes il ne se mêla jamais ni indécence, ni ironie'). En fait, les motifs scatologiques forment entre 1 et 2% des drôleries et sont inégalement répandus selon les manuscrits, beaucoup d'entre eux n'en comprenant aucun. Le jugement de Mâle et celui de Camille sont donc également erronés. L'ouvrage plus récent consacré au psautier Luttrell est sensiblement plus épais, mais il souffre des mêmes défauts et ne remplace pas l'excellente petite monographie de Janet Backhouse.[14]

Au risque de sembler injuste, il faut admettre que peu d'études récentes ont vraiment fait avancer la recherche sur les manuscrits à drôleries. Du point de vue de l'histoire du genre, le compte-rendu du livre de Randall par Nordenfalk est certainement la contribution la plus importante malgré sa brièveté.[15] Il a le mérite de poser sérieusement la question de l'origine des drôleries, en apportant du matériau neuf. Les plus grands services sont rendus par des études dont les drôleries ne sont pas le sujet, comme l'ouvrage de Branner sur l'enluminure parisienne ou, plus récemment, celui de Judith Oliver sur les psautiers liégeois.[16] Du point de vue iconographique, rares sont les travaux de bon sens. On marquera d'une croix blanche l'étude du *Roman de la Rose* fr. 25526 de la Bibliothèque Nationale de France par Sylvia Huot, un cas exceptionnel de rapport texte / image analysé avec compétence et ingéniosité, même si elle n'échappe pas toujours à la surinterprétation.[17] La plupart de ces recherches sont viciées par des a priori malheureux sur ce rapport et rappellent de près ou de loin les égarements déjà dénoncés par Emile Mâle. Plutôt que de les écarter par une autre pétition de principe, nous allons essayer de critiquer méthodiquement les principaux malentendus sur la nature des drôleries et sur leur rapport aux textes.

---

[13] Ibid. p. 152.

[14] Michael Camille, *Mirror in Parchment. The Luttrell Psalter and the Making of Medieval England* (Londres: Reaktion, 1998). J. Backhouse, *The Luttrell Psalter* (Londres: British Library, 1989).

[15] C. Nordenfalk, compte rendu de Randall, *Images in the Margins of Gothic Manuscripts*, dans *Burlington Magazine*, 109 (1967), 418-21.

[16] R. Branner, *Manuscript Painting in Paris during the Reign of Saint Louis* (Berkeley: University of California Press, 1977). J. Oliver, *Gothic Manuscript Illumination in the Diocese of Liège (c. 1250–c. 1350)* (Leuven: Peeters, 1988).

[17] S. Huot, 'Vignettes marginales comme glose marginale dans un manuscrit du 'Roman de la rose' au quatorzième siècle (B. N. fr. 25526)', *Littérales*, 2 (1987), 173–86; *The "Romance of the Rose" and its Medieval Readers: Interpretation, Reception, Manuscript Transmission* (Cambridge: Cambridge University Press, 1993), pp. 273–322.

Les limites de l'interprétation

La prolifération des études sur le rapport texte / image depuis une trentaine d'années mériterait une enquête sociologique sur les stratégies universitaires. Elle répond à l'injonction de pratiquer l'interdisciplinarité, c'est-à-dire de juxtaposer les approches de différents spécialistes sur des sujets qui exigeraient plutôt la pluridisciplinarité, la maîtrise par chacun de l'ensemble des méthodes requises pour appréhender l'objet. Il est à craindre que l'interdisciplinarité soit à la spécialisation aveugle ce qu'un emplâtre est à une jambe de bois, tout en permettant à des historiens et à des critiques littéraires de pontifier sur les images en ignorant tout de l'histoire de l'art et de ses méthodes.[18] Elle a cependant des origines plus lointaines dans l'iconologie panofskienne, parfois adaptée à des genres artistiques, comme les drôleries, auxquels elle convient mal. Même pour des gens qui savent regarder les images, faire de l'image l'illustration d'un texte rassure sur la pertinence de l'interprétation. Dans le cas des drôleries, ou bien on nie à la fois qu'elles aient un rapport au texte et un sens, comme l'avait fait Mâle, ou bien on voudrait leur trouver un sens dans un hypothétique rapport au texte.

L'article de Lilian Randall, 'Games and the Passion in Pucelle's *Hours of Jeanne d'Evreux*', est un bon exemple d'une interprétation de motifs apparemment profanes et anodins visant à leur donner un sens par rapport au contenu du livre d'heures.[19] Il a dans l'ensemble été accepté par la critique et ne présente pas de grosses invraisemblances. Aux folios 15^{v}–16 des Heures de Jeanne d'Evreux (New York, Cloisters, 54.1.2), Jean Pucelle a placé, respectivement sous le Baiser de Judas et l'Annonciation, deux cavaliers grotesques jouant à la quintaine avec un tonneau et des jeunes gens jouant à la grenouille, jeu qui consiste à frapper pour rire un personnage assis qui doit deviner l'identité de ses agresseurs (fig. 1). Constatant que les représentations du Christ aux outrages montrent parfois une parenté formelle avec celles du jeu de la grenouille et qu'il est fait explicitement allusion à ce jeu dans un *Livre de la Passion* à propos de la dérision du Christ, l'auteur voit dans la scène marginale une allusion à la Passion qui compléterait la trahison de Judas de la page précédente. En même temps, ce jeu printanier évoquerait l'époque de l'Annonciation, fêtée le 25 mars. Quant aux cavaliers et au

---

[18] L'interdisciplinarité étant l'alibi de la spécialisation aveugle, mettre en cause le rapport texte/image, c'est attaquer la routine universitaire dans ses fondements. Nous en avons fait l'expérience en soumettant au Fonds National Suisse de la Recherche le projet en cours. L'expert, une historienne de l'art américaine à laquelle le féminisme tient lieu de compétence, l'avait condamné parce qu'il affirmait que les marges à drôleries sont normalement indépendantes du texte. Il est à l'honneur de l'institution académique d'avoir accepté de financer le projet l'année suivante, après que je lui eus soumis une réfutation en règle de l'expertise au lieu de modifier le rapport.

[19] L. M. C. Randall, 'Games and the Passion in Pucelle's *Hours of Jeanne d'Evreux*', *Speculum*, 47 (1972), 246–57.

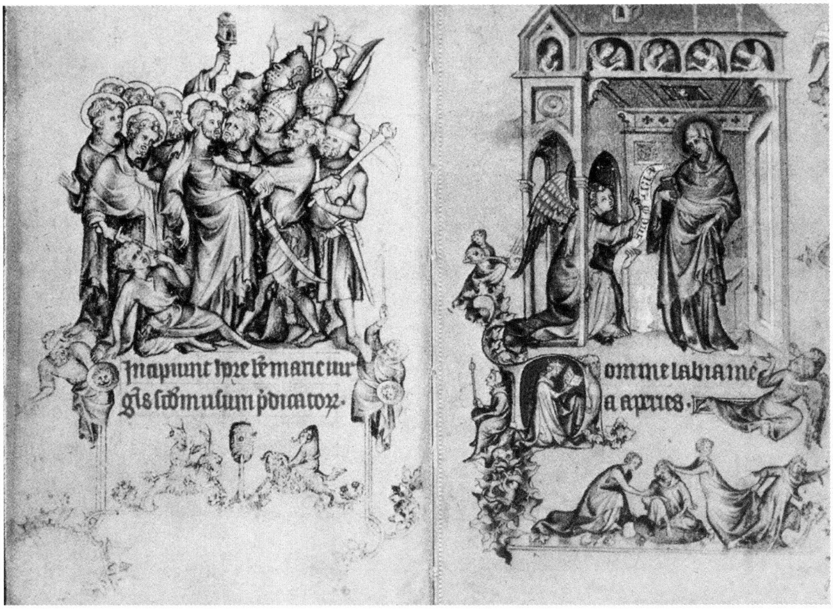

Fig. 1. Heures de Jeanne d'Evreux, New York, Cloisters, MS. 54.1.2, fols 15^{v}–16, 'Arrestation du Christ et Annonciation'. © The Cloisters, New York

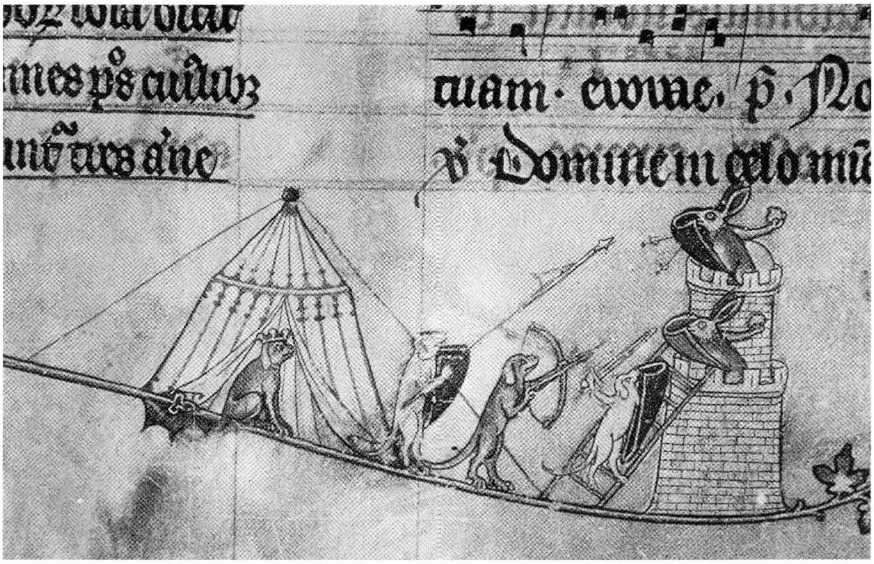

Fig. 2. Bréviaire de Renaud de Bar, Verdun, Bibliothèque municipale, ms. 107, fol. 138^{r}, 'Siège d'un château'. © Bibliothèque municipale, Verdun

tonneau sur la quintaine, ils feraient allusion au Juif errant qui avait frappé le Christ lors du portement de croix et au Christ lui-même, le vin du tonneau rappelant l'eucharistie.

On ne voit pas pourquoi chercher une allusion au Juif errant, mais il n'est pas impossible que la quintaine sous le Baiser de Judas soit un commentaire parodique de cette image, encore que la validité de l'interprétation serait difficile à établir. L'allusion à la Passion est en revanche très improbable dans le cas du jeu de la grenouille. Pour que le parallèle fonctionne, il faudrait que les yeux du jeune homme faisant office de grenouille soient voilés, comme cela est fréquemment le cas dans les représentations de ce jeu et dans celles de la dérision du Christ. De surcroît, on comprendrait mal pourquoi Pucelle a placé sa 'grenouille' sur un coussin et lui a donné comme seuls bourreaux des jolies filles qui semblent le titiller. S'il s'agissait vraiment d'une allusion à la Passion, le peintre aurait tout fait pour la rendre incompréhensible. En revanche, comme d'autres bas-de-page complètent incontestablement l'image principale dans ce petit livre, ainsi le Massacre des Innocents au bas de l'Adoration des Mages du fol. 69, l'allusion au printemps est très possible. De cet exemple, nous pouvons tirer une première règle d'interprétation trop rarement appliquée: NE FAIRE L'HYPOTHESE D'UNE ALLUSION QUE SI CELLE-CI A QUELQUE CHANCE D'ETRE PERCEPTIBLE.

La thèse de Sharon Davenport sur les manuscrits enluminés pour Renaud de Bar contient quatre cents pages consacrées à l'analyse des drôleries et représente la tentative la plus systématique que nous connaissions de leur donner un sens.[20] On y trouve bon nombre de renseignements précieux, parce que l'auteur montre une rare connaissance des *realia*, qu'il s'agisse du costume des jongleurs ou des religieux, de l'anatomie des animaux, de leurs moeurs réelles ou légendaires et des symbolismes sexuels qui peuvent leur être attachés. Mais elle pose le principe d'un rapport avec le texte liturgique et interprète pratiquement chaque drôlerie en ce sens, tout en multipliant les adverbes exprimant l'incertitude.

Voyons quelques exemples. Dans le bréviaire de Renaud de Bar (Londres, British Library, Yates Thompson 8, fol. 92), l'auteur renchérit sur Randall en interprétant le jeu de la grenouille et une lutte à califourchon comme des allusions à la Passion. Mais on peut se demander si la liturgie du quatrième dimanche de l'Avent que ces images accompagnent, toute centrée sur l'imminence des fêtes de Noël, est vraiment celle qui appellerait le mieux ces allusions. Au fol. 192, l'auteur a su identifier le thème du lapin, ennemi du tailleur qui s'intéresse à sa fourrure (plutôt qu'à sa viande), mais elle croit devoir le relier à l'abstinence durant le carême. Il arrive, ainsi au fol. 53, qu'un psaume faisant allusion à la musique soit décoré de musiciens dans les marges. Mais, si l'on prend en compte le fait que tous les psaumes sont des prières chantées, que

[20] S. K. Davenport, *Manuscripts illustrated for Renaud of Bar, bishop of Metz (1303–1316)* (thèse de PhD inédite, Courtauld Institute of Art, University of London, 1984), pp. 564 et ss.

beaucoup d'entre eux le rappellent explicitement et que les musiciens sont aussi innombrables dans les marges qu'elles entourent ou non des psaumes, il est plus raisonnable d'y voir une coïncidence. On fixera donc une seconde règle d'interprétation: LA POSSIBILITE D'UNE ALLUSION EST INVERSEMENT PROPORTIONNELLE A LA FREQUENCE DU MOTIF ICONOGRAPHIQUE ET A CELLE DU MOTIF TEXTUEL AUQUEL IL EST SUPPOSE SE RAPPORTER.

Toutes les interprétations de Davenport ne sont pas aussi incertaines. Comme elle le remarque, il est clair que l'un des peintres, celui qu'elle identifie comme la seconde main, a accès au texte latin, ce qui ne vaut sans doute pas pour tous les enlumineurs. Il remplace fréquemment les drôleries par des scènes bibliques en rapport avec le texte et quelques-unes de ses drôleries peuvent être légitimement soupçonnées d'y faire allusion. Dans la seconde partie du bréviaire de Renaud (Verdun, Bibliothèque municipale, ms. 107, fol. 137v), des lapins défendent un château attaqué par des chiens et on lit sur la même page l'antiphone: '*Expugna impugnantes me*' (fig. 2). Une coïncidence est possible, car le combat est un thème récurrent dans les psaumes et les prières qui en dérivent comme dans les drôleries. Mais, bien qu'il s'agisse de la troisième main, moins attentive au texte, l'intention est cette fois plus probable, car les marges et l'illustration du psaume 34, dont provient l'antiphone, montrent plusieurs fois une scène de combat.[21] Dans la première partie (Yates Thompson 8), deux allusions débusquées par l'auteur chez le second artiste sont très vraisemblables. Aux fol. 295v-296, un singe couronné est porté par deux lapins vers une tente où siège une guenon à son tour couronnée. Il s'agit de l'office de sainte Agathe et on y lit le répons: '*Ipse me coronavit qui per apostolum Petrum in custodia me confortavit*'. Le motif de la guenon couronnée est suffisamment exceptionnel pour justifier l'interprétation parodique du thème. L'intention est plus difficile à percevoir au fol. 308v, lorsqu'un homme nu vu de dos tient un tissu rouge muni d'un galon, à proximité de l'antiphone: '*Qui solebat in sericis procedere vestimentis, post in abjectis vestibus servit, pauper pauperibus*', mais l'allusion est difficilement contestable.

Il n'en reste pas moins qu'à vouloir systématiquement réduire les drôleries à des illustrations du texte, Davenport laisse échapper leur incongruité et leur impertinence. Les superbes marges du troisième peintre mettent l'accent sur les jeux guerriers, la fauconnerie et les jolies femmes, ce qui ne va pas complètement de soi dans le bréviaire d'un évêque et devrait poser quelques problèmes sur sa personnalité. Persuadée du sérieux des drôleries, Davenport en vient logiquement à défendre son évêque contre la réputation d'ecclésiastique indigne que les historiens lui avaient faite, en passant sans broncher sur des faits qui font réfléchir. La carrière de Renaud de Bar n'est portant pas très édifiante. Vers 1300, il est entre autres archidiacre à Bruxelles et à Besançon, chanoine à

[21] En particulier: Londres, BL, MS. Add. 62925 (Psautier Rutland), fol. 37; Paris, BnF, ms. lat. 1076, fol. 42; Cambrai, Bibliothèque municipale, ms. 87, fol. 132V.

Verdun et à Metz. Evêque de Metz élu en septembre 1302, il est consacré l'année suivante et ordonné prêtre à cette occasion. Il s'agit donc de la carrière typique d'un prébendier absentéiste qui ne s'est peut-être jamais assis dans les stalles d'un choeur. A partir de 1306, il passe son temps à guerroyer contre la ville, le chapitre et le duc de Lorraine. Rien n'indique le moindre intérêt pour les tâches spirituelles et, lorsque les enlumineurs plaçaient dans les beaux livres qu'il se commandait des images relatives à ces tâches, c'était probablement pour respecter la dignité de la fonction plutôt que celle de la personne.

La volonté de mettre à tout prix les drôleries en rapport avec le texte qu'elles décorent n'est pas le seul abus destiné à leur donner un sens. N'importe quelle histoire médiévale se présente, comme les fables, ou peut se présenter, comme les *exempla*, avec une moralisation. Chaque objet du monde extérieur, chaque événement de la vie peut devenir pour un esprit pieux l'occasion d'un petit sermon. Mais il va de soi que la moralisation n'est pas inhérente à l'objet ou à l'anecdote et que le même prétexte peut servir à des moralisations différentes. Comme on l'a déjà remarqué à propos de l'article de Randall sur les *exempla*, il est douteux que le bon tour de Renart faisant le mort pour attraper les oiseaux soit systématiquement destiné à évoquer les ruses du diable. Il est plus probable qu'une anecdote ou qu'une image quelconque ait été vue comme ouverte à l'interprétation, que ce même Renart ait pu évoquer à un dominicain le diable tentant les pécheurs et à un franciscain un dominicain plumant les dévotes. Un petit ouvrage comique comme *Salomon et Marcolfe*, où le roi et son fou échangent des maximes respectivement nobles et grossières, repose tout entier sur la possibilité d'interpréter les mêmes faits avec le sérieux du moraliste et la dérision du bouffon.[22]

Deux autres articles de Randall, malgré l'excellence de leur érudition, suscitent pour cela des réserves. L'un porte sur le guerrier terrorisé par un escargot (fig. 3).[23] L'auteur relève l'existence d'oeuvres littéraires où les Lombards sont supposés assez lâches pour fuir devant les escargots et interprète donc le thème comme une satire dirigée contre eux. Elle relève aussi que les Lombards n'avaient pas le droit de porter les armes dans le royaume de France, alors que les marges nous présentent des guerriers, souvent des chevaliers, armés jusqu'aux dents. Par ailleurs, le chevalier est fréquemment représenté, dans les cycles des vertus et des vices où il illustre la lâcheté, mais aussi dans le décor marginal, en train de laisser tomber son épée face à un lapin menaçant. On voit mal ce qui empêcherait quelqu'un qui en veut aux usuriers lombards d'identifier comme Lombard le chevalier au lapin aussi bien que celui à l'escargot, ou

---

[22] *Salomon et Marcolfus*, éd. W. Benary (Heidelberg: Winter, 1914). Cf. P. Lehmann, *Die Parodie im Mittelalter* (Stuttgart: Hiersemann, 1922; 2e éd. 1963), pp. 172 et ss.

[23] L. M. C. Randall, 'The Snail in Gothic Marginal Warfare', *Speculum*, 37 (1962), 358–67.

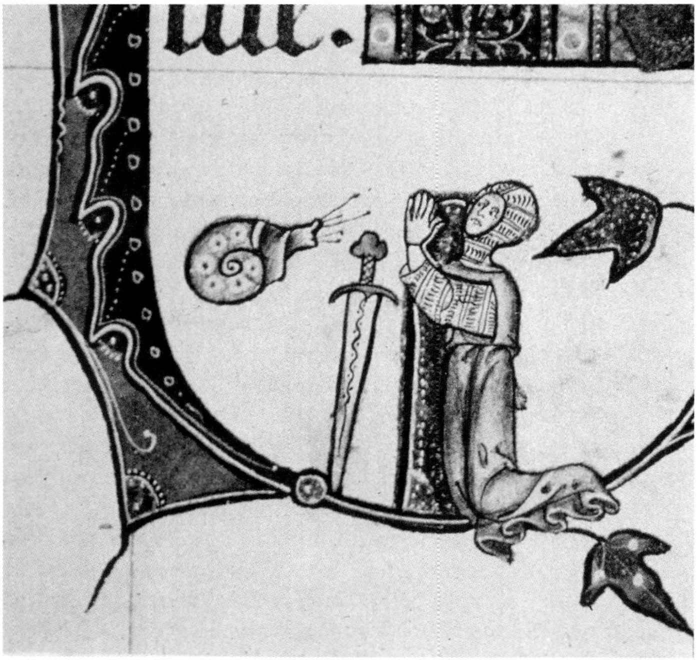

Fig. 3. Psautier de Gorleston, Londres, British Library, MS. Add. 49622, fol. 162^{v}, 'Chevalier effrayé par un escargot'. © British Library, London

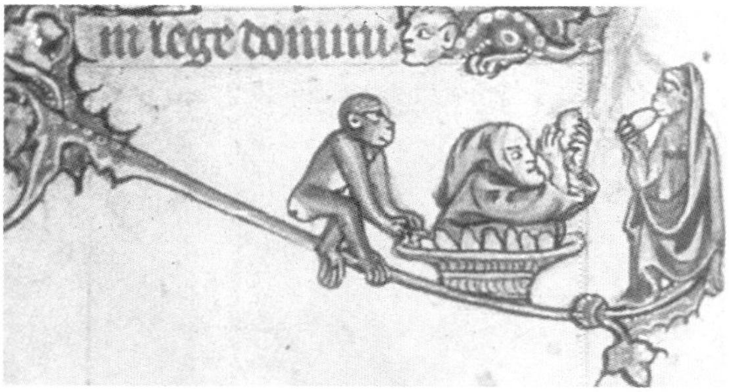

Fig. 4. Psautier gantois, Oxford, Bodleian Library, MS. Douce 6, fol. 92^{v}, 'Couvade'. © Bodleian Library, Oxford

encore ce qui empêcherait quelqu'un qui en veut, par exemple, aux barbiers d'identifier comme barbier le chevalier à l'escargot. Traitant dans un autre article de l'homme qui couve des oeufs (fig. 4), le même auteur présente plusieurs possibilités d'interprétation avant de conclure à une plaisanterie anti-anglaise.[24] Les Anglais sont en effet souvent supposés munis d'une queue et qualifiés de 'coués' depuis le XIIe siècle. Or, 'coué' peut faire jeu de mot avec 'couard', mais aussi avec 'couvé'. L'homme qui couve serait donc un Anglais efféminé, ce que confirmerait l'absence du thème dans les manuscrits d'outre-Manche. L'interprétation laisse à nouveau sceptique. Les manuscrits anglais sont aussi remplis de personnages coués que ceux du continent, peut-être plus, alors que le jeu de mot sur 'couvé', effectivement présent dans un texte anti-anglais, passe par la désignation des Anglais comme 'coués', tandis que la couvaison masculine ou couvade apparaît dans des contextes littéraires où il n'est pas question d'Anglais.

En cherchant des interprétations politiques, Randall tend à oublier un autre niveau symbolique plus général et dont la mise en oeuvre est plus probable. Le lapin qui fait fuir le chevalier est, en français médiéval un 'conin', ce qui fournit une mine inépuisable de jeux de mots obscènes. Qu'on se contente d'évoquer ici les aventures de Renart à la cour du roi Conin.[25] Or l'escargot, mou et visqueux dans sa coquille, suggère également le sexe féminin, comme l'a bien vu Camille.[26] Le tournoi et le duel sont des métaphores fréquentes du coït, dans la littérature comme dans les marges. Dans un fabliau comme *Berengier au long cul*, un chevalier fanfaron est mis au défi par sa femme, méconnaissable dans son armure, de jouter avec elle ou de lui baiser le postérieur.[27] Face au 'long cul' de son redoutable adversaire, le chevalier effrayé laisse tomber son épée, exactement comme s'il avait affaire à un conin ou à un limaçon. Pour ce qui est de la couvade, elle renvoie de manière non moins évidente à l'absence de virilité et on pense immédiatement au roi de Turelure en mal d'enfant qui scandalise le héros dans *Aucassin et Nicolette*. Il faut aussi remarquer, comme le fait Randall, que cette posture s'accompagne généralement dans les marges d'un geste caractéristique: le couveur lève un oeuf vers le soleil pour le mirer et vérifier sa fécondité. Le même geste apparaît non moins fréquemment dans ce répertoire pour le médecin qui mire les urines, une pratique qui servait de test de grossesse et qui est appliquée à des hommes supposés enceints dans le *Jeu de la Feuillée* d'Adam de la Halle.

---

[24] L. M. C. Randall, 'A Mediaeval Slander', *Art Bulletin*, 42 (1960), 25–38.

[25] *Le Roman de Renart*, éd. A. Strubel (Paris: Gallimard, 1998), branche 23, pp.751 et ss. (branche 22 de l'édition Martin).

[26] Camille (cf. note 10), pp. 46 et ss.

[27] *Nouveau recueil complet des fabliaux*, éd. W. Noomen et N. Van den Boogaard (Assen: Van Gorcum, 1983–98), IV, n° 34, pp. 247 et ss.

Pourquoi préférons-nous voir dans le chevalier qui laisse tomber son épée devant un escargot ou dans la couvade une allusion sexuelle plutôt que politique? Outre que, comme nous l'avons vu, l'interprétation politique est difficilement généralisable, remarquons d'abord que les deux interprétations ne sont pas exclusives, car elles ne se situent pas au même niveau. Pour la couvade, Randall comprend très bien que la virilité du couveur est en cause. En fait, l'interprétation sexuelle de ces thèmes est la condition de possibilité d'une éventuelle interprétation politique. Dans le cas de la couvade, elle est immédiate, puisque l'homme adopte un comportement des femelles destiné à la reproduction de l'espèce. Dans le cas du chevalier, elle semble bien se déduire du choix des animaux qui le terrorisent. La souris, la grue ou l'écureuil par exemple, qui métaphorisent le pénis dans les fabliaux, ne jouent jamais ce rôle, malgré le soin que prennent les enlumineurs à innover en variant les acteurs d'une histoire conventionnelle. L'interprétation sexuelle des deux thèmes est donc pertinente, tandis que leur moralisation politique ressemble fort à la projection arbitraire d'une moralisation. Si le peintre voulait proposer un sens moral, il aurait certainement trouvé les moyens de le suggérer. A titre d'exemple, pour identifier Renart prêchant aux poules à l'évêque, il lui donne une mitre. Il serait excessif d'en déduire que les représentations d'un renard non mitré volant une poule soient des allusions anticléricales, mais il est significatif qu'on ne donne guère d'autres attributs à cet animal que ceux du clergé, qu'il ne revêt jamais, à notre connaissance, la couronne royale ou le bonnet à grelots du jongleur. Il serait arbitraire de faire entrer tous les renards dans le clergé, mais il est raisonnable d'affirmer que cet animal rusé évoque en premier lieu le clergé. On peut ainsi poser une troisième règle d'interprétation: LA SIGNIFICATION D'UN MOTIF NE PEUT ÊTRE ÉTABLIE QUE SUR L'EXAMEN DE SES DIFFÉRENTES OCCURRENCES. L'état de la recherche nous oblige à formuler cette règle qui, comme les précédentes, devrait aller de soi.

Méthodologiquement proche du travail de Randall, l'article consacré par Howard Helsinger à l'illustration du psaume *Beatus vir* qui sert de frontispice au psautier est d'une rigueur inhabituelle.[28] Grâce à l'index de cette chercheuse, il peut faire intervenir des comptages et prendre en compte la fréquence des thèmes. L'analyse la plus longue et la plus minutieuse concerne la chasse au cerf. Il repère le thème dans huit frontispices du psautier et se demande si sa fréquence à cet emplacement est significative. Le cerf apparaît dans un tiers des manuscrits décrits par Randall, la chasse au cerf dans trois quarts de ces cas. Il considère néanmoins que la présence du thème au frontispice est significative, car il n'accompagne avec la même fréquence aucun autre psaume enluminé. Le psaume 41 ('De même que le cerf désire la fontaine des eaux, de même mon âme te désire mon Dieu...') et le Bestiaire qui signale l'hostilité du cerf envers le

[28] H. Helsinger, 'Images on the *Beatus* Page of Medieval Psalters', *Art Bulletin*, 53 (1971), 161–76.

serpent, inspirent la moralisation du cerf dans le commentaire biblique: il représente l'*homo viator*, le chrétien pérégrinant exilé dans ce monde. Les chiens de chasse qui poursuivent le cerf sont interprétés par les prédicateurs comme des figures du diable. L'iconographie reprend ces moralisations, déjà dans le psautier d'Utrecht (v. 820) où les chiens poursuivant le cerf illustrent le psaume 41. Si le thème décore le *Beatus vir* des psautiers gothiques, c'est parce que cette page sert de frontispice au recueil tout entier et que sa thématique n'est donc pas étroitement liée au contenu du premier psaume.

La démonstration semble à première vue indiscutable, car l'objection qu'on aurait tirée de la banalité de la chasse au cerf est réfutée par le repérage d'une fréquence anormale au frontispice des psaumes. Vérifions tout de même les chiffres: nous avons enregistré 356 cerfs dont 125 dans les psautiers et 60 dans les livres non liturgiques. Cela fait 2,9 % des fiches dans les psautiers comme dans les livres non liturgiques. Il est peu probable que l'égale fréquence du cerf dans les manuscrits non liturgiques et en particulier dans les manuscrits profanes soit due à une pieuse moralisation, mais cela ne contredit pas formellement la thèse d'Helsinger. Il est plus ennuyeux de constater que les psautiers ne se distinguent pas par l'abondance de ces animaux. Les singes, par exemple, font 13,6 % des fiches dans les psautiers et 12,6 % dans les livres non liturgiques. Les singes ont donc un rapport plus étroit avec le psautier que les cerfs. Surtout, l'auteur a oublié un paramètre essentiel: le *Beatus vir*, frontispice du psautier, est beaucoup plus souvent et plus abondamment décoré qu'aucun autre psaume. A l'exception du frontispice de la Bible, il s'agit de la page manuscrite la plus susceptible de recevoir un thème quelconque. Même si nous ne pouvons traduire ce dernier point en donnée chiffrée, il suffit pour considérer la chasse au cerf, décorant 8 frontispices sur les 102 psautiers et bréviaires pris en compte par Randall, comme assez peu fréquente à cet emplacement. Sa répartition dans les différents types de manuscrits laisse au contraire prévoir qu'elle est motivée par les goûts cynégétiques de la clientèle.

Helsinger repère 14 psautiers au moins où David et Goliath occupent le bas de page du *Beatus vir*. Il s'agit d'un pourcentage exceptionnel, mais le thème est motivé de manière cette fois évidente par l'attribution du psautier à David et par le contenu du psaume. Il note également neuf scènes de tournois sur cette page, ce qui n'est pas trivial. Le tournoi est déjà là dans le psautier de Saint-Albans (entre 1120 et 1130) où un commentaire, dû à l'enlumineur lui-même, en fait un symbole du combat spirituel, exégèse que Helsinger applique aux autres occurrences. Vérification faite, le tournoi occupe 0,36 % de nos fiches, 0,42 % pour les psautiers et 0,67 % pour les manuscrits non liturgiques. La part des manuscrits non liturgiques s'explique par le report en marge de scènes illustrant le texte dans les romans chevaleresques. Il reste que le tournoi est significativement plus présent dans le psautier que dans la moyenne des manuscrits. Mais faut-il nécessairement y voir une figure du combat spirituel? Dans le contexte monastique du psautier de Saint-Albans, cette moralisation explique vraisemblablement la présence du thème. Or les psautiers gothiques qui nous occupent ont souvent une ambiance très profane. Dans un psautier pris en compte par Helsinger (Oxford, Bodleian Library, Laud. lat. 84, fol. 19), le tournoi oppose un chevalier à une femme (fig. 5), tandis que dans le psautier-heures de Jean de Neuville (New York, Pierpont Morgan Library, M. 730), cette variante orne les bouts-de-lignes de manière récurrente, en compagnie de drôleries obscènes et scatologiques. Il s'agit à l'évidence d'une allusion aux ébats amoureux et il serait difficile, même à une oie blanche, de lui appliquer le sens d'un combat spirituel.

A défaut de convaincre, les études de Randall et d'Helsinger ne heurtent pas le bon sens. Il n'en va pas de même de l'article récent de Madeline Caviness sur les heures de Jeanne d'Evreux.[29] Selon toutes probabilités, le chef-d'oeuvre de Jean Pucelle a été commandé par Charles IV pour sa jeune et royale épouse en 1324. L'auteur part de ce fait et des présupposés ordinaires sur l'oppression des femmes au Moyen Âge, pour interpréter le décor marginal comme une série d'exemples moraux destinés à faire de la reine une épouse fidèle et une reproductrice soumise, une intention bien compréhensible après l'affaire de la Tour de Nesles où trois des brus de Philippe le Bel avaient beaucoup fait parler d'elles. Analysant la page consacrée à l'Annonciation qui avait déjà intéressé Randall (fig. 1), Caviness fait la pétition de principe que la reine prie dans l'initiale pour avoir un héritier mâle. La chandelle (en réalité une masse d'arme) que tient le garde qui la protège est donc un symbole phallique. En lisant la prière '*Domine labia mea aperies*', le mot '*labia*' occupant le milieu de la page, Jeanne pense aux lèvres de son vagin que son maître et époux se chargera d'ouvrir, sans toutefois lui procurer les plaisirs de la jeunesse auxquels renvoie le bas de page. Le chat dans le feuillage en dessous de l'initiale (si c'est bien un chat) est le *pussy* de la reine; la souris sous le jeune homme du bas de page (en réalité un lapin) représente à nouveau le pénis, le chien la fidélité conjugale et le reste à l'avenant. La page se partagerait entre les symboles des vertus demandées à la reine et ceux des vices dont elle doit se détourner. La même clé d'interprétation est imperturbablement appliquée au reste du manuscrit et l'auteur n'a pas de mal à conclure sur le caractère révolutionnaire de ses résultats. Considérant que ses conceptions de la recherche doivent être adoptées par l'ensemble du monde académique, elle s'insurge dans l'une des dernières notes de son texte contre un collègue qui avait osé proposer un cours sur l'art du XIXe siècle, fondé sur une liste d'artistes mâles de race blanche, en grande partie français, et se félicite que la menace d'un procès ait empêché cette infamie.

L'étude du statut social des deux sexes à travers l'histoire est un sujet qui mérite davantage l'intérêt qu'on lui porte aujourd'hui que l'indifférence dont les historiens ont trop souvent fait preuve à son égard. Mais cela n'autorise pas à se comporter comme si les opinions féministes garantissaient par avance la validité de l'interprétation. La méthode utilisée par Madeline Caviness permettrait de

[29] M. H. Caviness, 'Patron or Matron? A Capetian Bride and a Vade Mecum for Her Marriage Bed', *Speculum*, 68 (1993), 333–62.

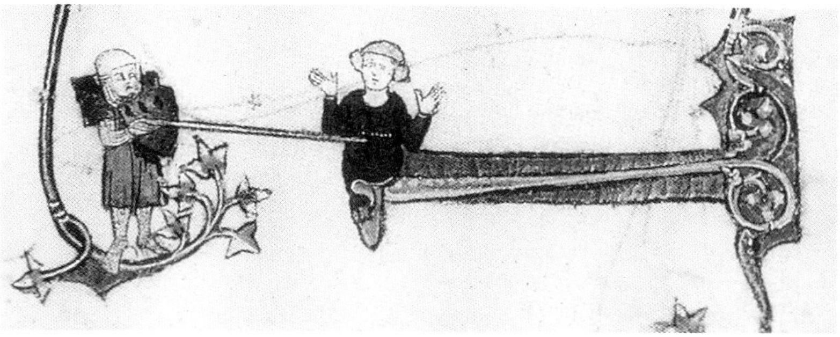

Fig. 5. Psautier, Oxford, Bodleian Library, MS. Laud. lat. 84, fol. 19, 'Initiale Beatus *'. © Bodleian Library, Oxford*

tirer les mêmes conclusions de quelque oeuvre picturale ou littéraire que ce soit. Toute histoire peut en effet être considérée comme un exemple à suivre ou à ne pas suivre, dans un livre d'heures comme dans un western, de sorte que les mêmes intentions didactiques et phallocratiques peuvent être infailliblement prêtées à n'importe laquelle. Appliquée au bréviaire de Renaud de Bar, cette méthode permettrait de prouver sans la moindre difficulté que l'évêque était une fille à marier. Il s'agit de ce que les anthropologues anglo-saxons appellent un *self-confirming system* et qu'ils croient trop souvent caractéristique des sociétés autres que la nôtre.

En appliquant la seconde règle d'interprétation que nous proposons, Camille aurait pu éviter l'une des hypothèses les plus discutables de son essai sur les marges.[30] Il imagine que certaines drôleries obscènes ont pu être suggérées au peintre par des jeux de mots sur le texte latin, comme la devinette bien connue qui fait de '*conculcavit*' le mot le plus poilu du psautier, puisqu'on peut y lire les mots français 'con', 'cul', 'cas' et 'vit'. C'est ainsi qu'un enlumineur ignorant le latin aurait pu lire l'anglais '*legs*' pour le latin '*lege*' et placer dans la marge une tête sur jambes. Pareillement, '*juvencularum*', décomposé dans le latin '*juvenis*' et le français 'cul', aurait pu inspirer à l'artiste du psautier Rutland le jeune homme nu à tête de Christ qui offre son derrière à l'agression armée d'un singe chevauchant une autruche (Londres, BL, MS. Add. 62925, fols 66^{v}–67). On ne peut rejeter formellement la possibilité qu'un peintre se soit un jour permis de rêvasser ainsi sur le texte du psautier et on conviendra avec Camille que le goût du jeu de mots n'a pas beaucoup de limites au Moyen Âge. Malheureusement, la langue latine est ainsi faite que les syllabes incriminées y prolifèrent et que le petit jeu lasserait rapidement l'obsédé sexuel le plus invétéré. Dans la seule double page du psautier Rutland qu'on vient d'évoquer, il y a, outre le mot '*juvencularum*', cinq occurrences du préfixe '*con-*' et, si l'enlumineur avait été

[30] Camille (cf. note 10), pp. 55 et ss., 61.

au courant des vilains mots aujourd'hui en usage, il aurait pu mettre à profit deux occurrences du suffixe '*-bit*'. Autant qu'à faire, ne serait-il pas plus vraisemblable que le bas de page ait été inspiré par le latin du psaume 67, verset 14: '*et posteriora dorsi eius*'? Mais, s'il avait vraiment procédé ainsi, le peintre aurait probablement réservé son bas de page blasphématoire pour le psaume 77, verset 73: '*Et percussit inimicos suos in posteriora; opprobrium sempiternum dedit illis*'.

L'éventualité que les drôleries reposent sur des jeux de mots ou, plus généralement, sur des allusions textuelles, dépend de l'accès que le peintre avait au texte, soit directement, par la connaissance de la langue écrite, soit indirectement, si quelqu'un lui apportait de l'aide. Il n'est généralement pas possible de trancher formellement entre l'accès direct ou indirect au texte et la prudence voudrait qu'on parlât, à la manière de Beat Brenk,[31] du concepteur des drôleries. Mais, dès qu'on s'est familiarisé avec le contenu d'un manuscrit, il devient le plus souvent évident que l'enlumineur possédait ou non une idée du texte. Voyons quelques exemples.

Le cas du bréviaire de Renaud de Bar a déjà été évoqué: l'un au moins des peintres l'illustre sans difficultés lorsqu'il choisit de le faire. Plusieurs psautiers ont été décorés dans les initiales à l'aide d'une liste qui circulait en latin et en français et qui était donc destinée à des enlumineurs capables de lire respectivement l'une et l'autre de ces langues.[32] Dans le cas du lat. 10435 de la Bibliothèque nationale de France, enluminé à Arras vers 1280, l'enlumineur utilise une liste française et ne connaît pas bien la Bible. Lorsqu'il lit l'indication 'moyses et aaron drescent l'arche', il ne pense pas à l'arche d'alliance et fait tenir l'arche de Noé à ces deux personnages, interprétant le français 'drescer' dans le sens de 'brandir' et non pas de 'bâtir', que suggère mieux le latin '*erigunt*'. Les indications de la liste ont été reproduites à l'encre rouge dans la marge, après le travail de l'enlumineur, jusqu'au folio 155^{v}. Il s'agissait d'une liste incomplète, à moins qu'elle ait été reprise à l'enlumineur avant la fin de son travail, car l'iconographie des initiales change alors de caractère et devient passe-partout: aux scènes bibliques succèdent des personnages en prière. On serait tenté d'en conclure que le peintre n'avait pas accès au texte. Pourtant, au psaume 127, '*Beati omnes qui timent Dominum*', il place des dominicains en prière dans l'initiale et un franciscain en conversation avec une femme dans la marge, laissant entendre que les premiers craignent le Seigneur plus que le second (fol. 158).

---

[31] B. Brenk, 'Le texte et l'image dans la vie des saints au Moyen-Âge', in *Texte et Image. Actes du Colloque international de Chantille* (Paris: Belles Lettres, 1984), pp. 31–39.

[32] E. A. Peterson, 'The Textual Basis for Visual Errors in French Gothic Psalter Illustration', in *The Early Medieval Bible. Its Production, Decoration and Use*, éd. R. Gameson (Cambridge: Cambridge University Press, 1994), pp. 177–204.

Le peintre ou son éventuel conseiller lit donc le français et assez de latin pour identifier l'incipit des psaumes, mais il est incapable de concevoir tout seul un programme d'exégèse par l'image. Son exemple paraît assez caractéristique de la culture moyenne des enlumineurs, mais les écarts peuvent être considérables des uns aux autres. Le livre d'heures lat. 13260 de la Bibliothèque nationale de France, à l'usage de Saint-Amand, semble avoir été décoré à Cambrai dans la dernière décennie du XIIIe siècle.[33] Le peintre a illustré les psaumes 1, 32, 45, 69, 73, 75, 101, 109 et 137, ce qui est inusuel, sauf pour les psaumes 1, 101 et 109. Comme l'a vu François Avril, l'iconographie est celle qui prévaut en France pour les psaumes majeurs. Or ce n'est pas le peintre, mais le scribe, qui réserve les emplacements destinés aux grandes initiales. On avait donc certainement prévu une subdivision originale du psautier, mais le peintre, faute de connaître ou de pouvoir inventer des iconographies conformes à ce choix, s'est contenté de reproduire celles dont il disposait, indifférent à leur emplacement.

Dans un livre d'heures à l'usage de Saint-Omer produit après 1318 et faussement identifié comme celui d'une Marguerite de Beaujeu (New York, Pierpont Morgan Library, MS. M. 754 et Londres, BL, MS. Add. 36684), trois plaisanteries blasphématoires montrent que le peintre (ou son éventuel conseiller) lisait et comprenait parfaitement les prières. Au fol. 27 du manuscrit Morgan, un singe tire le vin du derrière d'un manchot avec un fausset de barrique pour remplir un calice. Un peu plus loin, au fol. 35, un singe défèque dans un calice devant une dame et, au folio 48^{v}, un singe boulanger enfourne un derrière, tandis que son compagnon ramène des pains sur une planche tout en désignant le texte de l'index (fig. 6). Ces plaisanteries ornent l'office du Saint Sacrement et accompagnent pour deux d'entre elles le texte de la consécration eucharistique. La troisième correspond à l'hymne *Pange lingua*, le singe attirant l'attention sur les paroles '*mysterium corporis et sanguinis sui*'. Plus généralement, les marges de cet office sont décorées de nombreux calices comme celles de l'office des morts le sont de crânes et de squelettes. Le peintre ne devait pas être beaucoup plus pieux que la dame à laquelle le livre était destiné mais, à moins qu'un clerc ait veillé à côté de lui pour lui suggérer les mauvais coups, on admettra qu'il comprenait parfaitement la liturgie.

L'obsession du rapport texte / image a souvent fait ignorer aux chercheurs les rapports qui se tissent entre les marges et les images principales. Dans bien des cas où, à première vue, la marge se rapporte au texte, il est bien plus probable que l'artiste commente cette image ou s'inspire du répertoire auquel elle appartient. A titre d'exemple, l'illustration du psaume 52, '*Dixit insipiens*', se prolonge souvent dans la marge de manière évidente. On y trouve parfois un fou (Londres, British Library, MS. Burney 345, fol. 70; Copenhague, Kongelige Bibliotek, MS. 3384, fol. 98). Dans le psautier de Louis le Hutin, conservé à la

[33] *L'art au temps des rois maudits. Philippe le Bal et ses fils (1285–1328)* (Paris, 1998: Exposition, Grand Palais), n° 212, p. 313.

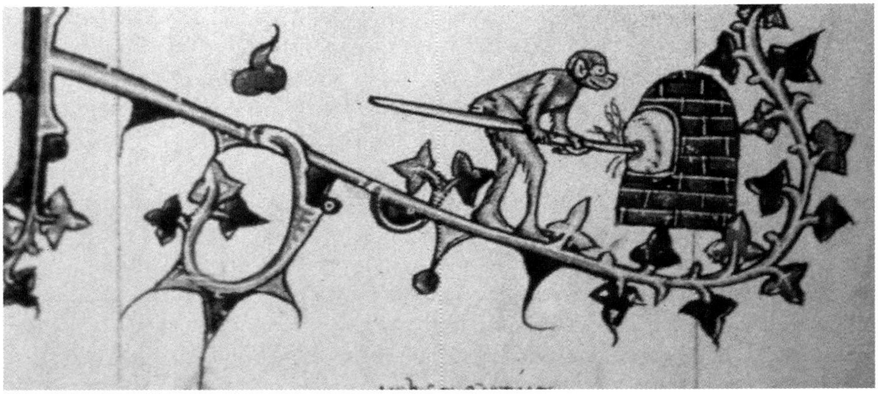

Fig. 6. Livre d'heures, New York, Pierpont Morgan Library, MS. M. 754, fol. 48ᵛ, 'Singes boulangers'. © Pierpont Morgan Library, New York

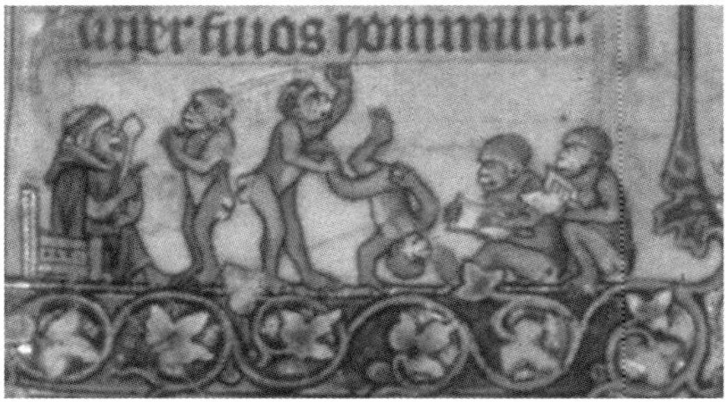

Fig. 7. Psautier gantois, Oxford, Bodleian Library, MS. Douce 5, fol. 146, 'Ecole des singes'. © Bodleian Library, Oxford

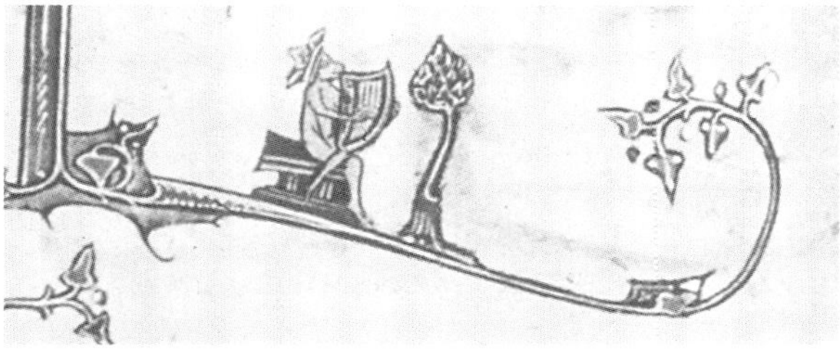

Fig. 8. Psautier-Heures de Geoffroy d'Aspremont et d'Isabelle de Kievraing, Oxford, Bodleian Library, MS. Douce 118, fol. 101ᵛ, 'David en singe couronné'. © Bodleian Library, Oxford

cathédrale de Tournai (fol. 92), un lapin mange un objet rond comme le fait souvent l'insensé du psaume. Dans le psautier gantois Douce 5-6, l'école des singes occupe le bas de page (Oxford, Bodleian Library, Douce 5, fol. 146) (fig. 7); il ne s'agit certainement pas d'une coïncidence, car l'enlumineur de ce livre a trouvé une iconographie marginale appropriée pour d'autres grandes divisions du psautier. L'exemple du psautier d'Ormesby (Oxford, Bodleian Library, Douce 366, fol. 72^{r}), est l'un des plus éclairants. En choisissant de placer les tentations du Christ dans l'initiale, l'artiste renonçait à y mettre le couple plus usuel du roi et du bouffon, mais il peint dans la marge une aventure du roi Salomon et de son bouffon Marcolfe.

Les motifs provenant des initiales du psautier envahissent souvent le psautier tout entier et, au delà, peuvent être utilisés pour décorer n'importe quel type d'ouvrages. C'est le cas du fou du psaume 52, mais aussi celui du roi David jouant de la harpe qui peut devenir un singe couronné, comme dans le psautier de Geoffroy d'Aspremont et d'Isabelle de Kievraing (Oxford, Bodleian Library, Douce 118, fol. 101^{v}) (fig. 8), tandis que sa victoire sur Goliath est parodiée par celle d'un lapin terrassant un chevalier avec une fronde dans le pontifical de Renaud de Bar (Cambridge, Fitzwilliam Museum, MS. 298, fol. 7). L'apparition de tels sujets hors contexte dans ces deux derniers exemples témoigne d'une forme d'indifférence au texte. Du reste, le peintre n'a pas besoin de s'intéresser au contenu des psaumes ou même de le connaître pour parodier dans la marge un répertoire d'initiales qui lui était de toute manière familier. Mais on comprend que ces pratiques puissent égarer les chercheurs: la thématique des psaumes étant répétitive (musique, prière, triomphe sur l'ennemi, angoisse face à ses succès, péché et pénitence), la tentation est grande de chercher une allusion chaque fois, par exemple, qu'il est question de combat dans le texte, tandis que des animaux s'affrontent dans les marges.

Face à ce risque, il faudrait non seulement vérifier les contextes dans lesquels un motif est récurrent, comme y invite notre troisième règle, mais encore la récurrence des procédés d'illustration à l'intérieur d'un même ouvrage. On ne peut pourtant faire de cette vérification une quatrième règle, car ce serait présupposer une consistance du décor qui ne se vérifie que rarement. Il y a dans les manières de faire médiévales une exigence de systématicité et un manque de systématicité dont la présence simultanée nous déconcerte. Le paradoxe prend souvent la forme d'un écart entre la cohérence du projet et les aléas de la réalisation. En l'occurrence, le décor marginal met en oeuvre des procédés systématiques et répétitifs, mais il est rare que le décor d'un manuscrit se poursuive de bout en bout selon les principes adoptés dans les premières pages. Les peintres avaient certainement des difficultés à planifier correctement leur travail, à prévoir le temps nécessaire à une réalisation et à la mener à terme sans se laisser distraire par d'autres tâches, afin de respecter les délais. Il se peut aussi que l'impatience des commanditaires ait contribué à des simplifications de programme en cours de route. Nombre de décors marginaux s'arrêtent brutalement, se raréfient progressivement ou deviennent de plus en plus répétitifs et sommaires vers la fin du livre.

Il est encore plus étonnant de constater que la programmation du décor marginal devait souvent être très lâche. Il est clair qu'on décidait au départ de la fréquence des marges enluminées. Il s'agissait soit de les décorer toutes, soit de concentrer le décor marginal à un certain niveau d'articulation du texte, par exemple aux grandes divisions du psautier ou aux pages initiales des livres de la Bible. En revanche, dans une majorité de cas, aucun choix ne semble avoir été effectué entre des drôleries indépendantes du texte, comme des scènes de chasse répétitives, des illustrations du texte qui pourraient tout aussi bien se trouver dans l'initiale, comme David et Goliath au début du psautier, des parodies de l'image principale, comme des animaux associant leur chant à celui des chantres du psaume 97, '*Cantate Domino*', des compléments de l'image principale, comme des bergers complétant ceux de l'Annonce aux bergers dans les Heures de la Vierge, ou enfin des scènes renvoyant à des textes autres que celui du manuscrit, par exemple au Bestiaire ou aux fables.

On pourrait y voir une inconséquence ou supposer que l'emplacement des marges en faisait une tâche secondaire et relativement indifférente, de l'ordre du remplissage. Il est vrai que l'organisation de la page subordonne naturellement la marge et que les programmes des images principales sont en général nettement plus codifiés. Inversement, il faut admettre que dans la grande majorité des cas, le ou les mêmes peintres s'occupaient des deux parties du décor: la qualité des drôleries est rarement inférieure à celle des images principales et le peintre semble le plus souvent le même, si l'on évite de supposer des mains différentes chaque fois qu'une réduction de l'échelle entraîne une simplification des formes. Plutôt qu'une tâche de rang inférieur, le décor de la marge est un exercice plus libre, une occasion de faire place au caprice, de laisser libre cours à sa fantaisie et de stimuler celle du lecteur. En conséquence de quoi, une drôlerie faisant allusion au texte ou à l'image principale dans un manuscrit n'implique absolument pas que d'autres le fassent et, inversement, une longue série de drôleries dépourvues de signification n'exclut pas un soudain clin d'oeil à un passage qu'on désire mettre en valeur.

Le problème de l'interprétation des drôleries est encore compliqué par un ingrédient qui défie le raisonnement iconographique: le recours délibéré au non-sens. Cela ne leur est pas propre, puisque les genres poétiques du fatras et de la fatrasies reposent entièrement sur le non-sens.[34] Dans les marges comme dans ces poèmes, aucun procédé n'est plus courant que l'*adynaton*, la représentation d'objets inexistants, comme les êtres hybrides, d'événements impossibles, comme la poursuite d'un chien de chasse par un lapin, et d'actes absurdes tels que l'utilisation d'une mâchoire d'âne comme archet pour jouer de la vièle. Ces

[34] Cf. L. C. Porter, *La fatrasie et le fatras. Essai sur la poésie irrationnelle en France au Moyen Âge* (Genève: Droz, 1960).

monstruosités peuvent être produites par substitution d'un objet à un autre, ou encore par inversion des rôles, ainsi lorsque le gibier chasse le chasseur. Il n'y aurait pas de difficulté, s'il suffisait de considérer le non-sens comme un non-sens, mais il n'en va pas ainsi, car ce qui n'a pas de sens littéral peut avoir un sens symbolique. Dans certains cas, il faut admettre que la conjonction de l'inconsistance du rapport texte / image et de la propension au non-sens rend impossible de décider avec certitude si telle rencontre entre le texte et l'image est intentionnelle ou relève d'une coïncidence. Nous avons donné un exemple de ce genre, celui des lapins attaquant un château dans le bréviaire de Renaud de Bar, que Davenport met en rapport avec le texte: '*Expugna expugnantes me*'. Le problème ne concerne pas que le rapport texte / image. Comme nous l'avons déjà remarqué, le nom de 'conin' donné au lapin permet un jeu de mot obscène qui explique certainement le motif du chevalier laissant tomber son épée, terrifié par un lapin. Mais faut-il prendre chacun des milliers de conins qui habitent les marges comme une allusion sexuelle?

De fait, le conin apparaît le plus souvent dans des scènes de chasse et la chasse est à son tour une métaphore fréquente du rapport entre les sexes. En même temps, il serait impensable que la chasse et les conins ne soient pensés que dans cette dimension et que leur représentation évoque systématiquement la sexualité plutôt que l'exercice physique en plein air ou le civet. Le simple bon sens fait supposer que d'une part le contexte plus ou moins érotique de la représentation, d'autre part la tournure d'esprit du lecteur du manuscrit, grivois ou naïf, influenceront la compréhension du motif. Mais ce constat ne mène pas loin. L'idée que la signification d'un thème iconographique n'existe pas absolument, ne dépend pas de l'intention de l'artiste, mais varie selon le contexte et selon la perception du spectateur est aujourd'hui courante; elle a été adroitement théorisée pour l'image liturgique chrétienne par Staale Sinding-Larsen.[35] Elle nous semble avoir le désavantage de conduire trop aisément au présupposé que toutes les lectures se valent et sont également pertinentes pour une oeuvre, qu'il n'y en a pas de bonnes et de mauvaises. Fait-il même privilégier la lecture de la personne à laquelle l'oeuvre était destinée? Et faudrait-il accepter aussi celle que fait aujourd'hui l'étudiant débutant, lorsqu'il confond les attributs des saints? Cette conception de l'iconographie pourrait être baptisée, de manière un peu malveillante, le point de vue du consommateur. Elle témoigne en tout cas d'un rapport à l'oeuvre qui privilégie le spectateur et la réduit à son utilisation, à sa consommation en somme. Deux ouvrages influents ont beaucoup fait, chacun à sa manière, pour légitimer cette attitude: la *Phénoménologie de la perception* de Merleau-Ponty et *Le musée imaginaire* de Malraux. Dans les deux cas, l'oeuvre est réduite à la perception d'un Français du milieu du siècle que son éducation pousse à fréquenter les musées.

---

[35] S. Sinding-Larsen, *Iconography and Ritual. A Study of Analytical Perspectives* (Oslo: Universitetsforlaget, 1984), pp. 147 et ss.

Même s'il était possible de spéculer avec quelques chances de succès sur la psychologie du spectateur médiéval, ce serait de toute manière secondaire par rapport à la compréhension de l'oeuvre comme un dispositif pensé par son auteur à l'aide de codes, pour être compris par des destinataires compétents. Cela ne signifie pas que l'artiste ait nécessairement prévu une lecture unique et univoque de l'oeuvre. Une représentation littérale du sacrifice d'Abraham doit être identifiée comme telle pour avoir un sens, mais elle peut se prêter à plusieurs lectures typologiques également acceptables. Le sculpteur d'un crucifix n'attend probablement pas les mêmes réactions des différents publics auquel il sera exposé. Pourtant, l'image est précisément codée et l'identification du supplicié comme le bon ou le mauvais larron serait une erreur inexcusable de la part d'un chrétien jouissant de toutes ses facultés. Cette affirmation ne nous contraint pas à considérer que chaque lapin est ou n'est pas un symbole sexuel. Il faudrait pour cela qu'un code ait été mis en oeuvre pour lever l'ambiguïté, par exemple qu'un attribut particulier soit affectée au lapin lorsqu'il joue ce rôle. On remarquera au contraire deux choses: d'une part, que l'attribution d'une valeur symbolique, sérieuse ou ludique, à un motif marginal, se faisait généralement sans crier gare; d'autre part, que la notion de symbole sexuel n'existait pas au Moyen Âge et que l'artiste ne risquait pas plus de signaler de tels symboles que de mesurer en centimètres les dimensions d'une enluminure.

Conclusion

Entre la négation du sens des drôleries par Mâle et la recherche d'un sens spirituel à chaque drôlerie par Davenport, il y a place pour une interprétation satisfaisante. Il faut partir du constat que la densité iconographique de la marge est le plus souvent faible. La grande majorité des motifs qui la peuplent évoquent le monde de la chasse, de la musique, de la danse et des jeux, dans le but de flatter les goûts d'une clientèle aristocratique dont ce sont les passe-temps. Dans certains cas, comme le psautier d'Isabelle de France, reine d'Angleterre (Munich, Bayerische Staatsbibliothek, Cod. gall. 16), le commanditaire semble avoir désiré pour un livre liturgique un décor plus conforme à sa fonction et demandé le remplacement total ou partiel des drôleries par des illustrations marginales. Dans d'autres cas, comme dans le psautier-heures de Jeoffroy d'Aspremont et d'Isabelle de Kievraing, une allusion au texte sacré de temps à autre semble servir de légitimation aux drôleries. Mais la majorité des allusions qu'on peut déceler dans les marges n'ont aucun caractère dévot et sont destinées à provoquer le rire ou le sourire, ainsi lorsqu'on se moque de la couardise du chevalier, de la lubricité du moine ou même du sacrement de la messe.

‘Primitive’ paintings: the visual world of populus rusticus

Helena Edgren

Most medieval pictures dealt with in (art) historical research and writing are bound together by one common trait: They are all part of the same European artistic tradition. The pictures may vary as to the degree of skill with which they have been executed, but they can all be thought of as fruits of the same tradition. The meaning of the pictures, their inner content, is not always clear and obvious, but each individual image can be studied by comparing it with other pictorial products of the same age, or through the use of literary sources. All of these works of art represent a common, Pan-European culture rooted in the civilizations of Antiquity and fostered by, or connected to, the Catholic Church.

Nevertheless, in the Scandinavian countries, as elsewhere in Europe, there also flourished another kind of medieval art, the so-called ‘primitive’ paintings, whose creators were not professional artists trained in the European painting tradition (fig. 1). This was a widespread phenomenon: Finland has about 100 surviving medieval churches, and roughly half of these contain ‘primitive’ paintings. In Denmark, ‘primitive’ paintings have been recorded from some 150 churches to date.[1] In both Finland and Denmark, ‘primitive’ paintings were

---

[1] Ulla Haastrup, ‘Danske kalkmalerier 1475–1500’, in *Danske kalkmalerier. Sengotik 1475–1500*, ed. by Ulla Haastrup (Copenhagen: Nationalmuseet, 1991), p. 26; Katrin Kröll, ‘Die Komik des grotesken Körpers in der christlichen Bildkunst des Mittelalters’, in *Mein ganzer Körper ist Gesicht. Groteske Darstellungen in der Europäischen Kunst und Literatur des Mittelalters*, ed. by Katrin Kröll and Hugo Steger Steen (Freiburg im

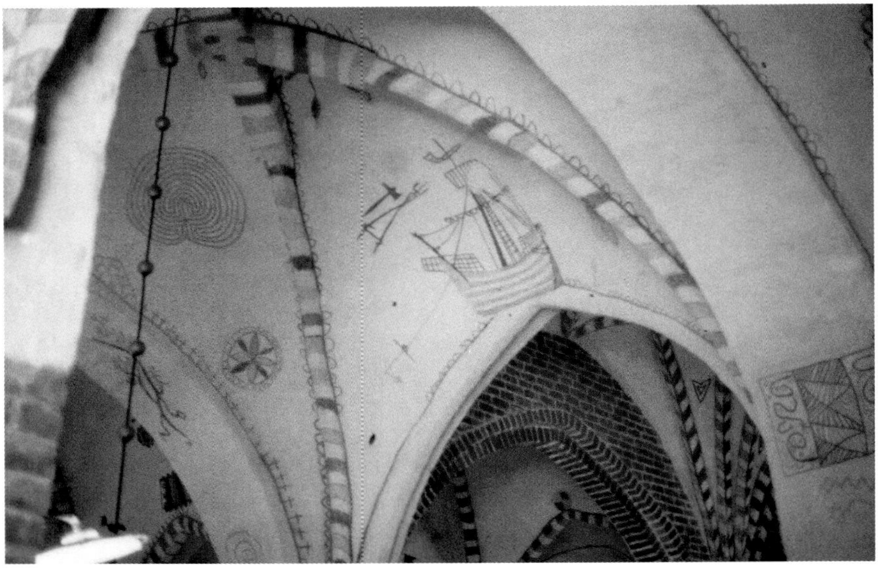

Fig. 1. Church of St Mary (Maaria), Southern Finland, 'Primitive paintings'. © Author

probably more numerous early on, but in the course of time they have been replaced by newer and more professionally executed illustrations. Many medieval church paintings are still to be found beneath the plaster. Accurate figures are not available for Swedish paintings, since they have not been studied as systematically as their Finnish and Danish counterparts. The 'primitive' paintings still suffer from the label of 'second-rate art' that they received a hundred years ago, and consequently they have not been able to compete with finer paintings for the attention of art historians. They are also much more difficult to interpret than so-called finer art. As a Swedish example of the genre one could mention St Birgitta's own convent church in Vadstena, where paintings classifiable as 'primitive' adorn the high vaults.

'Primitive' art, however, is not limited to paintings on the plastered walls of stone churches. A large number of carvings, found on the walls of Norway's wooden stave churches, belong to the same class of art (fig. 2). The Norwegian carvings have not been sketched on the wall with pigment but, rather, have been cut into the wall boards with a sharp utensil such as a knife. As the walls have become soiled and darkened during the centuries, the carvings have become very

Breisgau: Rombach, 1994), pp. 11–105; Steen Schjødt Christensen, 'Mysterious Images—Grimacing, Grotesques, Obscene, Popular: Anti- or Commentary Images?', *Medium Aevum Quotidianum*, 39 (1998), 55–75.

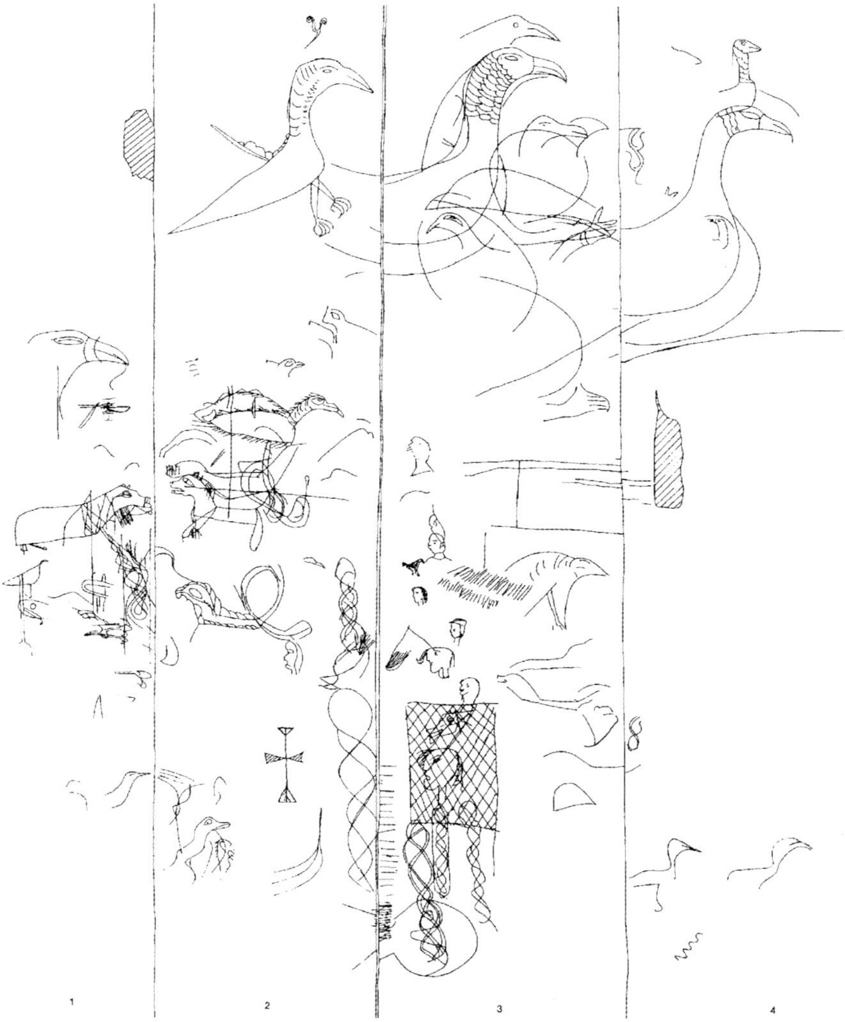

Fig. 2. Church of Borgund, Norway, 'Graffiti', from Martin Blindheim, Grafitti in Norwegian Stave churches c. 1150–c. 1350 *(Oslo: Universitetsforlaget, 1985)*

obscure. Their existence only became generally known in art-historical circles in 1985, when Martin Blindheim published his exhaustive study: *Graffiti in Norwegian Stave Churches.*[2]

[2] Martin Blindheim, *Graffiti in Norwegian Stave Churches c.1150–c.1350. Medieval Art in Norway* (Oslo: Universitetsforlaget, 1985).

A large number of similar carvings have been recorded in the churches of Gotland, where the figures have been scratched in the wall plaster. Carvings have been found mainly on the interior surfaces of the walls, but in some cases also on exterior surfaces.[3]

What, then, are these 'primitive' paintings and carvings? Who made them, and on whose order? What is their content? What do they tell us about the people who made them and perceived them, about how they conceived themselves and their world? Many questions concerning these pictures have yet to be satisfactorily answered. From the beginning, art historians have been totally baffled by these paintings. They have always been thought of as representing the 'others', the 'populus rusticus' who, in the Middle Ages, formed a group of their own, unreachable by ordinary research methods because they left such scant traces of themselves in written documents.

In Finland, the first 'primitive' paintings were discovered in 1880 (fig. 3). The study of medieval wall paintings had begun about ten years earlier and had produced some impressive results: paintings, which could not be compared to anything known thus far from the other Nordic countries. When paintings of a totally different kind appeared from under the plaster in 1880, art historians were both surprised and helpless; they felt totally incapable of interpreting and understanding this new art form (fig. 4). In his research report, one art historian described how impossible it was to describe what he observed: 'Formulating the description turned out to be somewhat more problematic than I had expected. Due to the extraordinary ornaments that differ from anything that one normally sees in *in secco* painting. [. . .] I had to try to develop a new kind of terminology in order to be able to give the reader at least some form of verbal description of what the eye perceived'.[4] Here was, in an extreme form, the art historian's perpetual problem how to render the visual world into words.

The first reaction of the art historians was not a clear rejection but, rather, a hopeful curiosity. Emil Nervander, one of Finland's leading art historians in the late nineteenth century, recorded the paintings carefully and even planned to publish them as a series of lithograph plates. He saw in them a trace of 'Irish style mixed with recollections of Swedish rock carvings' and dated them to the thirteenth century, when the Catholic Church finally had secured its position in Finland.[5] However, just to be on the safe side, he also wrote to the celebrated

---

[3] Uaininn O'Meadhra, 'Medeltida ristningar i Gotlands kyrkor', *Hikuin* 24 (1997), 229–31.

[4] Emil Nervander's 1900 report (on the wall-paintings of Pernå church) lodged in the topographical archive of the Helsinki National Board of Antiquities Department of History: *Berättelse om verkställ undersökning af Pernå kyrkas kalkmålningar afgifven af E. Nervander 15.1.1900*; Helena Edgren, *Primitiva målningar? Bild och känsla från antik till nyantik*, Picta Nr. 3 (Åbo: Åbo Akademi, 1994).

[5] Edgren (as in note 4).

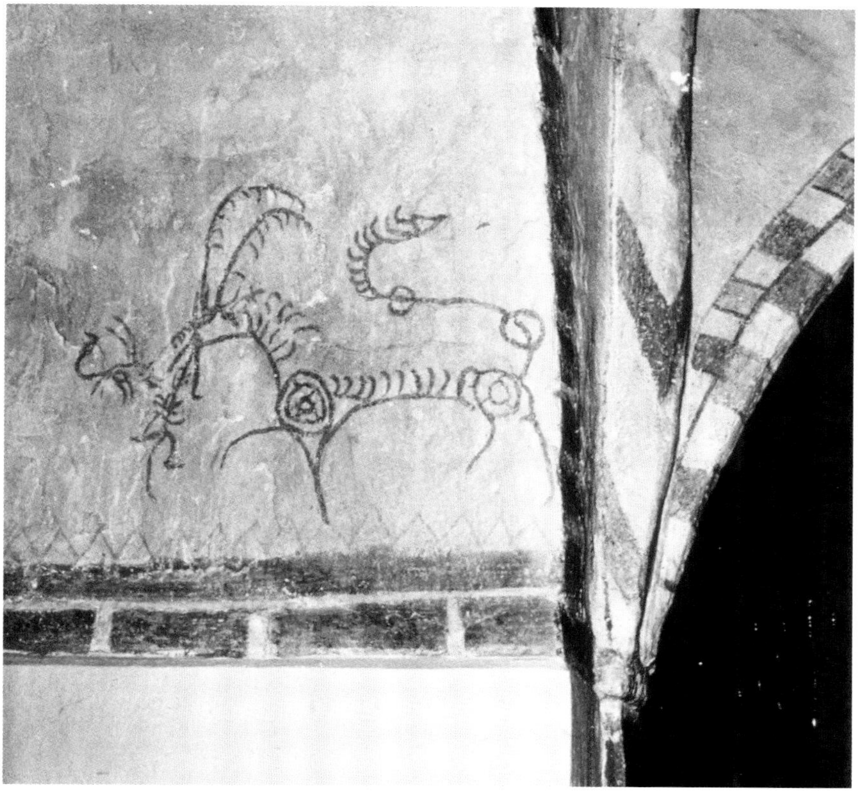

Fig. 3. Church of Nousiainen, Southern Finland, 'Primitive painting'. © National Board of Antiquities, Picture Archives

director of the Danish National Museum, Sophus Müller, and asked for his opinion on the paintings. Müller's answer was crushing. He saw no evidence of Celtic or thirteenth-century influence; instead, he thought the paintings were considerably later and totally unsuitable for publication or study. A few might be recorded as examples of the art form, but the rest were not worth wasting one's time on. Müller thought the paintings were extremely primitive, an appellation they have borne from that day onwards. Nervander, honest scientist that he was, published his correspondence with Müller and abandoned his project.[6] Müller's negative stance came to dominate the attitudes of later generations of art historians toward this genre, and in many cases has continued to do so to this

[6] Emil Nervander's report on Sophus Müller's 1903 comments on the wall-paintings of Nousis church, lodged at the Suomen museum in Helsinki: *Uttalande af Sophus Müller om kalkmålningarna i Nousis kyrka (Suomen museo, 1903).*

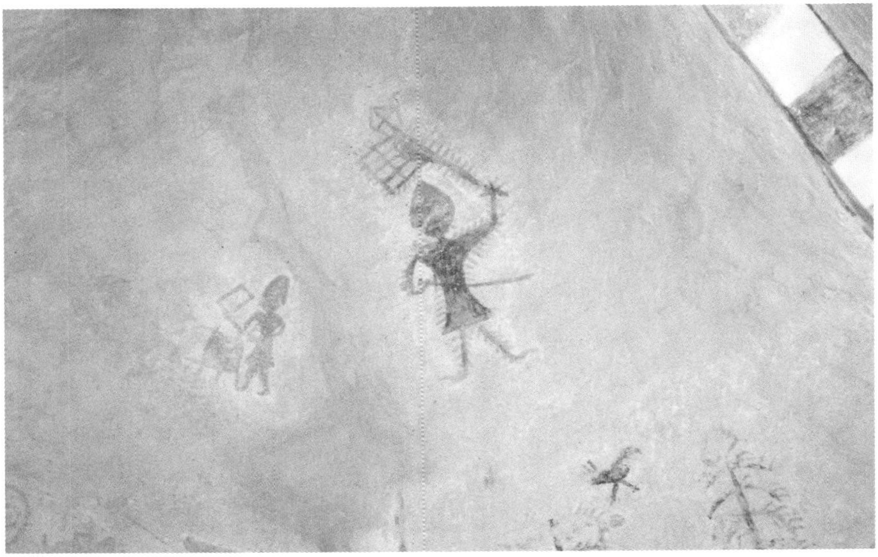

Fig. 4. Church of Nousiainen, 'Primitive paintings'. © Author

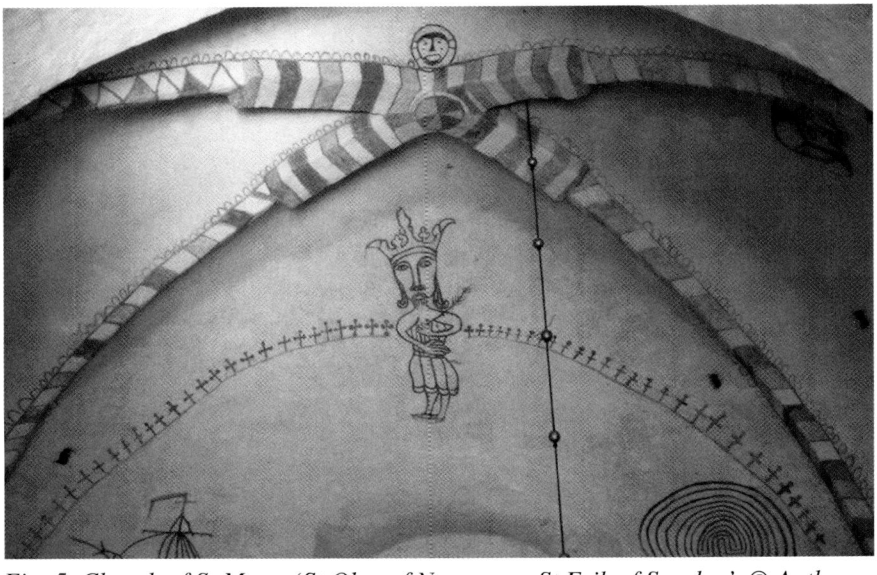

Fig. 5. Church of St Mary, 'St Olav of Norway or St Erik of Sweden'. © Author

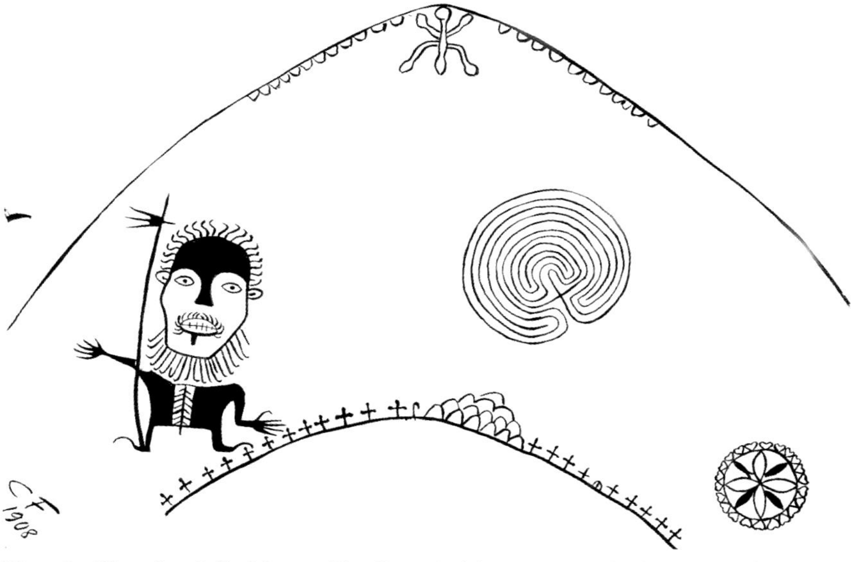

Fig. 6. Church of St Mary, 'Devil, primitive painting'. © National Board of Antiquities, Picture Archives

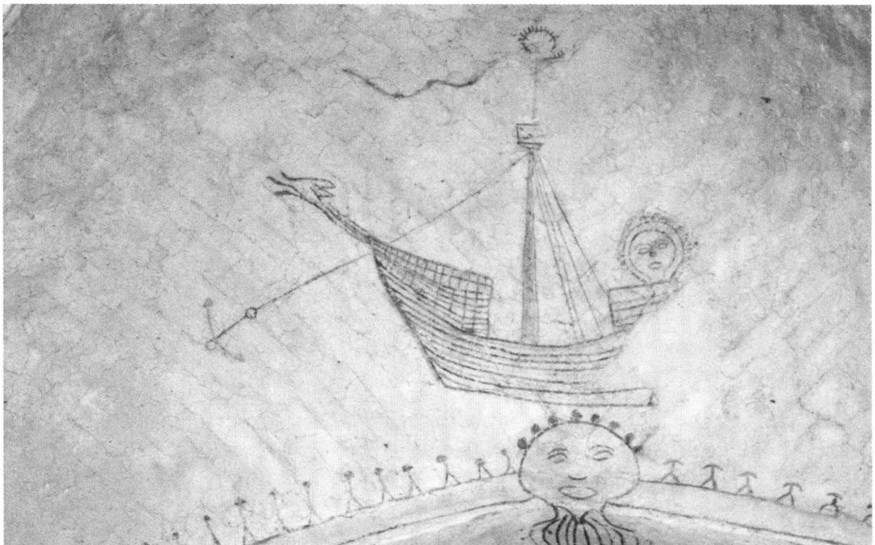

Fig. 7. Church of Korppoo, Southern Finland, 'Ship', probably depicting the journey of St Olav of Norway to Finland. © Author

day. Many of the 'primitive' paintings uncovered during the nineteenth century were actually recorded on paper or film but were afterwards covered up again.[7] Only towards the end of the twentieth century have we begun to uncover them once more from underneath the plaster. The 'primitive' paintings of Finland now have been added to an iconographic catalogue based on the standard Nordic model, though their description and classification continue to pose great problems. The first Finnish study on 'primitive' paintings was published in the 1970s,[8] but serious general art-historical interest in the genre has caught on only during the last decade. Previously, 'primitive' paintings received just a passing mention, if even that.

The motifs in these 'primitive' paintings and carvings were largely the same, but certain differences also can be noted. The differences are partly caused by the wide age distribution of the paintings and carvings. The carvings in the stave churches date from between 1150 and 1350.[9] The Gotland carvings date from the thirteenth century to the end of the Middle Ages and the beginning of the Modern Era,[10] and the Finnish and Danish paintings primarily stem from the late fifteenth century.[11]

The edging ornaments found on vault ribs appear only in painted form. These ornaments include different kinds of plant, cross, and roundel patterns. The diverse individual motifs, on the other hand, are shared by both the paintings and the carvings. These motifs include various kinds of human figures, such as clear representations of saints (fig. 5), musicians, soldiers, artisans, and other less easily interpreted figures. The individual 'personages' portrayed also include several unmistakable devils (fig. 6). The numerous animal figures include horses, birds, dogs, foxes, lions, and dragons. Of these, the horses and lions are especially typical in the stave church carvings. In Norway, horses have been thought to refer to the old Nordic horse cult, while the lions have been considered to reflect both the domestic tradition and a strong influence of the Romanesque art of continental Europe.[12] The motifs also include various kinds of ornaments and magical signs known from later folk art, including looped crosses and pentagrams. Other common motifs are labyrinth patterns and various kinds of ships and boats (fig. 7).

---

[7] C. Frankenhaeuser, 'Räntämäen kirkko II. Maalaukset', *Suomen museo* (1910), 9–12.

[8] Anna-Lisa Stigell, 'Kyrkans tecken och årets gång. Tideräkningen och Finlands primitiva medeltidsmålningar', *Finska Fornminnesföreningens Tidskrift* 77 (1974).

[9] Blindheim (as in note 2).

[10] O'Meadhra (as in note 3), p. 227.

[11] Ulla Haastrup, 'Danske kalkmalerier 1475–1500', in *Danske kalkmalerier. Sengotik 1475–1500*, ed. by Ulla Haastrup and Robert Egevang (Copenhagen: Nationalmuseet, 1991), p. 26; Edgren (as in note 4); Steen Schjødt Christensen (as in note 1).

[12] Blindheim (as in note 2), pp. 60–63.

Rune texts also are found in Denmark, Sweden, and Norway. Some of these are clear textual wholes, often with a religious content. Others are individual runes, which have been considered magical marks used to ward off evil. In Finland, where runes were not used, known texts were written in the Latin alphabet. These also included both actual texts and others that try to look like text but are unreadable, as well as individual characters, such as Virgin Mary monograms (fig. 8).

'Primitive' art also employs a large selection of Christian symbols, such as the Tree of Life and various types of crosses. Coats of arms are also common (fig. 9). All of these have been studied to some extent using art-historical methods, that is, analyses of content, contacts with other forms of visual art, and style, so I will not dwell upon this aspect any further. I will instead attempt to set myself outside the sphere of actual art-historical research and use the paintings as historical sources. In other words, I shall present a few attempts at interpreting whose worldview this form of art reflected, who painted them, who determined their content, and what sort of spiritual contacts the pictures describe. In order to achieve this goal, one must first reject the tenacious preconceptions concerning the reception of the paintings during the era in which they were originally painted, in other words, what the medieval person would have thought of them. The traditionally doubtful and negative attitude and the strangeness or 'otherness' of the 'primitive' paintings have the effect that art historians sometimes, even nowadays, find it hard to believe that they have not always been looked upon with a similar feeling of disdain. As late as 1997, a publication on the Gotland material poses questions like 'Who has doodled and sketched on the church walls during the Middle Ages, and why? How could it have been allowed? Was it done in secrecy, or with the permission of the priest?'[13] When one looks at 'primitive' paintings without preconceptions, however, it seems clear that they were as accepted in their own time as any other form of ecclesiastical art. This, at least, was the situation in Finland.[14]

The situation can be illustrated by a few examples. Perhaps the most convincing of these is the fact that 'primitive' paintings are found even in Finland's central shrine, the bishop's own cathedral in Turku (fig. 10). It is quite inconceivable that images not approved by ecclesiastical authority could have been painted in a cathedral where the bishop and his clergy celebrated mass daily, and where devotional activities continued at the numerous altars almost without break from dawn till dusk. If any inappropriate paintings had appeared on the cathedral walls, one cannot doubt that they would have been promptly removed. The 'primitive' paintings, however, are still there.

There are also cases where the 'primitive' paintings that had been acquired in

---

[13] O'Meadhra (as in note 3), p. 234.

[14] Edgren (as in note 4).

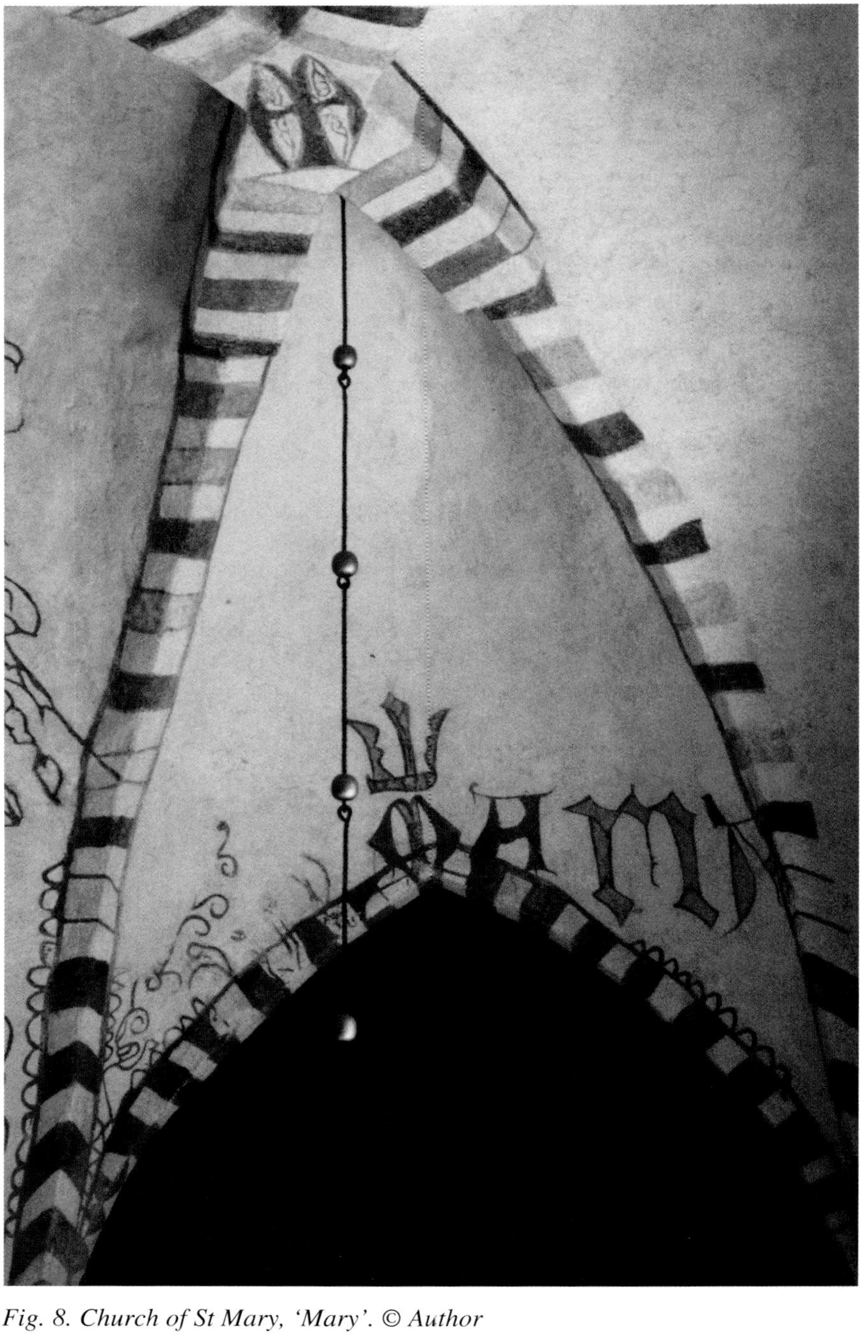

Fig. 8. Church of St Mary, 'Mary'. © Author

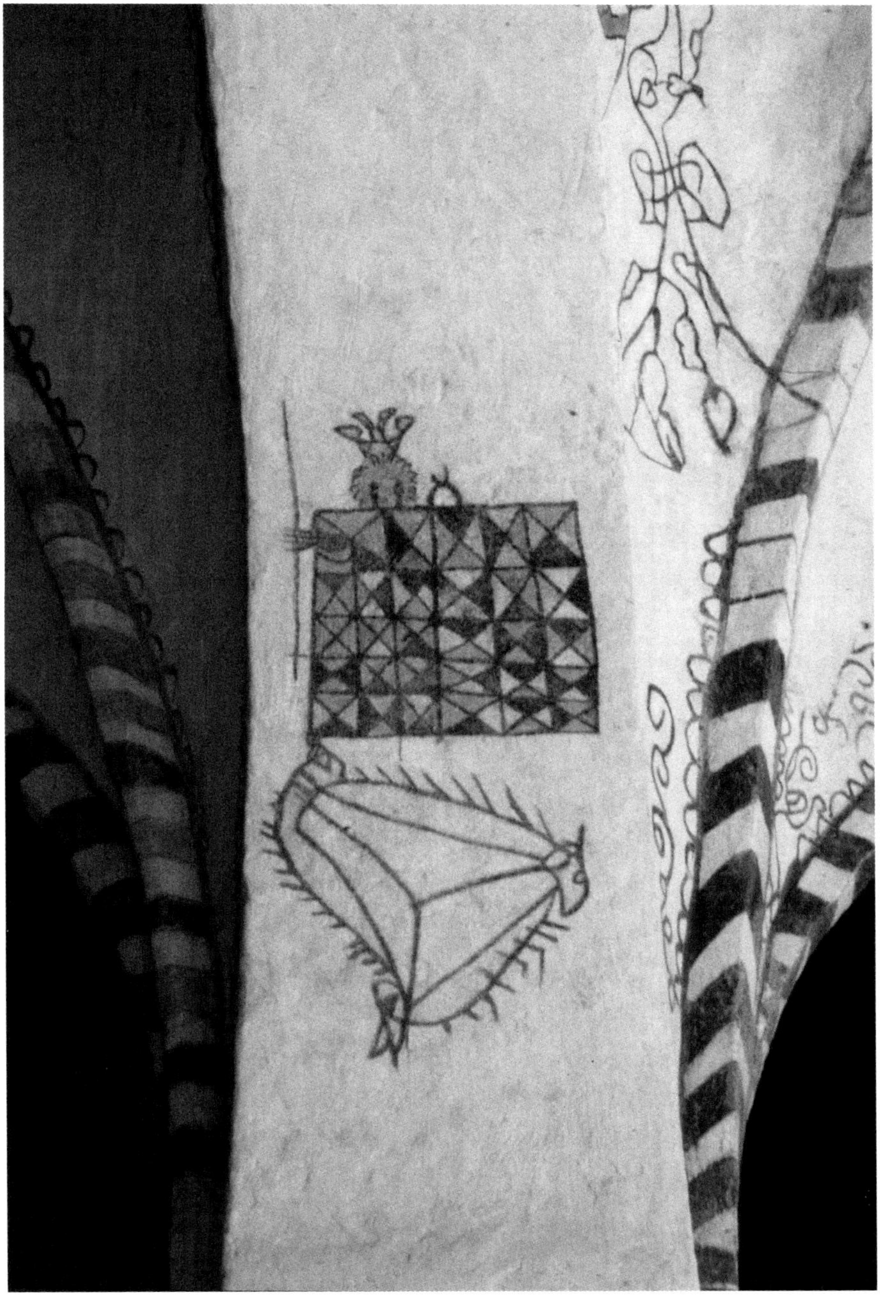

Fig. 9. Church of St Mary, 'Coat of arms'. © Author

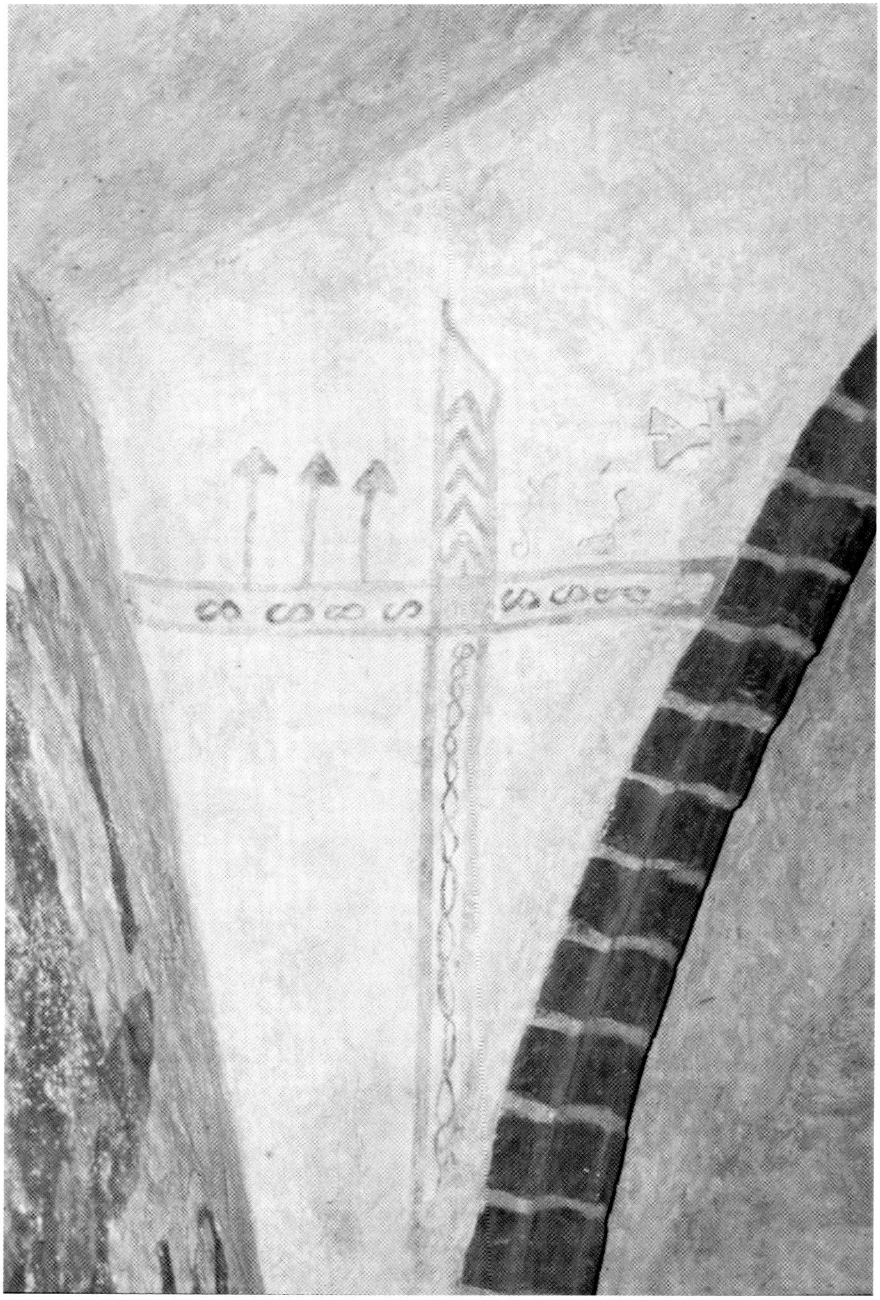

Fig. 10. Cathedral of Turku, 'Primitive painting'. © Author

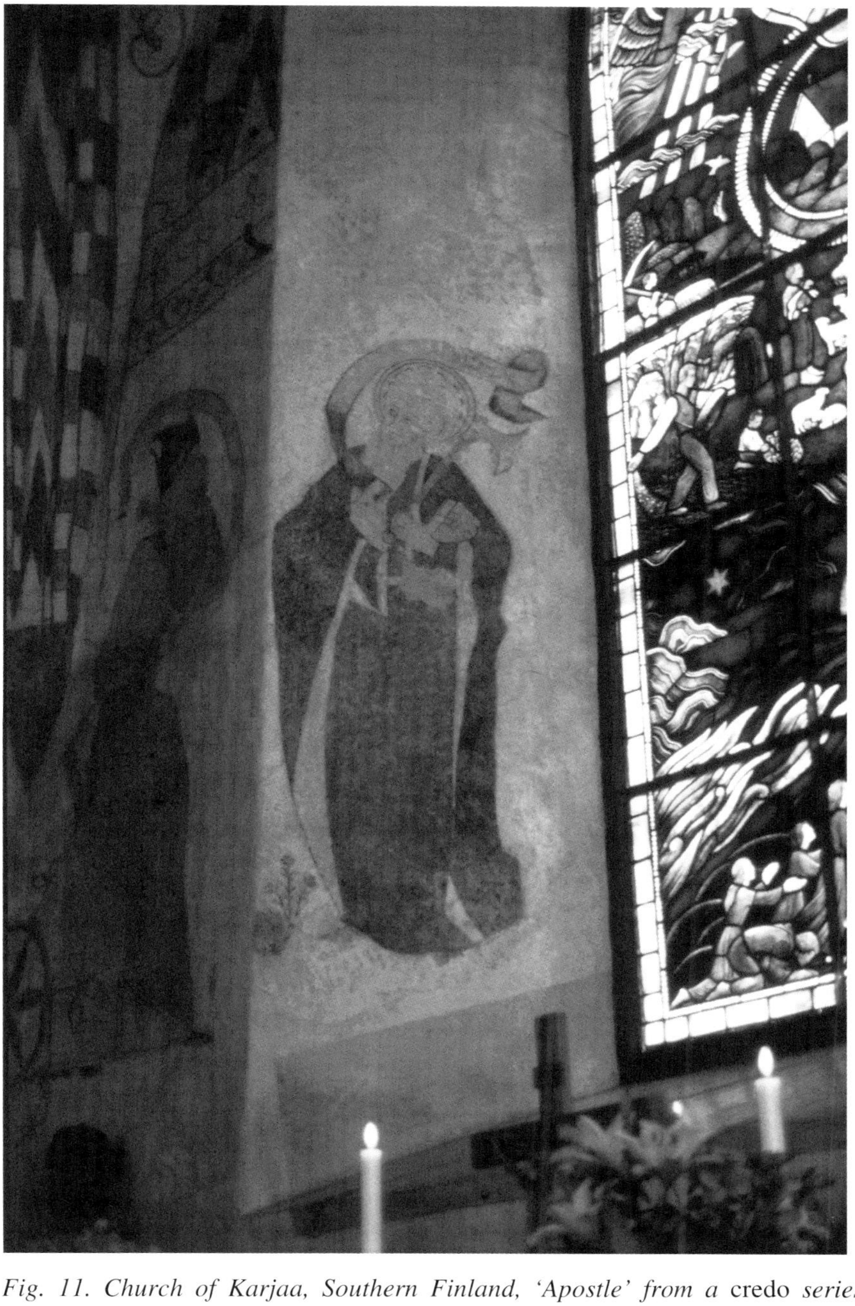

Fig. 11. Church of Karjaa, Southern Finland, 'Apostle' from a credo *series.*
© Author

connection with the building of the church or the erection of the ceiling vaults remained uncovered when so-called finer paintings were ordered. This is the case in, for example, the Karjaa church on the south coast, where 'primitive' paintings adorn the vaults while finer paintings cover the walls. The situation at Karjaa is exceptional in the sense that both series of paintings have been executed on the same plaster surface. Their age difference cannot therefore be very great, and both in fact have been dated to the 1470s based on a painted date that appears among the 'primitive' paintings. We are thus dealing with a case where someone, perhaps a member of the building team, finished the work by decorating the vaults with 'primitive' paintings. As soon as the congregation's finances allowed it or a suitable painter was found, the walls were decorated with an impressive *credo* mural (fig. 11). The 'primitive' paintings, however, suffered no harm because of this operation; instead, the two series of paintings form a single entity. The local patrons thus accepted both equally as decorations to their church.

Danish art historians have wondered why the churches should have suddenly been content to have *in secco* paintings composed of scattered, apparently meaningless ornaments and figures, even though instructive and content-charged murals were being created at the same time. How could such pictures have satisfied patrons whose taste, under the influence of a lengthy tradition, had become accustomed to images with a clearly defined theological content?[15] One possible answer lies in recalling the generally known fact that the primary value of the paintings lay not in their aesthetic appearance but, rather, in their symbolic meaning. One also can ask, what was the aesthetic training of the medieval person? Most people, including the clergy and the lay public, had none at all. The visual arts were not represented in any way in the curricula of medieval schools and universities.[16] The wealthy, and those who had studied abroad, might have seen fine art, but this hardly applied to the domestically trained rural clergy or the lower nobility. Educational books were normally cheap copies with no illustrations. Illustrated versions were available only to the wealthy few. For most people, the only contact with the visual arts was through cheap woodcuts, which were also often extremely clumsy. At least in Finland, only the richest and best-trained classes had permanent access to the products of the European painting tradition. Judging from heraldic church paintings (coats of arms) (fig. 12), they were also the people who ordered most of the high-quality paintings.[17]

---

[15] Haastrup (as in note 11), pp. 27–28.

[16] Jussi Nuorteva, *Suomalaisten ulkomainen opinkäynti ennen Turun akatemian perustamista 1640* Suomen kirkkohistoriallinen seura (Helsinki: Suomen kirkkohistoriallinen seura, 1997).

[17] Camilla Ahlström-Taavitsainen, *Vapenbilder bland kalkmålningarna i Finlands medeltidskyrkor* in *Publikationer utgivna av konsthistoriska institutionen vid Helsingfors*

The 'primitive' paintings, however, also include a large number of coats of arms and ownership marks. That indicates that both the clergy and the local persons of note wanted to be remembered for their part in building and decorating the churches and, as Ulla Haastrup has noted, to be symbolically present at the celebration of Mass.[18] The paintings therefore cannot be connected with only the lowest class. Rather, they represent the common aspirations of the whole congregation.

There are cases from both Finland and Denmark where a construction team that had been working on a church painted 'primitive' decorations on the walls and vaults as a parting shot, as it were.[19] By the late fifteenth century, the paintings had become such an essential part of the church interior that the church was not considered 'finished' without them. Both countries also had identifiable groups of painters who worked on several different churches. The Danes have even started to refer to 'primitive' paintings as 'murermesterbemalinger' (master mason paintings).[20] In Finland, however, this explanation does not cover the whole field. For instance, some churches have 'primitive' paintings dating from periods that cannot be connected with any notable construction episode. In one case, several images of ships have been painted on the same place on the church wall, so that the older figures were superimposed.[21] These are votive paintings, forerunners of the later custom of giving ship-models to the church as votive offerings.

Although a local building team might have executed the paintings, this does not mean that the team or the master builder made the final decision on the choice of motifs and the meaning content. Even when the paintings are purely ornamental decorations devoid of figurative representations, the paintings may nevertheless have a deep religious significance.[22] This is the case in, for example, the church of Finström in the Åland Islands, where the clumsy stars in the vaults portray the history of the world, from the Creation to the Last Judgement.[23]

Even in cases where it is difficult to see any coherent plan and the placement of the paintings appears totally fortuitous, one must take into account the general rules and regulations concerning the acquisition of pictures by churches. One

---

universitet. 8 (Helsingfors: Helsingfors universitet, 1984).

[18] Haastrup (as in note 11), p. 26.

[19] In Denmark, see Haastrup (as in note 11), p. 28. In Finland, e.g., Karjaa church, Southern Finland.

[20] e.g. Haastrup (as in note 11), p. 26.

[21] Maaria (St. Mary) church in Finland proper.

[22] Compare Niels M. Saxtorph, 'Markblomstmaleren, nogle værksteder', in *Danske kalkmalerier. Sengotik 1475–1500* (as in note 11), p. 89.

[23] Valdemar Nyman, *Ålands medeltida kyrkokonst. Det åländska folkets historia 1,2.* (Mariehamn: Ålands kulturstiftelse, 1980), p. 98.

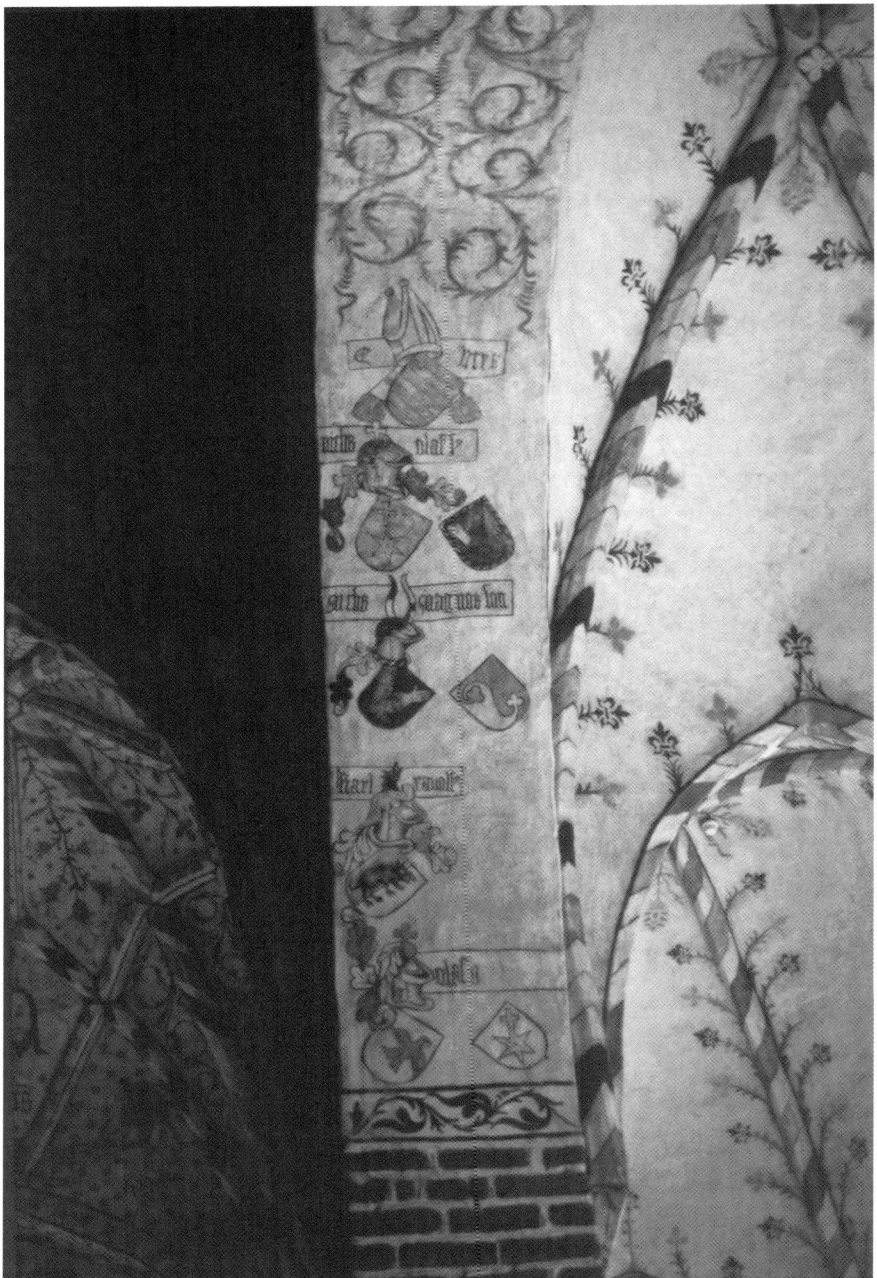

Fig. 12. Church of Taivassalo, Southern Finland, 'Coat of arms'. © Author

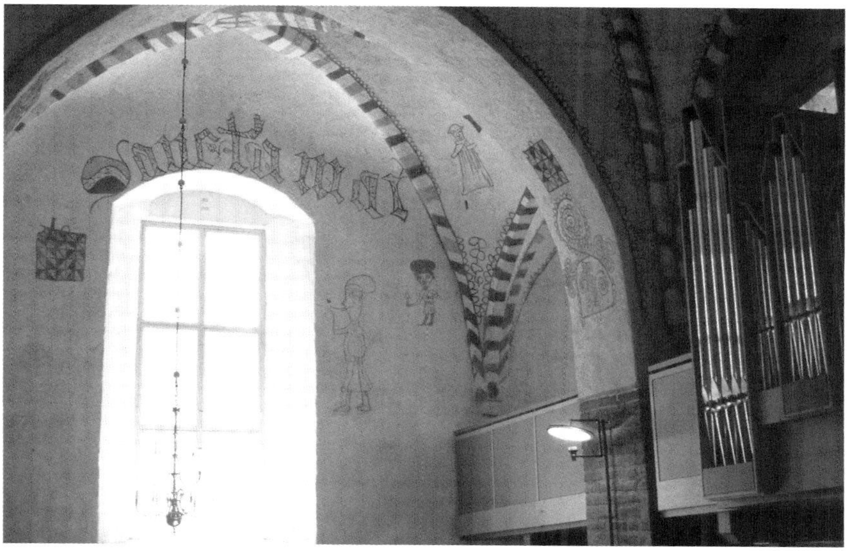

Fig. 13. Church of St Mary, 'Master mason and his assistant'. © Author

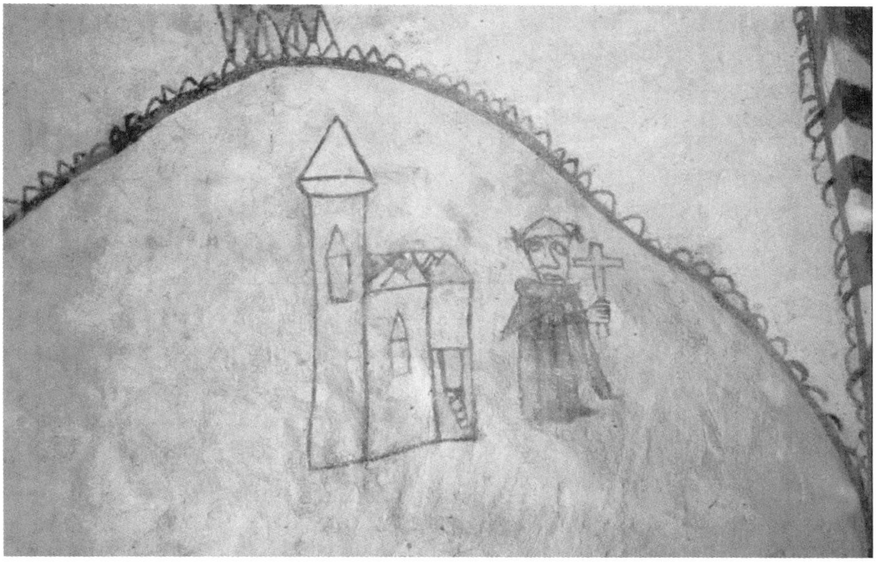

Fig. 14. Church of St Mary, 'Dominican friar'. © Author

Finnish example of control by ecclesiastical authorities dates from the 1480s, when the bishop and chapter of Turku forbad the churches to hire artisans, including painters, without the chapter's approval. Not even votive offerings could be brought to the church without the local priest's permission.[24] This order sometimes has been considered to reflect the clergy's negative attitude towards 'primitive' paintings,[25] but it is, in fact, just one of a series of medieval statutes also known from other countries besides Finland. Whatever the nature of the 'primitive' paintings, we must assume that they were approved at least by the local priest or clergy, who also, most likely, had a say as to their content. The background of the rural parish priest was probably only a little different from that of his parishioners, and their worldview would have been largely identical, characterized by the same traditional beliefs and notions.

Finally, I would like to present two Finnish churches as examples of the wide range and variability of 'primitive' paintings. One is the church of Maaria in western Finland, dedicated to St Mary, and the other is the church of Pyhtää in eastern Finland, consecrated to St Henry of Finland. Maaria church lies only some ten kilometres from Turku, the country's medieval centre, and thus was located within the immediate sphere of influence of the bishop himself. The church building has been thought to emulate Turku Cathedral in its vault structure. Nevertheless, the paintings in this church represent the 'primitive' style in its most disorganized form. The walls and vaults are full of individual figures. Most of these have a Christian content, but their mutual placement does not appear to be governed by any clear principle. Some of the figures also represent a pictorial world that has no connection with Christian tradition.

The decoration of the third vault of the north aisle has the clearest structure. The vault panels contain both texts and monograms that refer to the Virgin Mary, and in all probability the vault has been the site of an altar consecrated to Our Lady. On the north wall, two human figures are clearly benefactor portraits (fig. 13). They are probably the master builder of the church and his assistant, who have placed themselves under the perpetual protection of the Holy Virgin.[26] Another vault contains a different 'portrait', a Dominican friar standing in front of a small church and holding a cross in his hand (fig. 14). The Dominicans were the most prominent ecclesiastical order in Finland, and the sight must have been familiar to all parishioners.[27] The paintings also include several obvious

---

[24] *Finlands medeltidsurkunder*, ed. by Reinhold Hausen, 8 vols (Helsingfors: Statsarkivet, 1910–35), *IV: 1451–1480*, document 3853.

[25] Tove Riska, *Keskiajan maalaustaide. Ars. Suomen taide 1* (Helsinki: Weilin & Göös, 1987), p. 144.

[26] Helena Edgren, *Donatorsfrågor* (Helsinki: Suomen museo, 1989).

[27] Helena Edgren, 'Dominikanbrodern i S. Marie kyrka', in *Den monastiska bildvärlden i Norden, Föredrag vid det 10:e nordiska symposiet för ikonografiska studier*

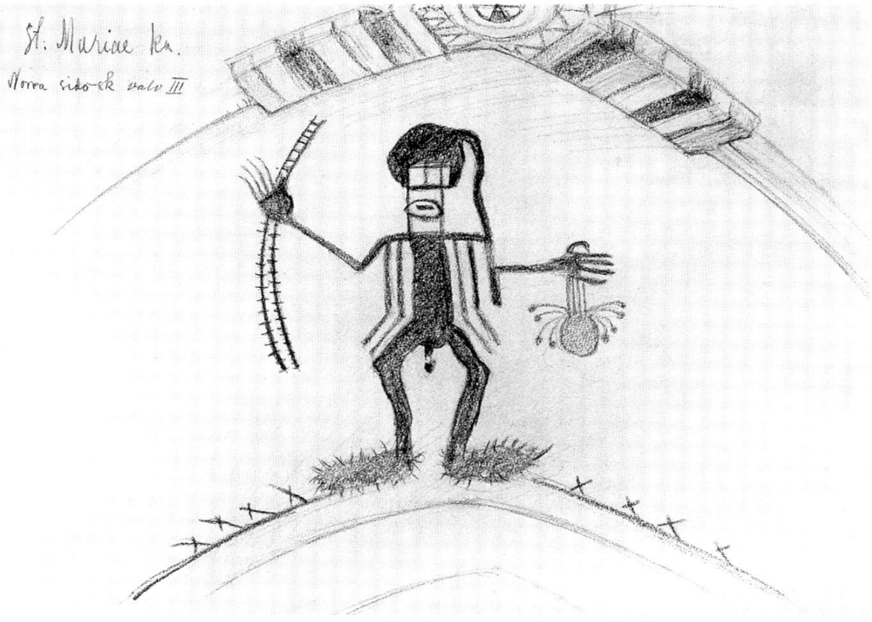

Fig. 15. Church of St Mary, 'Devil'. © National Board of Antiquities, Picture Archives

references to saints, including a ship with crew presumably portraying the journey of St Olaf. A song describing this journey was a part of the standard repertoire of pilgrims visiting the grave of St Olaf in Trondheim.[28] Perhaps the most striking of the figures nevertheless may be the Devil (fig. 15), who undoubtedly has been included as a warning against the greatest temptations of the male world: the excessive craving for money and sexual pleasures. In 1910, when the paintings were studied for the first time, the figure was considered so indecent that it was immediately covered up.[29]

In the church of Pyhtää the situation is totally different. In spite of their 'primitive' nature, the paintings form a coherent whole with a lucid theological content. In this case, the guiding influence of a trained theologian, the local vicar, is indisputable. Among the 'primitive' coats of arms, one might have belonged to the vicar who was in office when the paintings were made. The Pyhtää church

---

i Vadstena 1986, ed. by Ann Catherine Bonnier, Mereth Lindgren, and Marian Ullén (Stockholm: ICO/Riksantikvarieämbetet, 1990), pp. 11–16.

[28] Lindgren, Mereth, 'St. Olav in der mittelalterlichen Malerei Mittelschwedens. St Olav, seine Zeit und sein Kult', *Acta visbyensia* VI. *Visbysymposiet för historiska vetenskaper* (1979).

[29] Frankenhaeuser, *Räntämäen kirkko* (as in note 7).

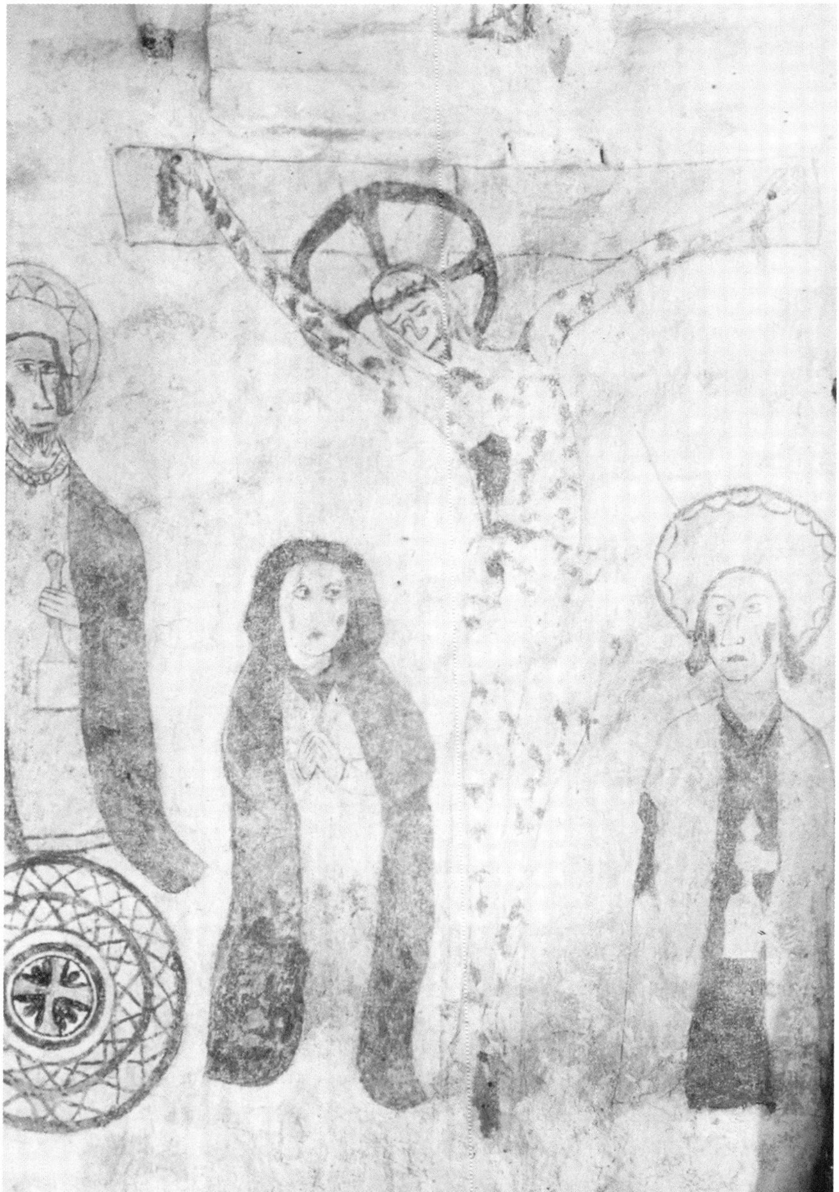

Fig. 16. Church of Pyhtää, Southern Finland, 'Figures from a credo *series and Christ on the Cross'. © Finnish National Board of Antiquities, Picture Archives*

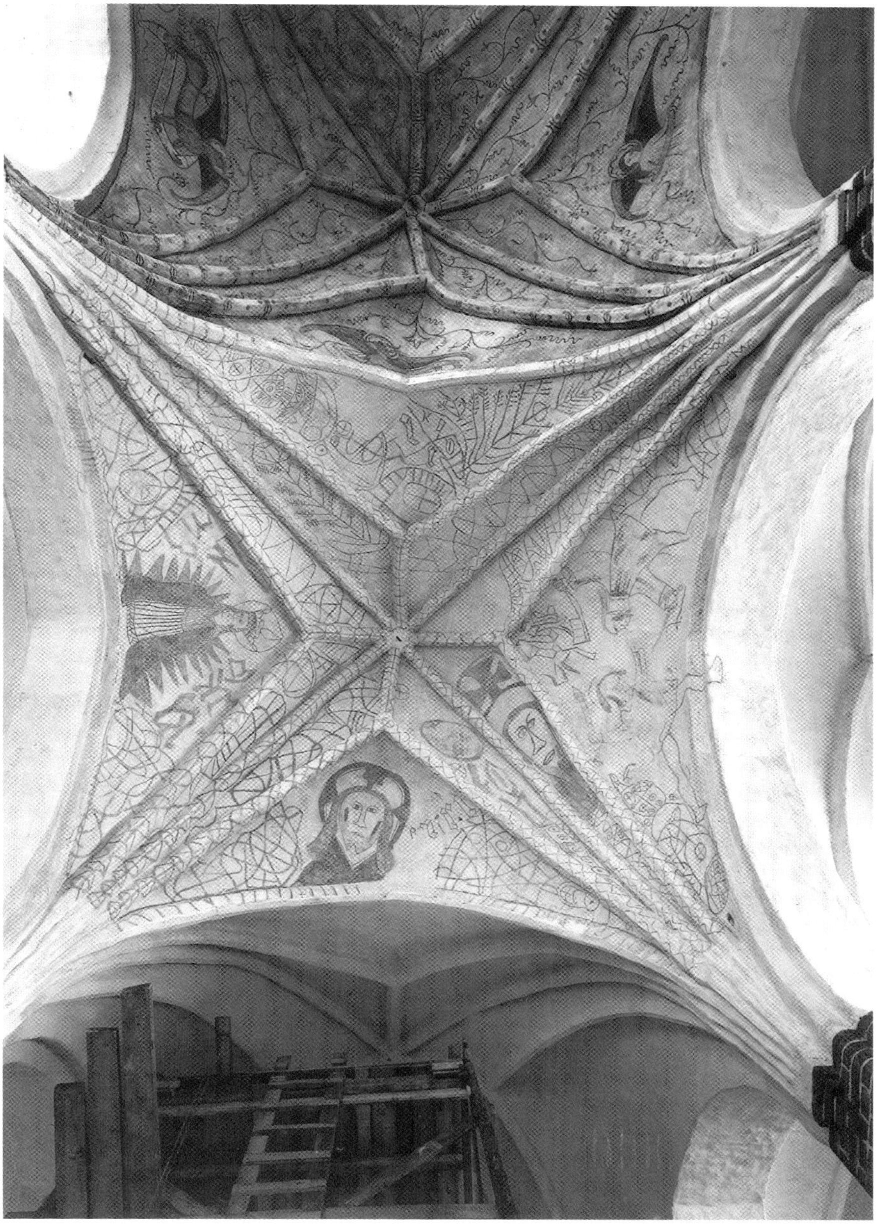

Fig. 17. Church of Pyhtää, 'The Apocalyptic Madonna and other paintings'. © Finnish National Board of Antiquities, Picture Archives

also contains finer paintings in addition to the 'primitive' set. The most extensive mural in the Pyhtää church is the so-called credo suite, the twelve apostles portrayed on the church wall. In accordance with Church tradition, the first in the series is St Peter, the leader of the apostles, who at Pyhtää has been placed next to the most important painting, the figure of the crucified Christ (fig. 16). The apostles have been placed next to the consecration crosses, as was the custom. There are also other saints depicted on the walls, including an almost six-metre-high representation of St Christopher, protector from the calamity of sudden death.

The crucified Christ is portrayed with bleeding wounds in the tradition of the late medieval Passion mystery. The emphasis on the role of the Virgin Mary, both as the mourning mother at the foot of the Cross and as the Apocalyptic Madonna (fig. 17) in the ceiling vault, is totally in accordance with the spirit of that period.[30] The face of the Saviour portrayed in the adjacent vault resembles the indulgence icon popular in St Birgitta convents.[31] The battle scene placed next to the Apocalyptic Madonna may symbolize one of the medieval cardinal sins, Ira (anger), so it also conveyed a clear moral message. Certain other figures, such as the trumpeter—known also from other churches—are more difficult to interpret. As a whole, however, the decorations of the Pyhtää church definitely represent a striving towards the same overall effect as in more artistically decorated churches, even though the style was what we term as 'primitive'.

As we have seen, the variability of the 'primitive' paintings is great, and they reflect the spiritual influences through which individuals have constructed their worldviews in very different ways. The Pyhtää suite is dominated by a lucid and comprehensive theological idea, which shows that the designer was well in touch with the theological currents of the times. In the Maaria church, in contrast, motifs from folk traditions and beliefs are much more evident. Their pictorial world can be compared to the world known from Finnish oral tradition. Folk epics and spells; a world based on the same unique admixture of pre-Christian beliefs and Christian influence, even though the folklore was not recorded until almost four hundred years after the paintings were made. The common people, including the priests who often came from their ranks, changed their conceptions of the world extremely slowly, especially in the road-less forests of Finland. The inhabitants of these backwoods would undoubtedly have nodded in common understanding of many paintings that remain unreadable mysteries to us.

---

[30] See, e.g., Helena Edgren, 'Mercy and Justice. Miracles of the Virgin Mary in Finnish Medieval Wall Paintings', *Finska Fornminnesföreningens Tidskrift 100* (1993), 28–33

[31] Sixten Ringbom, 'Bild och avlat', *Iconographisk Post. Nordic Review of Iconography, 3–4* (1983), vol. 3, pp. 8–16; vol. 4, pp. 1–14.

Man and picture: on the function of wall paintings in medieval churches

ANNA NILSÉN

The interiors of medieval churches were often covered with paintings, sometimes at considerable expense. In Denmark, Sweden, and Finland we are lucky to possess a great many series of pictures, a majority of them from the late Middle Ages and some of them still in a very good condition (fig. 1).[1]

Continuous picture programmes covering the whole of the church interior are seldom found in the larger churches, such as cathedrals and monastic churches.

---

[1] For Sweden, see, e.g., Henrik Cornell and Sigurd Wallin, *Schwedische Kirchenmalereien des 16. Jahrhunderts* (Stockholm: Humanistiska Sällskapet, 1954); idem, *Schwedische Kirchenmalereien des 16. Jahrhunderts 2* (Stockholm: Humanistiska Sällskapet, 1960); idem, *Stockholmer Malerschulen des 15. Jahrhunderts* (Stockholm: Humanistiska Sällskapet, 1961); Åke Nisbeth, *Bildernas predikan* (Stockholm: Gidlund, 1986); Anna Nilsén, *Program och funktion i senmedeltida kalkmåleri. Kyrkmålningar i Svealandskapen och Finland 1400–1534*, Kungliga Vitterhets Historie och Antikvitets Akademien, Diss. (Stockholm: Almqvist & Wiksell, 1986). For Danish wall paintings, see, e.g., *A Catalogue of Wall Paintings in the Churches of Medieval Denmark 1100–1600*, ed. by Knud Banning, 4 vols (Copenhagen: Akademisk Forlag, 1976–82); *Danske kalkmalerier. I (1080–1175); II (1175–1275); III (1275–1375); IV (1375–1475); V (1475–1500); VI (1500–1536)*, ed. by Ulla Haastrup and Robert Egevang; *VII (1536–1700)*, ed. by Eva Louise Lillie (Copenhagen: Nationalmuseet, 1985–92). Overviews of wall paintings in Finland may be studied in Nilsén (as above); and in Tove Riska, 'Keskiajan maalaustaide', vol. I of *Suomen Taide* (Helsinki: Kustannusosakeytio Otava, 1987), pp. 116–78.

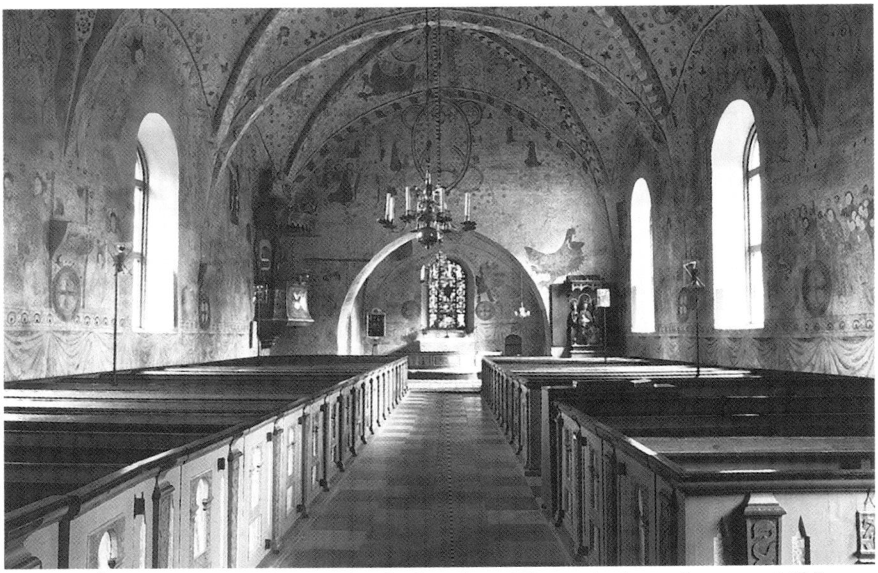

Fig. 1. Ärentuna church, Uppland, Sweden. The paintings from c. *1435 are among the best preserved in Sweden. The Passion series on the north wall, today damaged by the widening of the wall for the present large eighteenth-century windows, was probably well lit by one or two windows on the southern side. It has a devotional character. However, the picture programme in Ärentuna is, as a whole, of a mainly descriptive and didactic type. © Author*

Usually there are different programmes for each chapel or section of the interior, whereas in country churches the whole interior normally was covered with paintings in a single campaign.[2]

Since there are both architectural and liturgical differences between these churches on the one hand and the country churches on the other, and since there is a larger number of paintings preserved in the latter type of churches, their paintings thus forming a more homogeneous material, I shall base my discussion mainly on these country churches.

A natural question in connection with medieval Scandinavian wall paintings is whether they had more than purely decorative functions. Where any inscriptions, connected with the paintings and mentioning their purpose, survive, these inscriptions state—I think without exception—that the paintings were

[2] The picture programmes of the late medieval wall paintings in Middle Sweden and Finland have been studied in Nilsén (as in note 1). All programmes seem well conceived from a theological point of view. They are, up to *c.* 1450, mostly descriptive and epic in character, and after 1450 mostly composed with a leading idea, a main theme. Here there is a difference between Sweden and, e.g., northern Germany.

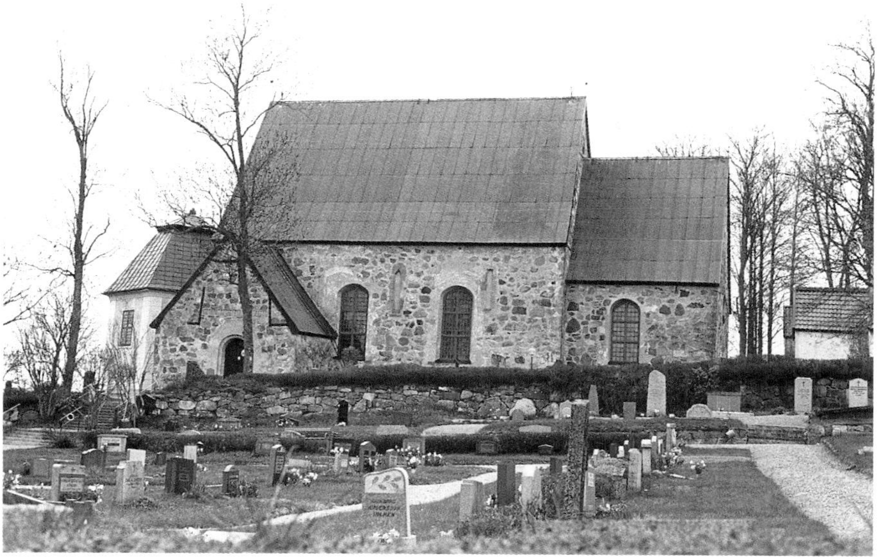

Fig. 2. Roslagsbro church, Uppland, Sweden. The original church consisted of the present nave, built in the latter part of the thirteenth century. The choir and the porch were added around 1400. Up to c. *1470, the probable year when the brick vaults were built, the church had a wooden ceiling. The original, very small, thirteenth-century windows, walled up in the fifteenth century, when a couple of somewhat larger ones were made, may still be seen on the southern wall. The fifteenth-century windows—one of them visible on the wall, close to the porch—were replaced in the eighteenth century by the present windows. On the northern wall there were no windows in the Middle Ages.* © *Author*

made to the honour of God and to embellish the church. But, of course, we need not and should not accept these statements as the only truth. They may just represent a generally accepted standard formulation. A widespread opinion is that medieval wall paintings were mainly intended as a pedagogic aid to be used by the clergy in their sermons. Hans Belting, for instance, concludes that since the sermons mostly took place inside the churches, where both priest and congregation could see the paintings, the priest must have taken advantage of that situation and referred to them in his sermons.[3] The opinion that the function of the wall paintings in medieval churches was mainly instructive derives from general statements by early Christian authorities, as for instance Gregory the

[3] Hans Belting, *Das Bild und sein Publicum im Mittelalter. Form und Funktion früher Bildtafeln der Passion* (Berlin: Mann, 1981), pp. 244–51.

Great (*c.* 540–604), repeated by later authors through time. However, throughout the Middle Ages there were many and varying reasons for providing churches with paintings, which, as we shall see, also entailed many and varying functions. In some quarters, though, there was no enthusiasm at all for providing churches with pictures. St Bernard and St Birgitta of Sweden are well-known examples of this attitude.[4]

The idea that the medieval parish priest referred to the pictures around him when preaching is anachronistic and based on a modern idea of preaching and teaching.[5] Against such an opinion there are several important arguments, of which the impossible pedagogic situation is among the weightiest. It is hard to imagine a good pedagogue trying to make his audience understand which one of all the pictures on walls and vaults he is referring to, in a badly lit and probably also crowded nave, especially when he was preaching in many cases far away from the picture referred to, and only a few persons would have a chance to come close enough to the pictures to be able to see them. The Swedish country churches of the Middle Ages had few, and small, windows, in order not to let in the cold during winter (fig. 2). This meant that the interiors of the churches were much too dark for the whole body of paintings to be identified by the congregation. Only in the porches and a few places inside the churches was there good light, and there are very often to be found didactic pictures, mostly of a moralising character. Devotional pictures, too, and series of the Passion of Christ were in general placed on well-lit walls (figs. 1 and 3).[6]

---

[4] Bernard of Clairvaux, *Apologia ad Guillelmum, Sancti Bernardi Opera*, vol. 3, ed. by J. Leclercq and H. M. Rochais (Rome: Editiones Cistercienses, 1963), p. 106; Birgitta of Sweden, *Revelationes extravagantes 31*; cf. Lennart Hollman, *Den Heliga Birgittas Reuelaciones extrauagantes*, Samlinga utgivna av Svenska Fornskrifts-Sällskapet, ser. 2., Latinska skrifter, band 5. Diss. (Uppsala: Almqvist & Wiksell, 1956), p. 145. A similar attitude towards paintings in churches is discernible in 'Pictor in Carmine' by an unknown author of the Romanesque era, possibly Adam of Dore, an English Cistercian; see M. R. James, 'Pictor in Carmine', *Archaeologia*, 94 (1951), 141–42. For the reference to the article by Dr. James I thank Dr. Phillip Lindley, Leicester.

[5] This was first argued in Nilsén (as in note 1), pp. 507–15, where the functions of the paintings in relation to the beholder and other relevant parties are discussed (German summary, pp. 529–30).

[6] Candles were expensive and used with economy. Indirect information on the use of candles is sometimes given in the provincial laws. Both the older and the younger version of the law of Västergötland, for instance, mention candles in two places, at the front and at the back of the church, and probably concerning those of the main altar and the one at the baptismal font near the exit; see *Svenska landskapslagar*, ed. by Åke Holmbäck and Elias Wessén, 5 vols (Stockholm: H. Geber, 1933–46), IV, pp. 14 (note 27), 206. But even if candles had been used more lavishly, this would rather have added to the mystical atmosphere than given a good overall light.

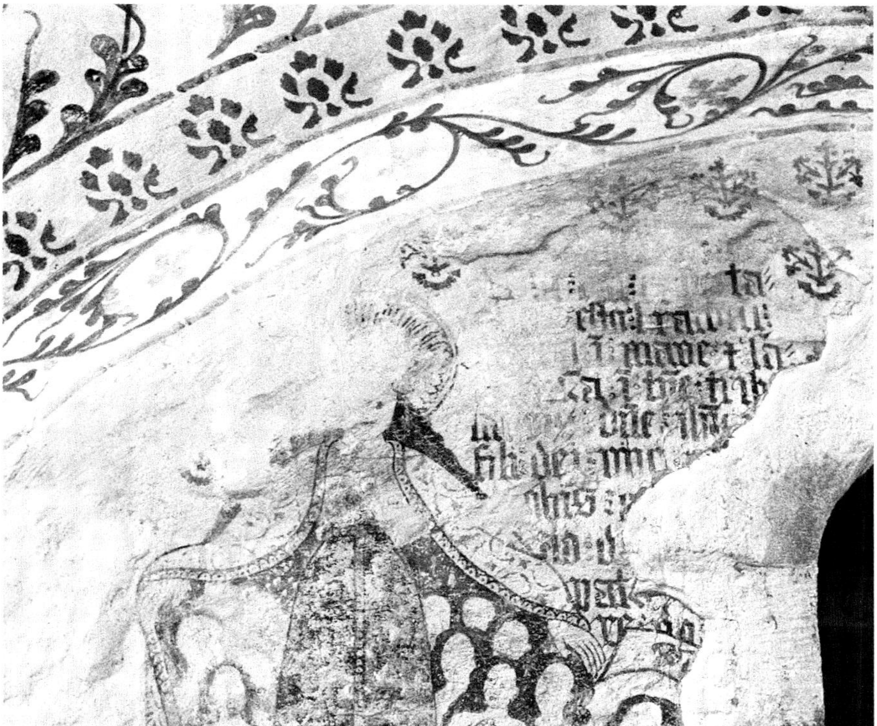

Fig. 3. Roslagsbro church. The visitor was met in the porch by the picture of Mater omnium with an accompanying prayer in Latin. © Author

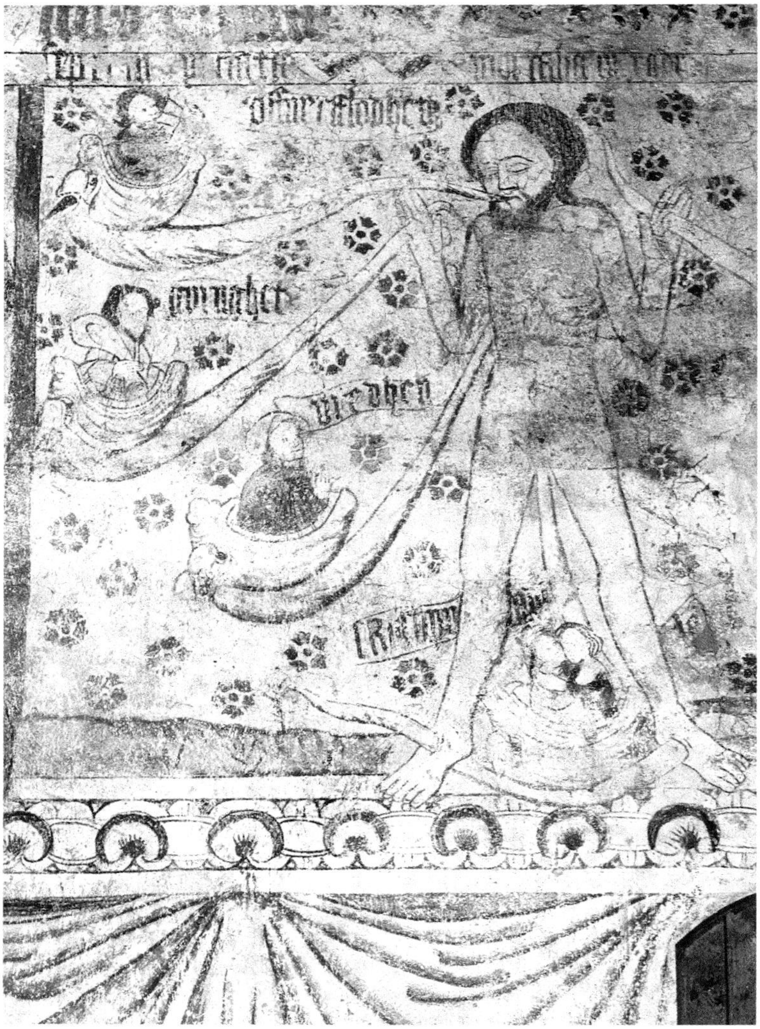

Fig. 4. Ärentuna church. c. *1435. 'The seven deadly sins with their roots'. The headline over the picture says 'Septem peccata mortalia cum radice', meaning 'The seven deadly sins with their roots'. The instructive picture shows us the sins and their places in the body of man, their 'roots'. Each sin is represented by a monstrous head with a sinner in its mouth and is also accompanied by its name in Swedish. The right portion of the painting is damaged. From the figure's left hand came Invidia, and from his backside the sin considered as the ugliest sin of all, Superbia. The representation is on the west wall at the end of a series depicting the Ten Commandments. © Author*

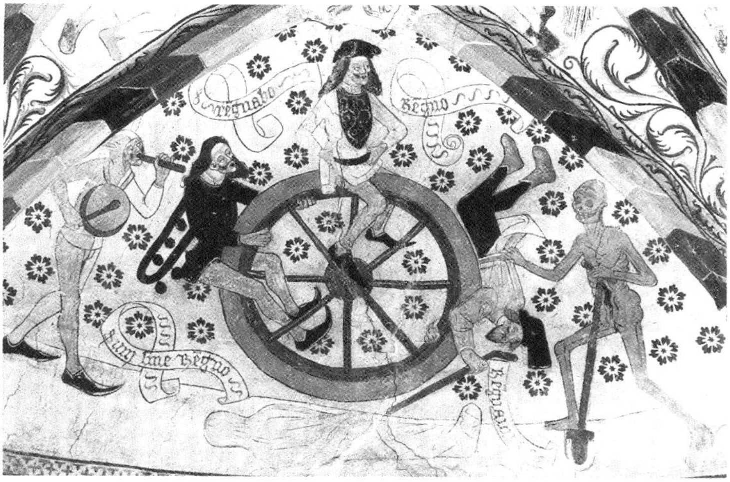

Fig. 5. Härkeberga church, Uppland, Sweden, c. *1485. 'The Wheel of Life', a 'memento mori' motif showing the inevitable destiny of all and also the vanity of earthly endeavour.* © *Author*

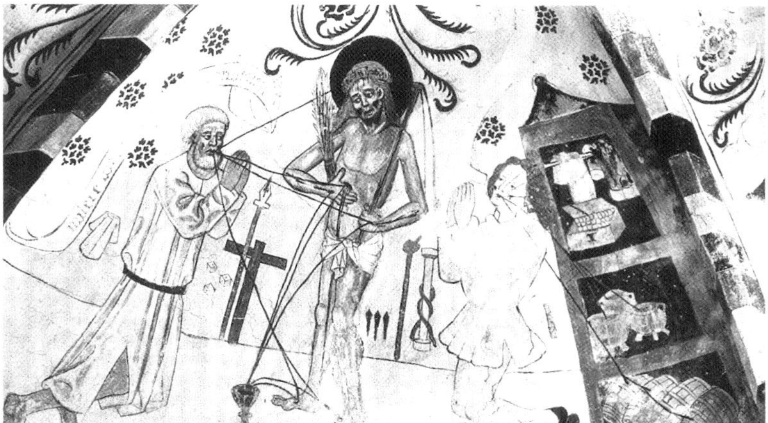

Fig. 6. Härnevi church, Uppland, Sweden, c. *1485. 'True and false prayer'. How you should pray is illustrated in the porch of this church and many others. The old, simply dressed, barefoot man on Christ's right has all his thoughts on Christ's wounds when praying, while the thoughts of the fashionably-dressed young man on Christ's left go to worldly goods, to his riches, to food and to drink: it follows that Christ turns his face away from him.* © *Author*

There are indeed instructive pictures in our medieval churches, but these pictures are overly explicit in character and need no intermediary to be understood (figs. 4–6). Nor do there seem to be any references to paintings in the sermons handed down to posterity. Very much of this material, of course, has disappeared, but if references to pictures had had any importance or been general, it certainly would not have been difficult to find a few examples of such sermons. Nor do the ecclesiastical sections of the provincial laws of the Middle Ages mention paintings among the things necessary to a church, and there are, indeed, churches, which have never had any paintings as well as churches with mostly or only ornamental decoration. The closest we come to any mention of paintings in medieval churches at all is a document from 1480 concerning the diocese of Turku (Åbo) in Finland, saying that the parishes were not allowed to engage any painter (or other craftsmen) without first asking the bishop and chapter.[7] Many of the Swedish parish priests were of rural origin, with just a rudimentary education.[8] These priests can hardly be believed to have practised any more advanced pedagogical methods to capture their audience.

Michael Baxandall has, before Belting, touched upon the function of pictures in churches during the Middle Ages. In his book *Painting and Experience in Fifteenth Century Italy* (1972), he devoted a chapter to the function of religious pictures, where he refers to the thirteenth-century author, Giovanni Balbi,[9] who in his *Catholicon* gives three reasons for providing churches with pictures:

1. They were for the instruction of simple people, because these are instructed by the paintings, as if from books;[10]
2. They should revive the memory of Christ's passion and the examples set by the saints; and
3. They were painted to excite the feeling of devotion.

---

[7] *Finlands medeltidsurkunder*, ed. by R. Hausen, 8 vols (Helsingfors: s.n., 1910–35), vol. IV, *1451–1480* (1924), pp. 525–26, document 3853. It says: . . . 'Item statuimus, quod nullus curatorum assumat sibi muratores, vitrifices, pictores, carpentarios aut ceteros officiales ad notabile edificium ecclesie spectantes sine speciali nostra vel nostri capituli licencia, sub pena xl marcharum'.

[8] *Svenska kyrkans historia. II: Den senare medeltiden, 1274–1521*, ed. by Yngve Brilioth (Stockholm: Svenska kyrkans diakonistyrelses bokförlag, 1941), p. 726; Bertil Nilsson, 'Om rättigheten och skyldigheten att predika', in *Predikohistoriska perspektiv*, ed. Alf Härdelin (Uppsala: Skeab Verbum, 1982), pp. 56–57; and Sven-Erik Pernler, 'Predikan ad populum under svensk medeltid', in ibid., pp. 81–82.

[9] Michael Baxandall, *Painting and Experience in Fifteenth-Century Italy* (Oxford: Oxford University Press, 1972), p. 41.

[10] This was certainly true for some pictures, e.g., the moralizing pictures (figs. 4–6). However a good many pictures were too complicated to be interpreted by people without learning, or could not be well distinguished because of the distance or lack of light.

Baxandall finds it tempting to see the mentioned points as a brief for a painter,[11] and he concludes that 'preacher and picture were both part of the apparatus of the church, and each took notice of the other'.[12] Baxandall has seen a connection between painting and sermon, and he is right to do so. There is a connection. But this connection is mutual only to a certain degree. Thus, there is an instructive factor but just for a part of the picture programme: the one that was painted where it could be seen, consisting of pictures that could be understood by everybody. There is certainly also a mnemonic function, but of course not for pictures that could be neither seen nor understood; and there is finally also the emotional aspect, but it is applicable only to some of the pictures. Thus all three arguments are true only to a certain degree. A serious problem is that so many of the pictures painted on walls and vaults could not be seen or interpreted by the congregation. Those pictures could not function in any of the three roles mentioned.

I tend to see the connection between preaching and painting in another way. In my opinion the church paintings are not sermons in themselves but reflections of sermons, glimpses of what was being preached in the churches.[13] The series of events represented on the walls often covers the whole of the church year. It sometimes is possible also to trace certain preferences or tendencies, stressed by the choice of pictures or by the character of the pictures, reminding one of the leitmotifs of thematic sermons. In one church you may find the Virgin Mary's importance for the Salvation clearly outlined among the paintings. Another programme may stress the necessity of prayer. A third one will focus on the Holy Eucharist. Still another one may be moralising, warning against sin and contrasting good examples with bad ones and so on. There is a great variety among the picture programmes of the late Middle Ages, much more than during the Romanesque era or the High Gothic period, when the content of the picture suites had a more descriptive character and mainly represented biblical material.[14]

In Sweden, the change in character of the sermon, in favour of a thematic approach to preaching, takes place in the middle of the fifteenth century and coincides with the change of composition of the ensembles of mural paintings.[15]

---

[11] Baxandall (as in note 9), p. 41.

[12] Ibid, p. 48

[13] This aspect has been studied in Anna Nilsén, 'Paintings as a Reflection of Sermon', in *Ars Ecclesiastica. The Church as a Context for Visual Arts*, ed. by Arja-Leena Paavola (Helsinki: University of Helsinki, Department of Theology, 1996), pp. 14–33.

[14] Nilsén (as in note 1), particularly pp. 459–60; see also pp. 527–58 (Zusammenfassung).

[15] On the development of the sermon in Sweden, see Roger Andersson, *Postillor och predikan*, Diss. (Stockholm: Riksantikvarieämbetet, 1993). The above-mentioned change

The thematic sermon had developed centuries earlier. But this—often very elaborate—type of sermon mostly was addressed to a learned audience, though the same structure could be applied also in sermons to an unlearned audience with, however, a less sophisticated degree of complication than was used for a learned audience.

Let us return to the church paintings. As I have already pointed out, their functions cannot possibly have been the same throughout the Middle Ages, first of all since the cultural and spiritual climate was not the same all the time. One well-known change is that there was, during the Gothic period, from the thirteenth century onwards, a successively growing tendency towards a more emotional approach in worship. This certainly made the educational aspect of the pictures less predominant than it may have been earlier, while the third of the functions, mentioned by Giovanni Balbi, the one of inviting empathy, must have stood out as more and more important. This is reflected in the choice of motifs and in the way of placing them. New types of devotional pictures such as Mary of the Seven Sorrows, Mary of the Rosary, Mary as Mater omnium (fig. 3), the Man of Sorrows, the Arma Christi, God with his sacrificed Son (fig. 7), and other motifs—all with an emotive quality—appear in connection with altars, in porches, and wherever the congregation could have easy access to them. There had been, of course, devotional pictures earlier, but they were there to function more exclusively as receivers of prayers; in the late Middle Ages the function of devotional pictures was also to appeal to the onlooker's empathy, to arouse emotion.[16]

The three functions mentioned by Giovanni Balbi are certainly important, but they do not constitute the stimuli for providing churches with paintings. And how would one be able to explain all the pictures that could not be seen by anybody? First of all, I think we ought to believe what the inscriptions tell us about the intention and function of the paintings: that they were painted in the honour of God and to embellish the church. If the whole of the ensemble of wall paintings could not be discerned or interpreted, it could undeniably be appreciated for the beauty of its colours, which may have had the effect that abbot Suger of Saint-Denis rated so highly, an anagogical function, meaning that the contemplation of beauty could lift the soul from its dull ordinary state and give it access to the Divine.[17] However, paintings, like other adornments, could be

---

is discussed on pp. 192–93. For the change in the picture programmes, see Nilsén (as in note 1), pp. 459–60, 527; and Nilsén (as in note 13), pp. 22–24.

[16] On the development of the devotional image, see Sixten Ringbom, *Icon to Narrative. The Rise of the Dramatic Close-Up in Fifteenth-Century Devotional Painting* (Åbo: Åbo akademi, 1965).

[17] Erwin Panofsky, *Abbot Suger on the abbey church of St Denis and its art treasures* (Princeton: Princeton University Press, 1946), p. 21.

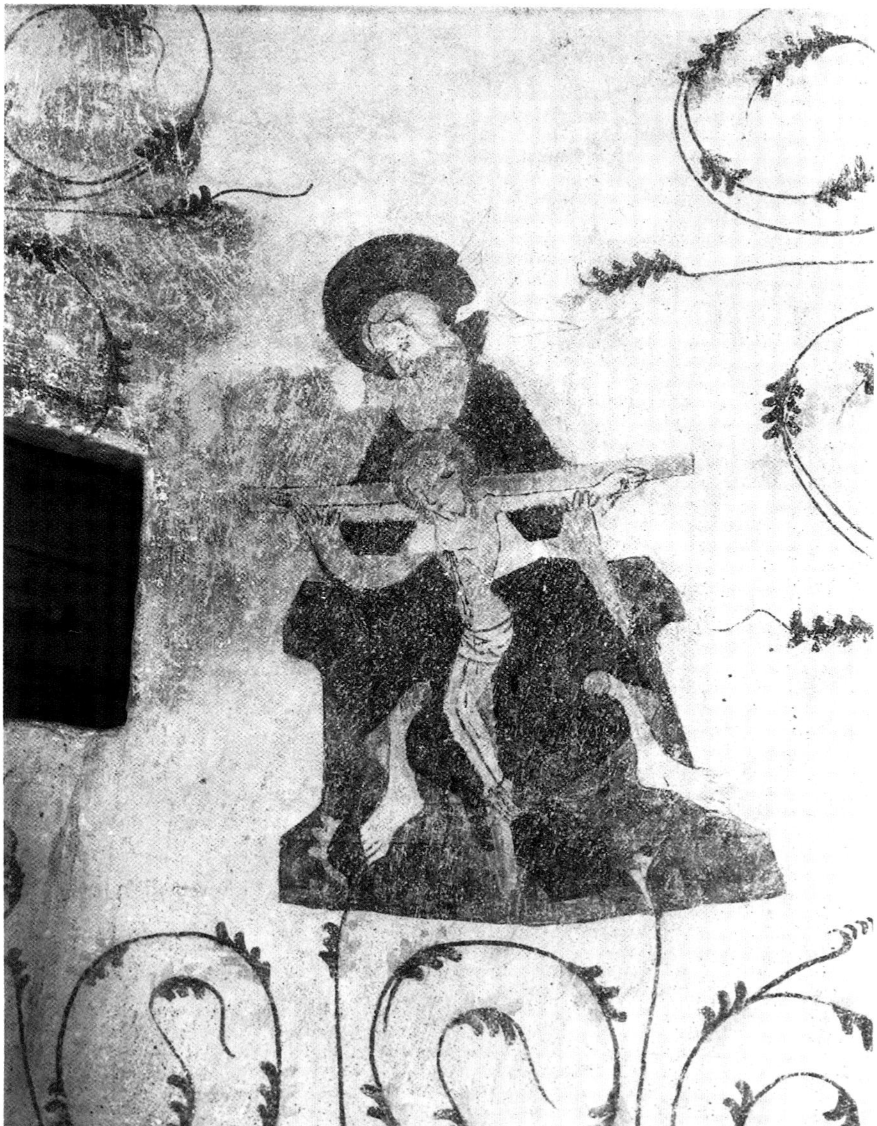

Fig. 7. Vendel church, Uppland, Sweden, painting in the porch, c. *1452. 'The Trinity'.* © *Author*

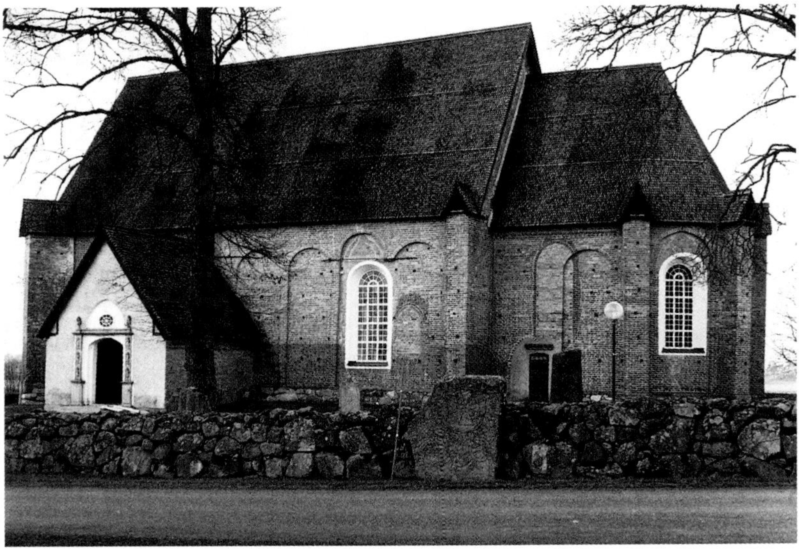

Fig. 8. Tensta church, Uppland, Sweden. End thirteenth century. 'Exterior from south'. This was no ordinary parish church but probably built by some among the foremost families of thirteenth-century Sweden. © Author

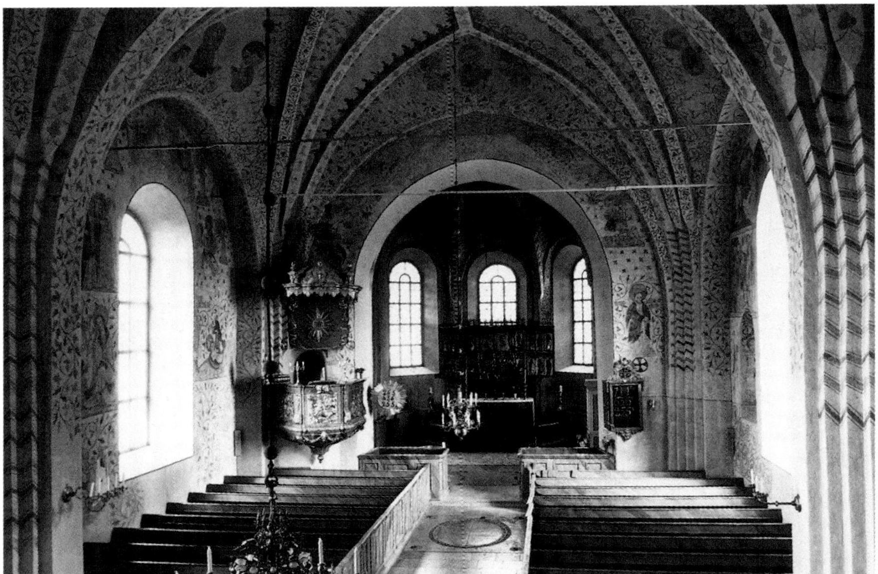

Fig. 9. Tensta church. Paintings from 1437–38. The painter was Johannes Rosenrod. © Author

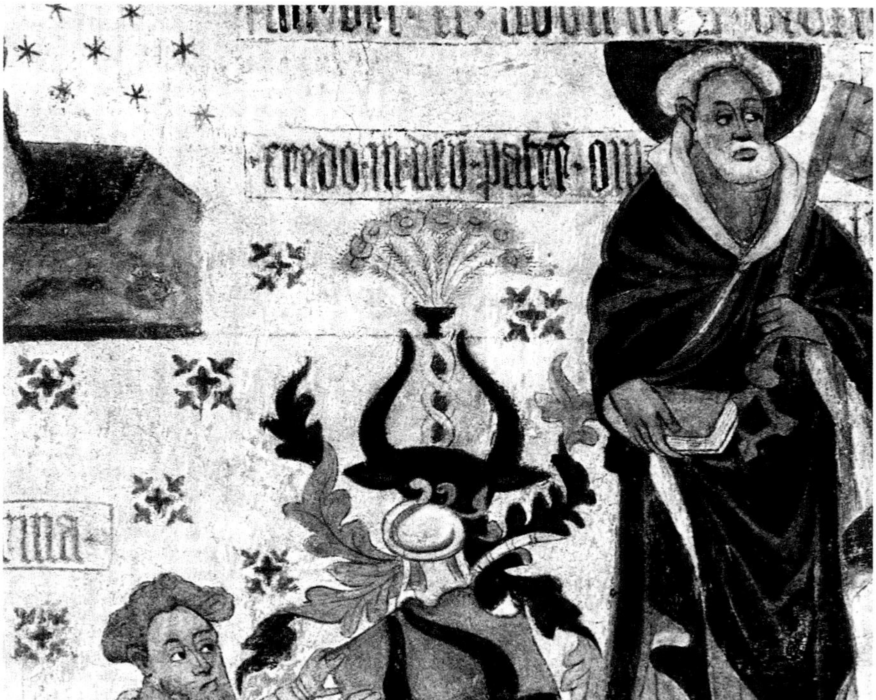

Fig. 10. Tensta church. 'Bengt Jönsson, the donor of the paintings, at the feet of St Peter'. © Author

given to the church for many reasons, very often for personal ones. In addition to the above-mentioned decorative function, which we should accept as the primary one, applicable to the whole ensemble of paintings, we may assume underlying functions, which are not always easily discovered. There are, as I see it, several possible types of such function, all of them referring to people involved: to commissioners, priest and congregation, and sometimes also to the painter. The officially documented generosity of the person who paid for the execution of paintings and sometimes also commissioned them could be useful in a personal career. It could add to a person's reputation or mend it. The votive aspect was probably very important. Many precious objects were given to churches as gifts to God to thank him for a success or in the hope of success. This certainly also applied to paintings.[18]

Let us study a case where we know a little more than usual of the paintings and the persons responsible for them and where more than one possible function may be assumed, though this is not evident at first sight. The paintings of Tensta church (fig. 8 and 9) north of Uppsala in middle Sweden constitute a good example.[19] We know the year the choir paintings were executed, which was 1437.[20] We know who paid for the paintings. The donor was one of the foremost men in Sweden of that time, Bengt Jönsson of the Oxenstierna family (fig. 10).[21] We also know the name of the painter, Johannes Rosenrod probably a German. For once we even know a little of the parish priest, whose name was Olof, documented as a member of the Corpus Christi guild of Stockholm.[22] First, a few words about the paintings and the picture programme. The figures and motifs are comparably large and distributed sparsely all over the interior, kept together in a tapestry-like unity by a vegetal ornamentation. Both the outline of the figures and the application of the colours are mostly of high quality, sometimes exquisite (fig. 11). Johannes Rosenrod was no doubt a skilled painter. The programme is thematic. Besides an evident reverence for the Virgin Mary, there are two clearly discernible main themes: one stressing the Eucharist and one focusing on the Swedish saint, Birgitta (*c.* 1303–73).

---

[18] Nilsén (as in note 1), pp. 507, 514, 515, 529–30 (Zusammenfassung).

[19] The programme of Tensta church has been studied in Anna Nilsén, 'Johannes Rosenrod—ein deutscher Maler in Schweden', in *Austausch und Verbindungen in der Kunstgeschichte des Ostseeraums. Homburger Gespräche 9: 22–25.11.1987*, ed. by Lars Olof Larsson and Jan von Bonsdorff (Kiel: Martin-Carl-Adolf-Böckler-Stiftung, 1988), pp. 43–60.

[20] The nave was probably painted the following year.

[21] See Hans Gillingstam, *Ätterna Oxenstierna och Vasa under medeltiden* (Diss.) (Stockholm: Hæggström, 1952), pp. 259–332.

[22] 'Handlingar rörande Helga Lekamens gille i Stockholm I: Gillesboken 1393–1487', in *Kungl. Bibliotekets handlingar, Bilagor, 2: 1–3*, ed. by Isak Collijn (Stockholm: Kungl. Bibliotek, 1921), pp. 48, 169.

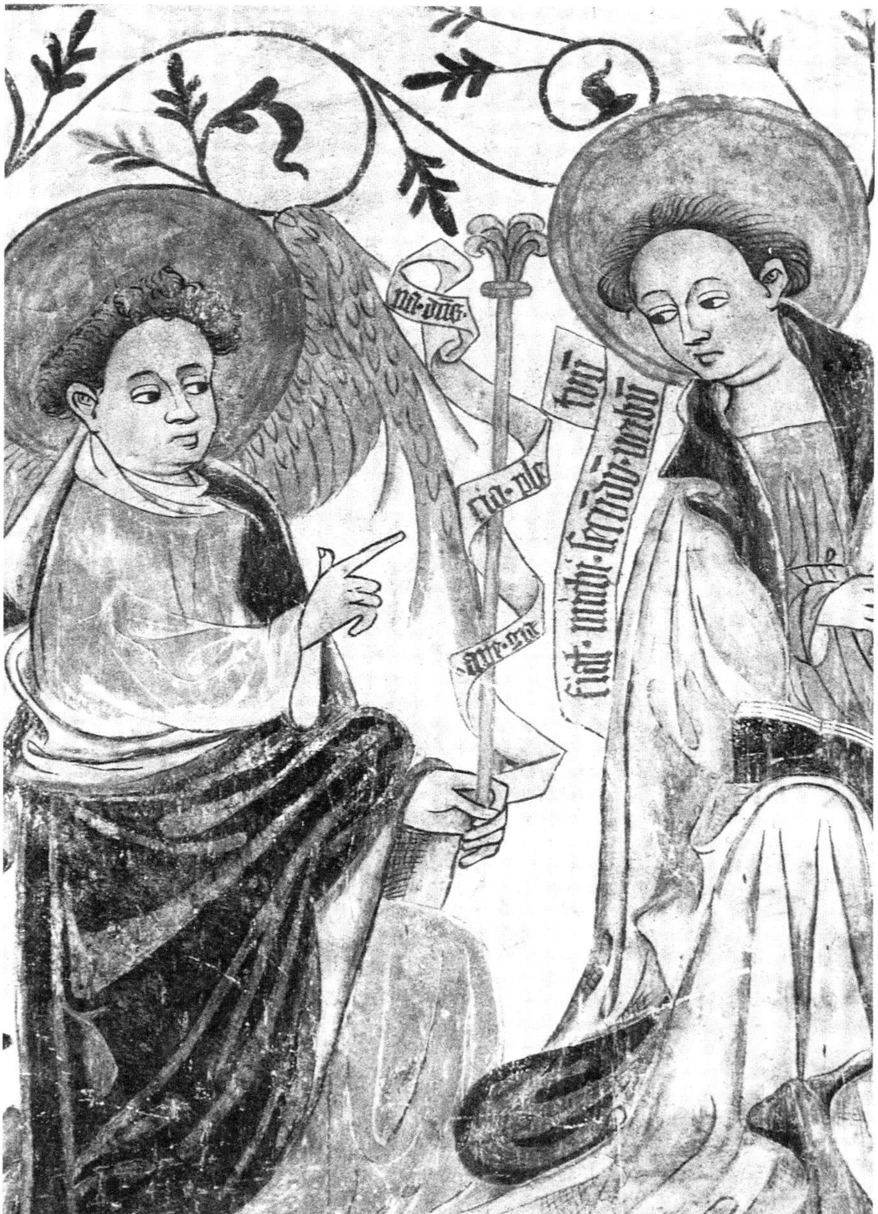

Fig. 11. Tensta church. 'The Annunciation'. © Author

The programme is well composed from a theological point of view and probably worked out by the parish priest Olof, who, in this church, under the patronage of Bengt Jönsson, was assuredly no ordinary, unlearned parish priest of rural origin but was an educated man. Many second sons among the nobility chose a career within the Church. The stress on the Eucharist in this programme may reflect Olof's own type of religiosity, indicated by his membership of the Corpus Christi guild. On the northern side of the nave, well lit, was (before the opening of the wall for a window in the place) a picture of the Man of Sorrows, surrounded by the Arma Christi, a devotional picture one would expect to find in connection with the Corpus Christi cult and certainly painted to serve those who wanted to exert their devotion and pray in front of it.

To judge from the content of the programme, it is also obvious that Bengt Jönsson himself influenced it, which one would expect, considering not only that he had spent a large sum of money on the project but also that he was an educated man and still striving towards the peak of his career. In 1437—the year of the choir paintings—he was already a member of the government council. From 1439 he was to reside over the provincial court of Uppland,[23] and in 1448 he was, together with his brother, for a short period governor of Sweden. During the same period his son Jöns Bengtsson made a rapid career within the Church. Jöns returned in 1437 or 1438 from Leipzig,[24] where he had studied at the university from 1434, and was almost immediately appointed dean of Uppsala Cathedral.[25] In 1448, finally, he was appointed archbishop of Sweden, the same year as his father was ruling over Sweden.

For a person with Bengt Jönsson's position and ambitions, we may suspect the paintings to have a propagandist function, and it is in such a connection that the remarkable series of pictures in Tensta, representing the most important events of Birgitta's life and deeds, should be considered. The series even contains a defence of her revelations, which at the time were under critical debate at a Church council in Basel, where it was maintained with some insistence that the visions of Birgitta were more likely to be inspired by the devil than by Christ and Mary (fig. 12). Birgitta was to be one of the most renowned saints of the Catholic Church. The importance of her person and of her revelations hardly can be exaggerated. In 1391 she had been canonized, and only a few years later she was mentioned among the Swedish national saints.

To call in an important painter and adorn a large church at one's own expense was doubtless regarded as an honourable deed and thus was certainly

---

[23] The Swedish term for this office was *lagman*, provincial judge.

[24] Gillingstam (as in note 21), p. 337 (*s.a.* 1438); Sven Tunberg, 'Jöns Bengtsson "Oxenstierna" ', in *Nordisk Familjebok* (Stockholm: Nordisk familjeboks förlags aktiebolag, 1914), col. 1149: *s.a.* 1437.

[25] *Gillingstam* (as in note 21), p. 337.

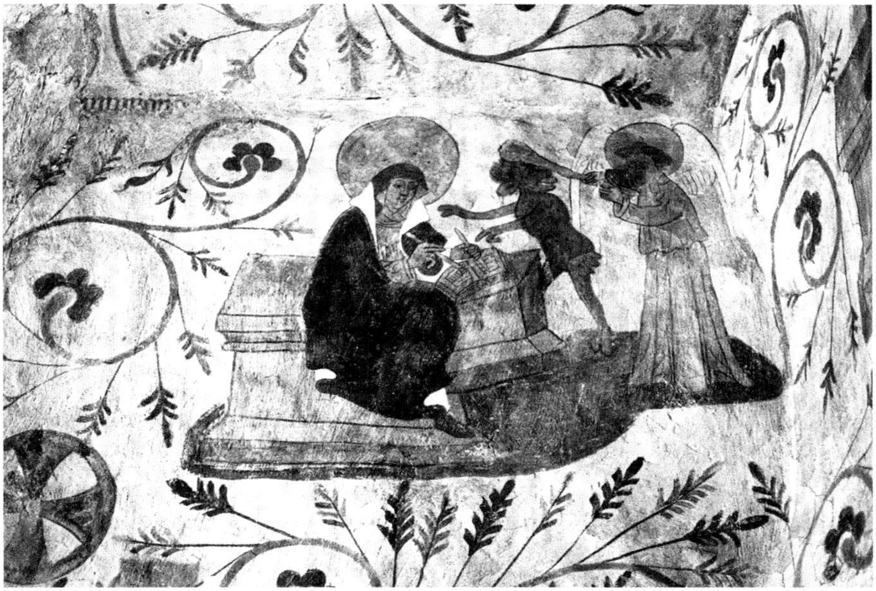

Fig. 12. Tensta church. 'Revelations of St Birgitta'. We here see a most effective defence of the Revelations of Saint Birgitta. The devil tries to instil in Birgitta a false revelation, but an Angel comes to her rescue and crushes his skull with a mace. How Christ and Mary inspire Birgitta's Revelations is shown in the following picture of the Birgitta series. © Author

propaganda in itself, but in the case of the Tensta paintings and particularly the Birgitta series the propagandizing function is, as we shall see, more explicit than this. From 1437 Birgitta was adopted among the patrons of Tensta church,[26] and this was certainly no coincidence. Bengt Jönsson was distantly related to Birgitta,[27] who was already in his time a national symbol. The connection with Birgitta indeed must have been something to manifest and propagate for a man with great ambitions, for both himself and his son. The depicted reference to the attack on her revelations, fresh in 1437, and the defence of them among the paintings, has no known precedents. This applies also to the rest of the pictures within the series. It thus may be concluded that it was specially composed for Tensta church, and there is little doubt that it was personally ordered by Bengt

---

[26] A medieval church bell, still in the church, mentions Birgitta among the patrons of the church; See Nils Sundquist, 'Tensta kyrka', in *Upplands kyrkor*, 42 (Strängnäs: Ärkestiftets Stiftsråd, 1970), p. 37.

[27] Nilsén (as in note 19), p. 46. See also Sigurd Rahmqvist, *Sätesgård och gods* (Diss.) (Stockholm: Historika institutionen, Stockholms universitet, 1996), pp. 242–43.

Jönsson to establish and proclaim his own and his family's connection with the national saint.

It is very seldom that the main themes of a picture programme are so easily explained with reference to identifiable contemporaries as in Tensta. We may conclude from the paintings of Tensta church that personal ambition sometimes may have resulted in the most beautiful pictures and that medieval wall paintings may have had other than instructive, devotional, or mnemonic functions—in other words, that there may have been functions of a less obvious character with reference to other parties than the congregation, such as the donor or the parish priest.

Representations of Jews in Danish medieval art— can images be used as source material on their own?

ULLA HAASTRUP *

This article deals with representations of Jews in medieval art in Denmark. I have selected a few examples from the wall paintings and altarpieces from the extensive material available. The images will show us how Jews were characterized as good, neutral, or evil in the period between the late 1080s and the Reformation in 1536. Jews never were depicted with photographic accuracy or through abstract symbolism. Their clothing, in particular their hats, always followed the norms of the medieval Jews themselves or, in particular, the norms demanded by Christian society. Jews had to differ from other citizens and must not be mistaken for Christians.

The images derive mainly from the art of the churches; they were commissioned by the Church and/or by secular donors. Since Jews were depicted in an attire similar to that of the contemporary European Jew, one must presume that the didactic and momentous pictorial message of the Church was understood by the spectator; otherwise the images would carry no meaning. If there were no Jews in Danish society, how would the congregations and the clergy immediately understand that a given figure was a Jew, depicted in the midst of an often densely populated scene? Would it be merely because of his hat, or because his face was in profile, denoting evil? Did all knowledge of Jews, their aspect, and dress derive from travels or from pictorial models? After presenting the various kinds of images, I shall discuss whether minority groups of Jews may have lived

* Translated into English by Elisabeth Kofod-Hansen.

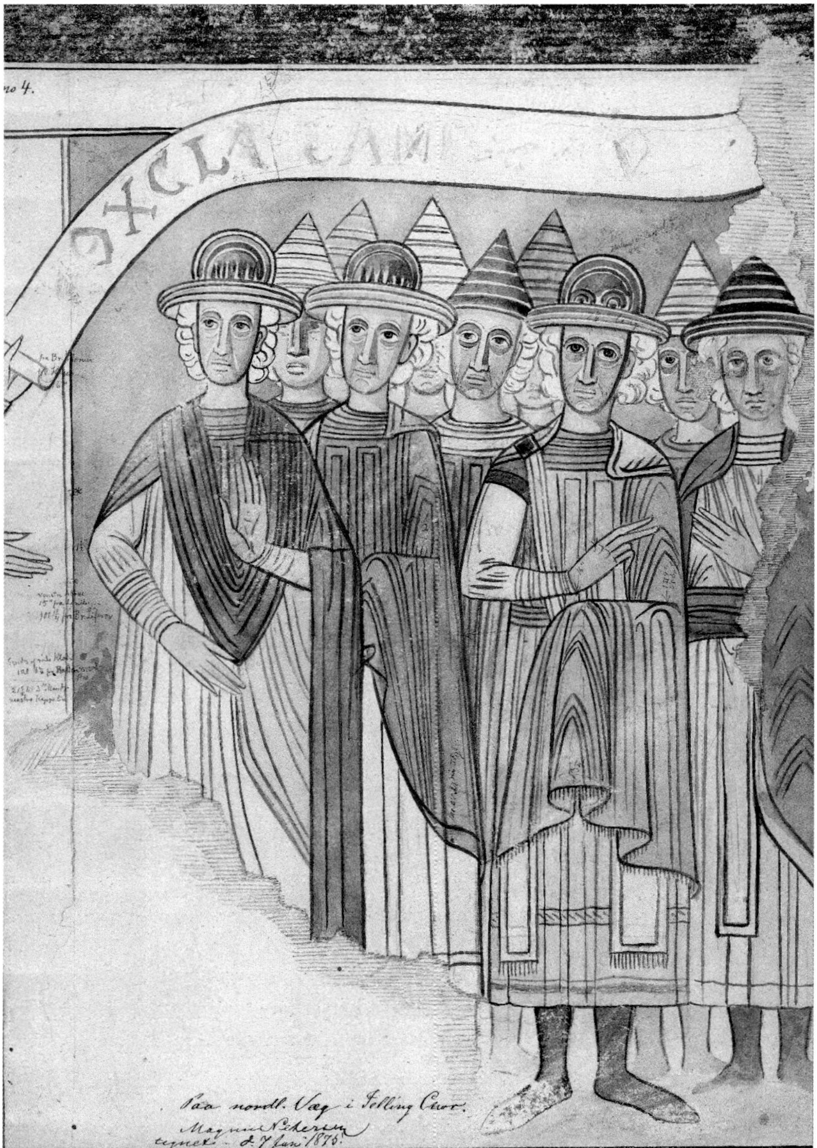

Fig. 1. Jelling church, fresco, 1080–1100, 'St John the Baptist preaching to a gathering of Jews', Watercolour by the restorer J. Magnus-Petersen 1874. © Nationalmuseet, Copenhagen

within the Danish realm during the Middle Ages. Information on this matter is, however, almost completely lacking in the few existing Danish written sources.

In Jelling church in Jutland, some extremely well preserved frescoes showing the Life of John the Baptist and the Baptism of Christ were discovered in 1874–75. Unfortunately, they were destroyed by humidity and were re-painted. However, the very carefully-executed water-colours by the restorer J. Magnus-Petersen show us, among other scenes, John the Baptist preaching to a gathering of Jews (fig. 1). The text scroll reads '. . . vox clamantes. . .'. The Jews are standing in rows, wearing brimmed hats with alternately round or pointed crowns. The position of the faces is neutral. From stylistic criteria, I would date the frescoes of the Jelling workshop to around 1080–1100.[1] The same characteristic hats are found in Reichenau, in the frescoes in the apse of the church of St Peter and Paul. The row of prophets in the lower parts of these paintings wear similar types of hat. Dendrochronological investigations have dated the frescoes to around 1104–15.[2] The early Romanesque stained-glass windows in the nave of the cathedral in Augsburg, Bavaria, show us, among other motifs, the prophet Daniel with a similar Jewish hat.

The frescoes from around 1125 in Råsted church in Jutland include the oldest extant depiction of an evil Jew in Denmark (fig. 2). He is shown in profile with a hooked nose, a short beard, and a Jew's hat. He is part of a painting showing, among other things, the Magi, who during their journey pay a visit to King Herod and his court in order to enquire about the newborn child. This picture and several other motifs in the extremely carefully prepared pictorial programme are directly in keeping with the liturgical plays about the Three Magi known abroad. At King Herod's court, the sage Judex Barbatus is asked what the scriptures tell about the king who is to come. In these particular Danish Romanesque frescoes, he stands out singularly in profile. All other figures in the church are painted in a three-quarter profile, and it follows that this is a marked characterisation of him as an evil Jew.[3]

---

[1] Poul Nørlund and Egmont Lind, *Danmarks romanske kalkmalerier* (Copenhagen: Selskabet til Udgivelse af Danske Mindesmærker, 1944), pp. 50–63, cat. 70; and Ulla Haastrup, 'Johannes i Jelling', *Skalk* 2 (1972) pp. 18–28. See also the following items in *Danske kalkmalerier, Romansk tid 1080–1175*, ed. by Ulla Haastrup and Robert Egevang (Copenhagen: Nationalmuseet, 1986): Ulla Haastrup, Introduction, pp. 24–26 and 39; Knud J. Krogh, 'En meget sørgelig historie', pp. 64–65; Ulla Haastrup, 'Johannes Døberens historie', pp. 66–69; Kirsten Trampedach, 'Gamle billeder på nye vægge', pp. 70–71; and Ulla Haastrup, 'Jellingværkstedets forbilleder', pp. 78–79.

[2] Wolfgang Erdmann, *Die Reichenau im Bodensee. Geschichte und Kunst*, 10th rev. edn. (Königstein im Taunus: Die blauen Bücher, 1993), pp. 22–25.

[3] Ulla Haastrup, 'Die romanischen Wandmalereien in Råsted. Ikonographie, Bildprogram und Theater', *Hafnia* (1972), pp. 69–138; Lise Gotfredsen, *Råsted Kirke—Spil og Billede* (Copenhagen: Akademisk Forlag, 1975); Ulla Haastrup, 'Liturgisk,

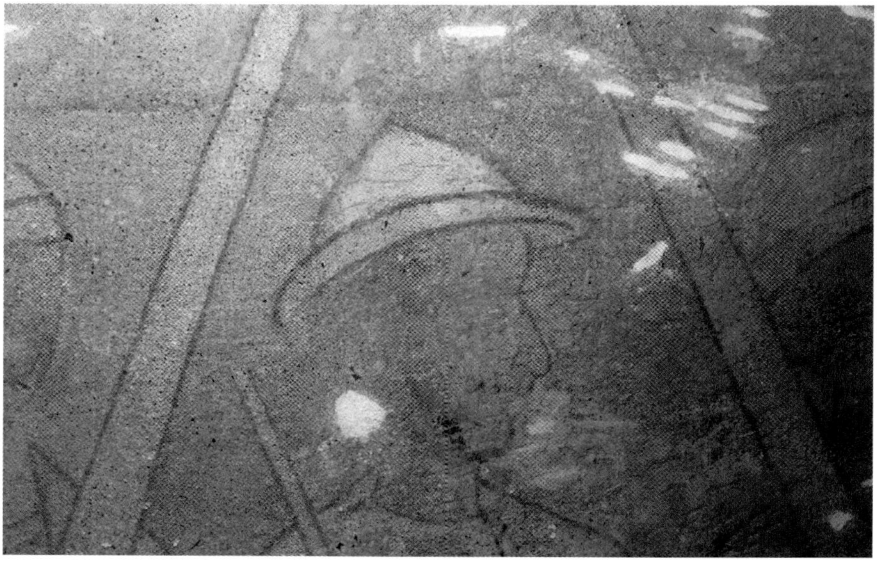

Fig. 2. Raasted church, fresco, about 1125, 'judex barbatus', in the scene of the Magi at the court of King Herod. © *Author*

Around 1275, the chancel vault in Strøby church on the principal Danish island of Sjælland was decorated with paintings. Prophets are depicted on the pendentives. One of them has obvious Jewish facial traits, but he is shown in a neutral three-quarter profile. In the paintings of the Passion of Christ at Strøby, the motifs are not framed but, rather, are intertwined with plant stalks and leaves. Here one finds in contrast to the Jewish prophet the oldest Danish examples of cruel Jewish executioners.[4] Their dress includes yellow coats or coats with broad stripes. On their Jews' hats there are stalks, their heads are mainly shown in profile with open mouths and tongues protruding, and they have hooked noses. They beat and torture Christ. Simon of Cyrene is pushing Him and does not assist in carrying the cross. The Jews in these pictures show strong hatred, as is the case in the rest of Europe at the end of the thirteenth century. A slightly later parallel is found in the large illustrated *Speculum humanæ salvationis* from

---

kirkeligt teater og Råsteds kalkmalerier', in *Danske kalkmalerier. Romansk tid 1080–1175* (as in note 1), pp. 84–87; Ruth Mellinkoff, *Outcasts: Signs of Otherness in Northern European Art in the Late Middle Ages* (Berkeley: University of California Press, 1993).

[4] Kirsten Trampedach, 'Nye iagttagelser, Strøby', in *Danske kalkmalerier. Senromansk tid 1175–1275*, ed. by Ulla Haastrup and Robert Egevang (Copenhagen: Nationalmuseet, 1987), pp. 184–85; and Ulla Haastrup, 'Representations of Jews in Danish Medieval Art', in *Danish Jewish Art: Jews in Danish Art*, ed. Mirjam Gelfer-Jørgensen (Copenhagen: Rhodos, 1999), pp. 153–54.

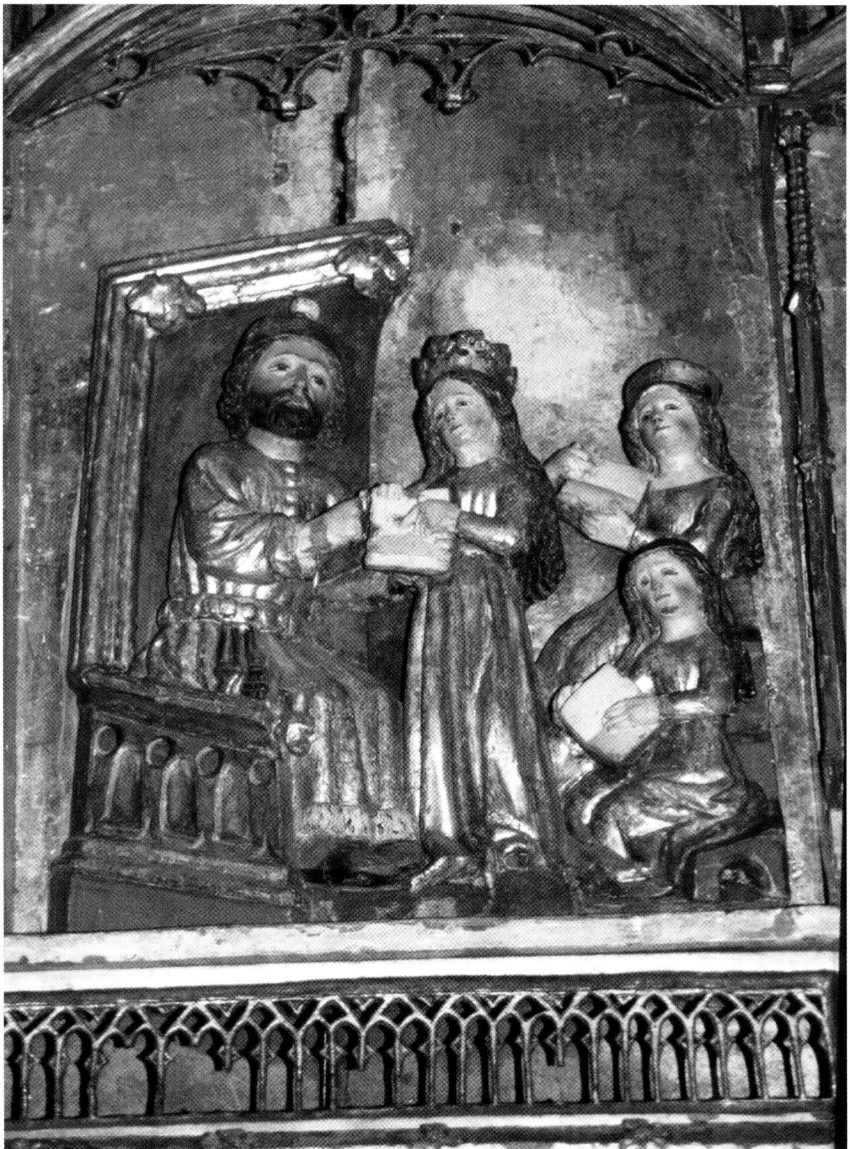

Fig. 3. Altarpiece from Boeslunde church, now at the National Museum in Copenhagen, about 1425–35, Lübeck. 'The Virgin Mary's Training in Reading'. © Nationalmuseet, Copenhagen

Kremsmünster of approximately 1325.[5] The executioners holding Christ before Pilate and the three tormentors in the scene of the Flagellation are also caricature Jews, in profile with open mouths and protruding tongues.

In 1980, wall paintings from the second quarter of the fifteenth century were discovered in Brönnestad church in Skåne, which belonged to medieval Denmark and now is part of Sweden.[6] From an artistic point of view, they rank among the best of late medieval Danish frescoes. They include several depictions of good as well as bad Jews. In the representation of the Infancy of Christ there are two motifs on the pendentives showing the Women with the infant Christ and Simeon and his assistant, in the Presentation in the Temple. Simeon is wearing the mandatory Jewish synagogue garb, the assistant wears a Jew's hat. In the depiction of the Miracle of the Cornfield during the flight into Egypt, the farmer wears a tall pointed hat—a peasant's hat or a Jew's hat? Pilate is wearing a similar hat in the depiction of Christ before Pilate. Herod wears a crown and Caiaphas a bishop's mitre. Pilate is often represented with a Jew's hat and not as a Roman governor. Brönnestad displays a rare motif where Judas receives the thirty silver coins from the high priests. Two Jews are shown, the high priest handing over the money and Judas opening his moneybag to receive them. Both are painted in evil profile, with Jewish traits. Some of the pendentives also display caricature-masks in profile. The one shown here must represent a spitting Jew if compared with Judas's profile.[7] However, even worse pictures of Jews occur in the main scenes of The Passion of Christ. The Flagellation is conducted by three tormentors, two of whom are shown as Jews with strongly caricatured traits. They are painted not in profile but with open mouths showing their teeth, which was considered highly indecent during the Middle Ages. Sadism and hatred radiate from their ugly faces.

The representations of Jews vary widely in character even in one pictorial programme. One cannot help but wonder at the vast shift in attitude from the depictions of the old Simeon to those of the tormentors of Christ.

Pictures of Jews are not found solely among the Danish wall paintings; they

---

[5] *Speculum humanae salvationis, Codex cremifanensis 243, Kremsmünster, Faksimili-Ausgabe*, ed. by Willibrod Neumüller (Graz: s.n., 1972).

[6] Torkel Eriksson, 'Nyframtagna medeltidsmålningar i Brönnestad', *Ale: Historisk tidskrift för Skåneland* 2 (1982), pp. 1–19; 'To usædvanlige motiver', ibid.; 'Bebudelsen og Jomfru Maria med barnet', in *Danske kalkmalerier. Gotik 1375–1475*, ed. by Ulla Haastrup and Robert Egevang (Copenhagen: Nationalmuseet, 1985), article 29, 30.

[7] Ulla Haastrup, 'Groteske Masken en face und im Profil. Die Bedeutung des Gesichtsstellung in der mittelalterlichen Symbolsprache', in *Mein ganzen Körper ist Gesicht—Groteske Darstellungen in der europäischer Kunst und Literatur des Mittelalters*, ed. by Katrin Kröll and Hugo Steger (Freiburg im Breisgau: Rombach, 1994), pp. 313–24; Haastrup, 'Representations of Jews in Danish Medieval Art' (as in note 4), pp. 132–37, et passim.

are also found on the winged, sculpted wooden altarpieces that furnished Danish churches in great numbers during the later Middle Ages. One of the major examples, the great winged altarpiece from Boeslunde church on Sjælland, can be seen at the National Museum in Copenhagen.[8] It is an imported work of art from Lübeck, dated about 1425–35. Following re-conservation in 1980, it is now to be seen with its original paint both on the sculptures and in the paintings. This altarpiece relates to the stories of Joachim and Anna and those of the Virgin Mary's visit to the Temple and her training in reading there (fig. 3). The teacher on the throne-like chair wears a Jew's hat. The paintings on the wings include the Passion where The Kiss of Judas shows a red-haired Jewish Judas in a yellow coat and Malchus, who is also depicted in the evil Jewish profile. The paintings on the outer wings contain detailed representations of Jews with different kinds of Jew's hat and the fur-lined garments of the wealthy.

Between 1460 to 1480, a large painting workshop was active in Sjælland. It worked with speed and therefore presumably made cheap wall paintings, covering the interiors in their entirety from chancel to tower bay in about thirty village churches in the northern part of Sjælland.[9] It worked from models, which we so far unfortunately have not been able to identify among preserved woodcuts. In this anonymous workshop, the 'Isefjords workshop', there was great consistency in the symbolism of the facial pose.[10] Three-quarter profiles alone are seen in depictions of ordinary people—and of Christ in epic scenes. Some people are shown in the evil profile: these are almost exclusively the cruel Jewish tormentors or, for example, Judas.

In Nørre Herlev church, the Jews flagellate Christ savagely. They are shown in profile with open mouths and hooked noses, and one has his chest bare in further mockery of Christ. In Mørkøv church one finds a painting of a similar flagellation, but in this case the executioner has loosened his hoses to mock with his bare behind. A similar detail is found in The Crowning with Thorns in Mørkøv, and in the same motif in Nørre Herlev the evil sneering profiles are the predominant feature. In Jörg Preus's paintings from 1502 in Stiftung Melk in

---

[8] Francis Beckett, *Altertavler i Danmark fra den senere Middelalder* (Copenhagen: Ministeriet for Kirke- og Undervisningsvæsenet, 1895); Ulla Haastrup, *Mariatavlen fra Boeslunde* (Copenhagen: Nationalmuseet, 1984).

[9] See the following entries in *Danske kalkmalerier. Gotik 1375–1475* (as in note 6): Niels-Knud Liebgott, 'S. Laurentius' legende', and 'S. Katharinas legende'; Bodil Franck, 'Moraliteter'; Dorthe Falcon Møller, 'Hyrdernes sækkepiber'; Ebbe Nyborg, 'Dommedag'; Ulla Haastrup, 'Restaureringsprincipper', 'Det bibelske verdensforløb', and 'Ødelagte kalkmalerier og restaureringshistorie'. See also Niels M. Saxtorp, *Danmarks kalkmalerier*, 2nd edn. (Copenhagen: Politikens forlag, 1997), pp. 22–23 et passim; and Jørgen Aabenhus, *En kalkmalers bibelhistorie* (Copenhagen: Religionspædagogisk forlag, 1999).

[10] Haastrup, 'Representations of Jews in Danish Medieval Art' (as in note 4), p. 132.

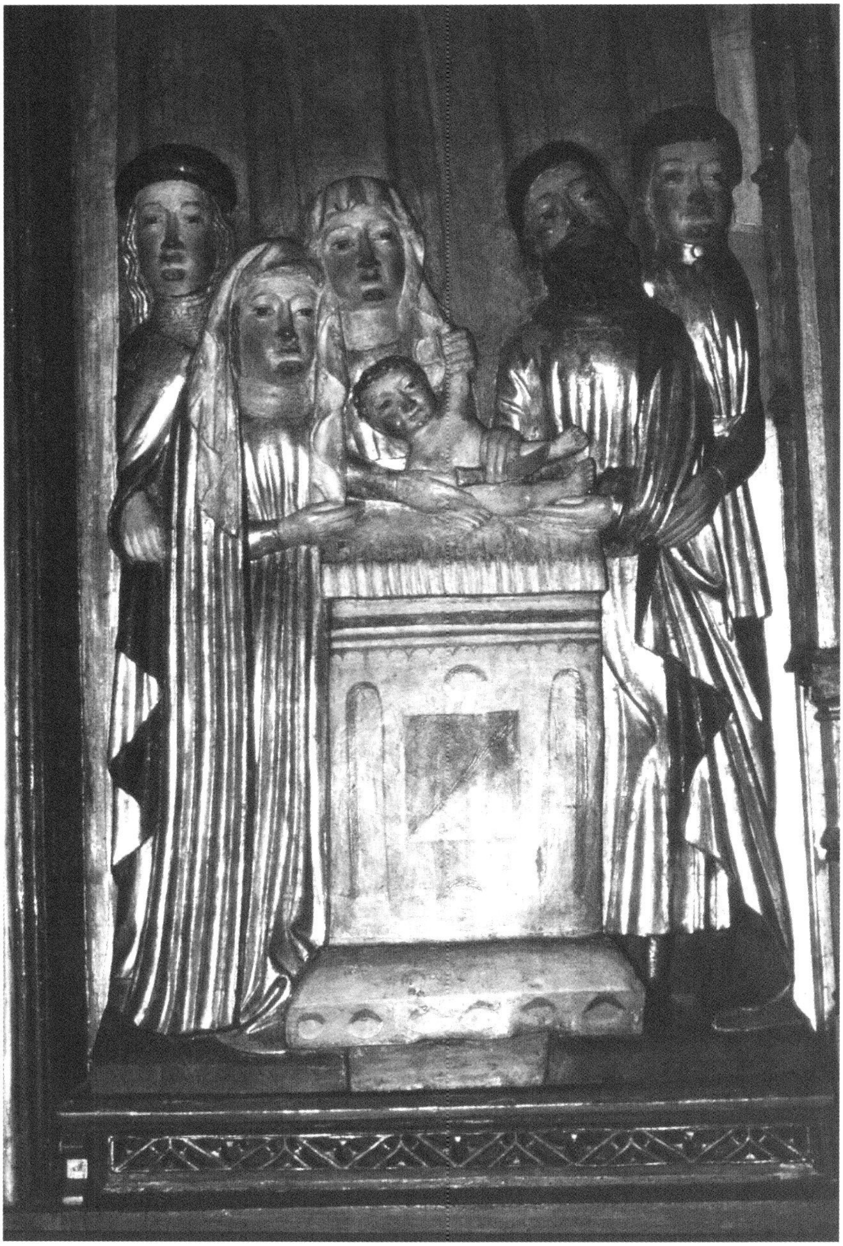

Fig. 4. Altarpiece in St Mary in Helsingborg, 1449–52. 'The Circumcision'. © Author

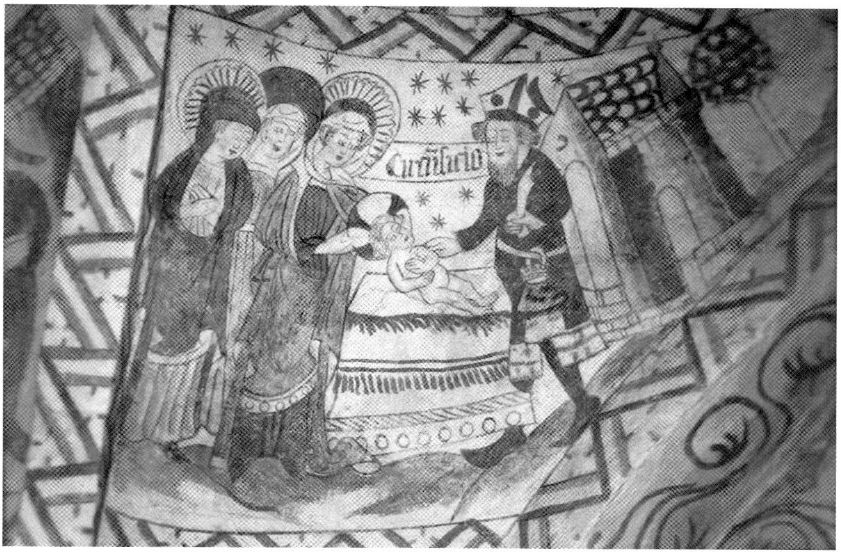

Fig. 5. Tuse church, wall painting, 1460–80. 'The Circumcision'. © www.kalkmalerier.dk

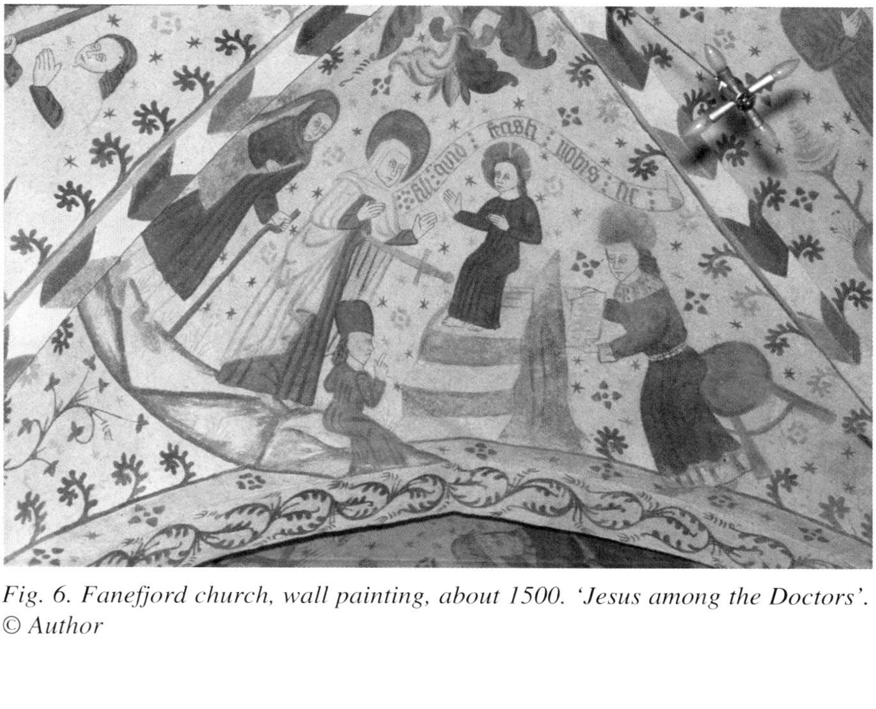

Fig. 6. Fanefjord church, wall painting, about 1500. 'Jesus among the Doctors'. © Author

Austria, we see the same type of mockery. Jews, however, were represented in a more neutral manner, as well-dressed wealthy men with a variety of types of Jewish hats. For instance, there is less drama in the rendering of the Expulsion of the Moneychangers from the Temple in Mørkøv church.

There were often many different types of Jewish hats depicted within one decoration or altarpiece. In the pictorial arts of the Middle Ages, each figure in the depictions of episodes from the Bible had to be painted in contemporary dress, so as to ensure that it could be easily identified. For that reason, even the dress of Jews changed and varied. The central panel of the winged altarpiece in Gudme church is taken up by a densely populated crucifixion scene. The group of Jews is shown with several different kinds of hats and beards. In the carved relief with secondary paint from the altarpiece in Brendekilde church, Funen, from about 1475, there is for instance a considerable number of Jewish hats in the scene with the Crowning of Thorns. Several Jews are wearing hoods or other pointed hats, with large upturned brims.

One particular motif is of special interest in this context; namely, the Circumcision and Naming of Christ on the eighth day as described in the Bible. In the Middle Ages, making a picture of the event as it had once occurred posed a problem. Should it be depicted as an analogy to the common practice of baptizing children inside the church, as an operation performed by a high priest looking somewhat similar to a bishop, or should it be represented in the manner in which the Jewish ritual of circumcision was carried out in the synagogue?

On the winged altarpiece in the church of Mary in Helsingborg, which is dated to 1449–52 on the basis of the coat of arms of the donor, the feudal vassal Joachim Flemming, the Circumcision is shown in relief on the central panel (fig. 4).[11] The small naked child is placed on a prominently placed altar. The infant Jesus is held by two women, while a bearded man and his assistant carry out the operation. Thus it is performed by two Jewish men with the holy women as participants. The altar receives the blood of Christ for the first time—a highly significant theological detail. The Circumcision by the Isefjords workshop in Tuse church, which is probably about ten years later, also depicts the child laid on a table. The Virgin Mary is holding the infant Jesus; behind her stand two women. The high priest stands on the opposite side of the altar with a knife in his hand. He is wearing a bishop's mitre, but his garb is nevertheless secular, with fur-trimmings on the borders of the knee-length coat. He carries a purse or bag in his belt (fig. 5).

Fanefjord church on Møn has an exceptionally large and detailed pictorial programme painted by the so-called Elmelunde workshop around 1500. Several of the motifs are copied directly from the forty-page edition of the *Biblia*

---

[11] Lena Liepe, *Den medeltida träskulpturen i Skåne. Produktion och förvärv*, pp. 154, 186, *Den medeltida träskulpturen i Skåne. En bilddokumentation*, fig. 153, Skånsk senmedeltid och renässans, vols 14–15 (Lund: Lund University Press, 1995).

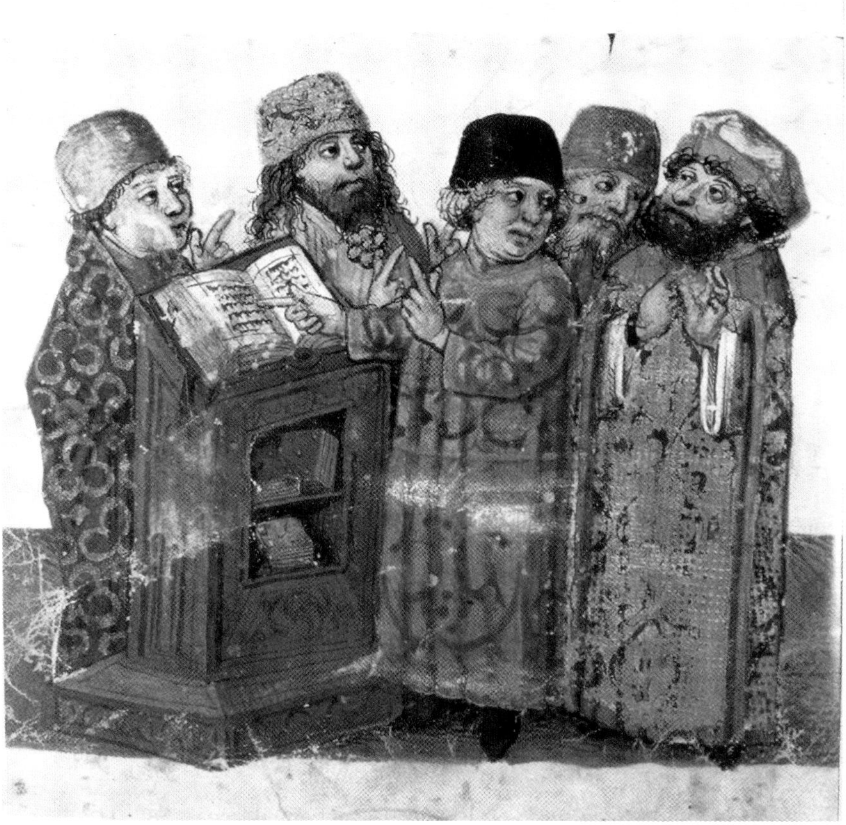

Fig. 7. Haggadah. German, c. *1460, London, British Library, MS. Add. 14762, fol. 7*v*. 'German Jews' (from Metzger:* Jewish Life *, fig. 175)*

Pauperum, as for instance David and Goliath and Samson slaying the Lion.[12] In the depiction of Christ, aged twelve, among the doctors in the temple there is no doubt as to who are the Jews. The two Pharisees wear tall hats with round crowns; the evil one shown in profile has a small pointed top on his hat, and the other one carrying a scroll wears a plushy grey hat. Similar plushy tall hats are worn by other evidently Jewish figures in Fanefjord, and such hats are found also

[12] Ulla Haastrup, 'Pictures in Both Books and Churches. Biblia pauperum and Speculum humanae salvationis as reflected in Danish ecclesiastical art', in *Living Words and Luminous Pictures, Medieval Book Culture in Denmark*, ed. by Erik Petersen (Copenhagen: Det Kongelige Bibliotek, 1999), pp. 127–44; Haastrup, 'Representations of Jews in Danish Medieval Art' (as in note 4), p. 132.

in a German Haggadah manuscript of 1460 (figs 6 and 7).[13] The Circumcision is painted in Fanefjord church as one of the scenes in the Childhood of Christ (fig. 8). A man wearing a red coat with a fur collar and brim is sitting on a turned wooden chair with the small naked child in his lap, Christ with the cruciform halo. The high priest is wearing not a bishop's mitre but a plushy Jew's hat. A kneeling young man with no headgear is performing the circumcision. Two women with haloes stand next to them. From an iconographical point of view, this is an unusual motif. The all-important altar is missing; instead, the Jewish high priest or godfather is sitting on a chair with the infant Jesus. In the forty-page edition of the *Biblia Pauperum*, the scene is missing. In the slightly more recent fifty-page edition, the Circumcision is depicted with a bishop at the altar where Christ is laid, exactly like the depiction in Tuse church.[14]

Where did the painters on Møn find their model? Turning to illustrated Hebrew manuscripts one finds close parallels (fig. 9). In a Hebrew manuscript from Naples, dating to the third quarter of the fifteenth century, there is an illustration containing the same elements as the mural in Fanefjord church. Godfather Sandaq or the high priest is sitting in a chair with the naked child in his lap, and the Jewish officiant, the Mohel, is kneeling in front of them while performing the operation.[15] On the altarpiece in Nürnberg, the Tuscher altar from the mid-fifteenth century, the Circumcision is painted almost as a 'photographic' rendering of the Jewish ritual (fig. 10).[16] The Virgin Mary and Joseph are seen at the furthermost back of the picture, looking in over a curtain.

Depictions with such realistic details cannot be found in Danish murals; they belong to quite another genre with other sets of rules for the symbolic rendering and with no use of spatial effects. When seeking depictions of Jews, one must make up one's mind as to what kind of pictures one should expect to find. Now we are approaching the core of my hypothesis. How could one depict the naming or baptism of Christ in a large Danish parish church as if it took place in a Jewish synagogue? In Nürnberg there were a lot of Jews, and one would understand the 'caricature' painting of the Circumcision; but what about in Denmark?

I have pointed out earlier the manner in which all biblical events were rendered in contemporary garb and with everyday objects. They should be quite

---

[13] Térèse and Mendel Metzger, *Jewish Life in the Middle Ages, Illuminated Hebrew Manuscripts of the Thirteenth to the Sixteenth Centuries* (Secaucus, NJ: Chartwell, 1982), p. 123, fig. 175.

[14] Knud Banning, 'Jesu omskærelse. En gennemgang af billedsiden i den 50-bladede Biblia Pauperum', in *Genesis Profeta. Studier i gammeltestamentlig ikonografi, 6, Nordiska symposiet för ikonografiska studier*, Gimo 1978, ed. by Patrik Reutersward (Stockholm : Almqvist & Wiksell, 1980), pp. 135–39.

[15] Térèse and Mendel Metzger (as in note 13), p. 225, fig. 333.

[16] Mellinkoff (as in note 3), vol. II, fig. II.23.

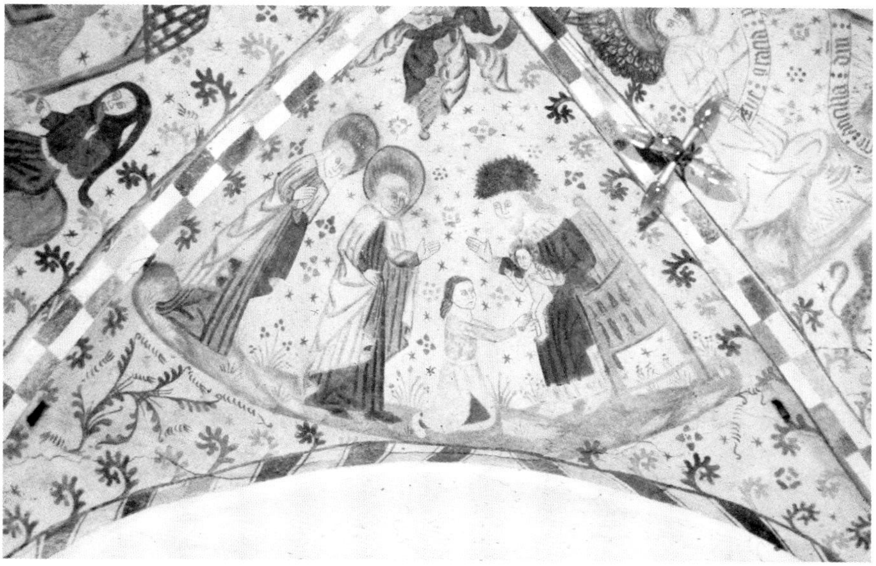

Fig. 8. Fanefjord church, wall painting, c. *1500. 'The Circumcision'.* © *Author*

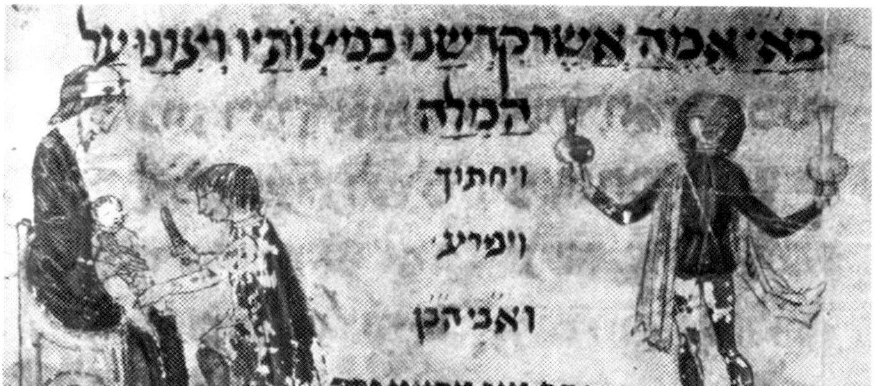

Fig. 9. Hebrew manuscript, Naples, Third quarter of the fifteenth century. Nîmes, Bibliothèque municipale, ms. 13, fol. 181v. 'The Circumcision' (from Metzger: Jewish Life, *fig. 333)*

comprehensible to the spectator. Nobody must be at a loss as to the meaning of the scenes or have any doubts about the identity of the participants. The clergy who approved and probably also determined the pictorial programs in the big rich church of Fanefjord must have had an immediate understanding of the depiction of the Jewish ritual of circumcision with the small Jesus-child with his cruciform halo, and so must their congregations. Could they fathom it, if they themselves were ignorant of contemporary Jews, their clothing and their religious customs? Would one for instance have to sail the short distance from Gedser to Rostock to see Jews?[17] Or might one in that period around 1500, so abundant in herring during the summer, have met Jews on Møn, Falster, and Lolland among the other foreign tradesmen from Germany, Norway, and the Baltic countries? If we seek such minorities in the Danish realm, we must expect to find them close to the king and close to centres of international commerce.

In Stege on Møn, where the king had a castle, the church was given a solid extension and was equipped with vaults in 1494 (fig. 11).[18] A series of names is painted on the western vault of the main aisle, and '. . . vi mormester alle evindelich meth Gudh' [. . . we the master-masons are all for ever with God]. The names of the guardians of the church are painted elsewhere, and on the northern wall of the second pier one finds some emblems and the designation 'Kristen Iude' (Christian Jew) next to a depiction of a man and a woman, each carrying a beaker and holding a jug between them. The man is wearing a pointed hood, and the caricature-masks on the pendentives are wearing extreme Jew's hats. Could Kristen Iude perhaps be a recently baptized Jewish artisan who took part in the building activities? In another significant Danish town, Nyborg on Funen, an account of about 1537 mentions the taxation with eleven marks of the booths in Jødestræde (Jews Lane).[19] The royal court at Nyborg Castle and the extensive sea trade from Nyborg counted among the most vital preconditions for a Jewish community to live here in the same manner as in other towns of Europe.

If historians read the old Danish written sources anew, then possibly several of the names with the surname spelled iude / jyde could be transformed from

---

[17] *Meklenburgisches Urkundenbuch*, vols 3–4 (Schwerin: Verein für meklenburgische Geschichte und Altertumskunde, 1865). For example, in 1279, the city of Rostock donates a burial-ground for Jews outside the town walls. In 1283, the Jew Salathiel's house and his children are mentioned. The following year, the city council receives a loan of four hundred marks from the same Jew and grants him the city's protection. I am indebted to Associate Professor Kurt Villads Jensen for drawing my attention to the publication of the Mecklenburg diplomas.

[18] Haastrup, 'Representations of Jews in Danish Medieval Art' (as in note 4), p. 161, notes 132–33.

[19] Lars Bisgaard, 'Gildernes religiøse rolle i det middelalderlige Svendborg—om en genfunden liste over altre i Sct. Nicolai og Vor Frue', in *Årbog for Svendborg og Omegns Museum* (Svendborg: Museumsforeningen Svendborg, 1996), pp. 42–63.

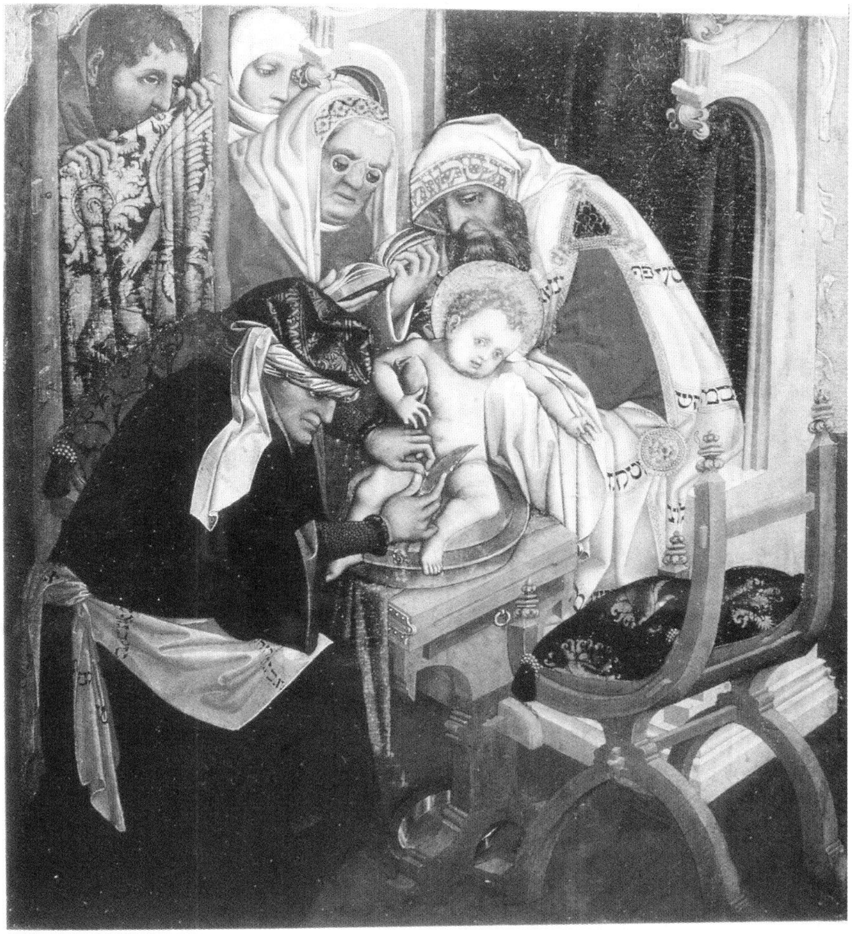

Fig. 10. Master of The Tuscher-altar, Nürnberg, c. *1450, 'The Circumcision'. Aachen, Suermondt-Museum, from Mellinkoff,* Outcasts , *vol. ii, fig. ii.23*

Jutlander to the minority, Jews.[20] The manner of spelling was the same until the early sixteenth century, only then *iøde* ['Jew'] was spelled with the *o* with a slash like the modern *ø*. When reading the religious medieval texts in the Danish language, there is never any doubt that the word *iude* designates Jews, even when spelled like 'Jutlander'. Medieval names as source material could possibly

[20] Haastrup, 'Representations of Jews in Danish Medieval Art' (as in note 4), p. 160, note 130.

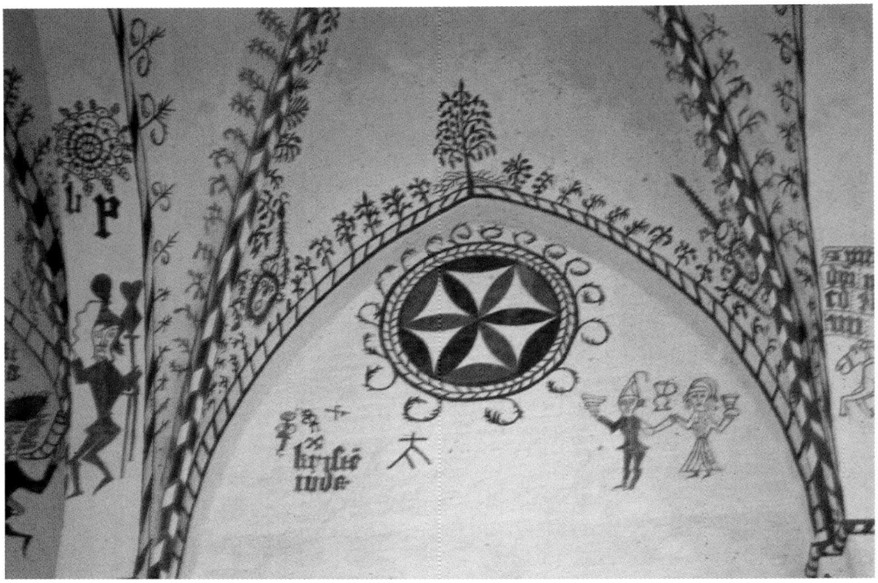

Fig. 11. Stege church, wall painting 1494. 'Kristen iude *and figures with Jewish hats'. © Author*

be exploited further. Old Testament names in Europe were usually names for Jews. Yet, accounts of Jewish history in Denmark always have as their point of departure that King Christian IV in 1622 summoned Portuguese Jewish goldsmiths to Altona and granted them freedom of religious practice.

After years of preoccupation with images of Jews in the Danish Middle Ages, I have found so many significant ones that I am no longer apt to believe the traditional statement of the Danish and Scandinavian historian that 'there were no Jews in Medieval Scandinavia'. I have been surprised by the many interesting depictions of Jews which neither I nor others had recognized before. Based on the pictorial evidence, historians must re-read the few written sources. Perhaps then accounts about Jews in Denmark may surface.

Why should there not, indeed, have been Jews in the Nordic countries? On all other levels, Denmark was an integrated part of the Catholic European society. Where are the arguments that permit one, based on a scanty and random written source-material, to claim that Denmark did not house a Jewish minority?

Anti-semitism, image desecration, and the problem of 'Jewish execution'

NORBERT SCHNITZLER

This essay deals with a sample of late medieval panel-paintings and woodcuts depicting the narrative of a miracle that allegedly took place in fourteenth-century Flanders, in the county of Hainaut. These pictures will be discussed from a historian's point of view, that is to say, they will be used as sources providing the basis for an investigation of medieval anti-Semitism, and especially of the impact of medieval legal theory on visual strategies of stigmatization and discrimination. From a quick glance at current debates on issues such as the modes of representation of reality or the relation between content and context, inaugurated by art historians and social historians as well, it seems clear that those debates which gave rise to a re-evaluation of pictures as historical sources require new methodological and systematic considerations, especially in the field of legal history.[1] More precisely, my argument

[1] N. Schnitzler, 'Picturing the Law—Introductory Remarks on the Medieval Iconography of Judgement and Punishment', in *Law and its Images in Medieval Europe* (special issue of *Medieval History Journal*, 3.1), ed. by N. Schnitzler (London: Sage, 2000), pp. 1–15; *Der Blick auf die Bilder: Kunstgeschichte und Geschichte im Gespräch*, ed. by Otto Gerhard Oexle (Göttingen: Vandenhoeck & Ruprecht, 1997); G. Signori, 'Wörter, Sachen und Bilder—oder: die Mehrdeutigkeit des scheinbar Eindeutigen', in *Mundus in imagine*, ed. by A. Löther et alii (Munich: Fink, 1996), pp. 11–33; H. Talkenberger, 'Von der Illustration zur Interpretation. Methodische Überlegungen zur Historischen Bildkunde', in *Zeitschrift für historische Forschung*, 21 (Berlin: Duncker & Humblot, 1994), pp. 289–313; G. Kocher, *Zeichen und Symbole des Rechts* (Munich: Beck, 1992); W. Schild, 'Nutzen und Wert von Rechtsarchäologie und Rechtsikonographie für die mittelalterliche Rechtsgeschichte', in *Rechtsarchäologie und*

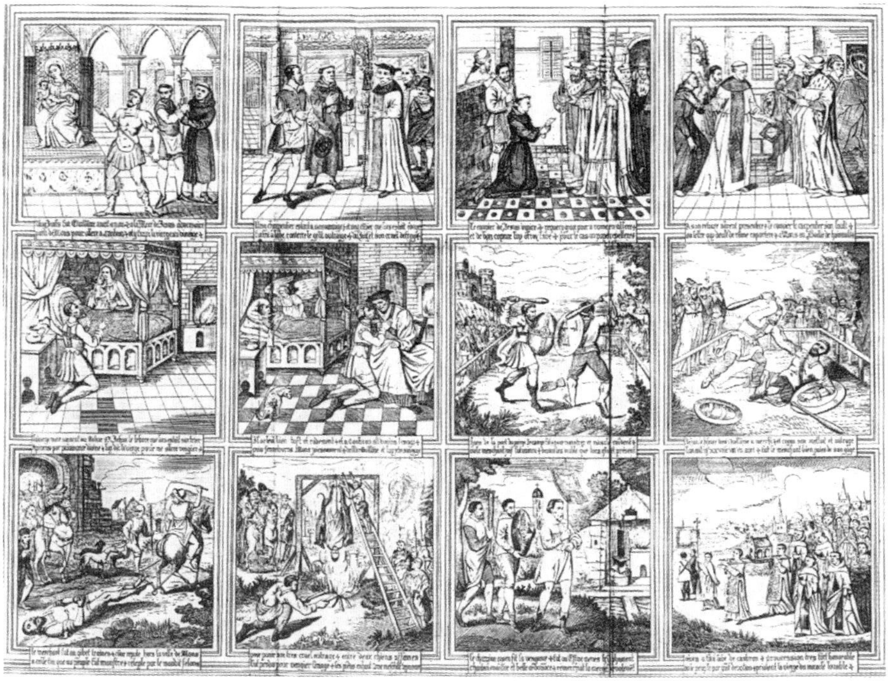

Fig. 1. Engraving representing the panel-painting with the Miracle of Notre-Dame de Cambron, c. *1890, J. van Péteghem, Brussels*

concerns the ongoing differentiation of the system of law in the later Middle Ages (i.e., the reception of Roman law, the generalization of legal norms, the regulations of proceeding) and its implication for the changing contents of images. This is to say the impact of penal law or the impact of juridical concepts such as 'deterrence' (or so-called juridical 'rituals of exclusion') on Christian iconography, especially on the representation of Jews. To a certain extent one

Rechtsikonographie. Eine Annäherung, Akten des Brüsseler Kolloquiums, Iuris Scripta Historica, 5, ed. by P. de Win (Brussels: Wetenschappelijk comité voor rechtsgeschiedenis koninklijke academie voor wetenschappen, letteren en schone kunsten van België, 1990), pp. 59–74; N. H. Ott, 'Der Körper als konkrete Hülle des Abstrakten. Zur Wandel der Rechtsgebärde im Spätmittelalter', in *Gepeinigt, begehrt, vergessen—Symbolik und Sozialbezug des Körpers im späten Mittelalter und in der Frühen Neuzeit*, ed. by N. Schnitzler and K. Schreiner (Munich: Fink, 1992), pp. 223–41; idem, *Rechtspraxis und Heilsgeschehen. Zu Überlieferung, Ikonographie und Gebrauchssituation des deutschen 'Belial'*, MTU, 80 (Tübingen: Niemeyer, 1983); *Text-Bild-Interpretationen. Untersuchungen zu den Bilderhandschriften des Sachsenspiegels*, MMS, 55.1, ed. by R. Schmidt-Wiegand (Munich: Fink, 1986).

could argue that reality occupies the sphere of pictorial tradition.

Our starting point will be a painting situated today in a small chapel about five miles away from the city of Mons (fig. 1). The chapel is dedicated to Our Lady of Cambron, which was the site of a former Cistercian convent another five miles to the north of Mons. The painting has been dated to the first half of the sixteenth century. Thus, most probably, it was part of the original inventory of the chapel, which was consecrated in 1483. The panel is sub-divided into twelve scenes illustrating the legend of an image-desecration fashioned as a late medieval curing-miracle.[2] If we confine ourselves only to the first frame, we may swiftly assume that it provides the pivotal scene (fig. 2). The panel shows the violation of the aforesaid cultic image of the Madonna and its moral and social impacts. The offender has to do penance for it, which means by his life. Just behind him a man, a carver we are told, already has brandished his axe to carry out this act of moral justice. But he is prevented from doing so, and this is the point where the actual version of the miraculous legend begins. Moreover, the following eleven scenes are dominated by the cultural strategies of honour and shame, as a closer examination will indicate.

In the field of medieval piety, the relationship between image and donor had developed in a specific direction. Obviously image and saint were almost completely identified with one another, that is to say image and saint were believed to be bound through heavenly ties.[3] This relation was conceptualized in

---

[2] Th. Lejeune, 'Notre-Dame de Cambron et sa légende', *Revue de l'art chrétien*, 7 (1863), 457–81; A. Klassert, 'Entehrung Maria durch die Juden', *Jahrbuch für Geschichte, Sprache und Literatur Elsass-Lothringens*, 21 (1905), 78–155. For the abbey of Cambron, see *Monuments pour servir à l'histoire des provinces de Namur, de Hainaut et de Luxembourg*, ed. by L. Devillers (Brussels: Publications de la Commission royale d'histoire, 1896), vol. III. A slightly extended German version of this article has been published in *Bilder, Texte, Rituale*, Zeitschrift für historische Forschung, Beihefte 24, ed. by K. Schreiner and G. Signori (Berlin: Duncker & Humbolt, 2000), pp. 111–38. For the history of the Jewish communities in Flanders, see C. Cluse, *Studien zur Geschichte der Juden in den mittelalterlichen Niederlanden*, Forschungen zur Geschichte der Juden, Abt. A Abhandlungen (Hannover: Hahnsche Buchhandlung, 2001).

[3] Some scholars have suggested the theological phrase 'real presence' to characterize the relationship between image and saint according to medieval pious imagination. This seems also to be true for the image of Notre-Dame de Cambron. Thus the notion of 'real presence' is addressed by the gesture of the Madonna in the first scene representing the image desecration: She points to the Christ-child who 'turns away' to escape the violent attack. Directly beneath that scene the Madonna appears in a vision (cf. fig. 3); interestingly enough, she is depicted not as a 'bleeding' sculpture but as a 'real' figure. P. Dinzelbacher, 'Die 'Realpräsenz' der Heiligen in ihren Reliquiaren und Gräbern nach mittelalterlichen Quellen', in *Heiligenverehrung in Geschichte und Gegenwart*, ed. by P. Dinzelbacher and D. R. Bauer (Ostfildern: Schwabenverlag, 1990), pp. 115–74; Robert W. Scribner, 'Das Visuelle in der Volksfrömmigkei', in *Bilder und Bildersturm im Spät-*

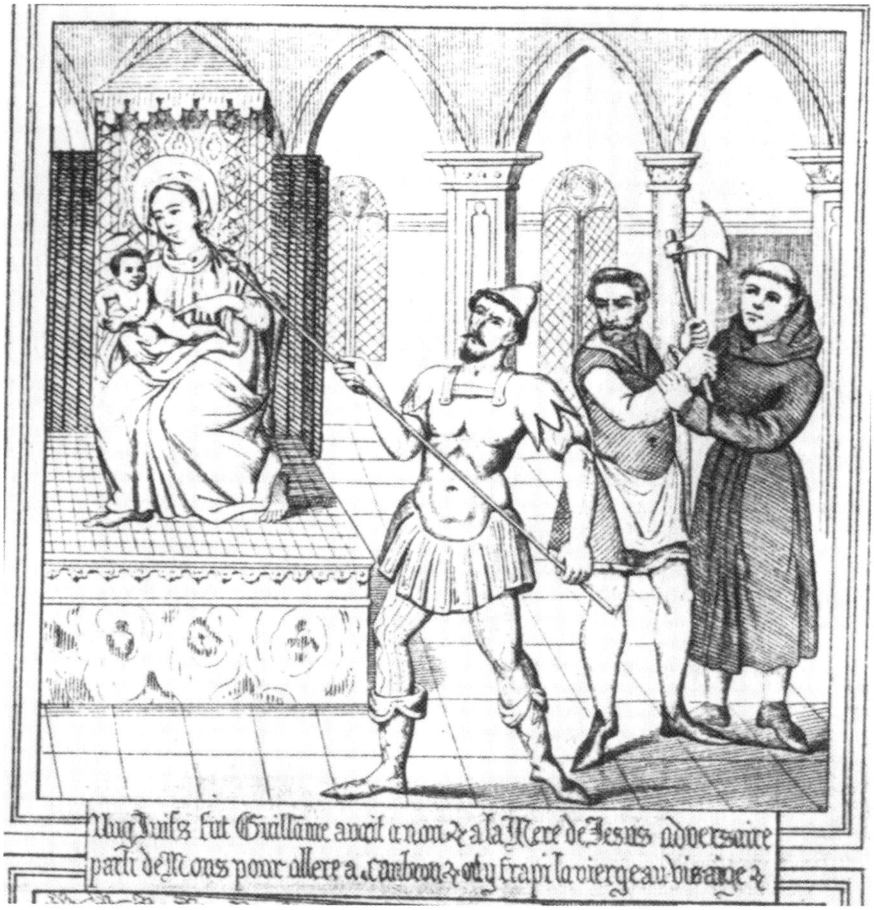

Fig. 2. First field of the panel-painting: The image desecration, detail, c. *1890, J. van Péteghem, Brussels*

terms of a moral economy depending on personal relations, based on an accumu-

---

mittelalter und in der frühen Neuzeit, Wolfenbütteler Forschungen, 46, ed. by R. W. Scribner and M. Warnke (Wiesbaden: Harrassowitz, 1990), pp. 9–20; G. P. Marchal, 'Bildersturm im Mittelalter', *Historisches Jahrbuch*, 113 (1993), 255–82; J. Hamburger, *The Visual and the Visionary: Art and female Spirituality in Medieval Germany* (New York: Zone, 1998). For a critical examination of the concept of 'real presence', see N. Schnitzler, 'Illusion, Täuschung und schöner Schein. Probleme der Bilderverehrung im späten Mittelalter', in *Frömmigkeit im Mittelalter. Politisch-soziale Kontexte, visuelle Praxis, körperliche Ausdrucksformen*, ed. by K. Schreiner (Munich: Fink, 2002), pp. 221–42.

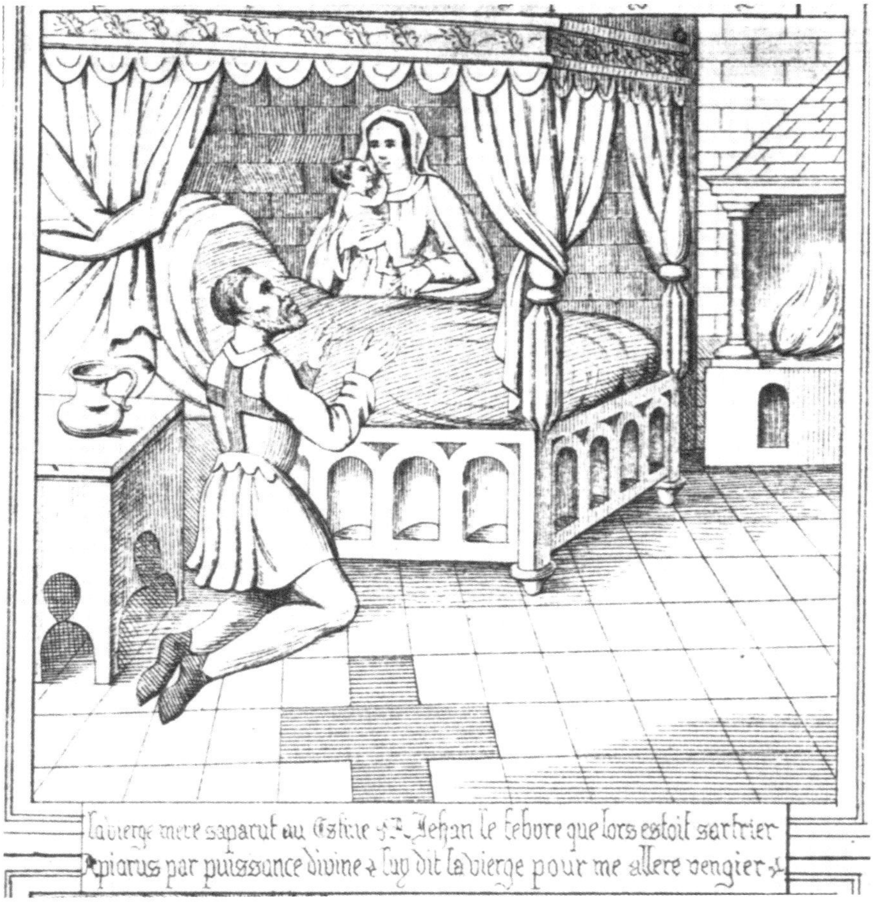

Fig. 3. Fifth field of the panel-painting: Mary appears in a vision to the blacksmith, detail, c. *1890, J. van Péteghem, Brussels*

lation of honour and prestige. According to this, one could suggest a triangular model covering saint, donor, and the image that determines the interaction of individual Christian believers.[4]

[4] H. Belting, *Bild und Kult* (Munich: Beck, 1990); R. C. Trexler, 'Florentine Religious Experience: The Sacred Image', in idem, *Church and Community 1200–1600* (Rome: Edizioni di storia e letteratura, 1987), pp. 37–74; idem, 'Der Heiligen neue Kleider—Zum Be- und Entkleiden von Statuen im Mittelalter', in *Gepeinigt, begehrt, vergessen—Symbolik und Sozialbezug des Körpers im späten Mittelalter und in der Frühen Neuzeit*, ed. by N. Schnitzler and K. Schreiner (Munich: Fink, 1992), pp. 365–88; Jeffrey Hamburger, 'The 'Liber miraculorum' of Unterlinden: An Icon and Its Convent Setting',

As the panel of the legend demonstrates, the Madonna of Cambron had been 'blasphemously violated' by a disbelieving offender, that is to say her 'virtue' [*virtus*]—the usual Latin term—had been tested. Besides the immediate effect (the image produces blood), the Madonna responded as an insulted medieval mistress would have done: she calls for a 'knightly' follower to take revenge for the degrading outrage.[5] Indeed, the fifth panel shows a male person—a blacksmith we are told, actually depicted as a knight—who is to play the part of the avenger (fig. 3). In a vision the Madonna urges the blacksmith to become her 'soldier' and to take revenge for the iconoclastic attack. The impact of our lady's claim is rather archaic, even in the social context of late medieval Europe. The 'knightly' blacksmith is designated to fight a duel, which in the legend is labelled as ordeal [*ordal*] that means a *judicium dei*, against the offender.[6]

The next scene from the cycle confronts the spectator with a terrifying representation of an execution (fig. 4). In the very centre of the scene, the blasphemous offender has been hanged from the gallows, with a pyre beneath him and two dogs hanging beside him. On the left, a group of noblemen, with the count in their midst, is watching the execution; in the background we detect traces of a city-skyline. The painted scene is accompanied by a verse quatrain, which reads as follows: 'In order to punish his most gruesome outrage / between two ravenous dogs / he was hanged to avenge the image / upside-down like a convicted criminal'.[7]

The term *avenge* might remind us once more of the suggestion that the former miraculous legend is mediated and at the same time transformed through the visual narrative into a story of honour and shame. Such an 'ethnographic' view is underlined by the extraordinary way the blasphemous offender was executed.[8]

---

in *The Sacred Image East and West*, ed. by R. Ousterhout and L. Brubaker (Urbana: University of Illinois Press, 1995), pp. 147–90.

[5] Lejeune (as in note 2), pp. 462–63. A similar case of denigrating an image of the Virgin is discussed in my article 'Geschmähte Symbole', in *Verletzte Ehre—Ehrkonflikte in Gesellschaften des Mittelalters und der frühen Neuzeit*, Norm und Struktur, 5, ed. by K. Schreiner and G. Schwerhoff (Cologne: Böhlau, 1995), pp. 279–302. In general, see: K. Schreiner, *Maria—Jungfrau, Mutter, Herrscherin* (Munich: Hanser, 1994); G. Signori, *Maria zwischen Kloster, Kathedrale und Welt. Hagiographische und historiographische Annäherung an eine hochmittelalterliche Wunderpredigt* (Sigmaringen: Thorbecke, 1995).

[6] Lejeune (as in note 2), pp. 464–66.

[7] Lejeune (as in note 2), p. 481: 'Pour punir son tres-cruel outrage/Entre deux chiens affamés/Fut pendu pour vengier l'image/Les pieds en haut comme meschant aprouvé'.

[8] The image represents an accumulation of the worst punishments of medieval penal law. The malefactor has been hanged from the gallows, the very act of earthly jurisdiction; this is accompanied by the stake, the most severe form of penance according to Church law. After this, to increase the degree of shame to its ultimate level, he has been

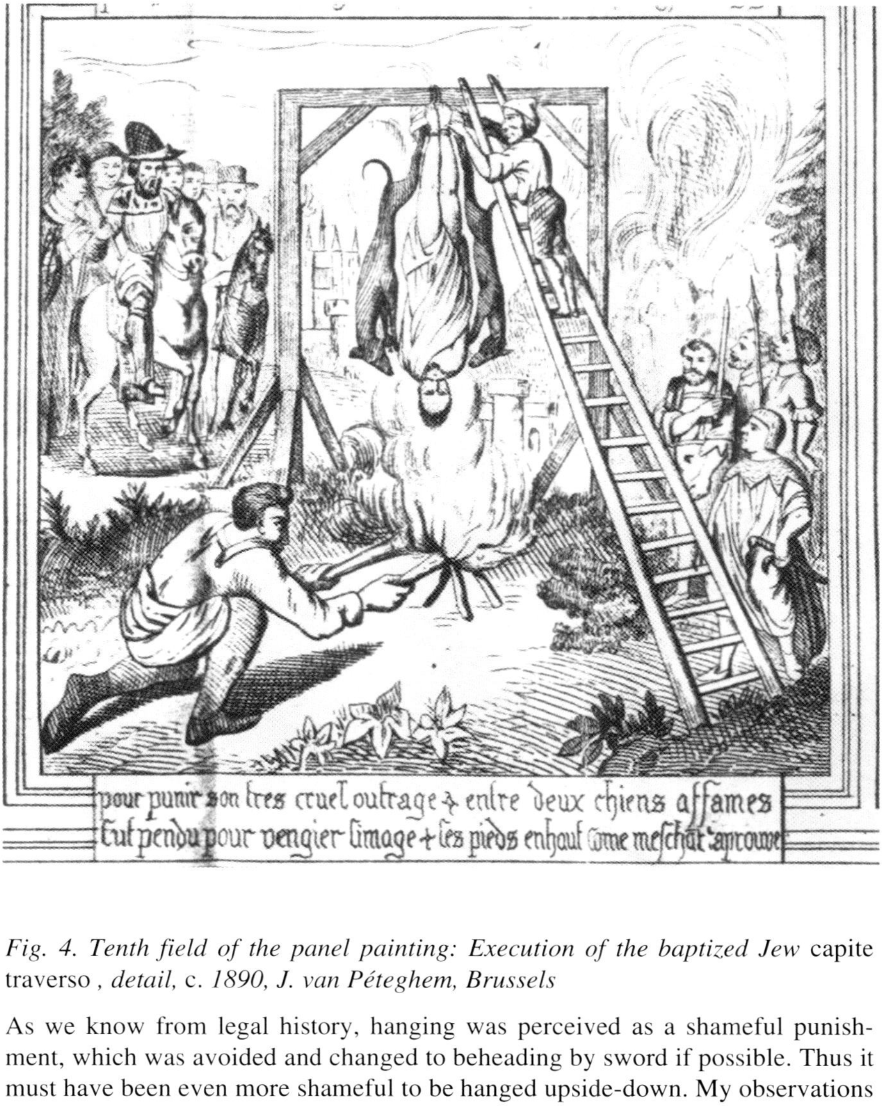

Fig. 4. Tenth field of the panel painting: Execution of the baptized Jew capite traverso *, detail,* c. *1890, J. van Péteghem, Brussels*

As we know from legal history, hanging was perceived as a shameful punishment, which was avoided and changed to beheading by sword if possible. Thus it must have been even more shameful to be hanged upside-down. My observations and remarks contain methodological implications and suggest mutual and com-

hanged upside-down, with two hungry dogs beside him. On medieval penal law in general, see: W. Schild, *Alte Gerichtsbarkeit* (Munich: Callwey, 1980), and by the same author, 'Verstümmelung des menschlichen Körpers. Zur Bedeutung der Glieder und Organe des Menschen', in *Erfindung des Menschen—Schöpfungsträume und Körperbilder 1500–2000*, ed. by R. van Dülmen (Cologne: Böhlau, 1998), pp. 261–80.

plex interrelations between a highly elaborated code of late medieval society (i.e., 'honour') and the iconographic representation of a miracle legend. As we will see, the painting from the chapel of Notre-Dame shaped the former legend and the historical events in a peculiar way. And, after all, there are further references to other contexts or discourses that we are compelled to reconstruct if we want to reach an historical level of interpretation.

The Legend of Cambron, or The Making of Cultic Imagery by Addressing Anti-Semitic Activity

Leaving the horrific details aside, I will concentrate now on another important aspect of the legend. As we learn from the verses beneath the scenes, the iconoclast is identified as a Jew. The visual representations of the panel seem to ignore this fact, because only the pointed hat, the *pileus cornutus*, refers to his Jewish identity. Yet the written sources are absolutely clear about it, and as other representations of this legend will indicate, it was precisely this anti-Semitic background that made this narrative attractive for authors and painters of the fifteenth and sixteenth centuries.[9]

The legend of the miraculous image of Cambron already had been established one hundred years earlier, in the mid-fourteenth century, most probably as a reaction to the first expulsions of Jews from France, in 1306 and 1321 respectively.[10] According to a Dutch chronicle from the 1350s, the iconoclast was a converted Jew from Mons named Guillaume who had been baptized by the count of Hainaut himself and who became one of his high ranking vassals.[11] During a visit to the monastery of Cambron (dated to the year 1322), he allegedly felt provoked to attack verbally as well as physically the image of the Virgin, yet he was able to escape the place unrecognized. It was only four years later that he was denounced by a Christian blacksmith. As we have learned already from the panel painting, he was defeated in a duel and consequently sentenced to death on the gallows. Thus, the written sources render the anti-Semitic origins of the legend perfectly clear.

---

[9] On the anti-Jewish image-desecration libel in general, see: N. Schnitzler, *Ikonoklasmus—Bildersturm. Theologischer Bilderstreit und ikonoklastisches Handeln während des 15. und 16. Jahrhunderts* (Munich: Fink, 1996), pp. 104–25.

[10] See G. Mentgen, 'Die Vertreibungen der Juden aus England und Frankreich im Mittelalter', *Aschkenaz*, 7 (1997), 11–53.

[11] Johannes de Beke, *Croniken van den stichte van Utrecht ende van Hollant*, ed. by H. Bruch, Rijks Geschiedkundige Publicatien, GS 180 (The Hague: Nijhoff, 1982), pp. 177–78. Some years earlier, about 1330, Wilhelm of Egmond briefly mentioned the Cambron event: *Wilhelmi cappelani in Brederode postea monachi et procuratoris Egmodensis chronicon*, ed. by Pijnacker Hordijk (Amsterdam: Mueller, 1904), p. 167.

This tendency also can be confirmed by two other arguments. First, we should keep in mind that during the fourteenth century the anti-Jewish image-desecration libel became an effective strategy to overcome Jewish adversaries.[12] Second, later commentators of the Cambron legend never forgot to add that the papal chamber hesitated to grant an indulgence to the monastery because its commercial aims were too obvious.[13] It therefore becomes clear that the attempt to establish the cult image of Cambron had incited as well as increased anti-Semitic feeling in the county of Hainaut. It was because of these anti-Semitic origins, as Eric Zafran has argued, that the Cambron legend reverberated (in written sources as well as in art) throughout the sixteenth and seventeenth centuries. Wilhelm Gumppenberg, for instance, the compiler of a voluminous collection of image-miracles, recounts the story in detail.[14]

In his study of the 'Iconography of anti-Semitism'[15] in the Middle Ages, Zafran took up an older reference to an early book-print of the first decade of the sixteenth century, entitled 'Dishonour and Disgrace displayed to Mary by the Jews', vaguely ascribed to the Strasbourg humanist Thomas Murner († 1537).[16] Compared to the panel of the chapel of Notre-Dame the anti-Semitic elements of these woodcuts appear even more drastic. As on the panel, the legend is represented in twelve individual woodcuts, which illustrate more or less the same episodes of the story. Besides stylistic aspects the woodcuts differ with regard to the number of offenders, which has now grown to five (fig. 2).[17] In other words, the insult has become an anti-Christian collective action. Furthermore, the scenes referring to the foundation of a pilgrimage are now replaced by two scenes presenting legal acts: an oath-taking and an application of torture.[18] Stigmatizing effects are evoked also by Hebrew letters on the garment, by headgear, and by the yellow badge on the clothes of the Jews.

---

[12] Besides the legends of violated statues of the Madonna, the legend of a crucifix attacked by a Jew was also very popular. See Schnitzler (as in note 8), pp. 107–10, 113–22; E. Zafran, 'An Alleged Case of Image Desecration by the Jews and its Representation in Art: The Virgin of Cambron', *Journal of Jewish Art*, 2 (1975), 62–71.

[13] Johannes Trithemius († 1516), *Chronica monasterii Hirsaugiensis, Pars II* (Frankfurt am Main, 1601), p. 216; Wilhelm Gumppenberg, *Marianischer Atlas von Anfang und Ursprung zwölfhundert wunderthätiger Marien-Bilder [. . .] durch R. P. Maximillianum Wartenberg in das Teutsch übersetzt* (Munich, 1673), p. 66.

[14] W. Gumppenberg (as in note 13).

[15] E. Zafran, *The Iconography of anti-Semitism* (D.Phil. diss., New York, 1973).

[16] Anonymous, *Enderung und Schmach Mariae von den juden bewissen* (Strasbourg, 1515?), ed. by Klassert (as in note 2), pp. 83–86; see also W. List, 'Ein seltener Druck aus der Offizin des Matthias Hüpfuff', *Centralblatt für Bibliothekswesen*, 4 (1887), 290–93.

[17] Klassert (as in note 2), p. 98–99.

[18] Ibid., p. 105–06.

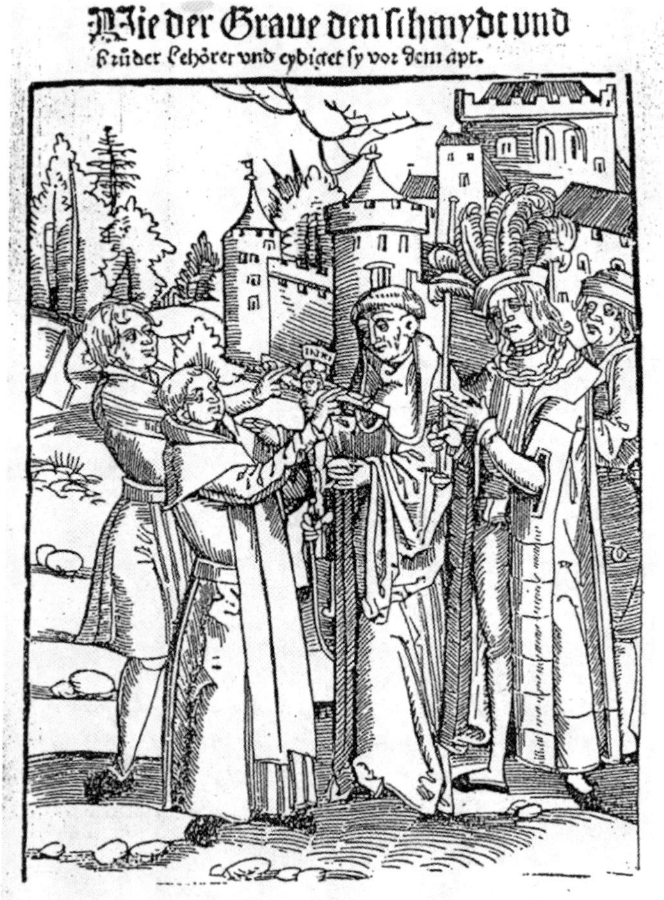

Fig. 5. Oath-Taking, from Enderung vnd Schmach der Bildung Mariae von den Juden bewiesen, *Strasbourg* c. *1515*

Zafran's main argument concerns the propagandist goal of the booklet to popularize the myth of Jewish iconoclasm, which he traced back to the early medieval period (figs 5 and 6). According to him, the booklet had been printed to strengthen the popular anti-Semitic sentiments of a wide audience. In addition, Zafran underlines an important remark by Murner stating that Emperor Maximilian had ordered the painting of these twelve woodcut-scenes on the walls of the Franciscan refectory in Colmar with the intention of strengthening the image desecration libel. Probably this was also a measure destined to legitimize the expulsion of Jews, which at the same time had taken place in the

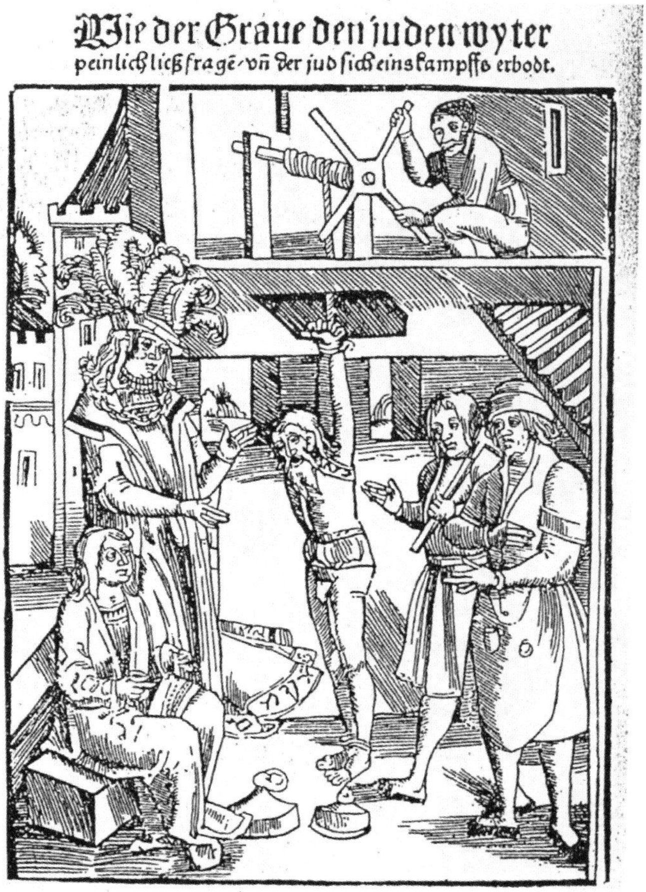

Fig. 6. Torture, from Enderung vnd Schmach der Bildung Mariae von den Juden bewiesen, *Strasbourg* c. *1515*

city of Colmar.[19]

In my view, Zafran has missed a central point of the printed legend. Of course, the woodcut-illustrations follow a narrative structure similar to the panel. But in contrast to the panel, the plot is not structured according to the contemporary discourse of 'honour'. The woodcuts are, rather, arranged according to the course of legal procedure, that is to say they affirm the logic of penal law.

---

[19] Zafran (as in note 12), pp. 64–65; For the history of the Jewish community in Colmar see *Germania Judaica*, 3.1, ed. by A. Maimon (Tübingen: J. C. B. Mohr, 1987), pp. 657–62.

The series starts with a crime and ends with the execution of the (main) offender. The different stations of legal procedures are systematically transferred to the field of visual narrative. Thus, I would assume that these variations were an effect of structural changes in the legal system itself.[20] The execution scene, above all, now is clearly intended not only as the story's climax but also as a climax of anti-Semitic propaganda (fig. 7). These arguments might become all the more convincing if we bear in mind that Murner, the presumed author of the booklet, was a well-known scholar of law and member of the emperor's 'Academy of Poets'.[21]

The text itself uncovers further dimensions of meaning, especially in relation to the unusually harsh form of punishment. It points to an anti-Semitic tendency of medieval penal law in general, which is confirmed by the application of a special sort of punishment against Jews. The heading of the image gives little more than a short description of the image: 'How the count ordered the Jew to be hanged together with two male dogs and to be burned by a fire beneath the gallows'. But the corresponding parts of the poem give a more extended version. The presumed reader is reminded that this horrific representation should be 'taken as an example / How all Jews are outlawed who commit such abominable outrage'. Moreover, it is said that the sacrilegious offence was no misdeed of an individual at all but, rather, an outcome of Jewish stubbornness: 'Although they are witness to such important miracles / They never learn from that / Therefore he should receive this penance / Burned and hanged as well'.[22] This is a clear statement. The author approves of the principle intended by penal law, which means he approves of the idea of deterrence.

In contrast the chronicles of the fourteenth century say that the Jew had 'only'

---

[20] E. Wadle, 'Die Entstehung der öffentlichen Strafe', in *Perspektiven der Strafrechtsentwicklung (Ringvorlesung im Sommersemester 1994 an der Universität des Saarlandes)*, ed. by H. Jung, H. Müller-Dietz and U. Neumann (Baden-Baden: Nomos-Verlags-Gesellschaft, 1995); *Die Entstehung des öffentlichen Strafrechts*, ed. by D. Willoweit (Cologne: Böhlau, 1999); G. Schwerhoff, 'Devianz in der alteuropäischen Gesellschaft. Umrisse einer historischen Kriminalitätsforschung', *Zeitschrift für historische Forschung*, 19 (1992), 385–414; R. van Dülmen, *Verbrechen, Strafen und soziale Kontrolle* (Frankfurt am Main: Fischer, 1990).

[21] *Thomas Murner—Elsässischer Theologe und Humanist 1475–1537. Eine Ausstellung* (Karlsruhe: Badische Landesbibliothek, 1987).

[22] The complete passage reads (my translation): 'The sentence was read out by the count / That the Jew should be put to death / As well as alienated from earth / by hanging upside-down / with two enormous dogs beside him / which should be taken as an example / How all Jews are outlawed / who commit such abominable outrage / And shame our religion day after day. Although they are witness to such important miracles / They never learn from that. / Therefore he should receive this penance / Burned and hanged as well / On account of his abominable crime', cf. Klassert (as in note 2), pp. 126–27.

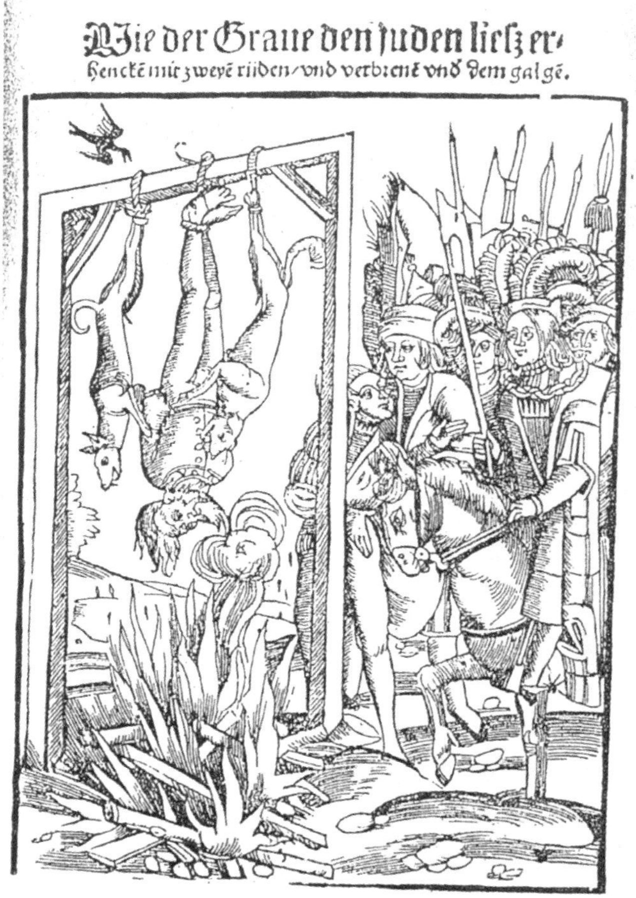

Fig. 7. Execution of the baptized Jew, from Enderung vnd Schmach der Bildung Mariae von den Juden bewiesen, *Strasbourg* c. *1515*

been burned at the stake. There is no mention of any degrading form of execution. However, hanging someone upside-down was not just a late medieval anti-Semitic fantasy. As we know from contemporary court-house records or legal ordinances, it became a common practice from the thirteenth century onwards, lasting well into the seventeenth century.[23]

[23] See N. Schnitzler, 'Juden vor Gericht—Soziale Ausgrenzung durch Sanktionen', in *Formen und Entwicklungen herrschaftlichen Strafens*, ed. by H. Schlosser, R. Sprandel, and D. Willoweit (Cologne: Böhlau, 2002), pp. 285–307; G. Kisch, 'The Jewish Execution in Medieval Germany and the Reception of Roman Law', in *L'Europa e il*

The Reality of Penal Law Against Jews

Evidence shows that the earliest testimonies of the application of hanging upside-down can be found in fourteenth-century France as well as in Aragon. The papal registers contain letters of remission, for instance one of a canon of the chapter of Beauvais from 1326 who applied to the pope for absolution since he had participated in stoning an executed Jew hanging upside-down on the gallows.[24] Earlier, in 1296, the annals of the Alsatian town of Colmar recount the case of a Jewish thief who had been sentenced to death, noting that he had been hanged upside-down on the gallows. Incredibly, the offender stayed alive for eight days and even was able to free himself, but because of his injuries he was unable to escape.[25]

A number of other cases demonstrate that the application of this form of punishment during the fourteenth and fifteenth centuries all over medieval Europe, including the imperial lands of Germany. But it should be noticed that in the majority of cases the punishment had been ordered against thieves, not against religious offenders.[26] This renders the case of the image-desecrator of Cambron unique.

Of course, there are other facts that might indicate a lingering tendency to enforce the rules of penal law against Jews. It was Ulrich Tengler († 1511?), a contemporary of the Alsatian humanist Murner and author of a highly influential book of law ('The Leyenspiegel' dating from 1511) who was the first to give a relevant (and explicit) definition of this special form of punishment: 'Jewish execution', he wrote, 'means to pull or to drag a Jew accompanied by two mangy dogs by chains or ropes to the common gallows place where he has to be hanged upside-down'. Such a description was quite common, but then Tengler added: '. . . and in this way [some] one who sticks to his Jewish heresy is put from life to death'.[27] From a juridical point of view, Tengler labelled it as a so-called 'arbitrary' measure. But due to the fact that he dedicated a complete paragraph to this form of punishment, it became an almost institutionalized element of the

---

diritto romano. Studi in memoria di Paolo Koschaker, II (Milan: A. Giuffrè, 1954), pp. 65–93.

24 S. Simonsohn, *The Apostolic See and the Jews*, Studies and Texts, 94 (Toronto: Pontifical Institute of Mediaeval Studies, 1988), pp. 348–49.

25 *Annales Colmarienses Maiores*, Monumenta Germaniae Historiae, Series Scriptores XVII, ed. by G. H. Pertz (Hannover: Hahnsche Buchhandlung, 1861), p. 222.

26 Schnitzler (as in note 23).

27 Ulrich Tengler, *Leyenspiegel* (Strasbourg, 1560), p. 118^{r}. It is also worth mentioning the term *iudicium iudaeorum* as it is used in medieval canon law; cf. W. Pakter, *Medieval Canon Law and the Jews*, Abhandlungen zur rechtswissenschaftlichen Grundlagenforschung, 68 (Ebelsbach: Rolf Gremer, 1988), pp. 47–67.

penal law code of the late Middle Ages. Tengler's comment emphasizes two aspects: first, he declared it a form of punishment exclusively reserved for Jews. Second, in his view it was an act of penance, which means a measure of Church law, resulting from the 'stubborn' Jewish 'heresy'. Therefore he never discussed the aspects of honour or shame.

It has been suggested that the reception of ancient Roman law was one of the main reasons for the transformation of the social status of Jews in late medieval times.[28] The present version of the image desecration legend and its presumed author Murner seems to confirm this suggestion. The original version of the image-miracle has been restructured in favour of legal aspects of the story. That also means a change in its visual narrative. The woodcut—a medium of the new printing technology—transformed the chronicler's story as well as the former visual narrative. Instead of these, it now is conceptualized from its end, the scene of execution. That means the author tried to resolve a problem, which may be phrased by the question: How to apply penal law against Jews?

The booklet marks some critical points of official law which—allegedly!—conceded a lot of privileges to Jews and saved them from being accused in court. At different levels in the legal procedure, the author demonstrates this problematic issue. His main intention can be derived from one central phrase of the lines: 'No Jew will be caught / due to the accusation by only one (Christian) man'.[29] This verse also is quoted in an abridged edition of Murner's booklet published some years later by Pamphilus Gengenbach in Basel.[30] Thus one can conclude that the booklet of the Cambron legend carries a clear didactic purpose which was at least influenced by the reception of Roman law. Its aim was to teach the audience how to apply public penal law to the members of Jewish communities.

Ritualistic Framework—The 'World Turned Upside-Down'

Another important aspect of the visual representation of hanging *capite traverso* can be detected if we take a look at iconographical parallels. As we know from Italian sources of the same period, this type of symbolic execution was also the usual way in which the Florentine city-state acted against traitors to the community. They were stigmatized as effeminate and dishonoured enemies of the commune, and this also was demonstrated on a symbolic level through propa

[28] Kisch (as in note 23), pp. 65–93.

[29] Klassert (as in note 2), p. 117. ['So grifft man nit den iuden an / vff reden eines eintzigen man'].

[30] Pamphilus Gengenbach, *Daz ist ein erschrockenliche historij von fünff schnöden juden [. . .]* (Basel, 1517).

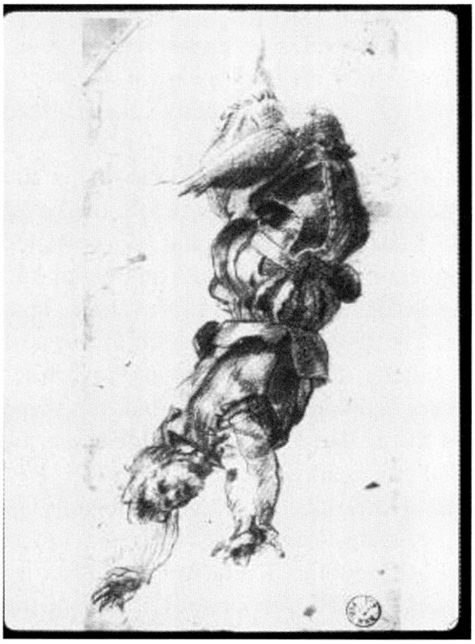

Fig. 8. Study of a man hanging upside-down, fifteenth century, Andrea del Sarto. © Gabinetto di disegni Uffizii, Florence

ganda strategies: the figures of the traitors were painted on an outside wall of the Palazzo Vecchio, hanging upside-down (fig. 8).[31]

As we know from studies of medieval popular culture, such a practice of symbolic inversion formed a general pattern of collective activity questioning the real impact of hierarchical order as well as the constraints of social roles. Nonetheless, the iconography of symbolic inversion received special importance or the members of medieval nobility. According to the customs for these high-ranking nobles, a shield with the arms of the family concerned was buried alongside its former bearer whenever the branch died out with him.[32] Regarding the shields hanging on the inner walls of churches, it had also become a useful and effective practice to turn round those owned by nobles who died a shameful

---

[31] W. Brückner, *Bildnis und Brauch—Studien zur Bildfunktion der Effigies* (Berlin: E. Schmidt, 1966), pp. 205–16; G. Ortalli, *'(. . .) pingatur in Palatino'—La pittura infamante nei secoli* XIII–XVI (Rome: Jouvence, 1979); S. Y. Edgerton, *Pictures and Punishment. Art and criminal Prosecution during the Florentine Renaissance* (Ithaca: Cornell University Press, 1987).

[32] V. Filip, 'Wappen', in *Lexikon des Mittelalters* (Munich: Artemis-Lexma, 1977-2000), VIII, cols 2031–34; R. Heydenreuter, 'Wappenrecht', in *Handwörterbuch zur deutschen Rechtsgeschichte* 5, ed. by A. Erler and E. Kaufmann (Berlin: E. Schmidt, 1998), cols 1139–44.

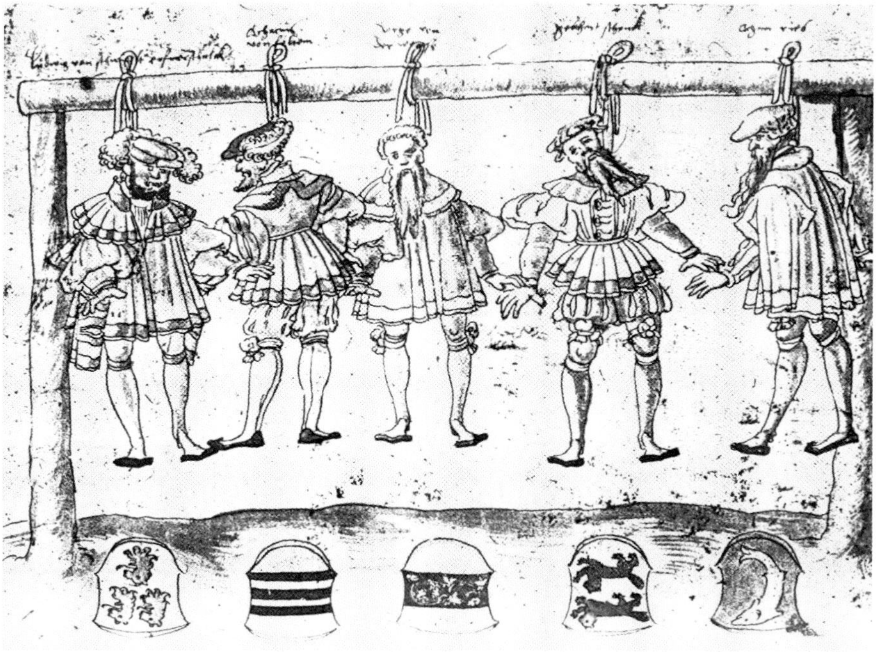

Fig. 9. So-called 'Schandbrief' by the nobleman Alexander of Oberg addressed to five noblemen who had answered for Duke Erich I of Calenberg-Göttingen as debtors; their arms are shown upside-down. About 1540, Niedersächsisches Staatsarchiv, Wolfenbüttel, Sig.: 1 Alt. 26. © Niedersächsisches Staatsarchiv, Wolfenbüttel

death on the gallows. That meant that they were even socially dead, without any *memoria* kept alive by family or by friends. To remove shields from their proper place on church walls or to publish illustrated letters with a nobleman's arms painted upside-down, proved to be an effective strategy. By its victims, it was perceived as a severe attack on family honour.[33]

The same is true for another form of medieval symbolic defamation, the so-called *libelli famosi*, which had been used to urge unreliable debtors to pay what was owing. From the fifteenth century onwards, through to the seventeenth century, the threat of becoming the subject of such a offending letter was obviously very effective in northern Europe (fig. 9). But—and this is of special importance—it was the visual rhetoric of these *libelli*, their use of denigrating symbols and metaphors, which made them work. The strategy of symbolic

---

[33] R. Quanter, *Die Schand- und Ehrenstrafen in der deutschen Rechtspflege* (Dresden: [s.n.], 1901), p. 149.

inversion could achieve its goal because the ties of honour that connected the families were strong. As the present example shows, the authors used different kinds of symbols, frequently highly-valued personal signs, as for instance seals, vestments, or the heraldic elements, to stigmatize their adversaries as disgraceful and unworthy debtors.[34]

Guido Kisch, the well-known scholar of medieval Jewry Law, already has pointed to the same conclusion. He likewise refers to the genre of *libelli famosi* as a key to explain historically the so-called 'Jewish execution'. In addition, he suggests an important link to the medieval legend of Judas Iscariot. As far as I know, the medium of *pittura infamanti* makes the only explicit reference to the avaricious traitor as personification of the Jews in general.[35]

Thus, it seems obvious that the code of honour marks a central point. It must be emphasized though that this was not a specifically anti-Semitic element but a symbolic strategy widely used to stigmatize an individual as an outcast deprived of any reputation or honour. Methodologically speaking, Murner's woodcuts refer to two sometimes conflicting discourses of late medieval society: on the one hand a highly elaborated academic discourse on law; and on the other hand a likewise elaborated elitist symbolic system of honour and shame.[36] Both of them dominated and transformed the traditional iconography of image miracles and image worship.

The Meaning of the Dog and Medieval Proto-Racism

A most interesting part of the debate on the so-called 'Jewish execution' focused on the symbolic value of the dogs. It has been argued that the execution of an offender along with animals was intended to express an affinity of both subjects, that is to say they both—man and beast—possessed the same bad and brutish character. This assumption has led to the suggestion that the intention to shame and to stigmatize Jewish offenders developed in consequence of the hegemony

---

[34] O. Hupp, *Scheltbriefe und Schandbilder—Ein Rechtsbehelf aus dem 15. und 16. Jahrhundert* (Munich: J. C. Manz, 1930); G. Schmidt, *Libelli famosi. Zur Bedeutung der Schmähschriften, Scheltbriefe, Schandgemälde und Pasquille in der deutschen Rechtsgeschichte* (Cologne: Lang, 1985); M. Lentz, 'Ehrverletzung als Rechtsbehelf? Zur Erforschung spätmittelalterlicher und frühneuzeitlicher Schmähbriefe und Schandbilder im Rahmen eines Entwicklungsgeschichte des Strafrechts', in *Neue Wege strafrechtsgeschichtlicher Forschung*, ed. by D. Willoweit and H. Schlosser (Cologne: Böhlau, 1999), pp. 55–81.

[35] Kisch (as in note 23), pp. 88–90.

[36] M. Dinges, 'Ehrenhändel als 'kommunikative Gattungen'', *Archiv für Kulturgeschichte*, 75 (1993), 359–93.

of Christian ideas in Europe, especially the idea of 'otherness' in respect of the Jewish population.[37]

With obviously denigrating words, a visitor at the Basel Council in 1430, named Gattaro, commented on the execution of two Jewish thieves by the city's hangman. 'They'd better ask for baptism', he wrote, 'unless they want to die like beasts'.[38] This was the same sort of remark that the chronicler of the city of Dortmund, Dietrich Westhoff, made when, in 1486, a Jewish thief was put to death outside the city walls, hanging upside-down between two dogs. Westhoff closed his report with the following words: 'Thus the three [*sic*!] dogs were hanging together on the gallows and in this way they also ended their lives'.[39]

But we also can find strong arguments that deny such an unambiguous interpretation of the symbolic meaning of dogs. In the context of penal law, for instance, the symbolic meaning of the dog was evident in the punishment of 'sacking' (in Latin: *poena cullei*). Perpetrators who had been placed in sacks together with dogs, cats, or snakes usually had been sentenced for the killing of their parents (in Latin: *parricidia*). Medieval glossatores who commented on Roman law gave the following explanation: the dog is attached to symbolize the offender, because he had violently attacked his parents like a dog, 'which is still blind for some days after birth, unable to recognize his parents'. What seems all the more noteworthy is the fact that this punishment was applied to both Christians and Jews.[40]

Another aspect of meaning can be gathered from the anti-Jewish polemics of medieval theology. Medieval churchmen and preachers used the metaphor of the dog to criticize Jewish 'stubbornness' and to stigmatize baptized Jews as alleged renegades, because they behaved like 'young dogs' which would not recognize their 'master' and always returned to eat their own vomit.[41] However this notion clearly referred to the religious differences between Christians and Jews and not to racial differences.[42]

---

[37] R. Glanz, 'The "Jewish Execution" in Medieval Germany', *Jewish Social Studies*, 5 (1943), 3–26. From a critical perspective see G. Kisch, 'Nationalism and Race in Medieval Law', *Seminar*, 1 (1943), 65–73.

[38] R. Wackernagel, 'Andrea Gattaro von Padua. Tagebuch der Venetianischen Gesandten beim Concil zu Basel, 1433–35', *Basler Jahrbuch* (1885), 49–52.

[39] D. Aschoff, 'Eine jüdische Hinrichtung in Westfalen 1486', in *Jüdisches Leben* (Aust.-Kat.) (Gütersloh, 1989), pp. 67–78.

[40] Tengler (as in note 27), 118^{v}.

[41] See, for instance, *Frutolfi et Ekkehardi Chronica*, Monumenta Germaniae Historiae, Series Scriptores VI, p. 208. For a revised edition (including German translation), see *Frutolfi et Ekkehardi Chronica necnon Anonymi Chronica imperatori*, Freiherr von Stein Gedächtnisausgabe, 15, ed. by F.-J. Schmale and I. Schmale-Ott (Darmstadt: Wissenschaftliche Buchgesellschaft, 1972), pp. 107–09.

[42] Kisch (as in note 37); cf. D. Nirenberg, 'Race as an Analytical Concept in the Study

Perhaps this discussion of the different symbolic meanings of dogs can also provide a starting point for developing a more pragmatic explanation for applying this unusual form of execution against Jews. Reports of Jewish executions that failed were frequently inserted into miracle collections. These legends gave accounts of Jewish convicts hanging upside-down who miraculously stayed alive for hours or even days and sometimes asked for baptism in order to die as Christians—which meant being executed by sword or dying in hospital. Nowadays, those fantasies may sound more or less cynical, but they may reflect the real intentions of contemporary judges and clerics to offer Jewish convicts a last opportunity to convert and to die as Christians.[43]

The medieval ritual of execution was thus not only expected to take effect on the audience in terms of 'deterrence', for instance, as our modern designation 'theatre of horrors' might suggest.[44] On the contrary, it was intended to affect the repentant sinner inwardly: during the execution his inner life should undergo a fundamental transformation. The goal of these forms of ritual acting was therefore either to bind or to dissolve, either to reconcile the repentant sinner or to dehumanize the perpetrator, and to exclude him from the binding ties of social community.[45]

However, we should keep in mind that in the context of the iconography of justice and law, the symbol of the dog always could convey multifold meanings. The 'sleeping dog' in medieval courthouse scenes, for instance, implied rather positive connotations. This is also true for these real-life dogs which were carried during rituals of submission by their masters, who walked in a sack-dress and with ashes on their heads, as symbols of penance.[46]

Visualizing Justice

As I have tried to demonstrate, Murner reshaped the story of the image-miracle in order to construct a new narrative grounded in the discourse of justice and law. Thus the focus of anti-Semitic implications also shifted from the image-desecration libel to the problem of legal privileges of Jews and how to overcome them. Therefore, the new (propagandistic) medium of printed woodcuts was

---

of Medieval Iberian Anti-Judaism', in *Jüdische Gemeinden und ihr christlicher Kontext in kulturräumlich vergleichender Betrachtung (5.–18. Jahrhundert)*, ed. by A. Haverkamp et al. (Hannover: Hahnsche Buchhandlung, forthcoming).

[43] See the Diary of Gattaro, in Wackernagel (as in note 38).

[44] This is the title of a book by the German historian Richard van Dülmen. *Theater des Schreckens* (Frankfurt am Main: Fischer, 1985).

[45] E. Cohen, *The Crossroads of Justice* (Leiden: Brill, 1993).

[46] B. Schwenk, 'Das Hundetragen. Ein Rechtsbrauch im Mittelalter', *Historisches Jahrbuch*, 110 (1990), 289–308.

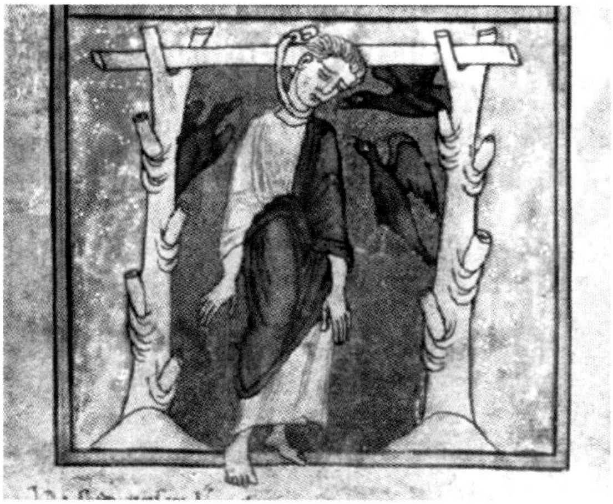

Fig. 10. Death of Judas, c. *twelfth century, from the so-called 'Hildegard-Codex'. © Bayerische Staatsbibliothek, Munich*

intended to emphasize an overall didactic purpose of the enterprise: to demonstrate the advantages and the power of public penal law.

Another corresponding example of shifting semantics can be found in the iconography of Judas's suicide, especially in the feature of the 'hanging tree'. During the thirteenth century, Judas not only became the paradigmatic figure of despair but also moved to the centre of the juridical discourse on suicide and the problem of guilt. The offence of betrayal and Judas' death at the rope—guilt and repentance, so to say—became the primary aspects of the scene. Thus the motif of suicide is transformed into an act of punishment.[47]

I would suggest that this development, which could be described as a sharpening of terminology through the aid of juridical categories and concepts, can be observed also in pictorial sources. In an illustration from a twelfth-century manuscript, the so-called 'Psalter of St Hildegard' (fig. 10), we see Judas hanging not from a tree but from the gallows. His hair is tousled, falling down his neck, and ravens are flying around his corpse. What we actually are confronted with is a scene of execution; nothing reminds us of suicide. The illustrator presents the image of a traitor who is put to death and at the same time figures as a spiritual idea, viz., the authority of *iustitia*, symbolized by the executed body. This meaning is underlined by the corresponding picture above. Usually the motif of Judas's death is accompanied by the 'betrayal in the garden' or by a representation of the 'crucifixion'. In this case it is a courthouse scene depicting Jesus, who is examined by Pilate, identified by his headwear, the

[47] N. Schnitzler, 'Judas' death—Some remarks concerning the iconography of suicide', in *Law and its Image*, ed. by N. Schnitzler (as in n. 1), pp. 103–18.

throne-like chair and his legs crossed like a judge.

Stating that pictures of medieval times are indispensable sources for the historian may sound like a truism, in particular for the ears of those working in the field of legal history. But asking for the shift of semantics, for the ways they affect the relation between text and image, for the tensions and reciprocal comments deriving from it, means to obtain methodologically important starting points for more reliable interpretations. It was my concern to demonstrate the mutual stimulations that in the late medieval period combined new juridical concepts such as 'deterrence' with corresponding concepts of representation. At least, the reader should keep in mind that the concept of public penal law in itself consists of a specific technique of visualization in which the body of the malefactor represents the projection-screen.

Framing history with salvation

SØREN KASPERSEN

A discussion of pictures and history, including pictures as historical sources, might well induce a mild attack of methodological vertigo at a time when perceptions of history and the question of the viability of historical reconstruction and the problems surrounding the contextual study of pictures are being debated exhaustively. According to Hayden White, 'the best grounds for choosing one perspective on history rather than another are ultimately aesthetic or moral rather than epistemological'.[1] I am basically in agreement with him, whether we are talking of the Middle Ages, whose view of history will here be considered from a history of art perspective, or of historical research in modern Western culture. It would be good if the way were cleared 'for the reconstitution of history as a form of intellectual activity which is at once poetic, scientific, and philosophical in its concerns'.[2] And is it not true to say that the humanities are actually poetic and philosophical by implication, and that they are at their most relevant when they are aware of these dimensions? The real touchstone of historical writing, therefore, is probably how it substantiates its claim to be a science. It is this that distinguishes it from the historical writing of other ages. But it is precisely the scientific nature of the humanities that has provoked a great deal of discussion and disagreement in these postmodern, deconstructivist and pluralistic decades.

To my mind, historical consciousness, as a separate scientific way of thinking, belongs to what might be described as 'the scientific turn' that is found in Kant,

---

[1] H. White, *Metahistory—The Historical Imagination in Nineteenth-Century Europe*, 2nd edn (Baltimore: The Johns Hopkins University Press, 1975), p. xii.

[2] See ibid.

the first philosopher to try to isolate the conditions for scientific cognition. This 'turn' marks the growth of a new culture, which now increasingly attempts to answer the great existentialist questions in a scientific way. This places us in a culture whose search for truth differs radically from that of the Middle Ages. However, at the same time, the status of the humanities has been seriously challenged. The natural sciences are making great advances on all fronts—in the study of the universe, the Earth, human beings, etc. These sciences in their examination and understanding of the origins of the universe and life, their building blocks and energy, the structures and processes of this incomprehensible cosmos, are so close to the deepest layers or secrets, as it were, that we must expect that the knowledge they will be able to reveal in the future is what earlier ages sought in myths and religion.

Although, as Hayden White says, the cognitive interests of the humanities are based on morality and aesthetics, this simply means that like all other scientific knowledge, they are related to the historically, socially, and psychologically determined creation of consciousness. And any radical difference between them and the natural sciences is probably due primarily to the fact that the main focus is not so much on epistemological and empirical relation between the subject and the world as on the education and experience of the subject in a particular cultural context. For example, when Panofsky referred to art history as a humanistic discipline, the subtext was that it is a discipline that by means of its models of interpretation would provide knowledge respecting a particular view of the individual and of the world, and which was thus concerned with specific historical circumstances and put specific questions to the material.[3] Since this ideal has vanished, and since the concept of educational formation has been heavily relativized and the differences between the actual education and cognitive interests of the subject have come to the fore, it is both natural and necessary for art history, and the humanities in general, to adopt a pluralistic approach in terms of methodology and theory of science and to concern itself with a broad spectrum of conditions that relate to the position of the subject and the formation of the consciousness of the age. In my opinion, these fundamental conditions do not prevent us from continuing to see the justification for the existence of the humanities in the scientific nature of the disciplines. Hayden White would probably have called the following discourse 'romantic' in its 'mode of employment', 'formist in its 'mode of argument', and 'conservative' in respect of its 'ideological implications'. But as far as its scientific credentials are concerned, you will have to judge for yourselves.

In Keldby Church on the island of Møn, in the High Gothic period around the

---

[3] See E. Panofsky, 'The History of Art as a Humanistic Discipline', in *The Meaning of the Humanities*, ed. by T. M. Greene (Princeton: Princeton University Press, 1940), pp. 89–118, reprinted in idem, *Meaning in the Visual Arts*, 2nd edn (Harmondsworth: Penguin, 1970), pp. 23–50.

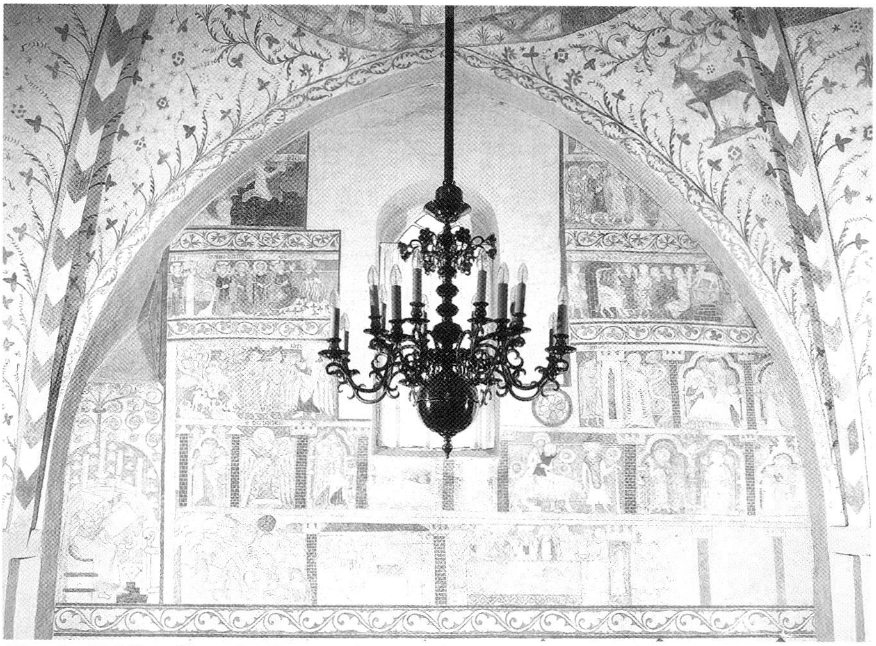

Fig. 1. Keldby Church. Decoration on the eastern part of the north wall of the nave, c. *1325.* © *Lennart Larsen, Nationalmuseet, Copenhagen*

year 1325, a large salvation history decoration was painted onto the walls of the nave, with a very elaborate Last Judgement scene as the unifying main theme on the Triumphal Arch.[4] At the eastern end of the north wall of the nave, large parts of a six-zoned decoration have been preserved, reduced by the vault which was a later addition. The three top friezes depict scenes from the Old Testament, the lower ones scenes from the story of Anne and Joachim as well as the childhood of Jesus (fig. 1). There must have been about forty episodes altogether in this section of the decoration, which made up about a quarter of the entire decoration on the south and north walls, and it is possible that the west wall, too, had narrative scenes in many friezes. Thus there might have been as many as two hundred motifs, and fragments on the eastern part of the south wall with scenes from the story of Adam and Eve indicate that the decoration started here. We do

[4] See J. Kornerup, 'Om Kalkmalerierne i Keldby Kirke', *Kirkehistoriske Samlinger*, 5 (1897–99), pp. 149–66; *Danmarks Kirker—Præstø Amt*, ed. by Nationalmuseet (Copenhagen: G. E. C. Gads Forlag, 1933–35), II, PP. 962–66 and fig. 5; S. Kaspersen, 'Kalkmaleri og samfund 1241–1340/50', in *Kulturblomstring og samfundskrise i 1300–tallet*, ed. by Brian Patrick McGuire (Copenhagen: C. A. Reitzels Boghandel), pp. 130–33 and figs. 16–18.

not know, however, to what extent the chronological order of the sequence was followed. Nor can we say for certain whether the new Covenant was confined to the last section of the north wall. If so, the Old Testament cycle would have been much more extensive than the New Testament series, but there is already an example of this kind of pattern in Pope Sixtus IV's (432–40) mosaic decoration in the church of Santa Maria Maggiore in Rome, and this weighting can also be seen, for example, in Master Bertram's high altar triptych in St Petri's church in Hamburg, to which we will be returning later.

Of particular interest in this context is the fact that a large rectangular panel has been inserted into the salvation history decoration in the middle of the north wall, at the same height as the three lower zones. The panel contains a circular composition with a broad frame like a mirror (fig. 2). The central scene shows two enthroned figures: a king with a lily-topped sceptre and a bird on his raised, right hand;[5] and a smaller figure, a woman with a crown, hands raised in front of her breast, the palms facing outwards to signify that some wonderful act is taking place, that something exalted can be seen. She is enclosed by a scroll, only a few letters of which, unfortunately, have survived. Similarly, only a small part of the inscription that surrounded the whole scene remains. In the frame immediately above the pair is another enthroned king *en miniature*, flanked by two courtiers, one with one hand grasped around the wrist of the other hand, in the manner prescribed in the Norwegian *Speculum Regale*.[6] The other figure is gesticulating and appears to be referring to a coronation scene to the right of the king: two bishops are crowning a standing figure, while an abbot or ecclesiastical helper carrying a crozier looks on. It is not possible to say for certain whether the central figure is male or female, though it does have short hair.

There can be little doubt that the scenes refer to historical characters and events. But is it a wedding, a coronation, or something quite different that is being depicted? There are theories that the 'royal couple' were Eric Menved and Queen Ingeborg, who were married at Helsingborg in 1296, long after Eric, as a

---

[5] The bird, dove(?), may have a purely symbolic meaning—see below—but it may also refer to a real insignia, most likely a sceptre with a very short staff or rather a long staff, now missing. E.g., two sceptres of silver are mentioned in connection with the crowning 1247 of the Norwegian king, Håkon Håkonsson, one crowned with a gold cross, the other with an eagle of gold; see Martin Blindheim, 'Spor av hersker- og kroningsinsignier i norsk middelalder', in *Kongens makt og ære—Skandinaviske herskersymboler gjennom 1000 år*, ed. by M. Blindheim, P. Gjærder, and D. Sæverud (Oslo: Universitetets Oldsaksamling, 1985), p. 65; and his *Soga um Håkon Håkonsson* (Oslo: Det norske Samlaget, 1928), pp. 244–45. An eagle of gold also is mentioned among the regalia of the Swedish king, Birger Magnusson, in 1311, but here as part of the coronation robes; see R. Cederström, *De svenska riksregalierna och kungliga värdighetstecknen* (Stockholm: Kungliga livrustkammaren, 1942), p. 10.

[6] See *Kongsspegelen*, trans. by A. Hellevik (Oslo: Det Norske Samlaget, 1965), p. 96.

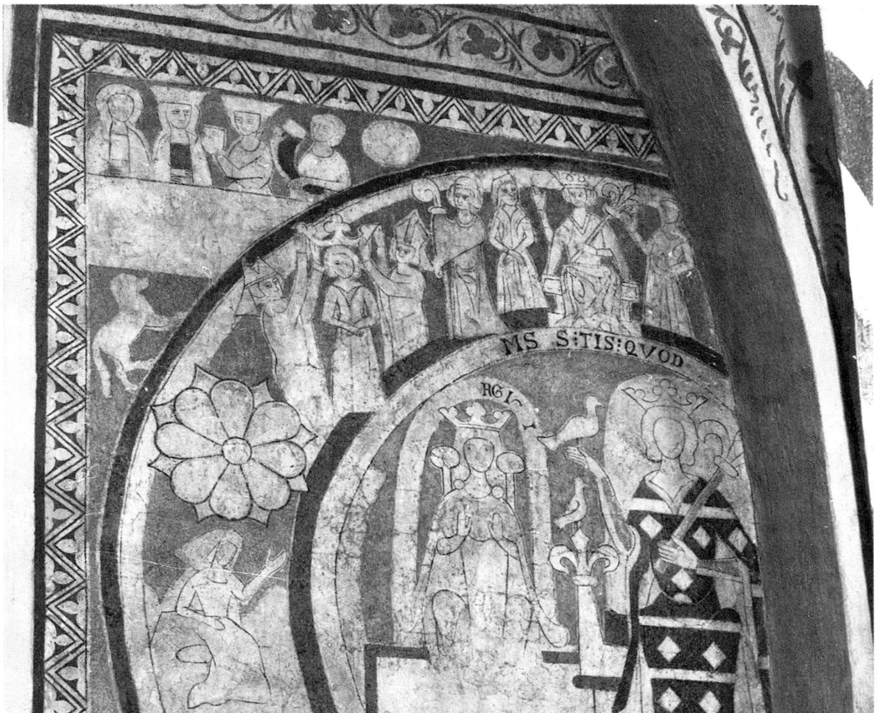

Fig. 2. Keldby Church. Decoration on the central part of the north wall of the nave, c. 1325. © *Nationalmuseet, Copenhagen*

child king, came to the throne in 1286,[7] or that it was Valdemar Atterdag, who married Princess Helvig of Holstein at Whitsuntide 1340 at Sønderborg Castle and who that same year was acclaimed at the Viborg assembly on St John's Eve.[8] But the first event seems rather early and the second one too late, in view of the general style of the paintings. The state of preservation, however, means that we have to operate within a wide range when it comes to setting a date. The only intermediate possibility is that the king is Eric Menved's younger brother, Christopher II, who married Euphemia of Pomerania before 1307 and succeeded Erik to the throne in 1320. But if it refers to that wedding there is no significant difference, as far as dating is concerned, from Eric Menved's wedding in 1296.

Two facts are significant for further determination of the course of events. First, the woman is clearly subordinate to the king. She is smaller than he and is sitting in a slightly withdrawn position. Second, what relation does the coronation scene have with the two enthroned figures? Why is the attention focused not on the coronation of the king, but on that of the queen or a third person? It is of interest here that in 1324, that is, four years after he came to power, Christopher II was anointed and crowned at Vordingborg, together with his son, Eric, by Archbishop Esger Juul. And at Christmas that same year, another important event in Christopher's reign took place. Count Ludvig of Brandenburg, son of King Ludwig of Bavaria, arrived at Vordingborg Castle to marry Christopher's young daughter, Margrethe. This alliance must have seemed a very promising move in Christopher II's attempt to strengthen his position and create a strong royal power in what must, in many ways, have been a very difficult situation.[9]

Thus, instead of representing a royal couple enthroned at their wedding and/or coronation, the decoration at Keldby might well be showing Christopher sitting in state with his daughter in connection with her wedding.[10] The bird in his right hand could signify a connection with the German ruler by reference to the so-called 'bird sceptre' in Aachen, a silver-gilt rod crowned by a dove from around 1220 or soon afterwards.[11] At the same time, the woman's gestures are rendered

---

[7] See Niels M. Saxtorph, *Danmarks kalkmalerier* (Copenhagen: Politikens Forlag, 1986), p.158.

[8] See *Danmarks Kirker* (as in note 4), pp. 965–66.

[9] See S. Tägil, *Valdemar Atterdag och Europa*, Bibliotheca Historica Lundensis, 9 (Lund: C. W. K. Gleerup, 1962), pp. 1–14.

[10] The crown of the female figure is then a bridal crown.

[11] The sceptre is part of a treasure that Richard of Cornwall as German king (1257–72) founded in the Aachener Münster. This kind of sceptre was otherwise unknown in Germany, while a 'Sceptre with the Dove' belonged to the insignia of English kings—as a sign of peace-keeping. See Karl von Amira, *Der Stab in der germanischen Rechtssymbolik*, Abhandlungen der Königlich Bayerischen Akademie der Wissenschaften [Philos.-philol. u. hist. Kl., 25.1] (Munich, 1909), pp. 119–21; Ernst Percy Schramm, 'Über die Herrschaftszeichen des Mittelalters', *Münchner Jahrbuch der Bildenden Kunst*, 3.1 (1950), pp. 45, 51.

more understandable as an expression of the marvellous event that is taking place, and it becomes clear why a scroll is needed around her. Thus, the episode at the top of the 'mirror's' frame then refers to the slightly earlier coronation of the son, Eric, attended and blessed by Christopher, whose succession is hereby formally assured. The seated, much-effaced figure with the head covering in the middle of the frame seems to be pointing towards the young princess, judging by the turn of the body and the uplifted left hand. Finally, the banquet at the top left corner of the rectangular panel might illustrate the wedding feast in an abbreviated form or another ceremonial meal connected with the function. Does the dog in front of the table signify that the bride will be a faithful wife?

This possible identification of characters and events can be corroborated by a number of accentuations and iconographic features in the remaining parts of the salvation history decoration. First, we note that the Trinity Judge on the Triumphal Arch, over and above a few individual figures, is flanked partly by two groups of apostles and then by male and female saints, and that the female saints are placed on the right hand side of the judge (fig. 3). The first is St Catherine, with a sword and a spiked wheel. The next is on a completely different scale: she stands upon a small, tortoise-like dragon, which extends across the border between the two zones. Above the vault, the top of a cross-staff and perhaps a crown can be discerned. The saint is undoubtedly St Margaret, the name-saint of Christopher's daughter. We can also see that the foremost figure in the corresponding group of male saints is not John the Baptist, as one might expect in a Last Judgement scene where Mary is praying so intensely and persistently that her knees are bleeding, but St Lawrence, the patron saint of the archdiocese and of the cathedral at Lund. Behind him stands John the Baptist. The order may have been a sop to Esger Juul for the coronation of Christopher and his son—despite the fact that relations with the bishop were strained. Or it might simply have been a mark of the special relationship with the patron saint of the archdiocese, which naturally came about through the coronation.

If we turn to the six-zoned composition on the north wall (fig. 1), it also reveals a number of interesting features. There are several breaks in the chronology. In the stories from the childhood of Jesus, scenes of the shepherds receiving the message of the angels out in the fields and their adoration of the Child have been moved to the lower zone, so that in the upper zone we jump directly from the Nativity, a scene that was greatly damaged by the later installation of the great window, to that of the Flight into Egypt. And this scene not only contains the apocryphal story of the arrival of the Holy Family at the town of Sotinen but also presents a very unusual version of the event. Beneath two arcades stand two figures, their right hands raised in greeting as the Holy Family arrives (fig. 4). The foremost, nimbed figure wears a long cloak, fastened across the chest by a

---

At the end of his article, P. E. Schramm emphasizes that 'Alles, was der König an Insignien und Gewändern trägt, hat einen Sinn oder strebt darnach, einen Sinn zu erlangen. Die Auslegung ist jedoch in ständiger Bewegung und wird nie eindeutig' [p. 59].

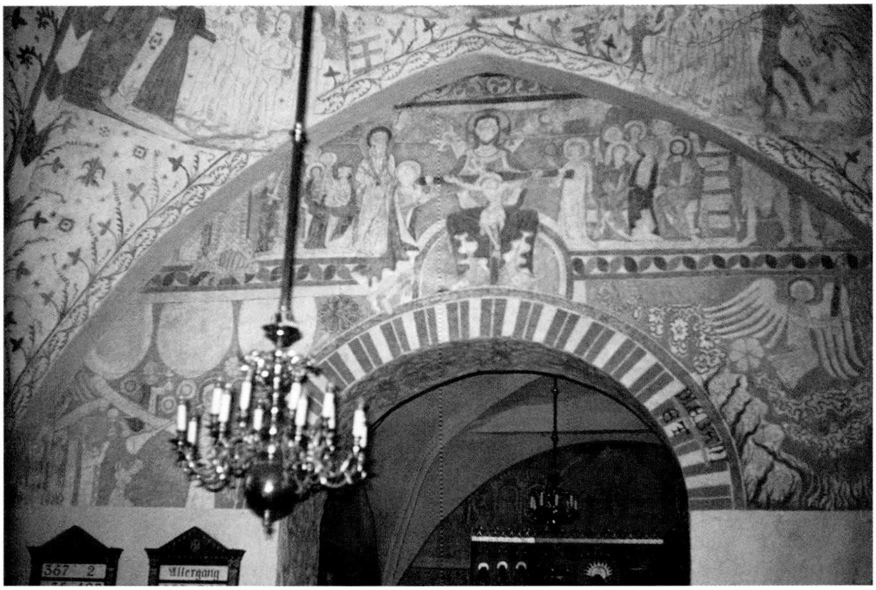

Fig. 3. Keldby Church. The Last Judgement on the east wall of the nave, c. *1325.* © *Author*

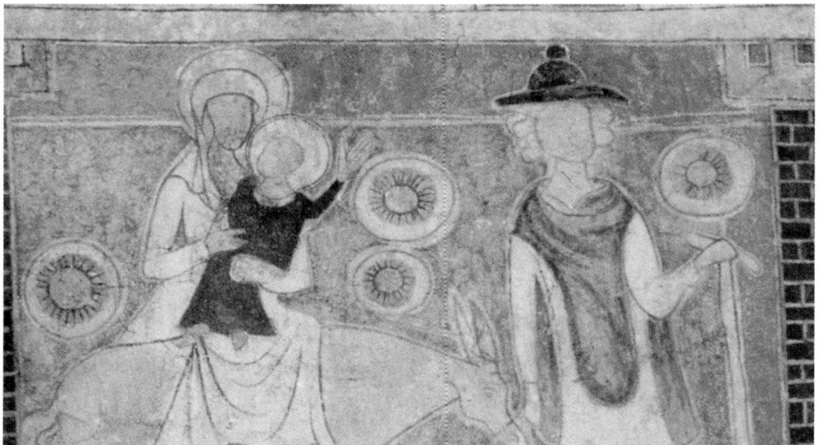

Fig. 4. Keldby Church. The Flight into Egypt/Sotinen, c. *1325.* © *Author*

brooch, and seems to be veiled. The other figure is obviously male. East of this there is a gabled arcade with a trefoil arch crowned by turrets, that is, like the canopy above Mary in the Annunciation. Beneath it a crowned virgin is seated, turning west, with a smaller figure kneeling in adoration in front of her and another behind her as well. Both these figures are rather fragmentary. She holds a small book in her right, raised hand, and she seems to open her arms towards the arriving family. The easternmost part of the canopy—and the last section of the scene(?)—is concealed by the vault.

This depiction of the town of Sotinen does not have much to do with the apocryphal text,[12] but since the story records that both ruler and inhabitants converted to Christianity when the Holy Family arrived, the nimbed figure and/or the crowned virgin might well personify Ecclesia, receiving Christ as her bridegroom.[13] This interpretation might be underpinned by a 'vertical' reading of the program (cf. fig. 1): the frieze above depicts the childhood story of the Virgin Mary, and the reception of the Holy Family to Sotinen corresponds with the Meeting of Anna and Joachim at the Golden Gate, while the panel just above the crowned virgin in Sotinen most likely depicted the Presentation of the Virgin to the Temple. One level up, the Adoration of the Golden Calf is represented in an Exodus-frieze just above the Virgin's Birth. The opposition of the newborn Mary and the new-cast idol may call to mind the contrast between the Golden Calf and Ecclesia in the *Bible moralisée*.[14] The apparent intertextual relationship, then, of the three pictorial sequences heightens attention to themes such as meeting and reception, bride and bridegroom, husband and wife, Mary and Ecclesia, the true Saviour versus false gods. At the same time, the unusual iconography of the Sotinen sequence seems to point towards a metaphorical reading of the scene or, perhaps, rather to indicate that it was dictated by the need to fulfil the requirements of a transposed reading: at Christmas, in 1324, the bride, Margrethe, welcomes her young bridegroom to Vordingborg.

Medieval thought was no stranger to this kind of blending of factual history and the salvation story, the procession of any ruler into a city could be and was

[12] For the gospel text of Pseudo Matthew, see *Evangelia Apocrypha*, ed. by Constantinus Tischendorf (Leipzig: Avenarius & Mendelssohn, 1853), pp. 84–87; *Apocryphical New Testament*, trans. by M. R. James (Oxford: Clarendon Press, 1924), pp. 75–76; or *Jakobs Forevangelium og Det uægte Matthæusevangelium*, trans. by Knud Banning (Copenhagen: G. E. C. Gad, 1980), pp. 31–36.

[13] On the triumphal arch of Santa Maria Maggiore in Rome, the Arrival in Sotina together with the Adoration of the Magi signifies the foundation of the 'church of the heathen'; see G. A. Wellen, *Theotokos: Eine ikonographische Abhandlund über das Gottesmutterbild in frühchristlicher Zeit* (Utrecht and Antwerp: Spectrum, 1961), pp. 97–116.

[14] See, e.g., *Bible moralisée—Faksimile-Ausgabe im Originalformat des Codex Vindobonensis 2554 der Österreichischen Nationalbibliothek*, ed. by Reiner Haussherr, Codices Selecti, 40 (Graz: Akademischer Druck- und Verlagsanstalt, 1973), fol. 25^{v}.

often seen in the light of Christ's entry into Jerusalem.[15] Therefore, when a son of Ludwig, king of the Romans, arrived at Vordingborg at Christmas to marry Christopher's daughter, it would have seemed obvious to seize on a parallel from the childhood of Jesus.[16] In fact, *tableaux vivants* representing the nativity of Christ were displayed during King Henry VI's first entrance to Paris on 2 December 1431,[17] and still later, when Louis XI entered Lyon in 1476 the day before the Annunciation, mystery plays about both the infancy of the Virgin and the childhood of Christ were performed.[18] We have no records of theatrical performances in Vordingborg 1326, and it is less than plausible that mysteries actually took place,[19] even if it is tempting to imagine that the unusual representation of Sotinen referred to some staged version which made it readable at that time.[20]

---

[15] See Ernst H. Kantorowicz, *Laudes regiae—A Study in Liturgical Acclamations and Medieval Ruler Worship*, University of California Publications in History, 33 (Berkeley: University of California Press, 1958); Idem, 'The King's Advent and the Enigmatic Panels in the Doors of Santa Sabina', *Art Bulletin* 26 (1944), pp. 207–31 and illustrations; Bernard Guenée and Françoise Lehoux, *Les entrées royales françaises de 1328 à 1515*, Sources d'Histoire Médiévale, 5 (Paris: Centre National de la Recherche Scientifique, 1968).

[16] See Guenée and Lehoux (as in note 15), pp. 202–03.

[17] See Guenée and Lehoux (as in note 15), p. 67: 'Et, a l'endroit de la Trinité, avoit escarfaulx moult richement aornez, es quel(e)z estoient, figurés de personnaiges vifz, les ystoires desmonstrans la Nativité de Notre Jhesu Crist; lesqueles personnes aucunement ne se mouvoient, et apparoient estre ymages, et estoient bien huit vins personnaiges'.

[18] See Guenée and Lehoux (as in note 15), pp. 202–03.

[19] The earliest French record of theatrical representations during a royal entry is from 1380, when Charles VI entered Paris—see Guenée and Lehoux (as in note 15), pp. 12 and 58.

[20] It is difficult to find comparative material to elucidate the depiction of Sotina in Keldby. When the Sotina-episode takes place as an adventus, it is normally, in Byzantine art, the personified Egypt, Aegyptika, who welcomes the Holy Family, while different models are used in Western art: Aphrodosius and his retinue, an anonymous group of inhabitants, a personification like Aegyptika etc.; see Karl Vogler, *Die Ikonographie der 'Flucht nach Aegypten'* (diss. Heidelberg; Arnstadt: Otto Böttner, 1930), pp. 16–19; Gertrud Schiller, *Ikonographie der christlichen Kunst*, I (Güthersloh: Gerd Mohn, 1966), pp. 128, 129, figs 310, 315; *Lexikon der christlichen Ikonographie*, I–VIII, ed. by Engelbrecht Kirschbaum, et al. (Rome et al.: Herder, 1968–76), II, cols 43–50, fig. 1 (C. Schweicher and G. Jászai); Marcell Restle, *Die byzantinische Wandmalerei in Kleinasien*, I–III (Recklinghausen: Aurel Bongers, 1967), II, figs 77, 153, 267, and III, figs 307, 386, 395; Kantorowicz (1944, as in note 15), pp. 220–21, [fig. 33a]. The triumphant character of the Flight into Egypt in its early phases is stressed by Hildebrecht Hommel, pointing out the ancient sources of the motif; see idem, 'Profectio Mariae—Zur Ikonographie der 'Flucht nach Ägypten'', *Theologia Viatorum*, 9 (1963), pp. 95–112 and ill. The nimbed, female(?) figure in Keldby Church is most likely a transformation of Aphrodosius or

Whether the unusual broadcasting of the glad tidings of the arrival of the Saviour by one of the shepherds in the lower register on a large horn, an 'Alpenhorn', also springs from the festivity of a princely *adventus* is debatable, of course. But it should be noted that the frieze contains a large banqueting scene as well, where Stephen the stable boy tells Herod of the newborn Saviour. In any case, the wedding was quite an event. The chronicle of Detmar tells us that many princes and noblemen were present and that the margrave stayed on until Epiphany.[21]

Linking the historical events and the salvation story in the context in which they appear to have been placed, there is a picture under one of the original windows whose connection with the two spheres is conspicuously ambiguous (fig. 5). Under a canopy that resembles a ciborium, a young man sits writing, reading, or leafing through a large manuscript. The cloak fastened in front of the breast with a buckle suggests that he is an ecclesiastical figure, but not least the round cap with a large turned-up brim argues against his being an evangelist. It must be either an Old Testament prophet or a contemporary chronicler, and his youthful appearance would seem to indicate the latter.

However, the somewhat unreal or, perhaps, allegorical nature of the scene springs from the lectern, which as a sturdy stem emerges from a compound of a triple corbel-stepped base, a rhomboid object—possibly a large precious stone—and a king's crown, culminating in a large laciniated 'leaf blade'. Perhaps even more important, in front of the domed baldachin with trilobed ornaments or perforations five staves (originally seven?) rise from the arcade arch, and three more (originally four?) appear behind the dome, together with a stem with winding offshoots bearing bunches of grapes. By analogy with 'barren' rods, the vine may be an allusion to Aaron's sprouting rod (cf. Numbers 17.17–26), which in turn is a prefiguration of the Virgin Birth, or to Joseph's flowering rod, when he was singled out for betrothal to Mary. The scene thus may be interpreted as both a prologue to and a symbol *of* the Incarnation, and as a wonderful statement about betrothal, about the blessing which, like a fruitful vine, will spring out of the union of the bride and bridegroom.

In the light of all this, if we turn back to the enthroned figures in the 'earthly

---

Aegyptika according to the ecclesiological symbolism of the scene, and the following male figure a representative of the inhabitants of Sotina. Yet, a single deputy is an unusual feature and the crowned, seated Virgin is without parallel, making the whole Sotina-depiction difficult to 'read' if it does not, e.g., refer to a specific, historical event. In fact, the whole 'adventus'-iconography is an early phenomenon and very surprising, at least in Western art as late as the fourteenth century.

[21] See *Die Chroniken der niedersächsischen Städte: Lübeck*, ed. by K. Koppmann, Die Chroniken der deutschen Städte vom 14. bis ins 16. Jahrhundert, 26 (Leipzig: S. Hirzel, 1899).

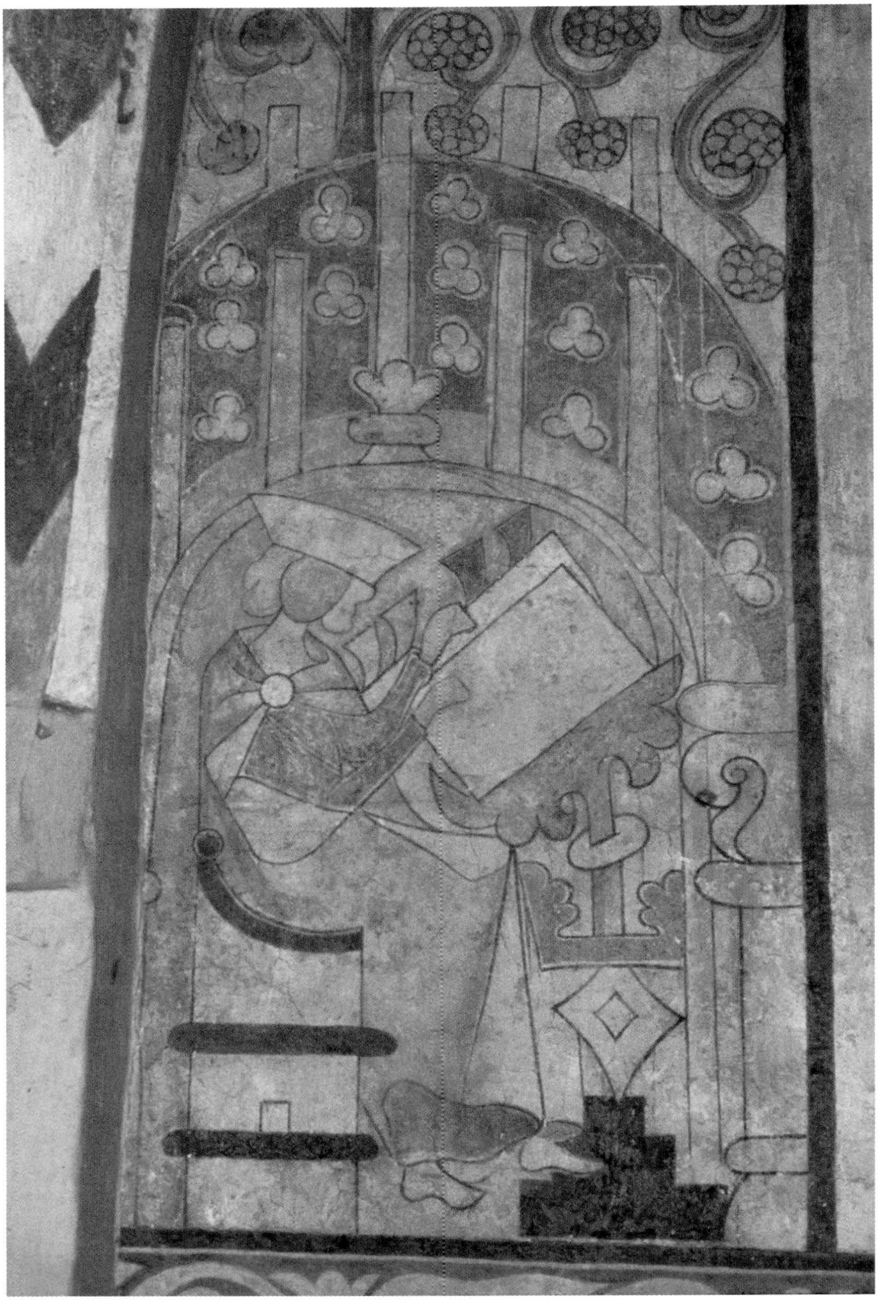

Fig. 5. Keldby Church. Prophet/chronicler? c. *1325.* © *Author*

mirror',[22] the king's dove-like bird and lily sceptre might well recall the Annunciation: to signal the arrival of the bridegroom, Christopher raises the 'dove sceptre' towards his daughter (fig. 2). Furthermore, the lily and bird motifs are repeated as ornaments on the seat of his throne. Finally, the dimensions between the king and the young woman, presumably his daughter, are *grosso modo* the same as between the archangel and Mary at the Annunciation, and the Virgin is crowned like the young bride.[23]

As the only iconic pictures among long narrative sequences, the two last-mentioned panels are like concentrates of the whole decoration: they mirror its character of annunciation, advent, and revelation. 'Ecce mitto angelum meum' (cf. Malachi 3.1) was one of the liturgical utterances employed at the reception of rulers in the Middle Ages.[24] In the present decoration, the Lord sends his angel both to Joachim and to Anna(?)[25] and to the Virgin and the shepherds; he reveals himself to Moses on Horeb, 'the mountain of God' (cf. Exodus 3.1) and originally also on Mount Sinai;[26] he allots Aaron to Moses as a spokesman and precedes him

---

[22] On the complexity and centrality of the mirror metaphor in the Later Middle Ages, see Herbert Grabes, *Speculum, Mirror und Looking-Glass—Kontinuität und Originalität der Spiegelmetapher in den Buchtiteln des Mittelalters und der englischen Literatur des 13. bis 17. Jahrhunderts*, Buchreihe der Anglia, 16 (Tübingen: Max Niemeyer, 1973).

[23] The crown is an unusual attribute for the Virgin at the Annunciation, but antecedents can be mentioned, e.g., a relief on Bamberg Cathedral from *c.* 1230–40—see Gertrud Schiller (as in note 20), I, p. 50 and fig. 89.

[24] See Kantorowicz (as in note 15), pp. 217–21; Malachi's prophecy continues: '. . . et praeparabit viam ante faciem meam; et statim veniet ad templum suum Dominator quem vos quaeretis, et angelus testamenti quem vos vultis' (3.1). The Lord, who suddenly will come to his temple, here refers to the second coming of Christ, and in that respect the Arrival in Sotina heralds the Last Judgement-scene on the east wall of the nave.

[25] The original, late Romanesque window easternmost on the north wall was situated on a level with the window above the prophet/chronicler and a little further towards east, leaving space for at least one episode between the Annunciation to Joachim and the Meeting at the Golden Gate. Following the chronology of pseudo-Matthew, it could have been the Sacrifice of Joachim during the angel's first visit or Joachim's Second Vision, both episodes known from the Arena Chapel, see *Evang. Apocr.* (as in note 12), pp. 54–60; *Apocr. New Testament* (as in note 12), p. 73 or *Jakobs Forevang* (as in note 12), pp. 31–36, and James H. Stubblebine, *Giotto—The Arena Chapel Frescoes*, Critical Studies in Art History (London: Thames and Hudson, 1969), pp. 75–77 and figs. 7–12; but most likely the Annunciation to Anna was represented, according to the chronology of *The Golden Legend* by Jacobus de Voragine; see ibid., pp. 118–20.

[26] Otherwise, the sequence with the Golden Calf seems unmotivated, and there was space enough for at least one episode between 'the Burning Bush' and the original window, followed by 'the Casting of the Golden Calf'. On Mount Sinai, God also promises Moses: 'Ecce ego mittam angelum meum, qui praecedat te, et custodiat in via, et introducat in locum quem paravi' (Exodus 23.20).

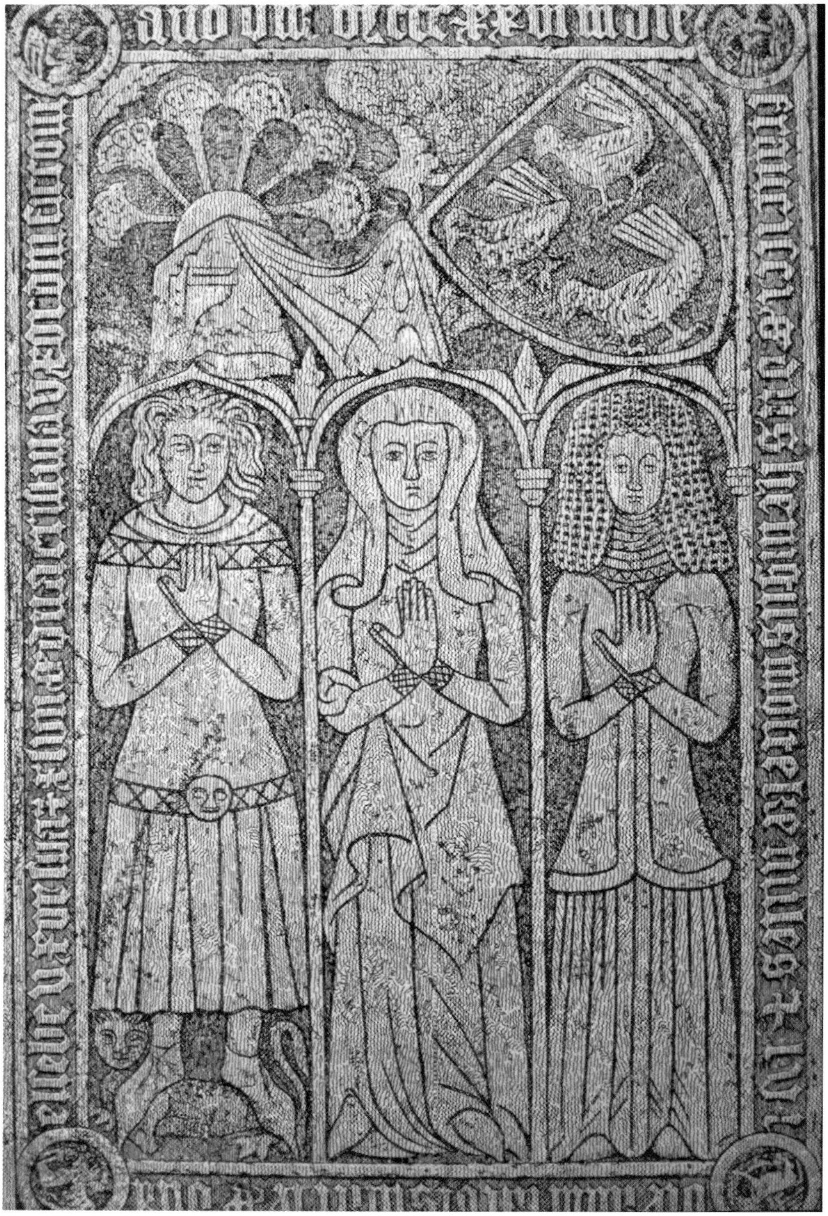

Fig. 6. Keldby Church. Tombstone for Henning Moltke, his wife and his daughter (?), 1355?/1360–70, from J. B. Løffler, Danske Gravstene fra Middelalderen *(Copenhagen, 1885)*

as a pillar of cloud or fire to lead the Israelites on their wandering in the desert (cf. Exodus 13.21–22). Finally, as the newborn Saviour he is acclaimed at the arrival in Sotina and proclaimed at the banquet by the vivified cock. All this gives the decoration a specific tone well suited to reverberate with the significance of the historical event and to invest it with profound layers of meaning.

In the Middle Ages, Keldby Church was approximately a day's journey from Vordingborg, just over thirty kilometres away. The size and content of the decoration are evidence of the status of the donors and planners. The Crown had long owned a number of properties on the island of Møn. For example, in 1177–78, three and a half 'bol' (*c.* 700 acres) in Keldby itself and one 'bol' in Tornby, a settlement that has now disappeared but which probably lay within the parish, were conveyed to Valdemar the Great by St Peter's Monastery at Næstved.[27] Furthermore, Keldby parish adjoins Stege, which during the thirteenth century flourished as market town, sheltered by a royal castle, Stegehus or Stegeborg, built by Valdemar the Great (1157–82). The castle and the landed properties on Møn were often mortgaged to North German princes.[28] But in May 1322, Christopher II repaid a mortgage on the island of two thousand marks of silver,[29] and the island appears to have been in his possession until May 1326.[30] In Keldby Church there is, furthermore, a tombstone showing the knight, Henning Moltke († 4.10.1326), his wife Elsebe († 25.3.1355), and their daughter(?), Lady Christina († 1347), originally erected in St George's chapel at Spejslsby in the parish by Lady Christina's husband, Fikke Moltke, knight and member of the royal council ('Rigsråd') (fig. 6). Henning Moltke stemmed from an old Wendic family, of whom, from the end of the thirteenth century, several members began to assert themselves in Denmark as royal officials, and as a knight Henning consequently also swore fealty to the king. Henning Moltke's wife, Elsebe, was most likely a daughter of Cecilie Jonsdatter Lille († 1307), a member of the once important Hvide family. Through her, Henning himself may have owned landed property on Møn, not least in the parishes of Keldby and Stege, where the Hvide family had had greater properties years previously, most recently known through the will of Cecilie's father, Jon Lille.[31] In any case, after 1360, Fikke Moltke

---

[27] See *Diplomatarium Danicum* (Copenhagen: Ejnar Munksgaards Forlag 1938–), 1.3, No. 67; and *Scriptores rerum danicarum*, ed. Langebek et al. (Copenhagen, 1772–1878).

[28] The earliest known mortgaging occurred in 1290; see Frede Bojsen, *Af Møns Historie*, I–IX (Copenhagen: Akademisk Boghandel, 1905–26), II (1906), p. 159.

[29] See *Dipl. Dan.* (as in note 27), 2.8, Nos 416 and 433; and F. Bojsen (as in note 28), II (1906), pp. 171–72.

[30] It was mortgaged to Henry II of Mecklenburg and Johan III of Werle 3 May 1326; see *Dipl. Dan.* (as in note 27), 2.9, Nos 261 and 278.

[31] See Erik Ulsig, *Danske adelsgodser i middelalderen* (Copenhagen: Nordisk Forlag,

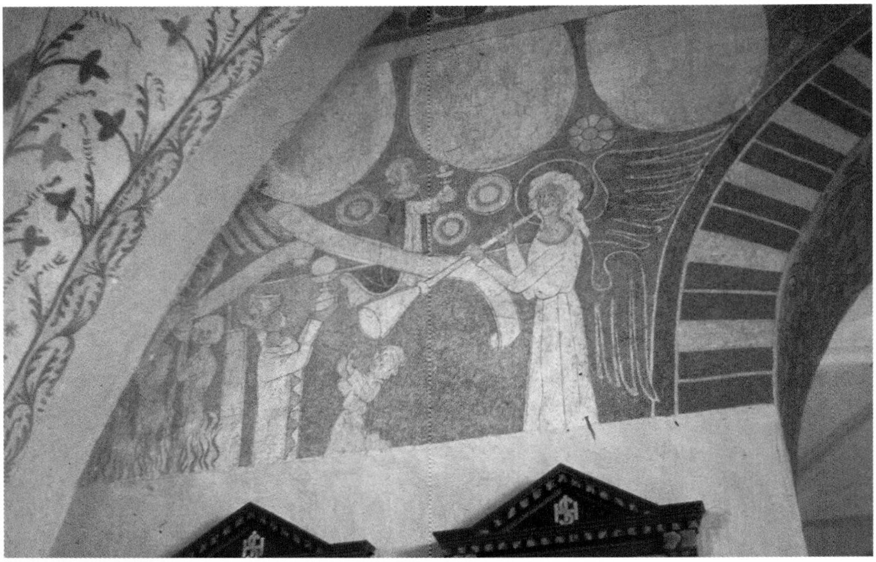

Fig. 7. Keldby Church. The Last Judgement: Purgatory, Resurrection of the Dead, and coat of arms, c. *1325.* © *Author*

(† 1371) designated himself 'of Møn', where the main part of his landed property, consequently, must have been situated, properties which he quite well may have inherited through his wife, Christina.[32] In Keldby parish there are remains of an old castle, called Gammelborg, which may have been a manor owned by members of the Moltke family.[33]

There are thus good grounds for assuming that Henning Molkte, as the king's vassal and someone who had a special connection with the parish of Keldby, planned and probably also donated the decoration in more or less close co-operation with the king himself. Unfortunately, the three great coats-of-arms in the Last Judgement scene on the east wall of the nave no longer have any blazoning, and among the risen, presumably the saved, we can see only a bishop with an elevated chalice and host, a kneeling and possibly tonsured figure facing the bishop, as well as, higher up, another clerical figure wearing a pluvial and again with an elevated chalice and host—perhaps, the parish priest, who was named in the inscription surrounding the chancel arch (fig. 7).[34] The kneeling figure could, of

1968), pp. 25–26, 37–39 (Jakob Sunesen and Countess Ingerd), and 55–58 (Jon Lille).

[32] See F. Bojsen (as in note 28), III (1917), pp. 13–14, 51, 184–88. Christina was a near relative of Henning Molkte and Elsebe, probably their daughter.

[33] See ibid., p. 14.

[34] Only a small fragment of an inscription in two lines with the word PLEBANI is preserved.

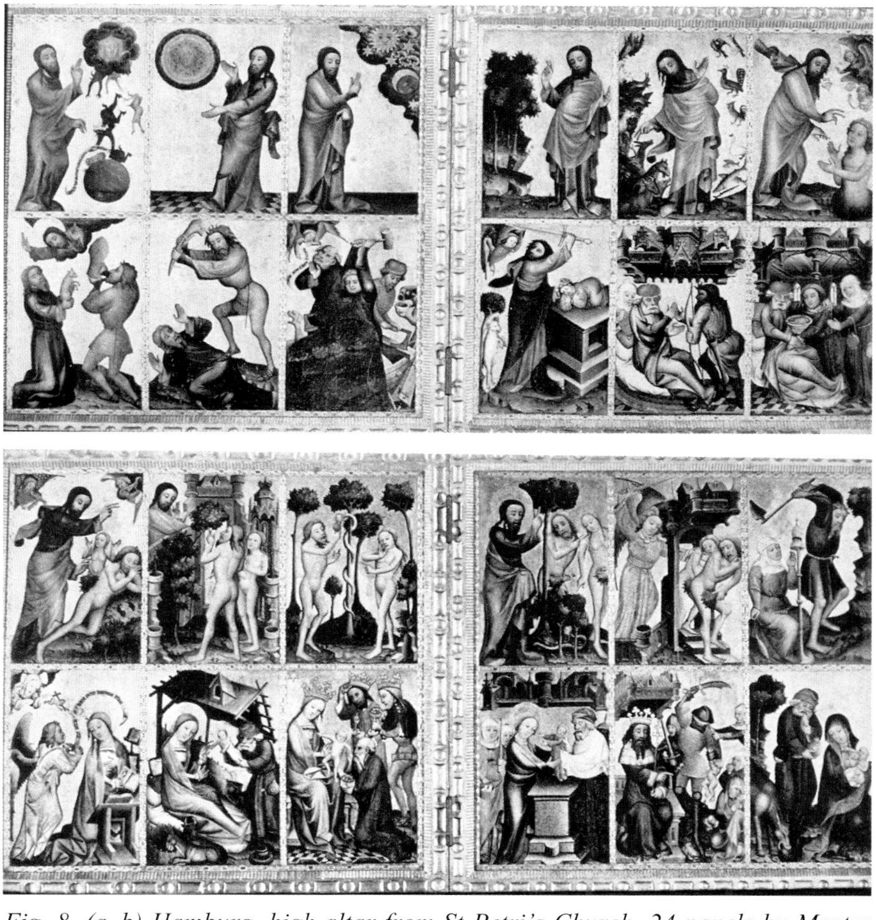

Fig. 8. (a–b) Hamburg, high altar from St Petri's Church, 24 panels by Master Bertram, c. *1379–83. © Kunsthalle, Hamburg*

course, be the vassal and the bishop of Roskilde, but the relationship between them and the portrayal of Purgatory just behind the bishop indicate, rather, that they illustrate the importance of holding masses for the dead.

At any rate, the decoration at Keldby Church seems to show us an exciting linking together of contemporary historical events and the history of salvation that provided at the time a framework for understanding the former, at least on a higher level. It is easy to pounce on the possible ideological, not to mention propagandist exploitation of this situation. However, it is more important here to establish that this linkage makes the Keldby Church decoration the kind of historical source of which very few survive from the Danish Middle Ages, a source that throws a rich spectrum of ideas and value statements over the events of 1324—if we have identified them correctly. It was probably a clerical brain that was behind the scheme, and there is not much evidence that Christopher II was a king whose thoughts were dominated by religious matters. He emerges from the sources as more of a practical politician, even a cynical power-seeker. But he clearly saw the importance—at least in a raw political sense—of being an ecclesiastically conescrated and crowned king. The broad dimension of salvation history in which his execution of government is placed in the decoration, possibly also springs more from power-political than from religious considerations. Taken as a whole, it may be seen as an impressive, rhetorical staging and invocation of the new alliance with the king of the Romans, *in spe* the Holy Roman Emperor.[35]

Finally, in order to elucidate this further, we will consider Master Bertram's retable for the high altar at the St Petri Church in Hamburg, dating from 1379 to 1383, just over half a century later.[36] This altarpiece, with a double set of wings, also depicts in the second position a salvation history cycle, here in two zones, comprising twenty-four panels in all (figs 8a–b). The series goes from the Creation up to and including the childhood of Jesus, although the Old Covenant, as indicated above, has been allocated the most space, constituting three quarters of all the scenes. It is a strongly structured narrative, permeated by inter-scene references, and this being so, numerous layers of meaning are unfurled, which intermingle and play together in a subtle way. It is primarily an Augustinian account of the two societies, of the City of God versus the City of Satan, from when they were predicted at the beginning of time through the split between the good and the bad angels—in the first scene of the upper zone—via their actual appearance on earth through Cain and Abel—in the first two scenes in the lower zone (cf. fig. 9)—to the time of the New Covenant, where the final scene of the Holy Family resting during the Flight into Egypt paints a picture of the City of God on pilgrimage through the world of sin and evil (cf. fig. 10).[37] One notes the dramatic juxtaposition of the Murder of the Innocents in Bethlehem and the fleeing family, and how Jesus' own sacrificial death on the Cross is anticipated by the malevolent donkey's attack on the green sheaf, which explains Mary's

[35] Ludwig was crowned as Roman king in Aachen on 25 November 1314, and as emperor in Rome on 17 January 1328.

[36] See, e.g., Christian Beutler, *Meister Bertram—Der Hochaltar von Sankt Petri: Christliche Allegorie als protestantische Ärgernis* (Frankfurt am Main: Fischer Taschenbuch Verlag, 1984); and S. Kaspersen, 'Grabower-alteret—En analyse af mester Bertrams frelseshistoriske cyklus', *Synligt og usynligt—Studier tilegnede Otto Norn*, ed. by Hugo Johannsen (Herning: Poul Kristensens Forlag, 1990), 27–48, including ill.; and 'Der St Peter-Altar zu Hamburg—Eine Analyse des heilsgeschichtlichen Zyklus Meister Bertrams', in *Der St peter-Altar zu Hamburg*, Verein für katholische Kirchengeschichte in Hamburg und Schleswig-Holstein (Husum: Matthiesen Verlag Ingwert Paulsen jr., 1993), pp. 8–44.

[37] See Kaspersen (1990; as in note 36), pp. 38–44, or (1993; as in note 36), pp. 23–36.

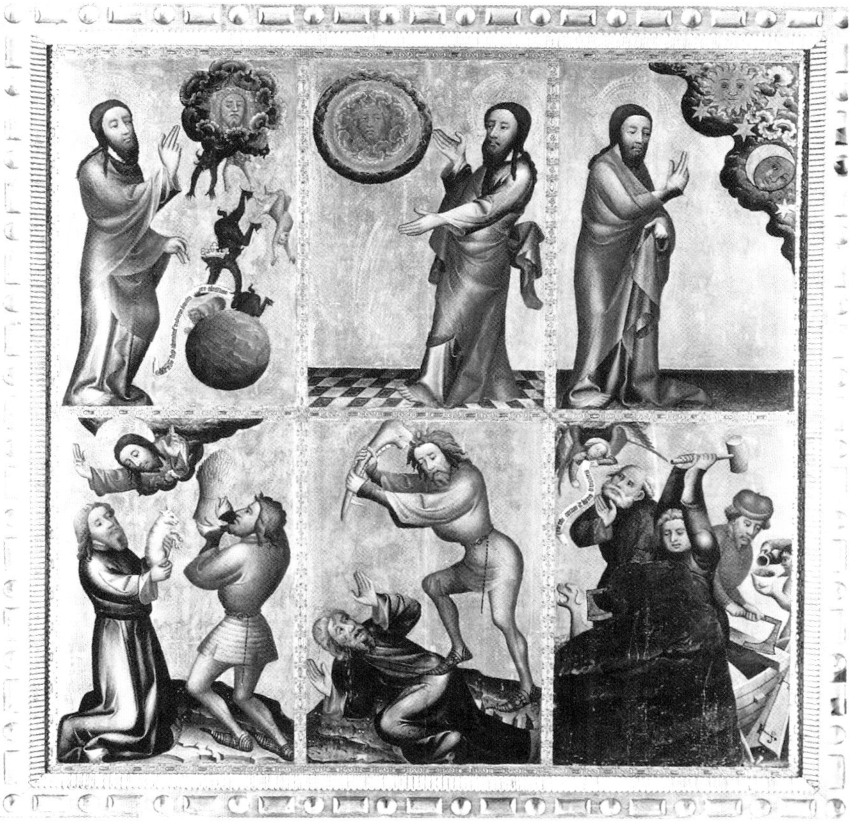

Fig. 9. Hamburg, six panels on the high altar from St Petri's Church, uppermost 'The Fall of the Rebel Angels', 'The created Firmament/ palatium *', and 'The Creation of Sun, Moon, and Stars', last 'The Sacrifice of Cain and Abel', 'Cain Slaying Abel', and 'The Building of Noah's Ark'.* c. *1379–83. © Elke Walford, Kunsthalle, Hamburg*

anxious look.

In this salvation history narrative, Mary is as much a bride as a mother and, as a bride, she also represents Ecclesia. It is she whom the Child Jesus points to every time—at the Nativity and the adoration of the three kings (cf. fig. 11), at the presentation in the Temple, and during the flight into Egypt (cf. fig. 10). The future union between Christ and his Church, the *magnum sacramentum* of Augustine, is foreseen already in the creation of Eve through her carnal union with the old Adam and her awe-struck spiritual union with the new Adam—music-making angels strike up at the great wedding feast (cf. fig. 11). And the bridal chamber or heavenly hall is ready from the dawn of time. In the second

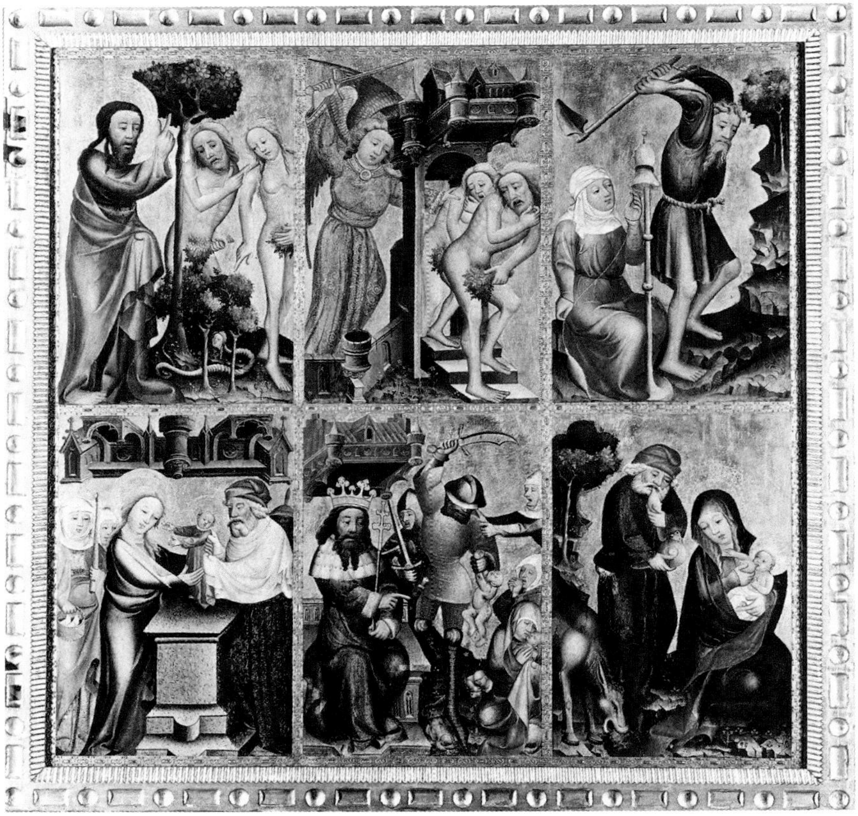

Fig. 10. Hamburg, six panels on the high altar from St Petri's Church, uppermost 'God's Curse on Adam and Eve', 'The Expulsion of Adam and Eve', and 'The First Labour', last 'The Presentation in the Temple', 'The Massacre of the Innocents', and 'The Rest on the Flight into Egypt'. c. *1379–83. © Elke Walford, Kunsthalle, Hamburg*

panel, the Creator stands on the firmament, according to Petrus Comestor called *coelum, quia celat*, because it conceals heaven above the firmament, which is the dwelling of the blessed, in Greek *uranon, id est palatium* (cf. fig. 9). By his use of gesture, the Creator indicates that this palace is now clean and adorned ready for the bride's unveiled meeting with the bridegroom.[38]

As a high altar, Master Bertram's work also alludes, of course, to the Eucharist, partly via sacrifices such as Cain and Abel's offering of sheaf and lamb and Abraham's surrender of his own son, and partly through various

[38] See Kaspersen (1990; as in note 36), pp. 30–32, or (1993; as in note 36), pp. 12–16.

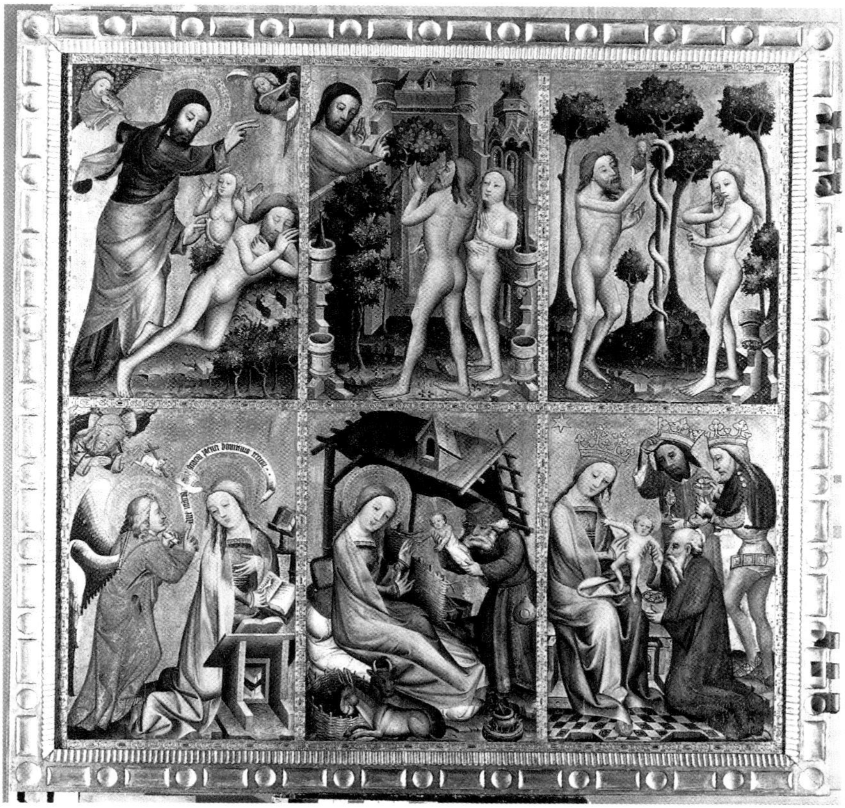

Fig. 11. Hamburg, six panels on the high altar from St Petri's Church, uppermost 'The Creation of Eve', 'The Admonition of Adam and Eve', and 'The Fall', last 'The Annunciation', 'The Nativity', and 'The Adoration of the Three Kings'. c. *1379–83. © Elke Walford, Kunsthalle, Hamburg*

emphases on food and drink as in the story of Jacob and Esau (cf. fig. 8a), emphases that are also statements that one can eat one's way to both salvation and damnation (cf. I Corinthians 11.29). This aspect is seen most clearly in the parallel drawn between God admonishing Adam and Eve and the birth of Jesus (cf. fig. 11). At the top, the Creator points toward the Tree of Knowledge, whose fruit is not to be eaten by the inhabitants of the Garden of Eden. At the bottom, Joseph holds the Child Jesus out to Mary, which is a very unusual feature in Nativity scenes, but which reveals the Child as the redeeming sacramental food, as the bread of life that has come down from Heaven. And the ox and the ass do not stand at the manger; they lie down by and nourish themselves from a *Gärtlein* with all its attendant connotations of Mary as the Mother of God and the Garden of Eden. It is hardly surprising, therefore, that food also has a central role in the final scene depicting the Holy Family at rest (cf. fig. 10).[39]

Master Bertram's altarpiece refers to a number of central aspects of the Christian universe in a detailed, differentiated way, and in that sense it is a hyper-iconographic or learned work, but it mediates its insights to a large extent through the basic idiom of style and composition, not least through countless inter-scene references of all kinds. The most important thing for us is to try to understand how a history of salvation cycle of this type found its way at all onto a high altar retable, for this is not at all usual. A slightly earlier silver frontal in the cathedral at Pistoia is possibly the closest parallel, but that was executed in several stages between 1357 and 71.[40]

It is my hypothesis that the scheme of the St Petri altarpiece is bound up with Hamburg's historical situation and that the most pertinent circumstance in the 1370s is the relationship with the Holy Roman Emperor, primarily, Charles IV of Bohemia. From the middle of the 1360s right up until his death in 1378, he attempted to involve the Hanseatic towns, especially Lübeck and Hamburg, more actively in the politics of the empire. As a trading town at the mouth of the Elbe, Hamburg was a kind of entry port to Prague, the new capital of the empire, via the river, and Charles wanted to turn the city into a centre for receiving and transferring goods from the entire northern European area to Prague and vice-versa.[41] The emperor's plans seem to have been received sympathetically in the city and to have been promoted with particular enthusiasm by the mayor, Heinrich Hoyer († 1375). Nothing concrete may have ensued from the various initiatives,[42] but Hamburg's involvement in the practical politics of that period is

---

[39] See Kaspersen (1990; as in note 36), pp. 36–37, or (1993; as in note 36), pp. 20–22.

[40] See Kaspersen (1990; as in note 36), p. 41, or (1993; as in note 36), pp. 28–29; and A. Venturi, *Storia dell'arte italiana* (Milan: Ulrico Hoepli, 1906), IV, pp. 940–52, incl. ill.

[41] See Heinrich Reincke, *Kaiser Karl IV. und die deutsche Hanse*, Pfingstblätter des Hansischen Geschichtsvereins, 22 (Lübeck: Verlag des Hansischen Geschichtsvereins, 1931). Charles had already granted Hamburg a privilege in 1359 to prosecute pirates and highwaymen, especially on and at the Elbe, and thereby strengthened the town's sovereignty over the river—see Horst Tschentscher, 'Die Entstehung der hamburgischen Elbhoheit (1189–1482)', *Zeitschrift des Vereins für Hamburgische Geschichte*, 43 (1956), pp. 1–48 (pp. 19–22); *Urkundenregesten zur Tätigkeit des deutschen Königs- und Hofgerichts bis 1451*, ed. by Bernhard Diestelkamp, VII: *Die Zeit Karls* IV *(1355 April–1359)*, ed. by Friedrich Battenberg (Cologne: Böhlau, 1994), pp. 350–51, no. 497; or *Hansisches Urkundenbuch*, ed. by Konstantin Höhlbaum et al. (Halle: Buchhandlung des Waisenhauses, 1882–86), III, pp. 225–26, no. 460.

[42] Yet, see Wolfgang von Stromer, 'Der kaiserliche Kaufmann—Wirtschaftspolitik unter Karl IV.', in *Kaiser Karl IV.—Staatsmann und Mäzen*, ed. by Ferdinand Seibt (Munich: Prestel, 1978), pp. 67–69. For a fine survey with further literature of Hamburg's political and social circumstances in the late medieval period, see Jürgen Sarnowsky, 'Die

evidenced, for example, by the fact that, at the end of the fourteenth century, the city had at least five altars and an important confraternity dedicated to the Bohemian Saint Wenceslas, the first martyr king of Bohemia and the name-saint of Charles IV's eldest son and successor.[43]

In the years when Lübeck and Hamburg were actively involved in practical politics, new life was probably breathed into a world of ideas concerning their importance in the empire, that is, their place in the *imperium christianorum* and its governance.[44] As a result of Charles IV's upgrading of their political importance, the towns could now regard themselves as the advocates of the empire, especially Lübeck, which was 'empire immediate' ('Reichsunmittelbar'). In an edict in German in 1374, the emperor elevates the people of Lübeck to deputies of the empire and to guardians against all harmful elements such as murderers and pirates, because he has learned about the particular trustworthiness, justice, and common sense of the mayor of Lübeck and because he has seen how the townspeople do their best to root out evil and protect the righteous, to the honour of himself and the Holy Empire and to the general good of the country and promotion of the peace. In all places, even in foreign parts, in all countries and towns with all kinds of rulers and forms of government, the people of Lübeck, on behalf of the emperor, are to pursue those who disturb the peace and try them in their own courts.[45] Lübeck's role in preserving the peace at land and sea was hereby elevated to a function of empire, and a Hanseatic naval power became the chief naval power of the empire. Even if the citizens of Hamburg were subordinate to the counts of Holstein,[46] they may well have entertained similar ideas about themselves in relation to the Holy Roman Empire.[47]

---

politische Entwicklung und die sozialen Strukturen Hamburgs im Spätmittelalter', in *Die Kunst des Mittelalters in Hamburg—Aufsätze zur Kulturgeschichte*, ed. by Volker Plagemann (Hamburg: Dölling und Galitz, 1999), pp. 97–108, ill.

[43] See H. Reincke (as in note 41), pp. 59–60.

[44] The Peace at Stralsund, 1370, had also considerably strengthened the position of the Hanseatic League.

[45] See H. Reincke (as in note 41), pp. 29–45 (40–41).

[46] And the emperor consequently supported the count against Hamburg's complaints and its claim for freedom; ibid., pp. 11–12.

[47] See above, n. 41. The relations between town and empire in the period generally were marked by clashes of interests; see Peter Moraw, 'Monarchie und Bürgertum', in *Kaiser Karl* IV (as in note 42), pp. 43–63 and notes. For a thourough investigation of the complex relationship between the Hanse and the empire in the fifteeenth century, see Horst Wernicke, 'Hanse und Reich im 15. Jahrhundert—ihre Beziehungen im Vergleich', in *Beiträge zur hansischen Kultur-, Verfassungs- und Schiffahrtsgeschichte*, Hansische Studien, X, ed. by Horst Wernicke and Nils Jörn (Weimar: Verlag Hermann Böhlaus Nachfolger, 1998), pp. 215–37. I have not had access to E. Voigt, 'Reichsgewalt und hansisches Bürgertum', *Wissenschaftliche Zeitschrift der Ernst-Moritz-Arndt-Universität*

Salvation history decorations, understood as events of the Old and New Testaments related to each other as parallel or continuous chronological progressions, are generally classed with didactic Christian art. They have no cult or devotional function but are considered to be 'painted likenesses, made for the instruction of the ignorant, so that they might understand the stories and so learn what occurred', as Pope Gregory the Great wrote.[48] However, such more or less extended Bible stories could evoke the conception of and be understood as a reference to Augustine's two *civitates*,[49] particularly when the emergence of these two 'cities' was emphasized so strongly, as is the case with Bertram's altarpiece in St Peter's church in Hamburg in which the unusual ending to the tale of the salvation story with 'The Massacre of the Innocents' and not least 'The Rest on the Flight'[50] also seems to conjure up a vision of the Church on a pilgrimage through the world of sin (fig. 10).

However, in the Middle Ages, the *civitas Dei* could hardly be conceived without intimating questions of how and by whom the Chosen People were to be led to salvation. And the same type of questions were likewise present in any reference to the condition and possible improvement of the *imperium Christianorum*:

Greifswald, Gesellschafts- und sprachwissenschaftliche Reihe, 12 (1963/65–66).

[48] See Caecilia Dawis-Weyer, *Early Medieval Art 300–1150: Sources and Documents* (Englewood Cliffs: Prentice-Hall, 1971), p. 48; Lately there has been much discussion of St Gregory's statements; see Lawrence G. Duggan, 'Was Art Really the 'Book of the Illiterate'?', in *Word and Image*, 5 (1989), pp. 227–51; Celia M. Chazelle, 'Pictures, Books and the Illiterate: Pope Gregory's Letters to Serenus of Marseilles', in *Word and Image*, 6 (1990), pp. 138–53; and *L'image—Fonctions et usages des images dans l'occident médiévale: actes du 6e 'International Workshop on Medieval Societies'*, ed. by J. Baschet and J.-C. Schmitt, Cahiers du Léopard d'Or, 5 (Paris: Le Léopard d'Or, 1996), pp. 7–26.

[49] For a comprehensive Scandinavian material and its conceivable political implications, see S. Kaspersen, 'Über spätmittelalterliche Genesis-Serien in der Kirchenmalerei der nordischen Länder—Eine politisch-theologische Skizze', in *Bild och Bruk*, ed. by Tove Riska, Taidehistoriallisia Tutkimuksia, Konsthistoriska Studier, 8 (Helsinki: The Society for Art History in Finland, 1985), pp. 115–41, incl. ill. Furthermore S. Kaspersen, 'Cotton-Genesis, die Toursbibeln und die Bronzetüren—Vorlage und Aktualität', in *Bernwardinische Kunst—Bericht über ein wissenschaftliches Symposium in Hildesheim vom 10.10. bis 13.10.1984*, ed. by Martin Gosebruch (Göttingen: Erich Goltze, 1988), pp. 79–103, incl. ill. (84–96).

[50] It is worth emphasizing the originality of Bertram's panel and the fact that the motif of the 'Rest' during the 'Flight' is relatively young and does not gain ground until about 1500; see Hans Möhle, in *Lucas Cranach d. Ä.—Die Ruhe auf der Flucht nach Ägypten*, Werkmonographien zur bildenden Kunst, 111 (Stuttgart: Philipp Reclam jun., 1966), esp. p. 17. According to G. Schiller (as in note 20), I, p. 132, the representation by Bertram is the earliest known example.

> weil die kaiserliche Herrschaft immer auch als weltliches Pendant zur geistlichen Herrschaft des Papstes in der ganzen Christenheit verstanden wurde. Die Verbindung des deutschen Königtums mit dem universalen Reich hat es mit sich gebracht, daß sich der deutsche Staatskörper von Anfang an nicht primär als politische, sondern als religiöse Ordnung verstehen konnte und sein Zweck nicht die Macht um der Macht willen, sondern die Vorbereitung des ewigen Heils für die Menschen war. So erweist sich die Staatsideologie des mittelalterlichen Reiches als religiös und individualistisch.[51]

Thus, when Hamburg, as a city on the empire's northern periphery, was unexpectedly drawn into imperial politics, new parameters were set for the doings of the city, which could now view its political, commercial, and religious activities even more strongly in the light of Salvation history. It had become a part of the City of God, which had from the dawn of time been on a pilgrimage toward the great wedding feast at the end of time. The high altar retable in St Petri, the townspeople's main church, showed the biblical prelude to the current situation and placed it in an overall framework. St Augustine divided world history into six or seven ages, corresponding to the six days of Creation and the six stages of life. The first age lasted from Adam until the Flood, and the sixth age began with the Incarnation and stretched out to Judgement Day. The seventh age was the seventh day, the day of rest, 'our Sabbath, whose end (finis) will not be an evening, but the Lord's eternal eighth day, sanctified by the resurrection of Christ'.[52]

Bertram's altarpiece begins with the days of Creation, which take up the first two 'sections', that is, six panels (cf. fig. 8a), and ends with the creation of Eve in the seventh (cf. fig. 11), a depiction that, as previously indicated, points toward the *magnum sacramentum* and eternal rest. It might also be said that among the first seven panels there are six panels dealing with the story of Creation, while the second panel in the row primarily depicts, as indicated, a state—that is, the established Kingdom of Heaven, the bedecked bridal chamber, which is now prepared for the great wedding (cf. fig. 9). In this sense, the first two panels encompass the entire history of the world from the dawn of time until its end. At the same time, the overall narration reaches the last and most important age, whose beginning—with the Incarnation of Christ—fills the final

---

[51] See Heinz Angermeier, *Die Reichsreform 1410–1555—Die Staatsproblematik in Deutschland zwischen Mittelalter und Gegenwart* (Munich: Beck, 1984), p. 16. For the indissoluble connection between reform of the Church and of the empire in the late medieval period, see, e.g., Tilman Struve, 'Utopie und gesellschaftliche Wirklichkeit—Zur Bedeutung des Friedenskaisers im späten Mittelalter', *Historische Zeitschrift*, 225 (1977), pp. 65–95: 'Die enge Verknüpfung von kirchlicher Reform und gesellschaftlicher Veränderung darf deshalb geradezu als Charakteristikum der Kaiserprophetie in Deutschland herausgestellt werden' (p. 88).

[52] Quoted from M. Gerwing, 'Weltende, Weltzeitalter', in *Lexikon des Mittelalters* (Munich: Artemis—Lexma, 1977–2000), VIII, col. 2169.

two 'sections'.[53] The 'clutch' between the days of Creation, which form the parameters of the chronology of salvation history, and the final, decisive age takes place through the linkage of the 'Creation of Eve' and 'The Annunciation', a comparison rich in revelatory, visual and symbolic-allegorical resonances (cf. fig. 11). At the same time, in an Augustinian sense, it can be said to be a juxtaposition of the original pattern of human community and the full appearance of 'the City of God' in its complete earthly manifestation through the incarnation of Jesus.[54] The creation of Eve depicts humanity in its original condition, turned towards its Maker and determined for eternal bliss. At the same time, her mutual bodily connection with Adam serves as the symbol of all symbols of the harmony and unity that should exist among people, and as a warning against the human inclination towards waste and strife.[55]

Thus, the question is what sort of framework can be imagined for such an Augustinian doctrine of two cities during the latter half of the fourteenth century. It can generally be asserted that the reception of Aristotle in the thirteenth century had a fundamental impact on the development of political and political-theological thinking in the late Middle Ages: for here begins not only 'die Vorgeschichte des Begriffs und der Vorstellung der 'bürgerlichen Gesellschaft' (*societas civilis*), sondern aller damit zusammenhängenden Begriffe und deren Verhältnisbestimmungen zu Glaube, Theologie und Kirche'.[56] John B. Morall calls the two centuries leading to Luther 'the age of ambiguity', and stresses how difficult it is to come to grips with and understand the various positions and developments during this period.[57]

There can scarcely be any doubt that the close ties between *regnum* and *sacerdotium* were in the process of dissolution during the late Middle Ages. Yet, the Hamburg altarpiece directs us to look at things in a historical perspective in which all events are understood in relation to eternal salvation, and it thereby sets a limit to Aristotelian-based thinking in which the worldly regime is entirely

[53] The altarpiece does not show all six ages but, instead, focuses on the patriarchs Abraham, Isaac, and Jacob in these three panels between the first and sixth ages.

[54] See Wolfgang Stürner, *Peccatum und Potestas—Der Sündenfall und die Entstehung der herrscherlichen Gewalt im mittelalterlichen Staatsdenken* (Sigmaringen: Thorbecke, 1987), pp. 67–85 (pp. 68–70, 82–83).

[55] See *De civitate Dei*, XII, 22: 'But he created man's nature from the one original man'. Augustine, *Concerning the City of God against the Pagans*, trans. by Henry Bettenson, ed. by David Knowles (Harmondsworth: Penguin, 1972), pp. 502–03. For a Latin edition, see Corpus Christianorum, Series Latina, XLVIII (Brepols: Turnhout, 1955). See also ibid., XII, 28: 'For the human race the union of man and wife', p. 508.

[56] See Ulrich Duchrow, *Christenheit und Weltverantwortung—Traditionsgeschichte und systematische Struktur der Zweireichelehre* (Stuttgart: Ernst Klett, 1970), p. 398.

[57] See John B. Morall, *Political Thought in Medieval Times*, 2nd edn (London: Hutchinson, 1960), pp. 119–20.

liberated from such religious goals. The Christian empire is distinguished by its special sacral dimension from the *regnum* in general. Within the bounds of hierocratic-curial and theocratic-caesaropapist modes of thinking, the late Middle Ages was characterized by hard-hitting and consistent theories of the papacy's superior position, and particularly in the so-called 'Augustine School', such figures as Aegidius Romanus and Jacobus de Viterbo denied any place at all to the state in *civitas Dei*, because of its lack of righteousness, which is why *plenitudo potestatis* went to the pope as the representative of the Church.[58] But even within this strongly hierocratic camp, it could not be imagined that the papacy could do without the emperor or that these two powers were to be separated. And the idea of a Christian state in which *imperium* has an important role in the interplay of these two powers lives on in such thinkers as Dante, William of Ockham, and Nicolaus of Cusa.

At the same time, at the beginning of the fourteenth century, new parameters were being set for the relationship between the *regnum (imperium)* and *sacerdotium* after Pope Boniface VIII's defeat by King Philippe IV le Bel, resulting in the transfer of the papal seat to Avignon in 1309. The final great struggle between the papacy and the Holy Roman Empire was played out by John XXII (1316–34) and Louis IV of Bavaria. The relationship between the two powers may now be said to have taken on a more pragmatic character, even though the papacy continued to champion its hierocratic point of view. All of this means that the doctrine of two states fits into a broad spectrum of ideological viewpoints, which were coloured by their factual circumstances and whose vitality can only be understood in light of their interplay with political and social reality.

The sources do not tell us who was responsible for the theological programme for the high altar of St Petri, but Christian Beutler has suggested Wilhelm Horborch (*c.* 1330/32–*c.* 1384), a theologian and lawyer, who was dean of the cathedral chapter in Hamburg from 1363.[59] In 1371, he was summoned to Prague by Charles IV to establish the law faculty at the new university, and in 1375, Pope Gregory XI made him the youngest of the twelve members of the highest papal court, the Rota Romana. He won international fame for his collection of papal rulings, *Decisiones Rotae Romanae*. He was in Charles IV's party at a meeting in Lübeck in 1375, and his brother Bertram, who was also linked to both pope and emperor during his thirty years as mayor, led the Hamburg delegation at the same meeting.[60] In such circles, one could easily surmise an Augustinian world view

[58] See, e.g., ibid., pp. 86–89; and A. Zumkeller, 'Die Augustinerschule des Mittelalters: Vertreter und philosophisch–theologische Lehre', *Analecta Augustiniana*, 27 (1964), pp. 167–262.

[59] See Chr. Beutler (as in note 36), pp. 66–72.

[60] See Wilhelm Mantels, 'Kaiser Karls IV. Hoflager im Lübeck vom 20. bis 30. Oktober 1375', *Hansische Geschichtsblätter* (1874), pp. 109–41, reprinted in idem, *Beiträge zur Lübisch-Hansischen Geschichte: Ausgewählte historische Arbeiten* (Jena: Gustav Fischer,

activated in the form of a salvation history decoration.

If we look at Emperor Charles IV himself, he was clearly a great admirer of St Augustine of Hippo, and promoted the Augustinian canons and the Augustinian anchorites in Bohemia.[61] The first convent for the Augustinian canons was founded in 1333 by the bishop of Prague, John IV, in the city of Raudnitz on the Elbe, where the bishop's castle was located. According to reliable tradition, at its dedication in 1340, on the day of the Ascension of the Virgin, the canons were brought there from the canonry at San Pietro in Ciel d'Oro in Pavia, where the relics of St Augustine were kept. Charles had stayed there for a while in 1331 during his first mission to Italy—for his father, King John VII—and re-established a convent that had been banned by Louis VII of Bavaria.[62] The summoning of the Italian canons must certainly be seen in the context of the negotiations of King John, Charles, and the bishop with the curia in Avignon to have the archbishopric established in Prague. St Pietro at Ciel d'Oro was a northern Italian centre for the reform of the Augustinian order based on Pope Benedict XII's constitution *Ad decorem ecclesie* from 1339. And with these canons, Raudnitz became a centre for a reform movement, which, among other things, promoted, a *devotio moderna* similar to that of the Windesheim congregation.[63] The second major monastery involved in the Raudnitz reform was Karlshof, which Charles IV established in Prague in 1349 in connection with the great expansion of the city and which was now to be not only the capital of Bohemia but also the centre of the Holy Roman Empire. And in 1358 Charles called the Augustinian canon and reformist preacher Konrad von Waldhausen to Prague from Vienna to stimulate the new movement of piety.

Thus, the Augustinians made up an important element of the spiritual milieu that surrounded Charles IV. What impact this had on his understanding of himself as a Christian ruler may be more difficult to pinpoint.[64] However, it may be

---

1881), pp. 287–323. Concerning the ties between the chapter and the Town Council it is worth mentioning that St Petri's, like the three other parish churches in Hamburg, was incorporated in the chapter and that the Council renewed itself by cooptation every year on the feast of St Peter's Chair (*St Petri ad cathedram*), i.e., 22 February. See J. Sarnowsky (as in note 42), pp. 99, 103–04.

[61] See Joseph Hemmerle, 'Karl IV. und die Orden', in *Kaiser Karl* IV. (as in note 42), pp. 302–04; and Franz Machilek, 'Die Augustiner-Chorherren in Böhmen und Mähren', *Archiv für Kirchengeschichte von Böhmen-Mähren-Schlesien*, 4 (1976), pp. 110–21.

[62] See *Vita Caroli Quarti—Die Autobiographie Karls IV.*, ed. and trans. by Eugen Hillenbrand (Stuttgart: Fleischhauer & Spohn, 1979), p. 90, 91.

[63] See I. Zibermayr, 'Zur Geschichte der Raudnitzer Reform', in *Mitteilungen des Instituts für österreichische Geschichtsforschung*, supplementary vol. 11 (Innsbruck, 1929), pp. 323–53; and Johanna Schreiber, 'Devotio moderna in Böhmen', *Bohemia—Jahrbuch des Collegium Carolinum*, 6 (1965), pp. 93–122.

[64] Unfortunately, I have been unable to consult Zdenek Kalista's account of Charles's

ascertained with relative certainty that, to a very high degree, Charles tried to live up to the ideals of a *rex justus*. In his two 'mirrors for princes,' *Majestas Carolina* [65] and *Vita Caroli Quarti*,[66] he paints a picture of a God-fearing ruler whose goal is to create peace and security for the empire's inhabitants through a just regime, based upon good advisers, in which evil is punished and goodness rewarded. And he lived up to those duties that the spiritual advisor of his youth, the abbot Pierre de Fécamp, now Pope Clement VI, enumerated for a Christian emperor in connection with Charles' assumption of the Roman throne/as a Roman king in 1346,[67]—for example, he attempted to propagate Christian doctrines, that is, the Church of Rome, by an appeal to the heathen prince of Lithuania[68] and by the establishment of a Slavic monastery in Prague.[69] He also fought against heresy[70] and provided something of a defence of the Church by supporting—to the extent possible—papal authority in its difficult circumstances in Italy.[71] Ritually, he displayed his willingness to defend the Gospel by participating actively in Christmas services in all his trappings of office and swinging the sword of state three times during the chanting of the Christmas mass.[72]

---

relationship to Augustine in idem, *Karel IV.—jeho duchovní tvár* (1971), p. 51 ff.

[65] See E. Werunsky,'Die Maiestas Karolina', in *Zeitschrift der Savigny-Stiftung für Rechtsgeschichte*, 23, Ger. Abt., 9 (1888), pp. 64–103; R. Schneider, 'Karls IV. Auffassung vom Herrscheramt', *Beiträge zur Geschichte des mittelalterlichen deutschen Königtums*, Historische Zeitschrift, Beiheft 2, ed. by Theodor Schieder (Munich: R. Oldenbourg, 1973), pp. 122–50; and Bernhard Töpfer, 'Zur Staatsideologie in den Prooemia der Konstitutionen von Melfi und der Majestas Carolina', *Karl IV.—Politik und Ideologie im 14. Jahrhundert*, ed. by Evamaria Engel (Weimar: Hermann Böhlaus Nachfolger, 1982), pp. 150–57. I have not had access to *Majestas Carolina*, ed. by H. Jirecek, Codex juris Bohemici, 2.2 (1870).

[66] See *Vita Caroli Quarti* (as in note 62).

[67] See Schneider (as in note 65), p. 147. Here, too, he is to reward and honour the good and drive out the bad through the exercise of justice and, with his power, he is to aid the oppressed and annihilate *tyranni*.

[68] See K. Conrad, 'Litauen, der Deutsche Orden und Karl IV. 1352–60', *Zeitschrift für Ostforschung*, 21 (1972), 20–42; and H. Grundmann, 'Das Schreiben Kaiser Karls IV. an die heidnischen Litauer-Fürsten 1358', *Folia diplomatica*, 1 (1971), 89–103.

[69] See M. Paulová, 'L'Idée Cyrillo-Méthodienne dans la politique de Charles IV et la fondation du monastère Slave de Prague', *Byzantinoslavica*, 11 (1950), pp. 174–86.

[70] See A. Patschovsky, 'Straßburger Beginenverfolgungen im 14. Jahrhundert', *Deutsches Archiv für Erforschung des Mittelalters*, 30 (1974), 56–198.

[71] See Ludwig Schmugge, 'Kurie und Kirche in der Politik Karls IV., in *Karl IV.—Staatsmann und Mäzen*, ed. by Ferdinand Seibt (Munich: Bayerische Nationalmuseum—Adalbert-Stifter-Verein, 1978), pp. 73–87, et passim.

[72] See Franz Machilek, 'Privatfrömmigkeit und Staatsfrömmigkeit', in *Karl IV* (as in

It is significant in our context that Charles' vision of the Christian ruler harkens back to the great imperial tradition in his promotion of the cult of Charlemagne, which was performed primarily by the Augustinian canons at Karlshof in Prague.[73] Moreover, he interlinked his understanding of the Christian ruler in the introduction to his autobiography with themes and texts on the Ottonian crown of state,[74] designating, for example, the ruler as Christ's vicar on earth ('cuius typum et vices geritis in terris').[75] In this way, Charles IV anchors and takes his starting point in the classical period of political Augustinianism—in the period in which the Holy Roman Emperors understood themselves to be the leaders of the City of God in its totality.

Certainly, there is no direct linking of the autobiography's 'mirror for princes' to *De civitate Dei*, but the entire introductory text deals with the two societies, the God-fearing and the Godless.[76]—indeed, it could be said to be an elaboration of or exegesis on Psalms 1.[77] Through a reference to Luke 10.27,[78] Charles also indirectly characterizes the two societies, 'the heavenly city' and 'the earthly city', in an Augustinian way: composed respectively of those who love God and those who love themselves.[79]

---

note 42), p. 100; and Hermann Heimpel, 'Königliche Weihnachtsdienst im späteren Mittelalter', *Deutsches Archiv für Erforschung des Mittelalters*, 39 (1983), pp. 131–206.

[73] See, e.g., J. Hemmerle (as in note 61), p. 302–03.

[74] For the following, see *Vita Caroli Quarti* (as in note 62), pp. 27–30 (Intro.), 72, 73–76, 77 and ill.

[75] Corresponds to the plate of Christ enthroned and with the inscription: 'Per me reges regnant' (Proverbs 8.15) on the Ottonian crown.

[76] 'Wenn ihr nun in der Furcht Gottes wandelt, wird dies der Anfang eurer Weisheit sein, So werdet ihr nicht vom Wege abirren, weil der Weg des Herrn gerade ist Die Gottlosen werden vor euch niedersinken, die Gerechten aber werden frohlocken'.

[77] Charles specifically refers to this psalm when he admonishingly writes: 'Meidet also von Kind an jede Sünde, Wandelt vielmehr ohne Makel im Gesetz des Herrn, So seid ihr wie ein Baum, geplanzt an strömendem wasser, der seine Frucht trägt zur rechten Zeit und dessen Laub nicht welkt' [see Psalm 1.3]; see *Vita Caroli Quarti* (as in note 62), pp. 79 and 81.

[78] Von besonderer Bedeutung aber ist jenes Gebot, Gott den Herrn zu lieben aus ganzem Herzen und aus ganzer Seele und den Nächsten wie sich selbst.

[79] See *De civitate Dei*, XV, 1 (as in note 55). In light of all this, it is quite understandable that there are statements in the autobiography that are reminiscent of the narration in Master Bertram's altarpiece—most clearly, the quotation below, which corresponds to the introduction to the lower and upper zone, that is respectively, the story of Cain and Abel and that of the Fall of Satan and the Rebel Angels followed by the celestial aula; 'Neidet einander nichts, sondern habt Liebe zueinander, denn Neid gebiert Haß, Wer haßt, wird nicht beliebt und richtet sich in seiner Raserei selbst zugrunde. . . Will euer Herz sich erheben, so erniedrigt euch, . . . Der Stolz ist dem Schöpfer verhaßt

The whole of Charles IV's religiosity—his name policy, his promotion of the cults of saints and relics, coupled with his spectacular staging—has most often been viewed as a particularly politically motivated piety—Rudolf Chadraba calls it a *devotio antiqua*, which has much more to do with 'mit seiner welthistorischen, von ihm geglaubten Sendung als mit privat-religiösen und ästhetischen Interessen im modernen Sinne'.[80] It would also be a mistake to underestimate this view, since it is such an obvious and important part of Charles' talent as a Christian ruler.[81] However, Heinrich Neureither seems correct in his emphasis on Charles IV's personal piety, viewing his particular brand of religiosity as an intersection between his inward piety and his political understanding of the significance of the cult of the Christian ruler.[82] For example, even as a child in the court of Charles the Fair in Paris, he read 'die marianischen Antiphonen des Stundengebets und las sie, als ich ihren Sinn einigermaßen verstand, in meiner Kindheit von Tag zu Tag lieber',[83] and throughout the rest of his life, he regularly continued to observe canonical hours as a priest.[84] As a six-year-old, he experienced a sort of religious awakening as a result of a sermon by Pierre de Fécamp,[85] and, later in his life he also had 'visions'.[86] Moreover, his theological training and knowledge of the Bible was far above the norm for a secular ruler.[87]

In this light, it is telling that Charles IV exhibited an intense, inner piety in taking the sacrament of holy communion.[88] For in this sacrament, there is an

---

und allen, die guten Sinnes sind. . . . Gott aber wird am Ende den Stolz brechen, er wird die Mächtigen vom Throne stürzen und die Niedrigen aus dem Staub erheben . . .', *Vita Caroli Quarti* (as in note 62), p. 79 (cf. Luke 1.52, and I Samuel 2.80).

[80] See Rudolf Chadraba, 'Kaiser Karls IV. devotio antiqua', *Mediaevalia Bohemica*, 1 (1969), pp. 51–68.

[81] See Fr. Machilek (as in note 72), pp. 87–101, 441–43; R. Schneider (as in note 78), esp. pp. 126–33; and Jirí Spevácek, 'Frömmigkeit und Kirchentreue als Instrumente der politischen Ideologie Karls IV', in *Karl IV.—Politik* (as in note 65), pp. 158–70.

[82] See H. Neureither, *Das Bild Kaiser Karls IV. in der Zeitgenössischen Französischen Geschichtsschreibung* (diss. Heidelberg University, 1964), pp. 18–203.

[83] See *Vita Caroli Quarti* (as in note 62), p. 83.

[84] See Johan von Jenstein's funeral sermon for Charles IV—*Fontes Rerum Bohemicarum*, III (Prag: Nákladem Nadáni Frantiska Palackého, 1882), p. 429: 'nam horas eciam suas canonicas, sicut unus sacerdos dicebat'.

[85] See *Vita Caroli Quarti* (as in note 62), pp. 43, 86.

[86] See Fr. Machilek (as in note 72), pp. 88–89.

[87] See ibid., pp. 87–88.

[88] In his funeral sermon for Charles IV, Johan von Jenstein enumerated seven points that demonstrate the emperor to be *beatus*: 'Quinto fortissime plorabat, cum corpus dominicum sumebat et alios ex devotione adducens'; see *Fontes Rerum Bohemicarum* (as in note 84), p. 429.

important intersection between personal piety and institutionalizing liturgy. By receiving the body of Christ, the believer becomes incorporated into the Church, understood as the mystical body of Christ, the inward remembrance of the Redeemer and His acts of redemption fused with the sacramentally established institution of salvation.

Perhaps this eucharistic piety was also Charles' way of accommodating the most radical of the papal apologists, who, for example, re-interpreted Romans 13.1 as reading that such authority 'as comes from God is ordained' ('que autem sunt a deo, ordinata sunt'), that is, more explicit a hierarchical interpretation in which secular power does not derive immediately from God but is only conveyed through the spiritual powers. In *De ecclesiastica potestate*, Aegidius Romanus contributed the view that only through the sacraments of the Church could a secular ruler be free from original and actual sin, that is, only by subordination to the highest power [i.e., the Church] could one become worthy of the office, which de facto derived from God.[89] But through his intense participation in the sacrament of Holy Communion, Charles might well have believed that a good Christian ruler could stand in direct relation to the King of Kings and, in this way, make the more subtle arguments of superiority and subordination uninteresting.

Undoubtedly, the most interesting thing for us is that this aspect of the Eucharist appears directly in Charles IV's understanding of the Christian ruler. His autobiography opens with a discourse on the two forms of temporal life related to the sacramental nourishment: bodily food is transitory and leads to death. But we learn from the Saviour: 'Wer mein Fleisch ißt und mein blut trinkt, der bleibt in mir und ich in ihm.' Further:

> Die von solcher geistigen Speise leben, bleiben in Ewigkeit Wer aber jene geistige Speise ißt, von der die Seele lebt, muß dieser Mensch nicht in seiner Seele ein Verlangen empfinden, diese Speise begierig aufzunehmen und in hingebender Liebe zu umfangen, Doch viele essen die geistige Speise ohne Verlangen und Begier und speien sie aus ihrem Herzen aus. Weh ihnen!

'They eat their way to punishment and damnation. Instead, one should seek spiritual nourishment, the bread of heaven, which is both 'flesh' and 'word', the Saviour continues, and:

> Durch jenes Brot hat uns Christus selbst das neue und ewige Testament bekräftigt. Jenes Brot stärke eure Herzen und Seelen in heiligher Zuneigung und Liebe zu ihm, damit ihr stark genug seid, das Zeitliche zu durchwandern, ohne das ewige Reich zu verlieren. Amen.[90]

This discussion of Jesus' body as sacramental bread and of eating one's way to salvation or damnation brings Bertram's altarpiece to mind. The panels can be

[89] See U. Duchrow (as in note 56), pp. 405–06.

[90] Four quotations all from *Vita Caroli Quarti* (as in note 62), pp. 67, 69, 71, 73.

said to make the same connection between the story of the two societies and the sacrament of holy communion that Charles IV makes in his autobiography between heavenly and worldly nourishment on one hand and of the god-fearing and the godless on the other. This is far from saying that the panels must be understood as a simple illustration of Charles IV's conception of the Christian ruler. Rather, it implies that they were created in an environment in which Charles' idea of the *regimen christianum* was one among a wide range of conceptions, more or less related to one another, that is, there was a spectrum of possible frames within which the altarpiece may delineate a certain configuration of ideas. What is essential is not that the statement of the altar-piece can be compared with a specific, written source but the kind of conceptions the painted program in its interaction with the general ideas and prevailing mentalities is supposed to reflect and evoke. The hypothesis of the politico-theological meaning of the high altar may be supported by other sources in future investigations, but, for the moment, Master Bertram's panels, like the wall paintings in Keldby Church, stand out as a potential testimony about certain opinions and expectations, as a possible source for insights which may be otherwise unaccessible.

We have now had a closer look at two examples of a painted salvation history and have tried to substantiate that they were closely related to specific historical events. In both cases, the use of pictures as historical sources is placed in the context of intellectual history. But to understand history in a frame of religious salvation was at the same time quite customary, one might say a fundamental aspect of the medieval outlook, the medieval mentality. There are no clear and distinct boundaries between intellectual history and the history of mentalities. For example, the politico-theological meaning of the high altar in St Petri may include many specific ideas and concepts. However, it also is rooted in views that were common in the Middle Ages, in conditions of life that the individual internalized more or less unconsciously or to which, at least, the individual was forced to adapt in one way or another, if not to revolt against them. The Hamburg citizen, the merchant or the shopkeeper, the artisan or the day labourer may not speak of an Augustinian world view or be acquainted with the different positions and arguments of the curial and imperial camps, but they would most likely have been familiar with the idea of the two cities, of the opposition between those who love God and those who love only themselves and worldly things, and, just as certainly, they would have considered both the Church and the empire to be important communities or institutions for attaining salvation.

I think it is in the context of the history of mentalities and intellectual history or ideology that pictures have their greatest importance as historical sources. It is true that this study, unlike the Annales school, is concerned with specific, historical episodes, with the narrative of events, but it also concerns important modes of thought and belief systems. The course of events is interpreted within these greater structures and these corroborate the readings. In Keldby Church, the exegesis, of course, is very involved with and dependent on the identification of the official royal act, but it is still grounded in general structures. In St Petri's, Hamburg, there are no immediate links between the altar-piece and the political history of the decade. The hypothesis can be supported and made probable only by references to certain modes of thought. In relation to the actual events, one may even point out that Charles IV might have been dead before the altar-piece was begun or, at least, that it was not finished until five years after his death, in 1383. Therefore, a closer look at the acts of King Vencelas may seem natural. But according to the basic premise of the present interpretation, it was Charles IV who formed the framework. One may ask whether Vencelas met the expectations of Hamburg,[91] or whether the somewhat sombre issue of the salvation story on the altar-piece reflects anxiety about the future.[92] But such minor, socio-psychological fluctuations are difficult to determine with any certainty.

The important thing is that pictures constitute their own kind of historical source. They make statements according to their own linguistics—for example,

[91] The question is not followed up here. In passing one may notice that an important part of the imperial politics, the King's Peace (der Landfriede), which Charles IV had extended to the northern region of Germany, soon crumbled under Vencelas's government; see Heinz Angermeier, *Königtum und Landfriede im deutschen Spätmittelalter* (Munich: Beck, 1966), pp. 266–317. In general, King Vencelas was severely critized as a regent by all contemporary and later chroniclers; see Klaus Schreiner, 'Correctio principis—Gedankliche Begründung und geschichtliche Praxis spätmittelalterlicher Herrscherkritik', in *Mentalitäten im Mittelalter—Methodische und inhaltliche Probleme*, ed. by Frantisek Graus (Sigmaringen: Thorbecke, 1987), pp. 224–31. For one thing, Vencelas was accused of inebrity (see ibid., p. 224) and there may be a connection between this and the unusual setting off of Ham as a drunkard in the panel with The Building of the Ark. But it is a somewhat daring assumption since the surprising iconography merely may arise from an allegorical understanding of the salvation story on a religious level. Finally, it can be mentioned that St Vencelas does not appear, at least today, among the many sculptured saints of the shrine; see *Goldgrund und Himmelslicht—Die Kunst des Mittelalters in Hamburg* (exhib. cat.), ed. by Uwe M. Schneede (Hamburg: Dölling und Galitz, 1999), pp. 101–11, incl. ill.

[92] The statement of Bertram's cycle on the position of the secular ruler in salvation history is ambiguous. Certainly, we see the three holy kings worshipping the Christ Child just below the depiction of the Fall, which made secular authority necessary; see W. Stürner (as in note 54), but in the following and final 'section', secular power is presented in the role of tyrant—in the form of Herod, and the cruelty of his action intrudes itself on to the Holy Family, with the mourning morthers continuing 'behind' the framework of the scene. Furthermore, it may be ascertained generally that the altarpiece's program of salvation history is being used not to tell the story of the Chosen People's leaders or to depict rulers under the Old Covenant—Moses, Joshua, David, Solomon, etc.—but, rather, to tell the story of the patriarchs, who, according to Augustine, designate the City of God before the coming of Christ, together with the prophets; see ibid., pp. 81–82, and *De civitate Dei*, XVII, 16 (as in note 55).

programmatic and iconographic rules—and they have their own syntactic structures determined by space and surface, colour and line, light and shadow, etc.—their own rhetoric of invention and composition. These latter aspects of figurative language are easily utilized in an investigation of mentalities and may even be relevant in the context of a more specific intellectual history. For example, conceptions of the *regimen christianum*, of the *regnum* and its place in salvation history, have an organologic aspect, which is interesting in relation to corporeality in Master Bertram's panels.

It was a stock in trade in the Middle Ages to compare the relationship between *regnum* and *sacerdotium* and the structure and the ideal function of society with the human body. In the High and Late Middle Ages, a proper organologic conception of the society or 'State' developed.[93] The different parts of the organic society in the early period were distinctly subordinated to one head; *regnum* and *sacerdotium* co-existed within Ecclesia; the 'State' was conceived as a function of the Church as the mystical body of Christ; and the relationship between the secular and the spiritual was typically compared with the mutual dependency of body and soul. However, the emphasis shifted in the later period: the earthly institutions of Church and 'State' broke away from each other and became self-contained bodies within the *corpus Christi*. Salvation was no longer, as a matter of course, the immediate or determinative objective of the *regnum*. The superiority of the head was now relativized into a large number of highly differentiated members, and their perfection and harmonious interaction became the central theme of the 'state'.

Within the figurative arts, this process may be compared to the general development of the depiction of the human body from a general model, stressing the head and the importance of the soul through prominent eyes and eloquent hands, to another model, stressing corporeality and giving other parts of the body greater importance and equality. One may argue, then, that the dichotomy between a distinct corporeality and the incorporeal gold ground in Master Bertram's panels reflects and comments on the tensions in the late Middle Ages between organologic and secular-oriented conceptions of a realm of estates, on one hand, and, on the other, an understanding of the *regnum, in casu imperium christianorum*, as an integral part and function of the *corpus Christi*, as a community or corporation determined by its eschatological goals.

I think this kind of analogy can be worked out in greater detail with advantage and become thereby a more subtle tool for the analysis of the specific language of pictures. I also think that such analogies can be corroborated by a theory that makes the structure of human society a determining factor not only for the organologic conception of the 'state' but also for the scientific understanding of

---

[93] See Tilman Struve, *Die Entwicklung der organologischen Staatsauffassung im Mittelalter*, Monographien zur Geschichte des Mittelalters, 16 (Stuttgart: Anton Hiersemann, 1978).

the human body and its functioning and for the mind's apprehension of space, of its continuum and its relation to solid bodies. Here these final remarks merely provide a hint of the potentials of figurative language, to suggest a final aspect of the use of pictures as historical sources in their own right.

On the epistemology of images

LENA LIEPE

Introduction

On the frontispiece of a 1452 French translation of Aegidius Romanus's *De regimine principum* (*Government of Princes*),[1] we see a detailed and colourful depiction of the presentation of the volume that contains the illumination to the patron who commissioned it (fig. 1). The translator himself, Jean Wauquelin, kneels in front of the duke of Burgundy, Philippe le Bon, and the court. He holds out the open book in both hands. This miniature will serve as my point of departure in this investigation of images as source material. The main question will be: how and on what—or on whose—premises, should images be interpreted as historical sources? I will promote an art-historical claim that images can and should be used as sources in their own right, according to the distinctive nature of their visual characteristics: that the main potential of images as historical sources lies precisely in their visual formation.

Everything that has survived from past times can be defined as historical source material if it is used functionally, that is, to answer questions about what once happened and how things once were. When historians treat images as sources, they naturally handle them similarly to other kinds of sources. The images are viewed instrumentally, as something that is used to reveal information about something else. This means that the main interest of the historian does

---

[1] Brussels, Bibliothèque Royale Albert Ier, ms. 9043. For a detailed description of the manuscript, see Frédéric Lyna, *Les principaux manuscrits à peintures de la Bibliothèque Royale de Belgique tome III*, ed. by Christiane Pantens (Brussels: Bibliothèque Royale Albert Ier, 1989), pp. 279–83.

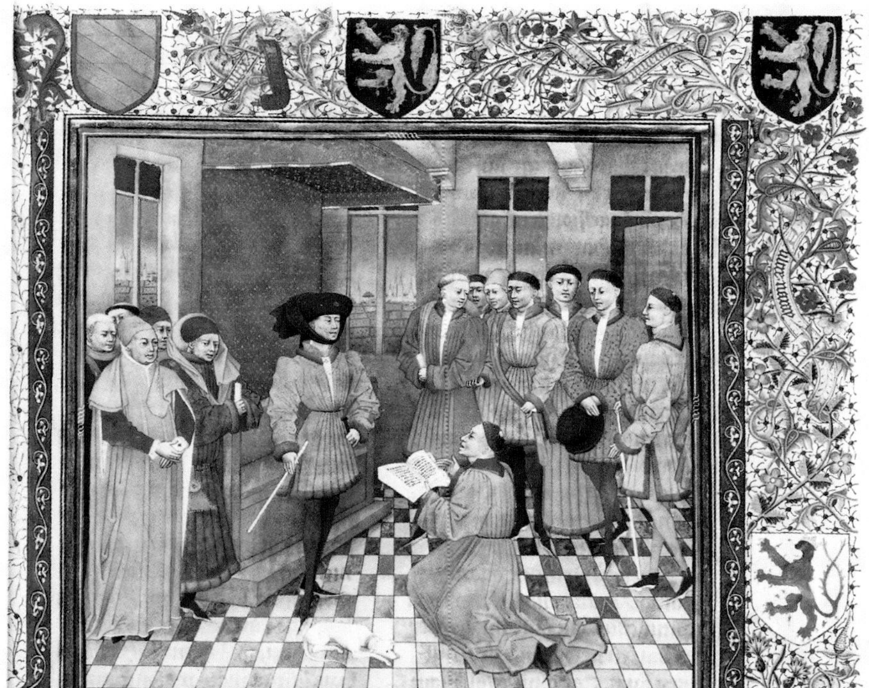

Fig. 1. Unknown artist: frontispiece, Aegidius Romanus, De regimine principum, *translation to French by Jean Wauquelin, copy from 1452 by Jacques Pilavaine. Brussels, Bibliothèque Royale Albert Ier, ms. 9043 fol. 2^{r}. © Bibliothèque Royale Albert Ier, Brussels*

focuses not on the image as such but on the image as a means of understanding the past. Art historians, on the other hand, often work the other way round; our aim is to reconstruct an historical context in which to situate the image, to understand it better. This approach appears to me as problematic, because of its tendency to relegate the image to a secondary position while the historical context becomes primary. The interpretation of an image becomes synonymous with the mapping of the historical situation: the economic, political, social, cultural, or intellectual circumstances that are chosen as relevant for the understanding of the image. When this historical context is completed, the image is brought in as a separate entity, as something that passively reflects the cultural processes of its epoch: 'the expectation is that context will *control* the text (the work of art); once their opposition is staked out the terms taken together are made to form an economy in which context is active and the text or work of art passive'.[2]

This will be one of my main points. Interpretations that aim at situating an image in its historical context are too seldom centred on the image as such, regarded as having a cognitive capacity of its own based on its distinctive character as an item of visual communication. An image is not just something that is understood by translating it verbally as completely as possible. An image also has its own visual language, its own rhetoric. Admittedly, that aspect of the meaning of the image is accessible to art historical discourse only verbally, through the use of words, but this does not mean that the image should be seen as nothing more than an illustration of an historical situation that has been established *a priori*.

In the first part of this chapter, I will discuss the conditions under which an image can be interpreted as an historical testimony: the extent to which images have to be subject to the same critical examination as, for instance, a text, with regard to the where, when, by whom, and, above all, why they have been produced. I then will concentrate on my main issue, the inherent epistemological value of images. Presupposing that images are powerful carriers of meaning which participate in the shaping of a wider social and cultural context, and that the main potential of images as historical sources lies precisely in their visual formation, I will suggest possible readings of images as visual configurations.

The Historian and the Image as Source Material

If we look at the miniature from *De regimine principum* as an historical document, what kind of information does it yield? If I were to interpret it as a snapshot of an actual historical event, as a peephole through the parchment to

[2] Norman Bryson, 'Art in Context', in *Studies in Historical Change*, ed. by Ralph Cohen (Charlottesville: University Press of Virginia, 1992), pp. 18–42 (p. 19).

the scene that is depicted, it would tell me that at a certain moment a clerical person presented a volume to a secular person in the presence of several other people, both clerical and secular, but all of them male. This took place in a stately room in a building situated at some distance from a town and, considering the stars in the sky, it happened in the evening or early morning. There was also a dog present, albeit sleeping.

Now, this is a reading that is rather meaningless. From the perspective of the historian, the information that the miniature itself can give us is minimal. To be able to situate it in time (middle of the fifteenth century), to locate it geographically (to Burgundy or its territories), and to define its historical context, it is necessary to turn to external sources. Even the identification of the persons as clerical or secular requires the use of a general cultural knowledge that transcends the information content of the painting. In the classical interpretative scheme of Erwin Panofsky, this means going from the first, pre-iconographical level to the second level of interpretation, the iconographical level.[3]

More important, however, is the fact that the miniature does not give us any information at all about past events, since it is not a snapshot or a peephole back into history. It cannot be used as evidence of how, where and in the presence of whom the volume was presented. The only thing that this painting tells us is that somebody once had reason to depict, or arrange to be depicted, a presentation of a volume in this way; but how it actually happened, if at all, is a totally different thing. Images, like texts, are historical products manufactured for certain purposes. This means that the instrumental use of images as source material necessitates the analysis of the image itself as an historically defined product. This is an ordinary, old-fashioned critical approach to sources: when, where, by whom, and why was this miniature produced? The answers to these questions determine the instrumental value of the picture.

A brief summary of the historical setting of the illumination would look as follows.[4] The text, *De regimine principum*, was translated in 1450 by the author, translator, and scribe Jean Wauquelin († 1452) for Philippe le Bon (1396–1467,

---

[3] Erwin Panofsky, *'Introductory' in Studies in Iconology. Humanistic Themes in the Art of the Renaissance* (Oxford: Oxford University Press, 1939), pp. 3–31.

[4] My account is based on Alain Arnould and Jean Michel Massing, *Splendours of Flanders. Late Medieval Art in Cambridge Collections* (Cambridge: Cambridge University Press, 1993); Otto Cartellieri, *The Court of Burgundy. Studies in the History of Civilization* (New York: Haskell House, 1925); Georges Dogaer, *Flemish Miniature Painting in the 15th and 16th Centuries* (Amsterdam: B. M. Israël, 1987); Georges Doutrepont, *La littérature française à la cour des Ducs de Bourgogne* (Paris 1909; Geneva: Slatkine reprints, 1970); *La librairie de Philippe le Bon. Exposition organisée à l'occasion du 500e anniversaire de la mort du Duc*, ed. by George Dogaer and Marguerite Debae (Brussels: Bibliothèque Royale Albert Ier, 1967); Richard Vaughan, *Philip the Good. The Apogee of Burgundy* (London: Longmans, 1970).

duke of Burgundy 1419–67). Philippe le Bon is among the most prominent of the Burgundian rulers of the house of Valois. Unlike his predecessors, he maintained peace with the French king and refrained from threatening French territory, expanding his duchy in other directions through purchases, alliances and conquests: Namur (1421), Hainaut (1427), Brabant (1430), Holland and Zeeland (1424–33) and Luxembourg (1433). Philippe le Bon manifested his rule in an extravagant court life, part of which was his patronage of art and culture on the highest level: artists such as Jan van Eyck and Rogier van der Weyden were among those engaged by the duke. The rule of Philippe le Bon has been described as 'l'âge d'or de la littérature bourguignonne',[5] and his collection of manuscripts was one of the largest and finest of the Middle Ages; it had been founded by his grandfather, Philippe le Hardi who ruled 1363–1404, but was much enlarged by the grandson. When Philippe le Bon died in 1467, it comprised close to nine hundred volumes. The duke spent considerable amounts on the acquisition of books through purchases and commissions; he regularly gave commissions to translators, copyists, illuminators and bookbinders and sometimes supervised their work personally. As a result of the patronage of Philippe le Bon, Burgundy in the later half of the fifteenth century became one of the most important art centres of Europe, second only to Paris.

There is no reason to doubt the genuine and dedicated enthusiasm of Philippe le Bon for art and literature, but through his patronage he also established and confirmed his political power and status, not least with the help of illuminated manuscripts. The collection of art and literature was a political and social means of influence among the highest levels of the Burgundian society: 'art functioned as a passport to the ruling elite'.[6] The example of the great-uncle of Philippe le Bon, the French king, Charles V, who reigned 1364–80, clearly shows the potential of the art of illumination as ideological propaganda. The king made strategic use of words and images to strengthen the position of the French monarchy, by commissioning translations of carefully chosen texts on royal power, furnished with illuminations showing himself in different contexts, but primarily as 'le roi sage'.[7]

The text in question here, *De regimine principum*, was written in 1277–79 in Paris by Aegidius Romanus (1243/47–1316) as a political and moral guide for Philip the Fair, future king of France (reigned 1285–1314). The text was translated into many languages (in French as early as 1282) and was read by rulers all over Europe well into the sixteenth century. It became one of the most widespread mirrors of princes of the Middle Ages and one of the most frequently

---

[5] Doutrepont (as in note 4), p. 480.

[6] Arnould and Massing (as in note 4), p. 143.

[7] Jonathan J. G. Alexander, *Medieval Illuminators and Their Methods of Work* (New Haven: Yale University Press, 1992), p. 143.

read texts of the period as a whole.[8] Today it is preserved in about 250 copies in eight different languages. The translator of this particular edition, Jean Wauquelin, was Philippe le Bon's principal scribe. In 1441, he set up his atelier for the production of manuscripts in Mons. Wauquelin's *Le Gouvernement de Princes* was by no means the only didactic text available to Philippe le Bon: George Doutrepoint, who has studied the literature of four generations of Burgundian rulers, enumerates a considerable number of mirrors of princes that belonged to the ducal library, among them several copies of *De regimine principum*.[9]

This manuscript from 1452 is the only extant copy of the 1450 translation made by Jean Wauquelin. The scribe responsible for this copy is Jacques Pilavaine, who took over Wauquelin's atelier on the death of the latter.[10] Accounts testify that Pilavaine did the calligraphy and decorative ornamentation, but the name of the artisan who produced the presentation picture—the only pictorial scene in the manuscript—is not known.[11] This kind of division of labour in the making of a manuscript was not unusual: in the middle of the fifteenth century the production of illuminated texts was a highly specialized craft, and the best illuminators were responsible for the most important pages and the pictorial scenes, while assistants took care of the ornamentation and decorative frames and copyists the calligraphy. The different artisans were seen as similar to other craftsmen and sometimes formed part of the ducal household together with other servants, as 'valets de chambre'. Philippe le Bon, however, did not keep a regular scriptorium of his own for the manufacture of illuminated manuscripts. He gave commissions to ateliers as far apart as Paris, Dijon, Mons, Lille, Brussels, and Bruges, and the volumes were sent among scribe, illuminator, and copyist to be edited, illuminated, and engrossed.[12]

All this is circumstantial information not directly related to the image in question. In an instrumental interpretation of the kind an historian would find

---

[8] Wilhelm Berges, *Die Fürstenspiegel des hohen und späten Mittelalters. Schriften des Reichinstituts für ältere deutsche Geschichtskunde.* Monumenta Germaniae historica 2 (Stuttgart: Hiersemann, 1938), p. 211.

[9] Doutrepont (as in note 4), pp. 290–319, 488; Dogaer and Debae (as in note 4), pp. 72–73.

[10] *Dictionnaire des lettres françaises. Le Moyen Age. Encyclopédies d'aujourd'hui* (Paris: Fayard, 1992), pp. 543, 713.

[11] Dogaer (as in note 4), p. 61; Dogaer and Debae (as in note 4), p. 73; Lyna (as in note 1), p. 280. He has been given the anonymous name Master of the Gent Privileges, and several more paintings in illuminated manuscripts have been attributed to him; see Friedrich Winkler, *Die flämische Buchmalerei des* XV. *und* XVI. *Jahrhunderts. Künstler und Werke von den Brüdern van Eyck bis zu Simon Bening* (Amsterdam: B. M. Israël, 1978), p. 31.

[12] Cartellieri (as in note 4), p. 167; Doutrepont (as in note 4), pp. 457–58.

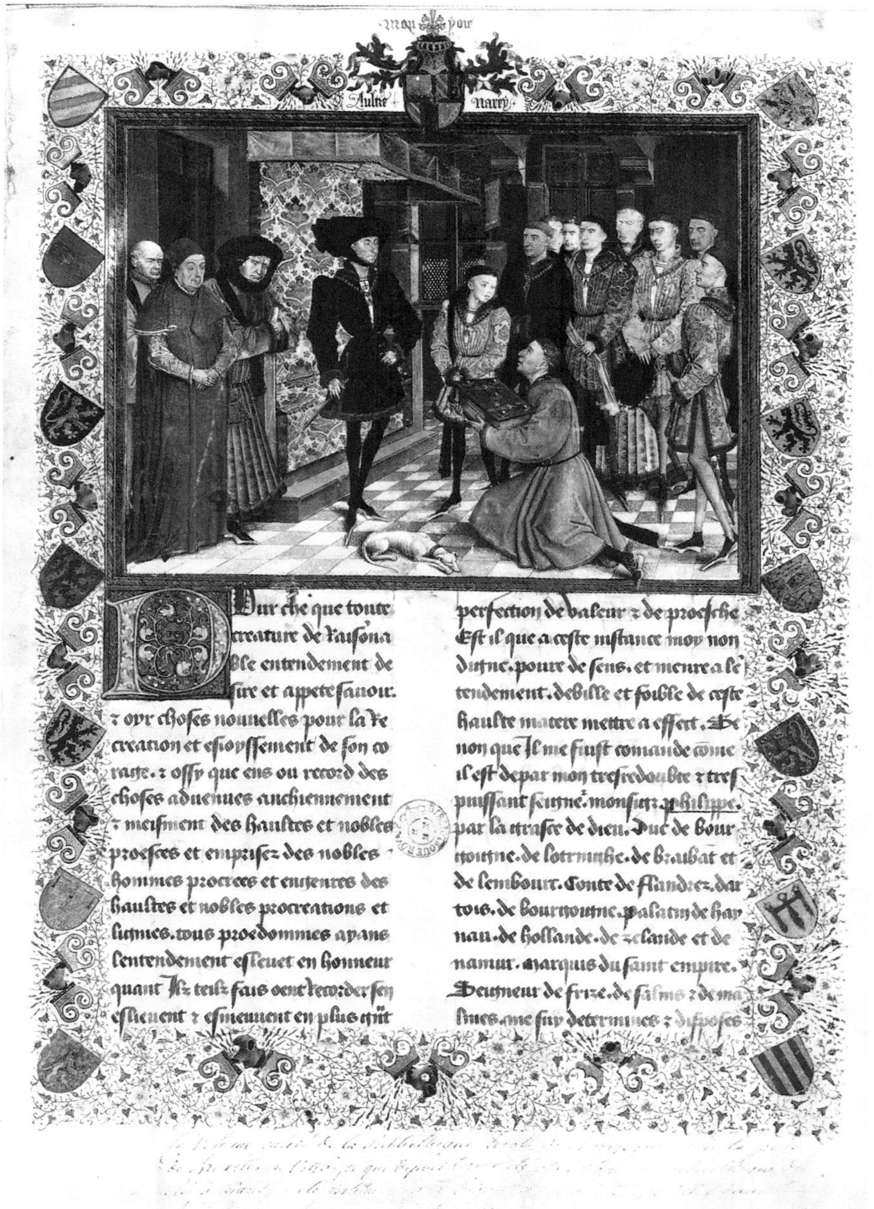

Fig. 2. Unknown artist: frontispiece, Jacques de Guise, Annales Hannoniae, *translation into French by Jean Wauquelin, copy from 1448 by Wauquelin and Jacotin du Bois. Brussels, Bibliothèque Royale Albert Ier, ms. 9242 fol. 1r. © Bibliothèque Royale Albert Ier, Brussels*

interesting, the evidence of the miniature itself has to be supplemented with external information to be of any use; after all, it is not the image itself that interests the historian. The miniature has a confirming function: it affirms what we already know about Philippe le Bon as a commissioner of manuscripts, or at least does not contradict it. The illumination informs us that Philippe wished to demonstrate his role as collector and patron visually. Actually, the painting takes its design from a slightly older presentation picture: a well-known miniature in a translation of *Annales Hannoniae*, an historical chronicle written in the fourteenth century by the Franciscan Jacques de Guise († 1399) and translated by Wauquelin for Philippe le Bon in 1447–48 (fig. 2).[13] This painting has been used as the model for several presentation pictures in manuscripts ordered by the duke, and the miniature in *De regimine principum* follows it closely, with certain variations: here, the group of people to the right of Philippe le Bon consists of seven, not eight, persons, as in the *Annales Hannoniae*; the boy immediately to the right of the duke (his son and future duke, Charles, who reigned 1467–77) is in the later painting shown as being a few years older; the colouring is partly different; the volume in the hands of Wauquelin is open and not closed; and the illuminator of *Gouvernement de princes* has added a view through the windows.[14]

Although the more recent miniature is thus made according to a model from another text, it brings with it some information to its new surroundings. There is, for instance, no reason to doubt that the translator, according to the painting, was a cleric (in the preface he calls himself the 'clerq et serviteur' of Philippe le Bon), although there is a record of a widow making demands for unpaid remunerations after the death of Wauquelin.[15] The obvious effort to give individuality to the features of Philippe le Bon corresponds approximately with other contemporary depictions and descriptions of him as tall and lean with a bony face, protruding nose, and wide mouth.[16] One can also assume that the painting shows contemporary dress fashion more or less accurately. However, this last statement has to be made with a certain reservation: depending on the use of models, or on pictorial conventions, or for other reasons, images can show people in old-fashioned or archaic dress. Thus, the man immediately to the left

---

[13] Brussels, Bibliothèque Royale Albert Ier, ms. 9242 fol. 1^{r}.

[14] On the *Annales Hannoniae* manuscript, see Dogaer (as in note 4), p. 63; Dogaer and Debae (as in note 4), pp. 125–26; Lyna (as in note 1), p. 281; *Rogier van der Weyden—Rogier de le Pasture. Official Painter to the City of Brussels. Portrait Painter of the Burgundian Court* (Brussels: Maison du Roi, 1979), p. 172.

[15] Doutrepont (as in note 4), p. 22–26.

[16] Vaughan (as in note 4), pp. 127–28; Francis Haskell, *History and Its Images. Art and the Interpretation of the Past* (New Haven: Yale University Press, 1993), pp. 491–92.

of Philippe le Bon, chancellor Nicholas Rolin, following identifications made of the individuals in the original miniature, is conservatively dressed according to 1430s fashion, rather than to that of the late 1440s.[17]

Furthermore, the miniature informs us that the presentation of a manuscript was an occasion of a certain formality that could take place in the presence of a larger company—or at least that this was the way it could be visually represented. Also, one can note not only what the picture shows but also what it does not show: obviously dogs were not considered out of place when manuscripts were presented, but there are no women present. There certainly were women at the Burgundian court, and records of female commissioners and owners of manuscripts during the Middle Ages tell us that women were not *per se* excluded from the world of books and reading.[18] A possible explanation would be that the text in question is a mirror of princes, a political and didactic text on the art of ruling, that belonged to a sphere in which women had no place. To confirm this assumption one would have to compare this miniature with other presentation pictures. A comparison to some other manuscripts from the Burgundian court shows that the design of the presentation pictures follow a general scheme, but for all we know this may be due rather to the fact that the pictures adhere to a conventionalized formula than to the fact that this was how presentations were actually performed at the court.[19]

Thus, in using images as historical sources, one needs to take into account the degree of representativity of the individual picture. Does this miniature represent a unique instance, or does it have a more general validity? The answer is simple: without comparisons with contemporary images from the same historical setting it is impossible to decide if a specific picture is unique or in accordance with a prevailing visual tradition. It is vital to be careful in attributing authority to an

---

[17] On Burgundian fashion and the dress habits of Philippe le Bon, see Margaret Scott, *Late Gothic Europe, 1400–1500*. The History of Dress Series, ed. by Aileen Ribeiro (London: Mills & Boon, 1980).

[18] John Bartier, 'Art Patronage in Van der Weyden's Time', in *Rogier van der Weyden—Rogier de le Pasture* (as in note 14), pp. 24–35 (p. 27); Susan G. Bell, 'Medieval Women Book-Owners: Arbiters of Lay Piety and the Ambassadors of Culture', *Signs. Journal of Women in Culture and Society* 7 (1982), 742–68.

[19] See Dogaer and Debae (as in note 4), pl. 1, 42, 43, 47, 49, 61. In a presentation picture from 1403, showing Christine de Pisan presenting her *Le livre de chemin de longue étude* to Charles VI, the author herself is the only woman present (ibid., pl. 23). Cf. Dogaer and Debae on the standard design of manuscripts ordered by Philippe le Bon: 'Au début du manuscrit se trouve un prologue dans lequel l'auteur ou le traducteur dédie son œuvre au Duc. Ce prologue est généralement accompagné d'une belle miniature où l'on voit Philippe le Bon en costume d'apparat, entouré de dignitaires de la Cour, recevoir un manuscrit des mains de l'auteur ou du traducteur. Les armoiries, la devise et l'emblème du Duc sont parfois peints dans cette miniature frontispice' (ibid., p. 5).

individual image that lacks comparable counterparts. The issue of representativity is central, but far too seldom critically evaluated, when dealing with fragmentary source material such as that of medieval imagery. In this case, when the relevant comparable material consists of illuminations from the same milieu and derived partly from the same model, it is necessary to take into account the possibility that, rather than reproducing actual circumstances, the visual formation depends on a conventionalized formula.

To summarize this part of my argument: what I have tried to do so far is to indicate some of the conditions for the use of images as historical sources. An image, as are all other artefacts, is a product of what Michael Baxandall terms a 'situational intention': at a certain moment, somebody found reason to make it, or have it made.[20] The image is the result of certain choices made in a certain historical situation, and this insight is fundamental for the use of it as a source. Actually, an image cannot tell us very much about a specific historical event other than that somebody has seen occasion to depict this event in a certain way. In addition, I have pointed to the necessary awareness of the fact that pictures follow formalized conventions in their representation. This assertion is valid for the imagery of every historical period, not solely for the late Middle Ages and for all types of pictures: portraits and 'realistic' genre paintings, as well as glorifying historical paintings or allegorical motifs. An image can never be trusted as a testimony of anything other than the intention of its instigator.

The Art Historian and the Image as Source Material

So far, I have focused on an instrumental use of images. As an art historian, however, I am more concerned with the question of the inherent epistemological value of images. In a post-structuralist and materialist theory of visuality, images are seen as agents in history, as articulations of social processes that in themselves constitute and influence those processes. Images are formed by the cultural system they represent, but they also partake in the formation of this system, a formation that works as an ideological authorization. This means that images should be interpreted not only as mere illustrations reflecting historical processes; they are in themselves historical processes that contribute to the culturally defined self-comprehension of an epoch. According to Griselda Pollock: 'Culture can be defined as those social practices whose prime aim is signification, that is, the production of sense or making orders of 'sense' for the world we live in. Culture is the social level in which are produced those images of the world and definitions of reality which can be ideologically mobilized to

[20] Michael Baxandall, *Patterns of Intention. On the Historical Explanation of Pictures* (New Haven: Yale University Press, 1985), chaps 1, 2.

legitimize the existing order of relations of domination and subordination'.[21]

All images, not only those with an overtly ideological propaganda objective, can be taken to interact with the cultural system of their setting in one way or another. Even a picture that seemingly makes no impression whatsoever in its time works as a focal point where different ideologically defined discourses are confronted and visualized. The production and reception of an image as a concrete manifestation in visual form of the social processes of a certain time and at a certain place means that those processes are being worked upon.

At several points already I have defined images as products. This implies an approach to images as being manufactured in specific historical situations, subject to social and economic relations among the different agents and institutions, for instance the patron and the artist or, in this case, the artisan and his atelier. Speaking of images as products also makes way for the concept of intentionality: the images are systems of meaning, made to be read and internalized as part of the ideological process that constitutes a culture. The images can function in accordance with the dominant ideology or against it, but they always are related to it in one way or another, a feature that they share with all other contemporary discourses. The distinctive characteristic of images, of course, is that they are non-verbal, and in the following, I will concentrate on the visual communication of meaning, again with the Burgundian miniature as my object of investigation.

To structure my analysis I will take up different aspects separately. I will begin with the *production aspect*: to what extent does the miniature reveal the condition of its manufacture? This question is connected with the *temporal aspect*: in what ways is the making of the painting during a certain span of time visible in the finished result? Next comes *the spatial* or *visual aspect*, by which I mean the co-ordination of picture and picture surface and of picture and ornamentation. This leads me to *the textual aspect*, the relationship between the pictorial elements and the text and finally to *the functional aspect*, the function of the illumination in the manuscript as a whole. I do not claim to present an analysis that is either unique for this miniature, or of general validity for late medieval illuminations in general. My purpose is to verbalize and exemplify conditions for a reading of images that is grounded in the epistemological value of their visuality as such.

First there is *the production aspect*. This miniature, as most illuminations in general, manifests itself as something strikingly costly and precious with reference to the time and labour spent in manufacturing it, as well as to the value of the materials used. Even without any more detailed knowledge concerning the process of making a fifteenth-century illumination (the design is planned and the

---

[21] Griselda Pollock, 'Vision, Voice and Power: Feminist Art Histories and Marxism', in *Vision and Difference. Femininity, Feminism and the Histories of Art*, ed. by Griselda Pollock (London: Routledge, 1988), pp. 18–49 (p. 20).

page ruled, the pictorial elements are sketched with a hard pointed stylus or in graphite and then drawn more elaborately in coloured ink, the gilding is applied, and then the colours and finally the shadings and other finer details are executed; also, somewhere in the process, the text is engrossed) it is obvious for the viewer that a single page like this one requires a considerable amount of time to make, with its degree of detail and its intricate ornamentation in miniature scale. This means that the illumination presents itself as the visual result of great effort—and Philippe le Bon as the person who can afford to pay for this effort. The materials used send the same signals, especially the gilding and the lavish use of blue pigment that defines the manuscript as a markedly valuable item.[22]

There is a contradiction, however, between the time and effort that have been invested in the making of the illumination and the temporality of the finished result. The presentation scene and the ornamentation manifest themselves as completed works: none of the previous stages in the production of the miniature show in the finished result, apart from the thin red underlining of the dark letters of the text. The presentation scene, as well as the miniature as a whole, is fixed and frozen in a present that lacks a past, as a closed and finished fact that bears no testimony to its history of production.[23] The effort required to make the illumination is manifested not as the work of the different artisans but as something for which Philippe le Bon has had the capacity to pay for. The production process is not visible in itself, other than as the finished result.

Next comes what I have called *the spatial aspect*: the organization of the visual elements on the page as a whole. The presentation scene naturally draws most attention, but on closer examination there is a striking degree of integration of the different parts of the composition—the pictorial scene, the flowery ornamentation, the frames, the coats of arms, and not the least text—into a tightly knit unity. In the overall composition, the presentation scene functions as the main centre of gravity, while the text area and the more sparsely decorated left margin provide some breathing space on the otherwise very dense page. The vegetative ornamentation (consisting of acanthus leaves, vines, strawberry tendrils, small thorny fruits, and various flowers: roses, columbines, corn flowers, and carnations) along the margins functions as a compositional anchoring of the totality: asymmetrical and graceful but at the same time rather firmly structured, a feature that is strengthened by the slightly irregularly placed coats of arms of Philippe le Bon himself, the duchy of Burgundy, Brabant (twice), Limburg, Flanders, and Hainaut. The text scrolls repeat the motto of Philippe le Bon: 'aultre n'aray tant que viveray' [as long as I live I will not have anything/anyone else].

---

[22] Alexander (as in note 7), p. 40.

[23] See Norman Bryson, *Vision and Painting. The Logic of the Gaze* (New Haven: Macmillan, 1983), chap. 5.

The different visual elements are clearly demarcated and separated by the frames. A hundred years later, in the middle of the sixteenth century, the epoch of illuminated manuscripts is definitely over, replaced by panel painting of the kind that is heralded by the presentation scene with its illusion of space in three dimensions. The illumination of *De regimine principum* represents a middle stage, an attitude of ambiguity towards the relation between picture and surface, with text and ornamentation obviously belonging to the surface of the page, while the presentation scene invalidates this two-dimensionality, as if the parchment has suddenly given way and we are seeing right through it onto a scene that is taking place beyond its boundaries. In the words of Otto Pächt, this change means that the pictorial field has become pictorial space: the illuminator, the scribe and the decorator 'each had an entirely disparate relationship to the page: looking and reading had become two essentially distinct activities [. . .] now the image was sometimes on 'optical' ground and at other times on a 'real' one'.[24]

As I see it, the combination of the illusionary space of the presentation scene and the framing that stresses the illumination as surface-bound underlines the representational character of the miniature. The intention is not to present an eye-witness account of an actual event but to provide a visual representation not only of the handing over of the volume but also of the validity of the text—Aegidius Romanus's *De regimine principum*—in relation to the rule of Philippe le Bon. The coats of arms in the margins are symbolical representations of social position with a significance that equals the figure of Philippe le Bon himself in the presentation picture. The coats of arms function as visual claims of territorial sovereignty and, thus, as a link between the presentation picture and the text. The coats of arms in the surface-defined part of the illumination are counterparts of the figure of the duke in the three-dimensional picture space ,and similarly the text of the manuscript has a real relation to the government of the duke; or rather, the coats of arms can be seen as a verification that the regime of Philippe le Bon should be interpreted in terms of *De regimine principum*.

This brings me to the *textual aspect*: the text as part of the visual as well as the verbalized meaning of the illumination. Visually it is obvious that the text is not the most important element of the page: the presentation picture dominates powerfully, the gilded frames only just shield the text area from the dense ornamentation and the text occupies no more than one fifth of the totality. Again, it is the representational character of the illumination that is brought to the fore:

---

[24] Otto Pächt, *Book Illumination in the Middle Ages. An Introduction* (London: Harvey Miller, 1986; orig. published as *Buchmalerei des Mittelalters. Eine Einführung*, Munich: Prestel-Verlag, 1984), p. 200. Pächt does not specify which is which. As I understand him, the text and the ornamentation are located on the 'real' ground, i.e., the two-dimensional surface that is the actual surface of the illumination, while the three-dimensional space of a miniature such as the one under discussion here belongs to the 'optical' ground, a picture plane that exists as an optical illusion but not in reality.

it is not the content of the text that is of importance, but rather the fact that it has been presented to Philippe le Bon.

The text of the treatise *De regimine principum* deals with the ruler as *rex quasi semideus*, meaning that he governs his subjects as God rules the world, through a combination of Christian doctrines and Aristotelian ethics according to which monarchy is the best form of government. The authority of the sovereign is absolute, the subjects' only duty is to obey. The text is divided into three books: on controlling oneself according to the four cardinal virtues; on the ruling of a household and a court; and on governing the state, with instructions as to how those duties are to be performed. However, the text of the frontispiece is not from *De regimine principum* itself; rather, it contains the dedication to Philippe le Bon:

> A son tresespecial seigneur, né de la royale et tressainte lignïe monseigneur Phlippe premier, engenré et hoir de Trescler, homme monseigneur Phlippe par la Grace de Dieu roy de France. Frere Gilles de Rome [Egidius Romanus] de l'ordre des freres hermites saint Augustin son devot orateur toute recommendation et luy meismes a toutes choses prest de servir. Mon treschier seigneur, la sentence des politiques dit que toutes princiés ne sont point de egale durée c'est a dire que elles ne durent point tant l'une comme l'aultre, et si ne sont point les regimes d'une chascune seignourie rieulés par ung meisme cours, mais. . . .[25]

After an introductory reverence to the duke, the translator continues:

> My dearest Lord, the judgement of the political historians says that not all periods of rule are of the same duration, that is they do not all last as long as one another; and nor do the forms of government in all countries follow the same rules.

Thus, the text of the page opens as a verbal counterpart to the presentation picture and then continues as a transition to the theme of the treatise itself, with an evaluation of different kinds of governments.

The last aspect is the *function* of the illumination related to the text and the manuscript as a whole. In her article *Reading Medieval Images*, Vera F. Vines sums up the functions of images in medieval manuscripts:

> They sharpened the visual interest of the page by interrupting the flow of the written word: cartoon-like, at times they provided the viewer with near-substitutes for the text; alternatively, they could communicate meaning by furnishing stories with descriptive explanations or moralizing commentaries, to heighten the impact of the text. Picture and word were in conversation with one another, collaborating in intricate ways'.[26]

---

[25] Translated by associate professor Trond Kruke Salberg, Department of Classical and Romance Studies, University of Oslo.

[26] Vera F. Vine, 'Reading Medieval Images: Two Miniatures in a Fifteenth-Century Missal', in *Medieval Texts and Images. Studies of Manuscripts from the Middle Ages*, ed. by Margaret M. Manion and Bernard J. Muir (Chur: Harwood Academic Publishers,

In this case it is hardly a question of the picture as a sharpening of the visual interest by interrupting the flow of text, since the presentation picture is the opening of the whole manuscript and furthermore is the only pictorial scene included. It establishes with a certain emphasis the terms of reading: that the relevance of Jean Wauquelin's translation of *De regimine principum* is to be related to the government of Philippe le Bon. The presentation picture constructs a relation between the duke and the text. The duke is the master of the situation: he is standing in the centre of the room in an attitude that signals sovereignty, and he is enclosed by empty space that creates a distance between him and the other figures. Wauquelin is the only person on his knees: the way Wauquelin is rendered, in a subordinate position in the composition as a whole, puts the emphasis on the duke on the one hand and the open volume, rather than its translator, on the other.

The presentation picture contextualizes the text. This brings me back to the definition of an image as an historical process, something that actively generates cultural self-comprehension. A picture such as this one visualizes and works upon mental structures connected with the conditions of power politics, social hierarchies, cultural education and political authority, and, more generally, the relation between reality and principles, between the actual rule of Philippe le Bon (manifested in the illusionary space of the presentation picture as well as in the coats of arms in the two-dimensionality of the margins) and the precepts for ruling as formulated in the thirteenth century by Aegidius Romanus and inscribed here as part of the totality of the page. The illumination has communicated its meaning to a larger public than the duke personally: I have already described the collecting of splendid manuscripts as a manifestation not only of cultural capital but also of political power and social status at the Burgundian court in the middle of the fifteenth century. To this can be added that the miniature has by no means ceased to create an historically defined understanding of Philippe le Bon and his rule: in fact, the potential of the image to set the terms for this understanding has been the core of my whole argument.

The Epistemology of Images

In this article, I have tried to formulate a reading of images that is not restricted to either pure form or pure content, that is, a reading that is more than merely a specification of the diagonals of the composition or a naming of the historical persons who can be identified. The interpretations that I have suggested have throughout been anchored in the visual properties of the illumination, according to the fundamental assumption that the image as such has a cognitive potential. I

1991), pp. 127–48 (p. 127).

have searched for meanings that can be detected in the illumination as a visually complex structure. Knowledge of the historical context has been fundamental, but at the same time the illumination has been recognized as a formative power in relation to this same context.

The question with which I began was: on what, and on whose, conditions should an image be interpreted? My answer is that, if an image is defined as an historical source, at the same time it is necessary to respect the epistemological value that is grounded in its visuality. To reduce an image to a mere illustration of historical conditions and at the same time to refuse to acknowledge it as a visual representation on its own terms, is to disregard its distinctive character as image. Ultimately I want to define this as a matter of ethics; it is about making it possible for an image to communicate as what it actually is: something that, at least sometimes, can have more to say than a whole lot of words.*

* This paper has also been read in Swedish, in a report from the conference 'De historiska vetenskaperna och bilden', Department of History, Lund University, February 1999.